The Haunting of
Twentieth-Century America

William J. Birnes

Worker in the Light: Unlock Your Five Senses and Liberate Your Limitless Potential

Journey to the Light: Find Your Spiritual Self and Enter into a World of Infinite Opportunity

Space Wars: The First Six Hours of World War III

Counterspace: The Next Hours of World War III

The Haunting of America: From the Salem Witch Trials to Harry Houdini

The Day After Roswell

The Riverman: Ted Bundy and I Hunt for the Green River Killer

Signature Killers: Interpreting the Calling Cards of the Serial Murderer

The Star Trek Cookbook

Star Trek: Aliens and Artifacts

The Haunting of the Presidents: A Paranormal History of the U.S. Presidency

Joel Martin

We Are Not Forgotten: George Anderson's Messages of Love

Love Beyond Life: Healing Power of After-Death Communications

Our Children Forever: George Anderson's Messages from Children on the Other Side

We Don't Die: George Anderson's Conversations with the Other Side

The Haunting of America: From the Salem Witch Trials to Harry Houdini

The Haunting of the Presidents: A Paranormal History of the U.S. Presidency

William J. Birnes
and Joel Martin

The
Haunting
of
Twentieth-
Century
America

A Tom Doherty
Associates Book
New York

THE HAUNTING OF TWENTIETH-CENTURY AMERICA

A Forge Book
Published by Tom Doherty Associates, LLC
175 Fifth Avenue
New York, NY 10010

www.tor-forge.com

Forge® is a registered trademark of Tom Doherty Associates, LLC.

Library of Congress Cataloging-in-Publication Data

Martin, Joel.
   The haunting of twentieth-century America / Joel Martin and William Birnes.—1st ed.
     p. cm.
  "A Tom Doherty Associates Book."
  ISBN 978-0-7653-2354-5 (hardcover)
  ISBN 978-0-7653-2785-7 (trade pbk.)
  1. United States—History—20th century—Anecdotes. 2. Spiritualism—United States—Anecdotes. 3. Ghosts—United States—Anecdotes.
4. Parapsychology—United States—Anecdotes. 5. Popular culture—United States—Anecdotes. I. Birnes, William J. II. Title.
  E741.M284 2011
  973.91—dc23

                                    2011019775

First Edition: September 2011

Printed in the United States of America

0 9 8 7 6 5 4 3 2 1

Dedicated to my wife, Nancy Hayfield, whose efforts as editor-in-chief of UFO Magazine make it one of the most popular magazines still in print, and to my grandchildren, Casey, Reese, and Marcus, for whom, I expect, what we call the paranormal will be completely normal.

—William J. Birnes

This book is dedicated to the memory of my wife, Christina Martin, with eternal love.

—Joel Martin

The authors also dedicate this book to the many generations of men and women whose courage and persistence, often in the face of unrelenting criticism and opposition, tell the true story of America's paranormal past.

History is a pact between the dead, the living, and the yet unborn.

—EDMUND BURKE

Contents

Acknowledgments

To our editors at Forge Books, Bob Gleason, Eric Raab, and Whitney Ross, and to our publisher, Tom Doherty, for their support and superhuman patience in the management of these manuscripts. To my coauthor, Joel Martin, who has tirelessly plied the field of the paranormal, debunking the frauds and establishing a scientific basis for what he believes is true. And to my wife, Nancy Hayfield, for her extraordinary patience as I traveled on the road for *UFO Hunters* and *Ancient Aliens* while working on all of my books. She is *UFO Magazine*.

—WILLIAM J. BIRNES

Many thanks to all those who helped this book become a reality, especially:

Kristina Rus, reference librarian, East Meadow (New York) Public Library, with deep gratitude for her loyalty and persistence. Her tireless and meticulous reference and research skills contributed to this book more than words can ever express.

Elise LeVaillant for enduring encouragement, inspiration, spirituality, knowledge, and love.

Margaret Wendt, my partner and dear friend for so many years. My love and thanks for guiding and sharing our journey to discover the "Spiritual Truth."

Catherine Erdelyi, thank you for your awesome assistance, brilliant organization, and computer skills.

Roxanne Salch Kaplan, with deep appreciation for years of friendship.

Max Toth, with thanks for sharing enormous knowledge of parapsychology and so much more.

Gaylon Emerzian, everlasting thanks for bringing Bill Birnes and me together to collaborate as authors.

Bill Birnes, with many thanks for sharing another complex and all-consuming book project with a deep knowledge of the subject and a keen eye for accuracy.

Special thanks to: Donna DiBiase, Salvatore Gambino, Patricia Ippolito, Nancy Kaiser, Arlene and Mike Rosich, Dick Ruhl, Vladimir Rus, Ph.D., Thomas Santorelli, Ruth Tanen, Al Ubert, Neil Vineberg, and the family of the late Hyman Berman.

All my love and prayers to my beautiful grandchildren, Cambria and Caleb Weintraub. May the world they live in be filled with peace, truth, and God's light.

At Tor/Forge, I am deeply grateful for the support we have had, and especially appreciative to our editor Whitney Ross, for her guidance and patience.

And finally, in everlasting and loving memory to: Evelyn Moleta, Stephen Kaplan, Bill Marshall, D. C. (Ben) Webster, Charles and Sadie Cohen, Mary Moleta, Shirleyann Martin, John Blake, Rick Moran, Len Jasen, M.D., Kathy Cashman, Aloysius J. Chirayil, and, of course, Father John Papallo. Lastly, John G. Fuller, my inspiration for writing about the paranormal.

—JOEL MARTIN

We have made every effort to present historical facts as accurately as possible. However, in the course of researching and writing, we sometimes discovered variations in details such as dates, locations, events, dialogue, and even spellings of names and places. To the best of our ability, we have consulted several authoritative references to provide the greatest historical accuracy possible. However, some variations proved unavoidable and are a reflection of incomplete, inadequate, or contradictory historical record keeping.

In some instances, some names have been changed to protect privacy. However, while certain identifying characteristics have been altered, the incidents and experiences described are genuine.

We can call the preceding century the Age of Science, but, in fact, it was actually an age in which the paranormal became the normal and science became more like science fiction. With the introduction of alternating current at the Chicago World's Fair just[1] before the turn of the century, the proof that human beings could fly heavier-than-air craft just a few years later, the splitting of the atom, and demonstrations that human beings could control events with their minds, the twentieth century marked the blending of the culture of rationalism and science, the culture of art, and the culture of the paranormal into a new concept of reality.

Even before 1900, in art and in literature, painters and writers depicted a world perceived through artistic vision if not through the realism of the middle nineteenth century. Cubist painters projected their vision of representing hidden angles and shapes within objects set in front of them. And Picasso, in his painting, *Guernica,* not only combined the symbolism of important Spanish cultural emblems—the bull and the horse—but drew these into a painting representing a very real event: the Italian bombing of a Spanish village in 1937 during the Spanish Civil War. The painting not only depicts the tragedy of war on innocent civilians but it shows the timelessness of the imagery of war. Thus, it is a four-dimensional narrative expressed in two dimensions. Picasso himself once said that to ask him to deconstruct his own work so as to examine particular imagery would be to ask him something impossible. Echoing Freud's statement that sometimes "a cigar is just a cigar," Picasso said that sometimes a bull and a horse are just a bull and a horse. Perhaps, he continued, the images came out of his "unconscious," but as far as he was concerned, he could not deconstruct his own work to ferret out what the various symbols might have represented.[2]

What was happening in art and the social sciences—a meaning and reality conveyed to the unseen world on a level greater than the world perceived by the five senses—was also happening in literature. For example, in the first volume of Marcel Proust's epic, *Swann's Way* (*Du côté de chez Swann*), the narrator has but to taste a small pastry and his mind is flooded with memories of things past. He has consciously forgotten these events, but, upon the taste of a madeleine, Charles Swann is transported. The past is alive again, triggered by visceral senses of taste and smell. It is as if all of his senses are flooded with living memory, memory that takes him over as if he's really there. In other words, what is unseen is perceived as if it were real. Reality lies in the perception of the unseen, not in the palpable world around us.

Interestingly, some forty years after the publication of *Swann's Way*, the first volume of Marcel Proust's epic *Remembrance of Things Past*,[3] Dr. Wilder Penfield in Canada conducted experiments on the surfaces of the cerebral cortices of individuals being treated for brain lesions and discovered that applying a mild electric current to these patients, he was able to stimulate memories so vivid, that the patients revealed they were at once living in the memory as if it were the present while consciously aware of being on an operating table in a hospital. This is a suggestive example of the world of the unconscious replaying a tape into the world of the conscious, scientifically validating both Freud and Proust at the same time.

In another twist on seeing the world through the prism of one's own perceptions, describing the world from different perspectives at the same time so that reality is a function of what the viewer sees—subjective—rather than an objective reality, English novelist and playwright Bram Stoker told the story of *Dracula* as a series of journals. What fascinated readers of this 1897 novel was not just the story of Dracula the vampire, who migrates to England from his native Transylvania by ship and inflicts a reign of terror on Edwardian London, it is about how the different narrators of the story, from Jonathan Harker to Dr. Van Helsing to Mina Murray, all tell the same story about seeing the same thing from their respective viewpoints. And in a classic carriage-chase climax, Van Helsing and his retinue of vampire slayers maintain their situational awareness of Dracula's whereabouts by a prolonged hypnotic session with once-bitten Mina, using her psychic connection with Dracula as a way to track him down even as he sleeps in his own earth. Again, Stoker is a product of the cultural zeitgeist of his time, translating an old Carpathian legend into a modern Freudian psychological thriller, which has since become one of the most classic horror stories in motion picture history.[4]

What Stoker accomplished in 1897, William Faulkner accomplished in 1929 with his novel *The Sound and the Fury*, describing the same story of the castration of the severely mentally impaired Benjy Compson after his sexual assault on a girl. In his twentieth-century representation of a multiple monologue satisfying the demands of classical drama's three unities, Faulkner is also a feature of the cultural outlook of the time: a subjective representation of an objective reality looked at from multiple viewpoints at the same time. It is at once Freudian and abstract, Cubist and classical.

At last we come to science, which was dominated at the turn of the twentieth century not only by the inventions of Thomas Edison, Nikola Tesla, and the X-ray photography of Wilhelm Röntgen, but by the theories of physical reality articulated by Albert Einstein and Max Planck. Here, in a confluence of intellectual discoveries, science itself revealed a truth behind the perception of the unseen. Röntgen showed that what could not be seen because it was inside the human body could be projected onto film by invisible rays from a cathode ray tube. Tesla demonstrated that an unseen stream of electrons could be projected across a distance from a tower to generate power and light. He invented the wireless supply of electrical current. Einstein calculated the relationship between mass and energy while Max Planck and later Werner Heisenberg postulated the characteristics of quanta of energy. In fact, Heisenberg, a product of the twentieth century, argued for a theory of physics that today is still at the center of the program of psychic spying developed by the CIA and the army in the 1970s: the theory of uncertainty.

Because, Heisenberg said, the very act of looking at either a wave or a particle of energy determines whether the object under observation will be a particle of energy or a wave, one can never determine exactly what the object is. The philosophical as well as the scientific implications of this theory are themselves overwhelming and, in a very real way, blend C. P. Snow's two cultures of science and the arts into a third and even a fourth culture comprising the science and the arts and the paranormal.

Imagine the concept that something exists in an observable form because it results from the observation itself. Imagine further that the act of observing is a predetermining factor of the form of the object's existence. This goes to the very heart of Existentialism, the nature of what and how things exist. But, theoretical physicists also suggest that in addition to quanta that can flip from wave to particle based on what the observer observes, quanta also have twins, doppelgangers, in the universe that flip whenever one of the quanta flips. Therefore, how one observes something not only can change the thing, but can cause its twins to change as well. This theory of Nonlocality also lies at the heart of the army's remote viewing program of the late 1970s and the remote influencing program, the subject of Jon Ronson's book, *Men Who Stare at Goats.*

In this way, in the world of the twenty-first century, science can demonstrate the reality of psychic phenomena. The abilities of the prophet Edgar Cayce can be said to have a testable scientific coefficient, and the entire world of Fortean story can have as an objective manifestation the real and reproducible results of scientific testing. The world has come full circle in the twenty-first century as science and the supernatural, Western objectivity and Eastern mysticism, and the normal and paranormal blend.

Perhaps, during the course of the next decades, someone, maybe in the heart of the Ozarks or in Delphos, Kansas, will come upon startling and irrefutable evidence that we have been visited by entities from another planet, another dimension, or another time. Maybe it will come as softly as a cat or as gently as the appearance of dew on the petal of a morning glory. It will be the revelation that life, maybe only microbial life or a single string of a colony of bacteria, exists in shallow underground streams on Mars or deep beneath the lunar surface. And suddenly the paradigm will have changed and everything we once believed will be wrong. And maybe it has already happened.

The Dark Side of the Paranormal: The Nazis and the Occult

If a way to the better there be, it lies in taking a full look at the worst.

—THOMAS HOOD (1799–1845)

There has long been speculation about what causes people to engage in evil. Is there a relationship between an actual devil or dark occult practices and killers and murderous dictators? Is the occult by its very nature evil? Is one of the most evil acts of the twentieth century, the Holocaust, explainable as a manifestation of evil occult forces or does that so demean it by removing culpability from Adolf Hitler and those who worked for him? Can we rationally explain Adolf Hitler and his Nazi cohorts exterminating six million Jews? Could "a conscious entity actively seeking entry into our world account for the nightmare of Nazism . . . ?" author Paul Roland asked in *The Nazis and the Occult*. The issue is "whether Nazi ideology was . . . rooted in occultism," Roland said.[1] In this chapter we'll examine the dark side of the paranormal and the effects it has had throughout history, with emphasis on the atrocities committed by the Nazis and what the connection was between the Third Reich and occultism.

At the core of Roland's thesis lies the question, "Do we consciously or subconsciously choose to commit harm or ruin when the opportunity presents itself, or is evil based on some malicious or egotistical motive?" Is it possible that some of us are caught up in evil because of something innate or in our genes or upbringing? That would imply that any one of us, at least in theory, is capable of committing a heinous crime against another person. Might there be cases in which malevolence is a supernatural force that attacks some people, so that a monstrous act can be attributed to the work of the devil? Are there individuals who encourage evil spirits or demonic forces to possess them? Therefore, is the power of evil beyond their control, or do we have the freedom to resist or reject wrongdoing? This, too, lies near the center of the theory of criminal law, a presupposition about the human capacity to consciously choose good over evil. This supposition goes all the way back to the Old Testament upon which much of Western criminal law is based. Rationalists believe that humans can choose and that there is no such thing as evil from birth. Recent brain research is contradictory, suggesting, on the one hand, that we may not have as much free will as we think, yet, on the other, demonstrating that the brain is plastic and can be trained to resist genetic predispositions.

Whether certain people are predisposed to evil or learn evil ways from their parents or teachers, society itself has its own demands. For society itself to function, the words of the German philosopher Immanuel Kant (1724–1804) still ring true: "Morality is an indispensable part of being human." Those who cannot discern right from wrong or who can make that distinction but cannot comport their behaviors to the law as a result of mental illness and commit violent crimes against innocent people are defined as criminally insane according to the federal penal code. However, that still leaves the question, is there an external agent—such as Satan—that can influence human actions? Many people believe exactly that, although most of us accept that the responsibility for crime belongs with the perpetrators, regardless of the underlying cause.

From the 1960s on, with a stepped-up interest in so-called New Age ideas, curiosity also turned toward the dark side of the paranormal. The turbulent '60s concluded with a savage crime that shocked the nation, the so-called "Manson killings," the work of a brainwashed cult led by the "devil-worshipping" and "Nazi-loving" Charles Manson, who had an admitted interest in the occult. Manson, imprisoned for life, went so far as to carve a swastika in his forehead. The bloody Tate-LaBianca slayings in Los Angeles left seven murder victims in all. The crimes sent waves of fear throughout the country, and incited debate about the psychology of evil, and whether an actual satanic force might have caused such savagery.[2]

Manson himself said that he was trying to create violent chaos to overthrow the established order. He described his mission as "helter skelter," a violent rage against the machine,[3] he told author and psychologist Joel Norris (*Serial Killers: The Growing Menace*, NY: Doubleday [1988]). Yet he also said that he was a child of Satan, born evil and destined to do evil throughout his life. He also said that he was contracted by dark forces inside the government to perform acts that no member of any governmental agency could be connected with. He admitted to being driven by the occult and occult practices. Is the occult, therefore, necessarily evil or is it deemed evil because it is so misunderstood even by those who adhere to it?

As the paranormal has become more accepted and understood in recent years—mainly since the 1970s—serious parapsychologists and a growing number of scientists have delved into what for centuries was wrongly called the "occult," as derived from the Latin word for hidden, secret, or mysterious. Too often it has been associated with phenomena that is considered evil, frightening, even satanic. The result has been media portrayals of psychic events that are heavily fictionalized and sensationalized. Adding to the confusion, mass media, some conservative theologians, and professional debunkers have lumped together ESP, astrology, UFOs, ghosts, Eastern philosophies, cults, paranormal research, monsters, witches, demons, mediums, and satanists into one category, inaccurately branding them all occult, and nearly always insinuating something malevolent. In this chapter, we'll largely limit our exploration of the occult to its dark side, the side most people associate with it: black magic, some forms of witchcraft, demonic or satanic worship and its rituals.

Few people doubt that evil exists. We see or read about evil people and sinister deeds in the news every day and night, the criminals, killers, and predators in our midst. There are terrorists who kill innocent people, many for invented political causes. There are the dictators whose monstrous acts live on in infamy: Hitler, Stalin, Pol Pot, Idi Amin, Vlad Tepes, Genghis Khan, and too many more to list.

In fact, evil dates back to the beginning of recorded human history. In the Old Testament, we are told that Eve succumbed to the serpent's temptation to eat an apple from the Tree of Knowledge. In turn, Eve tempted Adam. Later, Cain murdered his brother, Abel. In ancient Egypt, long before the birth of Jesus Christ, exorcisms were held to purge evil spirits, and in early Rome, many people were fearful of dangerous specters of the dead that lurked in the shadows. Some argue that war is always evil, while others, including President Obama in his acceptance of the Nobel Peace Prize, insist there are "just wars."

We like to believe what the Bible tells us: that all of us are born innocent. What then turns a young child into a murderous dictator, killer, or predator? Is there a genetic predisposition? Some studies have tracked criminal behavior within families from generation to generation so as to suggest some credence to predispositions toward criminal behavior. Other studies point to nurture, not nature, as the cause of criminal behavior. The truth is, we do not know. There are undoubtedly environmental reasons to explain why a number of people turn to evil, and there are genetic factors that may contribute to abhorrent behavior. Is it possible that some people are innately villainous? On the other hand, to borrow from Christian fundamentalist religions, and occult beliefs, might there be a genuine Satan and demonic forces that infest certain people who embrace evil or allow it to enter? Should we take the "dark side" of the paranormal seriously? Skeptics, of course, scoff at the occult, and the idea of Satan with his pitchfork in the fires of hell. Should we dismiss them as superstition? Or is there more to the subject than that?

Parapsychologists tell us that psychical phenomena are neutral. In other words, how we use the paranormal can be either positive or negative. Other researchers, especially those who worked in the army's remote viewing and remote influencing programs during the 1970s and 1980s, tell us that what people call the "paranormal" is less para than it is normal. By that they mean that the paranormal is simply an aspect of normality that we really haven't yet fully understood. For example, when Robert Louis Stevenson wrote *Strange Case of Dr Jekyll and Mr Hyde,* he used the character of Jekyll/Hyde to represent a spiritual duality in human nature, illustrating that both good and evil can exist inside the same person.[4] It was a magic potion that Dr. Jekyll devised to liberate his animalistic spirit, a concept of pure science fiction to enable the Faustian protagonist to reach for something that humans should not touch, just as Mary Shelley's Dr. Frankenstein did in her early nineteenth-century story.

Both Shelley and Stevenson are regarded as very early science-fiction writers. However, by the second half of the twentieth century, Wilder Penfield's experiments in Canada and later medical procedures in the United States showed that Stevenson's vision of a human spirituality duality was not paranormal at all, but very real science. In fact, in trying to treat serious grand mal patients whose seizures were so severe that they threatened to wipe out portions of the brain, doctors used a radical surgical procedure. They severed the thick bundle of neurons called the corpus callosum that runs from front to back between the left and right hemispheres of the brain, whose function it is to connect the two hemispheres. In the human brain, the left and right hemispheres—notwithstanding the plasticity of the human brain—have different gross functions. Connected by the corpus callosum, the two hemispheres communicate with each other internally. However, once the corpus callosum is severed, internal communication is cut off and the two hemispheres function as separate entities.

In research done on grand mal patients who, because their symptoms were so severe, received operations severing their corpus callosums, doctors found some astounding reactions. In one case of a Vietnam War veteran, it seemed to doctors that his logical, socially correct, and law-abiding left hemisphere had kept a more violent and impulsive side of him in check. In one instance, during a fight with his wife, he grabbed a knife with his left hand—the right hemisphere controls the motor functions of the left side of the body in right-handed people—and attempted to stab her. However, his right hand, governed by the left hemisphere, grabbed his left hand and stopped it before it shook the knife to the floor. What this told doctors was that he had become, in effect, two different people, each one governed by a different half of the brain. Does this not resemble the two different people chained together in Stevenson's novel, Jekyll and Hyde, freed from each other by the strange concoction brewed up by Jekyll?

Robert Louis Stevenson was writing a horror novel about a paranormal event. However, real science and medical research showed that what was paranormal and evil in the nineteenth century had become understandably normal, albeit bizarre, by the second half of the twentieth century. In addition, if stem-cell research continues and interspecies breeding is not made a criminal act by the federal government, who's to say that by the middle part of the twenty-first century Victor Frankenstein creations will actually become commonplace? If that comes to be, as it has with Jekyll and Hyde, then the paranormal will not be necessarily evil, only a lot less strange.

The paranormal became associated with evil because organized religion, beginning with Judaism, saw the paranormal as harking back to a pagan polytheistic past. Judaism differentiated itself from the pagan cultures the Israelites encountered by proscribing certain pagan practices, such as body piercing and painting, sorcery, soothsaying, divination, or prognostication. These were evil because the cultures within which they flourished could contaminate the culture of the Israelites as they traveled through the wilderness to the Promised Land.

What was in the Torah and the original Holy Bible found its way into the New Testament. As the world's three great religions—Judaism, Christianity, and Islam—took shape in ancient times it did not take long for the pagan ideas that preceded them to be branded evil, sacrilegious, or the belief of infidels and therefore prohibited. But the dissenters and nonconformists found a way to survive, by organizing into secret groups.[5] We should hasten to add that not all the clandestine assemblages were malevolent in nature or intent. But for centuries, the power of the Roman Catholic Church forced competing religious and mystical practices underground throughout Europe. Those who dared to step publicly outside Church-approved dogma risked being branded heretics and subject to torture and even execution.

It was not until the sixteenth and seventeenth centuries when the "two major secret societies . . . revealed themselves . . . in a public form," explained Michael Howard in *The Occult Conspiracy*.[6] The best-known covert societies were the Freemasons and the Order of the Rosy Cross or the Rosicrucians. A German mystic calling himself Christian Rosenkreuz, who had learned "magical arts" such as conjuring spirits and alchemy from North African occultists, founded the order. Alchemy was considered by many to be a form of magic, and some thought it was satanic in origin.

"Magic" as a concept is derived from the Zoroastrians, the priests, called the Magi, who performed supernatural rituals by means of various implements, such as wands. There is a rich cultural connection between the Zoroastrians and the Egyptians in terms of ritual and invocation of supernatural forces. Even the use of a magic wand harks back to the rod that Moses used to demonstrate to Pharaoh a far greater power than even Pharaoh's wizards could wield. Magic, whose history is far too involved and detailed to narrate here, transformed through the Christian Middle Ages and into the Renaissance and Reformation as a demonic force, purely evil, and ultimately anti-Christian. Even today, it connotes fraternization with the Devil or a demonic presence.

Freemasonry, according to one version, received its start in Germany with a guild of stonemasons contracted to build the Strasbourg Cathedral. Other sources place the start of Freemasonry as early as the late fourteenth century. Official histories place the beginning of the lodges in England, Scotland, and Ireland in the seventeenth century. Still other histories suggest that because Masons were also responsible for constructing magnificent Gothic cathedrals and churches throughout Europe in the late Middle Ages, they had to rely on Euclidian geometric equations even though Euclid, because he was pre-Christian, was banned by the Church as a source of information. Accordingly, Masons had to keep secret the fact that their brotherhood was relying on proscribed scholarship in order to do their work. The secret bonds of the Masonic society grew from simply sharing proscribed information to a fraternal organization with humanitarian goals. Freemasonry, therefore, was not to be confused with witchcraft or sorcery, which had its own separate source of influence in Europe and, especially, Germany.

Germany's interest in "magical beliefs and witchcraft" can be traced to ancient Teutonic mythology, a time before there was a single German national state.[7] Cathedrals and chapels contained numerous relics used to exorcise evil spirits. One example, dating back prior to medieval times, was the acceptance that the devil caused storms.

By the fifteenth and sixteenth centuries, witchcraft had been pronounced a crime of heresy by both the Protestant and Roman Catholic churches, and punishable by death, a decision that prompted widespread fear among most people. For a time, Germany led Europe in the number of alleged witches who were burned at the stake, and trials continued into the seventeenth century.

Following the Church's decree, a papal bull in 1484, that witchcraft was a capital offense, two German inquisitors, Jakob Sprenger and Heinrich Kramer, published a handbook titled *Malleus Maleficarum*, a comprehensive guide for witch hunters that all but guaranteed to prove the accused were guilty regardless of their actual guilt or innocence.[8] The German Lutheran Church agreed with the Catholic hierarchy in condemning sorcery and witchcraft, proclaiming them a grave threat, the Reformation's and Counter Reformation's version of political terrorists. It was only as the seventeenth century wound down that some critics mustered the courage to speak out against the Church's excesses and the torturing of countless innocent people.

Germany was also home to a number of mystical societies, and one of the most powerful mystics was Jakob Boehme (1575–1624), who wrote prolifically and then was censured as a heretic by the Lutheran Church. "Gnostic magical beliefs were espoused by secret societies," many "founded on those of the Middle Ages," according to the *Encyclopedia of Occultism & Parapsychology*.[9] In Gnostic belief, "spirit and matter were opposed to each other, matter being an interruption of the order of the cosmos—and therefore evil," explained Dusty Sklar in *Gods & Beasts: The Nazis & the Occult*.[10] "Matter was not the creation of the supreme god but of . . . an inferior divinity." Gnostic doctrine stated, "The . . . Jewish god was really the devil, responsible for all the world's evil." And so it began.

In the fifteenth century, occultists began employing a new name, the Illuminati, a reference to individuals "who claimed to possess light directly communicated from a higher source or because of abundant human wisdom," noted the *Encyclopedia of Occultism & Parapsychology*.[11] In modern ufological research and adjacent conspiracy theory, the Illuminati were also associated with a group called "The Nine," those in touch with an extraterrestrial race, which provides them with great insight, knowledge of the future, and the power to control events. The Illuminati are at the center of many modern conspiracy theories, but it's interesting to see that they had their beginnings in the very late Middle Ages and at the dawn of the Reformation, a time of great turmoil, pestilence, and social and intellectual foment in Europe.

Even as new scientific discoveries emerged in Europe, the occult continued to grow in strength and popularity throughout the eighteenth century. For example, by the mid-1700s, Rosicrucians and Freemasons were familiar in Russia, and "holy men and mystical cults" had become part of Russia's religious landscape. At the same time, scientists and philosophers who considered themselves rationalists angrily discredited occultism as the accumulation of centuries of superstition and ignorance.

In Europe, the years following the American and French revolutions were marked by new and shifting political alliances that would affect millions for generations to come. "Conditions were created that allowed the rise of the three major superpowers of the nineteenth century," according to Michael Howard in *The Occult Conspiracy*. They were "the Romanovs of Russia, the Habsburgs of the Austro-Hungarian Empire, and the Hohenzollerns of Prussia who became the Kaisers of Germany. Between these great European dynasties [what followed was] bloody conflict" that also involved Britain and France and the pressures ultimately led to World War I. However, history books typically omit or neglect the influence of occultism and secret societies on the rulers of that era. Howard pointed out "only by revealing . . . the occult conspiracy . . . can events be fully understood and placed in their true historical perspective."[12]

Russia was under the rule of the Romanov family for some three centuries, beginning in the 1600s, until the Bolsheviks ousted them in the Russian Revolution of 1917. Their adversaries accused the Romanovs of taking part in witchcraft and having "occult powers." For example, a century earlier, in 1805, when Czar Alexander I ruled, he considered war against Napoleon to be a "divine mission" since it had been predicted by a well-known psychic named Madame de Kruedener. The czar also joined the Habsburg emperor to prevent revolution in Italy. Both leaders were convinced such a revolution was spurred by a secret society named the Carbonari.

Michael Howard explained that Alexander's reason for invading Italy was "to counteract the empire of evil which is spreading by all the occult means at their disposal the satanic spirit which directs it."[13] Ultimately it was Austria that ended the Italian uprisings and sent the Carbonari back into hiding. In 1822, Czar Alexander I converted to Christianity, and believing there was danger to Russia from secret societies, banned Freemasonry and shut Masonic lodges.

After Alexander's death in 1825, his brother Nicholas, no friend of mysticism, assumed power. In 1855, Nicholas's son Alexander II became czar. Unlike his father, he was drawn to religion and the popular interest in spiritualism that had spread from America and England across the

European continent. By 1861, the czar and czarina participated in séances conducted by the famed medium D. D. Home, and joined by author Alexandre Dumas. Home later told of noticing that Czar Alexander had a personal library with "thousands" of books about spirituality and the occult.[14]

In 1872 the czar, Emperor Franz Josef, and Kaiser Wilhelm I joined in a pact that would eventually spell calamity for all three and take Europe on the dark and disastrous road toward World War I. Many historians have suggested that modern Germany was born when the German "nationalist movement" came into being in 1871. As Michael Howard explained, it was a dangerous jumble of "anti-Semitism, extreme nationalism, occult, anti-capitalist, and anti-liberal" dogma. By then there had been rumblings to unite "all German-speaking peoples of Europe."[15]

Also in 1871, King Wilhelm of Prussia became kaiser of the Second German Reich, which intensified the growth of a "pan-German nationalist movement" with its underlying mystical and occult beliefs, many drawn from secret societies. That, in turn, gave birth to National Socialism—the Nazis—during the 1920s. There is "unmistakable evidence of a direct relationship between the Nazis and occultism," Howard maintained.[16]

A strong impact was made on the German ultra-nationalistic and racist movement by Theosophy, founded by Madame Helena Petrovna Blavatsky (1831–1891), the Russian immigrant and controversial medium who settled in New York City and founded the Theosophical Society in 1875. Plump, hot-tempered, and untidy, Blavatsky cared little about Victorian-era propriety. She smoked cigars, used profanity as well as any man, and was obstinate but determined. Those who knew her agreed her outstanding physical feature was her penetrating and hypnotic eyes that people said entranced them.

As a teenager she'd been forced into an arranged marriage with an elderly Russian general whom she quickly left. Blavatsky then roamed through Europe and the East, especially India and Tibet, learning new philosophies, "ancient wisdoms," and taught herself to speak a number of languages. It was during her travels that Blavatsky learned of the Great White Brotherhood, "superhuman adepts or masters," believed by many Theosophists and occultists to have directed the development of humankind.

Blavatsky prophesized a future in which a "spiritually-developed type of human being" would come to be, Michael Howard explained. German nationalists embraced her racial ideas and distorted them into a combination of the occult drawn from Theosophy, virulent anti-Semitism, and the principle of Aryan racial superiority.

When Madame Blavatsky moved to the United States in 1873 one reason was to examine the widely popular interest in spiritualism that had captivated the attention of millions of Americans. Whether she had mediumistic gifts to the extent she insisted is questionable. Some psychic researchers considered her a fraud. Others maintained she had genuine powers. However, few could argue with her singular achievement: the creation of the Theosophical Society. It was a concoction of Hinduism, Tantric yoga, Gnostic belief, Western occultism, and the principles of the secret societies, and it ultimately attracted a substantial following and international influence, particularly in bringing Eastern beliefs to the West.

Among her best-known writings were *Isis Unveiled* and her voluminous *The Secret Doctrine*. She claimed spirit masters dictated her books from a higher plane. But there were those who criticized Blavatsky's occult philosophy for its unyielding hostility toward Christianity. Although she could not have known it in her lifetime, Theosophy was destined to exert a strong influence on the German nationalist movement that became the Nazi Party some thirty years after Blavatsky's death in 1891.[17]

What would attract some in the Nazi leadership to Theosophy? German nationalists eagerly embraced Blavatsky's racial prediction and distorted it into the infamous Nazi belief of Aryan racial superiority or "supermen." They also welcomed Darwin's theory of evolution which, when combined with Madame Blavatsky's racial beliefs, concluded that certain races would survive and evolve, while for other races, such as the Jews, their days were numbered. For the virulently anti-Semitic, racist theories couched in pseudomystical wrappings that supported their twisted thinking were well received.

Also inspiring Blavatsky were popular occult mysteries by author and occultist Sir Edward Bulwer-Lytton (1803–1873). Not only did the Bulwer-Lytton novels influence Theosophists, they also had an effect on the "mystical aspects of German nationalism," according to Howard. Bulwer-Lytton, a Rosicrucian, was a close friend of British Prime Minister Benjamin Disraeli who had a strong curiosity about the occult, secret societies, and conspiracies. In 1856, Disraeli cautioned the House of Commons that secret societies posed a threat to Europe.[18]

That brings us to the Vril Society.[19] In 1871, Bulwer-Lytton wrote an occult novel, *The Coming Race*. The book's plot concerns a "subterranean, socialist utopia ruled by superior beings who had mastered the so-called vril, or life force," Howard explained. As Bulwer-Lytton imagined it, vril was an inexplicable psychic energy that could be controlled by its masters to achieve skills including telepathy and healings. It was not unlike chi, the life force believed in by the Chinese, or prana, subscribed to by Hindus. The vril could also be used for "destructive" purposes such as a "death ray," not unlike the laser or the telepathic force made fun of—but all too real, according to its practitioners—in Jon Ronson's *Men Who Stare at Goats*.[20] The idea of a vril-like death ray also inspired the Serbo-Croatian and later American genius Nikola Tesla to design his own concept of a death ray, beaming high-energy power to distant locations. Tesla's death ray became so popular a concept in the 1930s that it was one of the inspirations for the death ray beamed at Earth from the planet Mongo in the 1936 *Flash Gordon* movie serials.[21]

It was the Vril Society that is credited with being among the early German nationalist organizations to employ the swastika as a symbol or emblem. But even before the vril became co-opted by the Nazis, it existed as a kind of pre-Wiccan society, created by a group of Russian women, who were the adherents to the supernatural theories of Madame Blavatsky. The vril, Bulwer-Lytton's mystical force, was the binding element of Vril Society founders, who claimed to have telepathic powers, and who also advocated the theory of the supremacy of the Aryan race.

As the group of German über-nationalists turned to mysticism and the occult for a source of power, the future Reichsführer Heinrich Himmler, looking for extrinsic evidence that the Aryan race was supreme and destined to rule the world, created the Thule Society, the group—loosely portrayed in the first *Indiana Jones* movie—sought to find evidence of the superiority of the Aryan race in distant corners of the world. They traveled to the Middle East, to India, and to the Arctic, looking for clues to the origin of the Aryans. And it was through their explorations into the mystical beginnings of the Aryans that they would later seek to blend occult with science in their attempt to develop the *wunderwaffe*, the super weapon that would guarantee them victory in the war.

Another one of the better-known occult groups was the Armanen-schaft originated by Guido von List (1848–1919) who fancied himself a descendent of a long heritage of "Nordic warrior magicians . . ." wrote Paul Roland in *The Nazis and the Occult*.[22] Von List had concocted his own premise of a "mysterious ancient race" called "Armanen," explained the *Encyclopedia of Occultism & Parapsychology*. Von List's society also used as its emblem the swastika, and began a "secret occult lodge." Numerous members were fanatical anti-Semites who were part of the "occult underground" that encouraged distorted Nazi racists ideas and fantasies of the Aryan *übermench* or "superman" of Nordic looks and ancestry with blond hair and blue eyes.

Von List also had an association with the Ordo Templi Orientis (OTO), the Order of the Temple in the East, begun between 1895 and 1900 by a pair of German Freemasons. In England, the occultist and magician Aleister Crowley became the leader of the OTO in the early 1900s.[23] Another occult association of note was the Ordo Novi Templi (ONT), the Order of New Templars, started in 1907. It also held malevolent racist attitudes. During the 1920s, as Hitler climbed to power, the ONT was the international coordinator for "far-right groups" in Europe and America. In the 1930s the ONT acted as a "front" for the outlawed National Socialist Party in Austria. Despite that, the ONT was banned by the Nazis in 1941 following the mysterious, failed "peace mission" undertaken by Hitler's Deputy Führer Rudolf Hess, a fervent devotee of astrology. The flight by Hess to Scotland in May 1941, and his capture by the British, infuriated Hitler who ordered a crackdown on occult practitioners throughout the Third Reich.

A branch of the Armanenschaft and the ONT was an occult group known as the "German Order," that began right before the First World War.[24] Like other similar groups, the German Order embraced virulent ultra-right, nationalist, and occult societies, anti-Semitism, and racist beliefs. The German Order was the model for the Thule Society that became a source of influence for the Nazi Party in its early days.[25] There was also serious interest in what was believed to be the "lost continent of Thule," described as the "Nordic Atlantis," supposedly where the Teutonic race began. Not surprisingly, the Nazis coalesced around the "mystical tradition of racial purity, neo-paganism, and Theosophical occultism," and targeted their evil, warped ideas at the masses of ordinary people in

Germany, and then throughout nearly all of Europe as their iron-fisted grasp increased.[26]

This occult tradition blended with the ultra-rightist political movements of the early twentieth century and with a political philosophy of German philosophers, who suggested that in order for the state to preserve its national identity, individual rights must be subsumed to the needs of the state. Foremost among the proponents of this view was German jurist Carl Schmitt, who ultimately became the president of the Nazi jurists, justifying the concept of the autocratic state under the führer as a political necessity, especially in the two decades after the Treaty of Versailles.

Before he left Germany and eventually wound up in the United States, teaching at the New School for Social Research and then at the University of Chicago, where he influenced a generation of American Neoconservatives such as former Deputy Secretary of Defense Paul Wolfowitz, Leo Strauss was one of the intellectual political philosophers behind National Socialism. In fact, it was Strauss's political legacy regarding the supremacy of the state over the individual that lay at the heart of the Neoconservative movement which drove much of the political policy of the early part of the last decade.

Even before political philosophers Strauss and Schmitt laid the groundwork for National Socialism, it was the secret occult societies that were surreptitiously at work to overthrow the "old European empires" that dated back to the early nineteenth century, Michael Howard explained. Historical events aided them at every turn. Between 1900 and the start of the First World War, Europe was thrown into turmoil. "The old alliances which had held nineteenth century Europe together" were collapsing. By the time World War I began, Russia and Germany were "bitter enemies," Howard noted. Efforts at various alliances to avoid war had failed, and Germany reached out to Rumania and Serbia hoping to secure itself.

But Serbia's participation resulted in the assassinations of the Archduke Franz Ferdinand and his wife in Sarajevo in June 1914. The assassins all belonged to a secret nationalist group fighting for Serbian independence. The consequence of the murders was global pandemonium and the outbreak of the First World War.[27]

Dr. Gérard Encausse was both a physician and occultist (1865–1916), born in Spain, and schooled in Paris. He'd briefly been a member of the

Theosophical Society, and was also a student of magic and alchemy. Before the Bolshevik Revolution in 1917, he conducted séances for the Russian rulers, Czar Nicholas and his wife, the czarina. Encausse was said to have communicated with the spirit of Czar Nicholas's father, Alexander III. Nicholas sought his late father's advice on how to cope with the rash of growing civilian and military disturbances in Russia. The spirit of Alexander III advised his son to be tough with the strife or it would worsen and endanger the czar's power.

Czar Nicholas was part of a growing trend of aristocratic occult enthusiasts. During the latter part of the nineteenth and early twentieth centuries, Russia's upper class was enthralled by spiritualism. Thus mediums, healers, prophets, and occultists were especially popular. However, Encausse came to the conclusion that Czar Nicholas was becoming over dependent on occultism. He was especially troubled by word that the czar and czarina had fallen within the spell of the mesmerizing and enigmatic Russian monk, Gregory Rasputin (1869–1916) who'd found his way into the royal court. Rasputin, the dark and brooding monk with the hypnotic stare, has become a legend and was popularized in motion pictures.

In 1912, the Tsarevitch, the hemophiliac young son of the royal couple, was accidentally injured and Rasputin miraculously healed the boy. While that endeared him to the czar and czarina, many people feared Rasputin had occult abilities. The eccentric, wandering, and disheveled monk went on to wield tremendous influence in the royal court of Nicholas II. Foes spread rumors that Rasputin had evil powers, favored Germany, and was a "secret agent" for the German kaiser. The mysterious monk apparently had a premonition that his life was in danger, and what that would mean for the fate of the Russian royal family, the Romanovs. True to his intuition, Rasputin was the victim of a conspiracy that assassinated him in 1916. Following his death, the Russian people regarded Rasputin as a martyr. The next year, Czar Nicholas II was overthrown in the Bolshevik Revolution.[28] The Romanovs were murdered and Russia evolved into the Soviet Union. The Soviet Union itself collapsed in the late twentieth century.

The defeat of Germany in 1918 by the British, French, and Americans ended World War I, but left Germany thoroughly demoralized. The country was in ruins, physically, emotionally, and financially. Returning soldiers, many of them wounded, barely recognized their devastated homeland. These were lost and disgraced men, hungry for a livelihood and purpose in life. In addition, the Versailles peace treaty that ended the war not only brought Germany to its knees, but the harsh terms of reparations—five billion dollars—a staggering sum to be repaid as punishment, which was overwhelming for a conquered country on the brink of starvation.[29]

The armistice, signed in 1919, called for Germany to disarm, eliminate nearly its entire military, agree to new border limits, acknowledge a new, independent Poland, and relinquish its colonies in Africa and elsewhere. "Germany [was also required] to acknowledge responsibility for the war and for all the damage caused by it," explained Edward Keleher in *Great Events from History*. It was known as the "war guilt clause." As a footnote, neither the United States nor Russia "officially recognized the treaty and [thus] played no role in upholding the peace" agreement, Keleher added.[30]

Both Germany and the Allies were bitter in the wake of the bloody and destructive war. American animosity toward Germany showed itself in small ways when the New York Philharmonic Society banned the playing of musical works by "living German composers." Politically, however, German Americans were subject to new scrutiny by the Justice Department under the supervision of J. Edgar Hoover. Called the "Palmer Raids," suspected German sympathizers were rounded up and investigated as agents provacateurs trying to establish a fifth column in America. Hoover would have similar fears about Germans just after World War II when former Nazi scientists were brought to America to carry on the German rocketry program.

The First World War had taken an enormous toll on populations in Europe and America. In all, 8.5 million people were killed, another 21 million were wounded, and 7.5 million were prisoners or missing. The total cost of the war was nearly $338 billion. The four allied nations that drafted the peace treaty hoped to thwart future German aggression by forcing the terms on Germany. But the humiliating loss and the conditions demanded by the treaty opened the gates that would unleash the fury of a group of right-wing military officers who sought as their spokesman a young and charismatic Adolf Hitler.[31]

Who was Adolf Hitler? How did he rise from virtual obscurity to become one of the most powerful, despised, and intriguing dictators the world has ever known? And as he emerged as the spokesman for a beaten German population, what part did the occult play in his ruthless climb to German chancellery and his ultimate step as the most infamous mass murderer in human history? Was Hitler actually psychic? Did he engage in the dark arts of satanism and black magic?

Many people believe Hitler was the work of the devil, while others concluded he was a psychopath who surrendered to his most primitive and evil impulses without any supernatural input. Did the devil grab Hitler or did Hitler reach out for the devil? Strangely, Hitler would later say he did not believe in the devil or the concept of evil.

What about the miscreants, misfits, and thugs who surrounded the warped dictator? Did they delve into the occult and the paranormal? Might they also have been creations of some demonic force? Or were they acting out of the darkest, most negative parts of their psyches? Is the relationship with Satan a psychiatric disease, a conscious or willful decision, or have some people allowed themselves to become portals for evil or negative entities? As the late Father Malachi Martin one showed, people can, indeed, turn themselves into portals for evil, allowing their bodies to be taken over in demonic possessions.

Adolf Hitler was born near Linz, Austria, on April 20, 1889, to Klara and Alois Hitler, whose last name is sometimes given as Schicklgruber. Alois, a fifty-two-year-old Austrian customs official, was twenty-three years older than Klara, his third wife.

According to Klara, Adolf was a "sickly baby," and a source of worry to his doting mother. However, a family maid recalled that Adolf was a "healthy and lively" child. Hitler's health in his early years may seem insignificant. However, if he suffered a childhood trauma to his head or an illness accompanied by one or more high fevers, it is possible that a part of his brain was activated or rerouted to cause or enhance psychic power. It is not unusual in the study of those with psychic or mediumistic abilities to find that some injury or insult to the brain has triggered ESP or some other form of paranormal aptitude. How the abilities are used— for good or evil—is another question.

Adolf was just three years old when his father, Alois, was given a job promotion that required the family to move from Austria to Germany.

"Living in a German city and playing with German children made a lasting mark on [young Adolf]," wrote John Toland in his highly acclaimed biography *Adolf Hitler*.[32]

Hitler's relationship with his mother remained close, until her passing from breast cancer in 1908 when he was nineteen. Klara's death left Hitler devastated. His relationship with his father, Alois, was another matter. Various authors and historians have described Alois as "authoritarian," "very strict," "exacting and pedantic . . . most unapproachable," Toland noted. Needless to say, father and son were not close. Alois wanted Adolf to make a career in civil service, as he had. But when Adolf was only eleven years old, he spoke up to his stern father in a confrontation that made it clear the boy had no intention of life as a government employee. In fact, Adolf was not motivated toward school or a serious livelihood, and resisted his father's wishes.[33]

As a youth, Adolf was already described as "resentful [and] discontented," wrote Robert Wistrich in *Who's Who in Nazi Germany*. What's more, Adolf was "moody, lazy, of unstable temperament [and] deeply hostile" toward his rigid father.[34] Hitler stopped attending school when he was sixteen. His dream then was to become a painter. Around 1908, he left home for Vienna, one of Europe's most cultured and cosmopolitan cities. He would remain there until 1913. His plan was to attend the Viennese Academy of Fine Arts but he was turned down. It was a refusal he took badly, blaming the school rather than what was viewed at that time as his lack of artistic talent.

Hitler's next five years in Vienna have been described in conflicting ways, depending on the historian or author explaining the events. The most common version is that Hitler's time in Vienna was spent in "misery and woe," leading to what Robert Wistrich described as a "bohemian, vagabond existence." Living from "hand to mouth," Hitler eked out a meager living by selling his sketches and postcards of Vienna's impressive architecture. When he wasn't selling his drawings in "low taverns," Hitler, discouraged and alone, found sleep in wretched men's hostels.[35]

He already was virulently anti-Semitic and anti-Marxist, and when able, he would visit inexpensive coffee shops and cafés where he'd expound his warped political beliefs to anyone willing to listen. Foremost was his hatred of Jews and mania with "purity of blood"—a lifelong obsession.[36] Whatever Hitler found wrong with German society, be it "corruption, prostitution, democracy, Marxism, culture, politics, or the economy," Wistrich wrote, it was the fault of the Jews for whom Hitler's "pathological hatred" shaped his worldview. In his disturbed mind, it was the "Jewish conspiracy" that would weaken Germany and destroy Aryan purity. Toland pointed out that Hitler had a morbid fear that one of his grandparents might have been Jewish.

The other, lesser-told version of Hitler's life in Vienna is not quite as desperate and poverty-stricken as the first description. According to this account, Hitler had sufficient money after his mother's death to live well. In fact, Hitler had considerable time to lie around, and indulge his distorted political positions and anti-Semitic vitriol. He also had ample income so that he was not forced to sell his postcard pictures.

We don't know which is the more accurate depiction of Hitler's Vienna years. However, author John Toland pointed out that Hitler preferred his cohorts and the masses, as he called Germans, to believe the first scenario. Why? It sounded more inspiring for people to believe that their leader struggled and starved on his climb to becoming the tyrannical leader—the Führer. In either case, Hitler finally left Vienna in May 1913 and headed for Munich, Germany, a hotbed for the German nationalist movement.[37]

In 1914, when war erupted in Europe, Hitler joined the Bavarian Infantry Regiment, and proved his bravery in battle. He was no coward, John Toland pointed out. Although Hitler received the Iron Cross for his courage, the highest rank he achieved was lance corporal. His military service was not without its dangers and injuries. He was wounded twice, seriously gassed, and hospitalized for three months as a result. As well, for a brief time he lost his sight.

On the other hand, Hitler's own psychic ability saved his life on more than one occasion, according to Toland, who shared the following incidents with coauthor Joel Martin in a rare interview years ago.

Toland said that one night during the First World War when the military unit Hitler belonged to bunked down for the night, Hitler moved a good distance from his comrades. He had a strange sensation that he'd face serious danger if he stayed with the other soldiers, as he usually did. As they all slept, a loud shattering noise shook the ground and awakened Hitler. When he looked in the direction of his fellow soldiers he saw the destruction. An allied shell had struck where the group slept, killing them. Hitler's prescience saved his life, as it would often in the years ahead.

Parapsychologists define such experiences as premonitions, while skeptics dismiss them as coincidental. Toland believed Hitler had a life-saving premonition, one of many Hitler had until nearly the end of his life. For those who associate such psychic incidents with religious belief, there is surprise that someone as hate-filled as Adolf Hitler would receive supernatural help. However, history and paranormal research have shown that many psychic events are neutral, and may occur to people whether their intentions are good or bad.

On an earlier occasion, when Hitler was still in Vienna, he went one day to a public lavatory, Toland explained. Once again, "something" inexplicable suggested to Hitler to move from one urinal to another. Hitler was proven correct in his caution. Moments later, a bomb or some form of explosive device detonated. Had Hitler not moved, he would have been seriously injured or killed. It appears Hitler's experience was a premonition.[38]

In the years following the war, and through the 1920s, Germany's lot did not improve, its strength and resources sapped by four years of bloody fighting. In this climate of physical and psychological humiliation, many Germans were ready for a mystical, mesmerizing, and strong nationalist leader to take advantage of the shambles that once was the great German nation of such notables as Beethoven, Bach, Schiller, Goethe, Planck, and Einstein. Now it faced unemployment and hunger. Hitler fumed about Germany's loss, as well as the failed German revolution at the time. He "was convinced that fate had chosen him to rescue a humiliated [Germany] from the shackles of the Versailles Treaty and from Bolsheviks and Jews," explained Robert Wistrich.[39]

Hitler's early sense of destiny has long been a subject of debate. Was he fated to rule Germany by some larger mystical or supernatural power? Or was his ultimate control of Germany caused by his own vision and will? As we shall see shortly, a number of psychics and astrologers had predicted that a powerful leader would emerge to raise Germany from the ashes of defeat. Was Adolf Hitler the one chosen for the monumental task of rebuilding the shattered nation? He certainly thought divine intervention had destined him to lead Germany. A number of world leaders and dictators have revealed having such sensations, but whether they are genuine or delusions is debatable.[40]

In Munich in 1919, Hitler, still in military service, was given the task to spy on political parties that were considered "nationalistic," a problem especially in post-war Munich. One of the gatherings Hitler was assigned to surreptitiously observe was a small group known as the German Workers Party. It had fewer than fifty members. Hitler was enthralled with what he heard, and soon after joined the group rather than spy on it. He soon changed its name to the National Socialist German Workers Party (NSDAP) and by July 1921, forced his way to the position of chairman. He also introduced a new salutation, "Heil," and a party symbol—the swastika. The groundwork was laid for the Nazi Party.

Meanwhile, with Germany in chaos, a new constitution was drawn that created a "liberal democratic regime," wrote Edward Keleher. It provided for a German president and a two-house legislature. It was the president who had the right to name the chancellor, Keleher explained. Because the constitution was written in Weimar, Germany, it adopted the name the "Weimar Constitution" and the "Weimar Republic."[41]

At the same time, in Munich, Hitler discovered that he had a commanding gift for public speaking. By November 1921, Hitler had become the leader—führer—of the group that had grown to a more imposing three thousand members. He also organized "strong-arm squads" for maintaining order within the party and to intimidate and disperse challengers and rivals. From these bands of coarse thugs developed the notorious Nazi storm troopers, and the dreaded SS in their menacing black shirts. When Hitler spoke to those assembled, he mainly railed against the Versailles Treaty, Marxists, and of course, his most hated enemy, the Jews on whom all of Germany's crises could be blamed.

The NSDAP priority was to merge "the myth of Aryan race supremacy and extreme [German] nationalism," explained Robert Wistrich.[42] Hitler's next goal was to overthrow the Weimar government that he believed was on the brink of collapse due to its own inability to instill a sense of national self-respect among the German people. Hitler also saw German society sinking into what he said was a moral decay of debauchery and sexual scandal.

In November 1923, with his sense of self-importance firmly in place, Hitler joined with other nationalist groups to lead what was known as the Munich Beer Hall Putsch, or violent uprising, hoping to bring down the Bavarian government in Munich. When the huge mob burst into the beer hall, Hitler shot his gun in the air and hollered that he was now in charge of a new interim government that would lead a revolution in opposition to what Hitler called "Red Berlin," a reference to the much-hated Marxists.[43]

But Hitler's plans went awry when the German nationalists were confronted by a large contingent of police who opened fire, leaving sixteen people dead. Hitler's Munich Putsch had failed. He was arrested, brought to trial in early 1924 and took the occasion to make a party line harangue in which he blasted the prosecutor and predicted he would emerge victorious. Then he was sentenced to five years in Landsberg Prison. This time it appeared that either no premonitions helped him—or he ignored them.

It was there that Hitler began work on a book that would become widely known as the "Nazi Bible," *Mein Kampf [My Struggle]*. In Landsberg, he dictated his manuscript to his obedient follower and sycophant, Rudolf Hess (1894–1987), an astrology buff, who would rise to become the deputy leader of the Nazi Party, even though he was described as "colorless and unassertive," by author John Toland. Hess joined the party in 1920 after hearing a speech Hitler gave and becoming deeply impressed. Hess, who had been with Hitler for the abortive Putsch, slavishly copied nearly every word for *Mein Kampf* that most historians have described as an unsophisticated, ill-considered jumble of primitive "Social Darwinism, racial myth, anti-Semitism, and *lebensraum* [living space] fantasy," in the words of Robert Wistrich. It was Hess who took the idea of *lebensraum* from a college professor. By 1939, *Mein Kampf* had sold five million copies, in a dozen languages, earning Hitler enough in royalties to make him a millionaire. Every German soldier was given a copy as "inspiration."

Hitler served only nine months of his prison sentence and then was released. He emerged from Landsberg quite differently than when he entered. He'd become astute, notably in the art of political strategy, a far cry from the vagabond that once wandered aimlessly through the streets of Vienna. Hitler now had made grandiose plans to control Germany. But this time, he told confidants, he would gain power by political means, and not by the kind of clash that ended in the failure of the Munich Beer Hall Putsch. Hitler's idea was to legally undermine the Weimar government. Then, as Hitler foresaw it, the government would be in his control. He could then assemble a "mass movement," combining legislative power with fear and intimidation enforced on the German people by his Nazi brutes.

In *Mein Kampf,* Hitler warned the world of his sinister plans. He was going to "destroy the German Republic, abolish democracy, stamp out workers' free-trade unions, establish himself as supreme dictator, and would 'settle' the Jews," famed author William L. Shirer wrote in *The Rise and Fall of Adolf Hitler.* Unfortunately, few world leaders bothered to read *Mein Kampf*—and they certainly did not take Hitler, with his Charlie Chaplin mustache, seriously. If they had, would world history and the coming carnage of the Second World War and Holocaust have been avoided?

One of the more credible prophecies in those years was offered by an apparition of the Virgin Mary in 1917 to three children in Fatima, Portugal.[44] During the famed event three predictions were made. One prophecy warned of a Second World War or conflagration to come unless people turned back to their faith in the Church. Obviously, the prediction fell on deaf ears. Interestingly the second prophecy concerned the spread of Communism, and the third, revealed by the Vatican in the past decade, described the assassination of the pope.

During the 1920s, the German economy rose and fell, then rose again. At times when life seemed to be improving, the Nazis' grip on the country weakened. It was when Germany's financial system plunged, resulting in steep unemployment and high inflation that Nazi policies seemed more appealing to the masses. So, "the world-wide depression which began with the Wall Street crash in 1929 gave Hitler the opportunity he'd been waiting for," Shirer noted. "The economic life of the West became paralyzed. Banks failed. Business firms went under. Trade came to a stop. Millions were thrown out of work."[45]

It was worse in Germany than in the United States, and that was precisely what Hitler needed. He was able to take advantage of the abysmal conditions with his plea to desperate Germans. Hitler countered efforts for a moderate German government by declaring that a Nazi government would refuse to pay reparations and what's more, it would shred the hated Versailles Treaty. He also promised that every German would have a job, and businesses would come back. The German masses were misled by Hitler's deceit, which elevated the Nazis to a position of political power they'd not known before.

However, in 1932 when Hitler ran for president against the popular elderly German war hero, Field Marshal Paul von Hindenburg, who faced reelection, Hitler lost. That only knocked Hitler down, but not out. Hitler would never gain the majority of votes he required to become Germany's chancellor, thus he resorted to trickery and pressure instead. The shadowy political deals he made eventually led von Hindenburg to legally name Hitler the chancellor of Germany in January 1933.

Hitler's dream had come true, and it would prove to be the world's nightmare. A month later, in February 1933, the German parliament or Reichstag was set ablaze. The Nazis blamed the "great Reichstag fire" on the Communists. It is generally assumed that it was the Nazis who set the Reichstag fire, however they managed to persuade the majority of Germans that the Communists were to blame.[46] Amazingly, Hitler believed God was on his side. In an odd synchronicity, Franklin Delano Roosevelt was inaugurated U.S. president on March 4, 1933. The next day, Hitler won absolute power over Germany.

Through more chicanery and coercion, Hitler soon purged his political enemies and became the sole ruler of Germany so that by summer 1933 only the Nazi Party remained. However, there was unrest and dissension within Nazi ranks. The storm troopers (officially the SA) were pressing for a "radical Nazi revolution," and then wanted to become the "new German army," Shirer explained. There were an estimated four million storm troopers by the close of 1933, too many to ignore.[47]

Finally, during the summer of 1934, Hitler beat back the disobedient storm troopers through a series of political machinations and initiated a "Nazi Blood Purge." He ordered the leaders of the storm troopers, including Ernst Röhm (1887–1934) and other enemies, to be executed. By the end of 1934 Germany was in the hands of only Hitler and those he deemed loyal. The Nazi Party could now get on with its other insidious goals, particularly persecuting Jews, promoting the concept of the "Master Race," Hitler's obsession with Aryan superiority, and planning for world domination.[48]

In the United States, there was relatively little interest in Hitler or Germany's internal politics. America, desperately trying to survive the Great Depression under President Franklin Delano Roosevelt's leadership and "New Deal" programs, gave scant thought to the problems of Germany. In fact, many Americans considered themselves isolationists and wanted no part of "entanglements whatsoever with foreign powers," wrote Robert Goldston in *The Great Depression*. Even in the late 1930s, "neither the Congress nor the American people were prepared to support a . . . program [to] contain European fascism," Goldston pointed out.[49]

The isolationists could boast such prominent names as Charles A. Lindbergh, Jr., Henry Ford, and Joseph P. Kennedy. FDR, however, was an "internationalist," and the Neutrality Act of 1935 became anguish for him and those wise enough to sense disaster ahead. Many American industrialists, business leaders, and bankers despised FDR for his New Deal programs. There was more than one attempt to overthrow the Roosevelt administration, and at least one attempt on FDR's life.

What's more, anti-Semitic and racist sentiment in Germany hardly caused a ripple in the United States. We had more than our share of both on this side of the Atlantic. Hitler didn't invent anti-Semitism; he merely took advantage of it. Even those in the United States who condemned Hitler's anti-Jewish edicts were reluctant to impose any sanctions against Germany. Names like Henry Ford and Joseph P. Kennedy, along with many Southerners in the Congress, fervently supported anti-Semitism and anti-Black racism. On radio, there were several anti-Jewish commentators in the 1930s, notably the out-of-control Father Charles Coughlin, the "radio priest."[50] In fact, the Nazi-leaning German-American Bund had many followers. Even in New York City with its large Jewish population, the Bunds could attract thousands to their anti-Semitic, pro-Hitler rallies and lectures.

For those who delude themselves in thinking the atrocities committed by the Nazis were unique to Germany, they could not be more mistaken or badly informed. In fact, John Toland told us that Hitler's evil plans for the "Final Solution," the extermination of millions of Jews, Gypsies, and homosexuals, "were inspired by the U.S. government's suppression of the American Indians."[51]

Throughout the 1930s, Hitler expanded his power. Anti-Semitism increased to a fever pitch, Jews were viciously persecuted and deported to die in newly built concentration camps, and German industry was secretly assembling a vast war machine, in defiance of the Versailles peace treaty and financed in part by loans set up by American financiers such as John Foster Dulles, Herbert Lehman, and Prescott Bush. In fact, Wall Street liked investing in Hitler's building of his war machine.[52]

As Hitler flexed his muscles in Europe, one after the other, European countries fell: Part of Czechoslovakia and Austria were the first to collapse under the Nazi terror in 1938, while England, France, and the United States looked the other way, buying into Hitler's claim of *lebensraum*— the need for more living space for German-speaking peoples in those countries. Appeasing Hitler's madness seemed safer than another war. It wasn't. Finally England laid down the ultimatum. Inasmuch as Chamberlain's "peace in our time" mission to Germany had failed, if Hitler invaded Poland, England would go to war against it. Hitler took the dare.

When Poland fell to the Nazis in 1939, it finally marked the start of World War II, just as the apparition had predicted in Fatima, Portugal, in 1917. Then Holland, the Scandinavian countries, Belgium, Luxembourg, and France fell under the steel fist of the Nazis, and on it went. Not since the Roman Empire had so many nations been under the domination of one power.

To secure his eastern flank, Hitler made an agreement with Josef Stalin for peace with the Soviet Union. In exchange, the Soviets would receive part of Poland. With his eastern front no longer a threat, Hitler was free to march west into France, flanking the Maginot Line by invading France through Belgium. France crumbled and England had to retreat, pulling its soldiers out at Dunkirk.

Hitler said that he never really trusted his general staff, calling them lazy, elitish, and cowardly. The German general staff had an equal contempt for Hitler. Hitler maintained throughout the war that his prescient abilities enabled him to see outcomes that his generals could not. For example, his general staff strongly advised him not to invade France, citing the weather and the terrain that would slow up the panzer division's armored columns. Hitler persisted, however, and forced his generals to invade. France fell very quickly.[53]

But if Hitler's self-described ability to see the outcome of his decisions well in advance succeeded in France, it failed utterly when he contemplated an invasion of the Soviet Union. His idea was to succeed where Napoleon had failed by advancing across a long front running north to south and seizing the European section of the Soviet Union. Even the timing, which Hitler thought would win him a victory before the winter of 1941, was a miscalculation. Stalin was quoted as saying that even as

Hitler advanced toward the Ukraine, Stalin's two strongest allies—January and February—would eventually defeat the Wehrmacht. And by the time the Japanese bombed Pearl Harbor in December 1941, and the United States declared war on Japan, Hitler, who then declared war on the United States, had calculated himself into his greatest blunder. If he had relied on any occult abilities, perhaps he had forced them or had led himself to believe that what he wanted was what his visions were telling him. By 1942, in what Winston Churchill had called "the hinge of fate," the tide had turned against the Germans on the eastern front, Montgomery was pushing Rommel back across North Africa, and Patton's army had joined the fight and was about to invade Sicily from Africa. By 1943, the German general staff knew the war had been lost.

John Toland shared with us several of Hitler's prescient experiences.[54] In 1939, a bomb exploded in a beer hall, right after Hitler had a feeling he should leave. A notable premonition occurred in July 1944, when the end of the war was only a year away and Germany had not yet been able to deploy any of its "wonder weapons." Hitler could not stand any criticism of his decisions, and it was obvious to those near him that he was in failing physical and mental condition, and the war was a lost cause. A group of Nazi officers secretly planned to blow up the table in Hitler's Reichstag war room where the führer obsessively pored over his battle plans with generals and other aides by his side. Thus, the Nazi regime would topple, and the agonizing war would finally end.

The explosive devices were placed in a briefcase near where Hitler always stood, and when the case detonated, Hitler would be killed. On the day the plot was to be carried out, for some inexplicable reason, Hitler walked to the other side of the large wooden table. The explosion ignited on time; however, Hitler suffered only minor injuries since his premonition told him where to stand in order to be safe. This is a version that traditional history books rarely allow to be presented. Such is the fate of the paranormal.

Even in the final months of the war, however, the German military machine was still hoping to deploy its most powerful new weapons: the atomic bomb, the guided missile, the sea-launched missile, and a weapon shrouded in mystery but colored, still, by the occult beginnings of Nazism on the Vril and the Thule societies. This weapon was called *"Die Glocke,"* or "the Bell."[55]

As historian and World War II researcher Igor Witkowski explained to History Channel's *UFO Hunters* in their episode about Nazi UFOs, the Bell, or *Die Glocke*, is one of the most mysterious stories coming out of the Wehrmacht's attempt to develop the ultimate weapon. What was it? According to Igor Witkowski in his book *Truth about the Wunderwaffe*, and author Nick Cook in *The Hunt for Zero Point*, as well as author J. P. Farrell, who cites Witkowski, the Bell was either a craft or an actual time machine that was powered by counterrotating cylinders containing a substance called Red Mercury. The Germans referred to it as Xerum 525. The radiation produced by the counterrotating cylinders was so intense, or created a torsion field that was so intense, that the German engineers had to enclose the device construction chamber deep inside the Riese Mine in the Owl Mountains in Poland, far away from Allied bombing raids that were destroying German factories and weapons plants.

There is much conjecture concerning just what the Bell was supposed to do or what kind of weapon it was or even what it looked like. Witkowski described the object as a ceramic-covered bell-shaped object about nine meters in size that enclosed two counterrotating cylinders. The energy field generated could have been strong enough to serve as an antigravity field, allowing the object to fly in completely unconventional ways. Witkowski also hypothesized to the *UFO Hunters* team that the energy field could have generated a time warp allowing the object to travel in time. Was that its true function? Could a weapon whose development consumed so many lives of concentration camp slave laborers and Nazi scientists themselves and still under development during the final weeks of World War II as the Soviets closed in on Berlin have been the very weapon that could have won the war by destroying the enemy before the war had actually begun? Imagine traveling back in time to assassinate Winston Churchill, Josef Stalin, or Franklin Roosevelt.

Or was the Bell an escape mechanism, a pod capable of space travel to evacuate the top Nazi leadership to the extraterrestrial home of the Aryan race, the planet Aldebaran? This planet, the Vril and the Thule speculated, was the real genesis of the Aryans. As the war closed in on the Germans and the scientists sought to preserve the secrets that they had so carefully protected during the final years of the war, escape to a distant planet, had that planet actually existed, might have been the plan.

Igor Witkowski suggested that the idea for the Bell arose from the

Thule Society's study of the ancient Vedic texts as they looked for clues to the origin of the Aryan race. They found the stories of the Vimana, ancient flying machines whose appearances dominate the epics of Indian legend. These two-storied windowed craft are so prevalent in Indian epic poetry that one has to wonder whether the poets actually saw these craft or learned stories in an oral tradition from those who had seen them. According to Witkowski, these craft were powered by Red Mercury, the heavy metal liquid that generated a radiation or torsion field so powerful, those inside the field were killed.

The members of the Thule Society actually traveled to India to study the Sanskrit and to examine the poetry for clues to the origin of the Aryans. Thus, the development based on the concept of the Vimana and the legends of Aldebaran, which, according to the Thule, was the real home of the Aryans. From Aldebaran, the Aryans migrated to Earth and made their home beneath the planet's surface in "inner Earth" and could be reached by secret passages beneath the poles. The Nazi Bell was said to have been the vehicle based upon these ancient legends.

There are so many theories regarding the real purpose of the Bell that even the researchers can't come to a single conclusion. Nick Cook suggested that it was turned over to the United States as part of a deal with Nazi scientists. Witkowski suggested to the *UFO Hunters* that it was an antigravity device that could deliver weapons of mass destruction to any enemy capital in the world. Farrell suggested that it was a time machine that turned up in rural Pennsylvania twenty years after the war. Still others suggested that whatever it was meant to be at its inception, the Bell, because it disappeared shortly before the end of the war, was an escape capsule. However, not even the Nazi scientists managing the project described the particular function of the Bell. The only complete description of the importance of the Bell was left by an SS officer who was tried by the KGB in Poland for war crimes. This officer, Jakob Sporrenberg, provided details of the Bell to Polish intelligence and was the only source of information regarding the Bell.

If the Bell was indeed the *wunderwaffe* with trememdous power, what happened to it? Did the Allies capture it? Did the Soviets get it? The fact that it seems to have simply disappeared without a trace also seems to belie its existence. Or does it?

While Igor Witkowski also maintains that the Bell was smuggled to

South America on board a huge Junkers transport plane, a German scientist named Axel Stuhl suggested to the *UFO Hunters* that the physics of the device would have lent credence to its function as a time machine. But if it were a time machine, where did it go? One clue might lie in the identity of one of the Bell's project managers who was secreted out of Germany as part of Operation Paperclip at the end of the war and turned up working for NASA in the 1960s.

This scientist and SS officer was Kurt Debus, an engineer by training, who was reputed to be one of the project managers on the Bell project in the Riese Mine. Debus was a developer of the army's Redstone rocket, the Atlas rocket, and the Saturn booster and became one of the officers at Cape Kennedy in the 1960s. He was a high NASA official during the time when a bell-shaped, violet-blue glowing object suddenly appeared in the skies over Canada in December 1965. The object, seemingly under intelligent control, crossed the American border and came to a crash landing in a rural town outside of Pittsburgh called Kecksburg. Many residents saw the object land and more than a few rushed to the spot where it came to rest. One truck driver, who talked to the *UFO Hunters* about his experience, actually stood next to the object, saw the violet-blue glow, and said he could make out strange lettering around the base of the object. He said that from the moment he stood next to that object to this very day, he experienced serious medical problems as a result of radiation exposure.

On the night of the Kecksburg landing, residents say the army arrived in great force, closing down the area and even turning away local fire-fighting and police units. A truck driver using one of the rural routes on the way to an early morning delivery said that he was stopped at gunpoint by a soldier and told to turn away. The other odd aspect to this entire incident is the reported presence of NASA personnel. More than one resident said that he could see NASA insignia on the jumpsuits people on the recovery team were wearing. They supervised the loading of the object onto an army flatbed truck and escorted it, with emergency lights flashing, out of Pennsylvania toward Wright-Patterson Air Force Base in nearby Dayton, Ohio. The NASA Cape Kennedy launch supervisor at that time was Kurt Debus, the very individual who was the supervisor of the Nazi Bell project in Poland. That doesn't seem like a coincidence.

Could it be that the Nazi Bell was never physically removed from the Riese Mine but, under its own power, managed to slip away through time, going forward twenty years until it was recovered by NASA in Kecksburg, Pennsylvania? If so, perhaps Kurt Debus, a prized asset in Operation Paperclip, was finally reunited with his project after twenty years, this time back in the United States where he could shepherd it through development. It could mean that the United States has had a time machine in its possession for over forty-five years, a machine so deadly, with such exotic technology that we don't dare use it. Or do we?

Despite the existence of Nazi superweapons, the Germans ultimately lost the war. Peace finally returned to a devastated Europe in May 1945 with Hitler's defeat, followed by Japan's surrender three months later. Hitler and his longtime mistress, Eva Braun, whom he married only the day before on April 29, took their lives in the führer's bunker under war-torn Berlin on April 30, 1945. Hitler shot himself. Braun took poison. She was thirty-three at the time. Their bodies were cremated and, it's believed, the Russians took the charred remains. The Third Reich, supposed to last a thousand years, collapsed after only twelve years. About that prediction, Hitler was dead wrong.

Obviously Adolf Hitler did not act alone. While the German people suffered mightily as a result of the Second World War, most Germans paid little attention to growing rumors of atrocities against the Jews. As John Toland explained, any questions were answered with Nazi lies created by its vast propaganda machine. But who were those deputies who conspired with Hitler? Who were his closest aides, and what was their connection to or involvement with the occult?

One of his close allies was Rudolf Hess. When Hess was still in college, he wrote a prize-winning paper detailing "how must the man be constituted who will lead Germany back to her old heights?" "Hess found his ideal in Hitler," Toland said.[56]

There is no secret that the reclusive Hess was a strong believer in astrology and the "influence of the stars on his personal and political life," according to Paul Roland, quoting a former professor of geography, Karl Haushofer (1869–1946), who taught Hess at the University of Munich.[57] Hess also had a fascination with ESP, especially clairvoyance, and was interested in alternative medicine. Some of his Nazi collaborators secretly laughed at Hess, tagging him "odd." Hess once asked for soil samples from throughout Germany in order to spread them under his baby's crib; it was supposedly a very old "magical blessing ritual," explained Roland. Hitler largely ignored Hess's paranormal interests as long as they were held privately. That later changed.

In May 1941, Hitler's deputy, Rudolf Hess, one night covertly borrowed a Messerschmitt 110 airplane and flew it to Britain. Hess crash-landed in Scotland and was immediately arrested. He explained he was on a self-appointed mission hoping to forge peace between Germany and England. No one has ever determined with certainty what prompted Hess's deluded plan, especially at a time when Britain was fighting for its very existence in the wake of the deadly and destructive Nazi air attacks on English cities. Hess was charged as a POW and imprisoned. He would spend the remainder of his long life in Spandau Prison in West Berlin, never repentant for any of his behavior. At the Nuremberg war trials Hess asserted, "I regret nothing." He died at Spandau in 1987, at the age of ninety-three.[58]

But, there still lingers the question of what motivated Hess to fly to Britain? An enraged Hitler snarled that Hess had "gone crazy," and blamed the bizarre event on astrologers who, because they opposed the Third Reich, purposely duped the gullible Hess. One possibility is that his former professor influenced Hess. Karl Haushofer claimed he'd experienced a vision of Hess in an English castle "bringing peace between the two great Nordic nations," as Paul Roland explained the strange story.[59] Haushofer had become disenchanted with the Hitler regime and that might have been the professor's intention for deceiving Hess, and embarrassing the Third Reich, but that was never proven.

After Hess's flight to England, Hitler became indifferent to astrology. Nonetheless he brooded about Hess's betrayal, and a month later declared a ban on every type and kind of "non-Aryan occultism." "Hundreds of occult booksellers, fortune-tellers, alternative medical practitioners, Theosophists," and others were dragged off by the Gestapo in the dead of night and grilled for hours to determine their loyalty—or lack of it—to the Nazi regime. Books, files, divination tools, and other psychic supplies were taken away. Some of the occult practitioners were freed but others whose answers did not satisfy the Gestapo were sent to concentration camps to die.[60]

Professor Karl Haushofer was also a clairvoyant. His wartime predictions included providing the exact time and place of Allied bombings that helped impede several attacks. Trevor Ravenscroft may not be a familiar name to most people. He was a controversial author who described Professor Haushofer as much more sinister and important to the Nazi cause than is generally recognized. "Haushofer awakened Hitler to the real motives of the Luciferic Principality which possessed him so that he could become the conscious vehicle of its evil intent in the twentieth century," Ravenscroft was quoted as saying.[61]

Some researchers and writers have described Haushofer as a "clandestine satanist" who taught Hitler a "secret esoteric doctrine," obtained, in part, from Theosophy and also from those German occult practitioners who particularly venerated the pagan deity Wotan.

However, in *Mein Kampf,* Hitler disparaged the "pseudo-pagan revivalists" whose satanic ceremonies included the burying of wine bottles in the shape of a swastika on a mountaintop, and swearing allegiance to the ancient gods. Hitler wanted action taken against Germans who dwelled on "mystical musings about the past," Roland noted.[62]

Also in *Mein Kampf* Hitler stated, "So-called religious reformers of the ancient Germanic type, I have the feeling, are sent by dark forces who do not desire the rebirth of our people. For their entire activity leads the *Volk* away from its fight against the common enemy, the Jew . . ."[63]

However, Roland writes that Professor Haushofer likely did not initiate Hitler into an "occult brotherhood." It is more probable that Haushofer influenced Hitler to become more pragmatic in his use of geopolitics. Remember, it was Haushofer who "introduced" Hitler to the theory of *lebensraum,* or living space, Hitler's pretext for expansion into other countries in his insatiable grasp for world conquest. Many historians suggest that Haushofer prepared Hitler for "public office," and through his student, Rudolf Hess, also swayed Hitler toward better personal habits. As a result, Hitler abstained from meat and alcohol. Curiously, Haushofer's wife was half-Jewish.

Another demented and slavishly loyal aide to Hitler was Joseph Goebbels (1897–1945), a genius at developing and ramming Nazi propaganda into the heads of the masses. As with other close supporters, Dr. Goebbels looked nothing like the mythic Aryan supermen the Nazis so worshipped, the fantasy of physically fit Nordic young men who were muscular, with fair skin, blond hair, and blue eyes. Self-conscious about his small stature and a lifelong limp from a childhood bout of polio, his inferiority complex made him a bitter and cynical person. His resentment of others was matched by their dislike of him. As was the case with his Nazi cohorts, Goebbels was a vicious anti-Semite whose career was entirely devoted to promoting Hitler's image. In 1922 he became a member of the NSDAP, and by 1926 he was a follower of Hitler. It was Goebbels who later created the "führer myth of the image of the Messiah-Redeemer," noted Robert Wistrich. To Goebbels, Hitler was "deep and mystical."[64]

Was Hitler's reign of terror predicted? When the famed sixteenth-century seer Nostradamus wrote in one of his enigmatic quatrains about "Hister," many modern translators of the prophet quickly thought the word was a corruption of the name Hitler. Could Nostradamus have predicted the rise of Hitler four centuries before he lived?

Hitler became personally interested in Nostradamus when Frau Goebbels, the wife of Dr. Goebbels, came upon Nostradamus's quatrains that seemed to apply to Hitler and showed them to her husband in 1939. Hitler seemed to recognize himself in the quatrains.

Beginning in May 1940, German planes were "dropping . . . forgeries of various quatrains . . . which predicted that Hitler would be victorious," Erika Cheetham wrote in *The Prophecies of Nostradamus*. "In retaliation, British Intelligence . . . spent an enormous sum on anti-German propaganda, carefully composing and imitating selected German Nostradamus quatrains which Allied pilots dropped over France and Belgium . . . as late as 1943."[65]

Cheetham continued, "One of Nostradamus's most remarkable series of quatrains [are those] with the name Hitler given in an anagram as Hister." In her opinion, "There can be little doubt that Hitler is implied." Goebbels put the quatrains to great propaganda purposes before World War II. Some researchers, however, concluded that Hister was from an old Latin name for the Danube River.

The following Nostradamus quatrain has been frequently quoted over the years:

> "Hunger-maddened beasts will make the streams tremble
> Most of the land will be under Hister
> In a cage of iron the great one will be dragged
> When the child of Germany observes nothing."[66]

The quatrains, of course, are open to different interpretations. However, more than one Nostradamus student has remarked that Nostradamus seemed to imply Hister—or Hitler—was "some kind of Antichrist," Peter Lemesurier noted in *Nostradamus: The Next Fifty Years*. The manipulation of Nostradamus's writings by both Germany and Britain represent what has been described as a good example of "psychological warfare."[67]

Hermann Goering (1893–1946) was second only to Hitler in power in the Third Reich. Goering held several top positions in the Nazi hierarchy, including head of the Luftwaffe, Reichstag president, and Hitler's "designated successor." Reichsmarschall Goering was a man with an enormous ego, but little if any conscience, typical of sociopaths. As with the others close to Hitler, he virtually worshipped the führer. Goering's anti-Semitism likely was the result of a deep concern that his mother had once had an affair with his godfather who was believed to be Jewish, John Toland explained.

No one ever accused Goering of being as good-humored or cordial as his smile made him appear, for behind that was a cruel and spiteful man who had distinguished himself as a fierce fighter and ace pilot. It was Goering who instituted the much-feared Gestapo, and put into effect the building of concentration camps.[68]

Strangely, Goering allowed his name to be associated with one of the most spurious occult theories to ever come down the pike, the so-called "Hollow Earth." It was in the seventeenth century that British astronomer Edmund Halley hypothesized that planet Earth was actually a unfilled globe surrounded by the "Earth's crust." Halley was serious about his theory, which he thought might help him understand the variation of the Earth's magnetic poles. He thought that perhaps there were two interior layers that rotated or revolved at dissimilar velocities. Halley conjectured that the Earth's poles were located in the inside layers.

By the twentieth century, the theory of the Hollow Earth had no scientific credibility. Nonetheless, a friend of Goering named Peter Bender, who'd been a World War I pilot, believed a race of people lived within the Earth. Goering, among other top Nazis, had little or no problem believing the preposterous story, which, according to legend was also ascribed to by U.S. Admiral Byrd.

In 1942, a group of scientists actually set out to the Baltic Sea to investigate the idea. They set up an experimental radar station that was supposed to propel infrared light beams to the sky, and then rebound to Earth at an angle in order to create a radar likeness of ships at a distance from the craft carrying out the test. Of course, the foolish experiment failed. When Hitler learned of it he was furious, for it had squandered personnel and supplies that were supposed to go toward the war effort. Bender and several of his associates were sent to concentration camps. As for Goering, he remained silent, apparently too humiliated for words.[69]

The second most influential—and feared—man in the Third Reich was the dour Heinrich Himmler (1900–45), commander of the dreaded Gestapo, the Secret State Police prior to the war, and head of the Waffen-SS, an elite force. It took only a mention of the name Gestapo to send terror through anyone within the Nazi sphere. Humorless and grim, Himmler had taken part in the failed Munich Putsch in 1923. Himmler fantasized "a race of blue-eyed, blond heroes," "supermen" who would be developed by the "laws of selection," explained Robert Wistrich.[70]

But Reichsführer Himmler also had a strong attraction to "philosophical mesmerism," the occult, homeopathy, and herbal medicine. In his insanity he boasted that concentration camps, where millions were ultimately murdered, were a means to "prove" genetic and racial laws, since the camps were designed to eliminate "inferior people," such as the Jews. Like other Nazi leaders, he was an uncompromising anti-Semite, and proud of it. He'd set up the first Nazi concentration camp at Dachau in 1933, and was the ultimate overseer of the "Final Solution." He also believed in racial selection by which women with Nordic qualities would produce offspring with SS men. But for all his crazes, Himmler could not bear to see an animal suffer, and he despised looking at blood, although he had no conscience about ordering the murder of millions.[71]

Himmler told of his interest and practice of the occult in *Zodiac and Swastika* by Wilhelm Wulff: "In the Third Reich we have forbidden astrology. We cannot permit any astrologers to follow their calling except those who are working for [the Reich]. In the Nationalist Socialist state astrology must remain a 'singular privilege' "; it is not meant for the "masses," according to Dusty Sklar in *Gods & Beasts*, who added the "Nazis took the occult seriously" and considered it a "potential threat," especially information that countered Third Reich propaganda, or predicted bad news for the Nazi regime.[72]

There is no disputing Himmler's strong interest in the occult. He found time to search for the Holy Grail, the cup Jesus was believed to drink from at the Last Supper, and which many believe caught drops of Jesus' blood at the Crucifixion, Paul Roland explained. Himmler's interest was based on the Nazi myth that Jesus was Aryan, rather than Jewish. To Himmler, the Holy Grail was a "vessel of occult power."[73]

He consulted astrological charts, and even had a favorite astrologer, Wilhelm Wulff, who'd also prepared astrology charts for Hitler.[74] Himmler considered the SS "the resurrection of the ancient Order of Teutonic Knights, and he was the grand master," wrote Robert Wistrich.[75]

Himmler once tried to ferret out unfaithful and traitorous individuals within the Nazi Party. Unable to find them, a troubled Himmler sought help from an Austrian psychic who described three men who'd conspired with a foe of Hitler, Otto Strasser, who had Communist leanings. When the British captured the once highly ranked Nazi at the end of the war, he committed suicide.

Himmler's interest in astrology and the occult was not an isolated circumstance. Many top Nazis shared similar interests. Skeptics who considered the occult to be "pseudoscience," blamed the fascination with paranormal subjects on either superstition or the dearth of strong scientists, such as Einstein, whom the Nazis forced to flee Germany. The occult, according to this somewhat cynical conclusion, filled the void left by the scientists who'd left Germany.

However, there is possibly a deeper and more insidious reason for the Nazis being drawn to occult practices. It is a theory suggesting that the Nazis were reaching deeper into the dark side for increased powers, especially from evil sources. They also wanted prognostications that promised victory over the Allies, something they were not always told. The masses were not to hear anything but triumph over the enemy. Although rationalists reject that supernatural hypothesis, it is worth exploring. There is no question that the Nazis delved seriously into the occult from the very beginning of their founding.

By 1919, when the Treaty of Versailles was signed and imposed on Germany, the Bolsheviks controlled Russia and were focused on inciting revolution anywhere they could in war-ravaged Europe. Meanwhile, President Woodrow Wilson's idea of the League of Nations he naïvely believed could someday handle any failings in the peace treaty was presented. By 1922, Benito Mussolini had become the Fascist dictator of Italy, and later would become an ally of Hitler. By now the Soviet Union was taking shape as a Communist regime under the rule of Nikolai Lenin. Banning "private ownership of property, nationalizing industry, and socializing state services," were all part of the new Soviet system that would remain in place for more than sixty years, George F. Putnam explained in *Great Events from History*.[76]

There has long been debate about the underlying causes of Hitler's "hypnotic hold over the German people," Paul Roland noted.[77] Some historians and researchers concluded that a supernatural reason was possible. One Swiss writer, Denis de Rougemont, felt that some force beyond our understanding could only explain Hitler's magical powers of oratory. If Hitler were a medium or channel for some supernatural force or discarnate entity it would not be unheard of in paranormal history. Could there have been a magical element at work?

Some of the reactions of Germans to Hitler's oratory remind us of the impact the CIA and other intelligence agencies hoped for in their mind-control experiments during the Cold War years in which attempts were made to hypnotize subjects for secret military and intelligence functions, such as spying.

The authors of this book have also studied several excellent psychic mediums who have been closely observed and tested. The differences in the medium before and during a period of spirit contact are often dramatic. The medium acts as a vessel for a spirit communication. However, when that occurs, the medium's manner of speech, personality, ideas, even vocabulary changes so that the spirit temporarily seems to take over. It's as if we are dealing with two entirely different individuals.[78] German politician Hermann Rauschning was one of Hitler's contemporaries who said, "One cannot help but think of Hitler as a medium."[79]

On the other hand, rationalists have concluded that Hitler's oratorical gifts were based purely on reason, with the Nazi leader drawing entirely from his own conscious thoughts or ideas. In our interview with John Toland, he suggested that Hitler's riveting and passionate speeches were often carefully planned beforehand, and then always analyzed afterward for their effectiveness. Hitler's well-known architect of the Third Reich, Albert Speer, attributed "Hitler's hypnotic hold over the German people to purely rational means."[80] The author, William L. Shirer, wrote that he'd heard "many of [Hitler's] speeches and perceived the magic of his spoken words. I saw him hold huge audiences in his spell. Only Winston Churchill in England was his equal."[81]

It is no secret that some mystics have been able to manifest the capability that Hitler could apparently produce subconsciously. One example was George Gurdjieff (1872?–1949), a mystic and spiritual teacher of Greek ancestry, born near the borders of Russia and Persia. He spent some twenty years in a search for the "esoteric truths of life," by visiting Tibet, India, and Arab countries. Although a somewhat baffling figure, the goal of his system was "to break habits of thought and emotion and awaken a higher consciousness, it was a kind of Westernized Zen," according to the *Encyclopedia of Occultism & Parapsychology*.[82] Gurdjieff was able to imitate Hitler's rhetorical wonders.

Did rationalists unfairly dismiss the supernatural explanation, as they so often do with paranormal explanations? Might those who were in the business of "Nazi myth-making" as Paul Roland called it, have been the creators? Or, is the original assumption correct, that Hitler's powerful and mesmerizing speeches to thousands of Germans at a time in giant theatrical and riveting rallies had help from some external supernatural, mystical, or demonic source?

There is an interesting footnote that adds to the mystery about Hitler's psychic ability. Even in childhood, Hitler could "change into another voice, whether from his own subconscious or an external source," Paul Roland wrote.[83] If true, that is a suggestion of mediumistic power on Hitler's part.

During the war years, the Nazis were secretly at work building rockets. Their efforts took place in Peenemünde, Germany, led by the brilliant scientist and rocket engineer Wernher von Braun (1912–1977) and his team of five hundred men. The rockets were to be developed as part of the Nazi weapons program. Von Braun's real interest, however, was in working on space flight, and as a boy was inspired by the writings of Jules Verne and H. G. Wells.

By 1930 von Braun was participating in a German group exploring the possibility for space travel by experimenting with small, "liquid fueled" rockets. When money ran out during the Depression, in 1932 von

Braun agreed to work for the German military where he continued to develop liquid-fueled rockets. In 1934, at the age of twenty-two, von Braun earned his doctorate in physics.

As the Nazis increased their power and laws against Jews, von Braun and his group moved to Peenemünde on the Baltic Sea in 1937, the year von Braun joined the Nazi Party and later became an officer in an elite unit of the SS. At Peenemünde he continued work in new quarters. By then, larger rockets were being designed, including the infamous German V-2. It was a highly determined effort, for the V-2 was designed to send a one-ton warhead a distance of 160 miles. The missile was 45 feet long. There were setbacks and technical problems before the first launch at Peenemünde in 1942. More unsuccessful launches caused more delays, and not until September 1944 was a "fully operational" V-2 rocket successfully fired. Between then and 1945, when the war ended, slave labor built six thousand rockets in an underground location known as Mittelwerk. Thousands of V-2 rockets were targeted at England, Belgium, and other locations in the Allied nations. Although the rockets von Braun developed killed many people, for the Nazis it was too late for strategic purposes, since Germany was losing the war. Still, the V-2 rocket demonstrated immense progress in rocket science.

Despite his Nazi background, von Braun planned his next move in 1945 when Germany lost the war. He and his workforce of hundreds surrendered to the Americans, rather than the Russians. It was a wise decision. The Americans were willing to employ former Nazis to work on U.S. "rocket development" at the White Sands Proving Grounds in New Mexico. They had at their disposal captured Nazi V-2 rockets.

When he moved to Huntsville, Alabama, von Braun continued his missile research that ultimately helped launch American astronauts Alan Shepard and Gus Grissom into orbit around the Earth in May and June of 1961. Von Braun continued to direct the design and development of missiles that continually advanced the U.S. space program.

"Another group of rockets developed under von Braun was the Juno series. "*Juno 1* . . . launched America's first satellite *Explorer 1* in June 1958." In 1960 von Braun joined NASA and was director of the Space Flight Center until early 1970.

Von Braun and his team achieved their greatest claim to fame with the powerful Saturn family of rockets that launched two American astronauts into orbit around the Moon and landed twelve of them on the lunar surface between July 1969 and January 1971. He is largely credited for developing the Saturn and Apollo programs.

In 1970, von Braun was moved to NASA headquarters in Washington, DC, where he was named deputy associate administrator. He eventually resigned from NASA for private industry and for the remainder of his life, von Braun continued to "promote human spaceflight." In 1975, he helped begin the National Space Institute and became its first president.

But, according to author Wayne Biddles, von Braun was no hero. In a new book on von Braun titled *Dark Side of the Moon*, Biddles demonstrates that von Braun, his devotion to rocketry and his love of science fiction notwithstanding, was nevertheless an SS officer and the overseer of a slave labor camp in which thousands of prisoners died even as they assembled the missiles that would drop out of the sky onto Allied cities. Unlike other concentration camp officers, von Braun was spared answering for his crimes because the Americans needed his rocketry expertise in the coming technology race with the Soviets.

Von Braun was one of many Nazi rocket scientists that the U.S. repatriated in order to build its missile program after the war. It was ironic, because according to Wayne Biddles, von Braun had an almost romantic attachment to rocketry because of the German fascination with it, but it was the American rocket scientist Robert H. Goddard, whose experiments in New Mexico on liquid-fueled rockets, who inspired a generation of German rocket scientists.[84] In a way, although von Braun and his colleagues are considered the fathers of modern guided-missile technology, it was Robert Goddard who was the grandfather, having launched the first liquid-fueled rocket in 1926. It was Goddard, also, who foresaw the liquid-fueled rocket as a potential weapon and a method for launching unmanned probes into space to circumnavigate the Moon, distant planets, and send messages through space to extraterrestrial civilizations. That was why it is even more ironic that in July 1947, not far from the very places where Goddard experimented, a strange craft—or two—crashed in Roswell, setting off the modern fascination with flying saucers and UFOs.[85]

The twentieth century began with a fascination for secret societies, a belief in the supernatural powers that membership in secret societies conferred upon its devoted members, and a very real belief that the world as people saw it through their own two eyes was not the real world at all. In art, science, social science, and politics, the world of the unseen became more important than the world perceived through the five senses. At the beginning of the nineteenth century Franz Mesmer showed that his subjects would react to things real in their minds if not palpable in the world of extrinsic reality. In the early twentieth century, Sigmund Freud demonstrated that events buried deep in one's psyche and not even perceived by his patients as extrinsic phenomena, could influence their behaviors in maladaptive ways. So began the modern medical practice of psychiatry: a delving into the universe of the unconscious mind that affected the world of the seen by a therapist's interpreting surface symbols as keys to what might lie beneath them.

All of this history considered, look at the rather peculiar timeline that took the world from secret societies, notably Theosophy, through occult and nationalistic groups, two world wars, and Nazis horrors that brought us several brilliant scientists such as von Braun and Willy Ley who played major roles in developing the U.S. space program. It is ironic that from the depths of the Nazis came rocket scientists who elevated us into outer space. And in outer space, not only lies our human future but the encounters with other life forces whose presence and existence will forever change our own.

2

New Orleans: A Haunted History

We all go die in the water, it's true; we all go die in
    the water.

—Nineteenth-century New Orleans Voodoo song

There has long been a certain spirit that permeated New Orleans, a kind of magic, many said, that drew millions. Perhaps it was the unique Cajun and Creole cooking, spicy and mouthwatering dishes such as jambalaya, crawfish, and gumbo. Few could deny the thrill of hearing jazz in its birthplace, or the melancholy and haunting strains of its blues music. Of course, New Orleans is the site of the annual Mardi Gras parade and celebration through the old French Quarter of the city; where there are streets named Bourbon and Canal with some of the loveliest old homes, distinctive architecture, and wrought-iron balcony grillwork in the entire country.

But another spirit and magic has long gripped New Orleans; one that is more tortured and terrifying than most people are aware of. It is the haunted New Orleans of Voodoo, vampires, and ghosts. What happens in a community where Christianity, the occult, and a long history of slavery, inequality, violence, and corruption collide? How does a city earn the dubious title, "Voodoo capital of America"? Is such a place fated to its own special and ignominious karma or destiny? Or are we dwelling on legend and superstition, as skeptics would argue?

"The city, known for its 'Cities of the Dead' because bodies must be buried aboveground, is somewhat otherworldly," wrote *Newsweek* magazine, not a publication partial to the supernatural. There was a "charm and beauty to New Orleans," author Susy Smith wrote several decades ago. But she hastened to add that New Orleans was "wrapped in somber garments of hate, fear, and misery."[1] The "spirit" of the city has never been easily defined or painted simply in one hue. But New Orleans' unique paranormal history cannot be ignored. It's often been called one of the country's most haunted cities, a reputation earned, in part, by the suffering of generations of its poorest and most deprived citizens.

Late August and early September typically bring about six inches of rain to New Orleans, a city familiar with heat and humidity, and built mainly below sea level; set between the mighty Mississippi River and the immense Lake Pontchartrain. But everything that was New Orleans— good and bad—began to spin out of control on Sunday morning, August 28, 2005, when the National Weather Service predicted an enormous storm named Hurricane Katrina, and the city that had mainly avoided the worst of nature's devastation until then was warned that this time the storm was on track to cause massive destruction. By late afternoon the rains were on their way and there was no stopping them. Lake Pontchartrain was rising steadily and dangerously, and would continue to, by several feet; citizens were advised to leave.

Then the news grew even worse when the city's aging system of levees and flood walls started to weaken, and breaches or breaks occurred in at least three places. There was no holding back the torrents of water that in the next several days left 80 percent of New Orleans a submerged city. New Orleans had been through storms before, bad ones, but nothing close to Hurricane Katrina. The floodwaters measured up to ten feet in some parts of the city. The Category 4 storm packed winds of 140 miles per hour when it slammed into the New Orleans area early the next morning. When Katrina veered east it caused enormous damage to Biloxi, Mississippi, and also struck Mobile, Alabama. The flood surge that battered the Gulf Coast reached nearly thirty feet, the highest ever recorded. The city of New Orleans, with some half a million people, continued an uneasy and controversial exodus, an evacuation fraught with delays and bureaucratic snafus, reported widely at the time by the media. "No major American city had been evacuated since Richmond and

Atlanta in the Civil War," reported *Newsweek*. It was no exaggeration when one network TV commentator described Katrina as a "hellish storm," while another reported "incalculable human suffering." Hardest hit were the city's poorest; about 20 percent of New Orleans' population is below the poverty line, and most of them are African-American, many too poor to own cars and escape the storm's fury and floods.

In the days ahead, floodwaters filling many streets became what one network news program described as a dangerously "toxic brew . . . of sewage, gas, and chemicals." Sewage bacteria levels in New Orleans' water were reported to be forty-five-thousand times the safety level. Utilities, of course, were out following the hurricane. When fires raged more than a week after the storm, there were no working hydrants. The death toll was about eighteen hundred; and those thousands more left homeless had to decide whether to rebuild their lives in New Orleans or elsewhere. The nation reacted with shock and horror at the devastation and suffering, and amidst the criticism of inept and slow government response, millions opened their hearts and wallets to contribute to the victims of Katrina, one of the deadliest natural disasters in American history. Incredibly, more rain and floods followed only weeks later when Hurricane Rita struck the beleaguered city.[2]

Had New Orleans done anything to deserve this? And why had the old French Quarter—where the most haunted houses, Voodoo shops, and even a Voodoo museum are located—suffered *less* damage than many other parts of the city?

Here's just a bit of background to set the story. Louisiana was founded as a colony in 1699, and New Orleans was settled in 1717. Only two years later, in 1719, the first French slave ship arrived, and New Orleans and the insidious slave trade were inextricably linked for the next century and a half.

Floods and hurricanes battered the city early in its history and two major fires ravaged it in the eighteenth century. Because of its closeness to swamps, epidemics were virtually an annual scourge. Between 1795 and 1905, some one hundred thousand people died from yellow fever, malaria, and cholera.

At various times in its early history, the colony was under either Spanish or French rule. Then in 1803, New Orleans became a part of the United States with the Louisiana Purchase. Louisiana became a state in

1812; and in 1815, the famed Battle of New Orleans ended the War of 1812. Two weeks later, the American victory over England was celebrated in the city's French Quarter, or Vieux Carre, its original name. Meanwhile, the slave trade—buying and selling black men, women, and children—thrived in New Orleans. By the early part of the nineteenth century, in addition to public slave auctions, much of the evil trade went on behind the closed doors of lovely and genteel Creole-style houses. In fact, for three decades before the Civil War, New Orleans was the "leading slave market in the U.S.," noted author Martha Ward.[3]

Black people, captured mainly from western Africa, brought with them their own tribal religions, such as the ancient Yoruba faith. Those vital religious beliefs helped sustain them spiritually and emotionally through the hardships and horrendous conditions they faced coming to America, packed in slave ships, and also offered hope when they were forced to toil on sugar and cotton plantations and farms.

Other slaves were brought to the islands of the Caribbean, particularly Haiti—or Saint-Domingue as it was originally called—which in the eighteenth century was France's most valuable agricultural colony. By the latter part of the century African slaves on Saint-Domingue numbered about a half million, and the religion they practiced, largely in secret, was Voodoo, also of African origin. It centered on spirit worship, especially of ancestors, with elements of magic including rituals, rites, spells, charms, sacrifices, possession, and its own terminology. The word *Voodoo* derived from an African term meaning "spirit," and has long been badly misunderstood by many who connect it entirely with black magic, sacrifices, evil spirits, and zombies—the "living dead."[4] But Voodoo's adherents say that the negative or dark side of the religion comprises only a small part of their beliefs, and has been wildly exaggerated into horrific myths and folklore. However, telling that to someone terrified by Voodoo is probably useless. On the other hand, for the slaves uprooted from Africa and forced to the New World centuries ago, Voodoo represented a link to their African traditions.

In addition to plantation owners' unspeakably brutal treatment of the slaves—chained, starved, and beaten—the Catholic Church stepped in to help eradicate Voodoo in Saint-Domingue since native religious beliefs were a potentially unifying force, and therefore a threat—the last thing slave owners wanted. The Catholic hierarchy had another motive, one that we've seen often throughout the history of the supernatural in America and Europe. For the Church, there was only one genuine faith: Catholicism. If you were not Christian, you were likely in league with the forces of evil; and so the Church associated Voodoo with devil worship, black magic, and curses. It did all it could to help eliminate the practice, but failed. Voodoo survived, and ironically, adopted aspects of Catholicism, as well as ancient African religions.

Voodoo first appeared in and around New Orleans during the late eighteenth century. At first, West Indian slaves were prohibited from the United States because of the fear they practiced "Voodooism" and therefore posed a danger. The ban was removed in 1803 at the time of the Louisiana Purchase. By the early 1800s, many black "free immigrants" or non-slaves migrated from Haiti to New Orleans in search of employment. White planters, who escaped war-ravaged Haiti, also settled in New Orleans, and brought their slaves.

With the thousands of slaves came beliefs in Haitian Voodoo that eventually developed into what author Erik Belgum called "a unique American version of Voodoo, often referred to as New Orleans Voodoo." It achieved its zenith during the first half of the nineteenth century, and women especially played a significant role as "Voodoo princesses," or mambos, engendering both admiration and fear. Magic was more of an ingredient in New Orleans Voodoo than it had been in Haiti, where religious rituals were more significant than they were here. There were two kinds of magic people believed in: white and black. White magic was meant to bring "good luck" or healing. In the language of New Orleans Voodoo, a juju was a "good luck charm"; and a mojo was a charm used for black magic or to issue a curse. Black magic was invoked to cause "bad luck," injury—or even death. In New Orleans Voodoo, "magical charms, potions, gris-gris bags, and Voodoo dolls," were widely employed, wrote author Shannon R. Turlington. There were also charms meant for protection. As well, live snakes became a part of New Orleans Voodoo rites. Some people were—and are—instantly repelled by the idea of snakes, especially within religion. However, in Catholicism there is a centuries-old story that St. Patrick drove the snakes from Ireland; and in the Old Testament, Moses performed a miracle in the desert when he turned his staff into a snake; and who can forget the serpent that tempted Eve in the Garden of Eden.

The practice of Voodoo, officially prohibited, was quietly condoned or ignored by New Orleans' authorities. On Sundays, Voodoo dance performances were held in an open part of the French Quarter known as Congo Square, an area that served as a gathering place. Whites often came to watch in fascination. As well, Voodoo dances of a more serious and scandalous nature were held clandestinely late at night along the shores of Lake Pontchartrain where the rituals included animal sacrifices, orgies, and nude dancing, performed by the light of bonfires.[5]

The most famous New Orleans Voodoo queen was Marie Laveau (c.1794–1881) whose reputation became legendary in her lifetime, and whose ghost is said to still haunt the city. Marie achieved status, power, and influence rare for a mulatto woman in a city and era of strict segregation. As a young woman she had the advantage of a quick mind and striking good looks, with black wavy hair and gleaming dark eyes that captured the attention of both blacks and whites. She was tall and carried herself regally; not a presence people could easily ignore. Marie was likely born in Saint-Domingue; possibly the child of a white plantation-owner father and a slave mother. As a result, she became a "free woman of color" and was never a slave. In 1819 she married a "free man of color," Jacques Paris, a quadroon from Saint-Domingue; but not long after he deserted her and probably returned to his native country.

Marie then found employment as a hairdresser for both affluent white and Creole women in New Orleans. It was the perfect setting for her to overhear the confidences her clients shared with each other about the secrets of their lives: marriages, finances, love affairs, paramours, husbands, and even the greatest fear many white women of the time had, that there might be "Negro blood" in their family ancestry. Marie had studied Voodoo by this time, learning from a powerful teacher named Dr. John, and the information she gathered from her customers became knowledge that she "later used to strengthen her powers as Voodoo queen," author Rosemary Ellen Guiley explained. How much of her insight about people, places, and events was the result of what she learned from patrons, and how much was obtained through "psychic powers" is open to debate; but her fortune-telling skills appeared uncanny. She was also considered expert at putting together and selling gris-gris (pronounced *gree-gree*) bags, Voodoo's most potent and costly magical charms made up of herbs and other ingredients in a small pouch. "Gris-

gris is a potion or spell to harm or help someone, a means to manifest your intention," explained author Martha Ward. Marie also prepared many love potions and invoked supernatural curses. There was no lack of people who sought her help, and she became prosperous by charging for her services.

Sometime in 1826, Marie and a man named Louis de Glapion, a quadroon also from Saint-Domingue, became lovers, and their relationship produced fifteen children. They lived together in New Orleans for nearly thirty years, until he died in 1855. Eventually Marie ended her career as a hairdresser for a full-time commitment to Voodoo, achieving a reputation as "Voodoo Queen of New Orleans" by the 1830s.

Despite the danger of white retribution, not all black people acquiesced to their status as slaves; there were many attempts to escape, as well as slave rebellions. For example, in 1811, the "largest slave uprising in American history" occurred in St. John the Baptist Parish, west of New Orleans. But many slave owners in the area needed to find a scapegoat to rationalize why masters and slaves were not getting along. The reality apparently never dawned on them that black people resented being chained and treated like chattel, and wanted their freedom. White owners found it more convenient to blame Voodoo and its practitioners for slave unrest. Some grew suspicious that women such as Marie Laveau could invoke the magical or supernatural powers of Voodoo to upset the "slave-master relationship."

In her book *Voodoo Queen*, author Martha Ward told of a well-known white doctor who advertised and lectured about "Negro fetishism." He defined it as "magic to help slaves escape or . . . improve their lives at the expense of their owners." He even offered medical evidence and advice about the "mystical connection between the Negro and the serpent" since Voodoo includes special regard for snakes because of their "close association" with the belief in the African "snake god," the creator of the planet Earth.

Could Marie Laveau's Voodoo love potions for ridding one of a bad spouse or ending an unhappy relationship have also been a cover for slaves to rid themselves of bad owners? It wasn't only Voodoo practitioners who believed this; many white slave owners were quite frightened by the power of Voodoo. The aura of mystery and secrecy surrounding Voodoo has always been one of its great strengths. Efforts by white authorities to eradicate Voodoo repeatedly failed, and prohibiting Voodoo only drew black people closer to one another spiritually and emotionally.

When Nat Turner led his famous though ill-fated slave rebellion in Virginia in 1831, he had fewer than eighty poorly armed followers, all of whom were killed as a result of the revolt; and thirty-one-year-old Turner was executed for leading the insurrection. However, he'd made it clear that he'd been a strong believer in the mystical and claimed to have "supernatural powers." "The uprising caused the entire South to tremble," William J. Cooper, Jr. wrote. For frightened and shaken white slave owners, magic, spirit contacts, and rebelling slaves all melded into one. Laws against blacks, both free and slave, tightened.

In New Orleans, while it was easy to lay blame for slave unrest at the feet of Marie Laveau and Voodoo, at the same time, even her enemies held her in awe for what were considered her powers, spells, and potions; and no laws or prohibitions against Voodoo could prevent her from practicing. In fact, many police and judges were too fearful to intercede; it was safer to turn their backs on her activities. As a result, Marie faced little official interference, and many came for her "magical" potions and counsel. Skeptics, then as now, could huff and puff that Voodoo was superstition and Marie was a charlatan, but few were willing to chance confronting her on the question. Even some white politicians and officials secretly sought her predictions for the future. Although there was a price for her services, Marie well understood the disparity in wealth between her white and black customers in New Orleans where the economic chasm too often reflected the racial divide. As a result, she rarely charged a fee to poor black people who came to her.

There are far too many stories about Marie's "magical powers" to recount them all. But a few examples will paint a fuller portrait of her, or at least show how her supernatural abilities were perceived—and feared—in her day.

In 1830, a young man from a wealthy, upper-class New Orleans family was charged with raping a girl. Authorities had substantial evidence against the suspect. According to the story told at the time, the young man's father sought Marie's help on behalf of his son. She first went to Saint Louis Cathedral to pray while she held peppers in her mouth. Somehow she next managed to secretly place the peppers beneath the judge's chair, and also put a gris-gris bag there that she'd prepared herself. As author Rosemary Ellen Guiley explained the incident, Marie then tacked a note to the front door of the building where the judge was certain to see it. In her message she proclaimed the young man's innocence.

Marie was in court during the trial at which the prosecutor pressed hard for a conviction. The Voodoo queen supposedly managed to flick one of her hairs onto the prosecutor's jacket, and his efforts to obtain a guilty verdict were in vain. The young man was acquitted; and his grateful father presented Marie with a new house in the French Quarter, not far from Congo Square, where she lived the rest of her life, and from where her Voodoo business was centered. The young man renounced his misguided and sinful ways, began attending church, and wanted to marry the young woman he'd been accused of violating. When she firmly rejected him, he went back to Marie Laveau for help. She told him the girl would agree to marriage within the next month.

Once again, Marie prepared a gris-gris bag, this one a concoction of powdered lizard eggs and animal hair; it was supposed to be a "love potion," for which she was particularly known. She then placed small pieces of the young man's hair on the girl's front steps.

It wasn't long after that the young woman fell as she exited church one day and sprained her ankle. The young man happened to be there and gently lifted her; took her to a doctor, and then home to mend. She kissed him gratefully, and they were married soon after. Was it all a result of Marie's Voodoo magic, a bizarre coincidence, or a tale—a fabrication—that spread? The answer depends on what one believes, as is so often the case with supernatural events.

In another incident, there was a rich elderly Creole gentleman who fell passionately for a young woman. Actually, he was old enough to be her grandfather, and she flatly declined his marriage proposal, even though such a union would have been of immense help to her father who faced serious money woes. But no amount of persuasion could convince the young woman to marry the old man, especially since she was already in love with someone her own age who at the time was traveling in the West Indies.

As you might expect, the elderly would-be suitor and the girl's father turned to Marie Laveau for help. Yes, she said, she could promise there would be a wedding between the old man and the lovely young woman. Marie prepared some kind of powdered love potion that the father was instructed to secrete in his daughter's meals. For the elderly man, she prepared a gris-gris that contained the "dried testicles of a black cat," Rosemary Ellen Guiley wrote. It was supposed to eliminate his impotency, and restore his procreative powers and masculinity.

A couple of weeks passed and inexplicably the young woman agreed to the marriage. Needless to say, the elderly groom was thrilled, and a wedding ceremony was held, followed by a lavish reception in his mansion. The newly married couple took the floor for the first dance when suddenly the old man's face flushed to a crimson color, and he fell dead. The young bride screamed in shock, a doctor was called, but the groom was gone.

Since the young woman was considered legally married, as the elderly man's widow she inherited his large estate and unexpectedly became a very wealthy woman. She was then free to marry the young man she truly loved, after a respectable mourning period.

Marie was asked about her role in the strange circumstances, and she had a ready answer. Yes, she acknowledged, her magical powers brought the unlikely couple together. But, she added emphatically that she'd agreed to make the *wedding* possible. She'd never promised anything beyond that.

There was one infamous incident in which a well-known New Orleans man, J. B. Langrast, who did not believe in Voodoo, dared to accuse Marie Laveau of thievery and murder, although there was no evidence of such crimes. In return, a group of Marie's outraged supporters retaliated by leaving gris-gris bags at his front door. It didn't take long for the man to flee New Orleans in terror. Whether as a result of his own fear, the power of suggestion, or something supernatural or magical, many said he'd gone mad as a result of the gris-gris.[6]

There has long been debate about whether the fear of Voodoo alone can psychologically induce injury or even scare a victim to death, or if there is, indeed, some potent magical force at work, such as Voodoo spirits, known as the *loa*, that causes harm. Casting a spell or curse is a part of black magic that even Voodoo practitioners know is best to avoid. "To curse others is to be cursed in return," Martha Ward cautioned in her book, *Voodoo Queen*. Nonetheless, Voodoo curses have caused victims to die, and while the precise reason remains a mystery, modern medicine and psychology have recently begun to look more seriously at the phenomena. Curses are not limited to those who practice Voodoo; the belief in them is found all over the world. If a curse is defined as wishing harm to befall someone else, there are many Americans who believe in the practice. A recent Gallup poll about the way we pray revealed that some fourteen million Americans—5 percent of the population—acknowledge they've prayed *against* someone.[7]

Dr. Larry Dossey, who has studied the subject, suggested the figures might even be much higher. He wrote in *Be Careful What You Pray For . . . You Just Might Get It,* "Some of these prayers appeared indistinguishable from curses and hexes—attempts to control the thought and behavior of a victim against his or her will."

Dossey, a medical doctor whose work on the relationship between prayer and healing has received national attention, said in a 2005 TV interview that he'd seen some "compelling cases . . . even in anthropological literature that suggests very strongly that people can harm and even kill others at a distance with hexes, curses, and spells."[8]

There are also references to curses in both the Old and New Testaments. For example, in Genesis, Noah placed a curse on his son Ham; and in Exodus, God ordered ten plagues on a stubborn pharaoh. In the New Testament, Jesus cursed a fig tree when it would not bear fruit.

Louisiana had been in the possession of Spain, then France—both Catholic countries—prior to the Louisiana Purchase, and so Catholic influence in New Orleans was disproportionate to what it was elsewhere in the American South which became predominantly Protestant. Marie Laveau was a bright and inventive woman who saw the value in connecting Voodoo with Roman Catholic symbols. In doing so, she helped move New Orleans Voodoo beyond mere superstition. For example, the Blessed Mother—the Virgin Mary—became an important presence in Voodoo, encouraged by Marie who always regarded herself as a devout Catholic and attended mass daily at the famed Saint Louis Cathedral in the French Quarter. Her status was such that she was even permitted to conduct Voodoo ceremonies behind the church, a landmark building that dated back to 1794. The cathedral that stood there prior to that time was demolished in a terrible fire that gutted much of New Orleans on Good Friday of 1788, destroying hundreds of buildings. And, ironically, the first church at that location was washed away in a hurricane in September 1722.

Every June 23, St. John's Eve, Marie oversaw an annual Voodoo ceremony at a place called Bayou Saint John, where she directed the dancing, always wearing a live "giant snake," named Zombie, coiled around her neck and body. On the Catholic calendar, June 24 is the feast day for the martyred St. John the Baptist. Among Caribbean people, the Eve of St. John was long an important celebration; and after the Civil War, it took on special significance in New Orleans among freed slaves.

Slavery's history was long riddled with efforts by the Catholic Church to force blacks to end the practice of their native religions, including Voodoo. But the Church failed when slaves cleverly included Catholic imagery and symbolism within Voodoo. For example, while the Church had its roster of saints, Voodoo had analogous spirits. So white saints were substituted for black spirits by Voodoo worshippers, and whites were none the wiser. If you've figured out that Catholicism became a useful cover for secret Voodoo worship, you're correct. As just one of many examples, St. Patrick was considered the equivalent of the African snake spirit Danbala. Other Catholic saints such as St. Peter, St. Michael, and St. Rita also had their equivalent Voodoo spirits. Catholic holidays were integrated within Voodoo, and slaves adapted the Catholic practice of communion into their native beliefs. Eating the communion wafer and drinking holy water became a way for slaves to protect themselves from danger, even witchcraft. Voodoo altars included Catholic crosses and candles. However, for slaves practicing Voodoo, the meanings of the religious objects were not the same as they were for unsuspecting white Catholics, although few probably realized it.

Strangely, when the "Voodoo Queen" died in 1881, some people were not aware that she had passed on. The reason was that one of her daughters, also named Marie, and who looked uncannily like her mother, stepped in; the younger Marie continued her mother's work until her death in 1897. The transition was so seamless that legends grew. One was that Marie Laveau could appear in two places at the same time. According to another tale, there was only one Marie who seemed to remain eternally youthful. Neither was true; it was mother and then daughter who created their own controversial legacy that spanned most of the nineteenth century and, many say, beyond the grave.

There has long been the belief that the elder Marie's ghost returns every year to guide the St. John's Eve ceremonies. Her apparition has also been reported at Saint Louis Cemetery Number One where she is entombed. What distinguishes her crypt from so many others in the crowded "City of the Dead" are the crosses, drawings, and writings on it, left there by visitors seeking favors and good fortune. Over the years, people have also placed small objects as offerings—flowers, fruits, coins, bones, candy, and beads, among other items—at her tomb, and then prayed for their wishes to come true. There is a story told that Marie's ghost once struck a man as he walked through the cemetery, and apparently ignored her stone vault.

The famed old cemetery isn't the only place Marie's specter has been seen. She'd lived at 1020 St. Ann Street in the French Quarter, and many say she still haunts her former home where her ghost conducts Voodoo rituals, joined by other spirit entities. She may also haunt another house where she once lived on Chartres Street where later residents reported witnessing her apparition poised near a fireplace. Anyone who has ever seen Marie Laveau's spirit materialize can quickly identify her from the distinctive seven-knotted *tignon*—a Creole turban made from a brightly colored handkerchief—she always wore in public.[9]

Not surprisingly, New Orleans has its own museum devoted to Voodoo and several shops specializing in Voodoo paraphernalia. In 1823 Louis Dufilho had an idea for the ground floor of his town house on Chartres Street in the Vieux Carre or French Quarter. Dufilho created the Pharmacie Dufilho, and he became the first licensed pharmacist in the country. The store, with its distinctive large front windows and mortar-and-pestle sign above the door, quickly became a popular establishment, filled with customers; while upstairs, Dufilho lived with his family.

Many patrons went to the pharmacy to purchase a variety of medicines and Voodoo-related items, such as ingredients for gris-gris bags, charms, and potions to create spells. In glass jars, there were various Creole remedies. Perhaps they were not all they claimed to be, but the state of traditional medicine in the early nineteenth century was no further ahead than many folk cures, in a city racked by repeated epidemics. Some of the surgical instruments of that era more closely resembled carpenter's tools or devices for torture than medical apparatus, such as an implement with sharp blades for "bloodletting," and a corkscrewlike contraption that was used to drill a hole into a human skull in order to cure headaches.

Following Dufilho's death the building had a long succession of owners. The store eventually became known as La Pharmacie Francaise, and then in 1950 a pharmacy museum where visitors could step back in time to see an array of "magical" Voodoo concoctions. It's also likely that some later customers glimpsed apparitions of patrons from a century earlier, since the pharmacy was designated as "officially haunted," according to author and researcher Dennis William Hauck.[10]

In more recent years, the red felt gris-gris bags, each tied off with a black ribbon were examined to learn what "secret" ingredients they contained. Traditional physicians found the gris-gris were typically comprised of "essential" or evaporating oils drawn from plants, and fragranced herbs. Other ingredients were sometimes bizarre, if not downright repulsive by modern standards, such as "sheep-manure tea, [and] moldy bread soaked in milk," according to the book *New Orleans Directions*.[11]

Could the gris-gris have some form of energy contained within its ingredients, that coupled with Voodoo chants and prayers really heal or help people? Whatever the answer, huge numbers of people over the course of many generations have believed in their potency.

Voodoo remains a genuine religion, and in New Orleans, is an important part of its past and present. Skeptics might find such ancient beliefs anachronistic and primitive in our technologically driven world. However, Voodoo's magical and occult practices fulfill a spiritual need for many people. How Voodoo dolls, gris-gris, charms, and love potions work are questions for scientists, religious experts, and parapsychologists to consider. To dismiss Voodoo as mere superstition is a mistake.

The history of haunted New Orleans may be all legend; skeptics would certainly agree with that. However, as with so many paranormal events, the sheer number of ghostly sightings makes that unlikely. Many of those over the years who'd reported apparitions were some of the most credible people one could hope to find. Throughout the history of the paranormal, one argument against haunting phenomena has been to relentlessly impugn those who've claimed they've had such experiences. Yet the large number and character of many of the witnesses contradict the likelihood that every one of them was fabricating or hallucinating. What if some energy survives physical death and clings to the place on earth it lived or died—especially if the death was violent, sudden, or unexpected? Could that account for the ghosts that people have witnessed and reported since the beginning of recorded history?

Madame Delphine LaLaurie represented antebellum New Orleans high society with a façade of wealth, beauty, and respectability. In 1831, she and her third husband, Dr. Louis LaLaurie, purchased an elegant three-floor, forty-room mansion at 1140 Royal Street in the French Quarter. The LaLauries were at the center of New Orleans social circles, and the parties they often gave for the city's elite were virtual extravaganzas. But behind the mask of glamour and allure, Delphine LaLaurie was a sadist and a murderess. In the history of New Orleans she is infamous, and her former mansion is considered the city's most haunted house, about which generations of people familiar with the story have said, "*La maison est hantee.*" Passersby have long reported the terrifying cries of mutilated and murdered slaves whose horrific apparitions some have claimed to see.

Madame LaLaurie had many slaves; dozens tended to her every need and whim, but within her lurked a hideous monster who derived sadistic pleasure from torturing them. No amount of pampering or exquisite living could appease or calm her barbaric urges, and her appetite for brutality seemed boundless; slaves were kept chained and secretly tortured, crippled, and disfigured in an attic room.

In one incident that occurred in 1833, Lia (sometimes spelled Leah), a young slave girl who was the madame's personal servant, was combing her mistress's hair when she accidentally snagged it. LaLaurie became furious, grabbed a whip she kept, and chased the terrified girl, who escaped to the roof of the mansion, where she was confronted by the deranged Madame LaLaurie who severely flogged the unfortunate child until her only escape was to jump from a balcony and to her death in a courtyard below. When Lia's body slammed onto the stone pavement it barely missed a man, possibly a relative of LaLaurie who'd just arrived by carriage; he notified authorities. This was one crime she could not hide. However, the penalty for Lia's death was only a three-hundred-dollar fine, a ridiculously small amount for someone as wealthy as LaLaurie, who was also ordered to sell her slaves. The punishment went beyond being lenient; it was virtually meaningless when someone close to the madame bought the slaves back at public auction, and returned them to the demented doyenne.

But even before Lia's suicide—or murder—there was gossip about the physical condition, and comings and goings of slaves in the LaLaurie residence. They seemed to remain for only a short while before they were replaced, and the madame never really explained where her servants mysteriously vanished. Even friends quietly agreed that the circumstances seemed peculiar when LaLaurie could not clarify the turnover or disappearances. She usually brushed aside the question. About Lia's death, the madame suggested that a slave girl was no more important than any other object or property one might use and discard. Even to some of the white gentry, themselves racist, that answer was unsettling; and several long-time friends of LaLaurie discreetly distanced themselves from her.

On April 10, 1834, Delphine LaLaurie's secret world of unspeakable brutality began to unravel. The madame had been entertaining a party of guests when fire broke out in the mansion's kitchen, which was actually separate from the main house. When the "fire brigade," as they were then called, responded, firefighters were startled to find two slaves chained to a stove. It was obvious the desperate servants deliberately set the small blaze to call attention to Madame LaLaurie's hidden house of horrors. An elderly black slave woman pleaded with the fire brigade to open the door of a particular attic room where, she said, people were chained and tortured.

Firemen located the room, found it locked and bolted, but from inside they heard moans and screams. It took a battering ram to break down the door, and when firefighters saw what was inside, even the toughest of them reeled, cried in horror and shock, and some retched from the sickening smell of death. None had ever witnessed such a scene. The room was a "chamber of horrors." There were at least seven slaves—possibly as many as a dozen—"horribly mutilated [and] suspended by their neck, with their limbs . . . stretched and torn from one extremity to the other," reported the *New Orleans Bee* the next day. So unspeakably hideous was the discovery that some newspapers preferred not to provide details of the heinous torture.

All the slaves were found naked, starving, and shackled to the walls, with "heavy iron collars" around their necks. Several women had been disemboweled; literally cut open. There were victims covered with insects; one woman's mouth had been filled with animal feces, and her mouth tied so it could not open. Another woman had her arms amputated, and her skin "peeled off." Newspaper accounts told of a female slave locked in a small cage; every one of her joints had been broken and reset in bizarre positions so that she was shaped like a "human crab."

Male captives were in even worse condition than the women. Men slaves had been mutilated and disfigured; their eyes gouged out, and fingernails torn off. Other parts of their bodies were deliberately cut or carved. The corpse of one man, still chained, was left hanging after a yawning hole had been made in his head. Another slave had his hand amputated and sewn to his abdomen, while others had their mouths secured shut. Some no longer looked human, they had been so terribly disfigured. Rescuers also found jars containing body parts. The torturing had been carried out so as to cause prolonged and painful suffering; the victims were not meant to die quickly. In fact, among those slaves found barely alive, some screamed in pain, pleading with rescuers to kill them and end their unimaginable agony.

New Orleans citizens were staggered by the extent of the depravity and butchery that had taken place behind the closed doors of the lavishly furnished and elegant Spanish-style mansion. Even for slaveholders, Madame LaLaurie had gone far beyond what could or would be tolerated. It didn't take long for an angry throng to gather; some had been guests at LaLaurie's party at the time of the discovery and rescue of the tortured slaves. The crowd grew much larger, ready to storm the house, and many shouted for the madame to appear. Had she fallen into the mob's hands, there is no telling whether she would have survived. No one could be sure how many slaves had been tortured, maimed, and killed; and still no one was certain where the LaLauries' slaves who seemed to disappear into thin air had gone.

Madame knew that she'd best leave New Orleans—and her mansion—once her grisly secrets were public; and she and her husband managed to flee the city by coach. Some said she made her way to Paris where she lived the rest of her life. That version of her fate was reported years later in the New Orleans *Daily Picayune*. Another story suggested she'd relocated to a different part of Louisiana, and some said, years later she actually moved back to New Orleans under an assumed name. As for earthly justice, there apparently wasn't any for Delphine LaLaurie; there is no record that she was ever charged or prosecuted for her ghastly crimes.

Whatever her fate, she left a monstrous legacy and the tortured souls of many victims who still haunt what was once her sumptuous mansion. Not long after the horrific discovery of her sadism, the LaLaurie place became simply known as the "Haunted House." Those who lived nearby insisted they heard crying and screaming from inside the house. Some attributed the eerie moans to superstition or fear. But many more remained convinced that the ghosts of tortured slaves clung to the site of their terrible ordeal, unable to find peace and move on to the other side.

The LaLaurie mansion remained empty for the next forty years. Eventually, the neighborhood became home to Italian immigrants, but the ghosts had apparently remained in the house. Long-ago residents reported seeing the specter of a man in chains, covered in blood, moving along the mansion's balcony. Children told of an apparition of a woman angrily shouting in French as she ran after them with a whip, likely the ghost of Madame LaLaurie. Some of the stories of hauntings were far more grisly. One resident told of witnessing a specter carrying his head in his hands. Others reported finding "decapitated animals" in a courtyard of the house. Not surprisingly, whether born of superstition or the supernatural, many accounts of hauntings had the predictable result: People eventually moved out, and the LaLaurie house was once again unoccupied.

Over the years the infamous dwelling was used for a variety of purposes. At various times it was a school, several kinds of stores and businesses, even a tavern. But no one stayed for very long; presumably the ghostly presences and unearthly voices frightened them away.

In the early years of the twentieth century, the old mansion, badly in need of repair, was refurbished and converted into apartments, and remains so today. When workmen tore up the original floorboards to replace them on the third floor where the slaves had been quartered, the remains of seventy-five people were uncovered. It was determined they'd been buried alive. That explained the terrible cries and screams that many insisted they'd heard after the fire in April 1834. The assumption then was that they were the moaning of ghosts. No one thought they were the cries of live people, slaves who'd been concealed and left to die by the madame. It was not a supernatural explanation, but it did answer the question of where so many of the LaLaurie slaves disappeared.

Many of the residents in the former LaLaurie mansion have had to coexist with spirits, some who reluctantly call the old place home. People say there continue to be encounters with apparitions of black men in chains, a white woman, and spectral beings dressed in cloaks and burial garments or shrouds. Some nights, they've heard the shrieks of a young girl falling through the courtyard. Others have heard the distinct sound of chains trailing down stairways. Over the years, not surprisingly, there have been frequent reports of loud, high-pitched, piercing cries of fear and pain coming from attic rooms, the rooms where Madame LaLaurie carried out her unspeakable brutality. The assumption is that the spectral screams and many of the apparitions are those of the slaves who'd been tortured to death. As for the madame's ghost, it might still be earthbound, her soul certainly not at peace; and she may still haunt the house where she caused so much misery and death.[12]

In New Orleans, phantoms have been seen, felt, or heard in more places than we could possibly include. No fewer than six well-known hotels are on record as being haunted, as well as many taverns and bars. Some of the experiences make a good argument that the French Quarter especially has long had many ghosts among the living. For example, the Hotel Provincial on Chartres Street was once a Civil War hospital. Ever since, ghosts of doctors and Confederate soldiers have been witnessed drifting through the hallways.[13]

One of the better-known haunted buildings in the Vieux Carre is the Lafitte Guest House on famed Bourbon Street, a four-story mansion built in typical eighteenth-century French architectural style with its distinct lacework iron balconies. No one is certain who the frequently seen ghost is; however, many presume it is Madame Geleises who lived there for many years with her husband during the early nineteenth century and suffered tragic loss when four of her eight children died, leaving her utterly grief-stricken. Just before the Civil War, Mrs. Geleises moved from New Orleans to the North, and after the war she sold the fourteen-bedroom house.

Actually it was a site that had known despair by the end of the eighteenth century when a "charity hospital" that served some of the city's poorest and sickest people was built there, only to be gutted by fire in 1809, killing all inside.

In a book titled *Ghostly Encounters: True Stories of America's Haunted Inns and Hotels,* Frances Kermeen devoted a chapter to the Lafitte Guest House. She quoted a former owner of the haunted house, Dr. Robert Guyton, a man trained in science who was highly skeptical of such paranormal phenomena as ghosts. But Guyton said that experiences in the house convinced him "there is indeed a departed spirit among us, and I believe it to be Madame Geleises . . ."

The doctor pointed out that he was not the only one to "feel the ghosts." He described an inexplicable routine in which the elevator went up and down by its own volition, and its doors closed, as the elevator rose by itself to the third floor. Then the elevator proceeded down to the second floor, opened and closed its doors, and returned to the first floor.

Guyton also reported that items on his desk moved about on their own, a form of psychokinetic (PK) phenomena reported frequently in connection with hauntings. Other guests also told of encountering phenomena in the Lafitte House. For example, a young woman said she'd heard persistent crying in the hallway outside her room. But whenever she went to look, the weeping ceased. Another guest was certain of a ghost in her room when various articles moved on their own. This guest had the presence of mind to quickly grab her camera and snap photographs in the room. One picture showed a "wave of energy" in one corner of the room, not unusual in so-called spirit photography; and after photographic analysis, determined not to be a camera imperfection or flaw in the picture. Ghostly phenomena captured on photographs, film, or videotape often appear as a hazy or vaporous form; while other times, spirits have taken the shape of balls of light or energy. Again, there are too many of them recorded and studied over the years to dismiss them all as photographic blips or chicanery.[14]

Across the street from the Lafitte Guest House was property that eventually became a "piano bar," that also was reportedly haunted. Witnesses told of the apparition of an elderly woman who energetically pounded away at a keyboard.

For Confederate General Pierre G. T. Beauregard, the Battle of Shiloh was a crushing defeat in 1862. Beauregard had become famous a year earlier, in April 1861 for ordering Confederate guns to open fire on Fort Sumter in Charleston, shots that began the Civil War. Dubbed the "Great Creole," he also led Southern troops to victory at the first Battle of Bull Run. But Shiloh was a bitter loss with enormous casualties; in all, some twenty-five thousand lay dead and wounded, one-fourth of all the soldiers who fought there.

Beauregard survived the Civil War, and once it was over, the Louisiana native moved to 1113 Chartres Street in the French Quarter where he lived, a "broken, disappointed, bitter" man, in the words of Southern author Stanley C. Arthur. The house, years later, became officially known as the Beauregard-Keyes House, for a later resident, a well-known novelist, Frances Parkinson Keyes (pronounced KIZE) who made her home there from 1944 until 1969. Of the more than fifty books she wrote, one titled *Madame Castel's Lodger* was about Beauregard; she may well have been aware of his ghostly presence.

The house's reputation for being haunted centered on accounts by many people who told of observing phantom troops, particularly in the dead of night. Some claimed they'd witnessed the specters of soldiers led by General Beauregard's ghost, re-creating the Battle of Shiloh in his former home. The "soldiers appear to materialize out of the paneled walls . . . on foggy, moonlit nights reminiscent of the bloody Civil War battle," Michael Norman and Beth Scott wrote in *Haunted America*.[15]

If you accept paranormal theory about the nature of hauntings, General Beauregard's specter remained on earth because during his life he never came to terms with the trauma of his crushing defeat at Shiloh. But there is no reasonable explanation why Beauregard's ghost should materialize with an entire spirit regiment in his former home, rather than on the battlefield at Shiloh where he lost to Union forces. Also disconcerting to some observers was glimpsing Beauregard's spectral troops in their familiar gray Confederate uniforms that then transformed themselves into bloodstained and threadbare remnants, perhaps recapturing the condition they were reduced to at the moment of their deaths at Shiloh.

In the early 1790s, a wealthy Turkish sultan rented a beautiful residence on Dauphin Street in the French Quarter known as the Gardette-LePretre House; and with him was his entourage that included his harem and eunuchs. The sultan apparently enjoyed entertaining; neighbors said they often heard outrageous parties and music late into the night. But one night, the sultan and his entire family, including his several wives, were viciously murdered while they slept. According to one version of events, assassins from an opposing sect had been searching for the sultan's brother to inflict vengeance, but then killed everyone they found in the house on Dauphin Street, as well as their intended target. When police arrived, they first had to break through doors that had been buttressed to strengthen them. Once inside they found those slaughtered in a virtual bloodbath.

The sultan's brother had been buried under a date tree in the courtyard of the house, and with his body was left the following message: "The justice of heaven is satisfied, and the date tree shall grow on the traitor's tomb." Not surprisingly, the grisly burial place became known as the "Death Tree." For years after the brutal killings, in addition to the apparition of a man in Eastern attire seen late at night, witnesses also told of hearing the strains of Oriental music, as if the ghosts of the murder victims were still holding their orgies. More frightening were reports of footsteps and terrifying screams that many concluded were the sounds of those as they were being killed.[16]

On Royal Street, in the French Quarter, witnesses have reported seeing a stunning young woman whose ghost has materialized clearly as she glides across the building's roof, and she is completely naked. The story is that she was a slave who'd fallen deeply in love with a Creole man. For reasons that are inexplicable, he promised they'd be wed, but only if she proved she loved him by spending a cold December night on the roof of his home; he insisted she not wear any clothing. Meanwhile he enjoyed the warmth of indoors where he remained playing cards with friends. Possibly the young man, not really wanting to marry her, demanded the dangerous test, never thinking the girl would actually obey him. But foolishly, she agreed, and the next morning her naked and nearly frozen body was found.

Those who've claimed to see her apparition tell of the unclothed specter, particularly on cold winter nights, re-creating her bitter ordeal.

Part of New Orleans' haunted history even included a place once called the "Devil's Mansion." The house, on St. Charles Avenue, was built in the 1820s, supposedly as a residence for a stunning young woman named Madeleine Frenau, who legend said was mistress to Satan, himself. But the mistress soon became bored and lonely, being left alone for long periods of time. She eventually took another lover, a good-looking young Creole man named Alcide Cancienne; and theirs was a sensual relationship that gave him great pleasure. However, Alcide did not know that Madeleine Frenau was in league with the Devil.

One evening on his way to the mansion, Alcide was startled to meet a strange figure on the street; a man dressed in a cape and hat. When Alcide introduced himself as Madeleine's lover, the shadowy stranger said he too was her lover. The stranger said he'd become tired of her company, and Alcide was welcome to her, providing they'd call themselves "Monsieur and Madame L." The stranger even offered the couple a large amount of gold if they'd leave.

A puzzled Alcide shared the experience with Madeleine. Reluctantly she told him the L was for Lucifer, and to be together they'd have to accept being the "Devil's couple." Madeleine pleaded with Alcide to take her away from Satan. But Alcide had no wish to marry her; she was his mistress and would never be more than that. Madeleine became so enraged she took a large napkin from the dining room table and quickly wrapped it around Alcide's neck, turning it so violently that she broke an artery in his throat, sending blood gushing from his mouth. He collapsed to the floor, dead in a puddle of his own blood.

Frantically, Madeleine went to clean the blood from herself and her clothing, but nothing would scrub it away. When the Devil returned to the mansion, she told him what had transpired. He unceremoniously lifted Alcide's body onto his shoulder, took hold of his struggling mistress, and up they went to the roof where Satan first consumed Alcide's corpse, then grabbed the terrified Madeleine to mete out the same diabolical vengeance upon her.

Not surprisingly, the legend of the Devil's Mansion was sufficient to frighten future residents away, and the mansion sat unoccupied for many years. The only beings reportedly seen there were the ghosts of Madeleine and Alcide, who repeatedly played the scene of her murderous attack on him. The only living persons to remain there, years later, were the daughter of the Civil War general Pierre Beauregard and her family. Somehow they were able to coexist with the unhappy ghosts. Another family subsequently moved in but found the specters more than they could handle, and soon left. They also reported the strong smell of something burning, invisible footsteps, and doorknobs that would turn on their own. Ultimately the most grotesque apparition that was ever seen there was the Devil's own head at an upstairs window or "gable." Some said they saw it grimace and growl, and reveal blood-drenched, pointed teeth. The Devil's Mansion was razed many years ago. Whether the story is fact or fiction, the psychological effect on anyone who lived there was likely substantial; so much negativity cannot produce a positive or normal environment. No wonder that many people frightened by ghosts had exorcisms performed to spiritually cleanse their premises of presumed evil spirits.[17]

The legend of vampires is not unique to New Orleans, for the "undead," as they are called, date back centuries in many countries and cultures, and were popularly fictionalized in the Bram Stoker classic about Count Dracula in the 1890s, and later in numerous horror films, beginning in the era of silent movies, with *Nosferatu*. However, as with Voodoo and ghosts, New Orleans has had its share of chilling vampire stories. One of the foremost researchers on the subject was the late parapsychologist Stephen Kaplan (1940–1995). It was his conclusion that vampires were more than legend; there are those who live on the blood of others, he found.[18]

The oldest building in New Orleans is the Ursuline Convent, built for an order of French nuns who arrived in 1727, but the sisters did not move in until 1734. According to one Web site, when the nuns arrived, they were appalled at the large number of men who'd been convicted criminals in France, who were released if they promised to move to Louisiana, help build New Orleans, and marry convicted prostitutes. To the nuns, the situation was morally offensive, and further they were alarmed that the men far outnumbered the women. Their solution was to send for "morally proper" young women from France. Two Ursuline sisters returned to France expressly for the purpose of recruiting poor but honest girls, between the ages of fifteen and nineteen, to migrate to New Orleans. A group of about two dozen arrived during the summer of 1728. But the young convent girls mixing with some very undesirable men did not elevate anyone's morality. Instead, the girls were raped and forced into prostitution; some of them died. New Orleans remained a city not easily tamed by Church standards, and the girls had to be rescued and returned to France. According to one version of events, the girls carried with them tiny coffins when they left, perhaps containing the bodies of infants who'd been born as a result of rapes. But once back in France, there was such upset and commotion that the caskets were shipped back to New Orleans, and made the responsibility of the Ursuline sisters.

Suspicion grew that for some inexplicable reason the Catholic Church had secretly concealed vampires in the coffins returned from France. The Church vehemently denied the allegation of smuggling vampires to America, and the rumor of the so-called "casket girls" eventually petered out.

In 1892, however, the story resurfaced when the archbishop of New Orleans ordered that all the coffins be stored in the Ursuline Convent. The strange boxes were put in the attic and its windows were closed over with wooden shutters. However, in the years that followed, many eyewitnesses told of seeing the shutters open, but only in the dark of night.[19]

Then in May of 1978, two female students from Boston University were researching the peculiar legend of the "casket girls," and in the course of their paranormal project, visited the Ursuline Convent. The Boston students were found soon after outside a chapel attached to the convent. Both young women had been killed in what police first thought was a vicious attack, likely by wild dogs, although strangely, there was no blood near the bodies.

When the New Orleans coroner conducted autopsies, his conclusion revealed something truly disturbing and considered medically impossible: 90 percent of the blood had been drained from each girl's body. Was it evidence of a vampire on the prowl? Had it been someone who'd secretly slept by day, but lived by night on the blood of unwitting and unwilling victims?

The Church, of course, denied any knowledge or culpability for the savage killings of the two young women. But Stephen Kaplan's conclusion that the manner in which the girls died and had been depleted of nearly all their blood, bore the signs of what some in law enforcement and occult research recognize as ritualistic or vampire killings.[20]

While the thought of individuals who drink human blood to survive was long regarded as myth or folklore, Kaplan's many years of vampire research produced substantial contemporary evidence that more people than we think either desire—or require—human blood. The savagery of bodies found murdered and drained of blood, Kaplan concluded, was often the work of vampire who lurked secretly under the cover of night. How many vampires stealthily prowl the French Quarter or other neighborhoods of New Orleans is anybody's guess. But if occult experts are to be believed then real vampires—those who crave human blood—stalk the Vieux Carre. Ironically, New Orleans is home to famed novelist Anne Rice whose books about vampires became bestsellers, notably her *Interview with the Vampire* in 1976, the first novel in her series, Vampire Chronicles. In fact, at one time, Rice held an annual vampire convention in New Orleans.[21]

New Orleans has to be regarded as having a special place in America's paranormal history. Even Samuel Clemens when he was a young riverboat pilot on the Mississippi once stopped there to visit a fortune-teller named Madame Caprell. She predicted his future as a writer, well before he became famous as Mark Twain.

There's little doubt that when *Travel Weekly* described the city as a place where the "unusual is the norm" it was probably an understatement. Serious parapsychologists who'd studied New Orleans before Hurricane Katrina—and hopefully will again after the city is restored to its fame and infamy—will continue to research the huge amount of occult activities and incidents, and the impact they've had on the city and its residents.

Should the conclusion of visitors, tourists, or skeptics be that the relationship between New Orleans and some very strange supernatural events are mere fiction or legends from long ago, let's bring you up to date.

In the aftermath of Hurricane Katrina, news reports told of California National Guard units sent to the beleaguered city in September 2005 as part of the first search and rescue operations. Not only did they witness images of horrendous damage and misery caused by the storm and floods, some of the troops reported they'd encountered ghostly phenomena. San Francisco TV station, channel 5, headlined its story on September 16, "Soldiers Spooked by New Orleans Spirits." As is too often the case when reporting psychic incidents, the news anchor added the requisite skeptical aside, "This next story will cause some to snicker." The report then went on to explain that some of the troops told of being haunted by spirits. One soldier, a California National Guard sergeant, said that when he opened his eyes in the hallway of a New Orleans building he saw the specter of a little girl. The soldier hastened to emphatically add, "It was not my imagination."

A California National Guardswoman interviewed insisted she saw a "shadow" lurking that she was certain was an apparition. Another soldier told of sharing the feeling of many of the evacuated children who said they felt "they were not alone"; they'd sensed ghostly presences close by. Still another Guardsman reached out for religious help when he encountered a spirit. "In the name of Jesus, we command you to leave," he called out. The TV report concluded by saying the ghostly experiences have "made many a seasoned soldier a believer."

"Stories of hauntings in New Orleans are legion," wrote Andrei Codrescu in *National Geographic Traveler.* "This is a city where Voodoo is still practiced and where, if you believe Anne Rice, there are more vampires than you can shake a stake at." In the French Quarter, the "haunted heart" of the city, "practically every street has at least one building with a creepy story associated with it." Which brings us back to the question we asked at the beginning of this chapter: Why did the French Quarter suffer far less hurricane damage than other parts of the city? Perhaps the answer from a leading paranormal expert is cynical. She concluded, "The Devil takes care of his own."

The serious question that remains is whether a long history of dark and evil practices and summoning negativity can cause harm, psychically as well as psychologically. Few cities can match the paranormal and occult history of New Orleans. Rarely have communities celebrated their supernatural and magical side to the extent New Orleans has—a city where an infamous bordello, the House of the Rising Sun, once sat on Ursuline Avenue, named for the order of nuns.

A Christian psychotherapist of Caribbean ancestry said that darkness leads to sin, and sin brings evil. In turn, evil brings destruction. New Orleans has certainly had its share of that.[22]

On October 3, 2005, the Associated Press reported, "The bells of historic St. Louis Cathedral[23] rang out across New Orleans yesterday, calling the faithful to the first mass since Hurricane Katrina hit more than a month ago." The famed cathedral with its triple spires "was left virtually untouched by Katrina's fierce winds and high waters." The same day, not too many blocks away, "bawdy" Bourbon Street was returning to life with its bars, Cajun music, strip clubs, and nude dancers. And somewhere in the French Quarter, Voodoo was still being practiced.

3

The Age of Spiritualism and Predictions of Disaster

The distinction between past, present, and future is only a stubbornly persistent illusion.
—ALBERT EINSTEIN

Who wouldn't want a peek at tomorrow, a look into the mysterious, un-known, and uncertain future? It is understandably one of humankind's longest held desires and there have been people in every generation who've claimed the unique ability to defy time and space as we conceive them and psychically peer through the curtain that separates today from tomorrow. Since the dawn of recorded history, prophets, seers, and prognosticators have played a significant part in predicting fates, fortunes, misfortunes, and disasters. Simply defined, the paranormal ability to see into the future is called precognition; it includes predictions, premonitions, and prophecies. "More than half of all psychic experiences are precognitive—they convey information about an event that has not yet taken place," explained parapsy-chologist Dr. Richard S. Broughton.[1]

Prior to and during America's Great Age of Spiritualism—roughly through the nineteenth and early twentieth centuries—prophecies and predictions were as eagerly sought as they were at any other time in his-tory. The roots of prophecy date back many millennia to ancient tribal shamans whose abilities to heal, counsel, and foresee the future were re-garded as extraordinary gifts that earned them an esteemed position in their respective cultures. Shamans played a similarly important role in the history of Native American tribes. For example, if a shaman predicted famine, he also could foretell if and when it would end.

"O Lord, you are my God, I will extol you and praise your name," vowed the prophet Isaiah (25:1). Such biblical pronouncements were believed to be the divine word of God, delivered by Old Testament prophets, not so much as a predictor of future events but to provide God's instructions for the Jewish people and warn of devastation or retribution if His word was ignored. In fact, most of the prominent individuals in the Old Testament were prophets: Moses, Isaiah, Daniel, Samuel, Elijah, Ezekiel, Joel, and Amos, to name a few.

For Christians, the Bible is the "most prophetic book," and of all biblical prophecies, the "best-known ones [concern] the return of the messiah" who is Jesus. Jews predict their own promised deliverer, but reject the belief that it will be Jesus.

New Testament prophecies say the Second Coming of Jesus will occur only after the antichrist has led the world through the huge bloody battle or struggle known as armageddon, before the Day of Judgment. In the New Testament, Jesus exceeds all others in His prophetic gifts.

Mother Ann Lee (1736–1784), founder of the Shakers sect, was certain she was the "Second Coming of Christ." But her "utopian" settlements founded in America were doomed by her insistence on sexual abstinence among her followers; and without procreation, obviously no future generations would be born within Shaker communities, which reached their peak in the nineteenth century then declined and disappeared.[2]

While prophecy falls within religious perimeters, predictions that foretell future events are within the realm of psychics and mediums, presumably received through spirit communication, rather than directly from God. There are also premonitions, those vague presentiments or forebodings that many of us often spontaneously experience before a calamity; their origin remains a mystery. Although prophecy and prediction are not identical, we'll use them interchangeably as a matter of convenience and to simplify terminology.

By the early nineteenth century, America was infused with the fervor of the religious revival known as the Second Great Awakening; and as the country grew and moved westward, revivalist preachers eagerly sought converts. It was a time when the nation saw its "first outburst of sectarian development in American religious history," wrote Robert C. Fuller in *Religious Revolutionaries.* "Several wholly religious groups or sects emerged . . ." For revivalists, the "emphasis [was] upon personal encounters with God that often gave rise to ecstatic experiences and mystical visions that were readily interpreted as new revelations."[3]

Based largely on biblical prophecies in the Books of Daniel and Revelation, many revivalists eagerly anticipated Jesus' return to Earth [Daniel 7:13–14; Revelation 5:1–10]. That concept, known as "millennialism," the prophecy of the Second Coming of Christ, was a powerful component of several American religious movements established in the early decades of the nineteenth century, among them the Seventh-Day Adventists in the 1840s. The promise of the Last Judgment or Doomsday in the Book of Revelation, apocalyptic in nature, predicts "the end of the world." The world as we know it may end in cataclysmic destruction, but the return of Jesus, say Christian believers, will bring peace and salvation to the righteous who obeyed God's laws.

As the year 999 AD drew to a close in the West, and the new millennium approached, there was dread among many that the world would come to a sudden and violent end. The hellish scenario was fueled by a combination of prophecy, superstition, and an understandable fear of the unknown; the Church stepped in to try and calm fears and minimize widespread panic, although some historians say there may have been less anxiety at the time than is assumed. When the year 1000 AD arrived it did not produce the annihilation that many had foretold; life with all its trials, tribulations, and tragedies continued as before. Presumably that stilled the "widespread fear of the end of the world and the last judgment" that had been anticipated. It did not, however, discourage prophets of doom in every age throughout the centuries that followed from regularly predicting the end days; and each time, there were multitudes ready to believe the apocalypse was at hand. And fueling fears were the familiar symbols from the Book of Revelation: the Four Horsemen of the Apocalypse; the Sign of the Beast, 666; and the Antichrist.[4]

In addition to the word of the Bible and the preachers and prophets who kept alive apocalyptic fears, there were secular clairvoyants and seers, many whose stories we told in our previous book, and who became known over the centuries for their precognitive and prophetic powers. In fact, those who made prophecies and predictions have a long history.[5]

Among the best known was the woman of Endor in the Old Testament, who was actually a medium; the famed oracle of Delphi in ancient Greece; the Roman augurs and soothsayers, one of whom predicted Caesar's assassination in 44 BC.

Roger Bacon, a Franciscan monk who lived in the thirteenth century, foresaw such inventions as the telescope, microscope, flying machines, elevators, deep-sea exploration, and the steamship, centuries before their invention; of course, there was the clairaudient French peasant girl, Joan of Arc in the fifteenth century; and the visionary Leonardo da Vinci. There was also the medieval English prophetess, Mother Shipton, whose predictions have been questioned by many for their authenticity; Nostradamus, the famed sixteenth-century French seer; John Dee, the royal prognosticator to Queen Elizabeth I in sixteenth century England; and George Fox, whose seventeenth-century predictions included the Great Fire of London.

In the seventeenth century, the English philosopher and intellectual Sir Francis Bacon remarkably prophesied machines and "mass production," telephones, submarines, flying machines, the refrigerator, and "light intensified and thrown great distances," likely a reference to the laser, not devised until the 1960s. There was Swedish mystic and clairvoyant Emanuel Swedenborg[6]; and also the early nineteenth-century English prophetess Joanna Southcott.

Those seers who were not clergy but possessed psychic gifts often were forced to hide them from the wrath of the Catholic Church, especially during the centuries of the Inquisition and witch burnings that swept across Europe.

In Puritan New England, daring to predict future misfortune or adversity could result in severe punishment, even execution, when prognosticators were believed to be in league with the dark forces of the devil. On occasion, the accuracy was uncanny. You may recall the story we told in our previous book about one of the women condemned to the gallows as a witch in Salem, Massachusetts, in 1692 whose last words were to predict her executioner would choke to death on his own blood for taking her life. Years later, the eerie prediction came true when her Puritan judge died in exactly that manner.[7]

Americans in the nineteenth century were no different than anyone else in wanting a glimpse of tomorrow, whether the predictions came from a clerical or secular visionary such as the "Poughkeepsie Seer," Andrew Jackson Davis who predicted automobiles and airplanes in the mid-1850s, and even foresaw the computer. However, his prediction of intelligent life on other planets has not proven accurate—so far.[8] What was most important was being able to peer into the future with the help of someone who had that special power to see or sense what lay ahead; in that way, perhaps a person could change his fate or at least be better prepared for some impending crisis or disaster. Fortune-tellers, astrologers, and crystal ball gazers never went completely out of fashion, although the churches condemned dabbling in divination and the occult, while rationalists disdained the supernatural as a relic of ancient superstition.

In the eighteenth century, Italian Archbishop Prospero Lambertini, who later became Pope Benedict XIV, was one of the first and most important psychic investigators anywhere. Commenting on the centuries-old practice of seers and prophets who only revealed their predictions to kings, queens, and other powerful leaders, Lambertini concluded that common people, as well as the rich and powerful also had access to "knowledge of things to come." He found that when people saw future events, they were more likely to do so while sleeping than when they were awake; and often images of the future appeared as symbols. Lambertini observed that prophets frequently were unable to discern whether a prediction was coming from some supernatural or "divine" source or their own thinking.[9]

Small sects were the most likely to hold "millennial" or apocalyptic religious convictions. One of the more interesting American groups in this category was the Millerites; at the heart of their beliefs was the millennial concept.

William Miller (1782–1849) was a poor New England farmer who converted to the evangelical faith in the early 1800s after he came home discouraged following military service during the War of 1812, deeply shaken by the bloodshed, agony, and devastation he saw. He hoped for answers to his disillusionment through Christianity, and avidly began studying the Bible. His attention was especially drawn to the Book of Daniel and the last book of the New Testament, Revelation.

Miller fervently prayed for the Second Coming of Christ; his overriding objective was to determine when Jesus would make His reappearance on Earth to reveal His Last Judgment on humanity's fate. Miller became obsessed as he worked feverishly to calculate the date of Christ's return; and through his biblical and mathematical research he was certain that he'd actually computed the time of the Second Coming. He was stunned when he discovered the date would be between March 21, 1843, and March 21, 1844. He wrote that he made his startling find in 1818, and that gave the world only twenty-five years to prepare for the apocalypse. Unnerved by the realization that so little time remained for humanity on Earth, Miller checked and rechecked his figures, but for a long time kept them secret. No matter how often he scrutinized them, he consistently arrived at the same answer: 1843.

Miller's next problem was how to share the information with others. With that in mind, the bashful and unassuming farmer became a revivalist preacher in his own right. In 1831, Miller addressed a Baptist revival with a rousing lecture about biblical prophecy. The following year, 1832, he wrote and published a booklet with the lofty but appropriate title, *Evidences from Scripture and History of the Second Coming of Christ about the Year 1843*. He became an ordained Baptist minister and his apocalyptic prediction received increasing notice from both the public and clergy. Many were especially fascinated by Miller's seeming capacity to pinpoint the date of Jesus' return.

Joshua Himes, a Boston minister, was one of those intrigued by Miller's ingenuity in deciphering the "end times." Himes had a knack for generating publicity, and with his help, in 1839 Miller's millennial message gained wide attention across the country; it had become a national movement. Himes was so confident in the appeal of the prediction he purchased a huge tent that seated an audience of four thousand so the public could hear Miller speak. Himes also began publishing a newspaper, several newsletters, and magazines, all of them focused on the millennialism theme; the best known was *Signs of the Times*.

Great numbers became enthralled—and frightened—by Miller's prophecy. Soon there were no less than fifty thousand devoted followers known as Millerites and many thousands more were inspired by his prognostication. Even among those who did not believe the prediction, there was curiosity and debate. Some regarded the sect as "irrational fanatics," newspapers called the movement's leader "Mad Miller," and mainstream churches condemned him. But many others defended Miller and his adherents. His was "a message promising immediate and total resolution of the world's imperfections," wrote Robert C. Fuller. What's more, Miller's prophecy came following the "financial and economic panic" of 1837 that swept America causing "inflated land values, wildcat banking, [and] paper speculation," Bernard Grun wrote in *The Timetables of History*. As Fuller noted, "Miller's message was perfectly tailored to such spiritual and economic disappointments."

The multitudes now waited for the glories of the kingdom of God to descend—Christ's thousand-year reign on earth—just as it had been prophesized in Revelation 20: 1–5. As 1843 drew closer, millennialism reached a fever pitch among believers. There was such certainty about Miller's prediction that many of his followers willingly gave up all their worldly goods and belongings to await the Second Coming.

Finally, 1843 arrived and the faithful eagerly anticipated the momentous event; others looked skyward out of curiosity, if not because of religious conviction. The days, weeks, and months went by and then the year was over. But Christ never descended nor was His arrival preceded by the apocalyptic devastation that had been prophesied.

If Miller was discouraged he hid it behind a brave countenance. Back he went to his arithmetic and computations; he said he would correct his error and determine a new date. Soon he confidently announced the Second Coming would occur no later than October 1844. Once again the Millerites held their breath and waited; but October came and went quietly. There was no violent upheaval or disaster, and Christ did not appear. For the Millerites—and presumably other enthusiasts—the non-event became known as "The Great Disappointment." Not surprisingly, it was a major setback for both Miller's credibility and for the Adventist movement that was based on the belief in the coming of Christ. Hardest hit by the erroneous prediction and subsequent letdown was the Millerite sect, which lost many followers.

William Miller remained resolute; he refused to admit defeat, and contended his prophecy was sound. Then a woman who had long experienced visions came to Miller's rescue. Ellen Gould White was a "charismatic prophetess," and she said in no uncertain terms that her visions wholeheartedly supported Miller's prediction. She publicly pronounced that he had been correct about the date; but he'd misunderstood the meaning of the "end times." But make no mistake, she reminded, Christ was preparing to come back to Earth. She apparently helped Miller regain a measure of credibility.

Eventually her visions became the basis for the founding of the religious denomination known as the Seventh-Day Adventists, which had about 3,500 members in the 1860s, and a hundred years later grew to more than 500,000 adherents in the United States, and totaled 1.5 million worldwide. William Miller eventually faded from public attention, as did his movement.[10]

Several observations emerge from Miller's blunder into the world of prophecy. Something he and his followers may have overlooked appears in the New Testament. Matthew 24:36 quotes Jesus, "No man knows the day or the hour I am coming, not even the angels of heaven, nor the Son, but only the Father." In other words, neither Miller nor the prophetess Ellen White could have predicted precisely when Christ would make His return. If you believe in the Advent, it might be tomorrow—or a thousand years hence, although many suggest that prophetic signs—wars, epidemics, famine, comets, and natural disasters—indicate we now are living in the "end days." But haven't there always been disasters; and hasn't the end of the world been predicted countless times throughout history?

The second observation is that people need prophets. Humankind cannot function securely without some structure, and people require prophets and prognosticators, whether they consciously realize it or not. Time on Earth is, of course, artificially divided into past, present, and future. It is the unknown future that is the most frightening and challenging. We may not think of ourselves as prophets, but every time we make plans or decisions for something ahead, that is exactly what we become. Unless we are one of those rare and gifted individuals who can psychically see beyond today, the most we can do is make an educated guess about what will happen tomorrow, and then hope or pray for the best.

Life is always a calculated risk. Even so, when we are unexpectedly interrupted by tragedy we are dazed, stunned, even numbed, and invariably at a loss for a rational explanation. On September 11, 2001, terrorists killed nearly three thousand people in several locations including the World Trade Center. We had not in our wildest dreams planned for the enormity of that catastrophe. How were we supposed to prepare beforehand and then cope with the horrific aftermath? What do we do to ready ourselves for the next unforeseen attack? As we talked about in the opening chapter of our earlier book, after September 11 many people hurried to read Nostradamus. Others sought answers from biblical prophecies. Some claimed they had premonitions of death and destruction prior to September 11 but were not certain how to interpret them.

In July 1996, all two hundred thirty aboard were killed in the crash of TWA Flight 800, a jetliner bound from New York to Paris that went down over the waters off Long Island. Shock and grief overwhelmed loved ones of those on the doomed plane. Change the date, and consider family members in any past century or year who had lost someone in war, accident, earthquake, flood or fire, crime, political upheaval, disease, or any other natural or man-made tragedy. People are no more ready psychologically to face calamity now than they were in 1896, 1916, 1996, or 2001. In 1900, many Americans had apocalyptic fears when one of the worst hurricanes to ever hit this country struck Galveston, Texas, claiming eight thousand lives. Some will look at more recent disasters as the Asian tsunami in 2004, and the horrific Gulf Coast Hurricane Katrina in 2005, as prophetic signs of the approaching end times. But every generation throughout history has feared such omens; has been that way dating back to primitive societies.

Now introduce those who claim they have the special gift to predict or describe events that have not yet happened, but will. If someone can tell you what's coming tomorrow in a dangerous and uncertain world, would you reject the warning? In that way we have changed little from the ancient tribes that sought shamans to guide their lives. Seeking a way to ascertain future events is more than mere curiosity. It is a way to cope with a very significant human characteristic: fear of the unknown.

Skeptics entirely miss the point when they ignore our deep desire to know what tomorrow holds. More than superstition, it is a psychological need so strong that just because we may never find someone who can truly predict what is going to happen, doesn't mean we won't try. In as common an experience as watching or listening to weather forecasts— sometimes woefully inaccurate in spite of sophisticated meteorological instruments, radar, and computer models—we are seeking information about the future, even if it's only to learn how hot, cold, wet, or dry it will be the next day. Millions consult mediums, psychics, and astrologers, or at least steal a look at newspaper or magazine horoscopes.

William Miller was hardly the first or last prophet to be mistaken. If we cannot acquire knowledge of future events with any accuracy from self-proclaimed religious or secular seers, prophets, or psychics, many will unwittingly turn to false prophets. Our fear and insecurity about what will happen to us and our loved ones is too deeply rooted in our psychological and chemical makeup to simply ignore the need to feel safer by glimpsing ahead—if we can.

That brings us to the perplexing question of those rare men and women—and even children—who throughout history and to the very present have a gift or ability that allows them to cross the boundaries of time and space to provide some clue about the unseen and unknown future. Although many of us maintain a skeptical attitude, there is a long history of accurate prophecies, predictions, and premonitions; and there are people who either see or experience an intuitive awareness about events that have not yet occurred.[11] How do we know when to heed our dreams or uneasy feelings that sometimes reach beyond our five senses? And what can we learn from examples throughout history of forewarnings and forebodings that have proven uncannily correct? What makes the seers and psychics able to predict as they do? From where do they access information about the future, and do we all have some measure of precognitive ability if we are attentive and attuned to it? These are frustrating questions religion, science, and parapsychology still wrestle with.

There is arguably no prophet more uniquely American than Joseph Smith, the founder of the Mormon religion, known formally as the Church of Jesus Christ of Latter-day Saints.[12] Born in Vermont in 1805, Smith was raised in the small western New York State community of Fayette. It was the region that became a hotbed of religious revivalism in the early nineteenth century, not far from where spiritualism would be born with the help of the Fox sisters and their spirit raps years later.

Smith was a fourteen-year-old boy in 1820 when he developed a strong interest in Christianity, and especially "the salvation of his soul." One of his questions centered on the confusion he felt being surrounded by a growing number of religious denominations, each with some variation or different interpretation of the Bible. But, he wondered, which was the "true church of Christ"? He was in the woods not far from home one day when he seemed to receive his answer: He experienced "a vision of great light, and two glorious personages appeared before him and commanded him to join none of the sects, for the Lord was about to restore the Gospel, which was not represented in its fullness by any of the existing churches."

Three years later, in 1823 when Smith was seventeen he experienced another vision that dealt with the Second Coming of Christ. That was followed by the appearance of an angel named Moroni who told young Smith he'd been selected to reinstate "God's true church on earth." The angel also informed Smith that he would be directed where to find "golden plates" or tablets that would permit him to translate the Book of Mormon.[13]

Finally in September 1827, after he'd turned twenty-one, Smith received the golden plates from the angel. Eleven witnesses accompanied him to verify the event. The gold tablets contained writing in some unknown language that resembled a form of Egyptian. Smith had also been given two magical stones that he said enabled him to translate or decipher the words and symbols on the plates. They were supposedly "the sacred records of the ancient inhabitants of this continent," according to author Benson Landis in his book *World Religions*.

Smith explained it this way: "There was a book deposited, written upon gold plates, also there were two stones in silver bowls . . . the possession and use of these stones were what constituted 'seers' in former times." He dutifully translated the writing from the tablets and dictated it to several friends and early Mormon believers. When the task was completed in 1830, they were published under the title the Book of Mormon "which described the fate of the lost tribes of Israel that had, it claimed, emigrated to America in the centuries before Christ," wrote Tony Allan in *Prophecies*. This was a "new revelation," in Allan's words, and Joseph Smith had been its "latter-day prophet."[14] That bestowed him with the responsibility of leading the new religion with the sacred right to create a church in order to carry forth its teachings.

In April 1830, Smith and his group of followers formally established their new church in Fayette, New York. Smith was handsome, personable, and a convincing speaker, traits that helped him gain a growing number of followers and converts to the Mormon faith. The new religious denomination and Smith, who was described as an authentic "American prophet," made news around the country.

A Mormon community was established in Ohio, but Smith and his new religion faced animosity from "gentiles" who quickly opposed them. When the Mormons resettled in Missouri, they faced ill treatment that erupted into violence and even death. Apparently many feared their communities would be overrun by hordes of Mormons, and by 1833 Smith and his followers were forced out.

Next they moved to Illinois, but hostility and violence exploded when the number of Mormons swelled into the thousands. In June 1844, a mob attacked Smith and his brother, and both were shot and killed. Three years later, in 1847, the Church of Latter-day Saints had a new and forceful leader in Brigham Young who led the Mormons to what would become the location of their headquarters to this day: Salt Lake City, Utah.

Tony Allan summed up the Joseph Smith story by noting the irony of Smith's death at the hands of "gentiles" or non-Mormons that eventually helped boost the Mormon faith. "Like many prophets before him, [Smith] had become a martyr in his own cause."

From a paranormal or supernatural perspective, several elements of Joseph Smith's story parallel or overlap with psychic experiences, including his visions, angelic visitations, "magic" stones, and of course his prophecies associated with the founding of the Mormon faith. "Healing, prophecy, and revelation" are all components within the church. Mormon belief is "that life has neither beginning nor end but is a continuous existence which always was and ever will be," wrote Mark P. Leone in *Roots of Modern Mormonism*. That same afterlife belief is integral to spiritualism.[15]

The fact that psychic and religious phenomena often coincide does not surprise most parapsychologists. "Up to the nineteenth century, paranormal phenomena [was] inextricably bound up with religious beliefs," Richard Broughton wrote.[16] However, for many traditional Christians, the idea has long been anathema. Yet the difference between the two is often more a matter of semantics than substance. Fundamentalists question the source of psychic pronouncements and predictions, assuming they must be of some demonic origin, a contention long leveled against mediums, clairvoyants, astrologers, and those with a more spiritually liberal bent.

Since the dawn of recorded history, prophets and prognosticators have predicted the fates of world leaders. Remember the Old Testament story of Joseph's interpretations of Pharaoh's dreams of feast and famine?

There was also Daniel who experienced prophetic dreams and visions, and used his ability to tell the Babylonian king, Nebuchadnezzar, his dreams and their meaning. Prophets traditionally spoke to pharaohs, kings, or the powerful leaders of nations or city-states. So it is no surprise that those who've attained the American presidency have also been the subjects of predictions, and will probably continue to be for as long as there are presidents—and prognosticators.

Perhaps no prophecy affecting U.S. presidents is better known, more ominous, and at the same time more hotly debated than the so-called "presidential curse," laid upon then-governor William Henry Harrison by the Shawnee medicine man and shaman Tenskwatawa, which predicted the death in office of the president every twenty years. Skeptics and debunkers have long regarded the story as mere legend or superstition, but that does not alter its place within the history of the American paranormal, or the precognitive powers of Tenskwatawa who was known as the "Prophet."[17]

The so-called "curse" began in 1840, when Governor Harrison first sought the White House, as a direct result of his victory in a bloody military campaign—some would have called it a slaughter—against the Shawnee and their chief Tecumseh. It was then that Harrison became the victim of Tenskwatawa's curse, which some say may continue to haunt the American presidency to this very day.

William Henry Harrison's campaign slogan, "Tippecanoe and Tyler Too!" reminded potential voters that he had been a popular war hero years earlier, and the catchphrase attracted enormous attention, became wildly popular throughout the country, and ultimately helped propel Harrison to the presidency. Tippecanoe, in the Indiana Territory in 1811, was the site of a fierce battle between the Americans and Shawnee Indians, whose leader was the astute and charismatic chief, Tecumseh. Harrison, then territorial governor, led American forces in repelling the Shawnee, forcing them off land Harrison wanted for new settlements.

Tensions between white men and Indians over the ownership of lands, long strained, had worsened as Indians increasingly found their territories encroached upon by white settlers. Angry and frustrated at Harrison's incursions onto tribal lands, Tecumseh issued a warning to Harrison in 1810 that the Indians "were determined to make a stand where they were." To mount a united defense against the white men, he issued a call for a western confederation of Indians to deal with the U.S. government. But it was not to be. The loss at the Battle of Tippecanoe was particularly bitter and shattered Tecumseh's plans for confederation.

Tecumseh, one of the most famous of all American Indian leaders, and Harrison, a popular state politician, had become fierce enemies by the time the Battle of Tippecanoe was fought. The Americans were able to drive the Shawnee off the field of battle and humiliate Tecumseh, demolishing the Indian settlement at Tippecanoe, also called Prophetstown, in the process. Harrison had all but ended the western migration of Indians in America. For Harrison, the victory became a stepping-stone to an ambitious political career, which he exploited as much as he could after he became known as the "Hero of Tippecanoe."

On December 16, 1811, after Tecumseh pronounced an angry threat to make the "ground shake," the most severe earthquake ever to strike the United States hit with such tremendous force over an immense Midwestern region that the Mississippi and Ohio rivers flowed backward, entire villages and farms vanished, and the skies darkened for two full days as the result of dust from collapsing homes and trees. Vast areas of land sank and disappeared. Wild and domestic animals panicked. Even previously buried dead were jarred from their graves. Casualty counts were imprecise, however, the vast area was sparsely populated. Likely, at least many hundreds died. Had the region been dense with people, the death toll would have been catastrophic. The quake was so powerful that it could be felt in every direction for nearly a thousand miles. Indians knew that only one man had the power to predict or cause such a disaster: Tecumseh.

The great chief never lived to see his dream of Indian confederation come true; the idea died with Tecumseh in 1813.

Tecumseh's younger brother, Tenskwatawa (1775–1836), widely known among the Shawnee as the "Prophet," became a religious leader and medicine man with a remarkable gift for prophecy. His paranormal abilities intensified after he experienced a vision of a beautiful and peaceful heaven—the spirit world—following a serious bout of illness during an epidemic when he fell into a coma, during which he probably had a near-death event. The emotionally overwhelming out-of-body experience, which enabled him to reach a transcendental state, transformed him from an unpleasant and alcoholic braggart into a "holy man." Reacting to the encroachment of Indian lands by the Americans, Tenskwatawa admonished his followers to avoid contact with the white man, and pronounced Americans "the children of the Evil Spirit." Instead, he hoped his people would return to their traditional way of life and customs.

William Henry Harrison, however, branded Tenskwatawa an "imposter" and demanded that if he was a genuine prophet, to prove so. "If he is really a prophet, ask him to cause the sun to stand still. If he does . . . you may then believe that he has been sent from God."

To Harrison's chagrin, Tenskwatawa proved ready for the challenge when he announced his powers would "darken the midday sun." To the absolute horror of his superstitious tribesmen, he then accurately, if inexplicably, predicted a solar eclipse and claimed he had dimmed the sun. He followed one amazing prediction with another. After this Tenskwatawa was taken seriously, even by his enemies.

Most historians believe Tecumseh prophesied the monstrous December 1811 earthquake. However, sometime after Tecumseh's death, Tenskwatawa took credit for both predicting and supernaturally causing the earth to convulse, as it never had before.

Tenskwatawa's most enduring and best-known prophecy was his infamous "presidential curse." Incensed by the defeat at Tippecanoe, Tenskwatawa invoked a malediction on his archenemy, William Henry Harrison, and declared that the U.S. president elected every twenty years would die in office. "Harrison will not win this year to be the Great Chief. But he may win next year. If he does, he will not finish his term. He will die in office," Tenskwatawa proclaimed.

"No president has ever died in office," a visitor pointed out to the Prophet.

"But Harrison will die, I tell you," Tenskwatawa insisted. "And when he dies you will remember my brother Tecumseh's death. And after him, every Great Chief chosen every twenty years thereafter will die. And when each one dies, let everyone remember the death of our people."

Despite the Prophet's ominous forewarning, Harrison ignored the threat and when it came time to run for president, he eagerly embraced the popular campaign slogan, "Tippecanoe and Tyler Too!" which contributed to his winning the White House in 1840. By this time, Tenskwatawa had been dead for four years.

Harrison, who handily won the election, may have had a premonition of his fate when he said good-bye to friends and neighbors in Cincinnati, Ohio, on January 26, 1841. "This may be the last time I have the pleasure of speaking to you on earth or seeing you. I will bid you farewell. If forever, fare thee well," he told them. Harrison's words quickly proved prescient.

Inauguration day, March 4, 1841, dawned cold, windy, and rainy in Washington, DC. Harrison had made the grueling journey to the nation's capital from Ohio by stagecoach, boat, and train, and stopped frequently along the route to meet the throngs gathered to see and hear their new president. He arrived in Washington visibly tired and weak, but despite the ordeal of his trip, he gallantly rode with neither hat nor coat to his inauguration on a white horse, ignoring, to his peril, the foul and blustery weather. After taking the oath of office, Harrison delivered the longest inaugural address in American presidential history; it ran an hour and forty-five minutes.

Later that bone-chilling day, Harrison was drenched by a heavy rainfall and soon after complained of chills and fatigue. It was obvious the new president had caught a severe cold, and during the next four weeks his health worsened. By April 3, Harrison was drifting in and out of consciousness. Then on April 4, 1841, after spending the previous eight days in bed, William Henry Harrison succumbed to pneumonia at age sixty-eight, becoming the first president to die in office, an office he had held for only one month. Tenskwatawa's prediction had proven surprisingly accurate.[18]

Was this indeed, the very fulfillment of Tenskwatawa's prophecy, which, after Harrison's death, would continue every twenty years exactly as the Shawnee seer foretold?

Abraham Lincoln, elected in 1860, was assassinated in 1865. Elected in 1880, James Garfield was assassinated in 1881. William McKinley, reelected in 1900, fell to an assassin's bullet in 1901. Warren G. Harding, elected in 1920, died in office in 1923. Franklin Delano Roosevelt, elected for a third term in 1940, died in office in 1945. John F. Kennedy, elected in 1960, was assassinated in 1963. Ronald Reagan, elected in 1980, barely survived an assassin's bullet in 1981, making him seemingly, the first president to finally break the infamous curse 140 years later.[19] Some parapsychologists speculate that Reagan's surviving the attempted assassination may have been the result of First Lady Nancy Reagan's dependence on astrological charts for predicting the best—and worst—times for presidential appointments.

Had Tenskwatawa made good on his threat to reach out from the spirit world to invoke a terrible curse on the presidents?

While prophecy has long been associated with religious belief, predictions and premonitions are spontaneous events that can occur to just about anyone at any time; that includes those who consider themselves professional psychics and mediums as well as so-called average or everyday people, many of whom don't regard themselves as psychic; some who do not even believe that paranormal phenomena is genuine.

Parapsychologists have found that the majority of psychic experiences—some 60 percent—take place in dreams, or to be more precise, during the dream state; and most psychic dreams are about "future events," as Richard Broughton noted.[20]

One of the founders of the Disciples of Christ Church, Alexander Campbell (1788–1866), no friend or advocate of psychic phenomena, was himself precognitive. In 1807, Campbell experienced a vision that the *Hibernia,* the ship that he was to sail on to America, would be demolished. Shaken by the vivid dream, he shared it with his mother and sisters who were traveling with him. Exactly as Campbell foresaw, the *Hibernia* met with disaster when it foundered, although its passengers were all rescued.[21]

Those who've had premonitions of their own deaths include several presidents of the United States. James Knox Polk, the eleventh president (1845–1849), predicted his own death shortly before it occurred on June 15, 1849. The next president, Zachary Taylor, taken ill on July 4, 1850, made a similar prediction before he died of cholera. "I'll be dead in two days," he'd announced on July 7. He died on July 9.

In our previous book we described in detail a number of the paranormal experiences that Abraham Lincoln, our most psychic president had. We related the incident after he was elected in 1860 in which Lincoln saw two images of himself. His interpretation was that he'd be elected to a second term but would die in office.

You'll recall his prophetic dream that he'd been killed by an assassin's bullet, shortly before John Wilkes Booth murdered him in Ford's Theatre on April 14, 1865. Lincoln saw himself lying dead in a casket in the White House, while all around, throngs of people were loudly sobbing. That was the most vivid and disturbing of the premonitions Lincoln had concerning his own death. Considering that both Lincolns were strong believers in "prophetic omens," it is baffling that the president failed to heed the obvious warnings. Could his destiny have been changed, or was what he saw in his dream fated to occur no matter what action he took?[22]

In addition to the spontaneous premonitions that Lincoln had about his own death, there were also mediums who predicted his assassination. In 1863, while he was in France, the famed medium D. D. Home psychically peered into the future and told friends that President Lincoln would be killed in office. Mrs. Lincoln's medium, Nettie Colburn, said she also had a sense of foreboding when she visited with Mr. Lincoln, fearing that he would soon meet with some danger while still president, and that, sadly, she would not see him again. In March 1865, she told Lincoln that the spirit world had warned her of the danger hanging over his life. Lincoln did not register any surprise, as if he was resigned to his fate, and mentioned other mediums had made that same prediction. "The horoscope was cast, fixed, irreversible," he'd once told a close friend. Lincoln's former law partner William Herndon recalled that Lincoln often told him, "I am sure I shall meet with some terrible end."[23]

When Nettie Colburn was a teenager in the 1850s, and found she had mediumistic abilities and could induce spirit rappings, she'd made a psychic prediction that the winner of the 1856 presidential election would be James Buchanan. Her father, a staunch supporter of the opposing candidate, John C. Fremont, was surprised to hear his young daughter, with no knowledge of politics, foretell the outcome of the election the day before the voting when she grabbed a piece of paper. Nettie scrawled the name "Buchanan," and as she did "loud raps came upon the table." Her startled father asked, "Do you mean . . . that Buchanan will be elected tomorrow?" Nettie just nodded. The next day, her prediction proved accurate.[24]

The Civil War ended when Confederate General Robert E. Lee surrendered to General Ulysses Grant on April 9, 1865. Despite the president's many precognitive dreams and his aides' forebodings about his safety, Lincoln was in a celebratory mood; he accepted an invitation to attend Ford's Theatre on Good Friday evening, April 14, where he and Mrs. Lincoln would sit in a flag-draped "presidential box," to enjoy a play, the popular comedy, *Our American Cousin*.

Perhaps, as Herndon later said, the president "felt the nearness of the awful hour," and left his destiny in the hands of fate. Earlier that same day, Lincoln held meetings with his cabinet, other officials, and the victorious General Grant. It appeared the premonitions were on the president's mind; for three consecutive nights he'd dreamed that he would be assassinated. Several cabinet members thought Lincoln seemed unusually distracted and morose. At one point he described his recurring dream premonition in which he always saw himself in a boat or vessel that moved rapidly "toward a dark and indefinite shore." Now he told his cabinet officials that he'd had the dream again. Lincoln's interpretation was that "something extraordinary was going to happen, and that soon."[25]

The president had invited Grant and his wife, Julia, to join them at Ford's Theatre, as an honor rightly due him for achieving the victory that ended the war only days earlier. But that same morning, April 14, Mrs. Grant was seized with a terribly uneasy feeling; and she wanted the entire family to leave Washington, DC, that very day. When she first told the general, he explained that his schedule was filled; there was simply no way he could go. However, as the day wore on, her foreboding intensified, and so did her persistence. She repeatedly sent messages to her husband frantically imploring him to depart, regardless of his appointments.

Finally, under the barrage of Mrs. Grant's pleadings and stubborn resolve, General Grant gave in. After making apologies to the president, the Grants left Washington by train, and headed for their home in New Jersey. Only when they stopped in Philadelphia did they hear the dreadful news that President Lincoln had been shot by an assassin, the crazed actor John Wilkes Booth. Later Grant discovered his name was on a list of Booth's intended assassination targets. By heeding her premonition, Mrs. Grant undoubtedly saved her husband's life, and perhaps changed the course of American history; for in 1869, Ulysses Grant became the eighteenth president of the United States, and served for two terms.[26]

After the assassination, Lincoln's cousin traveled back to the Midwest to tell the slain president's elderly stepmother the news that he'd been murdered. The cousin was taken aback when Sarah Bush Lincoln already knew; she'd experienced a strong premonition that her beloved stepson had been killed.

James Garfield was elected the twentieth president in 1880; and in the wake of corruption in the Grant administration he sought the reform of civil service laws. It would ultimately prove to be a fateful policy, which antagonized many in both political parties along with those who sought patronage. Garfield's stance on the controversial issue, he privately admitted, was guided by psychic advice from his late father, who wanted him to reform government.

At some point during his short term in office, Garfield experienced a frightening premonition that he would be murdered. Possibly the information was also psychically communicated to Garfield by his late father, Abram. Unfortunately, the warning could do nothing to alter Garfield's fate. Nor could an unusual meeting Garfield held with his Secretary of War, Robert Lincoln, son of the late president. At the end of June 1881, Garfield called Robert Lincoln to the White House and asked him to describe in detail recollections of his father's assassination. Robert Lincoln, twenty-one when President Lincoln was shot and killed in 1865, met with an extremely attentive Garfield for more than an hour.

Only four months into his term of office, on July 2, 1881, and just two days after his conversation with Robert Lincoln, Garfield waited in the Baltimore and Potomac Railroad Station in Washington, DC, to board a train for a vacation when he was approached by a deranged, rejected office seeker named Charles J. Guiteau. The assassin, blaming the president personally for the political rebuff he'd received, fired two rounds into Garfield's back, and he collapsed on the floor.

Ironically, President Garfield, who had talked openly about psychic phenomena, was shot and mortally wounded by a self-described spiritualist. In his delusions, Guiteau was convinced he was fulfilling his role as "the hand of destiny." Several times the mentally troubled assassin rambled that "spirits" had instigated his murderous act, and that he considered Garfield to be the personification of evil. Not surprisingly, those who abhorred spiritualism seized upon the shooting to discredit the belief. Others, more realistically, viewed Guiteau as a crazed religious fanatic.

Garfield lingered on in terrible pain for several weeks while doctors tried to remove the bullets that had splintered his spine. But his surgeons made a grievous error when they failed to sterilize their medical instruments or sufficiently wash their hands before they probed the president's wounds. As a result, Garfield developed a serious infection that, likely in combination with blood poisoning caused by the bullets, proved fatal. Despite the prayers of the nation horrified by the shooting, James Garfield became the second president to die at the hand of an assassin when he passed on September 19, 1881, with his wife Lucretia at his bedside. Garfield was not yet fifty years old.[27]

Was the assassination a chance occurrence? Or had James Garfield become the third president whose fate had been predicted by the Shawnee prophet's curse more than sixty years earlier, and first visited on William Henry Harrison?

In 1896, William McKinley (1843–1901) was elected the twenty-fifth president. While serving in office, McKinley had a foreboding that he'd meet with danger. His wife, Ida, also had a similar nagging premonition; she was certain her husband would be killed. On September 14, 1901, while visiting the Pan-American Exposition in Buffalo, New York, Mrs. McKinley's worst fears came true when President McKinley was fatally shot by an assassin, an anarchist named Leon Frank Czolgosz. Again the question loomed, was it a random act or was McKinley another victim of the Shawnee prophet's malediction?[28]

When William Henry Harrison died suddenly in April 1841 after only a month in office, his vice president, John Tyler (1790–1862), was elevated to president of the United States. When Tyler's wife, Letitia, died in 1842, life in the White House became depressing and lonely. Then, the next year he met a beautiful and personable young woman named Julia Gardiner (1820–1889), thirty years his junior, and the daughter of a U.S. senator from New York, David Gardiner. Tyler was instantly smitten with the lovely Julia who, unbeknownst to him, was quite psychic. At first she resisted his entreaties, but a tragic twist of fate drew them closer.

On February 28, 1844, a public demonstration was held for a new type of naval cannon aboard the steamer *Princeton* anchored in the Potomac River. Among the hundreds invited were President Tyler, many government officials, military figures, and other dignitaries and their wives. Everyone aboard seemed to be in a festive mood with the exception of Anne Gilmer, wife of the secretary of the navy, who had experienced a terrifying premonition in which she envisioned her husband's death right there on the deck of the *Princeton*.

Another person who admitted to a frightening dream premonition the night before was Julia Gardiner, and she immediately shared the chilling specifics with her father. She told him the dream was more realistic than any she'd ever had. Julia described in detail the deck of the *Princeton*, although she'd never been aboard it. In the unnerving vision, she saw two white horses galloping toward her across the ship's deck. As they came closer, she could see that the riders were skeletons, death itself. Then one of the skeletons turned to look at Julia. It had the face of her father and stared directly at her.

She was so alarmed by the macabre vision that she pleaded with her father not to attend the ceremonies on the *Princeton*, fearing for his life. But Gardiner dismissed his daughter's concern, thinking it was humorous that she would take seriously what he discounted as "a silly bad dream." Senator Gardiner was adamant; he was not going to miss such a special occasion, especially when the president would be there, just because his daughter had suffered a foolish nightmare. Julia's pleadings failed, and she ultimately agreed to accompany him.

Once aboard the *Princeton*, she was terribly shaken by how precise her vision of the ship's deck had been. How could the image have been so accurate if it was only a "silly bad dream," as her father had said? Julia's usual lively mood darkened, and lifted only slightly when the ardent President Tyler approached and smiled warmly, obviously most pleased to see her.

But when a friend told her why Mrs. Gilmer looked so troubled because of her "dreadful dream," Julia was understandably upset; still worried about her own fearful vision the night before. She tried her best to dismiss her uneasiness, to trust the logic of her father, enjoy the festivities, and the persistent attention lavished upon her by an adoring John Tyler.

Julia waited belowdecks for luncheon to be served. Meanwhile, a crew prepared the big cannon for its next demonstration. It had earlier been set off successfully; now the heavy gun's power was to be displayed for the visiting dignitaries. As Secretary of the Navy Gilmer went to join the group assembled on deck, his sobbing wife pleaded with him to remain below. She tried to hold him back, but he broke free of her grasp, and she was left crying.

President Tyler, however, decided to forego the demonstration when he was invited to go up on deck. He'd already seen and heard all of the cannon he cared to, and preferred to spend time with Julia Gardiner. At his invitation, they sipped champagne together belowdecks. Meanwhile, Julia's father, despite her premonition and warnings, left for the demonstration.

As the president enjoyed conversation with Julia, they both heard a deafening explosion from above them and smelled acrid clouds of smoke that billowed through the ship. The president was startled by the intensity of the blast. Julia instantly knew something was terribly wrong. Then a voice shouted, "The secretary is dead!" This was her horrific vision suddenly come true.

As she rushed upstairs, someone physically restrained her from going topside. Julia learned that her father had been killed. "My dear child, you can do no good," the person told her. "Your father is in heaven." The shock instantly overwhelmed her and she fainted.

Julia's premonition had been chillingly accurate. The big gun had breach fired, exploded, broken apart, and killed those observers closest to it, including Senator David Gardiner and Secretary of the Navy Gilmer, just as his wife predicted. Now she stumbled amid the smoke and debris, crying in vain, "I knew it. I knew it! Why would no one listen to me?" In all, five people were killed, many more seriously injured, while others suffered less critical burns and shattered eardrums.

It was a quirk of fate that saved Tyler's life. Had he not remained below to be with Julia, the president would have been on the deck very close to the cannon and almost certainly would have been killed.

In the days that followed, as Julia mourned her father's ill-fated death, which her premonition had been unable to prevent, the president was caring and concerned.

Julia Gardiner and President John Tyler were married in 1844 and soon had a large family. She became the country's youngest first lady ever, at the age of twenty-four. After Tyler left office they retired to his Virginia plantation, named Sherwood Forest.

In January 1862, Julia experienced a vision of frightening clarity in which she saw her husband lying close to death in a bedroom in Richmond, Virginia. He had gone there on political business. Julia had no doubt what the premonition meant, and she rushed from their home to be by his side. When she arrived at the Exchange Hotel in Richmond, where Tyler was staying, he hadn't expected her and was pleasantly surprised by the visit.

"Are you well?" she asked urgently.

"Perfectly, my dear. Had you heard that I was ill?" he replied.

Julia was at a loss for a reassuring explanation. However, when she looked into his room she immediately recognized the same bed she'd seen him in during her dream, and her heart sank. Sadly, it wasn't long before her premonition proved accurate. That night, Tyler unexpectedly collapsed as a result of what his doctor called "bilious fever." On January 18, 1862, at the age of seventy-one, John Tyler died in the very same bed Julia had seen in her foreboding vision.[29]

Born in Florida, Missouri, in 1835, the year Halley's Comet made an appearance, Samuel Langhorne Clemens would become well known by his nom de plume, Mark Twain, one of the greatest literary figures America has ever produced; forever identified with the classic characters he created, Tom Sawyer and Huckleberry Finn. But little is ever mentioned about the psychic side of his life.

When Sam Clemens was just a young man of twenty he took a job as an apprentice pilot on the *Pennsylvania,* a Mississippi River steamer that ran between St. Louis and New Orleans. Sam's younger brother Henry Clemens also worked on the *Pennsylvania.*

One night in 1858, when Sam stayed at his older sister Pamela's home in St. Louis, he experienced a vivid and frightening dream vision in which he saw Henry, of whom he was very fond, "lying dead." Henry's lifeless body was laid out in a metal coffin that was supported by two chairs, and on his chest was a bouquet of white flowers with a single red bloom in the middle. The scene appeared to take place in the Clemenses' home.

The deeply disturbing dream was so realistic that Sam awoke disoriented and confused, bolted from the bed, quickly dressed, and hurried from the house, certain that what he'd seen was real. Shaken by the vision, Sam headed to where Henry was boarding, and worried how he'd face his mother with the news, he later wrote. He was an entire block from Pamela's home before he realized that he'd had a dream. Sam stopped to calm himself and then returned to his sister. He told her about his vision and how realistic it all seemed to be. "I went to see if Henry was dead. I never had such an experience before."

Pamela was sufficiently concerned that she insisted Sam repeat every detail of his troubling vision and then did her best to reassure her brother that what he'd seen was only a dream. Their conversation seemed to calm Sam somewhat. To his great relief, when he found that Henry was indeed alive and well, he tried his best to put the disturbing dream out his mind. He confided the incident to several friends, but was careful not to tell Henry.

Some weeks after Sam's inexplicable vision, he and Henry were again working on the *Pennsylvania* as it set out from St. Louis, down the Mississippi, bound for New Orleans. But once the steamer arrived, Sam was ordered to work on another steamboat, the *A. T. Lacey,* while Henry remained on the *Pennsylvania.* The brothers waved good-bye to each other, and Sam stood on the dock and watched as the *Pennsylvania* navigated back up the Mississippi River until it faded from view. Two days later, the *A. T. Lacey,* the ship Sam was now working aboard began its own trek, also heading up the Mississippi.

Meanwhile, as the *Pennsylvania* drew closer to Memphis, Tennessee, a sudden and terrible explosion ripped the ship apart, killing at least one hundred fifty people and injuring nearly everyone else on board including Henry Clemens, who was left severely burned by the exploding boilers and barely alive. Sam learned about the devastating accident even before the *A. T. Lacey* reached Memphis. Once he arrived, Sam rushed to Henry's bedside in a hastily improvised hospital where he kept a constant vigil. Six nights later, Henry Clemens died, and his body was placed in a room with other victims. Finally, exhaustion caught up with Sam and he fell into a few hours of uneasy sleep.

When he awoke, he headed for the mortuary where those killed in the accident were laid in plain, unpainted wooden coffins, to search for Henry's body. But as he numbly stared at the grim scene, he noticed a difference: Henry's casket was made of metal, unlike any of the others, and identical to the one he saw in his dream. Much to his surprise, Sam learned that some of the kindhearted women of Memphis, moved by the tragic accident, were so taken with Henry's youth and good looks that they'd purchased a more expensive metal coffin for him. Then as Sam watched in further amazement, an older woman approached Henry's casket and placed a beautiful bouquet of white roses upon his chest with a single crimson rose in the middle of the white flowers. The events were exactly as Sam Clemens had seen them in his dream premonition; virtually every detail had proven true, except that in Sam's vision, Henry was laid out at home, not in a mortuary or morgue.

How was such precise precognition possible? The usual answer from skeptics is to declare incidents like these coincidental or the result of anxiety. However, the clarity and number of accurate details Sam saw in his vision before the *Pennsylvania* explosion suggest the probability of chance or coincidence was highly unlikely. Not to minimize Sam Clemens's dream premonition, but his was only one example of countless such experiences throughout history, and which continue today in as great numbers.

Another important question raised by premonitions is, what purpose do they serve? Sam Clemens had seen the death of a loved one before it occurred; but he could not change what was going to happen. Premonitions, in addition to occurring spontaneously, have no regard for time. In other words, anyone may sense a future incident accurately, but exactly when it will occur is often difficult or even impossible to predict. Time is all one; past, present, and future exist as one, many physicists have theorized. Sam had tapped into a part of Henry's future and saw his fate. However, without knowing the circumstances leading up to Henry's death, Sam could not have changed his brother's destiny. One possible explanation for Sam's foreboding vision was his deep emotional connection to his younger brother; but the most his dream premonition could accomplish was to prepare him for the shock of Henry's untimely demise.[30]

By the time Sam Clemens became Mark Twain, and a famous writer, he had definite opinions about spiritualism and psychical phenomena, most of them negative. For example, when he wrote *Life on the Mississippi* in 1883 he upbraided the medium JV Mansfield, calling him by the fictitious name, "Manchester," in his book. Twain's animosity apparently stemmed from disappointment at not receiving any messages from Henry's spirit when he attended a séance conducted by Mansfield. In *The Adventures of Tom Sawyer* and *The Adventures of Huckleberry Finn* there are references to ghosts, spirits, and poltergeists, but Twain's tone in his books was to treat spiritualism with either humor or disdain. Although he was quite familiar with séances that were all the rage when he was a boy in Hannibal, Twain later grew disenchanted with the substantial allegations of fraud leveled against mediums during the nineteenth century. However, after Twain's "favorite" daughter Susie died in 1896, he and his wife were so grief-stricken they attended séances in hopes of receiving communications from her. Twain, for all his caustic remarks and cynicism about spiritualism, was no different from countless other bereaved parents in every generation who ache for a measure of comfort through mediums.

Finally, there is one last incident about Mark Twain and the supernatural, specifically a prediction he'd made for himself. In 1835, the year he was born, Halley's Comet was in view. Twain insisted that he would die when the celestial tailed object was again visible in the sky. "I was born with that comet and I'll go out with it," he predicted. Halley's Comet made its next appearance in 1910. Mark Twain died that same year. Had he willed his own death, was it coincidence, as disbelievers would claim, or did he harbor a premonition of his own passing?[31]

"Over the centuries two themes have appeared again and again in the broad text of prophetic expression: catastrophe and inventions," noted the book *Into the Unknown*.

On the night of April 14–15, 1912, the RMS *Titanic*, on its maiden voyage from Southampton, England, to New York, with more than 2,200 aboard moved steadily through the bitter cold and somber North Atlantic Ocean, probably traveling too fast at the speed of 22 knots. But those aboard had no reason for concern; the *Titanic*, the largest ship of its day, had been deemed "unsinkable," by its owners and builders; and at a length of 882.5 feet, of 66,000 tons displacement, and with 3 propellers, it made it an imposing sight. It was a vessel of "sumptuous luxury," author Tony Allan noted. Others described it as "lavish" and "extravagant," unless, of course, one was traveling in steerage, where passage was the least expensive, and amenities were decidedly modest.

Suddenly the calm was shattered by disaster when the *Titanic* struck an iceberg that ripped a long and deep slash in its side, and, over the next few hours, the great ship sank, claiming more than 1,500 lives, rich and poor, young and old, male and female. More lifeboats might well have saved more passengers, but the *Titanic* carried only a paltry 20 boats, an obviously inadequate number. Likely there was a degree of hubris or, as one author wrote, "overconfidence" in the *Titanic*'s design, construction, and technology. At the very least, there was a serious error made in overestimating the *Titanic*'s structural integrity and its capacity to navigate through the iceberg-laden waters of the North Atlantic.

When newspaper headlines screamed details of the *Titanic*'s calamitous sinking a number of people came forward to claim they'd had prophetic dreams, visions, premonitions, and other precognitive experiences warning them. What's more, some said they could prove their prescience. Many who claimed they'd experienced premonitions were surviving passengers. How many of those who died had uneasy feelings or forebodings they ignored we will never know, but some passengers actually declined to go aboard the *Titanic* because of their uncomfortable sensations that something was—or would be—amiss with the ship. One of those who canceled was famed American financier and banker J. Pierpont Morgan who was interested in both the supernatural and new technology. It was as if there were those who had "a sixth sense of impending doom," author Tony Allan wrote.

Some who canceled their travel plans to sail kept their unused passenger tickets to prove their claim of premonitions. Others produced credible witnesses who corroborated stories of the eerie forebodings that kept them off the *Titanic*. One American businessman changed plans to sail on the "unsinkable ship" after he received an urgent cable from his wife, frantic that she'd had a vivid dream in which she saw the *Titanic* sink. The husband took no chance that his wife was just suffering jitters about his voyage, and her premonition probably saved his life.

There was a report of another woman who watched as the *Titanic* was about to set sail from England. She became so agitated from a premonition she'd had that all she could do was cry, "That ship is going to sink before it reaches America!" She pleaded with others nearby to intervene and prevent the *Titanic* from sailing—but to no avail. There was a man who had not one but two prophetic dreams in which he saw the *Titanic* go down as he "floated" above the submerged vessel.

Passengers weren't the only ones with premonitions of tragedy; at least one crew member's foreboding caused him to leave before the ship sailed into the open ocean.

There is a record of at least one psychic, Vincent Turvey, who foresaw disaster for the *Titanic*. He described his vision of the huge ship sinking as being similar to watching a motion picture—of the future.

Many premonitions came in dreams; others while people were awake. An eleven-year-old girl, whose mother worked aboard the *Titanic* as an attendant, experienced a "strange sense of doom" before the ship sailed. However, the mother managed to survive. Another woman reported a lifelike dream in which saw her mother in an overcrowded lifeboat tossing to and fro on the ocean. The following day the woman was shocked to find her mother's name on the *Titanic*'s passenger list. The mother had wanted to surprise her family in America, and so never told her daughter that she was on the *Titanic*; fortunately she survived the sinking.[32]

There were, in fact, so many premonitions experienced before the *Titanic*'s voyage they could fill an entire book. Some who'd had that sense of doom canceled their trip; others ignored their forebodings and sailed anyway. Years later, Dr. Ian Stevenson, a respected parapsychologist and psychiatrist at the University of Virginia, undertook a careful study in which he discovered at least nineteen cases of verified psychic experiences associated with the *Titanic*'s tragic sinking.

Stevenson found that some people who had precognitive, telepathic, or clairvoyant experiences about the *Titanic* were relatives or close friends of those aboard the ship. However, others had no relationship or association with any passenger or crew member. The cases Stevenson studied were all experiences of so-called ordinary people, not those who described themselves as professional psychics or mediums. One conclusion Stevenson arrived at was the discovery of "evidence that dreams may be a route through which [psychic] phenomena can penetrate conscious awareness."[33]

In about 1888, British journalist and spiritualist W. T. Stead wrote a story about a giant ocean liner that sank in the mid-Atlantic after colliding with another vessel, and because there were too few lifeboats, many on board perished. "This is exactly what might take place, and what will take place, if liners are sent to sea short of boats," Stead wrote with eerie foresight. In 1910, Stead envisioned that he was shipwrecked, bobbing in the ocean, and crying for help. Several other people also warned him not to travel; one predicted the *Titanic* would sink. But Stead ignored every caution when he sailed on the *Titanic,* and lost his life.[34]

But no prediction of the *Titanic* tragedy could match a remarkably prophetic book titled *The Wreck of the Titan or, Futility* written by an American author named Morgan Robertson. What makes his novel incredible is that it was written in 1898—fourteen years before the *Titanic* sank. It remains one of the most intriguing, if inexplicable, examples of a prescient story ever written at any time in American history.

Morgan Robertson was born in 1861 in Oswego, a small northern New

York State community. His father was a boat pilot on Lake Erie, so it's little surprise that as a child Morgan was on the water, and while still a youngster, became a cabin boy. He developed a substantial knowledge and affection for the sea and sailing. For some years Robertson worked in the merchant service, the jewelry business, and also turned to writing short stories and novels about the subject he knew best: the sea. His stories, well written and published in both American and British magazines, never paid him enough to achieve a comfortable living, although he was prolific, and ultimately wrote over two hundred short stories and two novels.

Faced with financial woes and a disabled wife to care for, Robertson fell into depression and alcoholism, and was also limited by poor eyesight. But there was a paranormal or supernatural component to Robertson's life that may help explain how he was able to write a story in 1898 about the sinking of a giant ocean liner that proved remarkably similar to the *Titanic* disaster in 1912.

One of his problems was that he thought he was "possessed." He "implicitly believed that some discarnate soul, some spirit entity with literary ability, denied physical expression, had commandeered his body and brain," a friend of Robertson was quoted as saying in the *Mammoth Book of Prophecies* by Damon Wilson. Robertson considered the entity the "real writer," and that he was just its "tool." In his own words, the spirit was his "astral writing partner."

Skeptics and many psychologists would dismiss Robertson's claim of a supernatural or spirit "writing partner" as delusional or hallucinatory, either fueled by his alcoholism, mental illness, or his subconscious. However, in the annals of parapsychology, and even in some psychological studies, it is not unusual to find writers, artists, and musicians who claim they've been inspired by some inexplicable psychic or spiritual force— acting as a "muse"—that has helped foster their creativity.

The bottom line was that Robertson sincerely believed his inspiration to write came from some discarnate entity. Typically, the process began when Robertson induced a trancelike state; and during it he would write or type what the spirit being directed him to. Sometimes the entity's dictation might last for several hours. Other times, the "supernatural muse" would not be heard for long periods, even weeks. That would force Robertson to wait anxiously, hoping for the "communications" to resume. It was a difficult and frustrating way to work, and often not very efficient or productive.

Robertson was in one of his familiar trances when the idea came to him for a story he titled *The Wreck of the Titan or, Futility* about a huge ocean liner, larger than any he'd ever seen. In his altered state he saw its imposing name *Titan* with three thousand passengers and crew members on board when the huge ship struck an iceberg in the dark of night and sank. In his story, there were too few lifeboats—only twenty-four—to save many on board.

These are a few passages Robertson wrote in *Futility*:

She was the largest craft afloat and the greatest of the works of men. In her construction and maintenance were involved every science, profession, and trade known to civilization . . .

Two brass bands, two orchestras, and a theatrical company entertained the passengers during waking hours . . .

From her lofty bridge ran hidden telegraph lines to the bow, stern, engine room, crow's nest, on the foremast, and to all parts of the ship where work was done . . .

Nineteen water-tight compartments could be closed in half a minute by turning a lever. These doors would also close automatically in the presence of water. With nine compartments flooded the ship would still float, and as no known accident of the sea could possibly fill this many, the steamship *Titan* was considered practically unsinkable.

Built of steel throughout, and for passenger traffic only . . . She was eight hundred feet long, of seventy thousand tons' displacement, seventy-five thousand horse power, and on her trial trip had steamed at a rate of twenty-five knots an hour over the bottom . . . In short, she was a floating city . . .

Unsinkable—indestructible, she carried as few boats as would satisfy the laws. These, twenty-four in number, were securely covered and lashed down . . . and if launched would hold five-hundred people . . .

The only thing afloat that she could not conquer was an iceberg.

So, it was confidently expected that when her engines had limbered themselves, the steamship *Titan* would land her passengers three thousand miles away with the promptness and regularity of a railway train.

Then later in the book, with eerie prescience, Robertson wrote:

[A] shout from the crow's nest split the air.

"Ice," yelled the lookout; "ice ahead. Iceberg. Right under the bows."

Seventy-five thousand tons—dead weight—rushing through the fog at the rate of fifty feet a second, had hurled itself at an iceberg.

The book was published in 1898 but was not very successful, poorly received by many because of its negative and pessimistic tone, although Robertson found the story fascinating. But 1898 was a time when most Americans were in a hopeful and confident mood, especially about the promise that technology held for the nation's future, and further inspired by incredible inventions predicted in earlier stories by Jules Verne. Robertson's book contradicted the country's temper; he was implying technology's potential failure while Americans were living in an era of such remarkable inventions as the automobile; electricity to light homes, streets, and entire cities; motion pictures; even an airship named the *Zeppelin*, after its inventor; and the promise of many more scientific advances to come.

But "*Futility* was a depressing story of shipwreck and marine disaster," wrote author Damon Wilson. Few Americans wanted to think about the fallibility of technology in such heady and forward-thinking times. The book, although well written, was another bitter disappointment for Robertson. Some who knew his reputation speculated that perhaps he'd written *Futility* as the result of some liquor-fueled delusion. How could the ingenuity and genius that was bringing Americans new technological wonders on a nearly constant basis in real life fail the way Robertson conceived? In any event, *Futility* was no match for the science-fiction stories H. G. Wells wrote, or such Jules Verne classics as *Twenty Thousand Leagues Under the Sea* and *Around the World in Eighty Days*. So Robertson's book was quickly forgotten and he returned to his personal struggles with finances and alcoholism, and continued writing.

Fourteen years went by but Robertson's fortunes had not particularly improved. In April 1912, the ocean liner RMS *Titanic* had embarked on her maiden voyage from England, across the Atlantic, to New York. Notwithstanding those with frightening or discomforting premonitions about the voyage, there was considerable excitement. The great ship—at the time the largest ever built—was launched with more than two thousand passengers aboard. The *Titanic*'s captain, Edward J. Smith, his officers and crew were aware of the potential danger of icebergs in the North Atlantic, but because the ship was on a southerly course, they were confident there would be no problem, especially since the closest iceberg was estimated to be some 250 miles from the *Titanic*'s location. On the night of April 14, the great ocean liner was traveling fast—too fast—at better than 22 knots an hour; its navigators still certain they'd be able to avoid any icebergs, even in fog. Visibility was quite good; although there was no moonlight, it was a starry night, and the bitter cold waters were calm. Then the officers on the ship's bridge thought an iceberg they'd grazed caused no significant damage. However, the largest part of an iceberg sits underwater, and that was what ripped open a vicious 330-foot-long slash into the *Titanic*'s side, and the flooding began its irreversible course to disaster.

Robertson's 1898 novel had envisioned "completely sealed compartments" but that was not the case with the *Titanic*, which quickly took on water. He'd also foreseen in his book that too few lifeboats was a potential death sentence for many on board who'd be unable to escape. Robertson had envisioned an inadequate twenty-four lifeboats on his fictional *Titan*. The *Titanic* had a pitiable twenty lifeboats. He had placed three thousand on the *Titan*; when the *Titanic* struck the iceberg, there were more than twenty-two hundred aboard. He also predicted a huge loss of life. The *Titanic*'s sinking resulted in the deaths of more than fifteen hundred people. Among those who perished was Captain Edward Smith, the distinguished veteran of the sea; ironically, this was to be his last voyage before retirement. The details in *Futility* were chillingly close to the *Titanic*'s tragic fate, right down to the number of propellers—three, the similarity in the ships' names; and the *Titan*, like the *Titanic*, was traveling on its maiden voyage in the North Atlantic during the month of April.

Suddenly, Morgan Robertson's 1898 book was remembered, and fourteen years after it was published, its eerie prescience could not be ignored. In the wake of the *Titanic* sinking *Futility* became famous for the uncanny resemblances between Robertson's fictional story and the real-life tragedy. Indeed technology could fail, and it had, with catastrophic results, just as Robertson had predicted.

Although Robertson continued writing, his belated notoriety from *Futility* did little to improve his financial position, and at the end of his life, friends helped save him from the brink of poverty. Robertson was just fifty-four years old when he died of heart failure in 1915.

After his death, the debate began that continues to this day about whether Robertson had experienced one of the most remarkable precognitive episodes in American history. Was his foreknowledge a reflection of his lifelong familiarity with the sea, a bizarre coincidence, or a genuine premonition, based on a vision, as he'd originally claimed?[35]

Two of the most intriguing figures in the history of predictions were not scientists, parapsychologists, psychics, or mediums. They were novelists, but unlike Morgan Robertson's one startlingly accurate prediction, these two writers made seemingly countless visits into the future. Jules Verne and H. G. Wells were both born in the nineteenth century and their remarkably prophetic books have fueled imaginations and influenced generations of Americans.

"We will reach the Moon, we will reach the planets, we will reach the stars with the same ease, speed, and security with which we now travel from Liverpool to New York."

Who made that prediction? Could it have been a well-intentioned promise from a NASA spokesperson or a president of the United States in recent decades, before the first astronaut stepped on the Moon in 1969? Actually, Jules Verne (1828–1905) wrote it in 1865, more than a century before the first lunar landing. Born in France, where he lived all his life, Verne became the first author recognized for writing modern science fiction, although that term was not yet in use. But as his many accurate prophecies show, what was once thought to be "science fiction" eventually became reality. The question, of course, is how did he see into the future?

When he was twelve years old, Verne tried to ship out to sea as a cabin boy, but his father intervened to prevent him from leaving. Jules vowed to his parents that, "in the future he would travel only in imagination." In fact, Verne seldom traveled far from home during his life and was a rather shy and private man. He might be called an "armchair novelist," a term that describes people who write about places they've never been to. The "place" he wrote about was the future. He hadn't visited there—or had he?

His novels often were about "journeys and voyages," and he was especially fascinated about the possibility of space travel. He once went aloft in a balloon in Amiens, the town he called home for many years. In 1863, he wrote his first novel, *Five Weeks in a Balloon*; not surprisingly it was about flight, specifically, an excursion over Africa, then a largely mysterious and unexplored continent. The book was an immediate success in France, as were the next several. *A Journey to the Center of the Earth* (1864) was a riveting tale of explorers and scientists who travel down through a volcanic crater where they discover a subterranean world.

The *Adventures of Captain Hatteras* (1866) was about the exploration of the North Pole. Verne wrote his fictional account more than forty years before the feat was actually accomplished in 1909 by Robert Peary. Later, Admiral Richard Byrd acknowledged that reading Verne had been an inspiration before his first flight over the North Pole in 1926. Many others shared the opinion that Verne stimulated not only imaginations; he also spurred achievements.

How Verne was able to envision the future as few others could remains inexplicable. It seems from the record of his predictions that he had psychic or clairvoyant ability. He was, at the very least, a visionary; and it's difficult to conceive that he didn't have some sixth sense about "things to come." For instance, in 1865, he wrote *From the Earth to the Moon,* and its sequel *Around the Moon* in 1870. Of course he was not the first to imagine what it might be like for humans to travel into space. As far back as ancient Greece, and later in the musings of Leonardo da Vinci, the idea of man flying was thought about, although a long way from becoming reality, and travel to other planets was mere fantasy. By Verne's time, most nineteenth century (and earlier) fictional scenarios were still far off the mark. Verne, on the other hand, had a vision that came closest to the actual *Apollo 11* flight in July 1969, more than a century before it occurred, as well as foreseeing Americans on the Moon.

The story describes the adventures of two Americans and a Frenchman who are fired in a projectile from a huge cannon that sends them beyond Earth's gravitational field, and near the Moon. Verne accurately foresaw rockets used to move the spacecraft. He also predicted the "state of weightlessness" his fictional space travelers would face during their voyage, just as astronauts in our own time have. Even more remarkable, he placed his fictional spacecraft launch site in Tampa, Florida, only about 125 miles from where the real-life *Apollo* liftoff occurred from Cape Kennedy, on Florida's east coast. Verne accurately predicted the Pacific Ocean as the location where his space travelers would "splash down" when they returned to Earth.

But his most incredible prediction about man's first lunar adventure was the length of time the flight would take from Earth to the Moon. In his story, Verne projected that the journey would last ninety-seven hours and thirteen minutes. When the *Apollo 11* astronauts made their voyage to the Moon in 1969, it took them ninety-seven hours and thirty-nine minutes. Verne's calculation had been correct within twenty-six minutes. Later, in *The Clipper of the Clouds*, published in 1886, he predicted that "heavier than air machines" could fly, an obvious reference to aircraft of the future, nearly twenty years before the Wright brothers' first flight in 1903.

Verne's two most famous books, *Twenty Thousand Leagues Under the Sea* (1870), and *Around the World in Eighty Days* (1873), became literary classics, often described by critics as "masterpieces." *Twenty Thousand Leagues* tells the story of the fictional submarine *Nautilus*, obviously written many years before the development of nuclear-powered submarines. The book also inspired future "ocean explorations." *Around the World* is the tale of a stoical Englishman, Phineas Fogg, who wins a bet he's made to circumnavigate the globe in eighty days in an adventurous journey by hot air balloon.

Verne was prolific; he wrote close to eighty books. Readers could look forward to at least one—sometimes two—new Jules Verne novels annually. His popularity was enormous, as was his early faith and optimism about the good that technology could do for humanity. He predicted in his books such inventions as elevators and escalators, and air-conditioned skyscrapers, as tall as a thousand feet, long before the Empire State Building was built in 1931; it stands 1,250 feet. In 1875, he envisioned huge cities in America and Europe with populations as large as "ten million inhabitants." That same year, he predicted computers. He even foresaw advances in crime-fighting technology, via photographic enlargements, decades before it was developed. His prediction of "telephonic journalism" describes television and radio news reporting.

However, late in his life, Verne's novels suggest he had a serious change of mind, and he began warning of the dangers society faced from unrestrained technology. His youthful optimism had given way to a far more cynical—and realistic—vision of the future; his outlook was gloomier. He foresaw technology being used to build frighteningly destructive weapons, including those that could obliterate entire cities with a push of a button.

In 1889 Verne wrote for an American magazine his predictions of what life would be like in a thousand years, meaning 2889. Again, he showed the same remarkable prescience that was so extraordinary in his novels. He envisioned America as a "superpower," at a time when European nations dominated the world stage. He also predicted that media moguls and titans would have vast control and influence over society via their ownership of something he called "telephonic journalism." We know it better as broadcasting, or radio and television, much of which is now controlled by huge conglomerates. Another remarkable prediction was a contraption he dubbed the "phonotelephote." Verne described it as a machine that would make it possible for people to see and talk to one another, even over great distances. It bears a striking resemblance to e-mail, videophones, and videoconferencing. He foresaw an America traversed by vast networks of electrical wires, and gigantic advertisements that were "beamed up to the sky," Tony Allan wrote in *Prophecies*. Had Verne foreseen satellite communications? Unfortunately, he had a fairly negative scenario about the future quality of the environment.

Since past, present, and future are one, was Verne able to see through time to access what is yet to come? Verne's mistake was to foresee many of these inventions being developed in a thousand years. It has actually taken only a century or less from the time of his article in 1889 for the technology he envisioned to become reality.[36]

Like Verne, Herbert George Wells (1866–1946) was neither a scientist nor a psychic. But, also like Verne, his prophetic and prescient gifts were often so extraordinary that anyone reading his novels today has to wonder how he was able to predict the future, often with uncanny accuracy; from motor vehicles to robots to space travel. Unfortunately, no one really has an answer; but his writings have long gripped and inspired readers, and he is regarded as the "father of modern science fiction."

Born in 1866 to a poor family in England, H. G. Wells, as he became popularly known, had little schooling as a boy. Later, however, he earned a scholarship and attended the Normal School for Science in London. In his twenties, he turned to writing novels, and eventually wrote more than a hundred books, as well as many articles.

Wells had two strong areas of interest: technology and sociology. When they were combined with his imagination, remarkable prescience, and flair for realism, he'd made a mark with readers. Tony Allan explained in his book *Prophecies* that Wells, fascinated by technology, was particularly curious about how the "machine age" would evolve, "[and] also what its social effects might be." Wells apparently had keen powers that enabled him to foresee the future. While skeptics attribute his prescience to literary imagination, that explanation does not stand up to close scrutiny. He had to possess precognitive abilities, consciously or subconsciously, to envision inventions and ideas that were a long way from being developed.

In 1901 Wells wrote a novel he titled *Anticipations*. In it, he peered into the future to consider the impact of automobiles—then a new invention—just emerging as a form of transportation. How would motor vehicles impact or change our lives? Wells foresaw highways, some multileveled, as they crisscrossed and connected cities. As he looked ahead, he also envisioned large motor vehicles hauling cargo. Later generations would know them as trucks. In his mind's eye, H. G. Wells saw automobiles offering people independence to travel in a way they'd never before known. If you preferred public transportation, he also foresaw buses, some of which could go great distances.

When Wells visualized life one hundred years into the future, meaning the year 2000, he predicted working people in such large cities as New York and London would commute between cities and suburbs, and their daily trips to and from work might be lengthy. He also envisioned the so-called "megalopolis"—a huge area of population reaching from Albany, New York, to Washington, DC. Actually the heavily populated and continuous cities and suburbs stretch as one from Washington to Boston. As for all those commuters, Wells foresaw them as members of a growing middle-class population, a trend that began in the latter part of the nineteenth century.

Wells was not unfamiliar with psychics and mediums of his day. There was no secret that among his friends and acquaintances was the gifted Irish medium Eileen Garrett, then in London, and later in New York. She was to become one of the most tested mediums of the early and mid-twentieth century, and among those she socialized with at cafes and the London tearoom she owned was H. G. Wells. Whether they spoke about her psychic powers—or his—is purely speculation. But in the early twentieth century there were many visionary literary and intellectual lights of the time who might have crossed paths with Wells, including George Bernard Shaw, Aldous Huxley, Carl Jung, Arthur Conan Doyle, and William Butler Yeats, among others. In their day they could well be considered what we now call New Age types: avant-garde, progressive, visionary, and antiestablishment.

Wells's early novels reflected his intrigue with the future. In 1895, Wells wrote *The Time Machine*, the first instance such a device was employed in science fiction. He wasn't so much interested in the technology of traveling back and forth through time. He was far more curious about how we would evolve biologically and socially. In the book, Wells envisions life on Earth ending some thirty million years in the future. Apparently, he was pessimistic about humankind continually evolving. At some point, he predicted, advancement would cease, and humans would slip backward to a primal condition. Analogous to Darwin's theory of evolution, had Wells prophesied that human beings could ultimately face extinction? In Wells's day, that was not the prevailing mood among the Victorian gentry.

War of the Worlds was Wells's great classic, and probably the novel he is best remembered for. Published in 1898, it is the story of Martians invading Earth. Wells wrote it, aware of the popular interest at the time that intelligent life existed on Mars. He also hoped to remind his Victorian contemporaries that humans might not always be highest on the evolutionary ladder. In the book, extraterrestrials are bent on destruction as they land a spacecraft near London. When the cylindrical craft opens before crowds of curious onlookers, what emerges is a large, monstrous, and repulsive being that appears somewhat "octopus-like." Those watching are shocked by what they've seen.

Humans approach, hoping to communicate with the being. But instead a deadly beam or ray is emitted from the Martian cylinder that annihilates anything it strikes. Many people are killed, others flee, and human authorities realize the Martians have come to Earth to destroy it. Ultimately an army of Martian craft land, and the extraterrestrial beings set out on a course of death and devastation, as they survive by drinking human blood. There appears to be no way to stop the invaders; people's control of Earth seems to have ended. But then, surprisingly, the Martians begin to die; they have no immunity to Earth's bacteria. Humanity has survived—this time.

Wells made several prophetic warnings that apply to future generations. Despite the death of the Martians, humans had best not take their superiority for granted. If not for the Martians' lack of resistance to disease-causing germs, their weapons were far advanced, and they would have quickly taken over planet Earth. The invaders apparently thought of us a lower form of life, much the way we consider insects and other creatures. All of our technology and military might was not powerful enough to defend ourselves, and we were also lacking in spiritual leadership. As Wells envisioned the future, our overconfidence left us vulnerable to both outside attack and moral decay; and we need to always be on guard for the worst possible circumstances.

Wells had not painted a very optimistic picture in *War of the Worlds*, but it had several later media incarnations. Most notably, the 1938 radio adaptation by actor-producer Orson Welles that caused many Americans to panic when listeners thought Martians had actually invaded Earth. Hollywood has contributed two film versions, one in the 1950s, and more recently, a remake in 2005 that starred Tom Cruise.

Wells wrote that one of his goals was "to discuss sociology in fable." He had a political agenda that many disagreed with, specifically his belief in socialism, the antithesis of American political ideology. His views, shared by such fellow writers as George Bernard Shaw, were easier to accept in England where Wells and Shaw were members of the Fabian Society, a group of intellectuals who advocated socialism. Wells also foresaw changing sexual mores. He championed "women's emancipation" and "sexual liberation," in several novels prior to the First World War; ideas that came to fruition decades later. His influence was felt in the United States; he'd advocated contraception, lent support to Margaret Sanger's highly controversial battle for "family planning," and wrote the introduction to her book in 1923.

Wells's predictions also included such advanced technology as gas and laser weaponry and industrial robots. When he turned his prescience to social changes in the future, he envisioned a growing middle class and greater emphasis on public education and increased literacy.

He foresaw with remarkable accuracy a future in which science and technology would be utilized in homes. As a young man he lived in an era when housework was essentially hard labor and drudgery. But as Wells looked ahead in time he saw electricity being used to make housework easier. He envisioned the kitchen of the future with an "electric range" that even had a thermometer to control the temperature of foods as they were being cooked. Such a home appliance was unheard of in his day.

But future technology had its dark side, as well. Wells did not view the world of tomorrow through rose-colored glasses. He predicted military tanks at least a dozen years before their invention, but not knowing what they would be called, he dubbed them "land ironclads." He also envisioned more advanced weaponry, such as rifles with "cross-thread telescope sights." In 1913, he wrote *Little Wars* that called for man to end wars, before wars end them, to paraphrase him. He would later say, "History is more and more a race between education and catastrophe."

He wrote prolifically, some of his titles are self-explanatory—and prophetic: *The First Men on the Moon* (1901); *A Modern Utopia* (1905); *The War in the Air* (1908); *The World Set Free: A Story of Mankind* (1913); *The Shape of Things to Come* (1933). The latter was Wells's "history of the future." When that book was made into a motion picture in 1936, one of the first science-fiction films, it did poorly. In *The Shape of Things to Come*, Wells looked into the future to predict World War II. However, relatively few of his countrymen saw what he did; they did not share his fears, only three years before the Nazis invaded Poland in 1939, and war was declared.

Wells was in his seventies when he observed the savagery of the war that he'd predicted so exactly. During World War II, and the horrors of the Holocaust, he held on to his vision of a "world state" that he believed would guarantee human rights, and his idea of a "socialist utopia." His final contribution toward world peace was his membership on the Sankey Commission whose task was to develop the charter for the newly formed United Nations, once the war ended. Wells's suggestions to the commission influenced the wording of the United Nations Declaration of Human Rights, accepted in 1948. But Wells did not live to see that happen. He died in August 1946, in London, one month shy of his eightieth birthday. He was cremated and his ashes were scattered to the winds over the English Channel.[37]

Today, religious prophets warn us of ever increasing and ominous signs that the "end days" are drawing closer. Psychics, mediums, and astrologers are not the only ones in the business of making predictions. In recent years science has joined in the search for what is to come, and what society needs to be ready for—good and bad. This is the work of the "futurists," whose prognostications are aided by sophisticated computer programs, studies of trends, think tanks, knowledge of how certain events repeat, and projections based on past and present knowledge. Do the futurists have a better bead on tomorrow than seers, psychics, and visionaries have had throughout history? Time will tell if their track record—and influence—can equal Jules Verne and H. G. Wells.

Meanwhile, millions of Americans still seek psychics who claim to see the future, astrologers who chart horoscopes, and many read everything from the prophecies of Nostradamus, to the Book of Revelation, and current best sellers on the subject, such as the Left Behind series, as we face the anxieties of our time.

Two later prophetic novels, Aldous Huxley's *Brave New World* and George Orwell's classic *1984*, were so influential that their disturbing scenarios of the future entered the English language as metaphors for much that we find amiss today about government intrusions in our lives; the overuse of drugs to modify or control thinking and behavior, and the ubiquitous "Big Brother." The term "Orwellian" has found its way into our language and consciousness as a synonym for a totalitarian state.[38]

"Visions of the future do not only come in the form of predictions of future reality. Many prophets have preferred to describe mythical situations in mythical lands," wrote author Richard Lewinsohn.

Some writers fancied a world they called Utopia, "an imagined perfect place or state of things." The word, itself, came from the title of a sixteenth-century book, *Utopia* by Thomas More. For many later authors, the utopian concept was both idealistic—and naïve. By the late nineteenth century, many novelists believed a "one-state socialist system" would be the answer to society's problems. They envisioned economic equity between all people; as well as fairness and justice that they—unrealistically—believed would reign in a socialist state.[39]

One of the best-known American utopian writers was Edward Bellamy. In 1888 he published *Looking Backward 2000–1887*; it quickly became a best-selling book in which Bellamy looked back at the year 2000 and envisioned a socialist society where, as Joe Fisher wrote, "bounty and brotherhood" would prevail, and "the state becomes the sole employer."[40]

H. G. Wells and Jules Verne both foresaw their Utopia as a place where advances in technology would improve life. Most utopian writers were pacifists and some mistakenly thought that the more destructive weapons they'd predicted for the future would discourage war.

Wells and George Bernard Shaw (1856–1950) both favored socialism. In 1921, Shaw wrote a play titled *Back to Methuselah*; in it he considered how human life could be lengthened in the future, resulting in a kind of "biological Utopia."

If the utopian writers were often overly optimistic about the future, the American author Jack London (1876–1916) took an opposite position when he wrote *The Iron Heel* in 1907. In it he predicted a harsh and merciless dictatorship in America, complete with secret police, press censorship, and forced labor or concentration camps. Actually, London had uncannily prophesied the future Nazi, Fascist, and Communist systems[41]; and earlier, in 1892, the French scientist Charles Richet looked a century ahead and predicted that the United States and Russia would become the "two most powerful nations."

Surprisingly there were relatively few documented predictions or premonitions of World War I. The spark that ignited the conflagration was the assassination on June 28, 1914, of the Archduke Franz Ferdinand, of Austria-Hungary. The assassination set off a chain of events that quickly escalated into world war. Given the magnitude of the hostilities and the toll it took in lives, one would suppose there were many incidents of precognition prior to 1914 of the coming warfare. If there were, not many can be authenticated or proven. One exception was a series of visions experienced by Dr. Carl Jung in 1913.

Carl Gustav Jung (1875–1961) became a recognized psychologist and psychiatrist by the early twentieth century, and to his credit, never hid his deep interest in psychic phenomena and the supernatural. He began experiencing "visions" as a young boy in his native Switzerland, and reported many paranormal events during his life.

In 1913 Jung had a number of "daytime visions," and toward year's end, while he was traveling, he said he was "seized with the overpowering spectacle of nearly all Europe, except Switzerland, covered with a sea that turned to blood; on its surface floated the bodies of uncounted thousands." Then he heard a voice say, "Look, it will be so." That premonition, or some variation of it, was repeated at regular intervals until the next summer. Jung first thought he was on the verge of a nervous breakdown. "The idea of war did not occur to me," he said. But once World War I broke out, he realized he'd had prophetic visions of it.[42]

On May 13, 1917, three peasant children were tending sheep near the village of Fatima, Portugal, when they unexpectedly saw a "bright flash." As the youngsters looked up, they saw in the light, "a beautiful lady from heaven," who spoke to them. The apparition said she would come back, and did, on the thirteenth of every month until October when she promised a miracle would occur "so that everyone may believe." News of the visions spread and by October 13 there were some seventy thousand people gathered in heavy rain at the location where the children had first seen the "Lady." No one except the children could see or hear her when she told them she was the Virgin Mary, and gave them three secret messages predicting future events.

As the immense throng of people waited, the drenching rain suddenly ceased, the clouds vanished, and the sun shone brightly in a clear sky. Those watching were not only the Catholic faithful; there were also skeptics, as well as reporters present. Then they saw the sun wobble from side to side, as if it was "dancing," and it appeared to spin and fall toward Earth. The crowd that had gathered fell to their knees in fear and began to pray. The sun resembled a "spinning disc," not unlike a UFO, as it continued a downward spiral, stopped, then reversed its course back toward the heavens.

The three Fatima prophecies were given to Catholic Church officials by the oldest of the children, Lucia dos Santos, who was ten years old at the time of the vision. The two other children were cousins of Lucia, Francisco and Jacinta Marta, nine and seven. They both died of influenza within two years of seeing the "Lady." Lucia became a nun and lived to be well into her nineties.

The so-called "secrets of Fatima" went on to become world famous. The children had been shown a horrifying vision of Hell as an ocean of fire, and then were given the prophecies: The Great War would soon end, but if people continued to transgress against God, there would be another war the same year that Pope Pius XI was to die. The sign that the next war was near would be an unfamiliar light in the sky. The "Lady" indicated the way to avoid future evil was for Russia to accept Catholicism.

The First World War ended the next year, 1918; and Pope Pius XI died in January 1939, the same year World War II broke out. What about the inexplicable light in the sky that had been predicted?

Actually, it did occur, six weeks before Hitler invaded Austria in 1938, and made news around the world. The *New York Times* headline read "Aurora Borealis Startles Europe—People Flee in Fear."

The Vatican kept the third Fatima prophecy secret for many years, causing great speculation and debate about what it might have predicted. In 2000, Pope John Paul II finally allowed it to be revealed. It was a vision the children had seen of a pope dressed in white robes. As he and his followers knelt to pray on a hill at the site of a wooden cross, soldiers attacked them with guns and arrows. Pope John Paul II interpreted the vision as a prophecy that was realized when there was an attempt on his life in 1981. Significantly, the attack on the pope occurred on May 13, the same date the Virgin Mary first appeared to the children in 1917. Only two years after the assassination attempt, John Paul "consecrated Russia to the Virgin," as the Lady had asked.[43]

There is seldom a light side to predictions and prophecies, but some of the greatest inventors had so little foresight about their own accomplishments it's almost laughable. For example, Thomas Edison saw no "commercial value" in the phonograph he invented. And in 1901, the Wright brothers predicted that manned flight would take another fifty years to achieve. Two years later, they made their historic first flight. A chagrined Orville Wright said, "Ever since . . . I have avoided all predictions."

There's no question that many predictions, prophecies, and premonitions have been accurate, and some people have more precognitive ability than others. Getting a firm grip on the nature of precognition is another matter. The truth is that even after many centuries—and a multitude of theories—we are at a loss to explain, by the known laws of physics, how precognition occurs. What has not changed is that since the beginning of recorded history—and likely before—people have had their forebodings and hunches, even if they've been hard to prove in a way that satisfies science.

Ironically, in recent years, "end times" predictions have found a place in the secular world, as well as in Christianity. However, where the devout await the "Second Coming," those not concerned with religious belief predict doomsday will come as a result of human avarice, aggression, and irresponsibility. Many fear the threat of nuclear and biological weapons; war; terrorism; and environmental calamities, such as global warming and melting polar caps. As far back as 1895, H. G. Wells foresaw acts of terrorism from insurgent or guerilla movements. However, we have no better answer today than people had in past centuries about whether to act upon or ignore prophecies, predictions, and premonitions, nor are we certain that we have the free will to change the future, or if what has been foreseen is fated and immutable. As Ebenezer Scrooge asks the Ghost of Christmas Future about the events he's being shown: Are these events destined to be or by changing the present, can we change the future? The question remains.

4   *Edgar Cayce: The Sleeping Psychic*

In man's analysis and understanding of himself, it is
as well to know from whence he came as whither he
is going.

—EDGAR CAYCE (1877–1945)

Perhaps no modern psychic is more prominent, more celebrated and studied, and more controversial with respect to his accomplishments than Edgar Cayce. Just who was he, what did he do, and why has his name remained at the forefront of presidential advisors who dealt in the realm of the paranormal?

Edgar Cayce (pronounced *Kay-see*) is regarded as one of early twentieth century America's most famed psychics, often called the "Sleeping Prophet" for the thousands of clairvoyant readings he gave while in trance, many about health problems and various ailments. He was also a seer who made a number of predictions. His "life readings" frequently told people about their past incarnations, including any they may have had on the ancient lost continent of Atlantis. A total of more than fourteen thousand readings are on file at his foundation in Virginia Beach, Virginia, where he lived and worked for many years. His unorthodox remedies and treatments often flew in the face of traditional medicine, and earned him a place as a progenitor or forerunner of modern holistic health. His ideas have had a strong influence in recent decades; many have called him the "Father of the New Age Movement."

* * *

Edgar Cayce was born on March 18, 1877, one of five children, in the rural farming community of Hopkinsville, Kentucky. It was a modest and humble beginning in a place where people worked hard, and most were conservative, "God-fearing" fundamentalist Christians. Although Cayce would remain a Christian all his life, he had a special gift: clairvoyant ability that enabled him to perceive events in the future, and see beyond what is observable to the normal five senses most people are limited to. How he became psychic remains an unanswered question; but he was very young, not even school age, when he first told of "seeing" visions; and both heredity and injury to his head may have played at least a part in developing his psychic gifts.[1]

In a biography about Cayce written by Sidney Kirkpatrick there is a story about his grandfather Thomas, who was also reputed to be psychic. His wife, Sarah, Edgar's grandmother, always referred to the ability as "the gift of second sight," a term often used years ago to describe clairvoyance. However, Tom's ability was not talked about outside of the family.

But it was no secret that Tom was an excellent dowser or "water witch," one who had a special sensitivity for locating water underground in order to determine where to dig new wells. Tom employed the centuries-old technique of using a Y-shaped or forked tree limb, by holding a branch of it in each hand. When the limb began moving up or down, it indicated that he'd detected water beneath the surface.

Tom may also have had "psychokinetic abilities." Years later, Edgar recalled that his grandfather was able to place his hands close to or over a table, broom, or some other object, and it would move about on its own as if it was performing a little jig. If Tom had psychic gifts or powers, it might explain his grandson's predisposition to them. Certainly, even as a child, Edgar was aware of psychics and mediums. This was, after all, the 1880s and spiritualists were virtually everywhere in America, even in rural and small towns.

In his book, Kirkpatrick told of an incident in May 1880 that might also have contributed to Cayce's clairvoyant ability. Edgar was only three years old at the time, when he tumbled from a "fence post" and fell onto a board that had a nail jutting out. The metal nail pierced Edgar's skull, "puncturing his cranium and entering his brain cavity," Kirkpatrick explained. Edgar's father, who witnessed the dreadful accident, immediately rushed to pull the nail from his son's head. The wound was treated with turpentine and then bandaged. Remarkably, Edgar healed quickly and was soon up and about again.[2]

Whether the injury contributed to Edgar's psychic ability is not certain. But what has not been unusual throughout the history of the paranormal are claims that psychic abilities often develop or intensify following trauma to the head or brain.

Edgar was only four when his grandfather died in 1881. Tom had drowned when his horse bolted and he was thrown into a nearby pond. The horse's hoofs then came down upon Tom's chest, crushing him. Although Edgar was very young at the time, he'd been close to his grandfather, so relatives were somewhat surprised that the little boy accepted the tragic news quite calmly. The reason became clear not long after Tom's funeral when Edgar's parents found their son in a tobacco barn talking to his departed grandfather. Although later in life Edgar always insisted his gift came from God, and never defined himself as a medium, he apparently could see and communicate with the spirit world if he so desired. As a young boy he sometimes saw his grandfather in a "beam of light," he told his uncle and aunt with whom he lived for a short while. But Edgar's Aunt Lou was neither understanding nor open to such talk about spirits. "He's got the devil in him," she insisted. "No good can come of this," she warned, and urged that her nephew be taken to a doctor or a minister for help. Edgar's parents wisely ignored Aunt Lou's advice; for the most part they assumed their young son had a vivid imagination when he spoke to his "imaginary playmates" and deceased relatives.

One day in 1888, when Edgar was eleven years old and running in the woods, he accidentally fell on a pointed stick that caused a painful injury to his groin. Because an infection developed, the healing process was slow—the medications applied were simply old folk remedies—and Edgar was confined to bed for most of a year. He spent much of the time reading the Bible, especially chapters and verses about what we would consider "psychic or supernatural events," of which the Bible has many. Cayce's interest in Bible study would last all his life. Once he came to terms with his psychic abilities, he considered them a gift from God, although there were always those who mistook what he did for something occult or evil.

How Cayce personally came to reconcile psychic phenomena with Christian belief was the result, in part, of a life-changing experience that occurred at age twelve when he had an angelic visitation. The female figure emerged from what he described as "a glorious light" after he'd prayed for guidance about his future. Edgar had sometimes wondered, if God heard his prayers would He answer? Now He did through the celestial messenger: "Thy prayers are heard. You will have your wish. Remain faithful. Be true to yourself. Help the sick, the afflicted," she told him.

When Edgar eventually described the incident, he said it was very "realistic." People in many cultures throughout history have told of similar experiences, always portraying the encounters as lifelike, or some similar characterization. That is what separates the visionary experience from an ordinary dream, and young Edgar's depiction matches untold other accounts throughout history. Whatever it was that he saw, it was an instant that helped define his future. But because he did not want to face either ridicule or a barrage of questions, Edgar kept the angelic encounter to himself for a long while before he spoke to anyone about it. However, for the first time, he felt he had some understanding of what his life's path would be. He defined it as "God's work," although he was not yet certain exactly how he would best serve others. In fact, it must have seemed odd to some that a boy barely in his teens would wrestle with such adult problems. But remember, Edgar Cayce was raised at a time when many Christian religious revivals were taking place, and he was unlike other children his age when it came to thoughts and interests.

One aspect of his life that he definitely did not embrace was attending school. By his own admission he was not a good student, and struggled with schoolwork. Then, at age thirteen he found an unusual solution to his academic dilemma. All he had to do was literally sleep with his head on a schoolbook or allow his forehead to touch a book and somehow he could memorize every word written in it. For example, if he slept on his speller, words he hadn't been able to spell suddenly were correct. Not surprisingly, his grades showed a marked improvement. His father, Leslie, at first thought it was some sort of trick on his son's part. But once he became convinced it was genuine, Leslie asked Edgar to demonstrate this uncanny ability for others, thus there were plenty of witnesses to confirm it. But because he was so obviously different from his peers, Edgar felt like an outsider, something children then, just as now, didn't want to be.

Once, when Edgar was playing in the school yard, he was badly injured when a baseball struck him in the back. The accident caused him to temporarily lapse into unconsciousness. When he spoke again, still in bed, he inexplicably predicted the winner of the upcoming presidential election. "Hooray for Cleveland!" he blurted out. Edgar proved to be correct; Grover Cleveland won the presidential election later that year, 1892.

What about his spinal injury? Edgar took matters into his own hands when he asked his parents to make a "poultice" from a recipe he gave them. It was a combination of "herbs, cornmeal, and onions." The poultice was prepared by putting together the indicated ingredients until they formed a soft mound that was heated. The concoction was then wrapped in cloth and applied to the body to relieve soreness and inflammation. Fearful of what effect it might have, his parents refused their son's request. But Edgar's grandmother Sarah had no such qualms; she prepared the remedy and placed it on the back of his head, near his neck. The treatment worked—Edgar had psychically healed himself and was soon on his feet again.

But nothing could persuade him to remain in school or even think about attending college, despite his greatly improved academic record. By the end of grade eight, fifteen-year-old Edgar Cayce quit school, never to return. His decision might have been motivated more by his poor feelings of self-worth than his grades. He'd grown tired of taunts from classmates, and being labeled a "freak" by those who knew of his psychic abilities; school bullies were a problem in his day also. In fact, Edgar's own father had taken to calling him "strange."

He was about sixteen when he moved from his parents' home to live with his grandmother Sarah, considerably more tolerant and understanding about his psychic gifts than most others he encountered. She convinced Edgar that God wanted him to follow the path "the good Lord" had planned for him, and reminded him not to "misuse" his abilities. She said that if Edgar heard voices, "compare them to what Jesus says in the Bible." That way, she told him, he couldn't go wrong. He would heed all his life his grandmother's advice given him that June in 1895 when he was eighteen.

Only a month later, in July, Sarah died. Edgar was there, holding her hand when she told him that she saw his grandfather coming to take her to the Other Side. Edgar had no doubts about that, remembering that as a small boy he'd talked to his grandfather after he'd passed on, as well as to other departed relatives.

Edgar had tinkered with thoughts of becoming a minister, but when it came time to seek employment, the sixteen-year-old found work at a Hopkinsville bookstore, and then in the shoe department of a local dry goods store. Within a couple of years, he abandoned his idea of a career in the ministry. Two years later, in 1897, at the age of twenty, nearly six feet tall, lean, and pleasant looking, Edgar Cayce fell in love and proposed marriage to Gertrude Evans, a bright, attractive, and petite young woman with dark hair and warm eyes. She was from a prominent family; he barely had any money. Other jobs followed, including another in a bookstore, and positions as a traveling salesman and then as an insurance agent. Edgar and Gertrude would marry in 1903 when he felt he could support a family, and he eagerly embarked on a career as a professional photographer.

In 1901 Cayce gave his first psychic reading when he faced his own illness; he'd inexplicably lost his voice the year before. When doctors were unable to find any physical basis for his laryngitis, Cayce turned to hypnosis for help; it was a popular healing technique at the time, and he had a friend induce a hypnotic suggestion. However, it provided him with only temporary relief and the laryngitis soon returned. He still had to find a treatment for his paralyzed throat muscles in order to restore his voice.

Cayce recalled how he'd been able to enter a trancelike or "hypnotic sleep" in order to commit his schoolbooks to memory. So he had a friend named Al Layne induce a hypnotic state by using an appropriate suggestion, making it possible for him to solve his own health dilemma. Cayce psychically diagnosed and then prescribed himself the appropriate treatment for his voice to return; it was a "procedure of hypnotic suggestion to increase circulation to the affected area," wrote Harmon Bro, minister and author who later worked closely with Cayce. He had cured himself, an event unusual enough to be reported in the local newspaper, the *Kentucky New Era* in April of 1901.

Layne, who would go on to become a doctor of osteopathy, had been greatly impressed by what he saw Cayce achieve for himself. The two were friends, and so Layne asked Cayce if he'd be able to do the same for his longtime stomach disorder. Cayce agreed and once he was in a hypnotic or trance state he informed Layne what he should do medically to alleviate his abdominal problem. Layne took the advice and was healed.[3]

When word of Cayce's apparent self-healing spread through the community, several medical doctors from Hopkinsville and nearby Bowling Green sought his help in determining what ailments their patients suffered from. To the physicians' surprise they found that all Cayce required to diagnose someone was to be told the patient's name and address. From only that bit of information he was able to psychically "tune in" to a subject; they did not have to be present.[4] The distance between Cayce and the patient's location did not appear to make any difference, whether the individual was nearby or far away. He was given "no other information regarding any patient," said his son Hugh Lynn. Cayce would then prescribe unique remedies to treat a wide range of ailments and diseases through various combinations of herbs, teas, diet, voiding, assimilation, psychic techniques, physical therapy, osteopathy, homeopathy, chiropractic manipulation, low voltage electrotherapy, nutritional therapy, and psychotherapy. There were also Epsom salt packs, sand packs, gold treatments, and antiseptics, depending on the need. Sometimes he advised ultraviolet treatment, violet ray therapy, balsam of sulfur rubs, and exercise.[5] Cayce was even open to astrology.

By Cayce's definition, a disease occurred when "something in the structure and relationship of the body-mind-soul unit becomes unbalanced or disturbed," explained Dr. William McGarey, who wrote about Cayce's healings. Cayce maintained that while in trance he was "actually communicating with the unconscious mind of the patient," McGarey noted, and Cayce believed, "all healing came through God," no matter the treatment, whether it was medicine, herbs, surgery, or prayer.

When Cayce spoke about "directing the flow of energy in the body" he'd likely be better understood by psychics than he would by traditional physicians. He suggested that "we must learn to deal with the vibrational nature of the body," McGarey wrote.[6] The ancient Chinese technique of acupuncture also theorized that the chi or energy flows through the human body and links the different "organs and systems." However, that was a concept foreign to Western medicine, only accepted in recent decades in America.[7]

There were far too many healings and remedies over Cayce's forty-three-year career (1901–1944) as a medical clairvoyant to present even a fraction of them in detail.[8] But a few cases might be representative. To share some examples, we consulted several books about Cayce healings including the writings of Mary Ellen Carter, William McGarey, M.D., and our personal research of Cayce readings at his foundation in Virginia.

For instance, Cayce treated a young man with a ruptured appendix by advising dietary changes to include green vegetables, along with a combination of packs, antiseptics, and osteopathy. For a girl diagnosed with a thyroid condition, he recommended iodine in combination with rehabilitation to correct the body's functioning. For various abdominal and intestinal problems, Cayce often advised castor oil packs. Golden seal herbal tea was used as a "stimulant," and also helped relieve nausea and vomiting. Teas were a timeworn treatment in the history of many cultures; but Cayce found they worked, and that's what mattered to him.

In one reading, to reduce a baby's high fever, Cayce prescribed that "tallow, camphor, and turpentine" be rubbed on the child's feet. He also advised "syrup of squill [an expectorant and diuretic] to reduce fever, calcidin [a cough suppressant], and natural fruit juices," Mary Ellen Carter explained.[9] The little girl's fever came down; she'd been healed by Cayce's unorthodox remedy, no small matter in the early 1930s, prior to the widespread use of antibiotics. In another reading for the same child, who later developed an ear infection, Cayce recommended a mixture of specific oils; cleaning the ear with an antiseptic; Fletcher's Castoria, a commercially sold product; and massages with olive oil and tincture of myrrh. For other conditions he sometimes added various spirits to the treatments, such as turpentine, or spirits of camphor mixture. One common remedy was camphorated oil.

In a reading in 1932 for a girl suffering the agony of juvenile arthritis, Cayce's records show a prescription of milk and potato soup, apparently for the "lime content." Two years later, she apparently was healed, and sent him a testimonial letter both thanking and praising his work.

For infertility, in an era before drugs that are now readily available to cope with the problem, Cayce recommended enemas "to relieve pains from pressure in the intestinal system," McGarey explained. By 1930, Cayce was treating cerebral palsy with "manipulation" and "sand baths." He did not shy away from helping patients with paralysis or other difficult maladies. From cancers to colds; scleroderma to sciatica; the range of ailments and diseases he treated was extensive, the number of patients in the thousands.

For the common cold—the vexation of humankind for centuries—Cayce's trance advice was rest, lots of water, "eliminations"—components that appeared in nearly every Cayce remedy. Of course, this gave skeptics and other detractors the opening to question if some patients wouldn't have healed as fast and well without Cayce's treatments. Other critics pointed out that there were no accurate records of those who may have been misdiagnosed or for whom Cayce's treatments were ineffective.[10]

Cayce's recommendations were not haphazard. His prescriptions were exact; he'd instruct so many drops of this, or so many drops of that. Sometimes they were to be combined when administered, and on other occasions only "sipped" rather than swallowed at once.[11]

Cayce did not ignore the psychological components of healing. He understood the value of telling patients they would recover. In other words, those who were discouraged or frightened required encouragement in order to have "the will to live." He also advised patients to pray, not a new idea by any means. Even most traditional physicians were aware of so-called "miraculous healings" in which prayer seemed to play a healing role. Even when most of orthodox medicine scoffed at the idea, Cayce understood the connection between "the power of prayer and healing," a concept lost in twentieth-century traditional Western medicine, and only resurrected for serious study in recent decades, long after Cayce concluded that all life is "a oneness." He'd said, "All time is one, and all life is one." Thus, healing was affected through the body, mind, and spirit—since they are all one. And he added, "No healing is perfected without some psychic force exerted."[12]

McGarey pointed out one curiosity—some would say frustration—that while Cayce could tell psychically "what was wrong in the human body," he offered very little about how the disease "came into being."[13]

One of those who sought Edgar Cayce's early help was a youthful doctor named Wesley Ketchum who practiced homeopathy in Hopkinsville. When Cayce's psychic reading for Ketchum proved to be correct, he asked Cayce to help him with ailments that were the hardest to diagnose. Ketchum also wrote about what he'd witnessed and sent it to a medical research society for its consideration and publication.[14]

Cayce continued working as a professional photographer after he and Gertrude were married in 1903 and became a partner in two photographic studios in Bowling Green where the couple then lived. Unfortunately, fire destroyed both studios in late 1906, leaving Cayce with a mountain of debts that took three years to pay back. By then they had a one-year-old son, Hugh Lynn.

Cayce's reputation was growing as a trance healer whose clairvoyance could be applied to diagnosing and treating patients of any age, although he remained reluctant to accept fees for his ability. He'd already helped local police find missing persons, and lost items; and he'd psychically aided law enforcement in a homicide case. In 1909, among those who sought his help were doctors who asked him to aid in saving the life of an infant suffering from convulsions; the three-month-old baby was not expected to live.

As always, Cayce entered a "hypnotic trance," closed his eyes, and then after a brief silent meditation, was ready. He used no tools of divination; there were no tarot cards, horoscopes, Ouija boards, or crystal balls. Nor did he purport to communicate with the spirit world as so many self-proclaimed mediums of the time did. His biographers would deny he was a medium, and he claimed no spirit guides assisted him.[15]

Now Cayce faced the prospect of healing a three-month old infant, this man without even a high school diploma, and certainly no medical training. Even if, as skeptics claimed, he memorized every medical book he could secretly read, it did not explain his uncanny gift for knowing exactly what diagnosis to make, and what treatments to recommend. Also his use of medical terminology often seemed beyond what would be expected from someone other than a physician.

But Cayce, the non-doctor, could presumably access in trance the technical knowledge that seemed far above what one would suppose. Those who observed him with an open mind usually concluded that something more than mere memorization was going on. Cayce, in his altered state, was able to use clairvoyance to look inside a patient's body, and psychically probe organs, arteries, and blood vessels, often with the accuracy of the best medical diagnosticians of that era.

Still in trance, he diagnosed the baby's condition, and concluded that the infant's spasms were the result of epilepsy. Cayce recommended the child be given a carefully measured amount of belladonna. He also suggested the baby be swathed in a "steaming hot poultice made from the bark of a peach tree," author Sidney Kirkpatrick explained.[16]

When Cayce announced the end of the reading and emerged from his trance, the two doctors present concurred that the diagnosis made sense. However, both physicians were somewhat shaken by Cayce's treatment. Belladonna, or deadly nightshade as it's sometimes called, is from a highly poisonous plant. How could Edgar Cayce prescribe that for a frail and tiny infant who was so ill? The doctors were certain that belladonna would prove fatal to the baby.

The child's mother, however, insisted on following Cayce's advice, and her husband reluctantly acquiesced. Cayce was unable to provide any additional information or help after the reading because he insisted that he remembered nothing uttered while in trance. His medical acumen only showed itself when he was hypnotized; but not when he was awake. Doctors had also told the mother that she could not bear any more children. During the reading, however, Cayce predicted that she could look forward to becoming pregnant again.

Meanwhile, Cayce's peculiar remedy was prepared, according to his instructions, and the infant was given the belladonna. A short while after, the baby fell soundly asleep. The child awakened several hours later, perspiring profusely, but the convulsions had ceased, and he was breathing normally. Cayce had saved the little boy who went on to live a full and productive adult life, according to Cayce biographers.

In October 1910, Edgar Cayce's psychic abilities became nationally known when there was a prominent story about him in the *New York Times*, with pictures that accompanied the lengthy article, apparently spurred by Ketchum's earlier research paper.[17] As the name Edgar Cayce became known around the country, many described him as a "wonder," and were eager for his help. He joined with Dr. Ketchum, the homeopath, back in Hopkinsville, and gave readings every day, something he had never done before. His calling couldn't be denied; he was now a "Psychic Diagnostician."

Cayce turned thirty-four in 1911, a busy year that brought further achievements and also heartache. He went to Chicago where he gave

readings for the newspaper, the *Examiner*. But there was personal tragedy when Cayce's second son, Milton, was born. The baby became seriously ill with whooping cough and died when he was not quite two
months old. Cayce and his wife were grief-stricken; and Edgar was also
guilt-ridden, believing that he might have changed the outcome if he'd
acted quicker by giving the baby a trance reading.[18]

It wasn't long after the infant's death that Gertrude became ill, and
was diagnosed with tuberculosis. It was more devastating news, made
worse when doctors told Cayce that she was dying. This time he did not
hesitate; he gave Gertrude psychic readings in which he mapped out his
own "course of treatment" for her. She completely recovered. Of course,
news of this kind, especially in an age before antibiotics, created quite a
stir among those who believed in Cayce's abilities, as well as his detractors and skeptics. So Cayce apparently felt the need for a quieter and less
publicly tumultuous life when he decided to move his family to Selma,
Alabama. Once there, he stopped giving psychic readings, and opened a
photography studio.

But tragedy struck again and it was Cayce the psychic, not the photographer, who stepped in. One day in January 1914, six-year-old Hugh
Lynn Cayce was playing in his father's studio when the boy accidentally
set off "flash powder." Hugh suffered severe burns and injury to his eyes.
One eye was hurt so badly that doctors advised it be removed. That was
not the answer Cayce or his wife wanted to hear. Instead, Cayce went
into a trance state and gave his son a psychic reading. Once out of the
trance, Cayce, as always, claimed he had no recall of anything he said.
But the reading had been copied down as he gave it; and the remedy he
prescribed was carried out. It took several weeks for Hugh Lynn to heal,
but the boy made a complete recovery, thanks to his father.

Cayce continued his readings to help others; it was his destiny, and
there were no lack of people who wanted his aid. However, one problem
his patients invariably discovered was the unwillingness of many traditional doctors to follow through with Cayce's unusual remedies. And, as
you might imagine, there were many people fearful of even telling their
physicians that a psychic had treated them. Cayce began to think the
answer would be to build his own hospital. Then doctors and other
medical personnel of his choosing could follow through with his treatments. The idea wasn't far-fetched for Cayce had come to know many

businessmen and other prominent and powerful individuals who he was certain would lend their support and financial assistance.

Meanwhile he provided readings, most concerning health matters, while his dream of opening a hospital percolated in his mind; he also gave "business readings" and "life readings." Harmon Bro, in his biography of Cayce told the story of another Cayce friend, David Kahn, a successful New York businessman and manufacturer. Kahn once told Bro that he'd gone to Cayce for psychic counsel over the course of both world wars, and for business readings "to build his own fortune."[19] Kahn became a willing backer of Cayce's hospital. In later years, Cayce stopped offering business readings.

There was no question that Cayce had reached a level of national recognition afforded few psychics. One of the most curious stories concerned his readings for President Woodrow Wilson. When Cayce wrote his autobiography, *My Life as a Seer, The Lost Memoirs,* he told how he was secretly called to Washington, DC, to consult with the ailing President Wilson, who had suffered a debilitating stroke toward the end of his second term in office. What circumstances led the two to meet?

By the time Wilson was elected president of the United States in 1912, he'd already served as the governor of New Jersey and the president of Princeton University. He was a deep believer in prayer, and felt strongly that God personally guided and even chose him to be president. Wilson was reelected to a second term in 1916, with the help of his campaign slogan "He kept us out of the war." However, the next year, the United States entered World War I. Wilson was in the forefront of leaders who forged the armistice to end the war in 1918, conceived the idea for a League of Nations, and ultimately won the Nobel Peace Prize for his efforts.

But as the end of his final term in office drew near, in October 1919, Wilson suffered a disabling stroke that rendered him virtually paralyzed for many weeks. The truth was kept from the public; the press reported the president had "a complete nervous breakdown." There were also widespread rumors that his second wife, Edith Wilson, assumed many of the responsibilities of the presidency—a role no first lady ever found herself in before—while the truth about the dire circumstances of the president's health was kept hidden. Mrs. Wilson remained in charge of the executive branch for the last seventeen months of her husband's second term because he was never well enough to regain full command of the presidency. If Wilson's health crisis was shrouded in secrecy, it would make sense that when Edgar Cayce was summoned to the White House to help the ailing president, it also was handled surreptitiously. Cayce's relationship with Wilson would remain a secret for more than a decade.

In 1932, eight years after Wilson's death, Cayce wrote that he was once ". . . called to Washington to give information for one high in authority. This, I am sure, must have been at least interesting, as I was called a year or so later for the same purpose." According to Cayce's longtime friend David Kahn, "At one time we were asked to give a reading [for] President Woodrow Wilson. I believe this was during the time that he was in the wheelchair and incapacitated and Mrs. Wilson was looking after his affairs."

Kahn wrote that a Secret Service official who'd known Cayce from their childhood years in Kentucky arranged the meeting between Wilson and Cayce. Kahn explained that, although he was not present for the readings with Wilson, he learned that Cayce psychically determined the gravity of Wilson's health; then predicted the president would not recover and did not have long to live.

There was another aspect to Cayce's work that intrigued Wilson. Cayce, an avid reader, had earned a reputation as a seer or prophet, albeit somewhat reluctantly. Some years ago in an interview, Cayce's son Hugh Lynn reported that his father "disliked making predictions" because he believed in free will and preferred not to influence anyone who might be vulnerable to suggestion. Nonetheless, behind his gentle countenance and rimless spectacles, Cayce did offer predictions about significant world events and disasters, both natural and man-made, including coming wars, conflicts between nations, and earth changes. Wasn't Edgar Cayce the perfect person to provide Wilson with a look into the future, especially as it concerned the president's all-consuming dream for a League of Nations?[20]

Other books allude to psychic readings by Cayce for Wilson. In *Edgar Cayce, Mystery Man of Miracles,* author Joseph Millard said that Cayce was "mysteriously summoned to Washington" on two occasions. In *A Seer Out of Season,* author Harmon Bro maintained that Cayce was invited to give psychic readings in the White House twice to President

Wilson on the future of the League of Nations.[21] Although no written documentation of those psychic readings has ever been found, there is a record of Cayce's readings for a cousin of the president, a man identified as Major Wilson.

No doubt, the famed psychic was warned in no uncertain terms to maintain silence—a White House position consistent with the veil of secrecy that concealed details about the president's health and Mrs. Wilson's role as de facto president. There was fear that political and public reaction to meetings between a psychic and the president would raise uncomfortable questions about Wilson's religious beliefs and mental stability, and further complicate his tenuous situation. One can only imagine what scandal would have erupted had Wilson's relationship with Cayce been reported in the press.

Woodrow Wilson lived for three years after he left the White House in 1921, although he never fully recovered. Unfortunately, Edgar Cayce had been unable to help Wilson's condition. Most likely it was already too late to cure the president, whose neurological impairments were quite severe. Or perhaps Cayce's unorthodox remedies could have helped, but were ignored by Wilson's own physician, who, trained in late-nineteenth-century medicine, might have been afraid that he would harm his patient.

Wilson left this world for what Cayce called "God's other door," the afterlife, a bitter and disillusioned man whose intractable idealism remained unfulfilled. He never was able to garner Senate support for the League of Nations, and his dream to advance peace in the world or prevent future wars proved unattainable. Cayce's pessimistic—albeit accurate—prediction that the League was doomed to failure only deepened Wilson's disappointment that he could not fulfill his God-ordained mission to "save the world from war."

A third son, Edgar Evans Cayce, was born in 1918, and Cayce continued giving readings and lectures, while his desire to build a hospital remained, and in his travels he met men who could help him with financial backing. As he gave trance readings in many parts of the country, including New York, Birmingham, Pittsburgh, Dayton, Chicago, Kansas City, and Texas, Cayce made a momentous decision that the rest of his life would be devoted to only his psychic work. At the time Cayce, Gertrude, and their sons were living in Selma, Alabama, where their photography business had become successful. So it came as a surprise when he told Gertrude that they were selling the studio, and moving to Dayton, Ohio.

The idea of moving had come about after a prosperous printer from Dayton named Arthur Lammers had gone to Selma for a reading with Cayce in 1923. Lammers had a strong interest and was knowledgeable in various occult subjects such as the kabbalah, astrology, so-called "mystery religions," Theosophy, and Hindu teachings. He was impressed by Cayce's abilities but wanted more than health readings, as accurate as they were. He had questions about larger issues in life, such as "the nature of human existence," as Harmon Bro explained in his book. Lammers saw possibilities for Cayce well beyond clairvoyant advice about personal medical concerns. So he offered Cayce and his family the opportunity to relocate to Dayton, and was even willing to finance the move. Cayce agreed and his psychic readings would deal with the "body, mind, and soul" of those who came for help.[22]

In his reading, Cayce had employed astrology, and while in a deep trance remarked that Lammers "had once been a monk." Suddenly, Cayce had psychically entered, so to speak, an entirely different realm. It seemed out of character, at first, that he would refer to reincarnation, since he remained devoutly Christian and devoted to the word of the Bible. Cayce always insisted that his psychic gifts came from God, and he had no intention of misusing them. "Jesus was his companion," he felt.[23] But here he was in August of 1923 discovering that in a trance reading he'd talked about reincarnation, which was anathema to his fundamentalist Christian beliefs, although widely accepted by the Eastern religions, Hinduism and Buddhism.[24]

Remember that Cayce maintained he had no recall of anything he said while in his "hypnotic sleep."[25] So, this time, when he awakened and his stenographer read back the transcript of his reading, Cayce was stunned and even confused. He listened in amazement. In the reading he spoke emphatically about reincarnation. It was genuine, he'd said, not fabrication or fantasy. But as far as the "awake" Cayce was concerned, reincarnation was never a part of his religious convictions or his consciousness.

However, the subconscious mind was another matter. Cayce became alarmed, even frightened, at his own utterances. Specifically, he worried that his subconscious mind might have been taken over by something evil. He was troubled since he'd sworn never to use any psychic ability if he thought it was manipulated by anything negative or sinful. He went through a period of "soul searching"; his chief concern about new topics brought forth in his readings was whether they were consistent with his biblical beliefs, for now he was offering information about the past and the future, as well as answering questions in trance that delved into such subjects as human morality, the soul, karma, even God.[26]

Finally, Cayce came to the decision that everything was a part of "oneness," a view that embraced all religions and many beliefs. "All power is from one source: God," he concluded. In addition to his famous clairvoyant medical readings, he was now giving people so-called "life readings," as they came to be known, and dealt with a person's past lives, as well as their present and future. Later he offered prophecies about Earth changes, even cataclysms that he predicted would happen. He delved into the origins of the universe, religion, philosophy, and questions about death and the afterlife, or as he called it, "God's other door."

Cayce also gave readings that dealt with his subjects' dreams, and offered his psychic interpretation of what they meant. He "suggested that many dreams were related to improper diet, incorrect posture, or predisposition to some illness," Dr. Robert Van de Castle wrote in *Our Dreaming Mind*. In his "self-induced" trance state, Cayce offered both diagnoses and treatments based on people's dreams, and, as well, experienced his own past-life dreams.[27]

In 1923 Cayce met eighteen-year-old Gladys Davis, who lived in Selma, worked in a local store's office, and had studied shorthand in school. This was no small matter because Cayce badly needed someone reliable to transcribe his readings and then retype them. He'd tried other secretaries, but with limited or no success; this was in an era before sophisticated recording technology, and stenography was then the most reliable way of taking dictation to maintain written records. Although there were Dictaphones at the time, they were awkward to use and of poor quality for Cayce's purposes. However, Gladys Davis displayed an impressive talent for accurately transcribing Cayce's readings. His search for a secretary was over.

Prior to Gladys Davis, Cayce's record keeping and transcriptions of readings were haphazard at best. The unfortunate result from a psychic research perspective was that many early readings were lost or never accurately written down. So relatively few of those sessions are available for study. Davis remained with Cayce from 1923 until his death in 1945, and much of the thanks goes to her for painstakingly transcribing, typing, and cataloging thousands of his readings now at the Association for Research and Enlightenment, Cayce's organization in Virginia Beach.

When Cayce settled in Dayton, he struggled financially at first. But it was there that he mentioned reincarnation for the first time in a trance, and his frequent references to Atlantis in past-life readings became influential decades later during the "New Age" movement that began in the 1960s.

Was Atlantis only a fictional story about an imaginary ancient continent that was swallowed up by some terrible natural disaster? Atlantis was not a legend as far as Cayce was concerned; it was a genuine place with a technologically advanced civilization that was decimated by some unknown catastrophe many millennia earlier; possibly a volcano and tidal waves, as well as seismic upheavals, that claimed a large number of lives.[28]

One Cayce theory was that the destruction of Atlantis resulted from the misuse of powerful energy that emanated from a large crystal.[29] Cayce had spoken in trance about the Atlanteans' use of something called the "Great Crystal," that captured the sun's energy. The crystal, "tuned" correctly, had positive applications, such as communication with God, and the ability to heal and to enhance human longevity. However, if the crystal was misused, it had immense destructive powers. At some point, Atlantean leaders erred in their tuning of the crystal to a higher tone or pitch that proved so devastating it triggered volcanic movements and the resulting catastrophic flood that first destroyed Atlantis as one huge continent about fifteen thousand years before Christ. Atlantis then shattered into several smaller islands.

The ancient Greek philosopher Plato first described Atlantis in the fourth century BC in two of his dialogues, Timaeus and Critias; and ever since there has been debate about whether it actually existed, or had Plato created Atlantis for literary or dramatic purposes? Was it supposed to be an example of Utopia, an ideal or flawless community? Plato spoke of an "island continent beyond the Pillars of Hercules [the ancient name for Gibraltar] called Atlantis, the heart of a great and wonderful empire." The Greek philosopher described it as "an earthly paradise, with a large population, golden roofed cities, mighty fleets, and armies for invasion and conquest," wrote Charles Berlitz in *The Mystery of Atlantis*. Then, "in a single day and night it disappeared beneath the sea." Plato estimated that Atlantis sank some nine thousand years before he lived; that would date its flooding to about 11,500 years ago.[30]

Even among those geologists and marine scientists who allow that there once was such a continent, there has always been dispute about where Atlantis was and how highly advanced it might have been. But something about the idea of Atlantis as an idyllic paradise has long captivated the public imagination. Berlitz estimated that more than five thousand books and pamphlets about Atlantis have been published since the mid-nineteenth century. One book that should not go unmentioned predated Cayce's first past-life reading by more than forty years. In 1882, American author and one-time politician Ignatius Donnelly (1831–1901) greatly renewed interest when he wrote *Atlantis, The Antediluvian World*.

Donnelly's contention was that similarities in primitive civilizations on both sides of the Atlantic that had no contact with each other suggested there was a "common origin." He concluded there was a time when disparate cultures shared the boundaries of the continent of Atlantis before it sank. Those who survived then migrated to territories in both the east and west. For psychics, such as Cayce, Atlantis was a veritable treasure trove of pronouncements and attributions that could not be proven, especially when suggesting past lives there.

Exactly where Atlantis was located is still uncertain. Some have suggested it was in the Azores; while other researchers have concluded it was somewhere near Greece, in the Mediterranean, possibly the island of Thera, north of Crete. Cayce's readings placed Atlantis in the Bahamas or near Bimini, and he'd prophesied that an Atlantean temple would emerge in the vicinity of Bimini in either 1968 or 1969. There was a tantalizing clue around that time when "several underwater structures [were] actually sighted nearby," Berlitz wrote.[31] But others have been disappointed that no further evidence of Cayce's prediction has materialized.

Cayce seemed not to be concerned with scientific investigations about Atlantis. In his trance readings, his interest was to provide a description of a lost continent where he believed many people had a past incarnation.

An endeavor on Cayce's part in 1920 to raise money for his new hospital through oil drilling in Texas failed. Then in 1924 Cayce met a New York stockbroker named Morton Blumenthal who was willing to support and contribute to Cayce's plans for a national organization. The next year Cayce received advice in one of his psychic readings that he should permanently move his family and work to Virginia Beach, Virginia. Heeding the psychic guidance, he did just that, and the Cayces lived frugally in a rented house. By 1927 he and Blumenthal began construction of the Cayce Hospital in Virginia Beach. Now Cayce hoped to realize his dream of a medical facility with qualified physicians and other professional staff able to implement his unorthodox treatments. The next year, the hospital was dedicated, and Cayce also met with financial backers and other supporters to next discuss establishing a university.

In 1929, the Cayce Hospital officially opened its doors to patients, and from the beginning was successful. There were many people who wanted Cayce's remedies for a wide range of ailments. But many traditional physicians and researchers remained highly skeptical of Cayce's hospital, and some even traveled to Virginia Beach for only one reason: to expose Cayce as a fraud. However, after observing readings, treatments, and other procedures, many who'd gone with negative attitudes were stumped. There was no denying that patients often improved with Cayce's approach. There was also no scientific explanation for psychic or clairvoyant diagnoses, or his peculiar treatments composed of herbs, special diets, castor oil packs, homeopathy, and chiropractic manipulations, among others. It was not unusual for those who came to debunk Cayce to change their minds and leave impressed with the efficacy of his unorthodox methods.

Sidney Kirkpatrick was an author who approached Cayce's techniques with a skeptical eye in recent years. However, the more he learned from extensively poring through Cayce's readings, letters, and papers, the more favorably he viewed the psychic's work. He changed his mind sufficiently to write a largely positive book, *Edgar Cayce: An American Prophet*.

Atlantic University, Cayce's school, opened in 1930. Its first classrooms were located in hotels along the beachfront. But unfortunately, his dream of treating patients and teaching his remedies to others who shared his vision was short-lived. The year before, America had been shaken to its economic core by the stock market crash of 1929. Fortunes that had been made were lost overnight. Many financiers and wealthy businessmen were wiped out, including several who were Cayce's backers and supporters. With even millionaires like Morton Blumenthal facing bankruptcy, monies for the Edgar Cayce Hospital and Atlantic University were no longer readily available. So in February 1931, Cayce's hospital closed, and in December, the university folded. But that same year, Cayce set in motion plans with his supporters for a new organization to be named the Association for Research and Enlightenment (ARE) headquartered in Virginia Beach to house and study Cayce's readings and treatments, maintain other records and files, and engage in related psychic and healing research. It was incorporated in 1931.

Cayce had been badly shaken by the closing of Atlantic University, as he was when the hospital was shut months earlier. Adding to his frustration was embarrassment; why hadn't he foreseen the personal impact of the country's massive economic failure, the Great Depression, as he peered into the future?

He decided to make one more effort to secure funding for Atlantic University; and so he traveled to New York in October 1931 to meet prospective investors. He was still in New York in November, when a woman approached him and pleaded for a reading. In situations where people appeared desperate, Cayce had a difficult time turning them away, so he agreed to give the stranger a trance reading. Once the session was completed the woman identified herself as a plainclothes police officer and arrested Cayce, Gertrude, and Gladys Davis, and charged them with violating the local anti-fortune-telling law. Cayce was certain he'd been "set up" by someone disgruntled with whom he'd previously done business.

His longtime friend David Kahn was called to secure bail for them, and they were "bitterly embarrassed," Harmon Bro wrote, by the arrests and tabloid stories. The most vicious were photos that showed Cayce and his pretty blond secretary, Gladys Davis, together, the implication being that they were lovers. Tabloid news photographers had cleverly removed Gertrude Cayce from the pictures.

The case went to trial, but the charges were dismissed. Cayce's defense was that he'd been engaged in "psychic research" for his newly formed association. When readings were given, subjects were asked for their written "consent" beforehand. The undercover policewoman had granted her signed permission before Cayce's reading. That was sufficient grounds for the "fortune-telling" charge to be dismissed. Cayce's vindication was headlined in the *New York Herald Tribune:* "Research Plea Voids Charge of Fortune Telling." But the incident left Cayce upset, nonetheless.[32]

In November 1935, Cayce, Gertrude, Hugh Lynn, and Gladys were invited guests at the Detroit home of a family for whom Cayce's trance readings had been immensely helpful. Family members were well intentioned when they asked the famed psychic if he'd give a medical reading for a neighbor, a young girl who'd been taken ill. Cayce agreed without hesitation. However, because the child's father was not home, Cayce neglected to obtain his consent.

When the father returned and discovered that Cayce had treated his daughter without permission, he was furious, called the police, and the Cayces were taken into custody for "practicing medicine without a license." Once they were arrested, Cayce, his wife, son, and secretary were all jailed. The public would soon know the details when the story was reported in Detroit newspapers. One headlined Cayce's latest legal travail: "Police Arrest Four on Quack Charge." The following day, after they'd spent an uncomfortable night in jail, the four were freed on bail. The case went to trial, and charges were dropped against Gertrude, Hugh Lynn, and Gladys. Edgar did not fare as well; he was found guilty. However, the judge ordered him "paroled in his own custody," Harmon Bro wrote of the outcome. Not everyone was an Edgar Cayce fan or supporter.[33]

By the 1930s, Dr. J. B. Rhine and his wife, Louisa, had become nationally recognized for their ESP testing at Duke University. By then Cayce was also nationally known. The logical leap would be to assume serious scientists and parapsychologists, like the Rhines, would be eager to test his clairvoyant and healing abilities. But here was the problem they faced. Rhine had hoped to establish parapsychology's credibility. In order "to gain scientific acceptance," explained Harmon Bro, "Rhine [had] establish[ed] simple repeated phenomena with such targets as cards and dice used on . . . subjects . . ."

But was that the best way to study Cayce's psychic gifts? "Science proceeded by widely repeated experiments built upon hypotheses, predicting results, and then verifying or disverifying them," Bro wrote. The Rhines had not overlooked Cayce; they were seeking the best way they knew to study him. J. B. Rhine suggested that Cayce visit the parapsychology laboratory at Duke so he could be tested by the use of ESP cards that had been employed with his other subjects. But Cayce balked at the idea of guessing shapes on cards; that was not his ability. His mission was to heal the sick. Several other psychics and mediums had also been reluctant to be tested with ESP cards. Famed Irish medium Eileen Garrett had been one who'd hesitated at the prospect of Rhine's testing her with cards. Cayce insisted on being examined for what he did best: "serving the ill," Bro said. It was Cayce's son Hugh Lynn who encouraged his father to visit Rhine at Duke; but Rhine was not particularly impressed by Cayce's abilities.[34]

However, in return, Rhine sent an associate, psychologist Lucien Warner to observe Cayce in Virginia Beach. Warner then brought another highly regarded parapsychology researcher of that era to study the famed psychic and healer. He was Gardner Murphy, a Columbia University graduate, professor, psychologist, and for years, prominent in the leadership of the American Society for Psychical Research. Unfortunately, Murphy was involved in other projects at the time, and his study of Cayce was apparently never completed.

Cayce, of course, did not go unnoticed within the community of psychics and parapsychologists. Two other well-known figures of that era were the mediums Eileen Garrett and Arthur Ford.[35] Both had so-called "spirit guides" when they conducted readings; and they wondered why Cayce did not. If there was one label he wished to avoid it was being known as a medium. Cayce always contended that his ability was to reach into a "universal consciousness," rather than tap into the spirit world. Therefore, he had no need for a spirit guide. He had his clairvoyant ability and his deep belief and faith in God. This was a man who'd read the Bible from beginning to end—Genesis to Revelation—countless times, until he'd virtually memorized it.

There may have also been more practical reasons for distancing himself from mediumship. It is only speculation, but Cayce knew that too many mediums had been accused of fraud, or had engaged in some chicanery. The spiritualist movement in America had contributed to its own demise in the early decades of the twentieth century for just that reason. There was no benefit in being known as a medium.

There is no evidence that Cayce ever engaged in any fraudulent act. Even America's self-appointed psychic debunker, Harry Houdini, never was able to expose any deception on Cayce's part.[36] Also, as a lifelong Christian, Cayce was fully aware of the Old Testament prohibition on mediums. Even if he privately disagreed, nearly all of Cayce's life and career were spent in the South where fundamentalists were more accepting of a healer than they would be of a medium. However, there was little doubt that Cayce could communicate with the deceased if he wished.

Cayce was also called upon to help in two of the biggest news stories of the 1930s. On March 1, 1932, the infant son of famed aviator Charles Lindbergh was kidnapped from the family's New Jersey home. Cayce's friend David Kahn had arranged psychic readings with someone supposedly close to the Lindberghs, but there is no indication that Charles and Anne Morrow Lindbergh were aware of the readings, or would even have accepted any of Cayce's information. Kahn may have been motivated by a ten-thousand-dollar reward for the return of the baby, and the publicity that Cayce's involvement would attract. The extent to which Cayce provided law enforcement with any helpful information was never officially made public.

German immigrant Bruno Richard Hauptmann was arrested and charged with the kidnapping and murder of the Lindbergh baby. New Jersey governor Harold Hoffman put some two-dozen questions to Cayce about the kidnapping, including the big mystery about whether Hauptmann acted alone.

Cayce's psychic readings suggested Hauptmann had some involvement, but did not act by himself. Hauptmann, meanwhile, was found guilty and went to the electric chair on April 3, 1936. The official version was that he'd committed the crime alone, despite his protests of innocence. Cayce's family requested that the psychic's name not be involved, no matter the outcome. In recent years there has been substantial evidence that Hauptmann, whatever his involvement, was not the lone kidnapper, confirming Cayce's version of the events.[37]

The next year produced another major story that has never been officially answered: What happened to Amelia Earhart? The famed aviatrix had been the first woman to fly solo across the Atlantic in 1932. But in 1937, she'd taken off for a flight over the Pacific, and was never again seen or heard from. By the time Cayce was asked to help it was too late;

Earhart was already dead, although it was claimed that he was able to locate where her plane went down.

Cayce had an impressive list of celebrities to whom he gave readings. Sidney Kirkpatrick mentioned some in his biography about Cayce's life. There were such immediately recognizable names as George Gershwin, Irving Berlin, Gloria Swanson, and Ernest Hemingway's mother, who early in her son's career, worried about his future as a writer. Scientists included Thomas Edison, Nikola Tesla, and David Sarnoff. Nelson Rockefeller and labor leader George Meany both sought medical help from Cayce. Years later, screen legend Marilyn Monroe used "beauty aids" recommended by Cayce in trance.

After 1923 Cayce, even as his health readings continued, gave predictions that went far beyond treating individual ailments. These were prophecies about world events.[38] One of the best known was his foretelling of the Stock Market Crash in 1929. Cayce also foresaw the failure of Prohibition (1919–1933); predicted the beginning and end of both the First and Second World Wars; the creation of the State of Israel; race riots that ripped apart American cities during the 1960s; the emergence of China as a global force; the return of religion to the officially atheist Soviet Union; the huge Alaska earthquake of 1964; and damaging quakes in San Francisco in 1989, and Los Angeles in 1994.

An interesting Cayce prognostication made in about 1936 was in answer to which investments would be the most profitable in future years. The response from Cayce was "those that have to do with communications." He foresaw the immense future of television at a time when radio dominated. And he may have seen far enough ahead to mean anything or everything from satellites and cell phones, to worldwide computer networks, such as the Internet.

In one prediction that long predated the AIDS epidemic, Cayce said, "plagues will be eliminated, but not until tens of millions of lives have been lost around the world." He looked into the future to see population explosions, shortages of food, natural disasters such as volcanoes, "violent ocean storms, tidal waves, and climatic changes" that seemed to foreshadow the 2004 Asian tsunami, and the Hurricane Katrina disaster that devastated New Orleans and the Gulf Coast in 2005.

In a prophecy offered in 1941, Cayce went far into the future, predicting a "religious war" that some thought pinpointed the troubled Middle East. Could it have been a psychic impression of the long and bitter battle between Israel and the Arab nations? Or even Islamic fundamental terrorism?

Cayce also foresaw the melting of the North and South poles and global warming, a serious environmental concern. He cautioned about the "Vanishing Shield," a reference to the depletion of the Earth's ozone layer that would weaken protection from the sun's ultraviolet radiation, leading to more skin cancers. According to Cayce believers, a number of his predictions have already come to pass, while critics argue that many of them were ambiguous, at best. He also made prophecies that included the Second Coming of Christ, and predictions for the new millennium past the year 2000.

Cayce's clairvoyant medical readings were estimated at about 90 percent accuracy. What about Edgar Cayce the prophet and seer? His predictions touched on everything from wars to Earth changes, the origin of man, the life of Jesus, dreams, and the future of the planet. There was no limit to what people thought to ask, and apparently no restrictions on what Cayce, in trance, was willing to answer. Although Cayce claimed to foresee the future, he also insisted that human destiny could be changed; but if people did not heed the warnings, the future might be one of calamity.

As far back as the 1930s, Cayce predicted major, even catastrophic changes ahead for planet Earth. His prophecies were supposed to commence in 1958 and continue until 1998, wrote author Tony Allan, but the calamities never occurred.[39]

As Cayce looked toward the year 2000 and beyond—the new millennium[40]—he predicted that earthquakes would strike the Great Lakes, and terrible floods in America's farmlands could result in major "food shortages." He foresaw new "land masses" emerging in the Atlantic Ocean as the "end times" approach. According to Cayce, the newly discovered land would prove to be the lost continent of Atlantis. He made dire warnings of earthquakes and volcanoes in the Pacific, the Mediterranean sinking, and "new lands" emerging. He foresaw a large part of Japan topple into the sea; and "changes" in northern Europe, also a sign of the "end times." He psychically envisioned the breakup of continents, including South America.

But many skeptics and scientists over the years have contended that Cayce's prophecies of geophysical changes were considerably less accurate than his followers claimed.

About the United States Cayce had forewarned, "The greater change will be in the North Atlantic seaboard; watch New York, Connecticut, and the like. Los Angeles and San Francisco, most of all these will be destroyed . . . Portions of the now East Coast of New York or New York City itself will in the main disappear."

Cayce predicted California will see "many land changes" along the Pacific Coast that will occur as the end times near, and the catastrophic earthquake long predicted for California will follow.

Cayce prophesied changes in weather conditions and the earth's atmosphere, and he spoke in trance of global warming and pole shifts. He foresaw changes at the North and South poles, and warned that polar regions would be shifted so that, in his words, "they occupied more of the tropical and semitropical regions . . ."

Cayce's prediction dated the pole shifts occurring in about 2000 or 2001 AD; another end times warning sign. Cayce had predicted there would be "sudden shifts in the Earth's polar axis in 1998. He foresaw World War III erupting in 1999, and civilization destroyed in AD 2000," noted the *Encyclopedia of the Future*. None of these events proved accurate, however.

Did Cayce have the clairvoyant ability while in trance to predict or prophesy coming Earth changes? It depends on whom you ask. Skeptics argue that Cayce was wrong far more than he was correct when he played seer or visionary. Some critics and skeptics have pointed out that since the predictions failed to materialize, it has cast a shadow over Cayce's reputation as a prophet or seer. Although the prophecies and predictions made up only a tiny percentage of his fourteen thousand readings on file, they've attracted disproportionate attention in books and media.

It seems that after his success with medical readings, many sincere and serious people yearned to test the extent of Cayce's psychic abilities. His son Hugh Lynn admitted as much by the early 1930s; the pressure on Cayce to perform must have been immense throughout his entire career. He was not in a position to decline demands to make predictions. That would have unquestionably diminished his reputation, and he was not independently wealthy so that he could refuse those who wanted him to go further with his abilities. Still, many of his prophecies have proven to be accurate, and others may yet be.

Many people throughout history have committed the same error in evaluating psychic abilities as those who pressed Cayce to go beyond medical readings, his true expertise. Often, researchers have discovered that a psychic or medium excels in one aspect of paranormal ability, but not another. Yet, the long held—and mistaken—perception is that a psychic encompasses some all-seeing, all-knowing power. As history has shown us, that is not true.

An often-asked question put to Cayce was where would be the safest place to live after all the Earth changes and geophysical disturbances have occurred? "Don't worry so much where you live but how you live. Make the family of man your family as well," Cayce answered.

In 1939, a longtime family friend, and once Hugh Lynn's college roommate, writer Thomas Sugrue came to Virginia Beach to live with the Cayces. Despite being bedridden with crippling arthritis, Sugrue wrote the first biography about Cayce titled *There Is a River: The Story of Edgar Cayce*.[41] Published in 1942, it was Sugrue's hope that "scientists and theologians" would take seriously Cayce's ideas about "psychology, philosophy, and spirituality," as Harmon Bro explained. However, that did not happen. At the time the book was released, some reviewers were critical of Sugrue noting that he had paid glowing tributes to Cayce; his goal was not to debunk or attack Cayce's gifts, but rather to educate people about them.

One outcome of Sugrue's book was an increased demand for Cayce's readings, probably more than he could physically and emotionally handle. Meanwhile, Cayce's private readings for Sugrue included intense massage treatments that helped the writer to walk again, although eventually his crippling condition returned several years later.

Coronet was a popular American magazine for years, with a large readership for its stories accompanied by photos. It was compact in size, not unlike *Reader's Digest*. In September 1943, *Coronet* devoted an article to Cayce's work, titled "Miracle Man of Virginia Beach." That also brought an immense response from the public, and many more beseeched Cayce for his readings.

During the years of World War II, Cayce worked especially hard.

Virginia Beach was not far from the naval facility at Norfolk, and there was a constant military presence in the area. There were so many who needed his help on the home front, as well as the young men returning from the horrors of combat, many with shattered bodies and minds. Cayce wanted to do his part for what all Americans then called the "war effort." He was receiving between four hundred and five hundred letters a day requesting readings. Obviously, he could not accommodate them all. But he increased the number from his standard two readings a day to eight, an incredible strain.

By the end of summer 1944, he was not well, and in a trance reading he gave himself, he was told psychically that his choice was clear: either he must rest or he will die. On September 17, 1944, Cayce gave himself one last psychic reading. He'd become too ill to continue; physical problems and exhaustion had taken their toll. The next few months were a time of waiting for anxious family, friends, and admirers. But Cayce grew sicker, and before December was over he was in a coma. Now his lungs had filled with fluid; he'd developed pulmonary edema. In a sense, he was "drowning," which was the way he saw himself die in several previous incarnations.

On January 3, 1945, Edgar Cayce suffered a fatal stroke at the age of sixty-seven. His passing was duly noted in newspaper obituaries. He did not seem to have any fear of death, what he'd long called "God's other door." He'd believed he only had to walk through it. Without him, Gertrude, already in poor health, lost her will to continue. Only three months later, on April 1, 1945, she died of cancer, no doubt certain that she and Edgar would be joined again in the afterlife.

Cayce's sons kept their father's work and legacy alive. Hugh Lynn Cayce, although he was not the least psychic, was committed to research, and the ongoing work of the Association for Research and Enlightenment, until his death in 1982. Under his leadership, the ARE grew, prospered, and became internationally known. His son, Charles Thomas Taylor Cayce, succeeded him as president in 1976, and Hugh Lynn was named chairman of the board. Gladys Davis remained with the ARE her entire career, until her death in 1986.

In 1967, twenty-two years after Cayce's passing, a hard-nosed and skilled journalist and veteran reporter named Jess Stearn became sufficiently interested in Cayce's life that he wrote a book about him called

The Sleeping Prophet, a reference to the seer's deep trance states. The times couldn't have been more propitious; the 1960s were the dawning of the so-called New Age, and among the burgeoning interests were mysticism, holistic health, meditation, and psychic phenomena. *The Sleeping Prophet* became one of the bestselling books of the decade, and remained in print many years later; its impact was to awaken new generations to his methods and purposes. The Association for Research and Enlightenment in Virginia Beach saw its membership double, thanks to Stearn's book.[42]

But there were also Cayce detractors; many physicians and others in the medical and related fields vigorously denounced Cayce's medical clairvoyance during his lifetime and ever since. His unorthodox remedies were concoctions of herbs, various packs and poultices, unconventional medications, meditations, and manipulations that were quickly dismissed as unproven, ineffective, perhaps even unsafe. As traditional medicine advanced in the twentieth century, it left behind the folk remedies and healing methods of centuries past, discarding many of them as worthless; criticizing others as "quackery."

Modern doctors consider themselves professionals who trained and earned licenses to practice. Cayce, with little formal education, was certainly not one of them. His claim of diagnosing by clairvoyance harkened back to what skeptics considered superstition that had no place in "modern medicine" or any branch of science. There may have been many who believed in him, including nontraditional doctors; but he also faced frequent attacks by science, medicine, organized religion, and the weight of government eager to invoke penalties on someone who dared to make diagnoses and prescribe odd treatments on the basis of psychic trance readings.

The better-known Cayce became, the more the pressure on him. He worked tirelessly, made little money; lived modestly, did not exploit his ability for wealth; and seldom refused a patient who could not afford to pay. Privately, a gentle and quiet family man, who fervently read his Bible, he gave the appearance of a kindly small-town pharmacist, rather than a gifted and famed psychic and seer who dared to trespass into the often rigid world of orthodox medicine. So he frequently found himself the subject of controversy, but he stood his ground, and knew his own mind.

One favorite criticism by skeptics has long been their argument that

Cayce's ability to diagnose illness was not based on clairvoyance or anything psychic. The critics' accusation is that somehow, in private or secret, Cayce studied medicine avariciously, apparently more than anyone could imagine. After all, as a young man hadn't he worked in several bookstores with access to medical and pharmaceutical texts that he could have cleverly memorized? And, how many times was he incorrect about diagnoses, treatments, and cures? How could skeptics be certain that the more than fourteen thousand readings cataloged were accurate? Many of those arguments against him have proven to be specious, say supporters.[43]

But laying all that aside, for debunkers will never yield to the remotest possibility that Cayce was clairvoyant, his lasting influence on holistic health, alternative medicine, and the New Age movement cannot be denied. Nor can the research he left for future generations to analyze and study. His readings form perhaps the largest single documented body of work by any one American psychic. Cayce's ideas helped move the New Age forward. His foresight and influence were nearly incalculable. Consider the surge in recent decades in holistic health, alternative medicine, even crystal healing. Millions of Americans have sought help from nontraditional medical practitioners. Cayce's treatments are similar to homeopathy, while millions use chiropractic manipulation and osteopathy. Herbal and nutritional approaches, recommended by Cayce decades ago, are also widely accepted.

The New Age movement has embraced Cayce's ideas about Atlantis and past-life hypnotic regressions have become widely popular. His understanding of the "power of prayer" to heal is today one of the major issues in medicine, religion, and parapsychology. His embrace of spirituality and the "oneness" of life have come to fruition in the beliefs of many. Cayce "saw each person as a unit of energy on the earth, a creation of the Universal Force we call God. He saw each [person] as an eternal being born into the earth plane for a purpose. And he pointed the way to the realization of that purpose," author Jess Stearn wrote.

Even Cayce's sensitivity to the idea of spending more time with patients to offer them a psychological boost, lost in our world of modern medical technology, has made a return; he understood it a century ago. Friend, fan, skeptic, or foe; no one questions Cayce's lifelong commitment, his sincerity, or his place, in Harmon Bro's words, as "the Father of the New Age." He may, as some biographers have noted, stand uniquely for his contributions and influence on America's paranormal history; it's no exaggeration to say he was far ahead of his time. Edgar Cayce's readings remain in the library at the Association for Research and Enlightenment, in Virginia Beach, open for membership and to the public.

5

The Subconscious, Relativity, Surrealism, and the Paranormal

We must remember that the rationalistic attitude of the West is not the only possible one and is not all embracing, but is in many ways a prejudice and a bias that ought perhaps to be corrected.

—CARL GUSTAV JUNG, 1961

The modern medical practice of psychiatry came into being with Freud in late nineteenth- and early twentieth-century Vienna. But psychology itself, although a modern health care practice, had its antecedents dating all the way back to classical and even ancient civilizations. In fact, some of today's modern psychological symptoms, as set forth in the *Diagnostic and Statistical Manual of Mental Disorders* (DSM-IV), can be traced back to biblical times even though the symptoms were ascribed to different causalities.

Psychology, in the nineteenth century, gave birth to its own offspring: parapsychology. How are psychology and parapsychology interconnected, how do they differ, and can they together lead to a greater insight into the human psyche and deeper self-understanding? The late psychoanalyst and author of many books about the paranormal, Dr. Nandor Fodor wrote, "Sigmund Freud and Carl Jung were the two giants of [twentieth century] psychology."[1] But, Fodor said, Freud was "pragmatic" [and] Jung was a "mystic." Who were these towering figures and what were their contributions to psychology and parapsychology?

When Jung died in 1961 at the age of eighty-six, obituaries in America and Europe reported the passing of the eminent Swiss psychologist and psychiatrist. But the *Journal of the Society of Psychical Research* noted that little if any reference was made to his paranormal experiences—and he'd had many of them.[2] In fact, Jung had an interest or curiosity about virtually every facet of the paranormal. He believed in telepathy, was open to spirit phenomena, apparitions, I Ching, precognitive dreams, premonitions, visions, déjà vu, clairvoyance, psychokinesis, and unidentified flying objects, or "flying saucers," as they were once called; and he told of encountering poltergeist activity at home. He was the first to note the value of astrology as a means to better understand the human psyche.[3] He even suggested that his pet dog, a dachshund, was "sensitive" to the presence of psychic and ghostly phenomena.

He also formulated the theories of the "collective unconscious" and "synchronicity," that have both become valued concepts in parapsychology.[4] Jung's contributions to the paranormal have proved indelible; the fact that scant mention was made about them following his death seemed an intentional omission. After all, traditional psychology and medicine had no place for the "occult," as it was then often termed, typically dismissing it as superstition or evidence of delusional behavior; so Jung's lifelong and serious interest in the subject was, to say the least, unconventional and left unreported. He was sometimes accused of being unscientific, but he disagreed and considered parapsychology a science.

Born in Switzerland, Jung became a world-renowned psychologist; and also earned his medical degree from the University of Zurich. As a young child he had his first experiences awake and asleep with visions and dreams. His mother was highly psychic, his maternal grandmother regularly saw apparitions, and one cousin was a medium, suggesting a genetic predisposition to paranormal or supernatural incidents.

Not long after he began attending university, his father, a minister, died; and six weeks later, Jung said that his father came to him in a vision that recurred several times and encouraged him to first begin thinking about life after death. "My father appeared to me in a dream, saying that he made a fine recovery, and would shortly be home from his holiday," he recounted.[5] Jung became increasingly intrigued by spiritualism and the occult [the paranormal], and was especially interested in determining what applications it had within the field of psychology.

Once his appetite for psychical phenomena was whetted, he fervently read as many books as he could find on the subject, sat with mediums, and attended séances. His quest for evidence of the paranormal became a lifelong passion. True to his curiosity, Jung's first published work was his doctoral dissertation, *On the Psychology and Pathology of So-Called Occult Phenomena* in 1902.[6] The focus of it was the study of a young medium; she was sixteen, and a cousin of Jung. He claimed he received spirit communications from a departed relative through her, and later when she was exposed for fraud, Jung was shaken and deeply disappointed.

Jung's career began with the practice of medicine at a psychiatric hospital in Zurich; then in 1905 he joined the faculty at the University of Zurich. There he found himself attracted to a new therapeutic approach to treating mental disorders called psychoanalysis, the brainchild of a Viennese psychiatrist, Dr. Sigmund Freud (1856–1939). Jung eagerly became one of Freud's most accomplished adherents; and both agreed on the importance of understanding dreams and the unconscious. However, their association was short-lived. While Freud dwelt on repressed sexual problems as the basis of virtually all neuroses, Jung disagreed. Freud believed the answer to most difficulties lay in a person's subconscious, a dark and frightening part of the mind that he did not trust.

Jung, on the other hand, had a considerably livelier theory of what he called the "unconscious." He considered that part of the mind that is inaccessible to the conscious or waking mind, a genuine and essential part of a person's life, as much as the waking state is, and regarded the unconscious as a "great guide, friend, and adviser of the conscious," author John Freeman explained in *Man and His Symbols*. Parapsychologists have long been fascinated by the functioning of the unconscious, and the psychic information that may enter through that part of the mind. But until Freud's work, the modern idea of the unconscious mind, as we know it, was not understood; for that contribution he deserves much credit.

People mainly communicate with their own unconscious through dreams, and Jung went to great lengths to explain that the "language of the unconscious is symbols, and the means of communications [are] dreams," to paraphrase Freeman. Jung regarded symbolism in dreams as vastly important to understanding the human mind. His theory suggested that each person dreams in symbols that are specific to his or her needs, and then that individual must interpret what the symbolism means. Dreams, therefore, are "personal," according to Jungian theory.[7]

Jung recognized that primitive peoples lived in "two worlds," the "physical" and the "spiritual," and "one of the most important sources of the primitive belief in spirits is dreams." When early people saw deceased loved ones in their dreams, they assumed them to be spirits. That gave dreams an important purpose in ancient times, less so in Jung's era, especially when leading psychologists concluded that dreams originated in the unconscious.[8]

His theory about waking visions was that "spirits are complexes of the collective unconscious." Jung offered as an example St. Paul's conversion to Christianity when he experienced a vision of Christ on the road to Damascus. Had St. Paul, or Saul as he was then known, actually seen Christ in a vision or was it some expression of St. Paul's unconscious? The answer, of course, depends on whether one is coming from a psychological or metaphysical perspective.

Eventually, a substantial quarrel developed between Jung and Freud concerning the paranormal. Although Freud once expressed curiosity about psychic phenomena, and even engaged in several experiments, with time he increasingly rejected it, at least publicly, while Jung moved in the opposite direction toward a more intent interest in the so-called occult, especially after his break from Freud. Jung then gave more serious thought and examination to the role of the paranormal within psychology, as well as his own personal psychic experiences. Because of the divergent opinions it was inevitable that each man would go his separate way, and in 1913 Jung forever distanced himself from Freudian theory and originated his own school of thought that he called "analytic psychology."[9]

"There are many approaches to clinical psychology, and some are more sympathetic to apparent psychic experiences than others," wrote parapsychologist Richard Broughton, adding, "Jungian psychoanalysts tend to be willing to explore such experiences in some depth before making a diagnosis."[10]

"Two men may interpret the same idea in their own individual ways," said writer George Boas, an observation that summed up perfectly the differences between Carl Jung and Sigmund Freud.[11] For example, consider their very dissimilar beliefs about God. Freud was viewed as antireligious, and considered the "belief in God" to be a "wish fantasy for mankind for a protective father . . ." and as far as he was concerned, religion "should be disregarded." Freud added, "Religion is an illusion and it derives its strength from the fact that it falls in with our instinctual desires."[12] For Jung, however, "God was a vital psychic need," author and psychoanalyst Nandor Fodor explained.[13]

"Often I had the feeling that in all decisive matters I was no longer among men, but was alone with God," Jung wrote in his autobiography *Memories, Dreams, Reflections*.[14] "From the beginning I had a sense of destiny, as though my life was assigned to me by fate and had to be fulfilled. This gave me an inner security, and though I could never prove it to myself, it proved itself to me. I did not have this certainty, it had me."[15]

Significant to parapsychology was Jung's theory of the unconscious that he said was divided into two parts: the "personal unconscious" and the "collective unconscious." It was the latter, the collective unconscious that became a popular concept in both psychology and parapsychology.[16]

The collective unconscious was something akin to a "universal memory bank" that all humans have access to, comparable to what mystics have long called the akashic records. Jung observed that the "basic structures of many symbols and myths" appear to be virtually universal, even among cultures that have had no contact or "influence" on each other. For example, nearly all cultures have legends or parables about heroic figures, and the sky or heavens above represent or symbolize something supernatural or beyond human grasp. For instance, how does one explain the fact that an African tribe and an Indian tribe in North America—thousands of miles apart and having no connection to each other—both had nearly identical astronomical and religious symbols? Within the collective unconsciousness, Jung called these symbols and myths "archetypes." These "unconscious images [are] shared by the [human] race as a whole," explained Richard Woods in *The Occult Revolution*.[17] Jung even conjectured about the phenomenon of "flying saucers," as an archetype, and later in his life devoted a book to them.

Jung's theory of the collective unconscious has often been used to explain incidents that suggest a "spiritual dimension," including the implication of an afterlife. Probably the best example is the near-death experience. Why have millions of people from virtually every culture and continent reported nearly identical events during near-death experiences? How do we explain that possession and exorcism have been described with remarkable similarity in disparate societies throughout history? Jungians would suggest a possible answer lay in the archetypes that exist within the human mind, as opposed to the actual existence of evil spirits. Jung also theorized that spirit controls used by mediums may actually be evidence of the collective unconscious. "If Jung was correct, that would enable the medium to tap into a storehouse of universal knowledge that far exceeds her or his individual experience," wrote James R. Lewis. If Jungian theory sounds similar to the late Joseph Campbell's popular writing and public television series a couple of decades ago, *Man, Myth and Magic*, it's not coincidental; Campbell believed very much in Jungian thinking.

However, few parapsychologists accepted that Jung's theory is the only answer to the vast mysteries of the unknown. For example, what if stories about UFOs are not archetypes drawn from the unconscious mind?[18] What if they were—or are—genuine objects that people throughout the world actually observed in different times and places? What if the common characteristics of the near-death experience are not drawn from archetypes in the unconscious, but rather because the spirit body has briefly separated from the physical being, and many have actually glimpsed the next dimension and had a peek at the afterlife? Similarly, spirit phenomena witnessed over many millennia may not always be products of hallucination or the unconscious mind. Might some of the countless reports of apparitions actually be the observation of spirit entities?

When two events occur simultaneously, and in such a way that seems beyond coincidence or normal cause and effect, Jung defined it as "synchronicity." His concept of this idea of "meaningful coincidence" has appeared in recent years, notably in astrology.[19] It is also a frequently reported type of after-death communication, a term applied to direct contact from the deceased, as opposed to those who seek mediums to convey messages from the departed.[20] An example from the authors' files: a man who'd recently lost his younger brother, named Daniel, one day was overwhelmed with grief as he drove his car to an appointment. With tear-filled eyes, he thought he'd distract his anguish by turning on the car radio. Unexpectedly and inexplicably an Elton John song, "Daniel" began playing; it had been a particular favorite of the brothers; Daniel often played it on his guitar. Was the incident merely coincidence—or something more? Might it have been a meaningful synchronicity, perhaps a sign from the man's late brother, Daniel?[21]

There is a widely told incident of synchronicity that happened to Jung and it greatly impressed him. He was treating a woman patient whom he described as "psychologically inaccessible." She would always know more than anyone else, no matter what the subject was. Wanting her to accept the existence of her subconscious mind, Jung hoped he'd find a way to puncture the woman's "extreme rationalism." What he needed was for something unexpected and irrational to manifest.

One day she told Jung that she'd had a dream about the golden scarab, a type of beetle revered as an ancient symbol of immortality. Suddenly there was knocking on the window. Incredibly, it was an insect. Jung turned, opened the window, and in flew a small gold-green-colored beetle that looked just like the scarab the woman had dreamed of. Was it coincidence—or meaningful synchronicity?[22]

Jung's personal life was filled with paranormal experiences. One well-documented incident occurred in 1909 when he visited Freud in Vienna, and asked his host what he thought of precognition and parapsychology. Freud dismissed the subject as "nonsensical." At that moment, however, Jung said, "I had a strange sensation, as if my diaphragm had turned to iron; and . . . there was a loud report [banging noise] in the bookcase next to us, so loud that we both stared up in alarm, fearing the thing would topple over on us.

" 'There,' I said, 'that is an example of a so-called catalytic exteriorization phenomenon.'

" 'Oh come,' [Freud] exclaimed, 'That is sheer bosh.'

" 'You are mistaken, Herr Professor,' I replied, and to prove my point I now predict that there will be another loud report.' No sooner had I said the words than the same detonation went off in the bookcase. Freud stared aghast . . . To this day I do not know what gave me this assurance," Jung later remarked.

Freud wrote to Jung after that incident to admit that the experience had made a "powerful impression" on him; but he did not believe the event was of a psychic or supernatural nature, because the inexplicable noise was heard again after Jung's departure. He referred to Jung's "occult" explanation as a "spook complex" and "lovely delusion." He also wryly remarked that furniture is "spiritless and dead." However, Freud never conjectured about why the loud bang was not heard before Jung's presence in the room; nor did he attempt any natural explanation for it. One paranormal theory is that Jung had somehow exerted psychokinetic or PK power, causing the noises by the force of psychic energy, not unlike poltergeist activity. Some researchers have suggested that Jung innately possessed PK or telekinetic abilities.[23]

A few years later Freud "openly acknowledged the seriousness of parapsychology, and recognized the actuality of 'occult' phenomena." Some biographers have suggested that while it is true Freud eventually became more accepting of some paranormal events, he remained guarded—and conflicted—about the subject. In 1911 when Jung asked Freud to join him in a campaign for an understanding of the occult, Freud unhesitatingly declined; yet paradoxically he had an interest in numerology.

"One of the very curious features of Freud's character was his preoccupation with, and belief in, the occult influence of numbers," Nandor Fodor wrote.[24] He also revealed that Freud as a young man experienced "auditory hallucinations" that may have been psychical in nature; he'd heard an unearthly voice that called out his name. In addition, Freud became open to telepathy or thought transference, but was initially reluctant to consider it a paranormal phenomenon. He expressed regrets that he'd never had a "telepathic dream," and also lamented that he'd never had a patient with a "truly telepathic dream." But Freud took the phenomenon seriously enough to engage in experiments about telepathy; and at the beginning of his work with psychoanalysis tried to comprehend what telepathy might mean to an understanding of human consciousness. In 1922, Freud presented a paper titled "Dreams and Telepathy" to a committee of psychoanalysts. One passage from the paper summed up Freud's change in opinion after observing tests that demonstrated genuine telepathy or thought transference. "It no longer seems possible to brush aside the study of so-called occult facts; of things which seem to vouchsafe the real existence of psychic forces other than the known forces of the human and animal psyche or which reveal mental faculties in which, until now, we did not believe."[25]

Curiously, some authors have suggested that Freud did not anticipate any threat to psychoanalysis from the growing interest in the paranormal. To the contrary, he recognized that both often faced criticism and disdain from traditional science and could help each other. If Freud's pronouncements about the paranormal sound ambivalent, they were. Until later in his life, Freud stood firmly against psychic phenomena; then his thinking changed somewhat, and he acknowledged his "conversion to telepathy." Eventually Freud concluded that some of the incidents he'd experienced left no explanation but that they were occult or paranormal in nature. In one example that's often cited, Freud and several people were involved in a complex series of synchronicities and thought transference that went far beyond coincidence in their intricacy. He also observed that telepathy was common among children, foreseeing the long scientific debate about the innate psychic abilities of youngsters. Ultimately, Freud concluded that "by inserting the unconscious between the physical and what has hitherto been regarded as the mental, psychoanalysis has prepared the way for the acceptance of such processes as telepathy," Fodor explained.[26]

For Carl Jung, telepathy was both a curiosity and a concern. He understood, as did Freud, that the sleep state is conducive to paranormal experiences, such as telepathy. But if telepathic or other psychic dreams originated beyond the dreamer, say from some other unknown dimension or another person, wouldn't that put an entirely different spin on the way dreams were interpreted? In fact, genuine telepathic dreams could be a challenge to Freudian psychoanalysis—unless there was a way to "trace" the origin of the dream back to the dreamer's subconscious.[27]

Jung had ample personal experiences and conducted sufficient tests to conclude that mental telepathy was genuine; although the phenomenon raised more questions than it answered. Acknowledging telepathy did not satisfactorily explain how a thought or message was transmitted or where it originated. What did paranormal dream experiences imply for the workings of the human psyche? Jung posed the problem this way: "The limitation of consciousness in space and time is such an overwhelming reality that every occasion when this fundamental truth is broken through must rank as an event of the highest theoretical significance, for it would prove that the time-space barrier can be annulled."

But Jung, like Freud, first chose to look for psychoanalytic explanations for telepathic dreams, as did most other therapists. Suffice it to say here that no one conclusion explains the source of every dream, nor is every dream of equal importance. Jung was not wrong in suggesting that other possibilities, such as "hidden memory," within the dreamer's subconscious might explain a dream's symbolic content. For a therapist engaged in dream analysis, obviously more than psychic communication has to be considered. On the other hand, to ignore dreams that might be paranormal in origin is equally disingenuous for such dreams have therapeutic value in bereavement counseling, providing comfort through after-death communications, working out emotional conflicts and fears, or even offering a clue to the future.[28]

Human curiosity about the mystery of dreams is nothing new. There are many references to them in the Bible, especially throughout the Old Testament. In ancient Greece, Plato expressed interest in how people's lives were affected by dreams; and a physician and diviner named Artemidorus wrote outstanding books about dream interpretation as far back as the second century, AD. The big question then, as now, was whether the content of dreams originated in the dreamer's mind, or from somewhere outside, a stubborn enigma unchanged for thousands of years.

Eventually, however, the study of dreams fell out of favor around the time of the Renaissance, in about the fourteenth century when the upper classes derided them as mere superstition. Even Shakespeare disparaged dreams in *Romeo and Juliet,* calling them "fantasy" and "the children of an idle brain." Of course, most people over the centuries remained privately curious about what their dreams meant, despite the professed attitude of skeptics, disapproving theologians, and so-called intellectuals.

In the late nineteenth century, science finally turned its attention to dreams and tried to decipher their origins and meanings. Credit goes to Sigmund Freud, at the beginning of the twentieth century, for spurring serious interest in dream analysis and interpretation in a scientifically reputable way for the first time. Dreams were "the royal road to the unconscious," Freud proclaimed, and in 1900 wrote what was called his "masterpiece," *The Interpretation of Dreams.* But he insisted that there was unconscious sexual repression in virtually all dreams.[29]

Of more relevance to parapsychology was Jung's acknowledgment that some dream messages might originate from outside the dreamer. Throughout his entire life Jung was fascinated with what his dreams meant, and sometimes considered them guides for the decisions he personally made. The first dream he recalled from early childhood and one of his last before he died at age eighty-six both contained symbols that he believed represented birth and death.

While Freud considered precognitive dreams to be impossible, Jung theorized that dreams of "future events" were conceivable. Beginning in late 1913, Jung experienced a series of visions that we described in detail in *The Haunting of America* about predictions. He said he'd been "seized with the overpowering spectacle of nearly all of Europe, except Switzerland, covered with a sea that turned to blood; on its surface floated the bodies of uncounted thousands." He also heard a voice say, "Look, it will be so." The next year, 1914, World War I began; but Jung admitted that he did not associate his recurring premonitions with the coming world conflagration until after the war broke out. He said that often "it has happened that suddenly I know something which I really could not know."[30]

That same certainty resounded in a famous quote by Jung. To paraphrase, when asked if he believed in God and psychic events, Jung typically replied that he did not just believe in them; he'd answer, "I know" they are genuine.[31]

Another of Jung's theories concerned what he called the "shadow," a part of the unconscious mind that contains all we find negative or "wicked" about ourselves and will not acknowledge consciously.[32] But Jung felt it was necessary that people recognize both their "light" and "dark" sides in order to gain a more balanced life. "One does not become enlightened by imagining figures of light, but by making the darkness conscious." That concept also has implications for both religious and spiritual beliefs, for it is necessary to recognize both the negative and positive aspects of our being to better understand our consciousness in full. Jung is also credited with coining the terms "introvert" and "extrovert" to describe personality types.

As we mentioned in our earlier book, Jung's life was filled with paranormal encounters of various kinds: clairvoyance, telepathic dreams, visions, precognition, and déjà vu, among others. It's apparent that Jung was more sensitive to psychic events than most other people. One of his experiences involved déjà vu; the French word for "already seen." Many of us have felt the sensation of déjà vu; being somewhere new but feeling as if we had already been in that place or circumstance, even recognizing locations and people we'd never before seen.

Jung's déjà vu incident occurred when he visited Africa for the first time. He was traveling by train when he looked out the window and noticed a lone tribesman standing atop a cliff. Jung later wrote about the experience, "It was as if I were [at] this moment returning to the land of my youth, and as I knew that dark-skinned man . . . had been waiting for me for five thousand years."[33]

There is no single absolute theory to explain déjà vu. However, in 1895, psychical researcher F. W. H. Myers suggested that the unconscious mind recognized an event a moment before it reached the conscious brain. Another long-held popular belief is that déjà vu is some form of evidence of reincarnation.

One of the most interesting paranormal occurrences Jung had took place in 1944, when, nearing the age of seventy, he suffered a heart attack. While being resuscitated, Jung said he felt himself "transported far above the globe of the earth; and . . . was on the verge of entering an illuminated room in a temple . . ." when he heard his doctor "who told him he had no right to leave, and must return at once." Jung had described a near-death experience, although that term would not come into popular use until three decades later when Dr. Raymond Moody coined the phrase in 1975 for an event that millions of people have likely experienced since the beginning of time.[34]

On the subject of death and the afterlife, Jung wrote that "it is normal to think about immortality, and abnormal not to do so or not to bother about it." He was well aware of the spiritualist movement that began with the Fox sisters' spirit rappings in Hydesville, New York, in 1848, and he addressed the huge popularity it had gained in America and Europe.[35]

By the time Jung began investigating the paranormal, spiritualism already had a long history that unfortunately had been rife with fraud, and he recognized the problem, but added, "This psychological interest of mine has prompted me to keep track of persons who are gifted as mediums." As a result, he examined eight mediums in Zurich—six women and two men.[36]

Jung's advice is as valuable today as it was a century ago. "The total impression made by these investigations can be summed up by saying that one must approach a medium with a minimum of expectations if one does not want to be disappointed." He was not entirely convinced that mediums were all they claimed. Were they actually receiving spirit communications? His early conclusions about them were cautious at best, and speaking as a psychiatrist he noted, "Mediums are as a rule slightly abnormal mentally." He also found it "irritating nonsense that spiritualists brag about their scientific knowledge." Jung thought that such people knew little if anything about psychology. But despite that, he added this caveat, "So far as the miraculous reports in the literature are concerned, never lose sight of the limitations of our knowledge . . ." Jung was leaving the door open for the possibility that wondrous paranormal events could occur.[37]

Jung's assessment of spiritualism was a kind of open-minded skepticism. He acknowledged that a belief in spirits is virtually universal, dating back to prehistoric peoples, although by his lifetime, Western scientific and rationalist thinkers had since the eighteenth century done their best to stifle and dismiss "metaphysical beliefs." Jung noted that even in the increasingly commercial and acquisitive twentieth century, popular belief in spirits and hauntings was still very much evident.[38]

There is also the factor called "cultural conditioning" that Jung was well aware of. In many ancient societies and tribes, a person who heard voices and declared he saw spirits might well have become a respected shaman. In Eastern religions, psychic events have historically been more readily accepted than in our Western belief systems. Someone in America who claimed to witness an apparition of a departed loved one, or reported a clairvoyant or clairaudient experience, such as hearing a discarnate voice, would probably be labeled "weird" or "nuts," to use a couple of familiar unscientific terms.

Jung could not deny ghosts and hauntings as forms of "postmortem phenomena," and suggested they are "based on psychic facts which cannot be dismissed out of hand" and reported his own experiences as well as those his patients had. But unlike many scientists who feared such ideas were a return to the superstitious Dark Ages, Jung considered them a scientific search for answers to "ancient mysteries." In fact, he was impressed with learned men who had the courage to investigate spirit phenomena; and he was of the opinion that an "awareness of a spiritual world" was a positive attitude, a hedge against crass materialism.

Meanwhile, in the early twentieth century, "Sigmund Freud rose to prominence as a paramount social force through his unparalleled literary gifts, and surely not for his cockamamie and unsupported theories of the human psyche," wrote the late scientist and author Stephen Jay Gould in his book *The Hedgehog, the Fox, and the Magister's Pox*. In recent decades, others have also debunked or dismissed much of Freud's theories about the subconscious mainly because of his near-obsession with sexual repression as a cause for nearly every neurotic human behavior.[39]

Psychology, as academic disciplines go, is not considered very old; it emerged in the latter part of the 1880s. In 1893, before Freud appeared on the world stage with his theories, Thomas Jay Hudson wrote *The Law of Psychic Phenomena*,[40] a popular book that actually touched upon the new field of psychology and role of the unconscious. By the beginning of the twentieth century, psychology was already a firmly established branch of learning supposedly dedicated to helping provide explanations for human behavior, terming itself the scientific study of the human mind. But when an American author named H. Addington Bruce wrote about the unconscious, suggesting it opened us to "metaphysical planes," it was not a question science could answer.[41]

Although Jung was indisputably the originator of the concept of the "collective unconscious," the idea of the unconscious mind played a role way back in the early years of mesmerism. It is the mesmerists who really deserve credit for discovering the unconscious. When some subjects entered what appeared to be "sleeplike states of consciousness," their mesmeric trances were sometimes characterized by recalling long-forgotten events in their lives. Other subjects apparently fell into more intense states of altered consciousness in which they became clairvoyant, telepathic, or precognitive. "These deeper realms of the mesmeric state had a decidedly mystical element to them," Robert C. Fuller wrote,[42] adding that some who were mesmerized "felt endowed with omnipresent and omniscient mental powers."

Mesmerism led to the idea that during altered states of consciousness, psychic information and spirit contact were more accessible. You'll recall that those sleeplike states or trances became an integral part of the spiritualist movement when virtually anyone who purported to be a medium induced a trance state to access spirit communications.[43]

When psychical research became better established by the late nineteenth century, as we described in our first book, *The Haunting of America,* scientists, philosophers, and psychologists created organizations specifically for the purpose of serious and systematic examination of paranormal phenomena, such as the Society for Psychical Research (SPR) in England, and the American Society for Psychical Research (ASPR). In doing so paranormal investigators delved into theories of the unconscious, paving the way for psychology to follow. Psychic experiences and the unconscious remain inexorably connected.[44]

The SPR, which began its work not long before Freud did, found in its early investigations nearly one hundred and fifty cases of dream telepathy; and more than half of them were about the death of someone the dreamer knew. One might think that psychical research would become a part of psychology in exploring the depths of the human psyche. That's not exactly what happened. Instead, many in the emerging field of psychology turned their backs on the paranormal, forgetting or ignoring how much psychology owed psychic researchers for their investigations into the unconscious or the "secondary self," as some then called it, and the mesmeric state.

Those psychologists who saw value in the paranormal at the dawning of the twentieth century were decidedly in the minority. Of course, there were notable exceptions, even before Carl Jung. One of them, you may recall we talked about in our earlier book, was William James who had extensively studied the Boston medium Leonora Piper.[45] James, America's preeminent philosopher and psychologist in the latter part of the nineteenth century concluded that the unconscious mind was related to the altered or trance state. He also believed that psychic phenomena could contribute to psychology; he was right, but far ahead of his time, and he theorized that the unconscious was an intermediary that might bridge science and religion—still a controversial idea—that's grown in popularity in recent decades. "All our scientific and philosophic ideals are altars to unknown gods," he said.

The modern New Age movement has propelled millions in a search for personal spiritual meaning and enlightenment that cuts across all religious denominations. In this quest, many Americans have sought a better understanding of the unconscious mind and its role in greater self-awareness and spiritual growth. Since the 1970s the proliferation of books toward that goal seems endless. Authors such as Wayne Dyer, Leo Buscaglia,[46] Jean Houston, and M. Scott Peck are only a few of the many who've reaped huge readerships with their books that touch on America's need to reach some spiritual nirvana by learning to tap into the unconscious, and better understand what consciousness is.

While many psychics and parapsychologists describe the unconscious as including a realm sometimes referred to as the "higher self," and through which the human mind can access spiritual experiences, most traditional psychologists have long resisted that explanation. William James, however, considered the unconscious capable of allowing us entry to metaphysical and mystical thinking, areas not accepted by many so-called orthodox schools of psychology, such as the Freudians.

Science has difficulty testing or explaining behavioral and subjective experiences, such as consciousness, the workings of the unconscious, and myriad paranormal events; it deals best with the physical and material world, not the metaphysical. Scientists have never agreed upon an objective definition for the unconscious, or for that matter, consciousness. Perhaps with advances in neurosciences and medical technology we'll be better able to understand the state we call "self awareness," and by extension, the unconscious mind, and the connection between the two.

For parapsychologists and psychologists that might lead to answers about how the mind seems to sometimes go beyond the limits of our physical being to some other dimension or realm, defying the known laws of time and space. It takes us back to that vexing question of where psychic information originates. Freud and Jung wrestled with these dilemmas at a time in history when the neurosciences were yet to be defined and there was little if any technology to draw on. "Careful observation," wrote Jung's secretary Aniela Jaffe, was mainly the method for his study and conclusions about paranormal phenomena.[47] Jung also drew somewhat upon the statistics compiled by Dr. J. B. Rhine's ESP experiments at Duke University.

Of course, while convoluted theories about the nature and existence of the paranormal were disputed among scientists, psychologists, and skeptics, millions of people in every walk of life continued having psychic experiences. If, for example, some "expert" dismissed the possibility of communicating with the dead, or tapping into the future, it did nothing to help the widow in Boston who was certain she'd witnessed her late husband's apparition, the mother in Kansas whose premonition of her young child in danger proved uncannily accurate, or the woman in Ohio who awoke at the precise moment a loved one died many miles away. Those in positions to pontificate about the paranormal and demean it without close examination discouraged many Americans from sharing and understanding their personal psychic encounters.

Jung also connected spiritual phenomena with the existence of a soul. In *Psychology and the Occult,* William McGuire wrote that Jung was only twenty-two in 1897 when he spoke about psychology to a student club.[48] "The soul does exist, it is intelligent and immortal, not subject to [the laws of] time and space," he told his audience. "We are so convinced that death is simply the end of a process that it does not ordinarily occur to us to conceive of death as a goal and fulfillment," Jung said, adding, "the fact that we are totally unable to imagine a form of existence without space and time by no means proves that such an existence is in itself impossible."

Between 1902 and 1932, Jung wrote a number of articles and papers dealing with the "question of the soul's existence after death." Among the topics Jung considered were accounts by people who claimed they were in contact with the spirits of the deceased, as well as the psychology of the belief in an afterlife. Jung was ambivalent about survival beyond death, but never ruled out the possibility.[49]

Don't feel frustrated or confused if you sometimes find Jung's paranormal theories contradictory, such as when he posits that psychic experiences lead back to the unconscious. He himself was uncertain if every psychic message was conceived there or if some were transmitted through the unconscious, but originated somewhere externally.

Early in his career Jung argued that "spirits and other psychic phenomena" were projections of the unconscious; it was an entirely psychological explanation. But time and study changed his opinions. Years later Jung acknowledged that psychology alone could not explain such psychic events as precognition, the ability to see into the future. He also performed several experiments with mediums and found they each experienced a small but consistent weight loss of "several kilograms" during spirit contacts. Whatever the reason, he realized it was a physiological response that went beyond the unconscious mind.

Jung once witnessed the apparition of a recently deceased friend who clairvoyantly showed him five books with red bindings on a particular shelf; and the specter specifically pointed to the second volume. When Jung later called upon the man's widow, he found on her library shelf five books bound in red, exactly where and like the ones the apparition held. The second in the set was *The Legacy of the Dead* by Émile Zola. Presumably Jung had experienced an after-death communication from his late friend, and concluded it was a paranormal incident that required more than a psychological explanation.[50]

Carl Jung deserves great credit for his willingness to explore the psychic world, a mission that took courage and independence in the face of academic and scientific hypocrisy and rejection. Traditional science would not even acknowledge that such phenomena existed, let alone study and test it. Jung had a strong distaste for "rationalism,"[51] but respected his few fellow scientists who were willing to investigate spirit phenomena even if spirits proved to be "errors [or] self-deception." One of those he held in high esteem was the respected physicist Sir William Crookes (1832–1919) who had not shied away from investigating spiritualism. You'll recall his controversial examination of the medium Florence Cook that we described in *The Haunting of America*.[52]

Jung acknowledged that the human psyche often went far beyond our comprehension. "It contains as many riddles as the universe with its galactic systems." He made it clear that psychology "cannot establish any metaphysical 'truths'; nor does it try to. It is concerned solely with the phenomenology of the psyche."[53]

For Sigmund Freud the answer to questions about an afterlife was far less complicated than Jung's explanation. Freud did not believe life after death was possible.[54] Jung agreed that while "immortality cannot be proven," the "more important . . . the essential point . . . is the functional value of the idea." In other words, Jung saw the need for a belief in the afterlife even if "proof" was absent. "Reason becomes unreason when separated from the heart," he said. The sheer number of psychic incidents and events—in the many millions—suggests to parapsychologists that in addition to subconscious wishes, fears, and desires, we have the ability to access information from somewhere beyond ourselves.

It's not that most Americans are unfamiliar with the term "the unconscious"; Freud's theories have long been the subject of countless books and articles. But Freud was not inclined to commingle psychoanalysis with the supernatural. His goal was to treat mental illness or disorders by freeing sexually repressed neurotic notions. The truth is that the unconscious is still a mystery, more of an idea than an exact place, with many unanswered implications for behavior—and the nature of the paranormal. Jung was not able to provide any conclusive answers, but he maintained an open mind, and ultimately admitted that he did not know whether "the future is unconsciously prepared long in advance and can therefore be guessed by clairvoyants."[55]

Before his death in 1939, Freud urged colleagues and disciples to advance his theories of psychoanalysis. But Jung made a startling revelation in his autobiography, *Memories, Dreams, Reflections,* completed posthumously by his secretary after his death in 1961. Jung revealed that Freud's insistence was part of a larger hope to replace the religion and philosophy humankind had long known, with his own Freudian dogma. If that's true, and there's little reason to doubt it, it was a disingenuous, cynical, and shocking undermining of people's innate spiritual needs and nature. It also explained why psychic experiences were dismissed by Freudians, considered mentally unhealthy thinking, and of no positive use. It took decades, but eventually Freud's theories lost their grip. Not every dream is a subconscious journey through a dark tunnel of sexually repressed neuroses. Sometimes a cigar is a cigar—not a phallic symbol.

During his long career, Jung's thinking was often overshadowed by Freudian positions, and repeatedly denounced by Freudians. In recent years, however, while Freud has been increasingly criticized, Jungian ideas have seemed more relevant, especially when considering the role of the unconscious in paranormal events. But there is an odd and contradictory footnote that revealed Freud's inner conflicts about parapsychology. For nearly all his life, he professed that he was a "staunch skeptic of supernatural and occult beliefs," Dr. Dean Radin reminded.[56] So it was ironic that in his last days, Freud remarked, "If I had my life to live over again, I should devote myself to psychical research rather than to psychoanalysis."[57]

Who hasn't had a dream that is so incongruent with reality that it is either frightening or funny? Whatever our subconscious is trying to release or tell us, it does it with some very peculiar symbols. We may all wonder why our dreams contain strange images, but few of us will wake up and paint or write what we've dreamt, as have those artists, poets, and novelists who were inspired by their dream life.

During the early twentieth century, a movement developed in art and literature known as surrealism that attempted to express the subconscious mind "by the irrational juxtaposition of images," and it was strongly influenced by Freudian psychology. Surrealist artists and poets "sought to depict the activities of the unconscious mind by presenting experiences in a series of disordered, dreamlike images," Robert Moss wrote.

Arguably, its best-known exponent was the Spanish painter Salvador Dalí (1904–1989). If his famed paintings seemed somewhat bizarre, distorted, even unsettling—in other words, dreamlike—it wasn't merely coincidental. Flamboyant and eccentric, with a gift for calling attention to himself, Dalí became one of the century's most celebrated artists for his works that have often been called "dreamscapes." What he painted was not exactly what we'd expect to see while awake. His greatest works were completed during the 1920s and '30s and his best known, *The Persistence of Memory* is a vista of melting or "drooping watches," painted in 1931.

For Dalí and other surrealist painters, often what they dreamt found its way onto canvas. His imagination was vivid, to say the least, and sometimes deeply disturbing such as his depiction of an eyeball cut apart by a razor blade, which he created for a short film in 1929. Another of his masterworks was curiously titled *Soft Construction with Boiled Beans (Premonition of the Spanish Civil War)* painted in 1936.

When Dalí read and became familiar with Freudian dream theory, he excitedly described it "as one of the discoveries in my life."[58] Dalí's odd dreams were always a source of concern and wonder to him. Some thought him simply eccentric; others were convinced he was "mad." But when Freud's theories of the unconscious became well-known Dalí felt there was at least some reason for the bizarre images that could now be explained in a scientific way.

Freud's theories—right or wrong—did not change Dalí's work, they simply placed it in a context he was more comfortable with; at least he had an explanation for the peculiar, even grotesque pictures he saw when he slept. As far as Freudian psychoanalysts were concerned, they couldn't have been more pleased; Dalí might have seemed like a gift from God to Freud—if Freud had believed in God. Dalí's surrealistic paintings represented to the world an example of the workings of the unconscious, and he became the Freudians' "star attraction." His paintings "seemed to mirror the bizarre depths of his subconscious mind," the *Contemporary Hispanic Biography* explained.[59]

In 1935, the internationally celebrated Dalí spoke at the Museum of Modern Art in New York where he explained surrealism, and specifically the "dream symbolism" in his paintings. Dalí said he was "the first to be surprised and often terrified by the extravagant images that I see appear with fatality on my canvas." The next year the rakish Dalí appeared on the cover of *Time* magazine. His appearance was unmistakable: His intense dark eyes and pencil-thin waxed mustache became as recognizable as his surrealistic paintings; his large hats and capes, and other outlandish outfits added to the unconventional impression he made.

During World War II Dalí and his longtime companion and later his wife, Gala, sought asylum in the United States, where one of his more interesting projects brought him into association with legendary movie director Alfred Hitchcock. In 1945 Dalí created the famed "dream sequence" in Hitchcock's *Spellbound*. That crucial scene, as does the entire film, has strong Freudian undertones.[60] The dream experienced by Gregory Peck's character reveals clues that explain why he's lost his memory. The female psychiatrist and Peck's love interest, played by Ingrid Bergman, interprets the dream symbols that are connected with a murder Peck is falsely accused of.

The dream sequence begins on a steeply sloping roof that resembles a surrealist Dalí painting. There are too many details to recount in this brief explanation, but the important sequence sets the basis for Bergman's character to interpret the dream's symbolism so that it provides clues to solving the murder, eventually clearing Peck of the crime.[61] Dalí also employed images with Freudian sexual undertones, including one moment of the dream scene in which the beautiful Ingrid Bergman is scantily dressed. *Spellbound* is a veritable Freudian feast that deals with dreams, the subconscious, and repressed thoughts.

Although there are no direct psychic references in *Spellbound,* there is a question the dream scene brings to mind about the role of the subconscious and paranormal dreams. In Peck's dream, as conceived by Dalí, the symbolism represents past events long repressed that require dream interpretation. But what would explain those instances when the dreamer experiences a peek into the future? In other words, what we call precognitive dreams. Is there an explanation for what are sometimes startlingly vivid or lifelike dreams of departed loved ones or events that provide information the dreamer could not otherwise have known? Can we interpret psychic dreams of any kind by turning to Freudian theory? The answer is, probably not. Therefore, it seems that while the subconscious is often the source of a repressed problem, fear or desire, at other times it appears to act as a pathway for psychic images that communicate information about the past, present, and future. We'll talk more about recent ESP dream research in a later chapter.

To conclude our story of Salvador Dalí and other surrealists, not everyone was enamored with Dalí's "dreamscapes." One of the most outspoken was British author George Orwell who remarked in the 1940s that Dalí's surrealistic paintings were "diseased and disgusting." *Art Digest* magazine asked, "Is Dalí Crazy?" comparing his paintings to a circus act.

During the 1950s many Dalí paintings depicted religious scenes; in the 1960s, his works attracted a generation that saw him as a "celebrated symbol of eccentric nonconformity," to quote the *Dictionary of Hispanic Biography.* He died of heart failure in 1989, and as many who studied his life and work have concluded, "He was surrealism."[62] Perhaps the most fascinating aspect of surrealist art and writing from a paranormal as well as psychological perspective is the opportunity that surrealism offers us to view the images produced by the subconscious dreaming mind.

Another mystery about the subconscious that has yet to be solved is where creative ideas originate: in the mind of the dreamer or from somewhere beyond. Samuel Taylor Coleridge, an admitted opium addict, dreamed his classic poem "Kubla Khan."[63] The nineteenth-century writer, Robert Louis Stevenson's idea for *Strange Case of Dr Jekyll and*

Mr Hyde originated in a dream. In the 1960s, singer-songwriter Paul McCartney dreamed the melody for one of the Beatles' hits, "Yesterday." The composers Chopin, Stravinsky, and Saint-Saëns all dreamed ideas for classical compositions. Novelist Graham Greene dreamt ideas for books, and Mary Shelley created the classic monster Frankenstein following a nightmare. Film directors Orson Welles, Robert Altman, Ingmar Bergman, and Federico Fellini all found inspiration in their dreams. As well, several scientific discoveries have been credited to dreams, including Elias Howe's invention of the sewing machine.[64]

The paranormal question is obvious: What is the source of creative or inspirational dreams? Do they originate in the subconscious, or are they communicated to it from some as yet unknown dimension? By what means do the ideas "travel"? Is there some psychic force or energy that we've so far not identified?

For Freud the answer was simple—and consistent; he dismissed any link between the paranormal and creative thoughts. His explanation was that the answer lay in the unconscious mind where the artist or musician took their dissatisfactions and discontents and "sublimated" or channeled them through their particular talent. Jung, on the other hand, endorsed the idea of a psychic explanation for creativity. For him, "the source of inspiration and psychical experiences lay jointly outside conscious volition," Charles Panati wrote.[65]

One of Jung's patients was the famed Irish novelist James Joyce (1882–1941). Jung encouraged Joyce to focus or center on an "ancient occult figure" called a mandala, actually a "mystical diagram" in Eastern belief systems employed for meditation or to bring to oneself "spiritual power." Jung regarded the mandala as an "archetypal image from the deep unconscious mind," and likely influenced Joyce's novel *Finnegans Wake* written in what was called the "stream of consciousness" style.[66]

William Blake (1757–1827) was noted as a poet, artist, and was also a skilled engraver. Blake, who lived in London his entire life, began experiencing visions as a young child; many were of angels. Not surprisingly, spirituality and mysticism became lifelong passions.[67] Some critics have decried his visions as hallucinations, and others with a psychological bent later regarded them as products of his subconscious mind. However, few scholars allowed that perhaps Blake's visionary experiences were genuine encounters with angels or spirits; although one of his biographers, Alexander Gilchrist said Blake wrote and drew for "children and angels."

Blake insisted about the poetry he wrote, "It is not mine, it is not mine." Whatever the source of his apparitions, they colored his view of the world, and influenced his creativity and thinking. Blake's "waking life and dreaming life were closely intermingled," wrote Robert Van de Castle in *Our Dreaming Mind*.[68] By 1788, his spiritual muse had encouraged him to write two books, *All Religions Are One,* and *There Is No Natural Religion,* provocative and controversial titles—and ideas—even today. Among Blake's works were several termed "prophecies," about America and Europe, written in the 1790s, as well as poems and stories that have been read by generations of children.

Although his writings had relatively little influence during his lifetime, he became especially popular in the twentieth century. Psychologists, other writers, liberal theologians, those who embraced Eastern beliefs, and even some rock music songwriters and singers found an affinity with Blake, for both his writing and his radical philosophy that opposed virtually any restraints on political or personal freedom and thought. Blake the visionary was no conformist, and he made clear his opinion that children should have the right to "dream and imagine," just as adults ought to. His advice was to "cleanse, once and for all, those doors of perception that have been clouded for too long."

While Freud and Jung were redefining the mind, Albert Einstein (1879–1955) was reconfiguring time and space. Artists, writers, and poets for centuries had tapped into their unconscious for ideas that would cast humanity in a new and perhaps brighter light, while others turned their intellects toward a better—or at least different—view of science and the natural world. Some of their ideas would have implications for the paranormal. One of them was Einstein, the German-born physicist forever associated with his famous theory of relativity, $E = mc^2$.

Raised in a middle-class Jewish family, there was also a spiritual side to the great physicist, in addition to his monumental scientific achievements. "Science without religion is lame; religion without science is blind," Einstein said, perhaps to the chagrin of diehard skeptics and atheists. "I want to know how God created this world." These are not quotes most school science books emphasize, if they are even mentioned; as with spirituality and the paranormal, debunkers and so-called rationalists generally prefer to ignore that part of Einstein's thinking. On the subject of school, Einstein resented the strict Prussian teaching methods he'd faced as a student. For all his life, he was a pacifist who would carry a resentment and resistance to "authority." The absentminded genius found relaxation by playing the violin.

"Science never held such a grip on the world's imagination as it did in the first half of the twentieth century," George Pendle wrote.[69] "This was largely due to the work of one man: Albert Einstein." The turn of the twentieth century saw giant leaps in scientific discoveries. Among the notable examples were scientists Pierre and Marie Curie's discovery of radium, Wilhelm Röntgen's development of X-rays, and the discovery of the electron. In 1900 an American scientist "transmitted human speech via radio waves," and Marconi relayed telegraphic radio messages; the Wright brothers made their first successful flight in 1903, the same year the electrocardiograph was invented. The next year, the photoelectric cell and ultraviolet lamps were introduced.

Then in 1905, twenty-six-year-old Einstein challenged the long-accepted conclusion that the universe was comprised of two separate entities, "energy" and "matter" when he presented his special theory of relativity. He also "demonstrated that time is not absolute and universal. Time is . . . elastic and can be stretched and shrunk by motion," explained Paul Davies in *God and the New Physics*. Time and space are inseparably linked, he said.[70]

"Einstein's scientific papers stand at the beginning of the twentieth century as imposing intellectual monuments," wrote Fritjof Capra in his bestselling book *The Tao of Physics*.[71] When asked about how he developed his famed theories, Einstein must have surprised many when he answered that his ideas went beyond his obvious mathematical genius. "Einstein attributed his theory of relativity to a flash of insight, not to the cold rationalism of the data-oriented researcher in the laboratory," wrote Russell Targ and Keith Harary in *The Mind Race*.[72] "The really valuable factor was intuition," Einstein revealed.

Sometimes called a "sixth sense," intuition is regarded as a form of psychic ability, an understanding of ideas or concepts without conscious reasoning. Carl Jung was actually one of the first to conclude that intuition "involves, at least in part, ESP," explained parapsychologist Richard

Broughton.[73] Jung "saw intuition as the direct, nonsensory perception of a truth . . . a separate mental function," Broughton wrote. But intuition is a balance to the rational mind; it is not a replacement. Had Einstein accessed ideas not only from his enormous intellect, and his unconscious, but also from some inexplicable paranormal source outside of himself?

In 1995, *Intuition Magazine* wrote that a preponderance of Nobel prize–winning scientists admitted they obtained information by using their intuition. Even many "skeptical" scientists conceded some ideas could only be explained as intuitive.

Until Einstein, light rays were believed to be "straight." When, in 1915, he developed his general theory of relativity Einstein candidly stated that part of his revolutionary discovery about "bending light rays" was the result of utilizing "visualization" as well as his mathematical acumen. The great physicist said he mentally pictured or "visualized what it would be like to ride on a ray of light," Brian Hines wrote in *God's Whisper, Creation's Thunder.*[74] Typically, an image or representation comes to mind when one is in a state of deep relaxation or meditation. Einstein obviously had no difficulty employing a nontraditional method to reach a highly scientific result.

Albert Einstein was not unfamiliar or uncomfortable with psychic phenomena, to the chagrin of obdurate skeptics, no doubt. In fact, as a young man he attended a séance conducted by a Polish medium. Later in his life, he wrote the preface to Upton Sinclair's book *Mental Radio*, which dealt with the testing of Sinclair's wife's telepathic abilities. Einstein praised Sinclair's integrity and the value of the tests.[75]

"Einstein strongly believed in nature's inherent harmony, and his deepest concern throughout his scientific life was to find a unified foundation of physics," Capra noted.[76]

Einstein's theories revolutionized scientific thinking and rocked the long-held Newtonian model of the universe. Other physicists, such as Niels Bohr, "were revealing the mysterious world of subatomic particles," author John G. Fuller wrote. "Atoms were no longer solid. They were micro–solar systems composed mainly of empty space." Bohr said, "The atom is a ghost."[77]

Fuller noted that one of the most credible and famed psychic mediums of that time, Eileen Garrett, remarked about Einstein's theories, "the new physics was beginning to appear as mystical as the paranormal." Then, Fuller explained, came the next revolutionary scientific question: "Was the material world material after all?"[78]

The new conception of the atom led to further questions and theories from physicists who had once considered splitting the atom to be impossible. The supposition now was that within atoms were even smaller and smaller particles, such as the electron that had virtually no mass to it. Perhaps "particles" was not even the correct term. Maybe they were "packets of energy," without any existence of their own; they simply appeared and disappeared, Fuller wrote.

The new theories posed inconsistencies and unpredictability that led physicists to consider further discoveries in terms of "probabilities," rather than absolutes. As Fuller noted, it came down to accepting that what had been called matter was not a physical substance, but rather areas or "regions of space where the field was very intense." By that reasoning the "only reality" was the "field."[79]

New thinking about time, space, and matter did not escape the attention of serious parapsychologists; some sought a correspondence between the seemingly inexplicable paranormal and new scientific explanations. Could the long-held laws of physics, apparently turned upside down by Einstein's revolutionary theories help clarify the enigmatic nature of psychic phenomena? It was a fair question, but those who expected ready answers from physicists were destined for disappointment. Few scientists were willing or able to tackle the elusive paranormal. They had no immediate explanations or theories for psychical events, nor any ideas and little inclination how to test for them. Curiously, however, famed parapsychologist J. B. Rhine showed scant interest in how the new physics might be applied to the paranormal, as he went about conducting his ESP tests at Duke University.

Exactly how the mind generates psychic events remained a mystery, as did the relationship of the mind to the brain. For centuries there was scientific debate on whether "the mind is produced by the material brain," to quote psychologist G. William Farthing. Whether the mind or some form of consciousness survives the brain's death is the big question that has long been debated by psychics, scientists, theologians, skeptics, and just about everyone else.

New theories in physics were considered even when they dealt only in probabilities about minute particles that were literally invisible. Many parapsychologists held out hope but when queries about the unseen paranormal world were raised the frustrations were as they had always been. There were few if any answers; in fact there was precious little supposition to explain the paranormal, at least as far as most scientists were concerned, and psychic phenomena still carried the weight of centuries of stigma, suppression, and misunderstanding. Few scientists wished to spend time on mystical questions when the material ones were difficult enough.

The irony was that if one stopped to compare the paranormal and physics they were similar in many regards; both were fraught with mystery and contradictions. It had long been argued by mediums and psychics that "time, space, and matter" did not operate by the established scientific laws of earth. What was startling was that new theories of physics did not contradict the belief in the way the spirit world operated. "For us who are convinced physicists, the distinction between past, present, and future is only an illusion, no matter how persistent," Einstein said in one of his most famous remarks. That's what mediums and psychics had been claiming for centuries. For Eastern mystics, "being able to go beyond the ordinary state through meditation, they have realized that the conventional notions of space and time are not the ultimate truth," Fritjof Capra explained. "According to relativity theory, space is not three-dimensional, and time is not a separate entity."[81]

Physicists at the turn of the twentieth century had to be surprised when their "worldview [was] shaken by the new experience of the atomic reality," wrote Capra, adding, "they described the experience in terms which were often very similar to those used by [Eastern mystics]."

It also became apparent that as scientists and psychologists studied the potential of the mind and explored the universe, to paraphrase the prolific occult writer and Theosophist C. W. Leadbeater (1854–1934), what we perceive with our five senses is not the limits of all there is to perceive.[82] Consider that the extent of our sight reveals only a portion of the light spectrum; birds see a much larger field. Visible light comprises only a small part of the electromagnetic spectrum. As any pet owner knows, dogs hear a far greater range of frequencies than people do. We're often presumptuous, forgetting that our human senses are limited.

Physicists and psychologists never came as close to investigating the paranormal as many had hoped a century ago, despite the similarity between what are called "mystical experiences" and theories of "modern physics." But Einstein's theory of relativity and Max Planck's quantum theory, developed in 1900, at least sparked optimism among many early psychical researchers that eventually science would find answers to the mysteries of psychical phenomena. As John G. Fuller wrote about that era, "The atom was becoming as mystical as the sayings of the ancient Oriental sages."

Einstein's special theory of relativity was made public in 1905; a decade later he formulated his general theory of relativity, considered his "greatest achievement." Among the highlights, Einstein proved that Newton's law of gravity was in error; space has a "structure"; gravity and matter are connected, and gravity needs matter. He also made several predictions that could be tested and confirmed. In one he correctly foretold that the orbit of the planet Mercury was different than Newton had calculated hundreds of years earlier. In another, Einstein predicted the "curvature of space-time." He also theorized "gravitational waves exist and travel at the speed of light."

The general theory of relativity is comprised of complicated mathematical formulas and new ways of looking at the universe that are beyond the scope of this book. However, what is significant is the psychic component of Einstein's remarkable thinking; that is how he reached his conclusions. Consider what Banesh Hoffmann wrote in a book titled *Albert Einstein: Creator and Rebel.*[83]

"By what magical clairvoyance did Einstein choose [certain] principles to be his guide long before he knew where they would lead him? That they should have led him to unique equations of so complex yet simple a sort is itself astounding."

Einstein may have revolutionized the thinking physicists long held based on Newton's laws, but few people had any idea what he was talking about—or how it affected their lives. $E=mc^2$ was an equation that sounded deceptively simple; it was not. Eventually, Einstein was asked to clarify the idea of relativity and wrote an article for the *London Times* attempting to explain that, "energy is equivalent to mass."[84]

If one stretched their imagination, Einstein's theory meant, "that time could be made to stand still, and a human being living in a time warp could enjoy eternal youth," Frank W. Hoffman and William G. Bailey wrote.[85] It sounded exciting, even bordering on the supernatural to "defy time and mortality." However, to do so a person would have to be sent into outer space and travel faster than the speed of light, a scientific impossibility. It inspired generations of science-fiction writers, but in reality it wasn't exactly an immediate or realistic likelihood.

But there were other implications for the paranormal resulting from Einstein's new ways of looking at physics. "The notion of universal oneness [is] one of the theoretical cornerstones of parapsychology" observed Charles Panati in his book *Supersenses*.[86] It is not a new idea, dating back to ancient Greece in the writings of Hippocrates. Medieval mystics held the same theory that "all things are interrelated." In the 1960s, psychologist and author Lawrence LeShan wrote that, "It was impossible to differentiate the worldview of mystics from that of Einsteinian physicists."[87] The long-held philosophy has been that "there is one common flow, one common breath, all things are in sympathy," Panati quoted. Remember, before Einstein, all "physical existence" was believed to consist of two separate entities, "matter and energy." When Einstein proposed that the two were fundamentally the same, it was "a giant step toward oneness," Panati explained. It is an idea that recently more scientists are considering, called the "superstring theory."

"Many physicists think the superstring theory may be the ultimate unified theory of all physical phenomena," noted Stephen M. Barr, author of *Modern Physics and Ancient Faith*. "It may be that the superstring theory is the only mathematically consistent way to combine quantum theory and Einsteinian gravity."[88]

"The new kind of interconnectedness . . . not only enforces the similarities between the views of physicists and mystics; it also raised the intriguing possibility of relating subatomic physics to Jungian psychology and perhaps even to parapsychology," Fritjof Capra wrote.[89]

Einstein had yet another revolutionary idea he hoped to develop; he called it the "unified field theory." He conceived of the universe as a "four-dimensional continuum," LeShan explained. "Thus all man's perceptions of the world and all his abstract intuitions of reality would merge finally into one, and the deep underlying unity of the universe would be laid bare," LeShan said, borrowing from a book titled, *The Universe and Dr. Einstein* by Lincoln Barnett.[90]

But the unified field theory held more frightening implications if you consider the story of what has come to be known as the Philadelphia Experiment.[91] At some point during World War II the United States Navy purportedly undertook a test in teleportation, the paranormal ability to transport people or objects between one place and another, even at great distances. In other words, personnel were meant to disappear from one location and then reappear elsewhere. In this case, the navy was said to have caused a warship, the destroyer USS *Eldridge*, and its crew members to briefly become invisible. They and their vessel were then teleported from a Philadelphia location to the Norfolk, Virginia, area. The experiment, which lasted for only several minutes, had "disastrous long-term results," wrote author Daniel Cohen. It was, of course, top secret, and whose name later surfaced in connection with it? Why none other than the world-famous Albert Einstein, author of the unified field theory, who for a year during the war was a "scientific consultant" to the United States Navy.

Typically, accounts of teleportation throughout history were rare and attributed to saints of the Catholic Church and Eastern mystics. Invisibility has long been considered an "occult power" or one of the siddhis indicating spiritual growth among Indian yogis. During America's Great Age of Spiritualism in the nineteenth century, when various objects and apparitions appeared and disappeared, mediums claimed spirits materialized from a mysterious oozing substance known as "ectoplasm" that was found to be fraudulent in nearly every instance until it was eventually dismissed by serious parapsychologists. Science fiction fans of TV's *Star Trek* no doubt recall the show's "transporter," that was used for teleportation, and made famous the line, "Beam me up, Scotty!"

But 1943 was far from ancient and medieval times, and the U.S. Navy hardly portrayed itself as a mystical or spiritualist organization; it was fighting a real and ferocious war, using some quite sophisticated weaponry and technology for its day, such as radar. In 1939, American research began on the atomic bomb that eventually became the army's top-secret two-billion-dollar "Manhattan Project" whose purpose was to produce a bomb before the Nazis. They were already conducting experiments with atomic energy; the fear was Germany might have—and would use—the A-bomb first. Through no fault of his own, Einstein's famed 1905 mathematical equation, $E = mc^2$, would move far from the realm of abstract or theoretical ideas, and lead to the world's first "doomsday weapon," and the dawning of the Atomic Age, wrote Dr. Thomas M. Smith in *Great Events from History*.[92]

For a thirteen-month period between late May 1943 and the end of June 1944, Einstein was engaged as a scientific consultant for the navy. What were his responsibilities and contributions? Might the great physicist have engaged in researching or implementing a daring experiment in dematerialization and invisibility? Some have suggested just that. Consider the convoluted trail in one of American parapsychology's more bizarre episodes.

If accounts of the Philadelphia Experiment are to be believed, about half the crew members involved died. Of those who survived, many suffered various mental and emotional problems, some quite serious, and every surviving crew member was discharged as "mentally unfit." Some men went through periods described as "going blank"; others temporarily froze wherever they were. Apparently there was no certain treatment or remedy for most aftereffects. Supposedly touching a victim in a certain way was a cure—but it often failed.

The U.S. military's attempts at teleportation and invisibility first came to public attention in letters named for a shadowy figure, Carlos Allende or Carl Allen. Allende contended that when he was a "deckhand" on another ship in 1943, he was an eyewitness to the experiment that caused the *Eldridge* to vanish or dematerialize from a Philadelphia dock.[93]

In 1956, he contacted an astronomer, astrophysicist, and UFO researcher named Morris Jessup, who, a year earlier, in 1955, had written a book, *The Case for the UFO*.[94] That correspondence to Jessup became known as the "Allende letters." Then someone—presumably Allende—anonymously mailed a copy of Jessup's book to the Office of Naval Research (ONR) that contained numerous scribbled notes and explanations. Many of the comments were disorganized and confused; they referred to UFOs, extraterrestrial life, and the so-called Philadelphia Experiment that Allende supposedly witnessed. There were also references to his "fears" of Einstein's unified field theory. For its part, the navy denied the entire story, claimed it never occurred, and maintained there had been no experiments in teleportation.

"Jessup's first reaction was that the letter was either a hoax or the ranting of a crackpot," wrote Vincent Gaddis in *Invisible Horizons*. But eventually Jessup changed his mind, and did write about the puzzling letters. However, his conclusions were left unknown because in April 1959 Jessup's lifeless body was discovered in his car in the Miami, Florida, area. Police ruled it a suicide. Some maintained Jessup's unexpected death at age fifty-nine was part of a cover-up connected to whatever he'd learned about the Philadelphia Experiment. Others who knew Jessup said he'd had emotional problems and spoke of suicide.

Jessup's death did not end the questions and controversy about whether the navy had engaged in a secret invisibility project. Whether it was true or false, the story had taken on a life of its own. Over the years several books about the Philadelphia Experiment and the Allende letters were written, and also became the subject of a motion picture. One book, titled *The Strange Case of Dr. M. K. Jessup*, by UFO researcher Gray Barker was published in 1963. A later book by popular writer Brad Steiger in 1968 dealt in detail with Allende's letters.

Allende was miffed that he received no compensation from either book. That motivated him to take his story to Jim Lorenzen, then director of the Aerial Phenomena Research Organization, or APRO, devoted to UFO investigations; in 1969, Allende confessed to Lorenzen that he'd made up the tale, creating a hoax he hoped to profit from. But then the eccentric Allende recanted his confession. The dizzying and contradictory turn of events did not discourage Gray Barker from reproducing Jessup's book with the original Allende notes in them.

Lorenzen was a well-known figure in UFO circles for many years, and one of his most trusted associates was longtime APRO investigator Dick Ruhl. Despite their friendship and frequent contact, Ruhl said that Lorenzen "never once" mentioned Allende or the Philadelphia Experiment. Ruhl thought that Lorenzen rejected Allende's claims. However, "Jim Lorenzen had a top government clearance," according to Ruhl. We can only speculate, but might Lorenzen have not discussed Allende because he was forbidden to?[95]

Gray Barker's 1973 book breathed new life and interest into the then thirty-year-old story, and it did not escape the navy's attention.[96] In July 1976, the Department of the Navy's Office of Information issued a written statement denying the Philadelphia Experiment ever occurred. It read in part:

"The Office of Naval Research [ONR] has never conducted any investigation on invisibility, either in 1943 or at any other time ... In view of present scientific knowledge, our scientists do not believe that such an experiment could be possible except in the realm of science fiction. A scientific study of such import, if it had in fact occurred, could hardly remain secret for such a long time."

It seemed peculiar to some that the navy would go to the trouble of calling attention to the Philadelphia Experiment, at all. Charles Berlitz and William Moore didn't buy the navy's denials when they wrote *The Philadelphia Experiment: Project Invisibility* in 1979. In their book is reprinted the text of the strange letters to Jessup in which Allende took strong issue with Einstein's research into a unified field theory and the potential danger it posed to all of civilization, presumably if it was applied to developing weapons capable of cataclysmic mass destruction.

Einstein had been appalled that his theory of relativity, $E=mc^2$, contributed to the development of the atomic bombs that were dropped on Hiroshima and Nagasaki, Japan, to end World War II in August 1945 that killed and maimed hundreds of thousands instantly in blinding explosions on both cities. That his theories could result in death and devastation on a scale unprecedented in human history horrified and shook him to his core. They were his "worst fears" come true, his secretary later wrote.

In 1932, just before Hitler came to power, Einstein left Europe for America where he joined Princeton University, and would remain for the rest of his life. When he came to Princeton he was already a famed international figure, and with his distinctive, unruly mane of white hair and mustache, an immediately recognizable celebrity. Although he absolutely understood the need to destroy Hitler and the Third Reich, at heart he was still a pacifist who despised the idea of war.

Had the navy employed Einstein's scientific and mathematical genius for a misguided and disastrous experiment in teleportation? The so-called Allende letters are not easy to read; Berlitz accurately described the scribbled notes as "bizarre annotations." They appear to explain the "mysterious disappearances of ships, planes, and people discussed in Jessup's book, many of them within the area of the mysterious 'Bermuda Triangle.'" A brief verbatim portion of his strange writing follows, including its original grammar and punctuation.[97]

". . . Complete invisibility of a ship, Destroyer type, and *all* its crew, While at sea (October 1943). The Field Was effective in an oblate spheroidal shape extending one hundred yards . . . *out* from each beam of the ship. Any person within *that* sphere became vague in form But He too observed those Persons aboard that ship they too were at the same state, yet were walking upon nothing. Any person without that sphere could see Nothing above the clearly *Defined shape of the Ships Hull* in the Water, providing of course, that the person was just close enough to see yet, just barely outside of that field. Why tell you Now? Very Simple; If you chose to go Mad then you would reveal this information. Half of the officers & the crew of that Ship are at Present, & Mad as Hatters. A few, are even Yet confined to certain areas where they May receive trained Scientific aid when they either, 'Go blank' or 'Go Blank & Get Stuck.'

"If a man Freezes [can Not Move of his own volition] unless two or More of those who are within the field go & touch him, quickly, else he 'Freezes.'

"If a man Freezes, His position Must be Marked out carefully and then the Field is cut-off. Everyone but that 'frozen' man is able to Move . . ."

Allende went on to write: "Most went insane, one just walked 'throo' His quarters Wall in sight of His Wife & Child & 2 other crew members (WAS NEVER SEEN AGAIN), two Went into 'The Flame,' I.E. They 'Froze & caught fire . . .'"

Allende's ramblings continued, "Somehow, also, The Experimental Ship Disappeared from its Philadelphia Dock and only a Very few Minutes Later appeared at its other Dock in the Norfolk, Newport News, Portsmouth area . . . But the ship then, *again*, Disappeared And went *Back* to its Philadelphia Dock in only a Very few Minutes or Less."

By 1946 the experiments were discontinued, Allende claimed. The navy found them "impractical," he alleged. He concluded, "In short, Ignorance of this thing bred Such Terrors of it that, on the Level of attempted operations, with what knowledge was then available. It was deemed as impossible, Impracticable and Too Horrible."

In all, Jessup received three letters that were hoax, hype, or an incredible paranormal revelation. The question has never been answered to anyone's satisfaction—not an unusual outcome in parapsychology.[98]

It's easy to dismiss the Philadelphia Experiment, as skeptics obviously do. But what if Allende was telling the truth or if there was even a grain of veracity in his strange notes? Then the story reverberates back to Einstein's complex and controversial unified field theory, originally published between 1925 and 1927. Allende contended that Einstein at first "withdrew" the theory because he was troubled by how it could be misused if it fell into the wrong hands.

Although Einstein had finished a "version" of his unified field theory for gravitation and electricity between 1925 and 1927, he withdrew it after it had been published in German scientific journals. The only explanation he offered for his change of mind was that the new theory was "incomplete." It was not seen again until 1940, a year before the United States's entry into World War II, and the same year the navy allegedly commenced work on the Philadelphia Experiment.

As briefly and simply as possible, Einstein's unified field theory applied complicated mathematical equations to develop a "scientific law" hoping to clarify how the three fundamental "universal forces"—"electromagnetic, gravitational, and nuclear"—are related. It was "gravitational force"—the force of attraction between particles of matter in the universe—that was evasive. Einstein reasoned that the universe had an organization to it. "God does not play dice with the universe," he'd said, meaning there had to be an "orderly, coherent whole" that mathematics could somehow explain, Berlitz wrote.[99] Einstein was not content with the increasing popularity of quantum mechanics. The idea "of the unseen subatomic world as collections of probabilities disturbed [him]," Richard Broughton wrote. Not every scientist agreed with Einstein. Some thought his objective was impossible; that attempting to create "order from chaos" could not be achieved.

Might some of Einstein's theories have found their way into the development of the Philadelphia Experiment? He labored at his unified field theory until the very end of his life; in 1953, only two years before his death, he revealed some very persuasive findings toward proving that electromagnetism and gravity were linked. Allende's assertions about the unified field theory that Einstein made known in the 1950s were quite similar to his original draft of the theory back in 1925. If that was so, then the unified field theory was available in some form in 1940 had the navy chosen to apply it to an experiment in teleportation. What harm could there be in applying scientific theory to affect human cells and molecules toward teleportation and invisibility?

Might the enigmatic Allende have inadvertently observed a navy invisibility test that went terribly wrong? Allende's last letter to Morris

Jessup hinted that the navy's top-secret experiments might somehow be related to "UFO propulsion," Charles Berlitz suggested in his book *The Philadelphia Experiment*. Did the mysterious and elusive Carlos Allende actually witness what he claimed: the dematerialization of the navy destroyer *Eldridge* and its crew? Even if Allende was a "crackpot" as some have claimed, he did have extensive knowledge about UFOs, the paranormal, and the implications and potential dangers of Einstein's complicated unified field theory, suggesting he had a grasp of physics, and the properties and interactions of matter and energy.

It's no secret that Einstein wrote President Franklin Delano Roosevelt at the beginning of World War II to urge scientific research and there were many top-secret or "classified" experiments undertaken by the United States, in addition to the Manhattan Project. Might the great scientist himself have suggested—even urged—that his unified theory be applied to the war effort, in the form of the ill-fated teleportation experiment?

So was the Philadelphia Experiment fact or fiction? Had the navy employed Einstein's theory in a failed attempt at teleportation and "force-field invisibility"? Charles Berlitz suggested electromagnetic activity in the mysterious area known as the Bermuda Triangle where ships and planes supposedly disappeared at alarmingly high rates. Could planes and ships have passed into other dimensions of time and space from where they were unable to return? Might the navy have actually created "force-field invisibility"? Berlitz asked, "Did the Philadelphia Experiment perhaps provide evidence of the existence of other dimensions in time and space?"

Whatever one concludes about the veracity of the Philadelphia Experiment, a substantial amount has been written about it—yet another odd chapter in America's paranormal history, as it may have been applied to warfare. We'll let longtime UFO investigator Dick Ruhl have the last word on the navy's alleged teleportation and invisibility experiment. "We can't say they absolutely didn't try—and fail." The accumulation of evidence, which we've only had space here to highlight, suggests something happened in the Philadelphia Navy Yard in 1943.[100]

The Philadelphia Experiment would not be the only allegation of teleportation made by those devoted to investigating the paranormal and the U.S. military. Long Island, today home to nearly three million people, is crowded with suburban split-levels, shopping malls, and traffic congestion.

It runs for a distance of some ninety miles from New York City eastward to a place called Montauk Point where it ends. Montauk is noted for its landmark lighthouse, a well-known tourist attraction at the very tip of the island, surrounded by a rocky beach that faces the Atlantic Ocean; still a somewhat isolated area just beyond the glitzy Hamptons, summer playground of the rich and famous.

It seems an unlikely place for a covert project in teleportation. However, there was a time after World War II when few people ventured to eastern Long Island, and not many were aware of a place at Montauk known as Camp Hero. At one time, during the World War II era it was a U.S. Air Force radar installation; decommissioned and abandoned by 1969. Those who believe top-secret paranormal experiments continued there say that tests in teleportation, psychokinesis, and other psychic abilities were carried out literally concealed deep underground, at the long-abandoned radar site. One version claims that when the covert tests were resumed, they were not under government auspices, but who funded the experiments has not been made clear.

Some paranormal investigators, accompanied by a small number of scientists and engineers maintain they've researched Camp Hero and discovered that tests including teleportation and later mind control, were ongoing at the site from the 1940s until 1983. One project supposedly involved a psychic named Duncan Cameron, but something went terribly wrong, and the facility was destroyed. Of course, debunkers dismiss the Philadelphia Experiment and other teleportation experiments as mere legend. But for those who believe, the curious and persistent story became the subject of a popular book, *The Montauk Project*, and several sequels in the 1990s.[101] In a later chapter we'll delve deeper into the long history of the U.S. government's secret involvement in the paranormal, and the conspiracy to keep it hidden from the public.

The twentieth century opened with the promise of answers about the nature of psychical phenomena. The work of Jung, Freud, and Einstein revolutionized the way we looked at the universe and ourselves. Their influence was virtually unparalleled. But as R. Laurence Moore observed, the paranormal never found a "satisfactory hypothesis" despite startling breakthroughs in psychology and physics. Ironically, the "new physics" and parapsychology shared similarities; both disciplines assumed the existence of phenomena that could not be seen, and dealt in probabilities and "uncertainties." Time, space, and matter, theorized by Einstein and other new physicists, came closer to the idea of universal "oneness" that mystics and mediums had long claimed. The new thinking challenged the idea of "materialism" that in science regarded psychic experiences to be impossible. Materialistic philosophy maintained that every phenomenon is capable of being broken down into small particles, analyzed, and the interactions between them observed. Since psychic communication between people cannot be defined this way, it's not supposed to occur. The problem is that it does.

Freud gave dreams and the unconscious mind a scientific respectability; Jung dared to encourage new ways of thinking about paranormal experiences that motivated researchers. But despite rays of hope, and some progress, few traditional physicists or psychologists welcomed parapsychology, and the debate continued about where psychic phenomena belonged: within science, psychology, or its own separate field. The paranormal remained elusive, but increasingly evidence suggested it was a genuine, useful, and normal part of the human experience, although some people seemed to have more psychic ability than others. Whether the phenomena could be captured and controlled by science was another frustrating question that would challenge future researchers who sought to learn what connection existed between physics and the paranormal.

Science has always been interested in the relationship between the brain and the mind. So it was that when Einstein died in April 1955, his brain was preserved for scientific study. His theories had changed the world; would there be evidence of his genius in that mass of soft nervous tissue? At first glance, it looked like any other brain, concluded several doctors who saw it. Eventually, Einstein's brain was carefully examined and found to have an excess of what are called "glial cells" that feed and help neurons, the brain's basic cells. Glial cells are able to grow in number, notably if there is "increased mental activity." As some neuroscientists speculated, Einstein's brain did contain a greater number of glial cells in a highly evolved part of his brain, evidence of "greater intellectual processing," said Dr. Marian Diamond at the University of California. The implication for the paranormal is the startling progress made in recent years showing where in the brain intuitive and psychic states occur. This lies at the heart not only of the stories of the prophets and soothsayers of ancient times but of modern experiments in ESP, out-of-body, and remote viewing.

6 *America's Search for Past Lives*

I can read reincarnation into the Bible, and you can
read it right out again.

—EDGAR CAYCE

In 1956, Dwight Eisenhower was president of the United States, and a
young man by the name of Elvis Presley was singing his way to rock 'n'
roll fame. While the Cold War simmered, and a new Buick automobile
cost $2,490, Americans were suddenly captivated by a book about rein-
carnation titled *The Search for Bridey Murphy* that became a surprise bestseller. It purported to be a true story about the past life experience of a
twenty-nine-year-old Colorado housewife, who, when she was hypnotized, told of being an Irish woman named Bridey Murphy more than a
hundred years earlier. To say the least, the book produced a storm of
controversy and curiosity on its way to becoming "one of the most famous
cases of possible reincarnation" America had ever known. Reincarnation
had not played a substantial role in American culture, mainly for religious
reasons; Christianity disapproved of the concept, unlike Hinduism and
Buddhism which readily accepted reincarnation beliefs.[1]

The unlikely author of the book was Morey Bernstein, a successful young Colorado businessman with a reputation for integrity. A few
years earlier, in 1952, Bernstein began experimenting with his favorite
interest, hypnosis, at which he'd become quite an accomplished amateur

practitioner. And he was also knowledgeable about psychic phenomena, including the famed ESP tests conducted by Dr. J. B. Rhine at Duke University.

One Saturday evening in November 1952, Bernstein decided to attempt an "age regression." His subject was a woman he would publicly identify as "Mrs. Ruth Simmons," but whose real name was Virginia Tighe. She and her husband were friendly with Bernstein and his wife. Tighe was a "standout" subject, he explained. "She had the capacity, that is, for entering immediately into a deep trance." He'd hypnotized her on a couple of previous occasions, at first to help her stop smoking. In an earlier session when Tighe was hypnotized she'd remembered events from infancy.

But now Bernstein said, "This time I would learn just how far back her memory could be taken." Once Tighe was in a trance, as Bernstein expected, she recalled "memories stored deep, past the reach of the conscious mind," including incidents when she was just one year old. Bernstein explained that he was trying something he had never before attempted. "I was going to make an effort to determine whether human memory can be taken back to a period even before birth," he said. "I had no clue as to just how far back the mind . . . can be regressed."[2]

Bernstein instructed Tighe to "try to go still farther back in [her] memory . . . back, back, back, and back . . . until oddly enough, you find yourself in some other scene, in some other place, in some other time, and when I talk to you again, you will tell me about it." Bernstein's goal was to learn whether she would have a reincarnation experience during the tape-recorded session. Would regressive hypnosis produce evidence for the possibility of a past life? He hastened to add that he had no idea what to expect.

When he asked Virginia Tighe, still entranced, what she saw, she began describing a young girl who'd scraped or "picked" the paint off her metal bed. Tighe went on to say that the grown-ups had just "painted [the bed] to make it pretty." That was her first memory.[3] It was a young child's story that seemed as if it came from some place long ago and far away, and she spoke in a gentle but distinct Irish brogue, to Bernstein's amazement. When Bernstein asked with whom he was speaking, he thought Tighe answered, "Friday, Friday Murphy." Actually she'd replied, "Bridey," not Friday.[4] She went on to explain that she was born in Cork, Ireland, in

1798 on the "twentieth day of the twelfth month." In the trance she was no longer Virginia Tighe, Colorado housewife, as she continued offering details of her life as Bridey, more than a hundred years earlier.[5]

So began the story of Bridey Murphy who supposedly was born and lived in Ireland during the early and mid-nineteenth century. Had the hypnotic regression made it possible to tap into Tighe's subconscious to retrieve memories that her conscious mind could no longer recall? Although Tighe said she had no personal interest in reincarnation, she'd agreed to Bernstein's request to be his subject as he sought to further "experiment" with hypnosis and reincarnation. In each tape-recorded session Tighe went into a deep trance state as Bernstein asked her to go back to "some other scene, some other place, some other time," and tell what she visualized.[6]

Bernstein realized that while much of Bridey's story was unverifiable, little more than interesting incidents, some of what she said seemed sufficiently detailed that perhaps it could be researched and confirmed. For example, she said she was born in Cork to a barrister and his wife. Bridey claimed she'd been married at a young age to a man named Sean Brian McCarthy, and the couple lived in Belfast until 1864 where she died at the age of sixty-six.[7] She also referred to several locations, as well as names and items that were too exact to have been guessed or concocted from mere imagination. Her phraseology and dialect were appropriate for nineteenth-century Ireland, but long out of date in America by the 1950s. It seemed unlikely that Tighe would be familiar with such antiquated and obsolete jargon, and she mentioned having red hair.[8]

Bernstein was fascinated by the responses he elicited from her in trance. For example, how did she know the exact denominations of money used in Ireland at the time she supposedly lived there? "Pound, penny, tuppence, sixpence, copper-half."[9] She also provided the names of two grocers where she did her marketing in Belfast: Farr's and Carrigan's. Later he found that both stores existed in the 1850s and '60s.[10]

In all, Bernstein conducted six private regressive hypnosis sessions with Tighe during a one-year period; all were tape-recorded, and attended by several witnesses. Tighe seemed just as surprised by her answers when she heard the tapes played back. Once he'd completed the six hours that she had agreed to, Bernstein wrestled with what to do next. Finally, he contacted several reporter friends in the Denver area, and also decided to hire "investigators" to look into Tighe's account of her past life as Bridey Murphy.

The name Bridey was actually a nickname for Bridget, but Bernstein's sleuths found no record of anyone by that name born in Cork in 1798. Nor did they locate the names she gave of her parents, Kathleen and Duncan Murphy, or the young man from Belfast she married, Brian McCarthy. Did that mean Tighe had fabricated her past life? Not necessarily, since Ireland kept no records of births, marriages, and deaths during the time Bridey would have lived. If no documents could be tracked down it was understandable. Bernstein also complained that the investigators did only a superficial job, not nearly what he expected.

By 1954 the story became the subject of a series of articles, serialized in the *Denver Post*. Then in January 1956, Bernstein's book *The Search for Bridey Murphy* hit bookstores and quickly caused a national sensation and heated debate. The public and press reaction was "all but overwhelming," wrote William Barker, the first to report on the case for the *Denver Post*. His story appeared in the newspaper's Sunday magazine throughout September 1954. "The great majority of readers, surprisingly, accepted the implication that Bridey was evidence that man lives many lives," despite opposition on religious grounds and skeptics who dismissed, out of hand, the possibility of reincarnation. Some clergy were infuriated, for the Bridey saga ran counter to the Christian doctrine that "a soul cannot be reborn"; it goes to heaven with Jesus, or to the torment of hell.

Still, Bridey Murphy's story captivated much of the country, a fact not overlooked by many major newspapers, and most took negative positions, as they did about anything that was paranormal. Accuracy and journalistic objectivity seldom applied to stories about the psychic or supernatural. Sensationalism sold more papers. Meanwhile, people were debating and even singing songs about Bridey. One popular fad it inspired was "Come As You Were" parties with past life themes.

Before January 1956 was over, the *Chicago Daily News* assigned its London reporter to Ireland to ferret out the truth about the hotly debated reincarnation claims. But the reporter found nothing in the few days he hurried through Dublin, Cork, and Belfast, and despite only cursory research, his story in the *News* was predictably critical of Bridey.

Also assigned to Ireland was *Denver Post* reporter and columnist

William Barker who said he approached the search for evidence about Bridey Murphy objectively. "I didn't take sides. I left the decision up to the jury, the readers," Barker wrote. For those with strict Western religious beliefs, reincarnation was "anathema." Barker explained, "It was vital in certain camps to destroy Bridey, because Bridey symbolized reincarnation."

In addition to religious hostility, many psychologists and psychiatrists rejected the belief in an afterlife or life beyond death. Reincarnation cut both ways; it suggested previous and possible future lives. So those therapists who desperately sought psychological explanations such as "mental instability" lined up against the Bridey Murphy story. There were a handful of psychiatrists in the 1950s quietly researching reincarnation, but the fear of ridicule and criticism by peers caused most to maintain a low profile.

Surprisingly, some mediums were also hostile to reincarnation. It had never been a strongly held conviction in America, not even during the Great Age of Spiritualism in the nineteenth century, except among Theosophists who embraced Eastern beliefs and mysticism. But there was also a practical—and economic—reason why many psychic mediums shunned reincarnation. If our souls reincarnate, what happens to the number of spirits on the Other Side? Reincarnation implied a potentially smaller spirit world, and therefore fewer to communicate through mediums. In other words, reincarnation could put a dent in their business.

The famed nineteenth-century medium, D. D. Home, was a strident critic of reincarnation. That put him at odds with Allan Kardec (1804–1869), the "father of spiritism," the French version of spiritualism. Unlike most American opinion, spiritism had as its paramount principle the absolute belief that "spiritual progress" was achieved through reincarnation; Kardec had no patience with those who disagreed. His reincarnation beliefs didn't make him many friends among American mediums in his day.

Yet as the initial reaction to the Bridey Murphy story proved, by the 1950s many Americans were intrigued—and perhaps comforted—by the idea that we'd lived before and would again. Morey Bernstein said he found "the most fascinating facet of hypnosis [was] concerned with the mysteries that have surrounded man for ages."[11] He seemed to have unleashed a new controversy about the oldest of human mysteries: What happens after we die? Does the soul return in a new body?

What were some of the details Tighe gave when she was in trance and regressed back to her life as Bridey Murphy? Her first memory was of scraping paint from her bed at age four. She said when she was seven, her baby brother died. She attended Mrs. Strayne's Day School where she studied ". . . to be a lady . . . just house things . . . and proper things." In 1818, at the age of twenty she married a young man of twenty-two named Sean Brian Joseph McCarthy, the son of a barrister, who attended school in Belfast. Their marriage was happy, but they had no children, and lived in Belfast, a city she did not like as much as Cork, a livelier place where there was more to do. But she made friends there, especially with a couple named Mary Catherine and Kevin Moore.

Although Bridey was Protestant, she said she attended St. Theresa's Roman Catholic Church in Belfast because Brian was Catholic. She recalled several places she'd known. In addition to the church, there was her childhood home in Cork, "The Meadows," and she mentioned a small town named Bailings Crossing. She remembered Caden's House, a woman's apparel store, and she also recalled Queens University where Brian taught, as well as a local newspaper, the *Belfast News-Letter* that she said he sometimes wrote for. A favorite dish of theirs was "boiled beef with onions," and to relax she played a card game called "fancy." Bridey said she read the works of the British Romantic poet John Keats, and described a number of Irish "customs and traditions," using phrases and vocabulary long out of date and unfamiliar to most Americans. For example, she said to "ditch" someone meant to bury them when they died. The cottage she and Brian lived in she called a "hut," and farming she referred to as "cropping."

During one session, Bernstein gave her a post-hypnotic suggestion to draw the location of her house on Dooley Road, in relation to St. Theresa's Church, which she did. Another time, while hypnotized, she danced the Irish "Morning Jig."

Bridey's memories included how and when she died on a Sunday in Belfast while her husband was attending church. The year was 1864 and she was sixty-six. Her death was the result of serious injuries to her hip she suffered from a fall down a staircase. In trance, she told Bernstein, "I was such a burden. Had to be carried out." Brian had taken good care of her, she said.

"Can you tell us what happened after your death?" Bernstein asked.

He'd hoped to learn where she was between lifetimes. But Bridey's answer dealt mainly with her concern—and apparent relief—that she was not going to purgatory. However, she said she saw some events after her death.[12]

Sometime later, Bernstein was on business in New York when he decided to take time out to research some of the information from the sessions with Tighe. For example, Bailings Crossing was not on any map of Ireland, despite Bridey's insistence. Bernstein doggedly persisted until he found someone who confirmed it once existed. At first, he could not locate a reference to St. Theresa's Roman Catholic Church. But his investigation turned up someone with knowledge that there once was such a church in Belfast.

One word Bridey gave was something she called a "brate." Bernstein had no idea what it meant, although Bridey described it as a small "wishing cup." Quite by accident, Bernstein met a British woman who had one in her antiques collection. The actual word was "quait," she told him. Perhaps he'd misunderstood Bridey's pronunciation. Another unfamiliar word Bridey used was "tup," when she referred to an unpleasant man. Bernstein eventually found a definition of the obscure word. It meant a "male, man, or fellow."

More problematic was Bridey's references in the taped sessions to a priest named Father John Goran or Gorman at St. Theresa's. He was the priest who married her and Brian, she said, but no one was able to find any record of a priest by that name.

The obvious question for believers and skeptics alike was whether the Bridey Murphy story was fact or fiction. Had Virginia Tighe fabricated a past life or had she actually recalled an earlier incarnation in Ireland, a country she'd never been to? In fact, Tighe had never traveled out of the United States. Most people were not certain what conclusion to draw about Bridey's existence. After all, anyone could claim a past life. Proving it was another matter.

As the Bridey controversy grew, a Chicago newspaper entered the debate. The *Chicago American* ran a series of stories that left no question it did not believe the reincarnation story was genuine, and was determined to debunk it. The newspaper claimed it could not find evidence that anyone named Bridey Murphy ever existed. Then came the *American*'s "bombshell." It reported that as a child Tighe lived for a time in

Chicago with an Irish aunt, Marie Burns, who often entertained her with stories about Ireland, and there was a neighbor, Bridie, whose maiden name was Murphy.

The newspaper's "exposé" explained that Bridey could not have lived in a wooden house because forests were scant in Ireland, most houses were built of stone. Nor could she have slept in a metal bed, as she'd claimed, since those were not then available in Cork. Further, Tighe had learned the Irish jig in school. The conclusion was that Tighe's knowledge of nineteenth-century Ireland was learned in her present lifetime. Might she have subconsciously absorbed information from her aunt or neighbor that became the basis of her past-life memories as Bridey Murphy? The phenomenon is known as cryptoamnesia meaning "hidden or unconscious memory," and skeptics and many scientists satisfied themselves with that explanation.[13]

By the time the newspapers "had finished their hatchet job, it seemed the highly suggestible" Virgina Tighe "was simply recalling hidden memories of long-forgotten stories she heard as a child but was able to recall only under hypnosis," wrote J. Allan Danelek in *Mystery of Reincarnation*.

The *Chicago American* led the pack of debunkers. The newspaper's self-proclaimed and poorly researched "exposé" of Bridey was accepted as the gospel by most other publications around the country with nary a blink. One headline read: "Hypnotist Morey Bernstein Hoaxed World with Search for Bridey Murphy." Another brazenly—but wrongly—boasted it had exposed the story that Tighe admitted it was a hoax. She did no such thing. To the contrary, Tighe said she was already eighteen when she came to know her aunt well, who was of Scottish-Irish ancestry, and never "regaled" Virginia with stories of Ireland. There was also a question about whether the neighbor Bridie Corkell's maiden name was actually "Murphy."

When the popular *Life* magazine reported the Bridey story nationally, it simply repeated the Chicago newspaper's conclusions with no questions asked.[14] Not surprisingly, the public lost interest in the Bridey Murphy past-life tale, believing it had been uncovered as a shrewd deception, or the result of Tighe's "hidden memories" that came to the fore under hypnosis.

Denver Post reporter William Barker later wrote *The Truth About Bridey*

Murphy recounting his own investigation. He noted that countless "exposés" passed off opinions as facts, in order to derail the reincarnation claims. Barker had traveled to Ireland in March 1956 to search for what he called "Bridey evidence," but he found few Irish people open to reincarnation, a reflection of their deeply held Catholic beliefs. Many documents he hoped to find were lost, discarded, or never existed. Despite missing records, he did locate some evidence to suggest that there once was a Bridey Murphy who lived in nineteenth-century Ireland, and he was told that many details Tighe gave when she was regressed were things "she could not have known."

Debunkers had picked on every detail they could to discredit the Bridey story. For example: Some insisted she could not have lived in a wooden house, there was no place in Cork called "The Meadows," and metal beds were unavailable when Bridey would have been a four-year-old in 1802. Barker found evidence to refute each of what skeptics branded "fabrications." Some dismissed as impossible a bedtime story Bridey said her mother read to her as a child, claiming the tale of "Deirdre, an Irish maiden" wasn't published until 1905. But Barker found it was in print a full century earlier, by 1805, when Bridey would have been seven. Other skeptics claimed St. Theresa's Church was not yet built in Bridey's lifetime; nor was there a Dooley Road.

One national magazine said Bridey's husband could not have taught law at Queens University in the 1850s as she'd said, since the law school was not yet in existence. Barker discovered the Belfast school was in operation by 1850. Even foods Bridey said she ate became a target for skeptics who insisted muffins weren't eaten in Ireland back then. Barker found that they, indeed, were. There was also criticism because Bridey said books could be borrowed from the library when she lived in Belfast. Some debunkers claimed there was no "lending library" at the time. In fact, Belfast had such a facility by 1788. Barker also took issue with a popular American magazine that claimed Bridey's "odd word usage" wasn't even Gaelic. But in the regressive hypnosis sessions, she had used many long-obsolete Irish colloquialisms, much as every generation and region has its peculiar localisms and slang terms.

"Bridey is an underdog almost without parallel," Barker wrote in frustration, "beleaguered by ancient dogma on one front, conservative science on another . . . and the inevitable skeptical press . . ."

Bridey named a number of places, including streets no longer in existence that had to be verified on very old maps, but no record could be found of the school she claimed she attended, "Mrs. Strayne's School." Barker suggested that perhaps some confusion in pronunciation or spelling might explain that. He was also at a loss to find any references to Bridey's father and husband holding the position of barristers, who were on a higher rung than solicitors or attorneys. Barristers were litigators—trial attorneys—a separate level of certification than solicitors. Could Bridey have exaggerated their status in her sessions with Morey Bernstein? Barker thought it more likely that her husband, Brian McCarthy, held some form of clerical job.

Barker did locate a reference to a "John M' Carthy" (sic) in the Belfast City Directories for 1858–59 and 1861–62. John would have been Bridey's father-in-law, and his occupation was given as clerk, then bookkeeper. Perhaps Brian worked with or for his father? During one hypnotic regression session, when Bernstein mentioned a business, "John Craig Hardware," that he'd randomly found mentioned in an 1847 Belfast newspaper, Bridey immediately recognized it. "Have you been looking at Brian's books?" she asked, suggesting her husband was in some record-keeping position.

Barker complained that *Life* paid no attention to his evidence supporting Bridey's claims. He'd found dozens of accurate responses she gave Bernstein. However, the magazine preferred to accept the *Chicago American*'s negative version that had been carelessly investigated and maliciously reported to discredit reincarnation. Barker also discovered that a Christian minister who strongly opposed reincarnation was brought in expressly to help prepare the newspaper's stories debunking Bridey. The *American*, owned by Hearst, distributed the misleading story to its other major newspapers including the San Francisco *Examiner* and the *New York Journal-American*. The purported "exposé" became a classic case of slanted and sloppily researched reporting. Even some skeptics agreed it was a sham.[15]

Whether the Bridey Murphy case was factual or not, most press coverage was so shabby and disingenuous, no honest appraisal could be made, one way or the other. "In summing up, I found neither for nor against Bridey," Barker wrote, and Bernstein never stated that the story was "proof of reincarnation," Barker noted.

What Barker found with respect to the Bridey Murphy story is what many UFO researchers find today with respect to the claims of debunkers. Similar to the Bridey Murphy debunking, most skeptics and debunkers start from a position of prejudgment rather than an open mind. They've made up their minds in advance and simply reject any information out of hand that doesn't fit into their mind-set. They rarely do their own investigations, simply relying on what others have said to bolster their position. As a result, a debunker is more like a member of a gang than an independent investigator. As it is with UFO debunkers, so it was with Bridey Murphy debunkers.

In academic and scientific circles there were a few open-minded to the Bridey story. One notable example was C. J. DuCasse, a philosophy professor at Brown University, who undertook a careful study of the case and then wrote his findings in *A Critical Examination of the Belief in a Life After Death*, published in 1961. His conclusion, to sum it up briefly, was that none of the debunkers or detractors had successfully disproved the Bridey story. "The reincarnation hypothesis" cannot be summarily ignored; in fact it made "sense," DuCasse said.[16]

What did the Bridey Murphy episode accomplish? It certainly left many provocative, if unanswered questions. In becoming the country's "all-time superstar," of past life regressions, as Time Life Books described it, Bridey's story raised America's consciousness about reincarnation to a new level, and sparked renewed interest in hypnosis, opening doors and minds to further exploration in the years ahead, especially about past-life regressions. It also revealed, again, the long-held hostility and shameful hypocrisy of the American press toward any evidence of a paranormal event. Nonetheless, Bernstein's book sold well over a million copies.

Years later, skeptics were still obsessing about Bridey Murphy. She must have made some impression on them. In 1996, a psychic debunker named Paul Edwards wrote *Reincarnation: A Critical Examination*, and concluded survival beyond death and reincarnation are "preposterous." He called Bridey Murphy "utterly worthless as evidence for reincarnation,"[17] and repeatedly referred to the paranormal as "occultism," a term not employed by serious parapsychologists in many years, and obviously meant to be derogatory. Another nationally known debunker, Martin Gardner had earlier branded Bridey's story a "worthless book designed to exploit a mass hunger for scientific evidence of life after death . . . and . . . modern huckstering to swindle the gullible, simple folk who take such books seriously."[18]

Gardner apparently forgot to mention that among those "gullible, simple folk" who seriously considered reincarnation were such famed Americans as Benjamin Franklin, Henry David Thoreau, Walt Whitman, Henry Wadsworth Longfellow, Oliver Wendell Holmes, Louisa May Alcott, Henry Ford, Charles Lindbergh, J. Paul Getty, and General George S. Patton.

The definition of reincarnation or transmigration boils down to the belief in the soul's survival beyond death and its rebirth in a new and different physical body. It accepts the theory known as "dualism," the idea that the mind and body are separate entities. The concept poses the fascinating possibility that human beings not only live on after physical death, but that they experience several—or even many—lifetimes.[19]

The belief in reincarnation dates back thousands of years; no one can say with certainty where and when it first began. But it probably predates the founding of the "world's major religions." However, the concept of reincarnation eventually took two very different roads, depending on whether one was in the East or West. It found its greatest number of adherents among Hindus, beginning around the sixth century BC. Closely related to the Hindu idea of the "rebirth" of souls is the principle of karma that teaches each incarnation is either a "reward or punishment" for how one behaved in an earlier life. Buddhism also developed reincarnation beliefs that taught the soul moves through a number of levels until eventually it becomes unimpeded on its path to reach nirvana or "perfection." From Asia, reincarnation ideas traveled to North America, and were embraced by some Native American tribes; while in Africa, some tribes also accepted rebirth beliefs.

Records about reincarnation date back to ancient Egypt, and the Greek and Roman civilizations held similar convictions several centuries before the birth of Jesus. Among the notable early Greek figures that subscribed to the theory were Pythagoras and Plato. "When the soul returns into itself and reflects, it passes into . . . the region of that which is pure and everlasting, immortal and unchangeable," wrote Plato (427–347 BC).[20] He also believed a person's soul could reincarnate into a "beast," and then be reborn again as a human. Later, the famed Roman poet Virgil (70–19 BC) said, "The great cycle of the ages is renewed. A new generation now descends from heaven."[21]

Once the early Catholic Church denounced reincarnation as inconsistent with Christianity, in the West the idea remained in the shadows for many centuries. But by the seventeenth century, the Dutch Jewish philosopher Baruch Spinoza wrote, ". . . we feel and know that we are eternal."[22]

The Bible, meanwhile, could be interpreted for or against reincarnation, as the famed American psychic and healer Edgar Cayce pointed out. In fact, one biblical quote often cited by those who believe in reincarnation begins, "In my Father's house there are many mansions." Even more controversial is a verse in the book of John in the New Testament in which Jesus said, "I assure you, most solemnly I tell you, that unless a person is born again, he cannot ever see the kingdom of God" (John 3:3). Christians believe the reference to "born again" means to be born in or accept the Holy Spirit of Jesus. But there are some who've argued that the phrase might be a reference to the concept of reincarnation, already a part of Hinduism by the time of Jesus.

While many Protestants and Catholics oppose reincarnation on theological grounds, few realize that it was an acknowledged precept in the first centuries of the Roman Catholic Church. Similarly, reincarnation is a precept in the Zohar, the book of Jewish mysticism in the Kabbalah. But despite early acceptance of reincarnation, the Church reversed its position with the Second Council of Constantinople in 553 AD. The council issued fourteen anathemas—doctrinal rejections or condemnations. One of them stated, "If anyone asserts the fabulous preexistence of souls, and shall assert the monstrous restoration which follows it, let him be anathema."[23] Ever since, Christian theologians have debated the concept of reincarnation. In the early centuries of the Church, expressing such beliefs could get a person executed.

In recent years, not all have flatly opposed the idea of the soul's rebirth. In fact, some liberal clergy have noted that Jesus never denounced reincarnation. Many suggest that Jesus realized it was an "accepted idea" in His time, and largely ignored it in His teachings, while both the Talmud and the ancient Jewish sect, the Pharisees, allowed for the existence of reincarnation beliefs, as did some Muslims.

There is a reference in the New Testament about whether John the Baptist was the reincarnation of the prophet Elijah (John 1:19–28). When John came before the Pharisees, "to witness for Christ," he was asked if he was Christ, to which he answered no. Then he was asked if he was Elijah the prophet (1 King 18:21), meaning was he reincarnated? John answered that he was not Elijah. He explained that he had come to baptize the people with water. But some believe that Jesus alluded to re-birth when He said, "John the Baptist was [the reincarnation] of Elijah" (Matthew 17:12–13).

To be accurate, according to medieval scholarship, there were three levels of interpretation to understanding the New Testament. On the first level of interpretation, a biblical passage was taken at its face value. On the second level, called "prefiguration," a passage in the New Testament directly correlates to a passage in the Old Testament because the Old Testament prefigures the New. For example, in a medieval carol, the verse reads: *"Ave fit ex Eva."* In modern English, the loose translation is that Mary, represented as Ave in Ave Maria, comes from Eva, or Eve. Mary, the mother of Jesus, is the second Eve, the mother of humankind. Eve prefigures the existence of Mary just as King David was the prefigu-ration of Jesus. Looking at biblical exegesis this way, the prophet Elijah prefigures John and, therefore, it can be said that John is Elijah, reincar-nated figuratively through an interpretation of how the Old and New Testaments relate to each other.

Many say the question of karma is also raised in the New Testament, in the Book of John. "As [Jesus] passed along, He noticed a man blind from birth. His disciples asked him, Rabbi, who sinned, this man or his parents, that he should be born blind?" Those who see that as a karmic reference conclude that Jesus was being asked about whether the man's loss of sight was a punishment inflicted for sins committed in a past in-carnation (John 9:1). Jesus answered that it was not. Neither the man nor his parents had sinned. Then Jesus "made mud and smeared it on [the man's eyes] and opened [them]." In other words, Jesus miracu-lously restored the man's sight (John 9:11–14). Jesus did not reprimand His followers for asking about karma or reincarnation. In fact, Jesus "never repudiated or denied it, or taught that it was false," wrote a Brit-ish minister, the Reverend Leslie Weatherhead. Even among those who do not accept the Eastern belief in karma, most people are familiar with the analogous biblical admonition, "Whatever a man sows, that he shall also reap."[24]

It's obvious that reincarnation's roots were in ancient religious teachings. However, as has often happened with other supernatural beliefs throughout history, somewhere along the way, reincarnation made the transition from a strictly religious concept to the paranormal. Likely, the Church's rejection of reincarnation was a "turning point."

About the only places where rebirth was accepted in the West for centuries was within secret brotherhoods or mystical cults such as the Knights Templar, Kabalists, Rosicrucians, and Freemasons. "America had Rosicrucians and alchemists before it had Methodists," noted religious historian Philip Jenkins. That probably explains why a "freethinker" such as the great American patriot, publisher, diplomat, and inventor Benjamin Franklin was open to the possibility of reincarnation, and wrote an epitaph for himself clearly referring to it.[25] Since many of America's Founding Fathers were Freemasons, it's likely they were at the very least tolerant of reincarnation, whether they believed in it or not.

Asian sects and gurus in America date back to "Thoreau and the Transcendentalists . . . in the 1840s," Jenkins wrote. "In . . . every generation since, there have been new infusions of Hindu and Buddhist thought." The New Thought movement of the late nineteenth century and Theosophy are two examples.[26] "With its cults, health fads, and wandering gurus, Boston in the 1880s [looked] a lot like San Francisco in the 1970s," Jenkins wrote.

Many great Western philosophers and thinkers also embraced reincarnation beliefs; Kant, Voltaire, Goethe, and Nietzsche, among them, as well as such famed writers as Sir Walter Scott, Victor Hugo, and Henrik Ibsen. The German philosopher Nietzsche (1844–1900) wrote, "All things return eternally, and ourselves with them; we have already existed in times without number, and all things with us."[27] He added, "The theory of reincarnation is a turning point in the history of man."

The famed psychotherapist Dr. Carl Jung, recognized for his openness to psychic phenomena, spoke and wrote about reincarnation, and considered it "an archetype and part of the collective unconscious." Although Jung never publicly proclaimed a belief in reincarnation, privately he was more open to "rebirth" than he let on, according to his colleagues.

In the latter part of the nineteenth century Americans were made more aware of Eastern teachings and mysticism by the controversial founder of Theosophy, Madame Helena Blavatsky, whose teaching also helped to inspire the Vril and Thule societies at the dawn of National Socialism.

Despite allegations of chicanery against her, Blavatsky has to be credited with stirring American curiosity in Eastern beliefs, including reincarnation and karma. Theosophists said we learn "new experiences" through repeated incarnations that help to develop the soul. You may recall that Blavatsky had traveled extensively to places such as India, Tibet, and Egypt to learn their philosophies; we'll leave the metaphysical complexities and technicalities to those who wish to explore them more deeply by further reading.

Following Blavatsky's death in 1891, the Theosophical Society came under the direction of her devoted and popular successor Annie Besant (1847–1933), British social reformer and Theosophist. The next year, 1892, Besant made her case in a small book simply titled *Reincarnation*.[28]

"Reincarnation is a truth that has swayed the minds of innumerable millions . . . and has [molded] the thoughts of the vast majority for uncounted centuries. It dropped out of the European mind during the Dark Ages," she wrote. "There is, of course, no doubt that the great historical religions of the East included the teachings of reincarnation as a fundamental tenet. It could scarcely be expected that a teaching of such vast antiquity and such a magnificent intellectual ancestry should fade out of the mind of mankind. The ignorance that swamped Europe carried away belief in reincarnation, as it carried away all philosophy, all metaphysics, and all science. The fundamental cause of reincarnation, as of all manifestation, is the desire for active life . . ."

The concept of reincarnation was also promulgated in America in the twentieth century by Edgar Cayce himself. One day in Dayton, Ohio, during the summer of 1923, American clairvoyant and seer Edgar Cayce gave a psychic reading to a man named Arthur Lammers who'd gone to the expense of bringing Cayce to Dayton from Selma, Alabama. Cayce had not dealt with past lives. His readings concerned the current psychological and physical health problems of his subjects.

Cayce self-induced a trance, reclined on a couch, and proceeded with the session for Lammers. When it was over, author Noel Langley said Cayce "received one of the greatest shocks of his life." Cayce always insisted he had no recall of what he said in trance. Now as he heard back the written transcript of the reading for Lammers, Cayce was stunned that he'd spoken about "the law of reincarnation," and pronounced it "a cold hard fact." He had clearly, if inexplicably, talked about past lives.

Cayce, you may remember, was born in a small, conservative Christian community in Kentucky in 1877. Reincarnation never figured in anything he'd been taught in his Bible-centered upbringing. As far as he was concerned, to believe in the rebirth of souls was "sacrilegious and contrary to all the teachings of Christ," Langley wrote in *Edgar Cayce on Reincarnation.*[29]

Nonetheless, despite his trepidations, Cayce proceeded with what at first he found abhorrent, the idea that people might live more than once, perhaps even many lifetimes. But he went further, perhaps driven by his own curiosity and Arthur Lammers's urging. Cayce allowed questioning to resume, with the understanding that he did not intend to contradict his Christian beliefs. He perused the Bible and noted the verses we mentioned earlier that could imply reincarnation, but said he would not proselytize on its behalf. Further, he agreed to give past-life readings only when asked to. Then it would be up to the subjects to decide if and how to use the information in their present life, Langley explained. It's estimated that between 1925 and 1944, more than twenty-five hundred people sought Cayce's past-life readings. In them he dealt with the problems people had coping with fears, marital difficulties, abilities, and aspirations.

Cayce saw "karma as a universal law of cause and effect which provides the soul with opportunities for physical, mental, and spiritual growth," his son Hugh Lynn Cayce wrote. He added that his father scrutinized "karmic patterns" that were the result of a person's past incarnations to help the individual cope with problems in the present.

What do we carry with us from past lives that we can use? In each incarnation the soul learns lessons that it then can apply to future lives. Might present attitudes, skills, or achievements have been influenced by past existences? Even for those who do not believe in reincarnation, strong affinities or yearnings for unfamiliar cultures, periods in time, or certain talents have long posed a mystery. Where and why do they originate? Is the answer in this life or in a past lifetime?

Once Cayce was in trance his "subconscious made contact with the subconscious" of the subject, Langley explained,[30] and Cayce went back further and further into a subject's past lives. He was able to describe when and where the person's earlier incarnations were and offered details— such as occupation, behavior, and personality traits—to better understand their effect or impact in the present lifetime. Cayce could even recount the way a subject died in a previous life.

"Each soul, as it reenters the earth's plane as a human being, has subconscious access to the characteristics, mental capacities, and skills it has accumulated in previous lives," explained Hugh Lynn Cayce. But the "entity" or soul must also fight the effects of negativity that have held back its progress.

Whether he was aware of it or not, Cayce was the forerunner of what would later come to be called past-life therapy. In Cayce's "life readings," he was the one who went into trance to recall a subject's previous incarnations. In more recent years, as the so-called "New Age" movement evolved, past-life therapists hypnotically regressed individuals to remember their earlier existences; not unlike Morey Bernstein's sessions with Virginia Tighe to recall her past life as Bridey Murphy. But Cayce took reincarnation a step further than merely satisfying someone's curiosity about who he or she might have been. Cayce explained the connection between present and past behaviors and traits.

Did it help? Yes, said those who heeded Cayce's advice, and applied past-life lessons to the present. For many there was therapeutic value in learning why we act certain ways based on who and what we were in former incarnations. The Bridey Murphy story occurred after Cayce's death, but it was certainly influenced by his earlier efforts. Cayce was the first in twentieth-century America to seriously explore the meaning of past lives; Morey Bernstein was the first to make reincarnation a national sensation with his book.

Sometimes Cayce's regressions took him back ten thousand or more years before the birth of Christ to the antediluvian civilization of Atlantis. Then he would tell a subject about a lifetime spent there, in what some called a magnificent and far advanced ancient culture. Of course, there was no way to prove what life was like in Atlantis—if it even existed. Skeptics derided the possibility that there ever was an Atlantis, branding it "a mythical island continent."

But "according to [Cayce's] readings . . . it was the cradle of our present civilization," Noel Langley wrote. No doubt, many who underwent Cayce's past-life readings believed what he told them. However, his greatest influence would come decades after his death when the New Age movement, particularly in the 1980s, developed a renewed curiosity about reincarnation and a passion for past-lives therapy. Many believed—or chose to believe—that they'd lived in ancient Atlantis.[31]

In *The Haunting of America,* we mentioned that the first references to Atlantis were in two of Plato's dialogues; from there, the legend continued to grow. Jumping ahead many centuries to 1882, an American politician and writer, Ignatius Donnelly wrote an influential book, *Atlantis: The Antediluvian World,* that renewed popular interest in the so-called "lost continent." Then, along came Theosophy's founder, Madame Helena Blavatsky, never one to be left on the sidelines. Borrowing from Donnelly, she incorporated Atlantis into her theosophical teachings. The next big step connecting Atlantis to reincarnation occurred in the early twentieth century thanks to Edgar Cayce.

Cayce's past-life trance readings described the Atlanteans as both "resourceful" and "aggressive" on a scale unprecedented in the world, Langley wrote.[32] They possessed ESP and telepathic powers; at its peak Atlantis developed and controlled modern technology eons ahead of its time. The source of their remarkable energy, Cayce said, was in a huge crystal, not unlike the modern laser ray. The crystal gathered energy from celestial bodies, such as stars, and in turn, projected the energy to provide power for Atlantean technology. They also understood the necessity for good health, exercise, and meditation.

But, according to Cayce, as Atlanteans captured and used their extraordinary source of power, so too did they eventually abuse it, and that was the cause of their ruination. Although Cayce claimed he knew nothing about Plato or Atlantis, he said in trance that the once great civilization disintegrated because of widespread "greed and lust for power." He saw the danger of modern man "repeating the tragedy of Atlantis," wrote Jess Stearn.[33] Cayce added that "the final destruction of Atlantis" came about when the "Great Crystal" was turned into a "death ray" whose energies were misused in an effort to control the earth.

"Cayce warned all this could happen again unless man considered the lessons of the past," Stearn wrote, adding that thousands of years later, like the Atlanteans, Cayce feared we would be the architects of our own destruction, despite our great knowledge, if we permitted greed and the misuse of power to overtake us.[34]

Cayce's pronouncements about Atlantis and reincarnation received derision from scientists, but Jess Stearn had a ready answer for them. He reminded readers about the long-held legend of "ancient Troy." A legend, that is, for many centuries until an enterprising businessman named Heinrich Schliemann unearthed remains of the ancient long-buried city in the 1870s.

Years after Cayce's death, the Association for Research and Enlightenment, the organization dedicated to perpetuating his name and work, published two books about his beliefs in Atlantis—one in 1962, another in 1968, a propitious time when many American youth began searching for alternative ways of viewing the world.

Cayce's teachings about past lives in Atlantis became an influential part of the New Age movement in the 1980s, as did the energy-emitting crystal that supposedly was the "heart" of Atlantis's technological power. It began the New Age fad called "crystal healing," a craze also credited to Cayce's past-life readings. The clear glasslike minerals were supposed to be able to heal a range of physical and mental ailments. However, with absolutely no medical research to support its claims, crystal healing was short-lived, and dismissed as a placebo. Still, there were many who insisted crystal energy could calm emotional stress.

Of Cayce's fourteen thousand psychic trance readings, more than twenty-five hundred were about past lives. Of those, about seven hundred told of prior incarnations in Atlantis; Jess Stearn found that many people carried memories of their Atlantean existence. In one example Stearn gave, Cayce's trance reading was for an eight-year-old boy who had a vague memory of a previous incarnation. Cayce found the child had a "technical background in Atlantis." In this life, the boy was a brilliant science student who later went on to become an electrical engineer. But during World War II, as a young man he refused to participate in developing atomic energy, because he considered it "destructive." Recalling his long-ago past life, he remembered how the misuse of powerful energy contributed to the annihilation of Atlantis. He wanted his present life to be one that was devoted to "constructive" purposes, Stearn explained.

Cayce always reminded people they had the free will to change. But he held fast to his belief that his visions of Atlantis were genuine, and "he warned people everywhere of the dangers of reliving the Atlantean experience, with the same disastrous results," Stearn wrote. Cayce's influence during America's New Age movement was palpable. By the 1980s, when spiritual journeys were beginning to outpace beliefs in long-held religious dogma among many young people, ideas inspired by Cayce resonated. Reincarnation no longer seemed so foreign or far-fetched.[35]

In America's search for past lives one name has long stood out, Dr. Ian Stevenson of the University of Virginia. He has been called "the world's foremost investigator of reincarnation" by other parapsychologists. Consider one of his best-known cases:

In 1926, Kekai Nandan Sahay, a prominent attorney in India was surprised when his three-year-old son, Jagdish Chandra, asked for an automobile, an unusual request in those years and in that region of India. Sahay explained to the little boy that he had no way to fulfill his wish right then and there. But the child was ready with a quick answer. "Get my auto at the house of Babuji in Benares." Benares was a city about three hundred miles from where little Jagdish lived in a town called Bareilly. Sahay asked his son who Babuji was, since it was not a name he recognized. Jagdish Chandra answered without hesitation, "He is my father."

Since this incident occurred in India, with its large Hindu population, and therefore a ready belief in reincarnation, Sahay was considerably more accepting of his child's unexpected statements than might be the case if the same scenario happened in America. Curious to investigate his son's remarks, Sahay questioned him further, and the little boy willingly offered more information about what seemed to be a past life.

For example, Jagdish Chandra said his name in his earlier incarnation was Jai Gopal, and he gave details of the house he'd once lived in and what it looked like. He said his family had two automobiles, horses, and a carriage, and he described his daily life and routines. He also revealed that Babuji's wife and two sons had died. Sahay investigated and discovered his child's statements were uncannily accurate, including the fact that Babuji did have a young son who died—and his name was Jai Gopal.

Not surprisingly, the story became the subject of considerable public attention, and was reported in Indian newspapers. Others soon came forward to further confirm Jagdish Chandra's claims. About a month after his past-life revelations, Sahay took his son to Benares. There the boy was greeted by a gathering of the curious as he moved easily through the maze of roads and paths until he came to Babuji Pandey's house. Young Jagdish had no difficulty identifying Babuji and other family members. The child seemed familiar with nearby places, one of them the Ganges River where he hurried to bathe, as comfortably as if he'd done it in the past.

The obvious question was whether Jai Gopal had reincarnated as Jagdish Chandra? What else could explain a three-year-old boy's "spontaneous" and detailed recall of people and places he'd never seen before?

By the time Ian Stevenson began investigating the case in 1961, Jagdish Chandra was in his late thirties. Stevenson went to India where he conducted interviews and paid visits to the homes of both families in an effort to verify the story. Noted parapsychologist Dr. Richard Broughton wrote that Stevenson considered this "one of the best authenticated of all reincarnation cases."[36]

Of course, as with anything purporting to be paranormal, this case also had its skeptics. Could there have been an explanation other than a past life to account for Jagdish Chandra's story?

A hoax was ruled unlikely because Sahay was a respected and successful lawyer with far more to lose than gain if he'd created or been part of a public deception. Could young Jagdish have had prior knowledge of Babuji's family or the city of Benares? The child had never been there, and it seemed far-fetched that a three-year-old would have access to such information or that he'd be able to recount it. In other words, Jagdish was too young to have the capacity to fabricate, read, or memorize such a detailed story on his own.

The examination of Jagdish raised another question: How did his past life affect or impact his later lifetime? Stevenson learned that Jagdish displayed certain "eating and dressing habits" characteristic of the Brahmins—a higher caste—something that would have originated in his past existence since Jai Gopal was apparently a more privileged child than when he reincarnated as Jagdish Chandra. As an adult, Jagdish retained his affection for automobiles, an affinity he carried from his earlier incarnation.[37] Eventually, Jagdish Chandra and surviving family members from his previous lifetime built a sufficient relationship to remain in contact.

What if this story had taken place in America? It would have been greeted by ridicule and derision, and branded a fraud by debunkers and the mainstream media, not unlike the Bridey Murphy case. "Was Jagdish Chandra the reincarnation of Jai Gopal?" asked parapsychologist Richard Broughton. Of course, for orthodox scientists mere "belief" is an inadequate answer; proving reincarnation is extraordinarily difficult and frustrating. It requires the dogged persistence of a detective as much as the skills of a psychic researcher. "Reincarnation is a treacherous phenomenon to investigate," wrote the late author D. Scott Rogo.

Whether you believe in reincarnation or not, Stevenson's work is difficult to ignore. For decades he has been regarded as the most notable researcher of reincarnation in the country. He earned impeccable credentials, including a medical degree, and was for many years a professor of psychiatry and director of the Division of Personality Studies (once called the Division of Parapsychology) at the University of Virginia at Charlottesville. He first joined the school in 1957.

Born in Montreal, Canada, in 1918, Stevenson built his reputation in the United States.[38] In addition to medical and academic qualifications, he was a member of the Parapsychology Association, and the American Society for Psychical Research, from whom he had support for his work. Stevenson first wrote about reincarnation in 1960, and went on to become a prolific writer and author on the subject for decades; his emphasis, he said, was on "the survival of physical death by the human personality." But he also wrote about various other aspects of the paranormal, including ESP, telepathy, and a study of psychic experiences, such as premonitions, connected to the sinking of the *Titanic*. His best-known book, *Twenty Cases Suggestive of Reincarnation* was first published in 1966, then a second edition "revised and enlarged" was issued in 1974.[39]

Notice Stevenson's use of the word *suggestive* in his title. Ever cautious, he never concluded that the cases he investigated around the world were the result of reincarnation; only that the evidence he amassed suggested that as a theory. He journeyed to several countries on the various continents to personally examine past-life claims. By the 1990s, he had extensively studied over twenty-six hundred cases. His was not the stuff of supermarket tabloids. For more than thirty-five years, Stevenson "maintained almost single-handedly the only contemporary research program on reincarnation," Broughton wrote.[40] His work again raised the age-old questions: What survives physical death? Does the soul "leave the body" and later return in a new body? Even if there are no absolute answers, as Einstein once said, "The most beautiful thing we can experience is the mysterious."[41]

One of the most intriguing examples in the history of reincarnation, also investigated by Ian Stevenson, was the case of Shanti Devi in India. Shanti was only three years old when she surprised her parents with memories of a past life in a town some eighty miles from where she was born in Delhi, India, in 1926.

Shanti Devi told of being married with children. She explained her husband's name was Kedar Nath, a "cloth merchant," and that they lived in Muttra. She described her "yellow stucco [house] with large arched doors and latticework windows," as well as a large flower-filled yard. "We often sit on the veranda, watching our little son play on the floor. Our sons are still there with their father," she said. Shanti seemed to know details that suggested she'd lived before. For example, she said her name had been Ludgi, she'd lost a child—a boy who died when he was only ten days old—and she described her own death during a "difficult pregnancy."

Shanti Devi was so persistent that eventually her parents decided to determine whether their daughter's past-life claims had any merit. To their surprise they found that a man named Kedar lived in Muttra, and wrote to him. More amazingly he wrote back, corroborating what Shanti said. He was also intrigued by this mystery, so he had a relative unexpectedly visit Shanti and her parents. The little girl instantly recognized the person from her past incarnation. Next, Kedar paid a surprise call upon Shanti's family. Without hesitation, Shanti identified him on sight. Once the story was reported in newspapers, it became one of the best-known reincarnation accounts in twentieth-century India. There was sufficient interest in her story that a committee was named to observe what would happen if Shanti went to the site of her alleged former lifetime.

Shanti was taken to the town of Muttra, where she recognized the house she said she lived in during her earlier incarnation, though it was now painted white, no longer yellow. She also identified both her parents and father-in-law from her past life. Although she was still a child, Shanti began behaving as both a diligent and attentive wife, and a caring mother. Once inside her former home, she was familiar with the various rooms and closets.

One astonishing incident occurred when Shanti went to the corner of one room where she said she'd kept money buried during her previous life. But when the spot was dug up, nothing was found—yet Shanti remained adamant that she'd hidden money there. Kedar admitted that after his wife died, he found the money and used it. Those who observed the event were astounded.[42]

When Ian Stevenson researched Shanti's answers to questions, he found them highly accurate; other remarks she made were also correct. If there was any misinformation given by the young girl, Stevenson did not specify it. "No instances of incorrect statements are recorded," noted John J. Heaney in *The Sacred and the Psychic*.[43]

Stevenson is credited with encouraging "popular interest" in reincarnation. He was especially intrigued by the reincarnation cases of young children whose memories of a recent past life were still vivid, and before they faded as the children grew into adulthood. Shanti Devi seemed to make a good case in favor of reincarnation; the evidence appeared compelling.

But not everyone was impressed by Ian Stevenson's research. Most parapsychologists simply distanced themselves from probing reincarnation claims. If survival research was extremely difficult to substantiate, verifying past lives seemed nearly impossible. One criticism against Stevenson was that he is "pro-reincarnation," therefore supposedly "biased," and not capable of maintaining scientific objectivity.

In America, past lives face a double whammy: Christianity deplores the possibility and debunkers who reject the possibility of an afterlife are equally hostile. But hiding their antagonism behind a façade of scientific correctness, debunkers lash out, accusing anyone who researches or makes a past-life claim of deception or deceit. So, in their view, subjects lie, they make errors in their recalls, they have financial motives, or they have faulty memories that result in "false statements and bogus identifications," as one debunker, Paul Edwards, wrote. In the case of three-year-old Jagdish Chandra, Edwards concluded that some adult, probably the youngster's father was the source of the child's reincarnation claims.[44]

Stevenson in tackling such a difficult area of the paranormal, distinguished himself with "the best contemporary attempts [in] psychical research to compile evidence on so complex a subject" commented the *Encyclopedia of Occultism & Parapsychology*.[45] But for all of his efforts,

Stevenson could not provide proof or a definitive answer to the mystery of reincarnation.

"Most of the best evidence bearing on reincarnation has come from spontaneous cases," Stevenson wrote.[46] He reminded readers that reincarnation research cannot be conducted in anything even approaching a laboratory or "controlled" setting. Only by verifying the information subjects give, that they could not otherwise know, can past-life evidence begin to be accumulated, and that requires "field study," something Stevenson did often.

Two of the ways we remember past lives are through regressive hypnosis and spontaneous recall. Stevenson considered spontaneous cases the most fruitful, and young children the best subjects. That position is consistent with near-death-experience research. Young children are less likely to have the knowledge that colors many adult preconceptions of the afterlife.

With reincarnation experiences, what explains how and why a three- or four-year-old child can spontaneously provide accurate details of some historical era or place that the youngster has had no chance of visiting, researching, or imagining? How do we account for a very young child's interest in a particular time or event in the past, even to the point where the little girl or boy provides specific names and locations that suggest another lifetime?

Such experiences do not happen to every child. However, they've occurred in sufficient numbers that the evidence suggests something is going on. Is it reincarnation? When a young child unexpectedly blurts out a story that he was someone else a long time ago, is it more than imagination? Should parents and other adults ignore or squelch the child's claims? What, in fact, do such experiences mean?

As an example, a few years ago, a network TV newsmagazine program devoted a segment to the story of a young boy, barely old enough to attend preschool, who surprised his parents when he told them that he was a pilot during World War II, nearly sixty years before his present lifetime. The little boy was even able to provide his prior name during the 1940s, explaining that he was killed when his plane was shot down in battle. The child in this life had an uncanny knowledge of aircraft, especially those of World War II vintage. There are too many specifics for us to provide them all here. However, the boy's description about what seemed to be a past-life recall was largely verified, and his parents were at a loss to explain their son's memories of being someone else many decades earlier. The TV reporter, feeling the urge to be the good skeptic, asked the father if he'd given his son the information. The father's look and tone of voice told viewers how ludicrous the question was. How does one prepare a child hardly old enough to read and write with a huge amount of detail about another era, including names and places? And why would one?

The late astronomer Carl Sagan (1934–1996) became widely known through his books, TV appearances, and his popular PBS series *Cosmos*. Sagan, who began with an open mind about the paranormal, subsequently became a devout skeptic, although he believed the universe abounded with extraterrestrial life. However, in his last years, Sagan surprised many— friend and foe alike—when he hinted that one area that might be worth examining was the question of young children who seem to profess past-life memories.[47]

Perhaps what we believe are reincarnation experiences are actually a result of genetics, brain organization, and DNA, even meditation, telepathy, spirit possession, or some other as yet inexplicable cause. There is no single way of searching for past lives. You need not approach it only as an Eastern belief or some article of faith. Whether one is religious or not, is of no matter.

"Andrew," from the time he was a toddler was attracted to any picture of mountains, and before he was old enough to attend school, was fascinated by snakes, although he lived his entire childhood and young adult life in city tenements, hardly a place reminiscent of mountains or reptiles. By the time he was in elementary school Andrew had acquired a vast knowledge of snakes, and swore that someday he'd travel west. Years passed, the interest remained, and Andrew, with a wife and child of his own, moved his family from the city he'd always called home. They now live and work in Colorado, in the shadow of the Rocky Mountains.

What would explain Andrew's long affinity for an environment so different than the only one he'd known as a child? Why the inquisitiveness about snakes, of all things? Some skeptics would suggest that he must have seen such settings on TV or film. Probably, but most children have. Few, however, develop a strong enough passion for the west and its wildlife that they relocate two thousand miles just to be close to it. Nor does it seem Andrew inherited his yearning, since his city-bred parents never had such interests. Might this be a memory of an earlier incarnation?[48]

Author Carol Bowman, who's written extensively about children's past lives considered that Ian Stevenson's "most brilliant innovation was to look to young children for evidence for reincarnation." He found that even children as young as between the ages of two and four have past-life recalls that he often referred to as a "previous personality."

"When a child speaks innocently and knowingly about living before, and so calmly describes what happens after death and on the journey to rebirth, it is firsthand testimony to the truth that our souls never die. These memories present perhaps the best documented evidence yet for reincarnation," Bowman wrote. She also uncovered past-life explanations for her children's phobias. Her young son's "terror" of loud noises was traced back to his life as a Civil War soldier.[49]

One troubling question about reincarnation beliefs is why people choose lives in which they suffer serious disabilities, pain, and sometimes even excruciating or violent deaths at young ages. The answer that some have karmic lessons to learn is scoffed at by skeptics, and even believers often have difficulty accepting that explanation.

Nine-year-old Jacob saw an illustration one day of the *Titanic*. He immediately asked his mother for every book and picture of the ill-fated ocean liner that sank ninety years before, telling her emphatically, "I was on that boat!" Might Jacob have had a spontaneous past-life recall? What "lesson" would have been learned if he had died, a *Titanic* victim?

Seven-year-old "Jimmy" one day collected some discarded feathers from geese nesting in a park. Once at home, the little boy took a pair of scissors and fashioned the tips of the feathers into pen points. He found black paint, mixed it with water and oil, and made what he said was ink. Then he took a lemon and squeezed drops of its juice on several pieces of writing paper. When it dried it resembled, albeit crudely, parchment. Now he was ready to write with a quill pen he'd fashioned from the feather, imitating the way people wrote in colonial times.

When his story was investigated, the conclusion was that neither his parents nor any teacher had shown him how to manufacture a colonial artifact. More curious was why he behaved as he did. When questioned, "Jimmy" insisted, "That's what I used to do before I was here." Further interviews with the child suggested an uncanny memory for life in Boston in the mid-1700s. By the time "Jimmy" was a young adult most of his colonial era recalls and yearnings had faded, typical of many children who have reincarnation experiences. One vestige, however, was a lasting love for early American furniture, and his career choice as a writer and reporter.[51]

Carol Bowman called Ian Stevenson's cases "detective stories." "A case is 'solved' when he finds a child with spontaneous and detailed memories of a past life and is able to match the child's memories to the life of one . . . deceased person," she wrote. "A verified case is one where both sides of the equation match convincingly."[52]

Not all children have past-life recalls or strong affinities. In many cases it is the lack of details that hamper investigations, yet there is enough information to stir a researcher's curiosity.

"Daniel" was in the second grade when he inexplicably began to display an intense interest in ancient Egypt. There was absolutely nothing in his suburban upbringing that could even remotely explain where and why his fascination originated. But by the time he was eleven and in the sixth grade he knew enough to instruct his classmates. Daniel's attraction to Egyptian civilization included knowledge of mummification, even the special jars or vases in which human organs were placed for use in the afterlife, the names and dynasties of Pharaohs, and the significance of the Egyptian gods. He drew pictures of "cat mummies," among other symbols such as the scarab, the sacred beetle of ancient Egypt.

Daniel's affinity was specific to the "Age of the Pyramids," (2560–2530 BC); later Egyptian periods with their Greco-Roman influences held no interest for him. Daniel has never undergone regressive hypnosis, so there is no way to know if more details might be revealed that could be further investigated. It is only conjecture, but could he have experienced a memory of a previous life? Might he have worked in the complex science of mummification in that long-ago incarnation? Today, Daniel is a young man whose career goal is in the field of chemistry, and whether there is a past-life connection remains speculation.[53]

"Elizabeth" was only nine when she and her two younger sisters had the pleasure of a European vacation with their parents. One of their stops in France was the palace at Versailles, near Paris, once the home to French royalty, centuries ago. Rather than being awed by the vast edifice and gardens, the little girl felt as if she'd already been there. She promptly told family members that she knew her way around, and proceeded to prove it by locating various rooms, corridors, and foyers, and how to get to and from them, including secret passageways in certain quarters. One surprise to her was that several pieces of ornate bedroom furniture were on display in a part of the palace where she insisted they did not belong. She remembered the furnishings being in another room and on another floor, in earlier centuries. The curator was startled that an American child correctly knew such details not on view to the public. If Elizabeth was experiencing a past-life recall, might deeper investigation have revealed evidence for reincarnation? Unfortunately, her parents, although puzzled by her knowledge, never considered further questioning their daughter along those lines mainly because of their religious resistance to the concept of reincarnation.[54]

While we're on the subject of royalty, a frequent criticism of reincarnation is that many people claim they were famous or important figures in past lives: Queen Marie Antoinette, Napoleon Bonaparte, Alexander the Great, Florence Nightingale, and the list goes on. That accusation is a creation of debunkers to derail any validity reincarnation might have. The fact is that very rarely does anyone recalling a past life claim to be someone of historical prominence. Overwhelmingly, whether through spontaneous recall, meditation, or hypnotic regression, individuals remember past lives that were generally mundane or routine for their time. Often lives of drudgery and violent or painful deaths are recollected, but rarely are there past-life memories of fame or great achievement. The closest I've ever witnessed was a young man who insisted he'd been presidential assassin John Wilkes Booth in a previous incarnation, more a life of notoriety and shame than accomplishment.[55]

Many women and men have affinities and memories that date back to ancient Greece, Rome, and the time Jesus Christ lived. Typically, people will recall they were peasants, simple merchants, farmers, craftspeople, or soldiers. The downside of their modest past lives is that tracing their stories is all but impossible; few if any documents or records exist to confirm assertions dating back to antiquity.

When a young woman named "Michelle" was hypnotized by an experienced past-life therapist, she was regressed to ancient Pompeii in the year 79 AD, gave many details of her simple life there, and described her death when the Italian city was decimated by the sudden volcanic eruption of Mount Vesuvius. Before she lost her life, she helplessly watched as the sky darkened, and many were killed. Her own home and family were destroyed as hot ashes and rocks fell upon Pompeii, burying it for centuries to come. In trance, Michelle explained her overwhelming grief for her loved ones and the thousands who panicked, suffered, and died from poisonous gas and burning cinders. Is it possible those memories are a link to Michelle's present career? In this lifetime she chose to work in the medical field and counsel the bereaved.[56]

Although Michelle, while in trance, told of her ancient Pompeii experience in modern English, there is another curious phenomenon sometimes observed when a person is regressed to what is presumed to be a past incarnation. The subject inexplicably begins speaking in the unfamiliar language of the time and place of their earlier life. The term given to this is xenoglossy, and while there are several theories for it, pro and con, there is no certain explanation how someone can speak in a language they claim not to know.

"Nicholas" never went beyond high school. And although raised in a New England town, since childhood his knowledge of ancient Rome has been remarkable, especially the military aspect of that once great civilization; he is certain he was once a Roman soldier. Growing up, he devoured every word he could find on the subject of Rome's battles, weaponry, and uniforms. What drove his affinity and the ease with which he accumulated knowledge on that one specific time and place in history? Might he possess either some genetic or past-life memory? As an adult, Nicholas made a career in the U.S. military, leading to speculation about whether there is a connection between his past and present lifetimes.[57]

Another issue raised in the search for past lives is why certain details from earlier incarnations are remembered while others are not. One often heard criticism is, "If you really lived during the Civil War . . ." or whatever period one believes they were in, you would remember everything about that lifetime. Whether you lean toward or away from a belief in reincarnation, the human memory is not as precise as we'd like it to be.

"Our conception of ourselves is strongly rooted in our memory of past experiences," wrote Paul Davies in *God and the New Physics*.[58] But, truthfully, how many of us can recall clearly everything we've ever seen or done in this lifetime? As we grow older, some memories fade and are replaced by others. You remember the names of the public schools you attended as a child. But do you remember the name of every classmate, teacher, or what seat you sat in? The point is why should we be expected to retain minutiae from a past life when we often struggle to recollect details from our present life?

Reincarnation remains at the center of debate about child prodigies. The most frequently cited example is the eighteenth-century composer Wolfgang Amadeus Mozart (1756–1791). At age six he was touring Europe as a wunderkind, a genuine "musical prodigy." By four he'd already composed "Twinkle, Twinkle Little Star." When he was eight years old he wrote his first symphony, and at age twelve his first opera was performed in Vienna. While his genius is undisputed, the question has long raged about how it developed. Were his prodigious talents purely the consequence of his DNA, brain chemistry, and genetics? Or did Mozart's extraordinary musical abilities result from his having been reincarnated? Might the remarkable musical gifts have been transmitted to Mozart's soul or mind from a previous incarnation?[59]

In 2004 on the CBS TV program *Sixty Minutes,* there was the story of an atypical twelve-year-old American boy named Jay who began composing music at age two, although neither of his parents were musicians. He was appropriately described as a "child genius" or prodigy, perhaps not unlike Mozart more than two hundred years earlier. Jay said he wrote compositions he'd not yet been able to play. Usually he composed on his piano, although he could also write music without an instrument. He explained that he hears the music in his head, sometimes even receiving multiple compositions. The work comes to his mind already written, and Jay said he "channels" what he hears, and that his hearing is "super-sensitive." Curiously, Mozart also had an unusual "auditory cortex." By age ten Jay entered the prestigious music school, Juilliard. And by the time he was twelve he'd written a dozen symphonies, one already performed by the New Haven Symphony Orchestra. His hero, he said, was Beethoven.

Is the child an example of someone who has inherited his talents from a past life? Might he have been Mozart? Or are Jay's musical gifts the result of fortunate if unusual "brain wiring," in other words, genetics and whatever cerebral activity account for prodigy? Might he be "hearing" the music already composed because it's being communicated from some other dimension, such as the spirit world? Debunkers pop their violin strings at the mere suggestion of any paranormal or metaphysical theory. As far as they're concerned all of the answers are within the brain. On the other hand, Carl Jung wrote, "I simply believe that some part of the human Self or Soul is not subject to the laws of space and time."[60] If we speculate about the reasons for child prodigies, shouldn't we also consider the possibility of a paranormal explanation? Even if sophisticated brain scans can show highly unique functions at work within a child prodigy, it doesn't necessarily negate reincarnation.

Both Ian Stevenson and Carol Bowman have authored substantial books on children's past-life memories, and there is much more to the subject if one wishes to research it further. The late Dr. Alex Tanous wrote that parents and teachers should regard a child's psychic experience "as a natural occurrence."[61] That's good advice for dealing with children's past-life claims, many would agree.

America rediscovered the Eastern concept of reincarnation during the coming of New Age culture in the last half of the twentieth century. The 1960s had been a time of the so-called "counterculture" generation. Many young people began to explore Eastern philosophies and religions, and there was no way to do that without bumping into reincarnation beliefs. Then from the late 1960s through the 1970s, American attitudes about discussing death and dying had begun to change—taboos were lifting. The first big breakthrough came with a book called *On Death and Dying* by Dr. Elisabeth Kübler-Ross.[62] Next, Dr. Raymond Moody made the "near-death experience" a virtual household expression with the success of *Life After Life* that brought another ancient concept up to date.[63] Soon millions of Americans were claiming in surveys and polls that they'd had such experiences, clinically "dying" but feeling as if they'd left their body for a glimpse of "heaven" or the afterlife.[64] Countless books by others followed.

By the 1980s interest in past lives was in vogue among Americans. A 1982 Gallup poll found 23 percent of Americans believed in reincarnation; conservatively, that's tens of millions of people. The late Joseph Campbell, respected mythologist, concluded that, "reincarnation suggests that you are more than you think you are."

Survey results also reported that 60 percent had déjà vu experiences, the strange sensation many of us feel of already having experienced a situation in a new or unfamiliar setting as if we'd been there before.[65] Some attributed déjà vu to the relationship between the brain's conscious and unconscious functioning; others claimed it was the result of a past-life memory.

Ever see someone for the first time, yet recognize the person and feel as if you've met each other before? There is an immediate connection that seems deep and intimate. That feeling is at the heart of what we call "soul mates," especially when two people in love are intensely and emotionally bonded to each other. Reincarnation experts suggest they may recognize each other from a past life; perhaps they had a relationship in an earlier incarnation. In one experiment, identical twin sisters were regressively hypnotized separately. In a previous life the girls were best friends who lived near each other in the 1870s. Had they chosen to reincarnate in this life as twins to be even closer?[66]

In 1983, motion picture star Shirley MacLaine literally went "out on a limb" in a book by that title in which she revealed her strong interest and experiences with psychic phenomena, especially concerning reincarnation. MacLaine learned about her past lives through acupuncture and consulting with trance mediums. She did not seek regressive hypnosis. In one past life she claimed she was beheaded in France during the eighteenth century by order of King Louis XV. In another incarnation, MacLaine was certain she'd been a prostitute. She also turned to Dr. Helen Wambach, a recognized expert on past lives and regressive hypnosis, to better understand reincarnation from a psychological perspective.[67]

More significant than MacLaine's past lives was her courage in daring to share her experiences in *Out on a Limb,* and several later books. Because of her status as a movie star MacLaine received a torrent of press and publicity for her "offbeat" beliefs. For late-night TV comics, the jokes were like manna from heaven, most ridiculing her. National celebrity and gossip magazines shared in the media hoopla. Few were complimentary, and debunkers mercilessly criticized MacLaine's past lives and metaphysical insights. In 1983 it seemed America's major media were not yet ready to seriously embrace what they labeled "far out" or "weird" paranormal claims. The most vicious critics disparaged the sensibility of anyone who could still "believe" in spirits, mediums, or reincarnation, branding them all quackery.[68]

But millions ignored the detractors, and in spite or because of them, her books became bestsellers, and a TV miniseries was based on *Out on a Limb;* MacLaine had touched a nerve in telling how she discovered "her own truth." She proved to be more in touch with a large segment of America than were her critics. With her books and public appearances, she'd opened the door wider to a second New Age; the first had been the Great Age of Spiritualism during the nineteenth century. Who knew so many Americans were searching for new spiritual paths, and moving away from long-held religious dogma that branded anything paranormal as the occult, or worse, demonic. MacLaine's message was that "we have the power to design the world in which we live, and the strength to remake ourselves in the image of our dreams."

MacLaine had sparked a renewed interest in past lives. She said it was not enough to know that she'd lived before. She had to know "how and why," and "what meaning it [had] for her life, and how it [would] shape her future." She also popularized "channeling," a variation of mediumship. We'll talk about that in more detail in a later chapter.

It was curious that so many Americans considered reincarnation some new discovery when its history dated backed thousands of years. With all respect to MacLaine she was not the first screen star to explore her past lives and psychic experiences. Mediums, psychics, astrologers, healers, gurus, and past-life readers all found a place in Hollywood from practically the beginning of the moviemaking industry in the early twentieth century, and they never left. "A whole new breed of radical metaphysical religions such as Christian Science, New Thought, and Theosophy had begun to take root alongside the mainstream beliefs," wrote George Pendle in *Strange Angel*.[69]

For many decades Maria Moreno was one of Hollywood's best-known mediums and a strong believer in reincarnation. Her list of clients read like a who's who of Hollywood names, and her story was told in Jess Stearn's book *A Matter of Immortality*. She'd been raised in Mexico, Catholic and poor. When the petite, dark-haired Maria moved to Los Angeles, she lived modestly and quietly, and never abandoned her Catholic beliefs. Although she knew the Church rejected reincarnation, Maria found references to it in the New Testament; she would readily quote Matthew 16:13 in which Jesus asked his disciples, "Whom do men say that the Son of Man is?"

"And they answered, Some say John the Baptist; others say Elizjah; and others Jeremiah or one of the prophets."

Maria concluded this had to be a reference to reincarnation, since those who thought Jesus might have been Elizjah or Jeremiah were al-luding to ancient prophets who lived and died long before Jesus.

Maria envisioned an afterlife in which the departed dwelt in other "planes and dimensions" while they readied themselves to return to Earth. She considered her most important message was that we survive physical death—we are immortal, and reincarnation is part and parcel of that belief. "It is a question of evolving spiritually," she said. "People must work out their karma, and by their choices they determine how they shall start their next life."[70]

One well-known figure from an earlier era with a strong sense that she'd been reincarnated was the bestselling novelist Taylor Caldwell, whose popularity dated back to the 1930s and continued for decades. In 1973, Caldwell shared a number of her previous incarnations in a book titled *The Search for a Soul* by Jess Stearn. After a series of hypnotic re-gressions, she came to regard reincarnation as "fact." Caldwell's past lives read like a travelogue. She revealed earlier existences in Atlantis, Jerusalem, Egypt, China, Mexico, Peru, France, England, and Italy.[71]

By the 1970s and 1980s, past-life therapy had become a more serious and focused endeavor, and with it came more questions about the soul, immortality, and "the meaning of life." The interest spurred a spate of books on the subject. Too many to name all of them here.

The late psychologist Helen Wambach wrote *Reliving Past Lives: The Evidence Under Hypnosis* (1978), and the next year, *Life Before Life*. Wam-bach's approach was to gather subjects in small groups. Each group mem-ber was given ten specific "past time periods," and asked to choose just one of them. The subjects were then questioned in detail about their lives during the period they'd selected. In one example, a subject recalled be-ing beheaded in a past life, and in this lifetime, the person was terrified by horror movies. Was there a past-life connection? Critics found the pro-cess "interesting," but subjects' memories could not be verified. Wam-bach also noted some people who'd taken hallucinogenic drugs such as LSD had "flashes" of past lives. In all, she estimated that up to 90 percent of those she worked with had some recall of a previous incarnation.

Edith Fiore wrote *You Have Been Here Before* and explained how re-gressions retrieved "past-life memories."[72] Dr. Frederick Lenz, steeped in Eastern religious belief, wrote *Lifetimes* about his studies of reincarnation experiences, noting memories can come "quite unexpectedly"; sometimes during prayer or meditation. He may have relieved many when he said we do not have to return in a new incarnation; it's up to each soul whether to remain in the "nonphysical world if it so chooses."[73]

Dr. Joel Whitton chose to focus on what occurs between incarnations in *Life Between Life*. What occurs from the moment of death? Once we are no longer "earthbound," what is "disembodied existence" like? In the "interlife," we have karmic lessons to learn and "self-exploration" before we make the decision to return to Earth. "Only through a relentless succession of exits and entrances can learning and growth be achieved," Whitton wrote. "The heartbeat of the soul is to be found in the interlife," he concluded.[74]

Dr. Raymond Moody, of near-death research fame, approached the question of past lives in *Coming Back: A Psychiatrist Explores Past-Life Journeys*, a 1991 book. His thrust was to look at the subject largely for its potential as a therapeutic tool, mainly through the use of regressive hypnosis, to cope with "present difficulties" that may result from unresolved problems in a past life.[75]

And just when you thought you'd heard all there was about reincarnation, along came Jenny Cockell, a British woman whose repeated dreams since childhood were actually memories of her past life as Mary Sutton, an Irishwoman who died in the 1930s, twenty-one years before Jenny was born. What made Cockell's story startling was that she had children from her former life who were still alive and older than her. She told the story of the search for her former family and the surviving children she found from that earlier lifetime in *Across Time and Death: A Mother's Search for Her Past Life Children* (1993).[76]

In the search for past lives some of us are quite content to learn that we may have lived previously, but with no reason or need to delve any further into reincarnation. However, many others want more than their curiosity satisfied. If you sense that you've lived before, do your past lives have any relevance to your present lifetime? Take that a step further and you've entered the world of past-life therapy. Perhaps your previous incarnations have impacted this life in some way, and through regressive hypnosis, the bridge between past and present can uncover the roots of problems and fears, and help to solve them.

When Edgar Cayce began offering "life readings" in the 1920s, he advised his clients how they could use past-life lessons and skills to help themselves in their current incarnations. Cayce was offering a form of past-life therapy, even if the term didn't come into popular use until decades later.

Regressive hypnosis has also been used to take patients back to earlier times in their present lives to determine the causes of deeply held fears and phobias. In the mid-1960s, a Boston psychiatrist, Dr. Benjamin Simon used the technique to uncover the reasons a couple named Betty and Barney Hill experienced sleeplessness and nightmares for two years until they finally sought help. While in trance, the Hills revealed an encounter in which they said they were abducted and taken aboard a UFO in 1961 in rural New Hampshire where they were subject to tests and examinations, presumably by extraterrestrials, although the Hills had no conscious memory of the incident. Only when they were hypnotized did the couple recall details of their unsettling experience.[77] With the use of regressive hypnosis, the Betty and Barney Hill case marked the beginning of the "modern history of [UFO] abductions," noted the late author and Harvard psychiatrist John Mack.[78]

One of the most popular past-life therapists to emerge in the 1980s was Dr. Brian Weiss whose book, *Many Lives, Many Masters* became a bestseller on the subject. Weiss was a practicing psychiatrist in south Florida. At one time he was chief of psychiatry at a major "university-affiliated hospital" in Miami, and he'd also written prolifically in his chosen medical specialty. Weiss maintained that he'd been "trained to think as a scientist and physician," a traditional one, at that. Parapsychology, he said, was "too far-fetched."

But Weiss noted that his thinking began to change after meeting a patient, a beautiful young woman he identified in his book as "Catherine." For eighteen months he employed the traditional therapeutic techniques to help her problems with nightmares, sleeplessness, and fears that led her to become increasingly depressed and suffer anxiety and panic attacks. She also admitted to relationship problems and told Weiss she was "frightened and confused."

When therapy and even medication failed to show any significant improvement in her condition, Weiss turned to hypnosis, hoping to regress Catherine to early childhood. Perhaps that would better locate the source of her psychological problems. Weiss explained that he'd often employed hypnosis in his practice; he found it "an excellent tool to help a patient remember long forgotten memories." It eased anxiety and phobias, and brought to the conscious mind "repressed thoughts."

To Weiss's surprise, once Catherine was in a hypnotic trance she began recounting "past life memories" that revealed the underlying reasons for her "symptoms."

The past-life therapy eased her problems and she was able to move on with her life. Weiss admitted that he had no "scientific explanation" for what had occurred with Catherine. But he wrote, "There is far too much about the human mind that is beyond our comprehension. Perhaps, under hypnosis, Catherine was able to focus on the part of her subconscious mind that stored actual past-life memories," or she'd reached into what Carl Jung called the "collective unconscious" for her memories.

Weiss said he was no less a scientist and medical doctor because of his new open-minded attitude toward survival after physical death and past lives. Still, the resistance by the traditional scientific community and many of his peers resulted in Weiss waiting four years to summon the "courage" to challenge scientific dogma that stubbornly resisted even the suggestion of reincarnation. Catherine, in revealing her past lives, also faced questions about the nature of life, death, and immortality.

We'll skip over the details of Catherine's problems and Weiss's therapy, not to minimize them, but so that we can briefly mention the links her past-life recalls had to her present lifetime.

Catherine followed Weiss's instructions that she "visualize a bright white light at the top of her head, inside her body." Once she was in a "fairly deep trance," Weiss assumed he'd regress her to early childhood to get to the root of her problems. He learned that at age three, her father, who'd been drinking, sexually molested her. With Weiss's help she worked through the fear of her father, their resulting poor relationship, and its deleterious effects on her later life.

But then when Weiss took Catherine's memory back before age three, he said later, he was "totally unprepared for what came next." In trance, she began describing a large white building with pillars. She said she was wearing a long dress "made of rough material" and that her blond hair was braided.

When Weiss asked her name, Catherine answered, "Aronda . . . I am eighteen." The year, he determined by her statements, was around 1863

BCE. Wherever she was, it was hot and desertlike. Water was scarce, and although there was a well, there were no rivers. Weiss asked Catherine to go forward a few years. She was now twenty-five and had a child of her own, but remained in the same past-life desert setting.

She explained that her daughter in that past life was now her niece with whom she was close. When Weiss reflected on what had just occurred he said, "I was stunned!" Was his patient describing her past lives? Thinking as a medical doctor, he did not feel Catherine was inventing what she'd told him. Could this have been a reincarnation experience on her part? She seemed "in touch with reality," Weiss noted. There were no signs of any psychiatric illness, hallucinations, delusions, or drug-induced behavior, he concluded.

Still in trance, Catherine recalled bits of two other past lives. One seemed to take place in the mid-1770s; her name was Louisa, she was Spanish, and ill with a fever. In another incarnation, her memory was of a life as a prostitute.

Weiss said he considered every possible medical explanation for her "vivid, immediate experience while hypnotized." Might this have been "fantasy" on Catherine's part? Before reaching that conclusion, Weiss reminded himself he needed to keep an "open mind; true science begins with observation."

There were more past-life regressive hypnosis sessions; yet in this lifetime she had no interest or belief in reincarnation. In fact, Weiss explained he felt the same way; he "never believed in reincarnation, nor did he give it much thought." But now he began to study the topic, and while he remained doubtful, he found the reincarnation research "overwhelmingly supportive."

What happened to Catherine? Weiss wrote that her "emotional" health showed improvement, and her long-held fears diminished. He discovered what many therapists have, that whether a patient's past-life memories are "vivid fantasies" or genuine recalls, past-life therapy can be very effective. For example, Catherine remembered a previous lifetime in which her father was an alcoholic and abusive to her mother. That provided clues from past-life traumas for Weiss to follow up with therapy to help Catherine in her present lifetime. He had found what he called "correspondences" between her current and past lives.

Catherine later also demonstrated the ability to receive messages from what seemed to be spirit masters. Her voice changed and became deeper, as if someone else was talking through her. Where were the voices coming from? One possibility was that "she could channel knowledge from the beyond," Weiss speculated. Hence the title of his book about his experiences with Catherine was *Many Lives, Many Masters.*

At one point, when Catherine had improved greatly, she visited a "well-known psychic astrologer who specialized in past life readings." To her surprise, the psychic "validated most of what Catherine had discovered under hypnosis," Weiss wrote. Other researchers have found similar results.

Obviously, past-life therapy is not a "cure-all" for every emotional problem. However, it has been used widely in America and proven to be effective in many instances. "Catherine had gotten rid of her distressing symptoms. She was healthy beyond normal," Weiss concluded. For her and others it has been a great help, whether the past lives of the patients can be proven or not and regardless of whether the therapist strongly believes in reincarnation or not. Many feel that America's search for past lives has resulted in a potent therapeutic tool to help with a range of emotional problems, traumas, panic attacks, and phobias. Even scars, birthmarks, and some physical ailments may be evidence of accidents, injuries, and maladies incurred in former existences.

As far as proving that reincarnation is genuine, although evidence suggests it, the question remains open, and perhaps future paranormal and scientific research will shed more light on the ancient and continuing mystery of past lives. The French philosopher Voltaire once said, "It is no more surprising to be born twice than it is to be born once."[80]

7

All the Presidents' Prophets: Americans and Astrology

There are more things in heaven and earth, Horatio, than are dreamt of in your philosophy.

—WILLIAM SHAKESPEARE, *Hamlet*, Act 1

There are few Americans who don't have an opinion for or against astrology, the study of the movement of the stars and planets and how they influence human behavior. Horoscopes in newspapers and magazines have been around for generations; it's estimated there are between five thousand and fifteen thousand full-time astrologers across the country, and some two hundred thousand more who engage in it part time. Polls show that as many as one hundred million Americans "believe in astrology," and many historical figures and events were guided by it. But apparently few thought about an astrologer working for the White House, especially by the 1980s, when science and technology were galloping forward at sometimes breakneck speed. It seemed a contradiction in a "modern age." Who would have believed that in modern America, a national leader would consult a soothsayer or prophet? But that's exactly what people would come to believe when an incredible story broke in the news.

The public learned that First Lady Nancy Reagan had consulted an astrologer while her husband, Ronald Reagan, was president of the United States (1981–89). The public learned it from one of Reagan's own staff-ers. And the consultation wasn't just a once or twice event, perhaps born from curiosity or entertainment. This was ongoing and serious business, and the media reaction was instant. What a story! The sensationalism was irresistible.

Nancy Reagan had a professional relationship with an astrologer named Joan Quigley, and it began a feeding frenzy when it hit the news-wires. The secret of how astrology influenced the daily routine of the Reagan administration burst onto the front pages in 1988 when former White House chief of staff Donald Regan authored *For the Record,* in which he claimed that the dictates of astrological predictions were a constant issue in planning President Reagan's schedule, and Regan had a distaste for astrology.[1]

With the exception of the Lincolns, no other first family was more fascinated by the workings of the paranormal than were the Reagans.[2] Perhaps first ladies before Nancy Reagan were more discreet or lived in simpler times when the media was less intrusive. That wasn't the case for Mrs. Reagan, and a flood of derision and criticism quickly followed:

"Good Heavens! An astrologer dictating the president's schedule?" roared *Time* magazine, adding, "New book tells of first lady's reliance on . . . seer."

"Astrologer Runs the White House," screamed a *New York Post* head-line.

The *Nation* magazine accused President Reagan of being "nurtured in . . . [a] . . . rich loam of folk ignorance [and] historical figment. . . ." The article went on to accuse Mrs. Reagan and her astrologer of "peer-ing into a crystal ball, guiding the policies of the U.S.," which the maga-zine charged was an "abdication of executive responsibility."

The *Economist* described "A star-crossed White House" and claimed "Americans are torn between shock and amusement at this bizarre reve-lation. It is the source of endless jokes and some chagrin. The religious right, thundering idolatry, is single-minded in its dismay." The article continued, "Both Mr. and Mrs. Reagan were known to be supersti-tious . . . but reliance on an astrologer to determine the American presi-dent's calendar is less endearing: it makes the administration look odd and rather silly."

The Federation of American Scientists, including five Nobel laureates, wrote to Reagan to complain they were "gravely disturbed." "In our opinion," they said, "no persons whose decisions are based, even in part, on such evident fantasies can be trusted to make the serious—and even life-and-death—decisions required of American presidents."

It was hard to say if some scientists thought the sky was falling, or if it was just that the planets and stars were moving dangerously close to the White House. This was not the first time in recent American history that science had confronted astrology. In 1976, goaded by a self-proclaimed psychic debunker, Paul Kurtz,[3] more than one hundred and eighty scientists including eighteen Nobel Prize winners, joined together to publicly pronounce that astrology had no scientific validity whatsoever.

They may have believed their word carried tremendous weight. It did not. Obviously millions of Americans either did not hear the scientists' proclamation—or ignored it. For in that same year, 1976, a Gallup poll found that more than 75 percent of Americans knew their astrological sign; an astoundingly high figure. Two years later, Gallup reported that nearly 30 percent of Americans "believed in astrology." Scientists and skeptics must have been devastated at the news; it was everything they had argued against. What happened to the Scientific Revolution that made Isaac Newton a hero in the seventeenth century? Hadn't we gone beyond divination, magic, and superstition? What happened to rationalism? But wait. Newton was not only a great physicist; he had also studied astrology.[4] It also became obvious that many modern American scientists and skeptics were not astute historians or psychologists. They failed to grasp the need that millions of Americans had for a sense of what might happen, a peek into the future. What made the first lady Nancy Reagan different than so many others?

In his book, Donald Regan charged that, "the president's schedule—and therefore his life and the most important business of the American nation—was largely under control of the first lady's astrologer." Regan said the astrologer's timing of events created havoc with White House and presidential schedules.[5] Although he insisted his book was not written with any animus or out of revenge or vindictiveness, not everyone agreed, especially Nancy Reagan. "I wrote about astrology because it was an essential truth about the way the Reagans operated," Regan insisted. The respected historian and author Richard Reeves came to a different conclusion. Donald Regan "had gotten even with Nancy Reagan by revealing her interest in astrology," Reeves wrote.

It was President Reagan's first chief of staff, Mike Deaver, Regan said, "who integrated the horoscopes . . . into the presidential schedule."[6] When Regan learned about astrology in the White House, he thought it was a joke, until it was made clear to him that it was not. Deaver's advice: Humor Mrs. Reagan. Although a skeptic, Regan said he tried, but remained troubled by the influence of horoscopes on the president's scheduling. But Regan approached the entire issue of the paranormal from the perspective of a political operative, an inside-the-Beltway professional, for whom anything that smacked of less than the smooth-running gears of a well-engineered administrative machine was something to be feared. Besides, he was right about one thing: You can't convince the president's sharp-toothed enemies just waiting to pounce that one can time the mechanism of a political administration to what he believed were the vagaries of a prognosticator's tossing of the celestial dice.

Regan didn't know it, nor might he have been able to appreciate it even if he did, but the Reagans' long interest in astrology dated back to the 1950s, not surprising considering their Hollywood background.[7] It is a place where sure things usually fail and only the most improbable, if not impossible succeed. In other words, Hollywood is home to an industry in which success is almost always built in the margins, not on the mainstream. Success in Hollywood has the architecture of a bumblebee, which from an engineering perspective, is not supposed to fly. But it does. That's what Hollywood is like, and those who've succeeded there, like Ronald Reagan and Nancy Davis Reagan, knew this as if it was their mantra. They looked for an edge to achieve success in any way they could, even when it came from the alignment of the planets.

Accordingly, Hollywood, even as far back as the silent movie era, became a place where celebrities, desperate to succeed, sought their career advice and answers in all sorts of extranormal venues, especially in the planets and stars. That's why, throughout most of the twentieth century, alternative cultures flourished in California, where many astrologers, psychics, and mediums have long thrived, and still do. When we mentioned a bit earlier that scientists who oppose astrology are poor psychologists that is exactly what we meant. It's easy to deride those who seek celestial counsel. However, the entertainment industry has always been filled with many creative but insecure people, laboring in one of the most uncertain businesses on the face of the Earth. Scientific skepticism is no match for the hundreds of astrologers, psychics, and mediums who can be found in Hollywood ready to offer advice and direction about careers and relationships that are often built on shifting sands and uncertain dreams. In that environment, guidance from a planet or a spirit is nothing to scoff at, as debunkers so willingly do.

Reagan biographer Kitty Kelley wrote, as a case in point, that in the late 1960s when Reagan became governor of California he took "his oath in the middle of the night, acting on the advice from an astrologer who said that was the most propitious time."[8] The Reagans were "devoted clients" of Hollywood astrologer Carroll Righter,[9] whose zodiac parties they regularly attended, and secretly consulted psychic-astrologer Jeane Dixon, until Mrs. Reagan lost faith in her abilities. Thus, it made perfect sense that Nancy Reagan would bring astrology to the White House from her background in the entertainment industry in Los Angeles, just as it made perfect sense for Mary Todd Lincoln, lonely and isolated and looking for some sign that her beloved sons were nearby, to have brought mediums and séances into the Lincoln White House.

Donald Regan, who only knew Joan Quigley as Mrs. Reagan's "friend" from San Francisco, admitted he was greatly frustrated coping with circumstances in which the president's schedule was decided by "occult prognostications." The astrologer "believed that the zodiac controls events and human behavior and that she could read the secrets of the future in the movements of the planets." It was a conviction Regan did not share, claiming Quigley was not always accurate, and complained that by humoring the first lady, "we had given her control."[10]

Regan found it useless to challenge the astrologer's advice because each time the president set foot out of the White House for an appearance or press conference, Mrs. Reagan insisted the times were to be approved by her "friend." Regan argued in vain that the president needed to be out meeting and talking to people, an opinion not appreciated by the first lady. When he asked whether it was possible that the astrologer was mistaken, Mrs. Reagan adamantly answered that "her friend" correctly predicted the assassination attempt on the president in March 1981, as well as several other major circumstances, even a premonition of "dire events" in November and December 1987. These "events" turned out to be the Iran-Contra scandal, which was an interesting spin on the concept of "events" inasmuch as the DEA investigators later learned, even though their files were "deep-sixed" by the CIA and NSA, that the Iran-Contra scandal didn't overtake the White House because it was planned from the Oval Office itself. Insofar as the Hinckley assassination attempt on Reagan's life was concerned, Quigley's critics pointed out that her assassination "prediction" was actually made after the event had already occurred.[11]

In the Reagan White House, even the reactions to world crises fell under planetary influences. For example, concerning the president's dealings with and comments about then-Soviet leader and party chairman Gorbachev, Mrs. Reagan's "friend" formulated horoscopes to help gain insight into Gorbachev's personality and likely actions. President Reagan's demand that Gorbachev "take down that wall," was subject to astrological timing too. Joan Quigley also scheduled the president's meetings with Gorbachev, particularly in Reykjavik, Iceland, after which Reagan revealed to the assembled press that he and Chairman Gorbachev discussed UFOs and threats from hostile extraterrestrials.

"I asked Mr. Gorbachev," President Reagan said, "what if we were threatened by aliens from outer space? Wouldn't we resolve our differences to resist a common enemy?"[12] President Reagan later made a very similar speech about UFOs and ETs to the General Assembly, whose timing was also scheduled by Mrs. Reagan's "friend." It is noteworthy that Ronald Reagan was only one of two former governors and eventually presidents who publicly reported having seen a UFO. The other governor was Jimmy Carter, whom Reagan defeated in the 1980 presidential elections.[13]

One question that's been raised about Gorbachev is what his reaction would have been had he known that at least some of Reagan's meetings with him were secretly scheduled by an astrologer. The answer is speculation, but consider the little-known fact that Gorbachev had a personal friendship with a well-known Indian guru whose home is in the United States. The guru, of Hindu faith, is open to virtually every aspect of the paranormal. He himself has psychic ability. It is difficult to imagine that Gorbachev would have objected to the discovery of a White House astrologer, since he maintained a longtime friendship with an Eastern mystic.[14]

Other political events, such as press conferences and major speeches, were scheduled according to Quigley's advice and held on what Quigley deemed to be "good days," even if a date had to be changed at the last minute, per the first lady's orders. Regan offered a glance at what were considered astrologically appropriate or good days as opposed to "bad days" for the president:

Late December thru March bad
January 16–23 very bad
January 20 nothing outside White House—possible attempt
February 20–26 be careful
March 10–14 no outside activity!
March 19–25 no public exposure
April 3 careful[15]

And so it went: the days best for presidential activity, and those when caution was to be exercised. Regan complained that the number of "dangerous or forbidden dates" permitted little leeway for scheduling. Still, astrology was an unspoken rule when Regan talked about the president's planned events. If there was a cover-up of the paranormal in the Reagan administration, it went far beyond the subject of UFOs or ghosts in the White House. It was to hide from the public that an official first prognosticator was casting the president's specific chances for success based on the alignment of celestial bodies. At least, some commentators said years later when the story finally came out, the pharaohs and other monarchs who reigned according to the advice of diviners or wizards looking at the stars were open about it. In the case of the Reagan White House, it was as if there was a black hole at the center of all events, distorting them according to an unseen physical force. That force was the advice of Joan Quigley.

There are many specific examples of last-minute schedule changes. In 1981, as Reagan and his top aides worked to free American hostages held by Lebanese terrorists, it became necessary for the president to address reporters. However, when Mrs. Reagan learned the date, she forbade him to do so, insisting that her "friend" deemed the timing wrong to talk to the press. When the president's surgery to remove a polyp in his intestinal tract was delayed in July 1985, Regan suspected it might have been because of astrological advice, a suspicion he never confirmed. Similarly, when Reagan and Gorbachev were to meet in Reykjavík, Iceland, for critical talks on arms reductions, the astrologer scheduled the date of the president's departure.

Regan wanted to bring these scheduling issues up with the president, but he could never establish to what extent the president himself knew of or relied upon his wife's dependence on astrology. However, the horoscope became so much a part of White House decision-making and scheduling that, for a time, Regan had on his desk a "color-coded calendar" with dates numbered this way: green marked good days, red indicated bad ones, and yellow for questionable days.[16]

Once when, by chance, Vice President George Bush raised the question of the president's many and seemingly arbitrary schedule changes, Regan revealed that the first lady's astrologer had determined them. Vice President Bush, surprised and dismayed, exclaimed, "Good God, I had no idea."[17]

If Regan stuck to working the president's schedule around the good days, as indicated by his color-coded calendar, he was able to avoid any conflicts with the first lady. However, if Quigley indicated that a particular day or week was "bad" for the president, his timetable was thrown into "a state of chaos," and any presidential appearances were subject to cancellation or strict limitations. As a result, the relationship between the first lady and Regan was often contentious, and when Regan left as White House chief of staff, no love was lost between the two. That's the story Donald Regan told about the first lady's astrologer. What was Mrs. Reagan's version of events?

When Regan surprised Mrs. Reagan with public revelations of the White House astrologer, the escalating criticism and ridicule forced the first lady to defend herself in her book, *My Turn: The Memoirs of Nancy Reagan*. She wrote, "Astrology was simply one of the ways I coped with the fear I felt after my husband almost died,"[18] a reference to the March 1981 assassination attempt by Bush family friend John Hinckley. She also admitted to her fear of the "twenty-year death cycle for American presidents," and was deeply worried that the attempt on the president's life might be an "omen" of even worse tragedy ahead.[19] Could a future attempt on Reagan be prevented? Mrs. Reagan said that in her emotional turmoil she turned to astrology, but in the spin on the controversy and in marked contrast to Donald Regan's version, she minimized her dependence on Quigley's advice.

It was talk-show host and entertainer Merv Griffin, a longtime Hollywood friend, who initially introduced Mrs. Reagan to Joan Quigley, a frequent return guest on Griffin's popular TV show in the 1970s.[20] Griffin, ahead of his time, often devoted programs to various paranormal themes. He told Mrs. Reagan that Quigley said, "The president should have stayed home [on March 30, 1981]. I could see from my charts that this was going to be a dangerous day for him." That explanation, which Quigley later repeated to the first lady, led Mrs. Reagan to believe she could have kept the president from heading to the site of the assassination attempt. Quigley also said she'd seen in her charts that Richard Nixon would easily win reelection in 1972. However, she also saw "trouble" ahead in his horoscope, which proved to be the Watergate scandal.

"My relationship with Joan Quigley began as a crutch," Mrs. Reagan said, pointing out Quigley's claim that she had predicted the assassination attempt before it occurred.[21] After the Hinkley shooting, Mrs. Reagan was very worried about her husband's safety; she said that Quigley's predictions and advice on good and bad days were just "one of several ways I tried to alleviate my anxiety about Ronnie." From her first conversations with Quigley, she said, astrology "had become a habit." While Donald Regan painted a picture of astrology as a pervasive influence in the White House, at least from his perspective, Mrs. Reagan downplayed Quigley's impact on presidential decisions.

Still, the relationship with Quigley deepened considerably after the astrologer said she could determine the president's "good" and "bad" days for travel plans and public appearances. Soon the two women were in regular telephone contact, and Quigley would tell the first lady which were "safe or dangerous" for presidential activities. The information given to Mrs. Reagan was forwarded to White House Chief of Staff Michael Deaver who would change a date or time if necessary. When Regan took Deaver's place, the same procedure was in place. According to Mrs. Reagan, if a schedule change could not be made, she acquiesced to Deaver or Regan.

"While astrology was a factor in determining Ronnie's schedule, it was never the only one and no political decision was ever based on it," Mrs. Reagan maintained.[22] Don Regan certainly didn't share that opinion and, in fact, saw the astrologer's role in the White House quite differently. While Mrs. Reagan and Donald Regan agreed that Mike Deaver accepted Quigley's scheduling, Regan never condoned the astrologer's influence and saw it at best as a disruption and at worst as the very kind of torpedo that could sink the entire administration. After all, at the core of Ronald Reagan's constituency were rock-ribbed religious conservatives whose leaders would bolt the Reagan majority if they thought their president was being controlled by a diviner.

Mrs. Reagan was obviously aware of the potential controversy if her use of astrology to influence the president's schedule became known so she took pains to cover it up. For one thing, since Mrs. Reagan didn't "think an astrologer should be sent checks signed by the first lady," Quigley was paid through a third person, chosen by Mrs. Reagan.[23] While Nancy realized news of a White House astrologer would be "embarrassing" to the president, she claimed she never realized "how embarrassing." But she said she never felt help from an astrologer was "particularly strange."

Mrs. Reagan insisted that, "Joan's recommendations had nothing to do with policy or politics, ever. Her advice was confined to timing, to Ronnie's schedule, and to what days were good or bad, especially with regard to his out-of-town trips."[24] To that, Donald Regan answered, "But he—or in this case she—who controls the president's schedule controls the workings of the presidency. It is the national chart of influence."[25]

In 1985, after having conferred with one another over the phone or through intermediaries, Mrs. Reagan saw Joan Quigley in person for the first time when the fifty-something attractive blonde was invited to a White House state dinner and she and the first lady met privately for tea.[26] At the time of the first lady's meeting with Quigley, did the president know about his wife's ongoing relationship with the astrologer? Probably not, according to Mrs. Reagan, however, he later discovered what was going on and accepted the fact.

One thing Mrs. Reagan said she never considered was that Donald Regan, despite their differences, would "take this information about my interest in astrology and twist it to seek his revenge on Ronnie and me." She said she was "shocked and humiliated" by the public revelation of Quigley, which Mrs. Reagan had done her best to keep secret. The first lady became, in her own words, a "national laughingstock . . . the butt of countless jokes."[27] At some point, she said she no longer paid attention to critics, while describing the ordeal as a "long nightmare." The relationship between the first lady and the astrologer was bound to come out because it was the kind of Beltway tidbit that reporters loved. Therefore, if Mrs. Reagan believed such news could be kept secret, she was naïve, although the American public itself was far more accepting of Mrs. Reagan's consultations with an astrologer than were the media. By the 1980s, psychic hotlines and professional astrological advice had become increasingly popular, and many mediums had their own cable television shows. For the Reagans, who were a very popular couple with American families, the revelations about Joan Quigley were not even an item. If anything, that was what people in La-la Land did.

In response to the media stories, the first lady said flatly the United States was never run by Joan Quigley, and insisted the horoscope was a personal way of dealing with "trauma and grief . . . the pain of life." Even Donald Regan did not say that astrology guided policy, per se. However, by timing presidential events, Quigley obviously influenced policy. Mrs. Reagan claimed the accusations of Quigley's impact were "distorted" by Regan. For her part, Quigley told *Time* magazine, "I don't make decisions for [the Reagans]. An astrologer just picks the best possible time to do something that someone else has already planned to do. It's like being in the ocean: You should go with the waves, not against them."[28]

After books by Donald Regan and Nancy Reagan on the subject, the third description of the controversy came from Quigley herself. In *What Does Joan Say?* Quigley told her version of seven years as astrologer to the Reagans: "What Mrs. Reagan omitted about the way she used astrology and my ideas would fill a book." It is a different story from what Mrs. Reagan presented, and some critics felt Quigley overstated her role, taking too much credit for Reagan's presidential accomplishments. According to Quigley, it was Mrs. Reagan who adamantly insisted the media must never know that the first lady had an astrologer: "This must never come out!" Realizing the potential media hostility and political fallout, the message to Quigley was clear: She was not to talk to reporters, and if any sensitive issue should be asked of her, Quigley was told, "Lie if you have to. If you have to, lie." Quigley said she did not follow those instructions. She would exercise discretion in her answers, but she would not lie.[29]

Mindful of the twenty-year presidential curse, Quigley was aware that if she did her job correctly—that is, if the president's horoscopes were accurate—Reagan would be the first president elected in a "zero year" to live through his term in office since James Monroe was elected in 1820. The fact is that after the March 30, 1981, attempt on the president's life, there never was another. "Was astrology one of the reasons?" Mrs. Reagan was asked. "I don't really believe it was, but I don't really believe it wasn't. But I do know this: It didn't hurt, and I'm not sorry I did it," she answered.[30] Quigley said she understood her awesome responsibility and placed the Reagans uppermost. "Nancy and I did work well. She trusted me completely and followed my advice absolutely."[31]

Quigley also wrote that Mrs. Reagan's "intuitions about the people surrounding [her husband] were almost preternaturally acute." It was as if "she had a sixth sense about the people around the president. Nancy, protective of her husband at every turn, was almost psychic in her awareness of his best interests and the motives of those surrounding him."[32]

Although Quigley understood that she would never receive acknowledgment from the first lady, she also realized the obvious: "I felt that doing astrology for a president would be a unique experience, insofar as we know, in American history. I would be able to contribute to protect and, at times, to influence this most powerful man."[33]

And exactly how did she help and influence the Reagans at the very outset of their relationship? The first lady's reputation was an immediate source of controversy because many people viewed her sometimes-imperial manner with disdain. The hyperbole reached the point where some compared her to Marie Antoinette, the reviled queen of France, when, during the rampant inflation of the early 1980s, she seemed to spend lavishly on personal items for the White House. As portrayed in a suspicious and openly hostile media, Mrs. Reagan appeared vain and haughty, concerned mainly with expensive china and her chic wardrobe. Stung by media criticism of her ostentatious style and tastes, in 1981 she asked Quigley to create "a new image" for her.

According to Quigley, she set about creating a new and improved persona for the first lady by giving her advice based on aspects of her astrological chart that stood the strongest possible chance of succeeding. The effects were almost instant and dramatic. Within the year, Mrs. Reagan began attending a number of charitable functions and became involved in a variety of public service projects, particularly antidrug efforts. As the AIDS crisis began to build and the federal government was accused of being close-minded about the medical issues surrounding the growing epidemic, Mrs. Reagan championed the plight of AIDS-infected children. Quigley suggests that, following the astrologer's very specific instruction, the first lady generally softened her image by being more accessible and sympathetic to causes ranging from the arts to broader health issues, and even poked fun at herself. The image transformation worked.

But Quigley was far more specific in her book about what she did and what brought her to the first consultations with the first lady. Quigley said she had been following Reagan's fortunes long before he became president. In 1976, Reagan unsuccessfully sought the Republican nomination, and Quigley foresaw that Gerald Ford would lose the election to Jimmy Carter by making an incorrect statement that would seriously strain his credibility. It happened in a dramatic moment during one of the nationally televised debates when Ford suggested that the Soviet domination of its Warsaw Bloc nations was less of an issue than the media made it out to be. Governor Carter jumped on President Ford, demanding that he "ask the people of Poland about that." Inside the spin rooms, the political aides and reporters could smell the blood. And the next day it spilled all over the front-page headlines from the *Washington Post* to the *San Francisco Chronicle,* screaming, "Ford Denies Moscow Dominates Eastern Europe." With inflation kicking toward double digits, the dollar was not even worth the WHIP INFLATION NOW button the president wore on his lapel, the Nixon pardon still an issue, and an American chief executive apparently not capable of taking a free swipe at the Soviets during an electoral debate, the voters threw Ford out after only a partial single term. Now it would be Reagan's turn, and in secret, Quigley began planning how she could help him.

When Quigley went to work on Reagan's horoscope, without his exact time of birth, she had to determine it astrologically, a process known as "rectification." Following that, to prepare the hundreds of astrological charts necessary, Quigley employed computers, without which she said, "The amount of in-depth work I did would have been impossible."

Reagan was born February 6, 1911, in Tampico, Illinois, one of the five presidents born under the sign of Aquarius, including Abraham Lincoln and Franklin Delano Roosevelt. It is an astrological sign, Quigley explained, distinguished by "humanitarian vision." From Reagan's charts, Quigley recognized the president's traits and leadership abilities. Without delving into details, one example, oversimplified here, is the presence of "Mercury in Capricorn, in conjunction with his Capricorn in Uranus," which Quigley explained accounted for Reagan earning the title, "the Great Communicator."[34]

"As with every human being, it was [Reagan's] destiny to undergo certain experiences," Quigley said. "Whenever . . . possible, astrology enabled him to avoid danger, to appear always at his best," she explained. "I believe that God intends certain experiences for each of us. Astrology is God's way of letting us read the overall plan for our lives."[35]

Quigley said she forwarded to the first lady her husband's horoscope with a detailed astrological forecast beginning August 1, 1980, and determined the best days and times for such activities as trips and campaign debates right up until Reagan's landslide win that November. She also claimed that Reagan's chart "indicated that he was vulnerable to assassination."[36] However, his horoscope showed that he had the strength to mend from the bullet wound suffered in the assassination attempt, as well as recover from two cancer surgeries and the stress of the presidency.

After Merv Griffin put them in contact with each other, Quigley and Mrs. Reagan consulted on a regular basis, sometimes as often as several times a day. According to the astrologer, for the seven years she served the administration, she gave Mrs. Reagan the best times for presidential press conferences, speeches, and public appearances and other "routine" appointments and activities, usually down to the minute, by using a "very complicated astrological technique . . . to predict what is happening." She also determined the best times and arrangements for long journeys, including "departure times of *Air Force One* when the president was aboard," and in the event of emergencies, was ready with astrological advice for the first family. "Astrology operates on many levels: physical, emotional, mental, and philosophical or spiritual. The Reagans took complete advantage of all these forms of assistance and advice," Quigley said.[37]

Quigley was also forced, during the publicity that followed the release of her book, to defend an issue many astrologers, professional psychics, and mediums find unfair. Can advice based on a supernatural or nonquantifiable source become addictive? Since you can't test it in a laboratory or point to a set of statistics to prove a point, is supernatural advice taken more on faith than on logic? And, if taken on faith, might it not run the danger of becoming addictive? How different is an astrological advisor from one of the pharaoh's sorcerers? Accordingly, in defending Mrs. Reagan, Quigley confronted frequent accusations that the first lady couldn't make up her own mind or that she relied on the stars for everything. "In all fairness," Quigley said, "Nancy was in no way addicted to astrology,"[38] although she took it more seriously than her husband did. Quigley explained that the first lady only contacted her when it was "necessary." She did not seek help about "frivolous matters," and only occasionally asked for help with personal and family problems. The hand on the nation's tiller, Quigley tried to make clear, was not that of a soothsayer, but that of the president.

Did Quigley know whether President Reagan was aware of her advice? She believed he "had to have known about me and the advice I was giving Nancy. He must have been aware and acquiesced when I gave instructions concerning the timing for certain congressional arm-twisting."[39] Quigley claimed that she also advised the president he needed to order a thorough investigation into the space shuttle *Challenger* disaster, which exploded shortly after takeoff on January 28, 1986, killing the seven crew members aboard.

When Reagan said he was looking for information in advance that would help him prepare for a 1986 summit meeting in Reykjavík, Iceland, with Gorbachev on the thorny and sensitive issue of an arms agreement, Quigley was again consulted. She advised Reagan to press hard for negotiations to every extent he could. She also took credit for urging the president to stop referring to the Soviet Union as the "Evil Empire." His softening his tone toward the Soviet chairman was one of the ways the two leaders were able to create a path of trust between them that ultimately wound up easing the way toward the end of the Cold War.

The Iceland trip was particularly important and required that Quigley also cast Gorbachev's horoscope. Quigley said she also charted Gorbachev's horoscope so the president would have a better sense of the man he was negotiating with. She astrologically determined Gorbachev was "very tough" and because of the influence of Gemini, a talkative individual, "highly intelligent," with the "Aquarian vision of the brotherhood of man that he shared with Ronald Reagan." In their horoscopes, Quigley said she saw chemistry between the two leaders, "one which I then believed could change the face of modern Russia and relieve the world of the threat of nuclear disaster between the superpowers." Suggesting a past life connection between the two, Quigley wrote, "The friendship that developed between Reagan and Gorbachev in this life is a continuation of a friendship from the past."[40] Gorbachev, also interested in the paranormal, was believed to have secretly consulted a clairvoyant in the Kremlin to learn his future.

Quigley said she also became involved in advising the president on the most difficult and possibly the most dangerous scandal during his administration, the Iran-Contra scandal. This potentially devastating affair, which some people believed began inside the White House and led all the way up through Vice President Bush to President Reagan himself, pit cabinet members and federal law enforcement agencies against one another and involved the U.S. government in the middle of a drug-trafficking network and money-laundering ring. The danger of a continuing investigation existed right through all the remaining years of the Reagan administration and was put to an end only when President George H. W. Bush pardoned Caspar Weinberger, thereby eliminating the possibility that Weinberger's notes—notes that might have incriminated Bush—would find their way into court. Through it all, President Reagan seemed a man at the mercy of events. Caught up in the affair and amidst damaging revelations involving his National Security staff and the CIA, Reagan sought to learn when the scandal would end and, perhaps in desperation, asked Mrs. Reagan, "What does Joan say?"

Although not involved in the Iran-Contra scandal, Quigley claimed she predicted it "in a roundabout way," and gave Mrs. Reagan advice on the best way to handle the embarrassment that Quigley said was in the president's chart when Uranus and Saturn "turned against him." Quigley said Reagan's problems in the scandal were fated and thus could not be prevented, explaining, "when the cosmic forces turn against one, it is best to run for cover, and insofar as possible, to conceal oneself until the fury abates." At some point, "malevolent planets had turned against Reagan, and there was no way for him to prevail," she said.[41] Therefore, Quigley's advice centered on making sure that whenever the president spoke, which should be as infrequently as possible, it be only on good days. Much of the work had to be left to subordinates, and the affair would eventually play itself out. Quigley's advice and predictions were accurate, and when Iran-Contra was finally over, the president phoned to thank her.

Ronald Reagan's tenure has been dubbed the "Teflon presidency," for despite Irangate and verbal blunders, his popularity remained largely intact through two terms. Did the astrologer deserve much of the credit for this feat? "Until I took over the task of guarding President Reagan's tongue by astrology, he had a tendency to come out not infrequently with real bloopers and other remarks better left unsaid."

Answering Donald Regan's charge that she'd chosen good days and excluded from consideration bad ones, Quigley said her task was far more complicated, for she also had to provide the exact time an event should take place. For example, Quigley provided times and locations for two debates between Reagan and Democratic presidential candidate Walter Mondale in 1984. She admitted to an error in her advice for the first debate, giving the advantage to Mondale, who, according to the media analysts, handled Reagan quite well. However, she corrected her information for the second debate, to Reagan's benefit. Quigley also astrologically timed Reagan's presidential addresses, including his State of the Union addresses to the exact second they had to begin.

Quigley found: "Reagan had configurations in his horoscope very much like Lincoln's in several important respects." Reagan, like Lincoln, was elected in a "zero year," so there always existed a danger. "While Reagan had times when he could have been assassinated, I was always able to protect him," Quigley said. By contrast, Lincoln's murder was "absolutely fated." Not "even the finest astrologer could have prevented [it]. Astrology, like life, is a rather fascinating combination of fate and free will."[42]

When Reagan was required to attend performances, Quigley checked "his special indicators with extra care." Had there been imminent danger, she would have forcefully insisted the Reagans not go. Where the president's safety was concerned, Quigley said she "stood guard astrologically."

Reporters who covered Reagan were curious why the presidential plane, *Air Force One,* departed at "unusual times." For example, it might have been twenty after or before the hour, no one knew why. Quigley said the times were astrologically determined with Reagan's safety in mind.

In addition to the president's safety, protecting his health was also a major issue for Quigley. For example, in July 1985, when Quigley prepared the president's charts, she realized the horoscope revealed surgery in his future. With a "Scorpio ruler," Reagan had a tendency for tumors, she explained. A polyp had been removed in 1984. The next year doctors discovered a second polyp. Surgery was set for July 10. However, Quigley informed Mrs. Reagan that July 13 at noon was a better time: "It was because of me that the operation was successful and there was no recurrence of cancer between July 1985 and the time Reagan left office in 1989."[43] What would have been the result if surgery had been performed before the day and time Quigley suggested? She said doctors would have chanced not fully excising the cancerous growth. To base medical procedures on astrological timing seems extremely unscientific in today's high-tech medical environment. However, for centuries astrology and medicine were inextricably related, as in the case of Nostradamus, who was both a physician and astrologer.

"Long, complex trip[s]" were an especially important responsibility for Quigley, she revealed. One such trip was Reagan's tour of the Philippines, Japan, and South Korea in November 1983, which also took the president on a number of "side trips and appearances." His travels required precise timing by Quigley, particularly where meetings might have touched on issues that related to the president's foreign policy. Among other presidential journeys was Reagan's visit to the Tokyo Economic Summit in 1986, for which Quigley also carefully chose the president's departure time. When Reagan and Gorbachev met for their historic Geneva Summit, Quigley advised the best times for sensitive meetings between the two.

Quigley determined the absolute best time for Reagan to announce his reelection plans for a second term in 1984. When the Reagans wanted to make the announcement in December 1983, she convinced them that late January 1984 was a better time: "I felt if he declared his intention to run at the time I chose, he was a cinch to win the election." She determined 10:55 P.M., Sunday, January 29, 1984, was best. "The planets were grouped in the part of the chart that referred to the person making the declaration to run. It was sort of like sitting in a poker game and holding a royal flush,"[44] Quigley explained. Did anyone know just how much the president's astrologer determined the exact timing of the reelection announcement? "It was common knowledge among those in the astrological community and others," she said.

In spring 1985, shortly after the beginning of his second term, Reagan became embroiled in controversy when he laid a wreath at Bittburg, a cemetery in Germany where soldiers from the infamous and dreaded Waffen SS unit were buried. Reagan's ill-conceived and ultimately awkward visit to the Nazi cemetery was bitterly criticized by Jewish organizations, especially Holocaust survivors who were victims of the SS. Quigley proudly took credit for timing Reagan's stop so the dispute would be minimized. "The Bittburg incident was brief, and the controversy soon died down. I had defused Bittburg for all intents and purposes," Quigley said.[45] As well, she timed another presidential visit to the Nazi death camp at Bergen-Belsen.

Quigley also studied the chart for Reagan's controversial Supreme Court nominee Robert Bork after he failed to obtain confirmation. "Bork was destined to be beaten," she concluded. When Anthony Kennedy's name was submitted next, Mrs. Reagan forwarded his name, birth date, and where he was born to Quigley. The first lady also asked the astrologer for the best time to announce that Kennedy was being proposed for the Supreme Court. Quigley chose November 11 at exactly 11:32:25 A.M. Kennedy's horoscope accurately predicted his confirmation by the U.S. Senate, which occurred on February 3, 1988.

In an ironic way, President George W. Bush owes Quigley some gratitude as well because it was Justice Kennedy who joined the majority in selecting Bush to become the forty-third president of the United States when he voted to shut down the Florida recount, effectively handing Florida's twenty-five votes to the governor of Texas.

"Choosing the appropriate time for an important beginning" is usually "the most difficult task" for an astrologer. "The times I set are always very exact. Presidential astrology has its advantages. The president can often command that things be done at a certain time in a way other people cannot," Quigley explained, adding, "An astrologer is not a magician. There are always limitations. An enlightened astrologer can help a great leader . . . harness the cosmic forces to his purposes, but only for a time. No one masters [them] forever. Sooner or later they turn against us, if only at the end."[46] As examples, consider the fates of Lincoln, the Kennedys, Martin Luther King, Jr., and Gandhi—all assassinated; Napoleon, who spent his last years in exile on St. Helena and died as a result of poison; FDR, who died in the arms of his mistress; and Nixon, who suffered an ignominious fall during Watergate.

Quigley admitted that her efforts for the Reagans were extremely time-consuming, and the seven years she served Reagan is something she would not do for a president again. When it was over, Quigley said, she "breathed a sigh of relief."

Did astrology help or hinder the Reagan presidency? The fact is that Reagan pulled through an assassination attempt and two cancer surgeries, broke the "zero year presidential death cycle," withstood the Iran-Contra scandal, negotiated the successful dismantling of the Soviet nuclear threat, and at age sixty-nine (the oldest man ever elected president), served two full terms. He was only the second Republican in the modern presidency to do so, after Dwight Eisenhower (1953–1961).

Was Mrs. Reagan an overprotective wife who meddled in presidential policies, or was she so astute in her use of an astrologer that she strengthened her husband's presidency? Whichever conclusion one reaches, it seems undeniable that many Reagan decisions were shaped by Quigley's advice, perhaps, in a way, not unlike the astrological advice given to rulers from the time of the pharaohs and through the Middle Ages.

Mrs. Reagan wasn't the first of the first ladies to consult an astrologer, and she probably won't be the last. Edith Wilson and Florence Harding both consulted regularly with Washington, DC, astrologer Madame Marcia Champney, who accurately predicted Warren Harding would die in office. President Teddy Roosevelt tacked an astrological chart to the underside of his chessboard, of all places, so he could refer to it. *People* magazine reported that Chicago astrologer Laurie Brady advised Betty Ford, who "mostly asked about her husband." In the 1984 presidential campaign, Democratic candidate Walter Mondale had an aide consult San Francisco astrologer Terrie Brill for guidance on choosing a running mate. However, Mondale dismissed the advice and selected Geraldine Ferraro against the astrologer's recommendation.

Skeptics contend that whatever successes Reagan achieved as president were in spite of astrological advice. But it appears his presidency was helped more than it was damaged, if we take Quigley at her word. Some have also raised ethical questions about the propriety of an astrologer in the White House, while supporters argued that it amounted to no more of an issue than any other paid consultant.

What would have been the outcome of the Reagan presidency without Joan Quigley? Of course we can never be certain, any more than we can be sure how history would have turned out if President Lincoln had not heeded the medium Nettie Colburn's advice to issue the Emancipation Proclamation. Apparently forgetting the spiritualist influence on the Lincolns, a political analyst on the Web site Parascope.com said about Quigley's work for the Reagans, "It is perhaps the only instance of paranormal forces having an undeniable impact on the course of U.S. history."

That some presidential decisions may have been based on paranormal advice does not lessen their impact or importance, and if certain events were predestined, then astrologers and psychics were simply discerning that which was already fated. Perhaps without supernatural intervention, American history would have unfolded differently and not as well. Of course, there remains the risk that if some psychic or astrological advice was erroneous, or even dangerously wrong, mistaken policies were formed in much the same way as presidents and advisors err without paranormal assistance. Still obdurate skeptics deny even the remotest possibility that in our high-tech scientific age, an astrologer or medium—regarded as forms of superstition or pseudoscience—might have helped or guided the country just as seers and stargazers had throughout the centuries.

Once, after a remarkable demonstration of astrology on Joel Martin's radio talk show, a respected astronomer was asked to scientifically explain how planets and stars are able to influence and affect our lives. Astrology, he said flatly, should not work. The only problem, he confessed, is that it does work.

Astrology dates back some five thousand years, despite its great popularity in the so-called "New Age" of recent decades.[47] Historians have described it as "the oldest of the occult sciences." Without belaboring the point, astrology has played a role in human life for so long, no one is quite certain exactly when it began. Historians have suggested that astrology is as old as humankind's interest in the heavens above and what connection there might be between the planets, stars, sun, Moon, and human behavior. Ancient civilizations were greatly concerned with the vast universe and how to best interpret and utilize it for life and work; from that came the creation of calendars and astrology, while comets and eclipses were omens or portends.

It was in Mesopotamia, the "cradle of civilization," that Western astrology as we'd recognize it was born, and practiced by the Babylonians or Chaldeans and the Sumerians. Ancient Greeks, probably introduced to astrology from Chaldeans around the fourth century BC, encouraged its study. At that time, astrology and astronomy were considered one discipline; in later centuries, astrology led to astronomy as a separate scientific field. Astrology "is also the origin of science itself," wrote historian Benson Bobrick. Among the famed Greek figures seriously interested in astrology was Pythagoras, and both Plato and Aristotle considered the question we still ask: How might the celestial world of stars and planets be connected to the earthly world? "As above, so below," Bobrick noted. "That is the sacred heart of astrology."

Astrology also had an impact on the study of medicine; the famed Greek physician Hippocrates (460–377 BC) demanded that his students learn astrology. So-called "medical astrology" related various ailments or diseases with the signs of the zodiac.

The Romans simply inherited and accepted the Greek zodiac and their astrological methods. Romans named planets for their gods or deities; those names are the ones we still use. "One of the most influential intellectuals in the history of Western astrology" was Ptolemy in the second century AD, wrote James R. Lewis, author and astrologer. Ptolemy's writings remained an influence for many centuries. For Ptolemy, "astrology and astronomy were two sides of the same coin," Bobrick explained. However, not everyone favored astrology in ancient Rome, although divination was widely used by soothsayers or augurs, as they were then called; some highly regarded "intellectuals," including Cato and Cicero opposed it; even ancient times had its skeptics.

Unlike today when we think of individuals seeking astrological help, in the ancient world, astrologers advised leaders, not private citizens. As the Roman Catholic Church grew and gained power in the centuries following the Crucifixion of Jesus, there was increasing disapproval toward the practice of astrology. Yet the Bible is open to interpretation on the subject, as it is on other aspects of the supernatural. The one unambiguous citation about astrology in the New Testament occurs when Christ is born. The Magi or Three Wise Men who had followed the Star of Bethlehem to the infant Jesus were astrologers and astronomers. Those who've studied the story of the bright celestial light they followed have generally agreed that the Star of Bethlehem was a conjunction of major planets.

Lewis wrote, adding, "the Magi believed, as do many of our contemporaries, that our planet was on the verge of entering a 'new age,' and this particular conjunction was taken to indicate the birth of a new world teacher."

Another often quoted biblical verse that seems to favor astrology is Genesis 1:14 which says, "God created lights in the heavens and He made them for signs and for seasons." Of course, not everyone leans toward that interpretation, pointing out that the Bible condemned all forms of divination that predict the future, astrology included. "You shall not practice augury or witchcraft" (Leviticus 19:26). In later centuries, the King James Version unequivocally rebuked astrologers. Other biblical references to astrology can be found in Isaiah and Daniel.

Eventually the study of the stars and the celestial world became the domain of astronomy, while astrology was denounced as pagan. St. Augustine in his influential book *The City of God* branded astrology as nothing more than "superstition." Finally, astrology and astronomy separated in the seventh century AD. But a century later, Arabic impact ignited renewed interest in astrology in the West. Although Christianity and Islam both objected to astrology, Muslim astrologers were astute practitioners.

During the Middle Ages, the Arabic system of astrology became a subject of interest in the Western world; it was even taught at such prestigious schools as Oxford University as a way of better understanding alchemy, medicine, and meteorology. At the University of Bologna, medical students took astrology courses during all four years of their study. But astrology faced an uphill battle where the Church was concerned. For example, although St. Thomas Aquinas in the thirteenth century believed there might be "indirect influence from the heavenly bodies" on thinking and behavior, he was against horoscopes.

Like a seesaw, the opinions about astrology among the great thinkers of their time rose and fell. For instance, Roger Bacon in the thirteenth century, regarded as the "greatest scientist of his time," was an advocate of so-called medical astrology, he said, in the interest of advancing science. The great Swiss physician and alchemist Paracelsus (1493–1541) argued, "In the heavens you can see man . . . for man is made of heaven."

In the fourteenth century, the hideous plague that became known as the "Black Death" devastated Europe, and astrology was called upon to explain the terrifying epidemic. The death toll was staggering: Between

1347 and 1351, the plague killed approximately seventy-five million people. In just one year, 1349, the Black Death claimed a third of the population of England, and then it reappeared there in 1361. But medicine at the time was so primitive that rather than approach the scourge from a scientific perspective, physicians looked to the planets and stars for answers. At the University of Paris some considered "conjunctions" of the stars responsible for the plague.

When another type of highly contagious epidemic raged throughout Europe in 1557, again doctors sought astrological rather than medical explanations. The epidemic became known as "influenza," from the Italian word for influence, suggesting the impact of the planets was responsible for the deadly outbreak that today we know is caused by a highly contagious viral infection. But we still use the term "influenza," from the old belief that a planetary alignment was responsible for the illness.

Throughout the Middle Ages, several well-known astrologers emerged, books on the subject were written, and astrology was taught at universities. Despite the fact that the iron fist of the Inquisition was under way to suppress heresy by any means necessary, including execution, some astrologers served monarchs and royal courts. Others were burned at the stake.

Later there was a shift in Church thinking and astrology was opposed only when it suggested an absence of free will; the Church stood firmly against what was called "fatalistic determinism." While in the fourteenth and fifteenth centuries, astrology was considered a legitimate science, with the Renaissance, there was another change, and many leading thinkers again branded it superstition. Still, astrology remained popular, and as printing techniques improved, more materials were published in quantity throughout the fifteenth century. But by the sixteenth century, the debate grew more heated, spurred by Copernicus's heliocentric theory that the Earth and other planets revolved around the sun. The Earth was not the center of the universe as had long been believed and supported by the Church. Later, Galileo concurred with Copernicus's theory; the English scientist Francis Bacon (1561–1626) also dismissed astrology as a superstition.

In the sixteenth century, the queen of France, Catherine de Medici turned to astrology, especially the noted French seer who became known as Nostradamus. His prophecies remain amazingly popular even today, as we explained earlier. In addition to what were apparently his clairvoyant abilities, Nostradamus employed divination, including astrology to foresee events. He was also a skilled physician who bravely saved lives during the plagues, and he considered astrology useful for "medical purposes." Also in the sixteenth century, Queen Elizabeth I employed the services of the gifted astrologer John Dee. During the Elizabethan Age, William Shakespeare made at least two hundred references to astrology in his plays. Astrology went through centuries of ups and downs; largely ignored during the eighteenth century, and despite the Enlightenment with its emphasis on "rational thinking," which failed to destroy interest in astrology.

Astrology arrived in America from Europe in the seventeenth century. The Rosicrucians were the first astrologers here, and it didn't take them long to get down to business. Their leader, Johannes Kelpius (1673–1708) founded a society and library devoted to astrology in the Philadelphia area. When Kelpius's organization folded, some who'd been associated with it moved on to become what were called "hexmeisters," or "folk magicians" who became popular in eastern Pennsylvania.

The best-known almanac in colonial America was *Poor Richard's Almanack* written and published by Benjamin Franklin for twenty-five years, from 1732 to 1757. On the cover were the signs of the zodiac, and readers were informed that included were "Astrological Signs, Planets, and Aspects." "Poor Richard," the name Franklin wrote under, was actually a reference to Richard Saunders, a seventeenth-century English astrologer. Franklin's almanac also became famous for his proverbs— "Early to bed, early to rise makes man healthy, wealthy, and wise," "A penny saved is a penny earned"—and so forth. But the almanac, a compendium of calendars, astrological and astronomical information, provided specifics about planetary positions, the times of sunrises and sunsets, lunar phases, when eclipses would occur, and even weather predictions. Farmers found the almanacs particularly useful, and "planting by the signs" was typical. Even Thomas Jefferson was familiar with astrology; in his private library was a copy of a well-known book by a British astrologer, John Gadbury.

It also was not unusual for ship captains to consult astrologers and have horoscopes drawn before setting out on the dangerous seas. Christopher

Columbus was encouraged by astrology when he made his historic voyage and discovered America in 1492; by then he'd read the works of a noted French astrologer, Pierre d'Ailly who'd advanced a theory of significant "planetary conjunctions" or combinations of Jupiter and Saturn at times of momentous world occurrences.

Another curiosity that few Americans are probably aware of are the number of zodiacs that decorate the nation's capital, including several in the Great Hall, the Library of Congress, the building where the Federal Reserve Board holds its meetings, and even the National Academy of Sciences, according to author and historian Benson Bobrick, who noted that outside of the Academy stands a bronze statue of Albert Einstein "contemplating a star-spangled marble horoscope."

It is also possible, according to Bobrick in *The Fated Sky,* that at least "some ceremonies in Washington would seem . . . to have been astrologically timed," including the laying of the cornerstone for the new Capitol building on September 18, 1793, by President Washington, who was a "Grand Master Mason." For the special occasion, Washington wore a "Masonic apron" given him by Lafayette. Among the symbols on the apron was "sacred astrological knowledge." Bobrick explained, "The sun was in Virgo, to represent the new nation's birth." There is also speculation that the Declaration of Independence may have been signed at an astrologically propitious time.

Throughout the 1700s and part of the 1800s, with the exception of the almanacs printed here, Europe was the source of astrology publications; interest in astrology dipped in America during the latter part of the eighteenth century. Its revival came around 1816 after a British astrologer, James Wilson wrote the *Complete Dictionary of Astrology.* For those interested in astrology, it provided information for readers to devise and understand their own charts.

In 1826, the first company in America devoted entirely to publishing astrology books was founded by Robert C. Smith. He printed an ephemeris, a kind of almanac that provided information needed to create an "astrological chart." The ephemeris gave "tables that indicated planetary positions on a day to day basis" so astrological charts could be computed. The book, published annually as *Raphael's Ephemeris* is still in use. By the 1840s, several astrology magazines and periodicals were also being published in America.

In the 1850s an Englishman named Luke Broughton (1828–1898) moved to America and began publishing an astrology journal, as well as distributing British books about astrology. He taught the subject to many would-be astrologers, and wrote about it. One of his most notable astrological predictions occurred in 1861 when he computed that the Civil War would take longer than most thought. The prevailing wisdom at the time was that the war would not last long. Broughton disagreed, for according to his computations, the war would drag on until 1865. He was, of course, correct. In 1864, he accurately predicted Lincoln would be reelected to a second term. However, he also warned of the threat of assassination. In early 1865, he calculated there was danger ahead, and that by mid-April, "some high official would die . . ." President Lincoln was assassinated on April 14, 1865.

Thanks to Broughton, astrology's popularity in America increased greatly by the late 1800s, but not without detractors. Where there were astrologers, there were also debunkers, just as there are today. One of the more formidable was the editor of the *New York Sun*, Charles A. Dana. But Broughton was up to the task of defending astrology and admirably debated many of the skeptics and self-appointed debunkers. No less a figure then famed American philosopher Ralph Waldo Emerson (1803–1882) remarked, "Astrology is astronomy brought down to earth and applied to the affairs of man."

By the latter part of the nineteenth century, America could even boast that it had several "astrological religions." One of the better known was the Brotherhood of Light that began in 1876 with the help of Emma Hardinge Britten, a popular spiritualist in her day. Another was called the Order of the Magi.

In the East, the Chinese and the Hindus long had their own systems of astrology, and by the late nineteenth century, the ubiquitous Theosophical Society that urged its members to learn Eastern philosophy also encouraged American interest in astrology. The fact that the appeal reemerged in the late nineteenth century at the same time spiritualism was still in vogue left no doubt that many Americans were drawn to the "occult," as the paranormal was then called, and it was then that science began to show serious interest in parapsychology.

One fascinating American was a Texan by the name of W. D. Gann, born in poverty in 1878. But Gann was a determined fellow who turned to astrology to make astronomical amounts of money on Wall Street; he'd moved to New York in 1903. Gann predicted the 1929 stock market crash, and by his use of astrological computations, he was unaffected by the economic collapse. During the Great Depression of the 1930s, when many investments and stocks were wiped out, Gann continued to amass a fortune by somehow mathematically determining certain "planetary aspects." Gann eventually was worth fifty million dollars, which today would be the equivalent of three or four times that amount.

The turn of the twentieth century was a time of remarkable advances and discoveries in science and technology: Edison's inventions; the Wright brothers' first flight; the discovery of X-rays and radium; telegraphy; motion pictures; sound recordings; advances in medicine, surgery, physics, and chemistry; names such as Freud, Jung, Einstein, Curie, and Planck. It was proudly called "the century of electricity"; there was an atmosphere of optimism in the country about all that science could do. Astrologers wanted in; they proclaimed theirs was "an exact science," and were eager to be regarded in the same category with the marvels of science, rather than relegated to some dark corner of the much-maligned "occult." If astrology could convince America of that, it would be taken seriously, after thousands of years on a bruising ride through a gauntlet of critics.

So astrologers touted themselves as practicing a science that they claimed, "described the nature of planetary influences on human life," James R. Lewis explained. Exactly how these "influences" occurred has never been made clear. "Most astrologers postulated a universe of heavenly correspondences to earthly conditions," he added. But astrology was an "occult science," many argued, since it "described the hidden forces of the universe," Lewis wrote. Astrology's problem has always been its inability to explain the exact "nature" of the relationship between the celestial and terrestrial worlds.

There really wasn't much difference in the practice of astrology in the twentieth century than there had been in Ptolemy's time, although modern astrologers considered the so-called "outer planets" to also be influential—the ones discovered long after ancient times: Uranus, Neptune, and Pluto. Still, astrologers were wise to insist they were engaged in a science; that minimized the controversy that left other forms of divination, such as tarot, numerology, palmistry, and scrying or crystal-ball gazing, trailing in popularity and more likely to be stereotyped as "fortune-telling." Americans embraced astrology far more than other types of divination. Astrologers who insist they are practicing an "exact science" answer their critics by pointing to scientific theories that suggest the possibility of so-called "subtle and invisible forces of [the] universe," to quote James Lewis. As one example, unseen radio waves support astrology's contention. However, in recent years, astrology has found itself more closely aligned with psychology than the so-called hard sciences.

The eminent Swiss psychoanalyst, Dr. Carl Jung, whose interest in the paranormal was extensive, had a great influence on "modern astrology"; he'd used it in his practice with patients, even preparing horoscopes for some. He was the first to note the value of astrology as a means to better understand the human psyche. Jungian concepts have been accepted by many astrologers, notably his theories of the "collective unconscious," "archetypes," and "synchronicity." Through his efforts, astrology became better integrated with psychology in the twentieth century, so that planets and signs were increasingly considered to correspond to a person's character or temperament. By comparison, conventional astrology, as it was practiced for centuries, dwelt more on predicting events and the time they would occur.

Just as other areas of the paranormal in America produced well-known figures, so too did several astrologers achieve fame. One of them was a remarkable woman named Evangeline Adams (1868–1932).[48] With her hair neatly pinned back, and her wire-rimmed eyeglasses, Adams's modest appearance might remind one of a stereotypical early twentieth century schoolteacher, rather than the most prominent astrologer of her time. Her lineage was also distinguished; she was a descendent of John Quincy Adams, the sixth U.S. president.

Adams, born in New Jersey, raised in Massachusetts, and educated both there and in Chicago, had her first exposure to astrology in Boston among members of that city's exclusive metaphysical circle, and she'd also had the opportunity to learn Eastern philosophy. But of everything she studied, astrology fascinated her the most, and it became her career.

She moved to New York in 1899 and took up residence at the Windsor Hotel, then a prestige address. One of her first astrological readings was for the Windsor's owner, Warren F. Leland. As she worked on his chart she realized there was catastrophe ahead. The conjunction of planets indicated an impending calamity, she was certain, and told him so.

It did not take long for Adams's prediction to come true. The very next day on March 17, 1899, the Windsor Hotel was ravaged by fire. The flames gutted the building and it was completely burned down. The Windsor blaze made page-one news, as did her prognostication when Leland shared it with reporters, and admitted he did not take Adams's warning seriously. Publicity of that kind in 1899 was just as valuable as it would be in our own time.

Adams immediately became well known as an astrologer, and from her office in New York's famed Carnegie Hall she prepared the horoscopes of many famous, powerful, and wealthy people. The entire list reads like a who's who of that era. Among her clients were King Edward VII of England; opera star Enrico Caruso; banker J. P. Morgan; silent screen stars Mary Pickford and Charlie Chaplin; J. Stuart Blackton, one of the founders of Vitagraph, an important motion picture company at that time; stage stars Tallulah Bankhead and Eva Le Gallienne; the writers Eugene O'Neill and Anita Loos; as well as two presidents of the New York Stock Exchange; railroad magnates; and several political candidates. She predicted the presidential elections of Warren Harding (1920) and Calvin Coolidge (1924). Her success as an astrologer was undeniable. Speculate for a moment about the influence she wielded that probably few Americans were even aware of, decades before the flap about Nancy Reagan's astrologer. How many decisions about business, finance, politics, and myriad other questions were based on the celestial advice Adams laid out for those powerful figures who controlled the destiny of millions of lives? Astrology was no "plaything" for many important individuals.

In 1914 Adams faced a challenge of another kind when she was arrested and accused of violating a New York state law against fortunetelling. She could have paid a fine to satisfy the charge; however, she refused and demanded a trial.

Adams arrived in court carrying her astrology books, and then carefully explained to the judge how astrology worked. She ended her remarks to the court by "reading" a horoscope for someone she did not know. That "someone" proved to be the judge's son. The judge, John J. Freschi, was favorably affected by her precision. Judge Freschi's comments have been quoted in many accounts of Adams's life and career.

"The defendant raises astrology to the dignity of an exact science," he remarked and then rejected the charges against her, saying, "no law had been broken and no fraud had been committed." Adams's attorney, Clark L. Jordan, also did an excellent job in presenting his client's position that astrology was "an empirical science." The law, as it applied to astrologers, was overturned, thanks to Evangeline Adams's ability.

Adams went on with her astrology readings, successfully wrote, and lectured to advance the public's understanding of astrology. She also penned a monthly periodical offering her political predictions; probably the most famous was made in 1931 that "the United States would be at war in 1942." We should note that during the 1930s, most astrologers on both sides of the Atlantic had predicted peace.

Then Adams made another breakthrough; in 1930 she became "the first astrologer to host a radio show," noted Benson Bobrick in *The Fated Sky*. It was broadcast three times weekly, and she was swamped with listener requests; in the next three months, 150,000 wrote in to have their horoscopes done. A year later, listeners continued to write at a rate of some four thousand letters a day.

There's one incident that showed Adams could not be easily tricked. A woman once came to her for an astrological reading, and Adams, presuming the horoscope was for a child, gave the reading. To make a long story short, the woman had purposely brought her dog's birth information, apparently to debunk Adams. However, virtually everything Adams told her applied to the dog and was accurate, even that he'd live to a "ripe old age." He lived to be eighteen, a good life span for a dog.

Evangeline Adams was an important force in making astrology popular with the American public. She'd long insisted that, "Astrology must be right. There can be no appeal from the Infinite." But, in what seemed to be a contradiction, she also said, "The horoscope does not pronounce sentence . . . it gives warning." Adams's death cut short her tireless efforts; she died of natural causes in November 1932.

Until the 1920s most astrology books were privately printed. But publishers took note when Adams's books became big sellers; her first was *The Bowl of Heaven* in 1924. That began a trend in publishing that continues to this day; Amazon.com carries more than three thousand titles about astrology.

* * *

Many parapsychologists do not regard astrology within their study and testing of paranormal events. However, what if there is a connection between psychic ability and astrological readings? Specifically, is it possible that some of those who appear to be gifted in astrology and other forms of divination are actually employing clairvoyance or telepathy, whether at a conscious or unconscious level?

One night during a live radio talk show Joel Martin hosted, the guest was a well-known astrologer who offered readings to callers. As each listener provided his or her birth information, Martin wondered why the astrologer ignored his charts, books, and ephemeris, although he did not raise the question on the air. However, after the broadcast, Martin confronted the astrologer about whether he was actually psychic. Although his answer was evasive, he insisted he was an astrologer practicing an "exact science," rather than be labeled a psychic. Perhaps for astrologers—as well as numerologists and others who practice divination—whether they are aware of it or not, might a measure of their accuracy be the result of psychic or intuitive ability?

Another important figure in America's history of astrology was Llewellyn George (1876–1954).[49] George, raised in Chicago, later settled in Portland, Oregon. His lifelong goal was to differentiate astrology from the stigma of the occult. In other words, George hoped to separate astrology from other forms of divination by insisting astrology was "scientific."

George compared astrology to "broadcasting; so every planet is a broadcasting station; and the nervous system of every person is a receiving set." The problem was that George's theory about "physical vibrations" or influences could never be found to explain "astrological effects," Lewis explained, adding, "Astrology was, and still is, intimately linked to the occult," to the frustration of many.

In 1923 Llewellyn George co-founded the American Astrological Society, and other astrology organizations followed; the most respected was the American Federation of Astrologers founded in 1938. He also established the Llewellyn College of Astrology in Los Angeles, and the Llewellyn Publishing Company in St. Paul, Minnesota, which continues to successfully publish books about many metaphysical and paranormal subjects.

* * *

There has long been speculation about what part astrology and the occult played before and during World War II. The answer is that "the Nazis formed a monstrous alliance with astrology," wrote the astrologer Zolar. Over the years the speculation grew into myth until it became difficult to discern fact from fiction. Some years ago, Joel Martin had a rare radio interview with John Toland, author of the highly regarded biography *Adolf Hitler*. Toland said unequivocally that Hitler and many in the Nazi leadership had been deeply interested in the occult, and that Hitler himself had psychic abilities.[50] There were a number of incidents in which Hitler displayed prescience, including premonitions and precognition that saved his life, until drugs and mental illness made him increasingly unstable. One of his first accurate predictions, made as a young man, was that the Allies would defeat Germany and win World War I.

Before World War I there had been occult societies in Germany, and some had become politically involved. Fear, inflation, and paranoia about a "Jewish-Masonic-Bolshevik world conspiracy," as author Jim Marrs explained, fanned the flames of anti-Semitism. Amidst Germany's widening political and economic disarray, extremist nationalistic right-wing groups attracted a following. One of the most important of the secret organizations was the Thule Society, founded in 1918. It had its roots in alchemy, astrology, and Rosicrucian beliefs; and was named for a mythical German island said to have once been a part of Atlantis. The island supposedly had been located in the north Atlantic, near the Scandinavian countries. The Thule Society adopted as its insignia the "twisted cross," better known as the swastika; its members included some of Bavaria's most accomplished and successful professionals and military figures.

One important member of the Thule Society was Dietrich Eckart whose strong interest in the occult motivated him to organize séances at which an elderly medium "predicted the rise of a messiah who would lead Germany to victory and world domination," Michael Howard wrote in *The Occult Conspiracy*.[51] The Thulists subsequently created the German Workers Party that by 1920 morphed into the National Socialist Party—the Nazis. Adolf Hitler became its leader, and there's no question he saw himself as Germany's messiah.

Hitler's virulent anti-Semitism was fueled, at least in part, by having read *The Protocols of the Elders of Zion*, a spurious book that alleged a "worldwide Jewish conspiracy" was to blame for Germany's defeat in World War I. *The Protocols* were proven to be a hoax in 1921, but that did not weaken their influence among anti-Semites for years to come. Hitler borrowed from *The Protocols* when he wrote *Mein Kampf.*

Hitler also loathed Freemasons, believing they had links to the alleged Jewish conspiracy to take over the world. It was likely that his deep hatred for Gypsies was motivated by concern that Gypsies had great occult expertise. The Nazis feared that knowledge could be used against them, although exactly how was never made clear. But they took no chances and rounded up some four hundred thousand Gypsies whom they killed in gas chambers.

In addition to Eckart, another occultist close to Hitler was Karl Haushofer, who'd served in the German military, and had learned Eastern philosophies in his travels. His son was an astrologer who studied the prophecies of Nostradamus. Another in Hitler's circle was an accomplished Russian occultist, George Ivanovitch Gurdjieff. Together they formed "a group of powerful occultists," around Hitler, author Michael Howard explained. Karl Haushofer knew Hitler's top aide, Rudolf Hess, who had a nearly fanatical belief in astrology that later spurred one of the most bizarre incidents of the war; we'll explain that in a moment.

Another Nazi official, virulent anti-Semite Alfred Rosenberg maintained, "The Aryan race had originated on the lost continent of Atlantis which was the source of all ancient occult belief," Howard wrote. The vicious Nazi thug Heinrich Himmler led the dreaded SS, in charge of the infamous concentration camps where millions died. Himmler's twisted "racial policies" also originated in his warped version of the occult.[52]

By 1937, the superstition-laden Nazis had banned several occult organizations and societies, including the Order of New Templars and the Theosophists, fearing that once their enemies learned of Nazi interest in the occult, those same "magical and psychic" methods would be used against the Third Reich. The occult had become a military and political weapon.

Although author John Toland said Hitler was a "practicing occultist," there are conflicting versions about the extent to which he delved into astrology. Most historians think his personal interest in the stars and planets was minimal. Yet the Nazis used astrologers; the best known was Karl Ernst Krafft. Another was Louis de Wohl who, in 1931, accurately predicted the war would begin with the invasion of Poland in 1939. He was also correct about the outcomes of several key battles.

It is also true that the Nazi leadership was deeply interested in the prophecies of Nostradamus. Nazi propaganda minister Joseph Goebbels considered them of such import that he ordered his astrologers to write a "pro-German" version of Nostradamus's prophecies to be disseminated among the Allies and other enemies. According to some historians, the Allies also used astrology as a propaganda tool; they created a rendition of the famed prophecies that was anti-German, in hopes of undermining the Third Reich.

Of all the Nazi leaders, Rudolf Hess was the one most absorbed with astrology. As a result, Hess became the center of one of the strangest episodes of the war. In May 1941, Hess—for reasons that are still disputed—took it upon himself to secretly fly to England on a self-appointed "peace mission," and it was connected to astrology.

One version is that the inexplicable event was spurred by the British Secret Service to "lure" Hess to Great Britain in the early summer of 1941, according to Michael Howard, who explained an astrologer working for British Intelligence fed Hess a concocted story that on a certain date, "the position of six planets in the zodiac sign of Taurus coincided with the full moon." Hess considered it a positive portend or "omen," and so decided May 10 would be the date for his so-called "peace mission" to England. He made his "ill-fated" flight in a small plane, parachuted into Scotland, and was arrested and imprisoned. Some in British Intelligence at the time suggested Hess be questioned about what part the occult played in the Nazi regime; but the idea was overruled and the interrogation never took place.

The Allies reported Hess's escapade as far and wide as they could; it was an obvious embarrassment to the Third Reich and a betrayal to Hitler who exploded in rage over the incident. Hess had been his closest and most trusted aide, and Hitler had no advance knowledge of the bizarre flight. The führer insisted Hess's actions were the work of one demented individual and blamed Hess's involvement in astrology and the occult for the harebrained scheme; while the Nazi press claimed Hess was mentally ill. That was undoubtedly true, but it was a bitterly ironic assessment from the Nazi madmen; some of the most deranged and twisted people to ever rule a nation.

Hitler's response did not end with his temper tantrums. In cruel retaliation, he ordered the Gestapo, his brutal secret police, to round up hundreds of astrologers, psychics, diviners, and fortune-tellers. They were mercilessly interrogated to determine if any of them knew Hess or other Nazi higher-ups. Astrology and the occult were banned, and many astrologers and psychic practitioners were thrown into concentration camps—including the astrologer Karl Krafft who died in Nazi captivity in January 1945.

When several astrologers dared to tell Hitler that invading Russia would result in calamity for the Nazis—comparing Hitler's fate to Napoleon's—the führer became so enraged that he had the offending astrologers killed.

Before the Hess flight, Hitler had approved of using psychics with "powers" to hinder British radar and thwart the RAF's bombing missions over Germany. There were rumors that the English were employing the same technique; British Intelligence was thought to have used psychics in an effort to avert German Luftwaffe attacks against English cities. There's no doubt that British Intelligence was curious about the Nazi fascination with the occult. Among the so-called occult practitioners the English pressed into service was an astrologer whose responsibility was to study Hitler's horoscope, and to report to the British War Office about what military recommendations Hitler was receiving from German astrologers. British Intelligence also had its astrologers fabricate bogus predictions that Germany could not win the war, and fake astrology magazines were secreted into Nazi-occupied countries throughout Europe with that message. The British had turned to the prophecies of Nostradamus, who in the sixteenth century, four hundred years earlier, predicted the rise and fall of a European dictator named Hister, an apparent play on the name Hitler.

As the Third Reich crumbled around him in early 1945, Goebbels found two horoscopes that de Wohl had prepared, one predicting peace by August 1945, and another that foresaw FDR's death in April of that year. Goebbels twisted the meaning in favor of the Nazis; he was wrong. The Allies crushed Germany and Japan, and World War II finally ended in August—just as the astrologer had foretold.

One prediction that fortunately did not come true was Hitler's boast that his murderous Third Reich would last "a thousand years." The Nazi butchers came to their ignominious end after only twelve years, still too long a time.

Britain's prime minister Winston Churchill kept information about the Nazis and the occult hidden. Exactly why is open to speculation but American Intelligence surely knew of the British position, and apparently agreed with it, for the American public was also officially kept in the dark about the "Occult Reich," although rumors circulated.

Consider the events that occurred after the war was over. The victorious Allies ordered the Nuremburg trials where the top Nazi echelon were tried as war criminals, among them astrology-obsessed Rudolf Hess. The Allies—that included the United States and England—did not permit any information about the Nazi involvement with astrology or any aspect of the occult to be presented at the trials. Why was that? The Allies trying the Nazi higher-ups responsible for the war and the Holocaust that killed millions had pressed for the death penalty against Hitler's captured henchmen. Prosecutors feared that if word leaked that the Nazi thugs had been deeply involved in the occult, consulted astrologers, and used psychics, there was a chance the defendants might have been judged insane and would therefore escape the gallows.

Whatever influence astrology and the paranormal had in the planning, fighting, and outcome of World War II was suppressed. Secretly, both sides in the war had sought to use the so-called occult, but publicly, they denied it. The obvious question is, if employing the paranormal or occult was such a grave sign of mental instability, why had so many political, military, and intelligence figures turned to it, especially in time of war? Could it be that astrologers, psychics, and mediums provided answers that were accurate and useful?

Where the paranormal was concerned, hypocrisy remained its yoke. Both Churchill and President Franklin Delano Roosevelt had privately consulted astrologers and psychics. In fact, in late 1944 and early 1945, only months before his death, Roosevelt sought advice from astrologer and psychic Jeane Dixon; among the questions FDR put to her concerned her predictions about postwar policy, and his dealings with the Soviet dictator Stalin once the war ended. FDR ignored Dixon's advice to not give too much of Europe to Stalin. In doing that, he allowed Stalin to gain control over much of Eastern Europe, which fell under Communist domination. That, in turn, led to the forty-year "Cold War" between the United States and the Soviet Union that ironically ended under the presidency of Ronald Reagan whose timing and tactics, as we explained before, may have been influenced by an astrologer.[53]

There had been popular horoscope columns in England before and after the war. Following the war American newspapers increasingly published astrology columns based on "sun signs," the simplest and some would say most generalized form of the horoscope, based on the sign of the zodiac a person was born under, for example, Capricorn, Aquarius, Pisces, Aires, Taurus, and so on. Professional astrologers dislike sun sign horoscopes; they are often not accurate, and ignore other "astrological influences." Thus, they've become an easy target for skeptics. Nonetheless, their popularity grew to the point where they became a feature in thousands of newspapers and magazines. For instance, the late American astrologer Sydney Omarr (1926–2003) reached millions of readers through his columns and books, and his horoscopes became "the most widely read in the world." His books "sold fifty million copies worldwide."

Another important figure in the history of astrology is Dane Rudhyar (1895–1985). Born and raised in France, Rudhyar moved to the United States as a young man. A prolific writer, as well as a composer and artist, Rudhyar became influential in a movement he called "humanistic astrology."[54]

Although much can be written about him, for reasons of limited space, his most significant contribution was his effort "that reoriented twentieth-century astrology from the predictions of events to its present emphasis on the analysis of personality," explained James R. Lewis.

Rudhyar, influenced by Jung's work, came to the conclusion that he could "develop a series of connections between Jungian concepts and a reformulated type of astrology." Rudhyar employed Jung's concept of "synchronicity" to propose that the planets and stars had no "direct effect" on people. Rather, he suggested that the "astrological chart" had a "coincidental relationship to the individual's psychological makeup," Lewis explained, adding that Rudhyar's conclusion was that "astrological forces do not determine but merely suggest a future with which the individual might cooperate." His perspicacity helped remove the stigma that lumped astrology with so-called "fortune-telling." He urged professional astrologers to move in the direction of helping people by integrating astrology with psychology, the idea that Jung had espoused years earlier. In a sense then, astrologers would function as "counselors."

Rudhyar's most famous client was Elvis Presley (1935–1977).[55] When Elvis burst forward in January 1956 with a song called "Heartbreak Hotel," he immediately became a national sensation. The strikingly handsome young man from Tupelo, Mississippi, and then Memphis, Tennessee, became an American icon; proclaimed the "King of Rock and Roll" with hit after hit, and a string of movies. But behind the celebrity and all its trappings, was another Elvis Presley, one few people knew. That was the Elvis who had a deep interest in metaphysics and "spiritual studies." He practiced meditation, was intrigued by numerology, and believed in reincarnation. He also held firm religious beliefs; he'd been raised as a fundamentalist Christian. He was a voracious reader about "spiritual teachings, philosophy, and esoteric arts," wrote his "close friend and spiritual advisor" Larry Geller in *If I Can Dream: Elvis' Own Story*. Eventually, Elvis accumulated a substantial private library of nearly a thousand books about a wide range of psychic, spiritual, and esoteric subjects, ranging from the writings of St. Augustine to Mary Baker Eddy and Kahlil Gibran's *The Prophet*.

Sometime in the early 1960s, Geller arranged for Elvis to have his "horoscope drawn." At the time, astrology was becoming increasingly popular, and so Geller introduced Elvis to a family friend and teacher of his, "world-famous astrologer" Dane Rudhyar who prepared a chart for Elvis that predicted "some kind of crisis after the age of thirty-seven," which would have meant 1972.

In 1972 Elvis referred back to Rudhyar's horoscope. "I mean, 1972 was the worst year of my life since my mom died in '58," Elvis said. Nineteen seventy-two was the year that his wife, Priscilla, left him for another man. Elvis was devastated by the breakup; Dane Rudhyar had been accurate. Elvis was twenty-four when he met fourteen-year-old Priscilla Beaulieu in 1959, and attributed his immediate attraction to her to reincarnation.

So is there any basis for believing astrology is genuine? To answer that we come now to one of astrology's most intriguing stories, which began in France before it became a scandal in America.

Michel and Françoise Gauquelin were both psychologists who worked in France. Françoise was also a statistician when Michel (1928–1991) acquainted her with his interest in a scientific examination of astrology. His curiosity centered around the age-old question of whether the heavenly bodies—planets and stars—had influence on human activity and behavior.[56]

For thirty years the couple worked together and the result of their efforts was something that became known as "the Gauquelin Mars effect with sports champions." But it wasn't only the planet Mars they studied; there was also Venus, Jupiter, Saturn, and the Moon, the "four most visible planets." Michel Gauquelin's specific goal was to determine if there was any correlation between the position of the planets and such aspects of people's lives as their occupation and disposition or temperament. Conventional scientific thinking, of course, was adamant that no such connection existed. But the Gauquelins ignored critics and skeptics as they methodically analyzed information and details gathered from some fifteen thousand skilled people. James Lewis explained the couple began by first amassing the birth information from thousands throughout Europe; then examined "natal planetary positions" with regard to "profession and personality."

To their surprise, the Gauquelins discovered that there were significant correlations between particular planets and certain professions, such as "athletes, soldiers, performers, artists, musicians, scientists, and politicians." For example, the planet Mars was frequently discovered to be close to the "meridian" in the birth charts of those who excelled in sports or athletic ability. That became known as the "Mars effect."

Examining other planetary correlations to careers, they found a "similar pattern" between noteworthy scientists and the planet Saturn. Creativity was related to the position of the Moon. The couple also examined about sixteen thousand "parent-child pairs" that revealed, "Similar planetary constellations preside at the birth of parents and their children in a statistically significant way," Lewis explained.

When the results were made public throughout the United States and Europe, skeptics and traditional scientists, bound in self-imposed straight-jackets of narrow scientific dogma, howled in protest. How could anyone find validity in astrology? Groups of scientists came together, formed committees, and challenged the Gauquelins' findings, certain they could be debunked. Orthodox science would save the world from astrology, but to their shock and frustration, traditional scientists found they were unable to discredit the Gauquelins' conclusions even after the strictest tests. In fact, none of the criticism or efforts to rebut the Gauquelins was successful; as one well-known British astrologer, John Addey noted, despite being "confronted by a mountain of prejudice against astrology in an age which demands secure empirical evidence." There were recurring efforts by antagonistic critics—mainly scientists—but they too failed to derail the Gauquelins. Later, Françoise Gauquelin conducted another study and found that the planetary correlations to certain vocations also applied to skilled people who were not well known. In all, the Gauquelins' collaboration lasted thirty years, until 1980. The full account of their work took up twenty-three volumes.

Although astrologers such as James R. Lewis proclaimed that the Gauquelins' research "provided the most rigorous scientific evidence for the validity of astrology," others have said the Gauquelins' results were not "traditional astrology." Aware of the severe criticism, they called their work "cosmobiology" or "planetary heredity," in an attempt to minimize the use of the term "astrology." Still, they were bombarded by attacks from skeptics and scientists.

To the chagrin of debunkers, their repeated efforts to discredit the Gauquelins failed. In fact, the skeptics strengthened the research by confirming the Gauquelins initial findings. "The significance of their work is such that no research validating astrology is more frequently cited," Lewis noted.

But the story of the Gauquelins did not go quietly into the night. What would the paranormal be without contentious debate? So it was, through no fault of their own, that the "Mars effect" became the subject of the oddly titled "sTARBABY scandal," a major embarrassment for skeptics. The term is actually a "play on words" that is an indirect reference to the nineteenth-century tales of Uncle Remus, written by the Southern author Joel Chandler Harris, the most popular of which was the story of Br'er Rabbit and the Tar Baby.

In the fable, Br'er Fox wanted to catch Br'er Rabbit, so the wily fox created something called the "Tar Baby," a sticky contraption he made from tar and turpentine, and set it in the middle of the road where the rabbit was sure to see it. When Br'er Rabbit came upon the Tar Baby he couldn't resist challenging it, but he was unable to force it to respond. So he struck the Tar Baby only to become caught in the gooey mess. The more Br'er Rabbit tried to move the Tar Baby the more he stuck to it and made his predicament worse.

The analogy to the debunkers was perfect. In their effort to discredit the Gauquelins, they found themselves mired deeper and deeper in a sticky fix much like Br'er Rabbit. Around 1975, a philosophy professor at the State University of New York at Buffalo, Paul Kurtz, an avowed debunker and atheist, gathered the support of 186 scientists to issue a strong denunciation of astrology. Then he published the statement in a magazine he edited, *The Humanist,* in the September–October 1975 issue. Astrology was described as an "irrational superstition," and all astrologers were labeled "charlatans." Kurtz made his diatribe available to others in the media. To his surprise and delight, the press lapped up the story and it was widely publicized. In fact, Kurtz was so pleased by the response, it motivated him to begin an organization in 1976 called the Committee for the Scientific Investigation of Claims of the Paranormal, a mouthful, better known in psychic circles by its acronym CSICOP.

In the same issue of *The Humanist* was another antiastrology article by Lawrence E. Jerome, titled "Astrology: Magic or Science?" In that piece, the Gauquelins' findings of "significant correlations" or "astrological relationships" between certain planetary positions at birth and the choice of profession were sharply denounced. It was hardly the first time the Gauquelins were attacked by the opposition, but Michel Gauquelin was particularly incensed with Jerome's article, and hinted he might bring a lawsuit claiming his work had been misstated in *The Humanist.*

That prompted Kurtz's next move; CSICOP launched a full-blown assault on the French psychologist and the Mars effect. Kurtz, brimming with self-confidence, threw a challenge to Gauquelin. Kurtz was certain that if the tests were done correctly, the Gauquelins' research would be debunked. *The Humanist* dared the couple to submit their findings to Kurtz to be "empirically tested"; the skeptics would compare the birth information of athletes to non-athletes. Gauquelin agreed and Kurtz and his self-satisfied fellow debunkers sat back, waiting to be proven correct.

But similar to Br'er Rabbit and the Tar Baby, that's not how the results unfolded. To the shock and dismay of Kurtz and his cohorts, *The Humanist* tests "confirmed the Gauquelins' original findings," Lewis wrote.

Kurtz was beside himself with frustration and humiliation. But what could he do now? He was a skeptic. His goal was to challenge their findings. Kurtz could not bring himself to publicly admit there may be some validity to the Gauquelins' theories. So he criticized "the validity of the Gauquelins' original sample of athletes," Lewis explained, and issued another challenge to them that resulted in yet a further test of the Mars effect under the auspices of CSICOP. One of the group's cofounders, Dennis Rawlins who specialized in planetary movement was placed in charge of computing the results.

However, Rawlins said he discovered the Mars effect seemed to be genuine. Rawlins later described Kurtz's reaction to that news as bordering on agony. It was another bitter disappointment for the debunkers. But, again like the foolish rabbit, Kurtz only plunged further into the tar. He gave Rawlins samples of athletes who demonstrated very low correlations with Mars; that, of course, would negate the original findings. Rawlins realized that Kurtz was manipulating samples to guarantee he could disprove the Mars effect.

Kurtz apparently misjudged Dennis Rawlins's integrity; he refused to participate in any CSICOP conspiracy to conceal or obfuscate the Gauquelins' results. Rawlins appealed to his colleagues, explaining his position. Their reaction was to expel him from CSICOP, rather than allow the truth to be told that the Gauquelins were right and the debunkers were wrong. But in his zeal, Kurtz published his own version of CSICOP's test results, telling readers that the Mars effect had absolutely been debunked.

Rawlins was furious with Kurtz's opinion. He chose *Fate* magazine for his reply about what he called the "sTARBABY exposé." It was published in the October 1981 issue of *Fate*, probably the most popular magazine in the country dealing with the paranormal. Rawlins also found support from another researcher, Patrick Curry, who would publish his positive findings about the Mars effect in a different magazine in early 1982. What followed was a commotion across the country among astrologers, parapsychologists, scientists, and skeptics, many of whom dubbed the sordid affair the "sTARBABY scandal." One of the most vocal and relentless critics of CSICOP's behavior was the late parapsychologist Stephen Kaplan (1940–1995). In hundreds of radio and TV talk show appearances he reminded the public about the "sTARBABY scandal," and the debunker he sarcastically nicknamed "Br'er Kurtz."

Eventually, Kurtz and CSICOP had no choice but to "sort of" confess. CSICOP would never admit to its own chicanery, but it acknowledged that it had "reappraised" some of the shortcomings in its tests. Of course, CSICOP could never bring itself to admit that whatever caused the Mars effect was anything "astrological."

Some concluded that the "sTARBABY scandal" revealed as much about the self-proclaimed debunkers as it did about astrology. The skeptics were quick to attack when they suspected psychic fraud, but CSICOP hurt its own credibility and revealed a stunning level of hypocrisy that hurt serious paranormal research. The debunkers showed their readiness to manipulate research findings if they did not conform to their expectations. We'll talk more about the role of the psychic debunkers and skeptics in a later chapter.

By the 1960s, astrology's appeal had widened in America, spurred by the "counterculture." The hit Broadway musical *Hair* featured the song "Age of Aquarius," which put the idea into the minds of millions who probably did not know what it even meant. Technically, the Age of Aquarius is one of twelve consecutive periods of 2150 years each, and each period coincides with one of the twelve signs of the zodiac. Some say in the new millennium we moved from the Age of Pisces that began in the time of Jesus and into the Age of Aquarius, while other astrologers disagree, claiming we have a way to go before we arrive. It all depends on how the dates are calculated. The Age of Aquarius supposedly will be more positive than the Age of Pisces. However, the oversimplification that any long period of time is all positive or negative is open to serious question, and whether any lengthy historical epoch can be controlled or heavily influenced by the supremacy of a certain astrological sign remains open to debate.

However, as a metaphor, the Age of Aquarius fit perfectly into the counterculture movement that began in the 1960s with hippies and "flower children," and then escalated into rebellions, protests, drug experimentation, and social revolution. That tumultuous decade did create a climate of change and open-mindedness that resulted in the so-called New Age, a broader term for what was initially dubbed the Age of Aquarius.[57]

Since the 1970s, polls estimate that anywhere from 30 to 40 percent of Americans "believe in astrology and think their lives are governed by the stars." That works out to at least one hundred million Americans. About ten million have consulted astrologers, nearly everyone knows their birth sign, and Internet sites devoted to astrology number in the thousands. "People want to believe astrology, they want to know their place in the universe," suggested author Peter Whitfield. "Astrology is deeply rooted in the human soul," concluded Carl Jung. Ironically, perhaps, the computer age hasn't dampened the interest; today many astrologers prepare charts with the use of sophisticated computer programs. Astrology—now referred to as "astral science" by some—has been found useful in meteorology. One example is that "planetary conjunctions and oppositions appear to affect the development of tornadoes," explained Bobrick. It's long been known that disruptions of the sun's magnetic field have influence on Earth; and who isn't familiar with the affect of the Moon on tides?

Meanwhile, "some investors are turning to astroeconomics, the art of using astrological cycles to predict financial asset prices," according to a *Reuters* story in 2001. In other words, many "traders and investors use financial astrology . . . correlations between past [stock] market events and the alignment of the planets, sun, and moon to predict market movements."

Yes, quite a few astrologers wrongly predicted John Kerry would win the 2004 presidential election. In their defense, astrologers point out that weather forecasting is sometimes equally inaccurate, and even wrong astrological predictions don't seem to damage its popularity. But studies continue: A poll taken in 2003 found that "Sagittarians and Scorpios speed more than drivers with other signs. Those born under Gemini love their cars the most, Pisceans are the most patient behind the wheel, and Librans are the least bothered by traffic jams."

While we continue to ponder and debate what invisible forces connect the earthly and heavenly worlds to make astrology possible, what about determining future events? How do we interpret Nostradamus, whose prophecies were a result of clairvoyance, divination, and astrology? For more than four hundred years, many have wondered about a puzzling reference he made to "rare birds [that] will cry in the air, 'Now! Now!' After that, there will be terrible battles, wars, and destruction, and the last coming of the Antichrist," he predicted. Did the sixteenth-century seer gaze into the future to see danger, and try to forewarn the world of a pandemic of deadly bird flu, and years of widespread terrorism and war? For critics who argue that it is easy to decipher such events after they have occurred, historian John Hogue had this to say: "As long as human beings are provoked into thinking about their tomorrow, they may find the courage to change today."

Meanwhile, astrology has withstood five thousand years of scrutiny. It "maintains an unshakeable hold on the human mind," said historian Benson Bobrick.[58] But astrology, once reserved for kings, queens, and the privileged, now is available to anyone from private citizens to Wall Street tycoons, celebrities, and, yes, even presidents of the United States.

8

Ghosts, Spirits, and Demons in America

Vision is the art of seeing things invisible.
—JONATHAN SWIFT

The Amityville Horror house on Long Island, made famous in the book and in the motion picture, may have become the most famous haunted house story in the country when it was the center of media attention, but it was hardly the only haunted house on the block. Throughout American history, there have been many prominent haunted houses, including the White House, that have hosted famous and not-so-famous spirits. There are so many haunted houses in America that many people plan their vacations around visits to haunted houses to see if the ghosts are still there.

In reality, despite thousands of cases, ghosts and haunted houses have gotten a bad rap, and either you believe in them or you don't. Few people are neutral on the subject. While ghosts are as old as humankind, you'll never learn about their long and sometimes dramatic history in school; they only get dragged out once a year at Halloween, and are wildly sensationalized on film and TV.

In our supposedly sophisticated and ever-advancing technological society, ghosts are supposed to be a vestige of more credulous and superstitious times. Although I'd hosted the *Joel Martin Show* on radio since

1972, which dealt with all manner of the paranormal, before 1997, I would have taken a very skeptical position on the timeworn question, "Do you believe in ghosts?" But what happens to that opinion if you encounter one—although scientists and debunkers say it's impossible—since ghosts do not exist? What if you saw a ghost, disembodied spirit, or the apparition of a dead person? Would you pass it off as imagination, hallucination, or the result of your own fear? Or might you begin to wonder if perhaps you'd witnessed a genuine phenomenon—whether you believed in it or not?

Joel Martin's Personal Experience

Here is my personal experience from the fall of 1997 in Bonn, Germany, on a visit with the wife of an old and close friend. He'd been ill for some time; now he was hospitalized, sadly in the last stages of terminal cancer. Bonn is a lovely old city, once the capital of West Germany. Largely untouched by World War II bombing raids, it has retained much of its noteworthy architecture. It is where the great composer Ludwig van Beethoven was born in 1770.

As is the case across Europe and other countries that are far older than the United States, some buildings date back nearly a millennium or more. The Bonn Basilica certainly qualifies; construction began on the magnificent Roman Catholic Church approximately nine hundred years ago, in the eleventh century. My companion, who is Catholic, and I walked there one day; a short distance from where we were staying in a nearby hotel. She'd asked if she could attend a midday Mass, and I, of course, agreed. Once inside, I was taken with the architectural detail, concrete spires, hand-carved wooden pews and "kneelers," marble floors, and beautiful stained-glass windows that surrounded the entire edifice. There were several altars in the majestic church, and with many of the furnishings made of various shades of dark wood it appeared unmistakably medieval. The lower floor was devoted to the relics of long-ago saints, their bones and other remains held in reverence; ancient burial tombs and caskets were also on view.

Bells signaled the start of the noon Mass, and we took seats in the last pew facing the altar and priest who conducted the mass in German; I sat to the right of my companion. Although I'm not fluent, I understood enough of what the priest was saying to follow the service. We'd been seated for about twenty minutes when I glimpsed someone to my right passing by in the distance; I assumed the person was difficult to see because of the way light and shadows cast through the church windows. Then as the figure moved in my direction, I realized it was not a person. It was a silhouette of a nun in a traditional floor-length habit, the kind worn for centuries. She was short in stature and not thin; that may have been her build, or a reflection of the folds or layers of the garment she wore. Startled and not knowing what to do, I sat very still. As she drew closer, I could discern no facial features. All I saw was a one-dimensional black shadow that appeared to be composed of tiny dots; it was not a solid form. The specter's movements were short and abrupt, yet the being seemed to glide forward, not what you'd expect from ordinary footsteps.

When the apparition was directly behind me, she placed an ethereal veil or shawl over my shoulders. In other words, there was no actual physical cloth or material, although it left the sensation of something gossamer. It also seemed to be composed of the same shadowy dots as the specter. Once the act of placing the shawl on me was completed, the apparition continued moving to my left, and literally disappeared into a wall that was at the end of the bench we sat on. With that, the silhouette was gone, leaving me with a feeling of calm and well-being. Nothing about the experience was "spooky."

After the unusual incident, I said nothing, preferring to first mull over as rationally as possible what had just occurred. For whatever reason, my friend had not seen or been aware of the apparition. I knew I had not been hallucinating or imagining, the usual accusations from skeptics. One of their explanations is to dismiss such experiences as "waking dreams." Whatever that means, I was fully awake, not daydreaming. It didn't take long to realize I'd witnessed a ghost or apparition. I knew all the debunkers' arguments about why this couldn't have occurred, and all the explanations given by psychics and mediums as to why ghosts and apparitions do appear. But until I personally had the encounter, I gave no thought that it would ever happen to me. I'd been hosting talk shows about psychic phenomena for twenty-five years, and never once had I observed a ghost or apparition until that moment.

It took me nearly three days to work up the nerve to tell my companion, a sensitive young woman and a devout Roman Catholic, about the incident. My first words were to swear to her that I was telling the truth; I raised my right hand as if I was taking an oath. We've been programmed so well in our society to believe that ghostly encounters cannot happen, that often our first reaction is denial. If we summon the courage to share our experiences, most of us tread cautiously and defensively in whom we tell, fearing ridicule, derision, or even condemnation from those who are deeply religious. Should we consider my experience religious or paranormal? Perhaps this was an example of the overlap between theology and parapsychology that Christian churches have long repudiated. There were many questions we could not answer with certainty.

It is impossible to investigate the long history of ghosts and hauntings and conclude that every experience is fraud or hallucination, when there are millions of such incidents in America and every other country and culture on the planet. Evidence exists that ghosts and apparitions are authentic phenomena, albeit badly stereotyped by the media, criticized as "demonic" by conservative Christianity, and dismissed by scientists. The only problem is that ghostly encounters abound, and genuine spirit phenomena has been captured on photographs, video, and audio recordings, providing what paranormal investigators term "objective evidence."

Before we go ghost hunting through American history, let's define exactly what we are talking about, since there has long been confusion regarding the terminology concerning ghosts. Even though some use the words interchangeably, technically, ghosts and apparitions are not identical. Both are souls that are "no longer living in a body," wrote Echo Bodine, psychic, author, and ghostbuster. However, ghosts are "earthbound," while apparitions are the equivalent of "free spirits" in their comings and goings, they have "moved on to the other side and [have] begun a new life there," Bodine explained. "An [apparition] can come to this side to visit, but it will return home; apparitions are not stuck here on earth. Ghosts are."[1]

A ghost is a "disembodied spirit," generally thought to be "a surviving emotional memory of someone who has died traumatically, usually tragically, but is unaware of his death," according to Hans Holzer, the author of many books about the subject. Holzer said that most ghosts "do not realize they are dead," and if they are aware they're deceased, they're likely "confused about where they are."[2] Some ghosts cling to the physical world because death interrupted or left undone some important work or task they were engaged in and feel the need to continue.

There has to be some "spiritual essence" in each human being that survives, suggested veteran writer Brad Steiger.[3] That essence is electromagnetic in nature. Since science tells us that energy cannot be destroyed, only transformed, energy survives the death of the physical body. Therefore, a ghost or apparition is comprised of electromagnetic energy that lives on; they are "electromagnetic fields," Holzer said.[4] Those who are religious may call it the "soul." The energy is supposed to make a transition to the next dimension, the "nonphysical" or spirit world. However, when it is not able to move on, it remains earthbound as a ghost.

Typically a ghost "haunts" some place it had an emotional bond to when it was in the physical body. In other words, a ghost is attached to a particular location—a house, or nearly any other building you can think of—as well as highways, byways, boats, planes, and trains. Most ghosts seem oblivious to those around them, and seldom do they interact with the living. Ghosts remain confined to one place, engaged in some repetitive behavior that we refer to as "haunting." Because ghosts have no awareness of time, a haunting can continue for many years, although not all last that long. The best we can say is that ghosts follow their own rules; they are not very dependable or predictable.

Usually when a person reports seeing an apparition, it is of a departed loved one—a relative or close friend—with whom there was a strong emotional attachment or connection, as opposed to a ghost who is usually someone we didn't personally know. Apparitions often appear vividly in the dream state, although some are seen by those who are fully awake. For our purposes, it won't be necessary to belabor definitions or quarrel about the imperfect vocabulary that has forever plagued the paranormal. Therefore the terms ghost, spirit, phantom, specter, wraith, or apparition may be used interchangeably. In recent years, many parapsychologists have preferred "apparition," as the term to encompass all spirit phenomena. The word *ghost* conjures up too many old stereotypes.

Poltergeists are an entirely separate phenomenon that we'll examine later in the chapter.

Sometimes ghosts appear as they looked in life; other times, people catch only a glimpse of a specter or silhouette. Often, they are transparent or translucent. They may manifest as a bright ball of energy, or streak of light, or a set of inexplicable footsteps. Ghosts can cause objects to move as if by their own volition, doors to open and close, utter moaning noises, or play havoc with electric lights and appliances. On occasion, the spirit presence is only felt or sensed, sometimes as an unexpected "cold spot" or breeze.

Understandably, most people are truly frightened by such encounters, although history shows they rarely need be, since a ghost's freedom of movement is greatly limited, but Echo Bodine cautioned, "Ghosts can actually feel your fear."[5] They don't travel from place to place, nor do they follow people, despite exaggerated literary and media portrayals exploding with special effects.

The numbers of people who have contacts with the departed are astounding. In 1993, four in every ten Americans "reported having experienced some form of communication or contact with the dead," according to the National Opinion Research Council of the University of Chicago. Among surviving spouses, the statistics were even higher: 65 percent of widows questioned said they'd "witnessed apparitions or had some form of post-death contact with their deceased spouses."[6]

Most ghosts or apparitions are "spontaneous," appearing when they choose, not necessarily when we ask them. However, some spirits may be "induced" to come forth, via drugs, hypnotism, or Ouija boards. For many centuries, people considered ghosts to be a forewarning of death.

Because they are "stuck" here, ghosts are the ones who haunt, and it is they who have long been the subject of books and films, many of them designed to scare readers and moviegoers "out of their wits" with help from "eye-popping special effects," as one movie reviewer described it. But the movies are fantasy; not meant to be taken seriously. Throughout history, some ghost stories have assumed the status of legends; that does not make them factual, such as the ghosts in Charles Dickens's classic *A Christmas Carol*, or the "Headless Horseman" in the famed Washington

Irving tale, *The Legend of Sleepy Hollow*. Incidentally, Irving's ghost was witnessed in the library of his Tarrytown, New York, home by several people after his death in 1859.

There's nothing new about the history of ghosts and hauntings; they date back to the ancient Egyptian, Hebrew, Greek, and Roman civilizations, and likely before. The Bible did not ignore ghosts; in the Old Testament, Job wrote, "Then a spirit passed before my face; the hair on my flesh stood up!" (Job 4:15) There is an Old Testament story of King Saul who visited the medium at Endor and ordered her to summon the spirit of King Samuel, despite Saul's own laws that prohibited the Hebrew people from consulting the dead.[7] There are also many references to the "spirit" in the New Testament. One example: "It is the spirit that gives life, the flesh is of no avail" (John 6:63).

In the Hindu religion, the concept of the human spirit dates back to at least 500 BC in the Bhagavad Gita: "These bodies are perishable; but the dwellers in these bodies are eternal, indestructible, and impenetrable."

Possibly, the first written ghost story is from ancient times, about the Greek philosopher Athenodorus. In the first century when he moved into a rented house in Athens that had a reputation as haunted, he saw the specter of an elderly man pass by him late at night, shackled to heavy chains that rattled as he dragged them. The moaning wraith directed Athenodorus to an exact location outside of the house where his bones had been carelessly buried, rusted chains and all. Once the skeleton was given a proper interment, the ghost was never seen again.[8]

The ancient Greek historian Herodotus, and Roman philosopher Pliny the Younger both left records, purportedly of genuine experiences with ghosts. What is most striking about their accounts from thousands of years ago is how similar they are to today's ghost stories.

There has never been a time in the world's history when people haven't reported ghostly encounters; they are a universal phenomenon. In England, where the history of ghosts and hauntings has long been a part of the culture, old homes, estates of the wealthy, and ancient castles are more likely believed to be haunted. "England is a country full of ghost stories," author Ann Elwood observed.[9] One of Britain's legendary ghosts is Queen Anne Boleyn, beheaded in the Tower of London in 1536 by order of King Henry VIII. Supposedly, her ghost, with severed head in hand, was frequently witnessed on the anniversary of her execution.

Another of Britain's famed apparitions is the "Brown Lady" of Raynham Hall, a large country estate. The transparent form was first seen by several people in 1835; years later, in the 1920s, a photograph taken in the house captured the ghost wearing a gown and veil as she "floated" down a flight of stairs. She has never been identified.[10]

Borley Rectory is said to be England's "most haunted house." A number of investigations were conducted there between 1929 and 1938 by famed British ghost hunter Harry Price who declared it "the best authenticated case in the annals of psychical research." The dreary nineteenth-century building has been home to several ghosts and a host of telekinetic and other paranormal events: objects moving, voices, strange noises, inexplicable footsteps, and temperature changes.[11]

Shakespeare described ghosts as "the sheeted dead [who] did squeak and gibber in the streets of Rome" in his play *Julius Caesar.* Apparently ghosts were never famous for being articulate. In fact, rarely have they been known for their speaking ability; that likely explains their long reputation for moaning and groaning. The famed playwright also included a ghost in *Hamlet.*

During the Middle Ages, Europeans ravaged by recurring epidemics of the plague and other contagious diseases sometimes danced in graveyards, hoping to fend off the evil spirits and ghosts they thought responsible for their plight.[12]

The Swedish mystic and clairvoyant, Emanuel Swedenborg (1688–1772) encouraged the belief and acceptance of spirits and apparitions, based on his visions and journeys to the spirit world where he claimed he saw the souls of the dead in the afterlife.[13]

Swedenborgian ideas and teachings became a strong influence on America's Great Age of Spiritualism in the nineteenth century. In fact, the Age of Spiritualism that began in March 1848 in Hydesville, New York, and swept across the country, was the result of "spirit rappings" reported by the young Fox sisters. Ruling out fraud or trickery, what were spirit rappings, if not the work of a restless or discontented ghost?[14]

The latter half of the nineteenth century in America was a time of great popularity for séances, mediums, spirit materializations, automatic and slate writing, and other ghostly manifestations.

However, it wasn't until 1882 that three founders of the Society for Psychical Research (SPR), asked some 5,700 people about their experiences with apparitions. The extensive project was titled *Phantasms of the Living,* and was published in 1886. Three years later, in 1889, the SPR undertook a second project that it titled a "Census of Hallucinations." Actually, the census asked just one question:

"Have you ever, when believing yourself to be completely awake, had a vivid impression of seeing or being touched by a living being or inanimate object, or of hearing a voice, which impression, so far as you could discover, was not due to any external physical cause?"

It does not appear from the wording that any distinction was made by the SPR between a ghost and apparition. In all, the SPR gathered 17,000 responses; nearly 10 percent of them replied yes. Next, a census was completed in the United States, France, and Germany. More than 27,000 answers were gathered, and nearly 12 percent responded yes. Based on the country's total population, about 10 percent of Americans in the late nineteenth century encountered an apparition. When the SPR repeated its census more than a hundred years later, in 1988, the results were very close to the original findings of the 1880s.

Spread out a map of the United States, close your eyes, and place your finger randomly on any state, city, or town and you've correctly chosen the location of a haunted house, cemetery, church, highway, school, theater, or other building that spirits call home. Wherever there have been people, there are ghosts. It's as simple as that to name the places in America that are haunted; there are far more than we could possibly count, they number in the thousands. Unlike Europe, America is a bit short on old castles; ghosts here have been reported in dwellings ranging from apartment houses, to suburban split-levels, and rural farmhouses in all fifty states. Anyone at any time may witness a ghost or apparition in almost any place. Libraries, bookstores, and Web sites offer such a large selection of ghost stories and related resources that you may hardly know where to begin, and many communities offer tours of their haunted homes and buildings.

There are certain haunted sites throughout American history that have withstood the test of time thanks to reliable witnesses, investigations, and even genuine photographic and recorded evidence. For serious parapsychologists, differentiating between natural and supernatural phenomena is a continuing frustration. Never knowing when a ghost will appear has made ghost hunting both challenging—and difficult. However, if even one ghost encounter or haunted location can be conclusively proven, consider the leap that psychical research will have made toward strengthening the case for the survival of the soul.

The most famous haunted house in the country hardly fits the stereotype of a "spooky, creaky old mansion." It is the White House in Washington, DC, of all places, home to the presidents and their families since 1800.[15] The number of psychic or paranormal experiences around presidents may seem surprising: ghosts of no less than twenty presidents have been seen or sensed in various locations around Washington or at historic sites, and at least seven ghosts have been witnessed inside the White House itself. The most frequently reported White House specter is President Abraham Lincoln. From George Washington to Bill Clinton, paranormal or supernatural incidents occurred in at least twenty-five presidential administrations, many of which directly involved the chief executives. Seven first ladies are reported to have returned in spirit form to haunt the White House, as well as other places, and at least fifteen presidents' wives have had a range of psychic experiences. In the first two centuries of the presidency, of forty-five presidential wives, nearly half had contact with the supernatural. Add to these numbers the ghostly apparitions of other presidential family members, including children of first families, and you have enough anecdotal evidence to argue that there are bizarre things going on inside the Beltway.

In addition, at least four presidents and six first ladies privately consulted at one time or another with a psychic, medium, astrologer, healer, or New Age advisor. The list includes not only Nancy Reagan, but also former first lady and U.S. senator from New York, Hillary Clinton, who channeled the spirit of former first lady Eleanor Roosevelt.

The White House has been home to every president and his family since the second president, John Adams and his wife, Abigail, took residence there in 1800, while construction was still under way. The new presidential mansion had just eight rooms, only four of them for living quarters.

Abigail Adams did her best to make the half-built, damp, and drafty house livable. When she discovered that the not-yet-completed East Room was the driest part of the building, she chose it as the place to hang the family's laundry. In fact, she spent a considerable amount of time in the East Room during the four months they called the "Presidential Palace" home. Despite the discomforts, she must have been very fond of the new Executive Mansion, for after her death in 1818 at the age of seventy-four there were stories that her ghost had returned there.

However, the first officially recorded appearance of Mrs. Adams wasn't until the twentieth century during the administration of William Howard Taft. By the time President Taft moved into the White House more than a hundred years later in 1909, official and state functions in the East Room had long replaced Abigail's family laundry. However, spirits often remember certain emotional or traumatic moments of their lives on Earth regardless of the passage of time or new uses put to original locations. Thus, Abigail returned to the East Room, a place for which she had a strong attachment.

Witnesses during the Taft years say they saw the specter of Mrs. Adams, in her familiar "cap and lace shawl," floating through the unopened doors of the East Room, her arms extended and laden with heaps of laundry. Some claimed they knew when Abigail's spirit was present, for it was accompanied by the slight scent of soap and wet laundry. The "oldest ghost" in White House history, Abigail Adams had not forgotten her makeshift laundry room, and even one hundred years after she left the White House, she still continued to do the family's laundry.

Another of the early first ladies whose ghost made a dramatic impression on the living was Dolley Madison, the wife of President James Madison who served two terms in office from 1809 to 1817. As first lady, Dolley was hugely admired and emulated, and had a unique attachment to the White House. She not only assisted in the design of the exterior landscaping of the grounds, but she also helped preserve the historic treasures of the White House when she and her husband were forced to flee the city as invading British forces advanced on Washington during the War of 1812. British troops set fire to the presidential mansion on August 24, 1814, destroying large parts of the structure. But because of Dolley's prescience, many important documents, artwork, and other items were removed before the English arrived.

Dolley especially loved the White House's enormous lawn, and there, behind the mansion, she patiently planted her garden, a gift to future first ladies. Some one hundred years later, First Lady Edith Wilson, President Woodrow Wilson's second wife, decided to make changes and instructed White House gardeners to dig up and relocate the garden. Mrs. Wilson's plans did not escape Dolley's vigilant spirit which became enraged that another first lady would undo what she'd so affectionately planned and tended. Unable to bear the affront to her landscape design, Dolley's specter materialized before the gardeners could touch so much as one flower or clump of earth. There was no mistaking the apparition, for Dolley was dressed in her familiar early nineteenth-century attire.

Dolley's ghost wasted no time angrily confronting the gardeners, and as the terrified workmen watched, her apparition stomped about wildly, her arms furiously gesturing them away. Then she scolded them in no uncertain terms. That was enough. The gardeners, sufficiently frightened and intimidated, tossed aside their tools and quickly fled, no match for the infuriated ghost of the first lady. According to White House legend, "hundreds of roses" were planted to calm Dolley's anxious spirit and the garden was never again tampered with. Today the famed White House Rose Garden continues to flower, just as Dolley Madison wished it, and in exactly the same place.

Dolley Madison was a vivacious and vigorous woman, and her spirit has been among the most energetic and lively in the nation's capital. Abigail Adams and Dolley Madison were two of the strongest and best known of our first ladies. Had their earthly exuberance translated into psychic energy that better enabled their spirits to materialize?

Thomas Jefferson, the great American patriot, our third president, served in office from 1801 to 1809, and after his death in 1826, did not forget his years in the White House. When his ghost returned it was to the Yellow Oval Room on the second floor of the White House, adjacent to the Lincoln Bedroom. As Mary Todd Lincoln, who moved into the White House more than fifty years later, once told a friend, "My, my, how that Mr. Jefferson does play the violin."

Indeed, it was in the Yellow Oval Room that President Jefferson years earlier received guests and relaxed with a favorite pastime, playing violin, an instrument at which he was quite accomplished. Mrs. Lincoln, an avowed spiritualist and sensitive to paranormal events, was certain she'd psychically detected Thomas Jefferson's spirit still enjoying his violin.

Andrew Jackson, the seventh president, held office for two terms from 1829 to 1837. He was the first president who'd been born in a log cabin, and became a hero when he led the fight against the British in the Battle of New Orleans during the War of 1812. Nicknamed "Old Hickory," he was, without question, one of our country's more colorful presidents—quick-tempered, tough, and highly intuitive. Before he was elected president, Jackson had the dubious distinction of encountering the infamous Bell Witch of Tennessee, actually a dangerous poltergeist that we'll describe a bit later.

President Jackson's spirit first returned to the White House in 1865, twenty years after he passed on. First Lady Mary Todd Lincoln said she confronted Jackson's cantankerous ghost in his former bedroom, the Rose Room, where she insisted she heard his spirit "stomping about" near his canopied four-poster bed. His fiery personality, which in life resulted in a number of altercations, even duels, must have remained intact because Mrs. Lincoln also claimed she heard Jackson's spirit swearing and "cussing" as it loudly stamped and stormed around the room.

One paranormal theory for the obstreperous behavior is that Jackson's ghost remained disturbed by political scandals that consumed his time and energy on Earth. Another theory concerns his run-in with the infamous poltergeist, the Bell Witch. Might Jackson's spirit have remained troubled even years after he departed this physical existence? Following Mrs. Lincoln's report of Jackson's ghost, Old Hickory's spirit quieted for many decades.

However, in the 1950s, Andrew Jackson chose to make his spectral presence known to a longtime White House seamstress, Lillian Rogers Parks, in the room that had been his as president.

By the 1950s, the Rose Room had earned a reputation as one of the most haunted locations in the White House because of frequent reports of an unexplained cold spot and the sound of loud laughter emanating from what had been Jackson's bed. One day, Mrs. Parks was alone in the Rose Room sewing when with no warning she felt someone's staring eyes boring into her from behind. The presence leaned over as she sat in a chair near Andrew Jackson's bed. Later, in her autobiography, *My*

Thirty Years Backstairs at the White House, Mrs. Parks described her experience:

"I remember that when I was working at the bed in the Rose Room, getting a spread fixed for Queen Elizabeth, I had an experience that sent me flying out of there so fast I almost forgot my crutches. [Parks had polio as a child.] The spread was a little too long, and I was hemming it as it lay on the bed. I had finished one side, and was ready to start the other, when suddenly I felt that someone was looking at me, and my scalp tightened. I could feel something coldish behind me, and I didn't finish that spread until three years later." Mrs. Parks concluded that the spirit presence in the Rose Room was none other than Old Hickory.

Years earlier, another White House maid also experienced a ghostly encounter in the Rose Room. She was busy with her chores when inexplicably she heard laughter in the room, which she said had a "hollow," or otherworldly quality. Was it Andrew Jackson's spirit?

In 1964, Jackson's ghost made its most recent White House appearance when an aide to President Lyndon Johnson reported he heard shouting and expletives that he believed were Old Hickory's still restless spirit.

Apparently, Andrew Jackson has had a difficult time finding peace in the hereafter, and his ghost has maintained definite elements of his earthly personality: restless, raucous, and coarse.

More recently, President George H. W. Bush may have witnessed a ghost in the White House, despite official denials. In 1993, a national tabloid reported that the elder Bush might have actually witnessed the apparition of President Lyndon B. Johnson. According to the newspaper, LBJ's spirit returned to the White House in 1991 when the United States was engaged in the Persian Gulf War. The timing of the ghostly visit by LBJ was no surprise, coming when it did, because Johnson's presidency was besieged by the bitter and divisive Vietnam conflict. The Gulf War, then the largest U.S. military action since Vietnam, drew his spirit back, some psychics said.

According to a "White House source," which was not identified by the tabloid, Bush was with Secretary of State James Baker and Defense Secretary Richard Cheney in a late-night Oval Office meeting about the Gulf War when a inexplicable chill whisked by, blowing papers and documents from the president's desk. Then the light flickered off and

LBJ's voice was heard, laughing heartily. The tabloid said Bush confided that he'd also heard "footsteps at night and [saw] a tall, gruff, big-eared ghost resembling LBJ."

But the senior Bush flatly denied to the media that he'd seen or heard Johnson's ghost. This is the same George H. W. Bush who was director of the Central Intelligence Agency in the 1970s, a period during which the CIA conducted covert psychic research into psychokinesis, teleportation, out-of-body experiences, and remote viewing. In 1999, Israeli psychic Uri Geller told *USA Today*, "George Bush, then head of the CIA, was very open-minded to the field of the paranormal." The CIA's response to Geller's revelation: "No comment."

There have been no reports of haunting or ghostly encounters during the administration of George W. Bush. However, it is safe to say that if any apparitions had been revealed in the White House, they would undoubtedly have been met with a terse denial; acknowledging ghosts does not boost presidential popularity.

No one has ever established with certainty what caused Abraham Lincoln to be our most psychic president or why he has been, without question, the most discernable ghost in the White House. His spirit has long been resident there, witnessed by presidents, members of first families, and the White House staff itself. Perhaps it was his assassination, maybe it was the unfinished business of Reconstruction, or possibly it was Lincoln's connection to the spirit world through his séances and communication with the spirits, but Lincoln's restless ghost is the longest occupant in the history of the White House, difficult even for skeptics to deny.

Lincoln's ghost seemed to live on in various manifestations. For several successive years, only on April 27, witnesses reported that a "phantom funeral train" traveled the same route taken by the "official funeral train," from Washington, DC, through New York State, and to Illinois. However, the ghost train supposedly never reached its journey's end, reported the Albany, New York *Evening Times*. Then one year the train failed to materialize. Eventually, after missing several more years, the ghost train was no longer seen. Some suggest the story of the phantom train was a legend; perhaps grief-induced hallucination and the trauma of Lincoln's murder are better explanations in this case than anything paranormal.

Lincoln's impact on American history was immeasurable. In 1864, when he sought reelection, he said, "I want to finish the job." When he was murdered, his plans for reconciliation between the states were abruptly interrupted, and his work left incomplete. Perhaps that is why his spirit has been seen and reported in the White House more than any other president's. Did his enormous psychic energy continue in the afterlife? Does that explain why Lincoln has been the White House's most conspicuous ghost?[16]

In the years immediately after his death, White House personnel reported mysterious footsteps in the hallways, believed to be Lincoln's. Years later, shortly after the turn of the century when President Theodore Roosevelt occupied the White House, Roosevelt admitted, "I think of Lincoln, shambling, homely, with his sad, strong, deeply furrowed face, all the time. I see him in the different rooms and in the halls."[17]

During the terms of President Calvin Coolidge (1923–29), his wife, Grace, was the first to report actually seeing Lincoln's ghost, dressed "in black, with a stole draped across his shoulders to ward off the drafts and chills of Washington's night air." She explained that, one day, as she passed by the Yellow Oval Room, she was startled to see Lincoln's apparition staring out a window in the direction of the Potomac, his hands behind him. The specter momentarily looked in her direction, then turned and departed. During his life, that room was Lincoln's library, and he often gazed intently through the window, deep in thought and contemplation, agonizing about the course of the war. At the same window in the Yellow Oval Room, adjacent to the Lincoln Bedroom, the late president's spirit has been seen or felt by others including Carl Sandburg, the poet and noted Lincoln biographer. President Herbert Hoover also admitted to hearing mysterious noises in the Executive Mansion. Although he never acknowledged it was Lincoln's ghost, Hoover left no doubt that he'd heard something he could not explain.

By the time Franklin Delano Roosevelt began his long tenure as president (1933–1945), Lincoln had been dead for nearly seventy years. However, his specter remained, unwilling or unable to leave the White House. During FDR's administration, Lincoln's ghost was at its most active, perhaps because of his steadfast concern about the perilous state of the nation during the Great Depression and World War II.

First Lady Eleanor Roosevelt never officially acknowledged that she'd seen Lincoln's ghost, but when she worked late at night she sensed Lincoln's presence as though he was "standing behind her, peering over her shoulder." She also acknowledged that she'd heard Lincoln's "footsteps in the second-floor hallways." One day as Mrs. Roosevelt's secretary, Mary Eben, walked by Lincoln's bedroom, she came upon the specter of a gaunt form sitting on the bed "pulling up his boots." The frightened young woman shrieked in fear and quickly fled the room. She was but one of many people, including—said the *Washington Star*—President Roosevelt's valet, who once ran from the White House, screaming in fear that he'd just witnessed Lincoln's ghost.

One of the most intriguing accounts came from Queen Wilhelmina of the Netherlands, who visited the White House during the war years, while in exile from the Nazis. Late one night, an insistent knocking on the Rose Room door awakened her. Thinking it might be an important message, she said, "Come in." When no one entered, the queen opened the door, and there stood the apparition of none other than Lincoln in his familiar stovepipe hat. Stunned, Queen Wilhelmina promptly fainted from fright. The next day, when she told President Roosevelt what happened, he said he wasn't surprised. Although he'd never seen Lincoln's specter himself, he said he had no doubts about Wilhelmina's vision because Mrs. Roosevelt often told him about reports of the ghost, especially in the Lincoln Room.

For Winston Churchill, England's wartime prime minister who displayed unflagging courage against the Nazi peril, appearances by ghosts was apparently another matter. Churchill, who had visited FDR at the White House on several occasions, slept in the Lincoln Bedroom only one night. After that, although he refused to discuss his reasons, he never slept in that room again. What caused Churchill's discomfort? Churchill never admitted it, but many people thought he'd been frightened by Lincoln's apparition.

Even President Roosevelt's dog, Fala, might have sensed the ghost. White House staff told of Fala's suddenly barking at something apparently only the dog could see, perhaps Lincoln's presence. What Fala might have seen also frightened Lillian Rogers Parks, the White House seamstress during the Roosevelt administration, who years later would also witness the ghost of Andrew Jackson. Mrs. Parks was working in a second-floor room one day when she heard someone repeatedly approaching the door, although the White House was quite empty at the time with the Roosevelt family at Hyde Park, along with most of their maids. Mrs. Parks went looking for the cause of the noise. On the third floor, she found a male servant she assumed was responsible for the footsteps. But the servant just arrived and hadn't been on the second floor. Then he realized what Mrs. Parks heard. "That was Abe you heard," he told her.[18]

Roosevelt's vice president, blunt-speaking Harry S. Truman, never claimed he'd witnessed Lincoln during his terms as president (1945–53). However, according to his daughter, Margaret, who acknowledged she'd sensed Lincoln's presence, Harry Truman did not deny the presence of ghosts in the White House, "so I won't lock the door to bar them either," he said. He wrote his wife, Bess, who often stayed at their family home in Independence, Missouri, because she didn't like Washington, "I sit in this old house, all the while listening to the ghosts walk up and down the hallway. At four o'clock I was awakened by three distinct knocks on my bedroom door. No one was there. Damned place is haunted, sure as shootin'!"[19]

During his presidency, Truman made the following entry in his personal diary, and in his own handwriting, about the ghosts he supposed haunted the White House:

January 6
Arose at 5:45 A.M. [,] read the papers and at 7:10 walked to the station to meet the family. Took 35 minutes. It was a good walk. Sure is fine to have them back. This great white jail is a hell of a place in which to be alone. While I work from early morning until late at night, it is a ghostly place. The floors pop and crack all night long. Anyone with an imagination can see old Jim Buchanan walking up and down worrying about conditions not of his making. Then there's Van Buren who inherited a terrible mess from his predecessor, as did poor old James Madison. Of course Andrew Johnson was the worst mistreated of any of them. But they all walk up and down the halls of this place and moan about what they should have done and didn't. So—you see, I've only named a few. The ones who had Boswells and New England historians are too busy trying to

control heaven and hell to come back here. So the tortured souls who were and are misrepresented in history are the ones who come back. It's a hell of a place.

Truman had been "much taken with the stories of Lincoln's ghost," wrote White House chief usher J. B. West. He said that one night the president decided to play a prank and frighten his daughter and three of her friends who were to sleep overnight in Lincoln's bed. Truman asked his doorman and barber, John Mays, a tall, thin gentleman, to don a stovepipe hat and "lurk in the corner of the bedroom." But on the day of the planned mischief, Mays declined, saying, "I didn't feel right about impersonating Mr. Lincoln." He was uneasy about the possibility that he might bump into the real ghost of Lincoln. It was the real ghost of Lincoln who also gave Rex Scouten, a Secret Service agent during the Truman years, the chills at night. "I go down that long hall and into the Lincoln Bedroom. I get a strange feeling," he admitted.[20]

Margaret Truman frequently heard knocking on her bedroom door late at night. However, every time she checked, she found no one. When she told her father about the clamor, he first suspected a "natural" explanation, perhaps some structural problem with the building, and directed the White House be inspected and, if necessary, shored up. Truman's decision proved to be no overreaction. The chief architect informed him that he hadn't acted a moment too soon, for the White House was in serious danger of a structural collapse. Was Lincoln's ghost responsible for the rappings as a way to caution the Trumans that the White House was close to falling down?[21]

During his terms in office (1953–1961), President Eisenhower made no effort to deny the experiences he'd had with Lincoln's ghost. He told his press secretary, James Haggerty, that he frequently sensed Lincoln's spirit in the White House. One day, Eisenhower explained, he was walking through a White House corridor when approaching him from the opposite direction was the specter of Lincoln. Ike took the incident in stride. Perhaps after the horrors of World War II, the apparition of the Great Emancipator was a comforting sight. Surprisingly, Haggerty disclosed President Eisenhower's ghostly encounter on a network TV program, despite the long-held White House position disavowing the presence of ghosts.[22]

Jacqueline Kennedy, who occupied the White House exactly one hundred years after the Lincolns lived there, admitted that she also sensed Lincoln's presence, although no record exists of John F. Kennedy ever reporting the famed ghost.[23]

Lincoln returned to haunt Mrs. Kennedy's successor in office, as well. One night in the old Lincoln Bedroom on the second floor of the White House as President Lyndon Johnson's wife, Lady Bird, watched a TV program about the Lincoln assassination, she was aware of the Great Emancipator's presence. Mrs. Johnson suddenly found herself drawn to a plaque on the mantel that described Lincoln's association with the room. As she read the inscription, she experienced a shudder, likely the result of Lincoln's ethereal presence. Most sightings of Lincoln have taken place in the so-called Lincoln Bedroom, which was actually his Cabinet Room, and where he signed the historic Emancipation Proclamation. It was dubbed the Lincoln Bedroom years later when his bed was moved there.

Mary Todd Lincoln had purchased the carved rosewood bed in the Lincoln Bedroom for some ten thousand dollars, a wildly enormous sum at the time. President Lincoln, at odds with Congress over Mary Todd's spending for the White House, was furious at his wife's extravagance, especially in wartime, and refused to sleep in the bed.

Notwithstanding official denials, members of first families continued to report Lincoln's ghost. When Gerald Ford was in office, his daughter, Susan, publicly acknowledged her belief in ghosts and made it clear she would never sleep in "that room." According to one account, Susan witnessed Lincoln's specter.

During the Reagan years, the president's eldest daughter, Maureen, and her husband, Dennis Revell, often slept in the Lincoln Bedroom when they visited the White House. Maureen, who died of cancer in 2001, claimed that, in the early morning hours, she and her husband sporadically witnessed "an aura, sometimes red, sometimes orange," which they believed was Lincoln's spirit. The couple once awakened in the Lincoln bed to witness his transparent specter at the window. Maureen later wrote about her experience: "I know it sounds hard to believe and weird as all get-out. Dad thought we were Looney Tunes." In 1987, Maureen confirmed to *Newsweek,* "I'm not kidding—we've really seen it."[24]

Despite President Reagan's initial skepticism, he later remarked in a Lincoln Birthday address that he'd begun to ponder the possibility of Lincoln's ghost in the White House. "Now, I haven't seen him myself, but I have to tell you, I am puzzled, because every once in a while, our little dog, Rex, will start down that long hall toward that room [Lincoln's Bedroom], just glaring as if he's seeing something, and barking . . . Funny thing, though, I have to feel, unlike you might think of other ghosts, if [Lincoln] is still there I don't have any fear at all. I think it would be very wonderful to have a little meeting with him and probably very helpful."

When Reagan's youngest daughter, Patti Davis, asked her father if he'd ever encountered Lincoln's ghost, " 'No,' my father answered, a bit sadly, I thought. 'I haven't seen him yet. But I do believe he's here.' "

First Lady Nancy Reagan's contact with Lincoln's spirit was less direct than that of her daughters or predecessors. Mrs. Reagan had to constantly straighten Lincoln's portrait, which she repeatedly found had tilted itself, possibly a result of psychic energy manifested by the unseen entity. She once said, "If Ronnie is away for a night or something, I can be here alone. I'm not afraid. I don't hear Abe Lincoln knocking on my door."[25]

There were no reports of Lincoln's ghost during the Bush administration (1989–1993). Both President and Mrs. Bush flatly denied ever seeing Lincoln or any other spirit in the White House. However, tongue in cheek, Mrs. Bush touched on the question in *Millie's Book,* which was supposedly narrated by the Bush's dog: "Although this is the room where the White House ghost is supposed to appear, the Bushes have not seen it nor do they believe in ghosts. I must confess that I have not seen one either."

During the Clinton years, there were at least two sightings of Lincoln's spirit. One encounter occurred to Roger Clinton, the president's brother, who claimed he'd sensed Lincoln's presence. In the second—perhaps it was a slip of the tongue when a Clinton aide admitted witnessing Lincoln's apparition—the story, reported briefly in the news, was quickly denied by the White House, and dismissed as a joke. During Clinton's second term, however, a scandal emerged concerning more than four hundred guests who, in many instances, made campaign contributions in exchange for overnight stays in the Lincoln Room. How many of those who slept in the famed carved rosewood bed sensed or saw Lincoln's apparition? How many of them will admit to a ghostly encounter? When Mary Todd purchased the famed bed, the angry president said, "It stinks in the nostrils of the American people!" How many visitors in the Lincoln Bedroom during the Clinton administration felt Lincoln's seething anger at the presence of that infamous bed or the sadness at having slept in the spot where young Willie Lincoln died?[26]

In *Ghosts: Washington Revisited,* author John Alexander told of President Jimmy Carter's young daughter, Amy, in 1977 and in the fourth grade, inviting several girlfriends to sleep over in the White House. Out of curiosity, the girls decided they would attempt to summon the ghost of Lincoln by bringing a Ouija board into the Lincoln Bedroom. However, they never communicated with his spirit, for Rosalynn Carter told her daughter and friends to end their adventure contacting the spirit world.[27] This was the same Rosalynn Carter who'd told *Good Housekeeping* in 1979 that when she and Jimmy Carter first married they'd lived in a haunted house in Plains, Georgia, where both had grown up. The plantation-style frame house was built sometime around 1850. She revealed to the magazine, "I knew about the ghost before Jimmy and I moved in. But I wasn't really afraid of it. I just never disturbed it by going into the 'haunted room' alone at night."[28]

Publicly, Richard Nixon professed no interest in the paranormal or supernatural. Privately, he had more contact with psychic phenomena than most people could ever imagine. Most startling was the revelation that while in office he'd consulted psychic and astrologer Jeane Dixon, whom he called a "soothsayer." A secret tape-recording of Nixon talking to his secretary of state Henry Kissinger about Dixon was aired in a History Channel TV documentary, *Presidential Prophecies,* in 2005.[29]

In the early 1970s, mired in the Watergate scandals, and facing almost certain ouster from office, might Nixon have had contact with Lincoln's spirit? Consider that the Lincoln Sitting Room was often a refuge for the beleaguered Nixon during times of crisis, especially during his final days, before his unprecedented resignation from office in disgrace on August 9, 1974. There are many who argue that Nixon's resolution to leave office had been arrived at through supernatural intervention.

Nixon's son-in-law Edward Cox revealed the president's state of mind during his final weeks in the White House. Nixon had been "walking the

halls . . . talking to pictures of former presidents [and] giving speeches."
Turning to the spirits of presidents past for advice, Nixon asked whether
he should fight on against his enemies or resign from office. Surely,
Nixon was unraveling emotionally. However, that did not negate his
psychic experiences. Only a short while after his "conversations" with
former presidents, Nixon made the difficult and unprecedented decision
to leave office.

Was it inspired by Nixon's affinity for the Great Emancipator or contact he'd had with the ghost? Lincoln's spirit has long had a reputation for
materializing during times of national difficulty or distress. What was a
more appropriate time than to resolve the crisis caused by Watergate?[30]

Ghosts of presidents and their families have not been restricted to the
confines of the White House. Presidential apparitions have also shown
up in former homes, where emotional attachments in life were strong.
Nixon's apparition has been reported at his birthplace and presidential
library in Yorba Linda, California. Dennis Hauck wrote in *Haunted
Places* that, "a night watchman has heard strange tapping sounds coming
from the Watergate Display Room, and the machines that play the Watergate tapes over and over have mysteriously malfunctioned."[31]

Richard Nixon was not the only president unable to resolve the disappointments he experienced in the physical world. President Woodrow
Wilson left office in 1921 after serving two terms and moved into a Washington, DC, mansion. By then he was suffering the effects of a stroke he'd
suffered while in office, and in retirement he managed to move slowly only
with the help of a cane. We've already told the story in *The Haunting of
America* about Wilson's secret consultations with the famed American
clairvoyant and seer Edgar Cayce. Wilson's bitterest disappointment was
that he'd been unable to obtain congressional approval for the United
States to join the League of Nations.

In retirement, Wilson was frequently depressed and confused and
given to "unpredictable crying spells." He died in the mansion in 1924,
but his troubled spirit remained in the house that later became a museum. After Wilson's death, a caretaker claimed he heard the "slow
shuffle of a man with a cane climbing the stairs," according to the book
Hauntings. Others reported they'd heard the sound of a man weeping.
There was a sighting of Wilson's spirit by a cleaning woman who said
she saw his apparition in his favorite rocking chair. Surprised by the

sight, she shut and opened her eyes quickly. When she looked again, the specter of President Wilson was gone, but the chair continued to rock back and forth on its own.[32]

From the perspective of the traditional historian, ghost stories about presidents, prominent political figures, and significant buildings are almost always ignored. But parapsychologists who've examined ghostly encounters in the nation's capital with a more open-minded attitude realize that something beyond fantasy and legend has been going on in Washington for more than two hundred years. What if some—or many—of the incidents are true? What influence has the spirit world had on the physical plane, even at the highest levels of government? The fact is that several presidents, their wives, and a number of lawmakers encountered ghosts and apparitions; others sought advice from mediums and psychics to contact the spirit world. That suggests spirit communications exerted influence on the lives and political decisions of leaders that, in turn, could potentially affect millions. That's a very different way of looking at American history.

There are dozens of significant haunted locations in and around the nation's capital, far too many to include here. But before we leave Washington, DC, let's briefly mention a couple of the best known.

The United States Capitol Building is a bustling place, especially when the House and Senate are in session. In addition to our legislators and their staffs at work there, a number of spirits or ghosts have also roamed the halls and offices.

Not long after George Washington laid the cornerstone of the U.S. Capitol in 1793, the building had its first ghost, that of a stonemason who was tragically plastered into a wall during construction, possibly by someone in an act of vengeance.

Among the best-known apparitions witnessed in the Capitol have been presidents John Quincy Adams and James Garfield, and the ghost of Garfield's assassin. The specter of the Unknown Soldier of World War I has also been reported. Others include the apparitions of two former speakers of the House of Representatives, at least one congressman, and Henry Wilson, President Grant's vice president.

In 1898, the Philadelphia press reported no fewer than fifteen ghosts haunting the Capitol Building; one of them was the famed architect Pierre L'Enfant who was personally chosen by George Washington to design the new "Federal City" in the late eighteenth century. L'Enfant's spirit had good reason to stalk the halls, because Congress, despite many promises, never paid the architect for his work. In his last years, he tried without success to get the money owed him. He was deeply embittered and died in poverty. His ghost remained bound to the Earth, still seeking its compensation. When L'Enfant's spirit was seen in the Capitol, witnesses said it was holding a parchment—the bill for monies long due him.[33]

One of the eeriest of ghost stories emerged from Ford's Theatre, scene of Lincoln's assassination. Obviously a place so emotionally charged from the heinous and violent act that it could not escape being haunted. The theater closed after the tragedy in 1865, and did not open again until 1968, as both a theater and museum. Actors working there complained of a reaction often associated with the presence of spirit phenomena, a feeling of bitter cold on one part of the stage.

Mediums who'd visited the theater determined the disturbances were the result of negative psychic energy that remained more than a century after Lincoln's death. The villainous assassin John Wilkes Booth who, after firing the fatal bullet, leapt to the stage, and hobbled across the floorboards to escape, was later trapped in a burning barn, and shot to death by a Union soldier.

But Booth's tormented spirit was apparently unable to make a transition to the afterlife. Mathew Brady, America's most famous photographer of the Civil War era, took pictures of the ill-fated box at Ford's Theatre where the president sat on the night of the assassination. When the photographic plate was developed, it was said to reveal the near-translucent presence of none other than John Wilkes Booth peering through the curtain at the moment he crept up behind Lincoln to fire the fatal shot into his head.

It has long been paranormal theory that the intense energy exuded by people at the moment of their greatest calamities can actually be recorded in photographs. Might the malevolent spirit of the demented actor, Booth, have burned its image into Mathew Brady's photograph?[34]

Washington, DC, is said to have many haunted houses where ghosts dwell. One notable example is the Octagon House, a beautiful Georgian-style mansion with six, not eight sides, only a couple of blocks from the White House. It was in the Octagon that President and Mrs. Madison

resided for a year while the White House was rebuilt following its torch-
ing by the British in 1814.

The Octagon was one of the first private residences in the new nation's capital. Built in 1800 by wealthy Virginian, Colonel John Tayloe,
the mansion became popular for social functions attended by numerous
dignitaries of the time.

The Octagon has also been home to tragedy, and as a result, several
tortured and earthbound ghosts throughout its long history. Many people
have witnessed specters on the mansion's towering staircase. In particular,
people have told of seeing the apparition of a very pretty young woman
either falling or leaping over the second-floor banister, and plunging to her
death. The ghost is probably Tayloe's youngest daughter who incited her
father's wrath by falling in love with a British officer. Tayloe thwarted
their relationship, and his brokenhearted daughter either deliberately
jumped or fell after a terrible fight with him. Many believe her apparition
haunts the Octagon House because her life was cut short at a moment of
intense energy and frustration.

But hers is not the only macabre phenomenon near the majestic
staircase. Witnesses have also reported hearing the plaintive cries of
another grief-stricken woman and the scuffle of unexplained footsteps.
Others have seen mysterious footprints suddenly appear on the floor.
Some have watched doors open and close by themselves, or were terrified by lights that inexplicably switched themselves on. At the bottom
of the great oval staircase is an area where visitors have reported a burst
of frigid air that they say has chilled them even on hot summer days.
Cold spots, sometimes called "psychic winds," are believed to be breezes
or gusts from another dimension that can be produced by a nearby spirit
presence.

Some psychics who'd visited the Octagon concluded that the spot at
the foot of the stairs is where Tayloe's other forlorn daughter plummeted
to her untimely death from an upper-floor landing. The young woman
either fell accidentally or took her life after her father blocked her attempt to elope. Although some historians consider the stories of the
daughters' deaths to be legend, Tayloe's own granddaughter wrote that,
after he died, house bells rung on their own, and "everyone said that the
house was haunted."

In the 1950s, a caretaker reported witnessing an apparition in early

1800s military dress. Then in the 1960s, an invisible presence turned lights on and off. In more recent years, witnesses and employees told of seeing and sensing spirits in the vicinity of the famed staircase, as well as on the upstairs floor.[35]

From the nation's capital, let's move elsewhere.

After relocating countless times during their married life, Mamie and Dwight Eisenhower were understandably excited by the prospect of finally settling down in a permanent home of their own. During her husband's long and distinguished military career Mamie lived in thirty-seven residences, most either government-owned or provided, as her husband moved up the ranks to become the Supreme Allied Commander leading the war effort in Europe. Their nomadic life was typical of many in the military. But as Mamie often said, no residence was really ever hers. Finally, after Ike's retirement, they bought a dilapidated nineteenth-century farmhouse in Gettysburg, Pennsylvania, in 1950, and renovated it. Mamie's dream of her own home finally came true. It had taken them only thirty-four years of marriage, she joked.

The farmhouse was adjacent to the famed Gettysburg battlefield, and the Eisenhowers ultimately restored it into a twenty-room Georgian-style residence. Mamie adored her new home, which she lovingly called her "dream house," in the gentle rolling hills of the southern Pennsylvania countryside.

But retirement was not immediately in the cards for the Eisenhowers. Ike was a genuine war hero and one of America's most popular figures. He was elected president in 1952, and again in 1956. While in office, their Gettysburg estate was turned into the "little" White House.

Finally, after two terms, Ike left the presidency in 1961, and the Eisenhowers wasted no time returning to Gettysburg where they spent their remaining years together. In 1969, Ike died of complications of congestive heart failure at the age of seventy-nine, the last president of the United States born in the nineteenth century.

Mamie Eisenhower spent the next, and final, ten years of her life bereft. Without her husband, she described herself as a "lost soul," but she would not hear of moving from her Gettysburg house. In 1978, she repeated what she'd so often said about Gettysburg. "We had only one home, our farm." The next year, she died of a stroke at the age of eighty-three.

After Mamie passed on, the Eisenhowers' Gettysburg home was designated a national historic site. Following her death, reports began of unexplained footsteps, voices, and a frequent rustling noise, which rangers assigned to the house could not identify. Lights in the front hall of the farmhouse blinked on and off, according to park rangers; engineers called to inspect reported there was nothing wrong with the electrical wiring to explain why the lights flickered at strange times for no apparent reason.

Rangers also told of hearing music inexplicably drifting through the hall from an unused guest room. At night, they reported "thumping noises." On other occasions, doors opened and closed, seemingly under their own power, one was a large stable door with hinges that made it impossible to open and shut quickly and suddenly. Yet the door loudly banged open and then slammed on its own. Needless to say, the incidents frightened some personnel, and two of three rangers assigned to the house threatened resignation if the strange phenomena didn't stop. But they did not stop. In fact, they got worse.

Mamie's spirit materialized to one of the rangers, who reported she'd witnessed the apparition on a number of occasions in a corner of the first lady's living room. The ghost seemed to know who the ranger was and appeared specifically in her presence.

Staff members weren't the only ones who reported strange phenomena in the Eisenhower house. Visitors also told of similar incidents in which objects seemed to move under their own power. However, National Park Service officials, when asked about the occurrences, flatly dismissed them as nothing more than hallucinations or pure fiction, ghost stories fit for Halloween, and not meant to be taken seriously. But those rangers who'd witnessed the unearthly incidents knew better, admitted they'd been made uneasy, and complained to their bosses about what they could not explain.

Eventually the unsettling paranormal activity in the Eisenhower home came to the attention of National Park Service official Priscilla Baker, special assistant to the director. Baker, open to the possibility of paranormal phenomena, was not against bringing a psychic into the house to help solve the mystery. However, she lacked the support of her superiors, who made it clear they would just as soon ignore the supernatural activity. Although Baker was criticized for her interest in ghost stories and apparitions, she persisted and invited a respected and nationally recognized medium named Anne Gehman to the Eisenhower home. Gehman's reputation was impeccable, her experience extensive, and she agreed to visit Gettysburg.

In 1982, Gehman arrived at the Eisenhower farm for a two-day visit. She entered the main door in the front of the house, accompanied by a small entourage of Park Service employees, other official attendees, and the park historian. Looking toward the stairwell, Gehman quickly determined the cause of the blinking lights by establishing a psychic connection with the spirit, who identified herself as Rose Wood, Mrs. Eisenhower's personal maid for many years. In life, Mrs. Wood had witnessed Abraham Lincoln's ghost and the apparition of President Andrew Jackson. The maid told Gehman she'd been at her happiest on Earth when she worked for Mamie. In fact, Mrs. Wood said, she never wanted to leave the house. But why had she turned the lights on and off? Her spirit communicated that she simply wanted people working there to know she was still present, but she promised to stop playing with the lights. True to her word, there were no further problems reported with electricity in the Eisenhowers' home.

Electrical disturbances are a common form of communication from the departed. Upon physical death, the spirit or soul survives as a form of energy, which we have yet to quantify. Since energy operates according to electromagnetic principles, it is reasonable that spirits are able to influence electrical equipment, such as lights, as a means of communicating to us, which Mrs. Wood did.

Gehman also tried to find evidence of Mamie Eisenhower's spirit. She walked around the house, both downstairs and upstairs, sensing spirit presences in various rooms. Finally she confirmed that Mamie's ghost was, indeed, present, especially in the living room and in an upstairs bedroom, where her apparition gazed out the window, as she often did in life. The ranger who'd witnessed Mamie's specter had no knowledge or expertise in psychic phenomena. She only knew that she'd seen Mamie's ghost several times in a corner of the living room. Gehman assured the park ranger that she was not suffering from an overactive imagination. Another ranger who'd seen Mamie's spirit, a veteran who'd served in Vietnam, literally thought he was losing his mind from post-traumatic stress disorder. No,

Gehman assured him, he was fine. What he'd witnessed was not a hallucination, but a genuine apparition.

When Mamie's spirit materialized, she communicated at least one reason why her ghost made its presence known to Park Service personnel. Mamie explained that she was concerned with the structural safety of the back stairs, which were used as an exit from the house. Her spirit insisted that the stairs "were not safe," and that by materializing she hoped to draw attention to the need for repairs. However, not all her supervisors at the National Park Service were as open-minded as Priscilla Baker. It took some time before she could convince her skeptical bosses to send structural inspectors to the house on the word of a psychic. But Baker persisted, and the back staircase was found in need of repair, just as Mamie's spirit had warned.

Her ghost also explained the rustling noise that park personnel had been unable to decipher. Mamie told Gehman that the noise was the crinkling sound of her taffeta dress, which she'd favored wearing when on Earth. In addition, the former first lady's spirit revealed she was upset about plans to rip up a portion of her yard for additional parking. This was something Mamie said she could not bear, and so her ghost materialized to discourage workers from making any change by frightening them. Quite possibly the Park Service heeded Mamie's apparition— although no one in an official capacity would admit it. The Park Service at the time did not replace that part of the yard with a parking lot.

Gehman also discerned the spirit presence of President Eisenhower, although not with the same degree of intensity as his wife's. Ike's ghost sat in his favorite chair in his study on the first floor of the house surrounded by many books. Still an officer and a gentleman, Eisenhower's spirit rose briefly from its chair, smiled, nodded, seemed to greet her, and then sat down again.

It's often easier to describe reports of apparitions than explain why they appear, but in Mamie's case, her spirit was drawn back to where she'd been happiest in the physical world, her Gettysburg home. Through Gehman, Mamie explained that, "she liked to check from time to time and make sure everything was O.K. in the house."

Outside the Eisenhower house, which adjoins the famed Gettysburg battlefield, Gehman psychically observed a line of ghosts. They were the apparitions of Civil War soldiers in tattered blue uniforms who had fought and died in the bloody battle and whose bodies, she thought, were buried in the national cemetery at Gettysburg. As Gehman watched the specters mournfully march by, she said the ghost soldiers rattled off their names to her, a roster of the walking dead. Gehman repeated aloud, as quickly as she could, what she'd heard clairaudiently to the park historian who'd accompanied her. He later checked the names of the soldiers she'd announced and verified her accuracy.

This bit of sensational information, although witnessed by a government official who followed up on data he'd received on the spot as it was being communicated to Gehman, did not make it into the historical record, presumably because its source was paranormal. Baker is convinced she was in the presence of ghostly apparitions. "Of course the spirits can come back. I have no doubt anymore. It's been proven to me," she said.

While we're in Gettysburg, let's talk about "battlefield ghosts." Where there is trauma, violence, or unexpected death, ghost sightings have been the most prevalent. "No more violent places exist than battlefields, and rare is the one not reputedly haunted by ghosts of the slain," wrote Rosemary Ellen Guiley, adding that "In the United States, there are numerous battlefields of the . . . Civil War."

The Battle of Gettysburg was not only a horror of bloodshed and violence, it also marked the turning point of the Civil War, and rightly described as "the greatest battle ever fought on the North American continent." It has long been regarded as one of the most haunted places in America, and if witnesses of that era are to be believed, one of the heroes was the specter of none other than George Washington.

Washington had been gone from Earth's plane for more than sixty years when, on the morning of July 1, 1863, Confederate and Union forces faced each other near the small Pennsylvania town, home to some 2,400 people at the time. What was strategically important about Gettysburg was its location, at the confluence of ten important roads, all from different directions.

The three-day battle began on July 1; by the next day, July 2, under the searing heat of the summer sun, 85,000 Union troops faced 75,000 Confederate soldiers. Eventually the two opposing armies amassed nearly 170,000 men in and around Gettysburg. Most significant from the

Union Army's perspective was to prevent the Confederates from breaking through Gettysburg, and therefore gaining a military foothold in the North. The goal was to turn back Confederate forces at all costs.

The Union Army's 20th Maine Regiment, under the command of Colonel Joshua Chamberlain, a theologian and college professor, but with no prior military leadership experience, had been ordered to march to Pennsylvania from Maryland. Although exhausted and with no accurate maps, the men under his command continued on through the dark and dismal night, not even certain they were moving in the right direction. Chamberlain rode ahead of his men until they finally came to a fork in the road, unsure which path to take. As they pondered their dilemma, the clouds broke sufficiently for the moonlight to reveal the outline of someone on horseback. The figure, dressed in a bright coat and tricorn hat, the kind worn during the American Revolution, sat atop an imposing light-colored horse. Then he galloped in the direction of one of the two diverging roads, waving for Chamberlain's men to follow.

The men thought that it was the figure of Union General George McClellan, who had recently been relieved of his command by President Lincoln. Then, someone realized it wasn't McClellan, at all. The mysterious figure on the giant steed was none other than George Washington! Word quickly spread through the troops that Washington's spirit had returned to lead them in the right direction. The sight of the apparition seemed a "divine intervention." Uplifted, the men marched with renewed confidence along the unlit road.

Once they arrived at the scene of the battle in Gettysburg, the 20th Maine Regiment received orders to defend a rocky hill known as Little Round Top, considered critical to a Union victory, and Chamberlain's men were in the best position to defend the strategically important hill.

The three-day battle with the Confederates, which began on July 1, 1863, was ferocious. The Rebels, from the 4th Alabama Regiment, on the offensive, overwhelmingly outnumbered the 20th Maine at Little Round Top. Making a bad situation worse, Chamberlain's soldiers, appallingly low on ammunition, believed they were surrounded by Confederate troops. There were frantic cries from the men for more bullets. Colonel Chamberlain thought that it was only a matter of time before his unit would have to forfeit their position and give up the hill. Faced with this extremely grave and dangerous situation, the men were understandably frozen with fear.

But rather than retreat, Chamberlain made a bold decision. He bellowed above the sound of exploding gunfire, "Fix bayonets. Charge!" Almost incomprehensibly he'd ordered his soldiers to advance, a command tantamount to virtual suicide given their situation. Would the men even obey?

Then something that can only be described as miraculous or supernatural happened. The same enigmatic specter on horseback, which led the men on the road to Gettysburg, again inexplicably materialized. Glowing and with raised sword, the specter urged the soldiers to follow him into battle. The sight of the ghostly figure on horseback inspired the 20th Maine to attack. Charging down the hill into the teeth of enemy fire, they completely surprised and overwhelmed the Confederates. Although both sides suffered heavy casualties, the bewildered Confederate defense lines were overrun. Survivors broke and ran for their lives, slipping and sliding along ground drenched with the blood of the dead and wounded. Confederate survivors from the 4th Alabama Regiment, who had faced Chamberlain's men at Little Round Top, later said, "They never were whipped before, and never wanted to meet the 20th Maine again."

Little Round Top proved to be one of the most unexpected victories of the Civil War and one of the most important at Gettysburg; Chamberlain's daring attack saved Little Round Top and helped maintain the Union defense. Many considered his accomplishment nothing short of a miracle—and perhaps it was. Considered a major turning point of the Civil War, the Union victory thwarted a Confederate effort to penetrate the North.

After the Battle of Gettysburg, accounts of Washington's apparition witnessed by hundreds of soldiers resulted in Secretary of War Edwin Stanton's asking the Union Army to investigate the incident. At least one general, as well as officers swore the ghostly image was that of George Washington's face. Chamberlain achieved the rank of general, and was awarded the Congressional Medal of Honor. Later he became governor of Maine.

Many years after Gettysburg, a reporter asked him about the story of

George Washington's ghost leading his troops at Gettysburg. Upon hearing the reporter's question, Chamberlain grew pensive, then answered, "Yes, that report circulated through our lines, and I have no doubt that it inspired the men."

Then after a pause, the elderly soldier added, "Who among us can say that such a thing was impossible? I do believe that we were enveloped by the powers of the otherworld that day and who shall say that Washington was not among the number of those who aided the country he founded?" Chamberlain added a final thought, "You could not say from what world they came, or to what world they go."

The ghost of Washington had materialized at a time when the United States was on the brink of dissolution. Might the outcome at Little Round Top have been different if Washington's spirit had not returned to lead?

Gettysburg, where more than fifty thousand men lost their lives, and many more were wounded in three days of brutal and bloody fighting, has been called the most haunted battlefield in the nation. It is said that the ghosts of soldiers who fell there still march in phantom formations across the field to this very day. And George Washington, it seems, who himself was inspired by an apparition at his army's darkest hour, was its most celebrated and important ghost.[36]

There are untold thousands of people in every walk of life who've encountered mysterious phenomena they cannot explain. When Donna and her six-year-old son, Dominic, moved to Franklin, Tennessee, in 2003, from another state, she knew absolutely nothing about Franklin's history, and had not an inkling that the town was inhabited by the earthbound spirits of many who died there in a terrible and bloody Civil War battle. When she purchased a lovely new home she had no idea that it was haunted; her house was only one of many where beleaguered neighbors whispered about bizarre paranormal activity.

Franklin, Tennessee, is a city of nearly fifty thousand people—and countless numbers of ghosts. The growing community is about twenty miles south of Nashville. Many neighborhoods, typically suburban-looking, and with so-called "big box" stores thrive. But picturesque and historic downtown Franklin, home to quaint old stores and buildings, is close to where one of the bloodiest conflicts of the Civil War was fought: the Battle of Franklin, on November 30, 1864. There are several versions of events, but there's no question about the outcome. Confederate forces attacked Union troops, and when the fierce fighting was over, two thousand Northern soldiers were dead, six thousand Southern men and boys lost their lives, and the Union Army had defeated the Rebels.

Some Franklin homes and stores were quickly transformed into makeshift hospitals during the fighting. At least five mortally wounded Confederate generals were taken to Carnton Mansion, an early nineteenth-century plantation. Not far from the house, a cemetery was hurriedly prepared for the mounting number of casualties. A mansion called the Carter House was a residence at the time, and around it much of the combat took place. To this day bullet holes and bloodstains remain in Carter House as mute testament to the Battle of Franklin. Some buildings, such as the public library, were constructed over a portion of the battlefield. Throughout the city there are other remembrances including historical markers and several cemeteries where soldiers were laid to rest. And there are the ghosts.

Donna discovered them accidentally, or rather they found her. Soon after she moved into her spacious new home, there were inexplicable voices and noises; glass objects that exploded; the family cat jumped and howled at something invisible; there were electrical disruptions—lights and the computer turned themselves on and off. Even the car lights blinked repeatedly. Donna saw the lighting fixture move by itself. A dead-bolt lock on a house door repeatedly opened on its own. Bottles mysteriously moved from one place to another. One day, she returned home to find an old metal pipe or bar inexplicably lying on the living room floor. A friend visiting from out of town also heard voices and swore she saw a shadowy form. Donna said she's often felt a male presence near her. When the incidents became overwhelming, she called local police to be certain no one had broken in.

She soon learned the reason for the disturbances; they were attributable to the ghosts of Confederate soldiers who died at the Battle of Franklin in 1864. She also discovered that she was not the only person in town living in a "haunted house." Many people in Franklin have had similar problems, although the topic is usually talked about in "hushed voices," Donna explained. One Franklin resident nervously told us the ghost stories were all "legends" with no basis in fact. Another individual who owned a beauty parlor in the historic downtown area was so plagued with disturbances, from bottles moving to hair dryers turning themselves on or off, that he closed and relocated to another less nerve-racking property.

One Halloween, Donna's son, Dominic, then eight years old, went trick or treating in their neighborhood. Donna bought an inexpensive disposable camera to take photos of the occasion. When she went to the store where they'd been developed, the clerk remarked to her, "You caught some spirits." Donna was stunned as she looked at the snapshots. In some of them, hazy forms can be seen surrounding Dominic and several other children. There are "orbs," or balls of energy, and a couple of faces can be discerned in the various white shapes and plumes that crisscross the photos.

In early 2006, the Nashville newspaper, the *Tennessean,* featured a story about a local woman, a psychic who has performed "cleansings," to rid homes of spirits; not everyone cares to have spectral activity where they live. Among her clients have been realty companies who employ her to clear houses of unwanted entities. She described herself as a "ghost whisperer," rather than a ghost hunter; she said she "talks" to the spirits to encourage them to move on to the afterlife.

Donna wondered if the historic re-creations that are held annually in Franklin to commemorate the long-ago battle "stir up" the ghosts. It's a good question, and a reasonable paranormal theory; some psychics believe that can occur. Meanwhile, historical markers, old battlefields, and cemeteries stand as reminders of the terrible carnage the Civil War wrought.

What should be of interest even to skeptics is the great number of ghost incidents reported, and the similarities between them. For example, Donna's account is not unlike events in an Ohio house where James Garfield and his wife lived many years before he became president in 1881.[37] In other words, people's experiences with ghosts share many commonalities, even when the subjects do not know each other, and are separated by time and distance. It suggests that something has long been going on that needs to be taken more seriously. It's absurd to conclude that millions of people are all hallucinating, lying, or misinterpreting their experiences.

As one can imagine, finding genuine "objective" evidence of ghostly encounters has been a major frustration to psychic investigators. Although spirit photography became a thriving business in America after the Civil War, there have always been questions about the authenticity of the pictures taken, such as the famous portrait of a widowed Mary Todd Lincoln, with the ghostly forms of President Lincoln and their son Willie behind her.[38] So much fraud permeated spirit photography that, even in the Great Age of Spiritualism, many recognized it as such—the product of double exposures, not spirit entities around the seated subjects. But while spirits defy easy capture on film or recordings, genuine spirit photography is not unknown. Spectral forms have sometimes made their appearance in photographs, videos, or film, and some photos reveal images that defy explanation. So fascinating is the subject that in 2006, New York's famed Metropolitan Museum of Art held a successful exhibit titled, "Photography and the Occult," that featured photographic images purporting to be evidence of the spirit world, many dating back to the daguerreotypes of the nineteenth century.[39]

So, can photography capture a spectral image? The answer is absolutely yes. Some of the best evidence has been caught on film quite accidentally.

In 1993, Tracy Abbott, a writer, paid a visit to one of her favorite historic buildings in New York City, the Old Merchant's House on East Fourth Street in lower Manhattan, not far from the Bowery, and open to the public. The Old Merchant's House, built around 1830, has uniquely preserved many original furnishings and articles of clothing. There is even a secret tunnel in the house that leads to the East River.

The impressive three-story brownstone was home to a wealthy hardware merchant named Seabury Tredwell, a stern and unyielding man. He and his wife, Eliza, had six daughters and two sons. One of them was Gertrude Tredwell, born in the house in 1840. She lived there her entire life until her death in 1933, at the age of ninety-three.

There are several versions of why Gertrude spent many years as a virtual recluse, rarely stepping out of the house. One story blamed it on her father, Seabury Tredwell, who broke up Gertrude's one romance, claiming her beau was more interested in Tredwell's considerable fortune than in Gertrude, a petite young woman with dark hair and blue eyes. In fact, Tredwell strongly discouraged any suitors he thought had designs on his money. Another account was that Gertrude had an unwanted child, and family reaction was harsh and disapproving. Whatever the reason, Gertrude lived a solitary life. Tracy thought about the irony; that in a house so beautiful, a woman spent such a melancholy existence.

Tracy walked through the downstairs rooms, then went upstairs to the third-floor bedroom where Gertrude had known many sad and reclusive years. All the while, Tracy snapped photographs with her 35-millimeter camera and its built-in flash. She also took pictures in the bedroom; one shot was of its white marble fireplace, upholstered chair, and a small wooden table with a Bible upon it.

When Tracy developed the roll of film, she was surprised by one photo she'd taken in the room where Gertrude was supposed to have spent considerable time. The picture showed a strange image she could not explain. It was unmistakably a white translucent plume that ran up and down the length of the photograph, but behind the plume, the furnishings and fireplace were still visible. No other snapshot showed the white vertical form. Although she could not figure out what it was, she joked that perhaps she'd gotten a picture of "Gertie's ghost."

Nearly three years later in a bookstore, Tracy happened to be browsing through a New York City guidebook. One recommended Manhattan sight was the Old Merchant's House. According to the book, the house "was alleged to be haunted by a spirit, assumed to be Tredwell's daughter; a white aura has been seen above the fireplace." Tracy was amazed. She wasn't serious when she called the white plume, "Gertie's ghost." But had she unwittingly caught Gertrude Tredwell's spirit in a photograph?

The photo has since been made available for experts to study, it has been written about, and seen on network television. If it is what it purports to be, it may provide objective evidence that something survives physical death.

Parapsychologist and author Hans Holzer also examined the Old Merchant's House for evidence of ghostly phenomena. In *Where the Ghosts Are*, he described manifestations in the house, and noted several on the ground-floor level in the rear of the house. "What used to be Gertrude's bedroom upstairs also has a presence in it from time to time," he wrote. "A presence has been observed in the Old Merchant's House by several reliable witnesses." Holzer added that when he and a professional photographer took pictures of the fireplace in the third-floor bedroom, both found that "there is a strange white area around it that cannot be accounted for."[40]

Another example of inadvertently stumbling upon a ghostly presence occurred in the early 1980s when a New York couple visited one of the several homes Edgar Allan Poe lived in during his brief and tortured, but prolific, life (1809–1849). Despite his immense talent for writing about the macabre, Poe sometimes found it necessary to keep a step ahead of the rent collector. He did that by moving when he had to. During one period, Poe and his young wife lived in a house in New York.

Steve, a fan of Poe's writing, was told that taking photographs was not permitted. But he and his wife were able to walk around, and into the room with a fireplace, near where the ailing Mrs. Poe, suffering from "consumption," sat in a rocking chair to warm herself and avoid the damp chill that often found its way into early nineteenth-century dwellings. Steve could not resist a memento. When no staff or other visitors were present, he quickly snapped several pictures of the room, the fireplace, and rocker; then hastily placed his small Instamatic camera back in his coat pocket.

About a week later when the photos were developed, Steve and his wife came upon one snapshot that at first left them speechless. There, seated in what was an empty rocking chair was, unmistakably, the silhouette of a slender young woman, wrapped in what was probably a quilt or cover. Had Steve, unknowingly, captured the apparition of the sickly Mrs. Poe sitting by the fireplace? The photo, examined by experts, has been deemed authentic.[41]

Attitudes toward ghosts and hauntings vary greatly from place to place. For example, the White House has long officially denied that it is home to any ghosts, while at the same time, many have called it "the most haunted house in the country." The National Park Service has stubbornly maintained that no ghosts exist in such well-known sites as the Gettysburg battlefield. Eastern Airlines adamantly denied ghosts were ever reported on any of its planes, despite many credible witnesses who'd insisted otherwise after a deadly crash in the Florida Everglades in 1972 that became the legendary story of *The Ghost of Flight 401*. The apparitions of the copilot and flight engineer were seen many times on other Eastern flights in the years immediately following their deaths in the crash, always on planes that had used parts from the downed Flight 401. Apparently, obstinate denials of the specters did the company no good; Eastern Airlines went out of business anyway. The story became the subject of both a bestselling book and TV movie.[42]

Many communities have seen the wisdom in embracing ghosts and the tourists they attract. For example, Fredericksburg, Virginia, is a charming small city that boasts many haunted houses, taverns, and churches. As a result, the local preservation society conducts a yearly tour of haunted places. They include buildings that date back to the eighteenth century such as the haunted home of Mary Ball Washington, the domineering mother of George Washington. The apparitions of two early presidents have also been reported: Thomas Jefferson and James Monroe, whose ghosts were spotted visiting the building where Monroe practiced law in the 1780s. Ghosts have been witnessed on streets and in at least three churches. Should you prefer Civil War to Revolutionary-era phantoms, there is Fredericksburg Battlefield where more than nine thousand Union soldiers, and some fifteen hundred Confederate forces, lost their lives fighting in December 1862. Witnesses have long claimed they've heard moans and seen apparitions of the ill-fated soldiers.[43]

Harpers Ferry, West Virginia, has been home to several specters; most prominent is John Brown, the fanatical abolitionist who was captured and hanged there in 1859, and many tourists make the trek, hoping for a glimpse of the distinctive ghost with his untamed white hair. New Hope is another popular tourist location in picturesque and historic Bucks County, Pennsylvania, that conducts an annual "Ghost Tour" every October.[44]

The Chicago area is chock-full of haunted places; among them the site of the old Biograph Theater where the apparition of Prohibition-era gangster John Dillinger has been witnessed; he was killed in a barrage of police bullets in 1934. Hull House, run by the great social reformer Jane Addams, has long had a reputation for being haunted by a "devil baby." The story dates back to 1913, and although it's been called legend, countless people have flocked to see the apparition of a child that supposedly looks like the devil. Several photographs purport to be of a mistlike or vaporous cloud that may be ghosts. On Clark Street, mysterious visions and voices have been reported at the site of the infamous St. Valentine's Day Massacre in 1929 where some of the Bugs Moran gang was mowed down by rival mobsters. Bus tours of haunted Chicago are available. If you get to the suburbs, there are several famous cemeteries where ghosts linger. At Bachelor's Grove Cemetery, for instance, there have been numerous ghosts and mysterious lights reported. The most frequently cited explanation is that the location was a "mob dumping ground" during Prohibition. The specter of that era's most infamous gangster, Al Capone has been seen at his grave site in Mount Carmel Cemetery.[45]

From the "Ghost Riders in the Sky" of Texas; to the spirit of naturalist John James Audubon, the famed painter of birds, at his Key West, Florida, home; and all the way to the Little Bighorn Battlefield in Montana, scene of "Custer's Last Stand" in 1876; ghosts have been reported in extraordinary numbers. There are even a couple of American communities that pride themselves on their huge spirit populations. In upstate New York, the nineteenth-century settlement of Lily Dale attracts large numbers of psychic mediums that gather during the summer and hold séances to contact spirits. No town is prouder of its spirit population that tiny Cassadaga, Florida, where virtually every one of the four hundred residents is a medium, and communicating with the dead is their principal occupation. Cassadaga attracts visitors year-round.[46]

The South has its share of haunted locales, and most tourism offices aren't shy about providing visitors with information about haunted former plantations, public buildings, and restaurants in their respective cities. Charleston, South Carolina, is home to a large number of ghosts, a reflection of its long history that included the tortures of slavery and the ravages of the Civil War.

In 1987, two young women, Sally and Annie, on vacation, came to Charleston to sightsee. They decided to spend a night in the city, and chose a lovely old inn called the 1843 Battery Carriage House. After dinner, they were relaxing in Room 10 when both saw the doorknob rattle a while and turn as if someone was about to enter. But neither of the women had heard anyone on the creaky staircase leading to their floor, and no one was outside the room. They were understandably frightened, but before they could decide what to do next, Annie felt "someone brush up against" her. Sally grabbed several towels, pushed them under the locked door, and spent a very uneasy night in Room 10.

The next day, still shaken by their encounter with the invisible, Sally asked some questions, and researched the Battery Carriage House. She and her friend were surprised to learn that many people had complained of similar ghostly presences. One spirit was believed to be a nineteenth-century gentleman who is only heard or seen when women are guests in Room 10. Some guests have reported the apparition of a man dressed in a Victorian-era suit and top hat. Others believe it is the spirit of a Confederate soldier who still has "an eye for the young ladies."[47]

What is noteworthy about this story is that there have been multiple and repeated witnesses to the same phenomena. The typical reply from obdurate skeptics that ghost encounters are all imaginary or coincidental falls flat.

Salem, Massachusetts, is America's quintessential ghost town, with its shameful history of "witch hangings." One of the strangest and most frightening of haunted places there is the House of the Seven Gables, made immortal in the novel by that name. Its author was Nathaniel Hawthorne (1804–1864), born in Salem, a direct descendent of one of the Salem witch trial judges; he always thought the gloomy family home was haunted. Hawthorne experienced one of the better-known ghost encounters in the early 1800s when, in the Boston Athenaeum library, he clearly saw the apparition of a minister he'd been acquainted with, every day for a week after the man died.

In addition to the reports of ghost sightings, every October, Salem holds a popular ten-day festival called "Halloween Happenings" that draws huge numbers of tourists.[48]

Head west and in Barstow, California, is the Calico Ghost Town, a "restored" 1880s silver mining town where tours are conducted. Its most famous ghost is, undoubtedly, Wyatt Earp who once lived there.

In Tombstone, Arizona, the local tourism office is not reluctant to tell you where you might see or hear a ghost, such as at the Bird Cage Theatre, built in the 1880s, and once a Wild West nightspot—dance hall and brothel—marked by many gunfights.[49]

The ego and drive one needs to become a motion picture star is enormous. Tremendous dedication, hard work, sacrifice, and tireless energy are required. So, when a well-known actor or actress dies tragically or is killed, their emotional state is sometimes so strong that death is a stunning interruption. Some have refused to move on in the afterlife, and instead remain here as ghosts. It's as if the spotlight that stardom brings is a stronger attraction than the light that guides the soul to the Other Side. Welcome to Hollywood, home to many celebrity ghosts, if countless witnesses are to be believed.

One of the best known is the specter of silent movie star Rudolph Valentino who died suddenly in 1926 at the age of thirty-one; his death was mourned by millions of hysterical fans all over the country. Valentino's apparition has been seen at Falcon Lair, his former mansion in Beverly Hills. Following his untimely death, Valentino's former wife, Natacha Rambova, self-proclaimed medium, claimed she was in contact with his spirit.

Another of Hollywood's legendary ghosts was a lovely young actress named Thelma Todd, who was found dead in her car in the garage of her Pacific Palisades home in 1935. The cause of her death remains a mystery. It was officially declared a suicide but bruises found on her body led many to think she was murdered.

Jean Harlow was a stunning blond star of Hollywood in the 1930s, and her tragic death at age twenty-six set off a string of supernatural events in her former Beverly Hills home that were uncanny. Harlow's death may have been the result of repeated beatings by her husband, agent Paul Bern, who killed himself. In the years after their deaths, voices and noises were reported that were believed to be the couple fighting.

But the story doesn't end there. In 1966, celebrity hair stylist Jay Sebring purchased the Benedict Canyon home. His girlfriend was the beautiful actress Sharon Tate. One night while she was alone in the house, she was awakened by the specter of Paul Bern, running wildly through her bedroom, banging into furniture. Frightened, Tate fled downstairs where she experienced a terrifying vision of Sebring tied to a wooden post; his throat had been slashed and he was bleeding heavily. At the same time, noises from the bedroom became louder. Tate was panic-stricken. The next day, she told Sebring about her horrific experience. He attributed it to her nerves or imagination. But in 1969, her ghastly vision came true when Sebring and Tate were among five people murdered by the deranged Charlie Manson family; both victims were found tied together to a living room beam.

If apparitional phenomena are hallucinatory, as skeptics insist, what explained Tate's chilling—and tragically accurate—vision?

Only several houses away, once lived actor George Reeves, better known to a generation of children in the 1950s as TV's "Superman." In 1959, Reeves was found shot to death in his bedroom. Although it was officially ruled a suicide, there has long been speculation that a girl-friend may have murdered him. After his death, there were many who reported seeing his apparition in and near his former Benedict Canyon Drive home.

Whether fact or fiction, the spirit of screen legend Marilyn Monroe has been reported in a couple of locations. One is near the mausoleum where she was laid to rest in Westwood Memorial Cemetery. Another place is her former home in fashionable Brentwood where Monroe took a fatal overdose of sleeping pills in 1962. To this day, there is controversy about whether her tragic death, at the age of thirty-six, was suicide, accidental, or the result of foul play.

One of the more credible ghost sightings concerns another beautiful actress, the late Jayne Mansfield. The blonde bombshell of the 1950s and '60s lived in a Bel Air mansion dubbed the Pink Palace, for the color she painted everything. Mansfield died dreadfully when she was decapitated in an automobile accident in 1967, a year after she joined the Church of Satan. But her ghost—looking beautiful—returned to her home. Among the witnesses to her apparition was singer Engelbert Humperdinck who later purchased the house.

One of the stranger stories to emerge from celebrity homes is the house where the movie star Joan Crawford lived many years ago. Her daughter said that voices were heard from within the walls, while phan-toms wandered around. Crawford was alarmed enough that she called in a priest to perform an exorcism. But after Crawford died, the wall be-hind her bed repeatedly and inexplicably burst into flames. Arson inves-tigators could find no earthly explanation. Later owners included several well-known actors who also experienced disturbing phenomena, and exorcisms were again performed.[50]

For anyone interested in celebrity ghosts there are books and Web sites galore. In fact, there were so many "visits" by Elvis Presley's spirit, after his untimely death from drugs in 1977, that an entire book, *Elvis After Life*, by Dr. Raymond Moody, Jr., was devoted to the subject. It included accounts of ordinary people who told of witnessing Presley's apparition, and raised both paranormal and psychological questions about the experiences.[51]

You'll notice the same pattern with the ghosts of the famous as those who were not well known. In most cases they were individuals who died tragically or unexpectedly, often at a young age. Ghosts are a part of American history not deemed worthy of serious consideration by scholars. Yet the number of incidents and witnesses suggests that something is occurring that should not be neglected. Perhaps people have a psychological "need to believe" in spirit phenomena. However, in turning a blind eye to ghosts, are we ignoring evidence of survival beyond death?

Alcatraz Island is only a short distance from San Francisco, but emotionally, it is a world away. Long ago, the Miwok Indians believed evil spirits possessed the island. But it was when the federal government turned the old army prison into a maximum-security penitentiary in the 1930s that it became infamous. In its day, Alcatraz was considered the toughest prison in America. Within its walls and drab concrete buildings some of the most dangerous criminals in the country were confined; perhaps the most notorious were Prohibition-era gangster Al Capone, and Robert Stroud, the famed "Birdman of Alcatraz." Conditions were bleak and brutal. Inmates were confined to tiny cells with the barest of amenities, and had little to do, except slowly waste away mentally and physically. Many a tough guy was broken by "doing time" there, and some went insane from isolation on the chilly, fog-shrouded island.

Finally, in 1963, Attorney General Robert F. Kennedy ordered the aging, decaying prison closed. But the ghosts of some tormented inmates did not leave, and there were inexplicable disturbances in several cell blocks. There were such frequent reports of noises, screaming voices, and crying that even the National Park Service, responsible for the island, and never a supporter of the paranormal, called in a California psychic, Sylvia Browne, for help.

Browne was able to communicate with the agitated and angry spirit of an inmate nicknamed "Butcher." He was just as bitter in the afterlife as he'd been on Earth. Prison records identified him as Abie Maldowitz, a mob hit man, who'd also killed another inmate while in prison.

Other cells were haunted and disembodied voices were frequently heard. One cell was bitter cold, even during the summer, and some visitors reported feeling "emotionally overwhelmed" there; it had once been the cell where a vicious killer named Rufus McCain spent three years in solitary confinement.

One of the most curious sounds reported has been banjo playing. It has been attributed to mobster Al Capone who played banjo when he was an inmate.

It obviously has been difficult for many of those imprisoned in Alcatraz to release their anger and bitterness, and move on to the hereafter. It's as if the souls of those once confined there remain imprisoned. Alcatraz has since become a popular tourist attraction, where visitors unwittingly walk among the spirits of some of the worst criminals in the history of the country.[52]

So is there a "most haunted house" in America, other than the White House? Some contend the title should go to the Whaley House in San Diego, California. In fact, the state has designated it an "officially haunted house." Built in 1857 by Thomas Whaley, the brick mansion was located in what was known as the Old Town section of San Diego. Whaley rented a part of the two-story house to the county for use as a courtroom and a place to store records. But problems arose when the Whaley House found itself at the center of a "power struggle" between Old Town residents and those who considered themselves "New Towners" and wanted county records stored in their part of the city.

Thomas Whaley was not home when a mob from New Town forced their way into his house, terrified his wife and daughter, pillaged, and stole county records stored there. Whaley was stunned and angered; he'd been wronged and demanded restitution from the county for the invasion. For twenty years, he attempted to collect monies he insisted were due him. But the county would not fork over a cent, and Whaley died bitter, never having been compensated.

Nearly a century went by until the county purchased the Whaley House and began to restore it. That's when strange events started. Workers reported seeing ghosts walking by on the second floor, alarms sounded without explanation, and windows opened on their own. Several of the apparitions have been identified as Whaley, his wife, and children. Another frequently reported ghost is that of a young girl who died accidentally in the house. Other phantoms are dressed in nineteenth-century clothing.

Some have claimed to see the specter of a man hanging in a doorway. Speculation is that he was someone convicted of stealing a boat in the early 1850s, and sentenced to the gallows, and hanged on Whaley House property.[53]

Today, the Whaley House is a museum, where psychic investigators have made audio recordings of spirit voices and mysterious noises.

Inanimate objects also qualify as ghosts. The *Flying Dutchman* is arguably the best-known ghost ship in the world. There are several versions told about the legendary vessel, depending on the country. But the problem seems to center around the deranged captain who "made a deal with the devil," for one reason or another. In exchange, the phantoms of the captain and his crew were condemned to sail for eternity.

The *Flying Dutchman* has allegedly been sighted all over the globe, including America. According to one author, the ghost ship was seen twice in Galveston Bay, Texas, in 1892, and more recently in other countries; if the ghost ship is seen, it is considered a "bad omen."[54]

And the stories keep on coming. In May 2006, a Staten Island, New York, mansion, already reported haunted by the spirits of two people who died in a fire long ago, became the scene of a mob hit.

What are you supposed to do if you confront a ghost, or if you happen to live in a house occupied by one or more of them? Since they are "earthbound spirits" whose time here has expired, most ghost hunters suggest they be encouraged to move on to the next stage of life, the other side, in order to "grow spiritually." There are a number of instances in which psychic mediums have been able to ascertain who is haunting and why.

Many people have simply learned to coexist with ghosts. If however, hauntings become too disturbing—or seem dangerous—then ghost hunters are sometimes called in. The hosts of the Syfy cable network TV series, *Ghost Hunters,* estimated that about 80 percent of the allegedly haunted houses they're called to investigate are explainable by natural occurrences, not ghosts. Sometimes, a noise in the attic is just a noise. But about 20 percent of hauntings are found to be paranormal.

Ghost hunters, with their array of equipment that can include meters to determine electromagnetic changes, compasses to discover magnetic fields, thermometers to measure any temperature variations such as "cold spots," a variety of still and film cameras including infrared photography, videotape and audiotape recorders with highly sensitive microphones, even night-vision scopes, claim they can locate the source of haunting phenomena. Web sites can direct you to ghost hunters; there are groups or individuals in many communities and every state in the country. Some charge for their services, others perform gratis. Incidentally, ghost phenomena are taken so seriously that some states, such as New York, have enacted laws that require someone selling a haunted house to inform a potential buyer in advance of the transaction.

In addition to ghosts of the kind we've just described, there are poltergeist phenomena. Technically, the word *poltergeist* is from German meaning "noisy ghost." Some consider poltergeists another form of haunting, while other parapsychologists are of the opinion that rather than being caused by spirits, mysterious disturbances are the result of psychokinetic effects from a living person, usually a child or adolescent. Whatever they are, spirits or some form of energy, most poltergeists are mischievous, although occasionally they've been known to be evil or dangerous. When poltergeist disturbances occur, objects are often flung from place to place, some fly through the air, then fall and break, and there may be inexplicable noises, sounds, odors, even strange lights, and apparitions. A bottle may pop its lid, or a chandelier might spin on its own. Poltergeists are notorious for interfering with electricity. Most incidents occur at night, and poltergeists can create a disconcerting ruckus. The activity seems to begin without explanation or warning, continues for days, weeks, or months, and then ends abruptly.

As with nearly every other paranormal phenomenon, poltergeist experiences have been reported for thousands of years, dating back to ancient Rome, through medieval times, and in many countries around the world. Serious psychic research about the cause and nature of poltergeists began in the 1890s. There are several theories, but no one can say with certainty what a poltergeist is. One interesting aspect is that in many cases, there have been multiple witnesses to the unsettling phenomena. For centuries, the devil or demonic forces were blamed. More recent theories suggest poltergeists may be an "involuntary or unconscious type of psychokinesis (PK) on the part of the living," wrote Rosemary Ellen Guiley. Might they be "sexual conflicts during adolescence," or "projections of repressed emotions, such as hostility or anger?" Guiley asked.[55]

One of the best-known poltergeist cases in American history occurred in the early nineteenth century in the tiny town of Adams, Tennessee, in 1817. Among the many witnesses to an infamous poltergeist called the Bell Witch was a famous general who went on to become the president of the United States, Andrew Jackson.

Adams, on the Red River, was home to a wealthy farmer, John Bell, his wife, Lucy, and their children. One hot summer day in 1817 Bell was stopped by the sight of a large and strange-looking creature in his corn-field. Several days later, Bell saw it again; it was a huge bird perched on a fence, staring at him. Badly frightened, the farmer fired a rifle shot at the odd creature, but missed, and the gigantic fowl flew off.

Never again, from that moment, did the Bell family know any peace. For the next three years, they were haunted and cursed by a sinister and demonic spirit, an evil force that came to be popularly known as the Bell Witch. Its behavior suggested that it was a poltergeist, capable of moving objects and people, even sending them flying. However, unlike mischievous poltergeists, the Bell Witch proved to be an angry and dangerous force.

The next incidents involved inexplicable banging and scratching noises on their door late at night. Each time the Bells were awakened and checked, there was no one outside. The family's nerves understandably became frazzled.

Then the strange scratching moved indoors, joined by the sound of rodents gnawing. There were choking noises, lips smacking, stones pelted their roof, chains were dragged, and furniture moved about. At first the Bells kept their supernatural experiences a secret, despite their fears.

A year later, events grew worse. The entire house shook as if an earthquake had struck. Some nights the children were terrified when the invisible force tore the bedcovers off them. One night, seven-year-old Richard Bell screamed in pain, when the unseen being became more aggressive and attacked the young boy. He said it felt as if someone was trying to tear his head off.

The witch seemed angriest with thirteen-year-old Betsy Bell, the only daughter of the eight Bell children still living at home. The poltergeist dragged the terrified girl out of bed by her hair. Then the demonic spirit cast spells that caused the child to lose her breath, and faint. Other times, the cruel invisible force smacked Betsy's face hard enough to leave red marks.

Finally the Bells realized their frightening encounters could not remain secret; they needed help. They first called a friend and preacher who performed an exorcism. "Stop, I beseech you, in the name of the Lord!" he commanded the evil entity. Incredibly, the exorcism seemed to work. For a time, things calmed in the Bell house, much to their relief.

But to their horror, the poltergeist returned, angrier than before. The entity seemed to calm when prayers were offered, but the force always came back. In one horrific incident, it caused Betsy Bell to throw up a medicine she'd been given to combat the witch's spells. The girl's vomit contained sharp needles and pins.

The unrelenting attacks were harshest against Betsy. Even when she was sent to live with neighbors, the spirit followed. There seemed no escape from the torment.

Eventually as news of the evil entity spread, the curious came in droves, hoping to witness the witch. The spirit seemed to oblige, especially when it began to speak. At first, it whistled, then whispered in a low female voice that soon grew clearer, although it would say nothing about its identity and purpose. However, the witch debated the Bible and scripture with visiting clergy. Not everyone believed what they heard; skeptics accused Betsy of ventriloquism. Yet when Betsy's mouth was covered, the entity's voice could still be discerned.

By the summer of 1820, the story had spread all the way to Nashville and newspapers reported the Bells' troubles. One of those who heard about it was none other than war hero General Andrew Jackson. He was curious enough to gather several friends and together they set out on the forty-mile journey from Nashville to the Bell plantation to personally witness the bizarre events. But Jackson was a skeptic and wagered the witch did not exist or engage in the terrible acts it was accused of. His opinion was that the story was either a hoax or the result of some natural phenomena.

Jackson's wagon was only a mile from the Bell home when inexplicably its wheels locked and would not budge. Jackson's men could not push it or get the horses to advance no matter how hard they tried. Jackson was amused by their predicament, and realized it was the work of the Bells' witch. The witch's voice answered, acknowledging Jackson was correct. "I'll speak with you again tonight," it snickered. "By the Eternal, boys, it's the witch!" Jackson exclaimed. Suddenly the wagon wheels unlocked, and Jackson and his group continued their ride to the Bell home.

John Bell played host to Jackson and his party that evening, as they sat around the fireplace talking, and drinking rum, waiting to see if the witch would appear as it promised. One of Jackson's men proclaimed himself a "witch-slayer" or exorcist. He boasted that he could rid the house of the noxious entity, by shooting it with a silver bullet. He loudly demanded the witch show itself; while Jackson was annoyed by his friend's bragging. Then the unseen being announced its presence. "Here I am as promised, General." The witch called the self-appointed exorcist a "bag of hot wind," angrily taunted him, and demanded he shoot. But the man's gun would not fire.

The Bell Witch went into action. The invisible force slammed the braggart into walls, furniture, and dishes; it dragged him by one leg, and finally grabbed his nose until he screamed in pain. The entity cackled with glee as the terrified man fled from the house, never to return.

Jackson had enjoyed the remarkable supernatural demonstration. When the witch announced it was leaving, and would return the next night, it could not resist a parting swipe at Jackson's wife, Rachel. The witch howled, "How's that fat old wife of yours? Think you'll ever get her carcass into the White House?"

Jackson, stunned and angered by the witch's unexpected and vulgar outburst, claimed he felt the entity brush by his chin. He was very protective of his wife; he'd once shot and killed a man for insulting her.

The next morning Jackson and his group left the Bell farm; he'd seen enough. Jackson returned home to Nashville, and never again spoke about his encounter with the Bell Witch. His last words on the subject were: "I wish no more dealings with that torment." That a national figure of Jackson's stature witnessed the witch added immensely to the credibility of the Bell family's claims.

John Bell's problems with the unseen force were not over. Her evil and demented antics continued against him, although the witch never bothered Mrs. Bell. The entity did reveal itself as someone named Katie Batts. No one could identify her with any certainty. But "Old Kate" promised to haunt John Bell until he was "dead and buried."

True to her word, John Bell took ill in the autumn of 1820. His tongue stiffened and became badly swollen, until he could barely speak or eat. Then he developed a facial twitch. Bell knew why. "This terrible thing, the witch is killing me," he told his son.

Finally, on December 20, 1820, Bell lapsed into a coma. The vindictive entity was ecstatic. She even bragged that she'd switched medicine given Bell with poison. The next day, Bell died. Even as the family grieved, the witch was heard laughing and singing. The Bell Witch pronounced her work done, and with that she was gone, as mysteriously as she first appeared.

No one has ever determined with certainty the Bell Witch's identity or what caused her malevolent behavior. True to the activity of most poltergeists, this one had centered its attention on a child, Betsy Bell. Unlike ghosts who typically cling to one location, poltergeists can move from place to place, and then eventually dissipate and leave.

One paranormal theory suggested that young Betsy was the "poltergeist agent" whose own telekinetic energy caused the horrific activity. Had Betsy, under emotional stress, acted out a subconscious resentment against her father that manifested itself as psychic energy to create the poltergeist's destructive behavior?

Skeptics blamed Betsy, accusing her of fabricating the Bell Witch phenomena, but that was never proven and Betsy refused to ever talk again about her family's "troubles." In fact, no one has ever established a definitive answer. Betsy Bell died in 1890 at the age of eighty-six. However, many Bell descendents met violent or untimely deaths. The Bell Witch holds the dubious distinction of being the only poltergeist in American history to ever speak to—and kill—someone. Poltergeist activity usually results in mischief, not serious harm. The Bell Witch proved the exception to that rule. Andrew Jackson had been one of the best-known and most credible witnesses to the country's most infamous ghost, although, as with other paranormal events, you won't find the story in most traditional history books.

Eventually the Bell house was torn down; although some believe the area remains haunted. On U.S. Highway 41, a Tennessee Historical Commission marker briefly tells the story of the infamous haunting. Close by is a monument dedicated to the Bell family, the only official monument to a ghost in the United States.[56]

More typical of poltergeist activity was the mischief caused in another famous case that took place in Seaford, New York, in the spring of 1958. At the time, David Kahn was a young reporter for the newspaper, *Newsday*. His assignment was to get to the bottom of one of the strangest incidents at the time. Something mysterious was definitely going on in the modest one-family suburban Long Island home of the James Herrmann family.

Years later, Kahn shared his memories of that experience on the *Joel Martin Show* from which this story is taken. It was later retold in the *Dead Zones*, a book edited by Sharon Jarvis.

Until the spring of 1958, James Herrmann's life was not unlike millions of other hardworking middle-class Americans. Jim was employed by a major airline; his wife was a nurse, and the couple had two children, twelve-year-old James, Jr., and thirteen-year-old Lucille. There was no way to imagine that inside their home, supernatural phenomena was occurring that would be the subject of worldwide attention.

The incidents began when jars and bottles literally started to pop their lids, and something unseen shoved them off shelves. As startled family members watched, glassware spun itself around. Religious objects also acted as if some invisible force was propelling them; a statue dangled in midair, while other figurines literally took flight.

Stunned and unnerved by the inexplicable activity, James Herrmann called the local police department for help; perhaps they would be able to find the source of the disturbances. Police took Herrmann's plight seriously, and even assigned a detective to the case. One suggestion was that the Herrmanns "install a draft mechanism on the chimney." That would eliminate any air currents in the house that might be responsible for knocking over bottles, jars, and statuettes.

They tried, but the draft mechanism was not the solution: bottle tops continued to pop, and flying jars interrupted the Herrmanns' daily life and routines. On one occasion, a perfume bottle flew through the air and smashed into a piece of furniture. Although the glass remained unbroken, when it fell, the perfume spilled all over the floor, filling the room with its aroma. Another puzzle was the surprisingly loud noises made by bottles and jars when they popped their lids or hit the ground.

One witness to the phenomena said, "They sounded like small

explosions, a louder noise than you'd expect from a bottle being hurled at a dresser and breaking apart. It was as if there was some explosive force inside the bottles."

The Herrmanns reported more than sixty incidents; all acts of mischief, none of them posed any danger or threat. The only commonality the strange events had was that the majority of them occurred near or around twelve-year-old Jimmy Herrmann.

The Herrmann house phenomena did not escape the attention of parapsychologists and psychic researchers, some of whom visited the house to investigate the phenomena. Was it something paranormal? One of the parapsychologists who sought answers was William Roll of the highly regarded Psychical Research Foundation in Durham, North Carolina. His first task was to rule out the "most logical and obvious possibilities: fraud, pranks, strings, tricks, mechanical devices, even pets or squirrels" that could have moved objects from one place to another in the house. He checked for any drafts or air currents that might be responsible for "movements and unusual sounds." Roll also considered "plumbing, underground river currents, even sonic booms." But after his exhaustive investigations, he was still unable to find any natural explanation.

There was no way to keep the goings-on in the Herrmann house private; it became an obvious source of public curiosity. It was soon after, that David Kahn was assigned to report the story for *Newsday*. "Get down there and catch the kid, Dave," his editor told him. The assumption was that twelve-year-old Jimmy Herrmann was somehow responsible; it was a popular theory that Jimmy was behind the peculiar incidents.

Kahn gave serious thought as to how he could uncover the cause of the Herrmann house events. Then he hit upon an idea. "Let me stay there one night," Kahn asked his editors. They and the family agreed. The Herrmanns hoped someone would find the answer to their peculiar circumstance.

Meanwhile, rumors spread through the community and in the media that some sort of spirit phenomena was at work. Might the Herrmann family be living in a haunted house? Was a poltergeist responsible?

Kahn was not inclined toward supernatural explanations, and did not believe in ghosts. His approach was more like a detective out to solve a case. He was searching for some rational and practical explanation; there had to be some logical reason for the strange activity. Kahn devised a plan. "I stationed myself in the living room," he recalled, "facing the young boy's room." From that vantage point, Kahn would be able to watch Jimmy's goings-on all night. "On one side was the boy's bed. In another part of the room was a globe of the world, which he used for school. As I sat there, suddenly the globe came pitching out of the boy's bedroom toward me into the living room.

"Of course, I dashed right into his room to see whether the boy had thrown the globe out in my direction. When I ran in, the boy was in his bed, with his covers drawn up. It couldn't have taken more than a second or two to get in there. So there was not enough time for him to get out of bed and go for that globe. Also he was a kind of heavyset kid, slightly overweight at the time, and not especially agile, I didn't feel. He would have to have been remarkably fast to have gotten that globe without my seeing him, because I was looking right at him. It just wasn't right from a ballistics standpoint, either.

"There didn't seem to be any kind of pattern to the occurrences. The detective once had the same experience I did. He was climbing the cellar stairs with the young boy right behind him when something, an object, suddenly went flying, and there was the popping sound again accompanying it. He spun around and the boy was right there. Maybe if the youngster had been like some comic book character with extraordinary agility and speed, he could have done it. But the detective didn't think the boy could have caused it, exactly the same way I didn't think so," Kahn concluded.

Meanwhile, other investigations of the house continued. Everything was scrutinized. Even the local utility company checked for possible electrical disturbances or alterations in "energy fields." But they found nothing out of the ordinary.

The story of the Herrmanns' spirit-racked house was now making national news. Then, as inexplicably as the mysterious phenomena began, it slowed down, and soon the chaos ceased. Once the disturbances ended, they never occurred again. Whatever had entered the Herrmann house was gone. "It died down by itself. It had gone away, and it was like it had never been," Kahn said. It was typical of poltergeist activity to abruptly appear and disappear, to mysteriously come and go.

Thirty years later, reporter David Kahn's opinions about what he observed had not changed. "There's no doubt that the phenomena were going on around James, Jr., and from my research of poltergeist incidents, in nearly every case a child or adolescent is involved.

"I still remain convinced that it was poltergeist phenomena. I don't have another explanation. I found no evidence of spirits. My conclusion about the whole thing is that it remains unexplained. I can only put it in the class of other still-unexplained poltergeist incidents that go on around the world."

The Herrmann house remains "one of the most thoroughly investigated poltergeists cases" in modern American history.[57]

When the Herrmann house story came to the attention of J. B. Rhine at Duke University, Rhine dispatched two psychic investigators to examine the poltergeist claims, J. G. Pratt and William Roll. Rhine's attention had been piqued because the case appeared to concern psychokinetic energy or PK, the "ability of the mind to act upon or influence the physical world." Prior to the Seaford case, Rhine's only way to study PK was in his laboratory with dice throwing experiments. He'd theorized poltergeist disturbances were similar. Pratt and Roll coined an expression, "recurrent spontaneous psychokinesis" to explain poltergeist cases. In other words, the activity did not have to be the result of spirit phenomena. Other parapsychologists disagreed, maintaining that spirits were responsible for the mysterious incidents.

Nine years later, in 1967, Roll and Pratt joined to investigate the "Miami Poltergeist." In that case, the pair sought an explanation for the cause of disturbances in a Miami warehouse of Tropication Arts, a company that sold novelty items to retailers. The poltergeist tumult resulted in inventory that inexplicably fell and broke. Even police called to investigate watched as items mysteriously dropped from shelves. Once natural explanations and warehouse personnel were ruled out as the culprits, ghosts were suspected. Media coverage brought the story to the attention of Roll and Pratt.

Their investigation led to the conclusion that the poltergeist or PK activity centered on a nineteen-year-old shipping clerk identified as Julio who eventually admitted to a deep-seated hatred of his employer, and serious family problems. Were Julio's anger, hostility, and other repressed negative emotions unconsciously responsible for the poltergeist force? In all, there had been more than two hundred separate incidents. But, once Julio left the warehouse, the phenomena stopped. Roll's conclusion was that PK was responsible for the poltergeist disturbances, rather than ghosts. For many years, Roll was regarded as the foremost expert on poltergeists in the country. Julio was tested by the ASPR and found to have an uncommon ability for PK.[58]

The late parapsychologist D. Scott Rogo had conjectured that "a poltergeist might be some type of apparition created or projected by" the individual around whom the activity occurs.[59] In 1973, several members of the Toronto Society for Psychical Research (TSPR) put that theory to a remarkable test in what came to be known worldwide as the "Philip Experiment." Their goal was to determine if they could collectively create an "artificial ghost" or poltergeist by intensely concentrating for a period of time. The eight people, under the direction of the TSPR directors, A. R. G. Owen and his wife, Iris Owen, concocted a ghost they named "Philip Aylesford," and created a fictitious history that he lived in the seventeenth century, served in the military, was a spy, and had an adulterous affair. In the make-believe biography, "Philip" committed suicide in 1654 at the age of thirty.

The TSPR group, none of whom had psychic ability, gathered to concentrate and meditate, hoping their creation would materialize as a ghost, but it did not, although several members said they'd felt a "presence" in the room.

Several months later, having had no success, the TSPR group resorted to the old spiritualist technique of placing their hands gently on the table, and then watching it tilt. At nineteenth-century séances, "table-tilting" had been a popular technique to receive what many believed was a response from the spirit world.

Eventually, at one of their sessions, TSPR members felt the table vibrate, then heard rapping and knocking noises. "Philip," although fictional, was able to answer questions put to him by rapping once for yes, and two for no. However, "Philip's" replies were not able to go beyond the information the group fabricated about him. At a later gathering, the table levitated off the ground. The group was never able to cause an apparition to materialize. However, TSPR members believed they'd successfully established that their collective subconscious was able to generate, through psychokinesis, some of the same physical phenomena attributed to poltergeists. They called their experiment "PK by Committee." Iris Owen later wrote a book detailing their efforts, titled *Conjuring Up Philip.*[60]

In 1531, a poor Aztec peasant named Juan Diego, a convert to Catholicism, witnessed an apparition that identified herself as the "Blessed Virgin Mary." In all, she appeared to him on five occasions. Juan Diego described her as a glowing figure standing in a cloudlike mist. It was during one of her materializations that the Lady instructed Juan to gather a species of roses not known in Mexico at the time. The peasant did as he was told, finding a garden that he'd never before seen. Next, the apparition told him to place the flowers in his cape and bring them to the bishop. Juan followed the Lady's instructions, and when the folded cape was opened there was an exquisite picture of the Immaculate Conception miraculously printed on the garment. The painting showed the Blessed Virgin in a celestial setting with an angel at her feet. The art did not resemble the primitive Mayan-Aztec style of the time, although the image of the Virgin Mary was dressed "like an Indian woman" and in the Lady's eyes was the reflection of a man, possibly Juan Diego.

Juan's cape, woven from a rough-hewn material called "cactus fiber," was not supposed to last many years. However, the painting of the Blessed Virgin imprinted in Juan Diego's sixteenth-century wrap survives to this day; it is on display at the church and shrine at Guadalupe, built to honor Mary's apparition, as she requested.[61]

The Roman Catholic Church has a long tradition of "religious apparitions" that theologians are careful to point out are not ghosts; the paranormal remains anathema to Christianity. Rather they are defined as supernatural or "mystical phenomena." Over the centuries, there have been countless thousands of "Marian apparitions," that is, visions of the Blessed Virgin Mary.

Officially, the Church has been very sparing in giving its approval to apparitions of the Blessed Virgin; only a few have been declared genuine. Typically, witnesses describe the apparition of the Virgin as a beautiful lady dressed in white, and shining or bathed in brilliant light. Often she brings messages and implores people to be more prayerful and reverent. It is not uncommon for the apparition to first appear to children.

Bernadette Soubirous was fourteen years old, and living in the small village of Lourdes in southern France in February 1858 when she first claimed she saw a vision of the Virgin Mary in a nearby grotto. Between February 11 and July 16 of that year, Bernadette reported seeing the vision of a girl or young woman a total of eighteen times. The apparition spoke on one occasion, and the last time she appeared she announced, "I am the Immaculate Conception."

Following the visions, Bernadette found a nearby underground spring whose waters were believed to be the source of "miraculous healings." The Vatican deemed Bernadette's visions authentic in 1862. A chapel was built there in 1871, as the apparition had asked. Bernadette of Lourdes was canonized a saint in 1933. Up to six million "pilgrims, invalids, and sightseers" visit Lourdes every year, including many Americans. Between 1878 and 1978, the Church had accepted just sixty-four cases of miraculous healings at Lourdes out of more than five thousand that were claimed.[62]

When it comes to investigating paranormal or supernatural events, the Church has long proven to be extremely thorough and, historically, not quick to accept miraculous claims as only a matter of faith. But in recent years, the Vatican has become more lenient; too many people regard the apparitions as a "special sign from God."

One of the most famous cases of a Marian apparition occurred to three young children in Fatima, Portugal, in 1917. Ten-year-old Lucia dos Santos and her two cousins, Jacinta, aged seven, and Francisco, aged nine, told of seeing a "young lady." The two girls also claimed the apparition spoke to them. The Lady appeared once monthly for six successive months. As word spread, thousands of the faithful came to the pasture where the children said they saw the vision. Her last appearance to the children, on October 13, 1917, drew seventy thousand people, despite heavy rains that day. The apparition identified herself as the "Lady of the Rosary," and asked that a chapel be constructed at the site to honor her.

Then the downpour unexpectedly ceased, and the sun peeked through the parted clouds. Suddenly, the sun began to spin, giving off an array of colored light. The gyrating sun looked as if it was coming closer and about to fall to Earth. Some said they could feel its heat, and many became panicky, fearing this was a sign the world was about to end. But then, inexplicably, the sun returned to its place in the sky. The phenomenon that day, witnessed by thousands, has become known as the "miracle of the sun."

The apparition also gave the children three messages. She urged greater devotion and prayer, accurately forewarned of another horrific world war, and also predicted Russia's conversion to Christianity. A basilica was later built at Fatima; the stories of Lourdes and Fatima both became major Hollywood motion pictures years later.[63]

Marian apparitions are not simply curious relics or tales from long ago; they continue to occur. On June 24, 1981, six teenagers—four girls and two boys—saw the apparition of the Blessed Virgin Mary on a hill in the mountain village of Medjugorje, in what was once Yugoslavia, and a decade later became the independent republic of Bosnia-Herzegovina, the location of a devastating civil war and brutal "ethnic cleansing." For the next eighteen months, one or the other of the young people saw the apparition every day. Since then there have been literally thousands of sightings, lasting anywhere from a few minutes to more than half an hour. Other miracles have also been reported, ranging from healings to the Croatian word for peace—*mir*—written across the sky during the summer of 1981. The sun has also been seen oscillating and revolving. The apparition's most significant message has been her call for peace, prayer, and a "return to God." Many Americans have made the pilgrimage to Medjugorje.[64]

What's arguably most significant about Marian apparitions is the profound effect they've had on those who've experienced them, whether they are church-authenticated or not. There have been many sightings in America, as well as in other countries. While atheists and debunkers scoff at the apparitions, the number of them has greatly increased in recent years. While it seems at first easy to dismiss religious apparitions as psychological or superstitious phenomena, perhaps a reflection of people's fears amidst growing world tensions, and a yearning for a spiritual sign from God, the huge number of witnesses makes it difficult to dismiss the phenomena as imaginary or meaningless. Marian apparitions obviously fulfill an emotional need; it is a "mother figure," noted one priest, Father Johann Roten, an expert on the subject.

There has long been debate about the reality of ghosts and apparitions, and the overlap between theology and parapsychology adds another element to the long argument. Meanwhile, as the "experts" engage in their polemics, people of all kinds continue to experience visions, regardless of what churches, scientists, psychologists, or skeptics tell them they can or cannot see.

By the late 1960s, American popular culture was paying little attention to the ancient belief in possession or exorcism, although you might have gotten a dose of vicarious evil from seeing the Roman Polanski thriller, *Rosemary's Baby* in 1968. The next year, ironically, Polanski's wife, the beautiful actress Sharon Tate was one of the victims slaughtered by the murderous followers of Charlie Manson, who boasted he was a satanist. As Catholics and fundamentalist Christians believe, there is a phenomenon in which the devil or demonic spirits can enter and take control of a person's mind and soul. Living in fear of the devil and his henchmen went on for many centuries. However, it wasn't exactly in the forefront of modern America's consciousness. Manson and his twisted, drug-crazed disciples were considered sickening aberrations. "Middle America" had espoused no interest in contacting the "dark forces." Few people wanted to tangle with the devil and his minions, notwithstanding skeptics and atheists who regarded the whole business as "superstition" that belonged to earlier centuries. Even some clergy dismissed the idea of demons running to and fro, creating evil.

Then, in 1973, *The Exorcist* hit movie screens all over the country. The story of a presumably ordinary twelve-year-old girl whose body becomes possessed by the devil was both riveting and frightening; chillingly enhanced by makeup and special effects that included the possessed child's spinning head, her vomiting green bile, mutilating herself with a crucifix, and levitating from her bed. All the while, a troubled priest tries desperately to face the hostile and defiant demon, and remove it from the tortured girl, played by actress Linda Blair. The deep and scratchy voice of Satan that spoke through the possessed child, actually actress Mercedes McCambridge, added another layer of terror for moviegoers.

Suddenly, possession and exorcism were on the front burner; pardon the pun. The number of Americans who thought demonic spirits possessed their homes increased greatly, and so did the call for exorcists. To add to people's fears was the reminder that *The Exorcist,* based on a book by William Peter Blatty, had been inspired by true events that occurred to a young boy, years earlier.

The message of the movie was that there "is still a force of supernatural and evil active in the world, and both science and reason were powerless against it," wrote Michael W. Cuneo in *American Exorcism*.[65]

Not all Catholic clergy found words of praise for *The Exorcist*. For instance, the Jesuit magazine, *America*, at the time berated it as "sensationalistic and sordid," Cuneo noted.

In 1949, Blatty was a student at Georgetown University when he read with fascination the story of a fourteen-year-old Maryland boy who had been demonically possessed and then exorcised. According to the *Washington Post*, the child had been tortured with a barrage of unseen and terrifying phenomena. Objects and furniture in the boy's room went sailing through the air; there were inexplicable noises, and the sound of "scratching" on the bedroom walls. The youngster was even pulled from his bed, and chilling was the description of the boy's bed moving itself from one place to another—with him in it. The child, tortured by the chaos, could find no rest or peace.

The boy's parents called a Protestant minister for help—one who claimed knowledge of both religion and the paranormal. But the disturbances did not abate, in fact they worsened. The family next sought medical attention for their child, and he underwent a battery of tests. But doctors were stymied; they could find no course of treatment or cure for whatever was wrong with him.

The boy's parents suspected an "evil spirit," and asked Jesuit priests for help. After observing the youngster and the mysterious phenomena, one priest was designated to perform a series of exorcisms on him. The *Post* story reported that the Jesuits, during a period of several weeks, carried out twenty exorcisms. With the exception of the last, during every other one, the boy broke into a "violent tantrum of screaming, cursing, and voicing Latin phrases . . . whenever the priest reached those climactic points of the twenty-seven page ritual in which he commanded the demon to depart," according to the newspaper article.

Finally, the exorcisms worked; it had taken two stress-filled months, but the boy was apparently well again and free of whatever had possessed him.

The story fascinated Blatty, who'd once considered becoming a priest. If there was truth to it, the concept of demonic possession and exorcism still had meaning in the modern world. Finally, in 1969, Blatty, by then a

Hollywood writer, researched Catholic demonology, and sat down to write a novel based on the once-possessed boy's ordeal.

With the help of the priest who'd performed the original exorcisms, Blatty gained access to a diary one of the Jesuits had kept about the troubling encounter. In the journal were entries about perplexing skin eruptions on the boy, furniture that shook and crashed, and a "nightstand" that lifted itself from the floor and levitated to the ceiling. Blatty's bestselling novel took a great deal of license to make diabolical events even more terrifying than they actually were; and the movie, *The Exorcist*, went still further in exaggerating demonic possession.[66]

One of those alerted to the original story in 1949 was respected parapsychologist Dr. J. B. Rhine at Duke University; the minister whose exorcism proved unsuccessful had called upon him. Rhine was particularly interested in what incidents might be a result of psychokinetic energy. Similar to poltergeist cases, Rhine theorized that the so-called demonic phenomena was actually attributable to the "power" of the boy's own unconscious mind.

The most successful follow-up to *The Exorcist* was a book by a controversial, former Jesuit priest named Malachi Martin (1921–1999). In 1976, he wrote *Hostage to the Devil*; the bestseller that claimed to be true stories of five possessed people kept exorcism in the forefront of American consciousness. Martin carefully spelled out how people fell into and then were helped out of their bondage to the devil.[67]

Thanks to—if that's the right word—*The Exorcist* and *Hostage to the Devil,* "in the 1970s and 1980s there were . . . more exorcisms taking place in the United States than the Catholic Church was . . . aware of," Cuneo noted.[68]

Ed and Lorraine Warren, touting themselves as the "world's most famous demonologists" found plenty to talk about; they'd supported the controversial supernatural claims made in *The Amityville Horror*; and investigated other cases where evil entities sent people in fear for their lives. In 1988, with journalist Robert Curran, they wrote *The Haunted*; it later became a made-for-TV movie. It told the story of Jack and Janet Smurl and their three children. The family lived in West Pittston, Pennsylvania, when to their horror they found their home overrun by evil spirits. The Smurls claimed they were both sexually attacked by oppressive demons. There were inexplicable "claw marks" and stains on walls and floors. Once, their TV set erupted into flames, and ghastly apparitions appeared in one daughter's bedroom. News of the family's difficulties attracted huge crowds. More than fifty others witnessed mysterious phenomena in the house. Although the Warrens investigated, and a priest exorcised the residence, the Catholic Church didn't buy their story, and distanced itself. In all, more than fifty exorcisms were performed in the Smurl house, until the family finally moved out in 1989, ending their supernatural torment.[69]

In April 1991, the ABC-TV newsmagazine show, *20/20* televised an actual exorcism of someone demonically possessed—a first in network prime time. Millions of viewers watched a severely troubled sixteen-year-old girl named Gina exorcised by a priest. The girl, restrained in a chair, shrieked, jabbered incoherently, and twisted her body, as she struggled to break free.

Exactly how the televised event might have helped anyone was not clear, but a New York priest, Father James LeBar, found himself defending the TV exorcism that he'd helped arrange. Other clergy were angered that demonic possession was being "glamorized." There was also serious concern that blaming demons would lead some people to conclude they were not responsible for their actions. LeBar's answer was that demonic possession had to be recognized as a "tragic fact of life even in the modern world."[70]

Some clergy continue to scoff at the idea of demonic possession. They maintain that evil spirits do not exist as little hobgoblins running around wreaking havoc. There is general agreement, however, that evil endures in the form of "negative energy," and few theologians deny there is a "dark side" to human behavior. The devil, or Satan, is considered by some to be a "bad angel." There are liberal clergy who regard demonic possession as "bunk." Some argue that possession and exorcism feeds into negativity. But other ministers and priests continue to exhort believers that the devil and his demonic cohorts are absolutely genuine. In fact, some ministers view exorcism as a useful form of therapy; there's no evidence that it can cause any undue harm.

The Roman Catholic Church does not have a monopoly. The growing Pentecostal movement is a firm believer in the devil, possession, and exorcism, although they remain virulent opponents of the paranormal. Born-again Christians recognize "gifts of the Holy Spirit," citing references from the New Testament. At prayer services, in some fundamentalist denominations, ministers perform exorcisms to "cast out demons." The Catholic Charismatic movement also carries out "deliverances," a form of exorcism.

So, who is responsible for the explosion of interest and belief in demonic possession and exorcism in America? If you look back at events since the 1970s, it has been the media, not the churches that have brought the devil into the glare of the spotlight. Whether you find that to be a positive turn of events depends on your point of view. It is also a matter of opinion whether you recognize or accept the overlap of theology and parapsychology. For skeptics and atheists, the idea of evil spirits hovering in our highly technological society may seem anachronistic. But, for a host of reasons, both paranormal and psychological, the belief in—and fear of—the devil appears to be here to stay.

The Catholic Church regards many, if not most possession cases, to have psychiatric underpinnings. In many instances, it reflects a person's "cry for attention." Often, demonic possession has been used as an excuse for abhorrent or even criminal behavior. "The devil made me do it," has been attempted as a legal ploy many times, but has failed far more than it has succeeded. In fact, in *The Amityville Horror* story, demonic possession was considered a possible defense for convicted mass murderer Ronald DeFeo, Jr. in a bid for a new trial, but the idea was dropped.

"The Church and its theologians are most cautious about attributing the cause of unusual phenomena to Satan," wrote John J. Heany in *The Sacred and the Psychic*.[71] So while some experts did believe that the child in the Blatty story was demonically possessed, others concluded he was ill, but not because of possession.

In the Catholic Church, the only Christian denomination to maintain formal rites of exorcism, experts will look for every possible "natural explanation," and only after ruling them out, will the supernatural be considered. Most trained exorcists, psychiatrists, theologians, and parapsychologists agree with that approach. Thus, out of thousands of cases of alleged demonic possession, the Catholic Church has, by its strict criteria, only classified a handful as genuine. One danger to people who are highly suggestible is that belief in demonic possession can cause it to occur.

The history of evil or demonic spirits is as old as humankind. A number of biblical passages refer to the devil and demons. For example, a man tells those gathered that he had been possessed, but that he was returned to health after Jesus drove many demons out of him (Luke 8:27–36).

Not many people want to confront the devil or demons as Jesus did, but the reality is that evil has been a part of human life since the beginning of time, and "denying the dark side of the Almighty is inconsistent with biblical teachings," Dr. Larry Dossey wrote. "I form the light, and create darkness: I make peace, and create evil; I the Lord do all these things" (Isaiah 45:7).

Whether you approach evil from a religious or a paranormal perspective, evil is a force to be reckoned with, since it cannot always be avoided. Carl Jung said, to "grow psychologically and spiritually," we need to confront the "dark side" in each of us. Jung's conclusion was that to be a "whole person," one had to have experienced both God and fought with the devil.

Actually, in the history of Christianity, good and evil were simpler to define. Any supernatural phenomenon not sanctioned by the Church was evil. Anything psychic or paranormal was branded the work of the devil, and that included prohibitions on communicating with spirits of the dead. Fortunately, Christian beliefs are no longer that oversimplified, and those suspected of being possessed are not executed, as they were for centuries. In fact, the late Pope John Paul II had performed three exorcisms, the "rite to cast out demons," during his long reign. One took place in September 2001 when he "sprinkled holy water and commanded the devil to leave the body of a possessed twenty-year-old woman," according to the New York *Daily News*. The report said the pope "first went toe to toe with Satan in 1982 when he exorcised a demon from a woman who began thrashing on the ground during a Vatican audience."

"Even saintly Mother Teresa reportedly underwent an exorcism after Satan invaded her soul before she died of a heart attack in 1997," the *Daily News* said. The Catholic Church, which still teaches priests about possession, regards four signs as proof of demonic possession: extraordinary physical strength, clairvoyant ability, blasphemy or profanity against God, and levitation.

In the Catholic rite, exorcism includes blessings and prayers, then holy water is sprinkled, followed by the priest/exorcist placing his hands on the possessed person, making the sign of the cross, and ordering the devil to leave.

For parapsychologists, the "devilish destruction of the soul," as Rosemary Ellen Guiley explained, is not necessarily their concern. The paranormal focus has been on how and why such spirit phenomena commands and enters the body. How do spirits become tangled within us? How do we expel them? Spirit possession can lead to a host of physical and mental problems: powerful headaches, insomnia, inexplicable voices, noises, and lights, even psychokinetic or poltergeist phenomena.

It's rare that a person would seek to become spirit possessed. The exception is mediums that, technically speaking, allow spirits to communicate through them. The same is true for channelers, a variation of mediumship. But even mediums must be cautious not to wander into the spirit world irresponsibly. Mediums only permit spirit entry for a very short period of time. Technically, any medium that permits a discarnate spirit to enter is engaging in possession, if only temporarily. Historically, people were cautioned against employing Ouija boards for much the same reason—one might unwittingly summon demonic entities.

In recent years, there has been both paranormal and psychological interest in schizophrenia as a possible form of possession. Traditional psychiatrists scoff, of course. However, is it plausible that the frightening voices schizophrenics hear are not hallucinatory or imaginary, but perhaps lower-level demonic entities? Many psychiatrists have observed some schizophrenics become highly psychic. Is there a link between schizophrenia and paranormal ability?

In recent years, the number of Americans who claim contact of some kind with the deceased has grown to more than a hundred million people. If we've become a more scientific and technically sophisticated society, why would more people believe in "contact with the dead"? Some frantic debunkers have warned that America is sliding backward to the "Dark Ages." Obviously that isn't the case. In fact, surveys have found that among those who've reported witnessing apparitions were a wide cross-section of Americans, including some of the best educated and most affluent. A more reasonable explanation than a return to the Dark Ages is that millions of people are finally coming forward to share their paranormal experiences, realizing that bumping into a ghost or spirit does not have to be at odds with science or "rational thinking."

There are several possible explanations: People have always created myths, especially to cope with intense fears, such as death. Have we created ghosts in our minds because we have a need to believe? Jungians might suggest ghosts are archetypes or universal symbols, but not necessarily genuine physical phenomena. There is a third likelihood: What if the appearance of ghosts and apparitions is genuine, and evidence of life after death? In that case, you need not believe in ghosts to experience them.

9

New Age, Psychic Dreams, and Revolutions

Everything has been thought of before, but the problem is to think of it again.

—JOHANN WOLFGANG VON GOETHE (1749–1832)

In 1956, nationally syndicated columnist Jack Anderson interviewed psychic-seer and astrologer Jeane Dixon for *Parade* magazine. He asked her to predict the future, especially what she foresaw for the 1960 presidential race, still four years away. Anderson wrote: "As for the 1960 election, Mrs. Dixon thinks it will be won by a Democrat. But he will be assassinated or die in office, though not necessarily in his first term."

It would become Dixon's most famous prophecy, although the first time she told anyone about the fate of the president who would be elected in 1960 was actually in 1952 when she predicted that John F. Kennedy, then a Massachusetts congressman, "would achieve political victory at the highest level, but would die violently." Dixon even predicted that the 1960 presidential candidate would have blue eyes.

Her 1952 prophecy, she said, was based on a vision of the White House with the numerals 1-9-6-0 above it, which then was blotted out by a "dark cloud that dripped onto the [Capitol] dome." Dixon explained that she psychically witnessed Kennedy in a doorway while a clairaudient voice impressed upon her that he would be elected president, and then be assassinated in office.

Several million Americans certainly read Dixon's prophecy in *Parade* in 1956. What was the public and political reaction? Not much; as far as most Americans were concerned, a prediction from a "fortune-teller" was not something many would heed—if they even remembered it in 1960, four years after Dixon foretold the event. Who in his right mind would seriously consider what some soothsayer said?

The 1960 Democratic candidate was, indeed, John Fitzgerald Kennedy, the youthful, handsome, and charismatic U.S. senator from Massachusetts, portrayed as a World War II naval hero when, as commander of the PT-109, he supposedly saved his crew. Kennedy's Republican opponent was Richard Milhous Nixon, who'd been vice president under President Dwight Eisenhower for two terms.

When the new decade, the 1960s, yawned its way in there was little reason to suspect how different it would be than the conformist 1950s. There were a number of so-called beatniks and "Beat" writers and poets, notably Jack Kerouac and Allen Ginsberg, who had gained a measure of influence. Kerouac's novel, *On the Road*, written in 1957, was a tale of someone wandering freely around the country, with no particular purpose or responsibility, except pleasure. The book represented the very opposite of traditional American values of hard work leading to success, but it would be a potent inspiration for many youth in the sixties. However, fifties' Beat writers were hardly considered mainstream; they epitomized defiance and rebellion against authority.

The United States, with a population of nearly 180 million, was no less a religious country in 1960 than it had been in the preceding decades. Arguably, the best-known religious figure here, as elsewhere in the world, was Pope John XXIII. During his relatively brief tenure (1958–63) he dramatically called for modernizing the Church; but it was the pontiff's kindly and warm demeanor that captivated millions. In fact, religion became a contentious presidential campaign issue that year. John Kennedy was a Roman Catholic, and no Catholic had ever been elected president. Americans were divided on the question of whether the country was ready for a Catholic president; would his first loyalty be to the nation—or the Vatican? Kennedy answered without hesitation, "I believe in an America where the separation of church and state is absolute . . ."

A Roper poll taken in June 1960 revealed that 35 percent of Americans did not favor a Catholic seeking the presidency. But in November,

Kennedy eked out a narrow victory. Some credited Kennedy's slim win to his articulate performance in the historic TV debates between him and Nixon; there were eighty-five million TV sets in the nation, and most were riveted to the debates.

Whatever the reasons, John Fitzgerald Kennedy had become the thirty-fifth president—only forty-three years old at the time, the first U.S. president born in the twentieth century, and the youngest ever elected to the office. The new first lady, Jacqueline Bouvier Kennedy, who turned thirty-one in 1960, sparkled with beauty and elegance. Together, the couple projected an aura of youth and confidence that seemed to invigorate the country, and the White House bubbled with the laughter and energy of their two small children, Caroline and John, Jr. When Kennedy proclaimed that we were on the verge of a "new frontier," millions of Americans cheered the idea.

"The 1960s began with a tremendous burst of excitement and optimism," wrote Stephen Feinstein in *The 1960s from the Vietnam War to Flower Power*.[1] The decade became a time for a reawakening of psychic and related phenomena, and had "enormous influence on the evolution of what [became] New Age thought," wrote Mary Olsen Kelly in the *Treasury of Light*.[2] Throughout the chapter we'll detail some key events and movements that millions of America's youth turned to, such as Eastern practices for spiritual and psychic enlightenment, including meditation, yoga, and Zen. Many were drawn to astrology, the I Ching, tarot, spiritualism, witchcraft, and even satanism. Some turned to cults and communes. Others thought the path to higher consciousness could be found through psychedelic drugs, especially LSD. There were even those who questioned whether God was dead.

Astrology drew millions of followers; one of the themes of the decade, from the Broadway rock musical *Hair*, touted the sixties as the "Age of Aquarius." The ideas of psychic-seer Edgar Cayce; dream-ESP research; a controversial televised séance with Episcopalian bishop James Pike; the founding of the Church of Satan; Hare Krishna; Scientology, which considered the value of past lives; new attitudes toward death, dying, and afterlife experiences; and even the "Jesus Freaks," a movement that attracted alienated youth were all a part of the sixties.

The so-called "American Dream" was intact, and conspicuous consumer consumption was a sign of America's robust economic health. For the poor and the underclass, many of them black, some dared to dream of a future of greater equality; the nascent civil rights movement boasted such dynamic leaders as the Reverend Martin Luther King, Jr. The fact that he was a minister, who had organized and conducted what was essentially a political movement, imbued the civil rights cause with a moral force and an underlying spiritual message of brotherhood.

In 1960, four black college students held a sit-in at a Woolworth's lunch counter in Greensboro, North Carolina, where blacks had been refused service. Violent retaliation from white segregationists only inspired black youth to engage in hundreds more acts of "civil disobedience," an idea promulgated in America more than a century earlier by such New England transcendentalists as Henry David Thoreau and Ralph Waldo Emerson, called in their time, "unorthodox dissenters," author William Hutchinson noted.

There were political missteps—the failed Bay of Pigs invasion of Cuba in 1961, and close calls—the Cuban Missile Crisis in 1962, that brought the United States to the brink of nuclear war with the Soviet Union. But Americans could look with awe toward the wonders of outer space, sharing President Kennedy's lofty goal to have a man on the Moon by the end of the decade. In May 1961, Alan Shepard became the first American in space. Then, in February 1962, astronaut John Glenn became the first American to orbit the Earth. There was exhilaration about travel to outer space shared by most Americans, regardless of wealth, politics, or position.

In December 1961, President Kennedy sent four hundred U.S. military personnel to South Vietnam, a place most Americans would have been hard put to find on a map. Ripples of coming events that would have devastating effects on the stability and social fabric of America, but were barely noticed at first.

Secularists, who abhorred the supernatural and aligned it with their animus toward religion, gave a rousing cheer to the U.S. Supreme Court's decision in 1962 that prayer in public schools was unconstitutional. Others bitterly remarked that, "God had been thrown out of the classroom."

By the spring of 1963, Americans watched deeply disturbing TV images of black men, women, and children attacked by fire hoses and police dogs during civil rights demonstrations in Birmingham, Alabama, by order of racist police chief, "Bull" Connor. For many, black and white, what they saw was etched into their consciousness. Only three months later, on August 28, 1963, more than a quarter of a million people gathered in Washington, DC, to hear Martin Luther King deliver his powerful and stirring speech, "I have a dream." In the famed address, King shared his vision for the future:

> I have a dream that one day this nation will rise up and live out the true meaning of its creed: "We hold these truths to be self-evident: that all men are created equal." I have a dream that one day on the red hills of Georgia the sons of former slaves and the sons of former slave-owners will be able to sit down together at a table of brotherhood . . .

By summer 1963, "Blowin' in the Wind," written by a young folksinger-songwriter named Bob Dylan, had catapulted to become one of the decade's greatest protest songs. The lyrics suggested the answer to many troubling social problems was out there somewhere: invisible to us, not unlike the power of the wind—or even something supernatural. The question was how to harness that energy to effect social change.

In early 1963, Jeane Dixon shocked several friends when she predicted that President Kennedy would soon die in office, the result of an assassination that would occur "down South." Denis Brian, in his book *Jeane Dixon: The Witnesses*, corroborated her prophecies by verifying witness accounts and other documentation. "All I can see is the casket over the White House," she said. "What I see is going to happen to the president himself and he cannot avoid it. It won't be long now."[3]

On Friday, November 22, 1963, Dixon lunched with two friends in Washington, DC. She'd already told them that, "someone is going to shoot the president," when an acquaintance approached to tell her that President Kennedy had been shot at 12:30 P.M. in Dallas, Texas, as he rode in a motorcade. When some early news reports said Kennedy might live, Dixon psychically knew the outcome. "No, he's dead," she said sadly, the color drained from her face. Dixon made clear that Kennedy's murder was predestined, and the outcome could not be changed, despite her efforts to warn him through intermediaries.

There were many predictions and premonitions prior to President Kennedy's assassination, from both professional psychics and mediums, as well as from ordinary private citizens. Some reported dream visions;

others simply experienced a "sensation" that tragedy surrounded Kennedy. By various estimates, there were as many as fifty thousand predictions of JFK's death. Even Edgar Cayce forewarned that a future president, after FDR, would not survive his term in office, a prophecy that aptly applied to Kennedy's fate.

Another renowned psychic who predicted President Kennedy's murder was trance-medium Arthur Ford whose controversial séance to receive messages from the spirit of the late magician Houdini is still being debated. In 1962, at a séance attended by U.S. senator McClellan of Arkansas, Ford experienced a vision that Kennedy would be assassinated. Ford also foresaw Lyndon Johnson's presidential win in 1964.[4]

The Kennedy administration had lasted only a thousand days, then "Camelot" as it was popularly called, was gone in the mad burst of an assassin's bullets. With his murder, the optimism that so many felt lay shattered. The 1960s would next enter a period vastly different than when the decade began; jolted back to a harsher reality. Kennedy's death was a blow to the utopian dreams some Americans held, and now clouded by disillusionment. How could a young leader's life be so senselessly snuffed out in a flash of lunacy? It was a despair the country hadn't experienced since President Lincoln was assassinated in 1865.

The metaphysical speculation about Kennedy's destiny vs. free will can be argued for eternity without arriving at an answer. The fact is that numerous premonitions did nothing to alter the course of events; perhaps making an argument that a predetermined national fate had to be fulfilled, no matter how wrenching and painful. America was about to experience extraordinary changes that would amount to social convulsions. How different it might have been had Kennedy lived, we will never know.

For psychical researchers, the early sixties were only marginally different than the fifties had been. Traditional Americans remained largely suspicious of the paranormal; it was still typically referred to in the popular media as the "occult" and few people had any inkling that the U.S. government, via its military and intelligence networks, was already involved in more than a decade of covert paranormal and mind control research and experiments. As far as most Americans were concerned, psychic phenomena and UFOs remained "fringe" subjects that appealed mainly to eccentrics, weird, and crazy people.[5]

Decades are seldom uniform or consistent in character. For example,

the forties were divided into the "war years" and the postwar era. The fifties portrayed as the first rock 'n' roll generation actually began in mid-
decade. Similarly, the sixties we identify with the so-called New Age or
"Age of Aquarius," the counterculture of hippies, widespread drug use,
race riots, and antiwar protests, emerged after President Kennedy's death.

The sixties did not spawn the New Age movement, as much as it became
fertile ground for a wide renewal of interest in metaphysical, occult, and
spiritualist beliefs. The social ferment and turmoil of the decade created an
environment that encouraged a revival and an exploration of ancient ideas
wrapped in glistening new packages. But the comparison to earlier times
was inevitable.

America's first "New Age" was, of course, the Great Age of Spiritualism that began with the Fox sisters in 1848 and stretched into the early
twentieth century, until it seriously damaged itself by tolerating exces-
sive amounts of fraud. Mary Baker Eddy's Christian Science posited new
ideas for healing illnesses through faith and prayer, sans medications.
The transcendentalists of the mid-nineteenth century, including literary
lights such as Ralph Waldo Emerson and Henry David Thoreau, defined prayer as a way to evolve spiritually and achieve "oneness with
God." Madame Blavatsky's Theosophy movement brought Americans a
new awareness of Hinduism and other Eastern philosophies. Ignatius
Donnelly renewed interest in the ancient lost civilization of Atlantis. For
the more scientifically minded, there were the parapsychology studies of
William James and the ASPR, and later, psychoanalyst Carl Jung who
embraced most psychic experiences.

During World War I, the Ouija board became a popular and lasting
parlor game that many took seriously as a means of communicating with
departed loved ones. Throughout the twenties and thirties, parapsychology hardly disappeared—from the controversial séances to reach
Houdini's spirit to the emergence of Edgar Cayce, the trance psychic-
seer and an inspiration for the later New Age to Evangeline Adams, who
brought new respect to astrology to Dr. J. B. Rhine's pioneering ESP
experiments at Duke University and Eileen Garrett and Arthur Ford
who earned national reputations as mediums. After World War II, the
government delved into covert psychic research, and in the 1950s, the
Bridey Murphy story brought Americans a new awareness of reincarnation and the use of regressive hypnosis as a tool to recall "past lives."

Divination, especially astrology, but also tarot, the I Ching, and witch-craft, became increasingly popular during the sixties. Such interests put many young people at odds with long-held Judeo-Christian tenets, setting up confrontations between generations that often frustrated dialogue. Arguments between parents and children about politics, war, and religion were plentiful, and the so-called "generation gap" was born. When opposition to traditional values seethed over, protests moved to the streets and campuses.

Music, hair, and dress became expressions of rebellion: many young men grew long hair and often beards, while women and girls sent their style in opposing directions. Some wore nearly floor-length Victorian dresses; others dressed "mod" in miniskirts. They quickly became the vogue, as did bell-bottoms, beads, and headbands that started with "hippies," and then went mainstream.

The Beatles launched a "British invasion" of America, that influenced rock music, culture, and tastes, while other musicians developed an edge; lyrics protesting the war and inequality became popular, by such artists as the folksinger Phil Ochs. While the Vietnam War intensified, and danger of nuclear annihilation was obviously a concern. Barry McGuire's hit song, "Eve of Destruction," in 1965, captured the dark apocalyptic mood that gripped many.[6]

Fifties rock 'n' roll had dwelled mainly on teenage love, with few references to society's ills and few lasting "protest songs" to urge on dissent. One notable exception able to transcend the decades with his socially conscious music was fifties folksinger Pete Seeger.

In their quest for new answers to eternal dilemmas, America's restless youth set out on unfamiliar spiritual paths. In doing so, Western religious dogmas and restrictions that bound kids to their parents' beliefs increasingly showed signs of strain. Eastern teachings became one popular avenue of exploration that included Hindu philosophy, Zen, yoga, and meditation.

Another road many young people chose led them to hallucinogenic drugs, such as LSD, and other mind-altering substances. The idea wasn't to escape reality, said the gurus of psychedelic drugs; one was Aldous Huxley, the visionary author of the classic, *Brave New World*. Ironically, Huxley died on November 22, 1963, the day President Kennedy was killed.

The purpose of LSD and other psychedelic drugs was ostensibly mind-expansion, to become open to new realities and spiritual dimensions, proponents claimed. Hallucinogenic drugs were supposed to allow one to see beyond the present, to view the future—perhaps, even experience God. A former Harvard instructor named Timothy Leary emerged to lead the sixties generation toward the LSD experience: "Turn on, tune in, drop out," he preached, and many listened to this charmingly glib but slightly mad Pied Piper, and alienation between generations grew wider over the issue of drug use, while a number suffered from "bad trips," and some died from overdoses.

For the long-haired and colorfully dressed hippies the counterculture revolution centered in the Haight-Ashbury section of San Francisco. Some went in the direction of communes and cults, seeking a utopian life, eschewing the materialism and affluence that was the measure of success for their parents. Dropping out of mainstream society, proselytizing for "peace and love," protesting the Vietnam War, and opposing the "system" or establishment appealed to many.

There were also the initial stirrings of the coming environmental movement after Rachel Carson wrote an influential book, *Silent Spring*, in 1962, that warned of serious, potential danger from pesticide use. Although her revelations were not directly spiritual or psychic, consciousness-raising about the environment led many toward a new way of thinking about ecology, an idea embraced by the emerging New Age.

Betty Friedan's 1963 bestseller, *The Feminine Mystique*, became the first step toward the feminist revolution. Even such sacred institutions as marriage were threatened, when more young men and women chose premarital sex and to live together "without benefit of clergy," a shocking affront to parents and long-held religious dictates.

"The sixties brought extreme confrontation with social, cultural, political, and personal values. This inspired an insatiable curiosity to learn more about one's inner life, and to satisfy some of the longings and need for spiritual connection that traditional religion had not been able to fill," noted Mary Olsen Kelly.[7] "A wholly new culture, based on a new spirituality," author Robert S. Ellwood wrote, seemed to be a goal of the counterculture. A new lexicon also came into being with such terms as: "hippies," "LSD," "acid trip," "pot," "anti-establishment," "generation gap," "flower power," "psychedelic," and "Zen," to name just a few. Hippies had their own jargon: "cool," "far out," "rap," "stoned," and "square."

Surely, in such an environment, there had to be a new openness toward psychic phenomena. The tireless efforts by the pioneers of parapsychology who fought a long, determined, but frustrating battle, in earlier years had laid a pathway to the sixties that brought a marked transformation in youth's attitudes toward psychical, spiritual, and metaphysical thinking and beliefs. Many of America's more idealistic young people were becoming increasingly disillusioned with the status quo.

New solutions were needed for a rapidly changing America in which the future seemed less optimistic after the president's assassination and an escalating war in Vietnam that was able to draft thousands to serve—and perhaps return them crippled, injured, or in body bags. While many obeyed the call to war, others protested on campuses, burned draft cards, and some fled to neighboring Canada, even Sweden. Many kids now suddenly began to contemplate their personal fate—and mortality. The generational divide had widened into a deep chasm. Where would millions of dispirited young people turn for faith and spiritual guidance amidst escalating war and social upheaval?

First called the "Age of Aquarius" during the 1960s, the term later evolved into what was popularly known as the New Age. "In astrology, an 'age' is defined by the location of the sun at the moment of the spring equinox each year," according to the *Encyclopedia of Occultism and Parapsychology*.[8] "Because of the tilt of the Earth's axis that sign changes approximately every 2,160 years. Depending upon the astrological system used, the sun was to make the transition from the sign of Pisces to that of Aquarius sometime" around the new millennium. "Pisces, the fish sign, is often associated with Christianity, in which the fish is frequently used as a symbol of Jesus. The passing of the Earth to a new astrological age would bring a new religion or spiritual perspective to dominance." That would explain the belief in the emergence of so-called "New Age" beliefs.

If such events can be dated, the Age of Aquarius officially dawned on October 17, 1967, with the opening of *Hair* on the Broadway stage. The self-described "American tribal love-rock musical" brought the counterculture uptown to the legitimate theater with its promising message of "peace, love, and harmony." It was also a spectacle of nude hippies chanting "Hare Krishna," a display of "sex, drugs, and dirty words," as more than one theater critic described it. Most reviewers agreed it was "vulgar." But it was the "Big Nude Scene," that drew audiences night after night. Among the most notable and enduring songs from the play's score was one with a clear reference to astrology: "Aquarius." The New York *Daily News,* reminiscing years later, recalled *Hair* as "rock, shock, and bare bottoms." Whatever it was that appealed to audiences, the play had a four-year run, not bad for a bunch of hippies singing about their horoscope.

Astrology's appeal during the sixties was rather obvious. Much like the hippies and other alienated youth, who saw themselves as nonconformists, astrology was also an outsider, on the fringe; belief in it represented a challenge to established scientific and religious orthodoxy. One of the decade's bestsellers on the subject was *Sun Signs* by astrologer Linda Goodman; there were estimated to be several thousand full-time astrologers across the country, as well as magazines and periodicals for hungry fans of the zodiac. Perhaps in uncertain times of social upheaval and war, the position of the stars and planets might hold an answer—or at least some assurance about the future?

Another important contribution in the early sixties was several books that shed light on the Kabbalah, ancient Jewish mysticism. For many centuries, "Jewish occultism" was kept secret, open only to a small number of mystics—special people who sought spiritual truths in Kabbalah's hidden meaning. "Words and numbers," as in numerology, have special power to Kabbalists; there was fear that in the wrong hands, Kabbalah's secret wisdom could be misused.

Author J. Gordon Melton wrote about a Hassidic rabbi who took LSD with Dr. Timothy Leary in 1959. The rabbi said the experience "caused him to seek greater spiritual depth in Judaism's tradition." During the sixties, that rabbi became "a much sought-after leader by New Age groups," Melton noted. A scholar named Gershon Scholem, highly respected for his writings, commented that Kabbalah was encouraged, at least in part, by yoga. Others have suggested that Kabbalah is equal with the body's "chakras or spiritual centers." Kabbalah also motivated some rabbis to examine psychic phenomena, healing, and vegetarianism, all New Age concepts. As you can see, in the sixties, psychic, religious, and mystical elements came together; even hallucinogenic drugs, legal in the early part of the decade, were not out of bounds for some on a path to greater enlightenment and enhanced psychic powers.

But for centuries, the occult nature of the Kabbalah fed anti-Semitism, perpetuating the myth that Jews were secretive and sinister, author Daniel Cohen explained. However, once the Kabbalah was accessible to the public in the 1960s, it quickly took its place alongside other mystical teachings popular with the counterculture and the emerging New Age. The Kabbalah's message, as Cohen explained, "is that things are not what they seem and . . . a hidden message can be found in everything." That was an appealing idea to many in the sixties counterculture, as was wearing Kabbalistic magic amulets to ward off evil.[9]

The 1960s provided the spark that ignited the second American New Age that continued to develop throughout the 1970s and 1980s. How did psychical research fare in one of the most tumultuous periods in this nation's history? Perhaps the same optimism that permeated much of the country's mood in the early sixties also energized some paranormal researchers. President Kennedy was still in the White House when Dr. Montague Ullman obtained grant money to scientifically probe the relationship between dreams and ESP.[10] The setting was a New York City hospital in a quiet residential Brooklyn neighborhood. Ullman was a forty-six-year-old psychiatrist when he founded the Dream Laboratory at the Maimonides Medical Center in Brooklyn in 1962. He sought answers to the age-old questions about the source and meaning of dreams: "What is real and what is symbolic?" he asked. Can dreams transcend "space and time"? Ullman hoped that carefully designed scientific experiments on the cutting edge of paranormal research would provide explanations that had eluded centuries of study and debate about dreams.

Prophetic dreams played a significant role in the Old Testament. Plato, in the fourth century BC, was interested in what influence dreams had on people's waking lives. Also in ancient Greece, the philosopher Democritus reasoned that the mind of a sleeping person might somehow be accessed, a profound insight made several millennia before modern ESP dream research.

Ullman made no secret of his serious interest in parapsychology; the native New Yorker was a trustee of the American Society for Psychical

Research (ASPR). He'd come upon paranormal incidents during his years of private practice that spurred his curiosity about ESP, and he began psychic research alongside Dr. Gardner Murphy (1895–1979), a respected psychologist and parapsychologist who was vice president of the ASPR from 1940 to 1962, and later became its president. Murphy was long a formidable voice for the paranormal. In 1938, at a meeting of the American Psychological Association (APA), many members were outspoken in their criticism of psychic research. It fell to Murphy to champion the subject; he did it so convincingly that he was elected president of the APA in 1944. As you might imagine, Ullman and Murphy were dauntless in their efforts on behalf of the ASPR; always an uphill battle against so-called traditional scientists and skeptics.

Ullman's interest in ESP's relationship to dreams was buoyed by the discovery in 1953 of "rapid eye movement" (REM), a "phase of the sleep cycle" in which there are "sudden bouts of rapid movements of the eyes horizontally and vertically," he explained. "The REM state is a distinct and separate phase of the sleep cycle." Although a person appears to be sleeping restfully, the brain is so stimulated that an EEG measuring brain wave activity "shows a resemblance to a normal waking record," Ullman said.

It is during the REM phase that most dreaming occurs, and dream recall is particularly notable in the early morning, "at the end of a night's sleep," he explained. His specific interest in the REM periods of sleep was to determine if ESP events occurred during those times. His question was whether "alternate states of consciousness, such as dreaming," were related to ESP.

Ullman discovered what other psychical researchers had: that although not all vivid dreams contain paranormal information, virtually every paranormal dream has been found to be vivid or hyper-real. He also found that "most paranormal dreams are precognitive," and predict or foretell "tragic events," Ullman said, concurring with the findings of other parapsychologists.

In American history, the best-known example of a precognitive dream associated with an impending tragedy was President Lincoln's dream predicting his assassination. There are literally thousands of dreams that eerily seem to transcend time and space to tap into the future. If you think back to some of the dreams you've experienced, you'll likely recall an ESP or paranormal dream you've had. The question is how and why do they occur?

Initially, Ullman obtained money from the respected Parapsychology Foundation (PF) and joined with two other well-known psychical researchers Karlis Osis, longtime president of the ASPR, and E. Douglas Dean to begin a series of experiments. When Gardner Murphy received a substantial grant, the Dream Laboratory, destined for national recognition, opened at Maimonides Hospital in 1962, with Ullman as the lab's first director. This marked the "most systematic study of paranormal dreams in a laboratory setting," Robert Van de Castle wrote in his highly regarded book, *Our Dreaming Mind.*[11]

The obvious value in such research was to better understand the dream process; if a psychic component could be determined, it would lead to a profoundly deeper understanding of what the human mind was capable of. Such conclusions would have substantial relevance for dream therapy as well as establishing a stronger case for evidence of ESP ability and a link between dreams and the paranormal. Ullman had no doubt that altered states of consciousness, such as dreaming, were related to ESP. His task now was to design carefully controlled scientific tests that would provide evidence to support his theory.

Another seminal figure in psychical research and the study of ESP dreams was Dr. Stanley Krippner, psychologist and parapsychologist.[12] He'd studied with such notable figures as J. B. Rhine and Gardner Murphy.[13] His lifelong interest in dreams, altered states of consciousness, and the paranormal began when he was a teenager in Wisconsin. Krippner was thirty-four years old when he relocated to Maimonides, and in the next decade worked with Montague Ullman, and then Charles Honorton, a thirty-year-old parapsychologist when he joined the Dream Laboratory; he'd also worked with Rhine at Duke University.

Perhaps it was a sign of the changing times. Rhine's methodology had been considerably more rigid, and Honorton was a part of a new generation, less willing to abide by the restrictions in experimentation that bound earlier parapsychologists. Honorton also was intrigued by ESP's apparent accessibility to the dream state. He surmised "that the dream state facilitated ESP simply because it is during this period that stimuli from the external world are markedly reduced and that the focus of attention during dreams is inward," Richard Broughton explained.[14]

Honorton would also be with Ullman and Krippner in receiving the first-ever grant for parapsychology research from the National Institute of Mental Health.

One of the oldest, most confounding questions the Dream Laboratory faced was how people were able to "tune in" to future events, especially a disaster that has not yet occurred, as happens in precognitive dreams. Debunkers have long dismissed such incidents as "coincidental" or "anecdotal," with little scientific significance. That is an inadequate explanation for one of the most perplexing and persistent of paranormal phenomena—why meaningful psychic information often is communicated through the dream state.

In our two previous books together we mentioned President Lincoln's precognitive dream of his assassination. We also told about the famed American author Mark Twain, when he was still a young man named Samuel Clemens, and dreamed that he saw his younger brother Henry's body laid out in a coffin with a bouquet of white flowers placed on his chest. Only days later, Henry was killed in a Mississippi riverboat explosion. When Sam found the funeral scene, it was exactly as he'd dreamed it. You'll recall that there were many precognitive dreams and premonitions prior to the *Titanic* sinking in 1912 that claimed more than fifteen hundred lives.

One of the best-documented cases in more recent times occurred in October 1966 in Wales. Robert Van de Castle described the tragedy in which a huge "coal tip slid down a mountainside and engulfed the Welsh mining village of Aberfan, killing one hundred and forty-four people, most of them schoolchildren." There were many people who reported premonitions before the tragedy that have been documented. In at least twenty-five instances, the forewarnings appeared in precognitive dreams.[15]

Paranormal or psychic dreams are remarkably "vivid and intense," Van de Castle noted. That's been the conclusion of virtually every researcher, including the authors of this book who've gathered hundreds of precognitive dream reports from all over the world. In fact, we opened the previous book with examples of such experiences many had prior to the 9/11 terrorist bombings of the World Trade Center.

Dream predictions, of course, appear in the Old Testament, and even further back in records kept by ancient and primitive societies. Ullman hoped to move beyond centuries of speculation and debate about psychic dreams; he and Krippner would devote a decade to researching ESP dreams. To do so, they developed an "experimental design," as Ullman explained to Joel Martin.[16]

While a subject slept in a soundproofed room, his or her "sleep stages" were monitored. Then another person in a separate room called an "agent" was instructed to "send" what was called a "target stimulus" to the sleeping subject during REM periods. The stimulus was actually a color copy of a painting or some artwork that the agent had concentrated on and attempted to send telepathically to the sleeping subject. A third individual was responsible for monitoring the EEG readings throughout the night to note the sleeping person's periods of rapid eye movements (REM).

The sleeping person was not told in advance what the art print would be. The test was designed to determine if he or she could telepathically determine the picture's details while in the REM periods of sleep. After ten to fifteen minutes of "REM activity," the sleeping subject was awakened and "asked to describe, in as much detail as possible," his or her dream. The goal was to determine how closely the sleeping person's dream matched the art reproduction he or she had been "sent" telepathically, but had never seen.

This is a very simplified sketch of the dream-telepathy experiments to give you some idea of what the Dream Lab tests were like. The actual procedures and logistics were considerably more sophisticated, and the sessions were tape-recorded. The lab's researchers then studied the results to determine how closely the subjects' dreams matched the "target picture." The results reveal statistically significant probabilities of dream telepathy. But, when experimenting with the paranormal, always be prepared for some scientists and skeptics to pounce on any findings that upset their narrow view of science; the paranormal simply doesn't fit in, as the Dream Laboratory learned.

If you've been with us this far on our bumpy, sometimes jarring, journey through the history of psychic phenomena, from prophetic dreams in ancient Babylonia, two thousand years before the birth of Jesus, to the Dream Laboratory in Brooklyn in the 1960s and '70s, you probably won't be surprised by some of the reaction to the new findings about ESP dreams.

There were serious, scholarly reviews of the Maimonides experiments. One of them, written by Dr. Irvin L. Child, chairperson of the psychology department at Yale University, appeared in the journal *American Psychologist*. He gave careful and deliberate attention to evaluating the dream-telepathy experiments Ullman and Krippner designed, especially the "statistical significance" of their results. This is a portion of what Dr. Child wrote:

"The outcome is clear. Several segments of the data, considered separately, yield significant evidence that dreams (and associations to them) tended to resemble the picture chosen randomly as target more than they resembled other pictures in the pool."

That was affirmation from someone in a prestigious academic position with outstanding credentials and certainly more to lose than gain by defending a study about dream telepathy. Child was a man of integrity and objectivity; something that could not be said of several others who reviewed the Maimonides dream experiments.

Robert Van de Castle explained in *Our Dreaming Mind* that Dr. Child "devoted several pages of his article to documenting how the Maimonides research program had been misrepresented or ignored in books by psychologists that could be expected to cover the topic of paranormal dreams."[17]

Child made it clear that he was frustrated by "some of those books" that had presented "nearly incredible falsification of the facts about the experiments; others simply neglect them." He added his opinion that many in the scientific community and psychologists sought only any "defect" they could find in the Maimonides experiments so that it could lead to the only acceptable conclusion: "fraud or inappropriate statistical reasoning."

In other words, many in traditional science and psychology were not beneath resorting to "inaccurate and biased reporting" about the work of the Dream Laboratory, Van de Castle remarked. President Kennedy's image of America as a "New Frontier" may have applied to reaching the Moon by the end of the decade; it apparently was never meant to include the paranormal. Anyone who expected the optimism of the early sixties to spill into parapsychology laboratories was, well, dreaming.

Here's how skeptics cleverly disputed statistically significant findings: If paranormal experiments failed, that proved there was nothing to psychical or psi phenomena. However, if there was even a glimmer of evidence for genuine psychic events, then the results must have been fraudulent, or the outcome of poorly controlled experimental conditions, therefore not statistically meaningful. Loser or liar—a parapsychologist couldn't win among the ranks of the closed-minded.

To their credit, Ullman and Krippner were braced for the inevitable antagonism and criticism from disapproving colleagues, and they persevered in spite of it. The Maimonides program also studied precognitive dreams and "obtained significant evidence of their existence under well-controlled laboratory conditions," Van de Castle explained.[18] Other experiments were designed to determine if two persons who were asleep could telepathically transmit dreams to each other—a phenomenon called "shared dreaming." Although the laboratory found evidence for paranormal dreams, most orthodox scientists stubbornly dismissed the possibility. Unfortunately, the Dream Laboratory closed in 1978.

What is especially frustrating was the unwillingness of many traditional scientists to explore the "invisible world" of the paranormal. Ironically, skeptics failed to realize their own contradiction. On the one hand, they could not accept the possibility of psychic communication—in or out of the dream state—because it could not be seen, measured, or proven. On the other hand, even the most obdurate skeptic would never doubt that we dream. But could you show someone your dream? Of course not; although dreams are also part of that invisible world, they can't be measured or proven, any more than a paranormal incident. Still we recognize the legitimacy of dreams as a shared universal experience. The Dream Lab had come tantalizingly close to bridging two parts of the invisible world: dreams and ESP. But orthodox science was unable to accommodate the psychic component of dreaming, and evidence that a certain amount of dream content came from outside of the dreamer. The Maimonides laboratory had run into the same stubborn resistance that has long plagued paranormal research. How much more could have been accomplished if the dream research was allowed to continue?

The 1960s may have held the promise of a more open-minded time, but the scientific establishment's opposition to the paranormal remained unyielding. In some ways parapsychology was not unlike the counterculture; both were on the fringe, heretics and outsiders with ideas that dared move beyond mainstream thinking and belief. It was no surprise that rebellious sixties' youth found an affinity for the so-called "occult."

On streets, college campuses, at parties and in coffee shops—wherever young people gathered in the sixties—there were fewer inhibitions about exploring new spiritual realms, and questioning one's place in the universe. Did the paranormal have a better chance of gaining greater acceptance among those who espoused nonconformity? This much was obvious: A "spiritual awakening" was under way during the 1960s. Many youths dared to venture along paths toward enlightenment that their parents and grandparents would never have even considered. Fewer young adults were willing to heed dogma-obsessed clergy, psychologists, scientists, and skeptics.

As the decade moved forward, "America in 1964 was a young person's land," Robert S. Ellwood wrote.[19] "The growth rate of the teenage population was four times that of the United States average; twenty-four million people were now aged thirteen to nineteen, one eighth of the nation." They were too many to ignored and were on their way to the forefront of New Age beliefs, as they would be in the civil rights and antiwar movements. For those of the "baby boomer" generation, the decades ahead would reveal how their attitudes toward the paranormal were influenced by consciousness-raising experiences of the 1960s.

Exactly what was so alluring about ancient Eastern beliefs to millions of American youth who came of age in the 1960s? Most had been raised with Judeo-Christian teachings. To the consternation of many parents, their sons and daughters, in the throes of rebellion, embraced religious systems completely alien to their upbringings and by 1964–65, declining church attendance among young people showed the effect of the shift. By the end of the sixties, there was an 11 percent drop in the number of young people attending traditional houses of worship.

Actually, Eastern philosophies arrived long before the 1960s; yogis, swamis, and gurus were here decades earlier. Americans were aware of Asian religions dating back to the early days of the country. In 1784, Hannah Adams, a cousin of John Adams, compiled *A Dictionary of All Religions*, in which she referred to Eastern faiths, albeit not in any detail. Asian beliefs were given short shrift in eighteenth-century America, and well into the nineteenth century, for they were alien, if not inferior, to Christianity.

One notable exception was the enigmatic and controversial Madame Helena Petrovna Blavatsky (1831–1891) the Russian immigrant who moved to America, and in 1875 founded the Theosophical Society. Blavatsky, by dint of her magnetic eyes, personality, and tireless energy, introduced Hindu and Eastern teachings to many Americans. She made no secret of her dislike for Christianity, while lauding the preeminence of Hinduism. Blavatsky, had she lived a hundred years later, would likely have been right at home as a leader of the counterculture.

Hindu, the world's oldest known religion, long predates Christianity, and is based on the Vedas, "sacred scriptures," more than three thousand years old. But unlike the tightly structured Catholic Church, and other Christian denominations, Hindus faced few restrictions about what to believe, notwithstanding faithfully upholding the Hindu social caste system. During the sixties, some young people were drawn to the esoteric teachings found in the "sacred writings" of the Bhagavad Gita. For many others, practicing meditation was as far as they were prepared to go on the road to nirvana. The writings of the gurus were increasingly available in bookstores and libraries from the mid-1960s on. Lectures and lessons were also available at ashrams or centers devoted expressly to Eastern practices.

Hindus have no difficulty accepting reincarnation, karma, astrology, and psychic abilities, ideas long anathema to hard-and-fast Christian dogma. Hinduism teaches the purpose of life is to ultimately attain nirvana or perfect bliss through continuing stages or levels of reincarnation. If you were a restless, alienated, and rebellious young American in the 1960s, how exciting to discover an enlightened approach that ran counter to everything your parents and church taught! Not only were you learning new ideas, you were demonstrating opposition to the dreaded "establishment," and you had plenty of gurus to choose from as you wandered freely along various spiritual paths, presumably in search of God.

At the heart of the teaching is yoga, the "Hindu system of philosophic meditation and exercise." Among the first to acquaint Americans with yoga was Indra Devi who wrote *Yoga for Americans* in 1959. She explained that, "the secret of yoga lies in the fact that it deals with the entire [person] . . . It also expands the power of the mind."[20] Throughout the sixties and beyond, yoga gained immense popularity in the United States—a surprise to many cynical observers who did not view materialistic and self-indulgent American youth as willing to practice strict self-discipline and abstain from freewheeling pleasure-seeking.

To keep definitions as simple as possible, one who teaches yoga is called a yogi, a Hindu spiritual teacher or head of a religious sect is a guru, and a Hindu male religious teacher is called a swami. One of the misunderstandings Westerners have about yoga is that it is a religion; it is not. Rather, it is an approach that teaches a person to elevate his or her capabilities by utilizing meditation, concentration, among other techniques, and "physical and mental" exercises. "The ultimate aim is to bring body and mind to the highest perfection," explained Nathaniel Lande in *Mindstyles/Lifestyles*.[21]

In addition to the benefits of physical, mental, and spiritual health there is a psychic component to yoga. It includes perception of the past and future, understanding of other people's minds, past incarnations, awareness of one's moment of death, knowing of things at great distances, and the aptitude "to see perfected beings beyond humanity," Lande wrote.

There are many branches of yoga, "spiritual paths leading to the same goal," Lande noted. Since there are limits to space, we'll offer just a few examples of some of the better-known types of yoga, rooted in ancient principles that became trendy from the sixties on. Probably the most familiar in the United States for many years has been Hatha Yoga with its emphasis on breathing techniques, yoga postures, concentration, and diet; its aim is to lead to better health.

Karma Yoga centers on karma, the "law of action and reaction." Those attuned to this approach are dedicated to "selfless service" as a means of purifying one's heart and mind. "Devotion to duty helps us in our spiritual progress . . ." according to the teachings of Karma Yoga.

Tantra Yoga is the only yoga whose center of interest is human sexuality. "Male and female partners . . . concentrate on the flow of energy between them, they become briefly but literally divine beings," Nathaniel Lande explained.

One more example is Kundalini Yoga that has as its aim the development and growth of psychic power. The ancient Hindu belief was that Kundalini was a "cosmic energy" within human beings. It emphasizes breathing practice and meditation with the goal of stirring the potent energy within the reproductive system so that it moves up through the body's higher chakras enabling one to attain "enlightenment." There are seven major energy centers or chakras within the body. Theosophy included the concept of chakras in its teachings; by the 1960s as Eastern practices were increasingly in vogue here, awareness of chakras became more prevalent, until they were widely accepted within the New Age movement—although there is still dispute about the "nature of them and what experiences they lead to," according to some parapsychologists.

Two of the chakras deserve special mention for their association with psychic ability. One is commonly known as the "third eye," between and above the eyebrows. The seventh chakra or energy center is said to be located at the "crown" or top of the head. Yogis have told of experiencing "perfect joy" and gladness associated with mystical states through the "awakening" of this chakra that is the highest point of the Kundalini.

For Americans drawn to Eastern philosophy and teachings during the 1960s, there was no lack of opportunity for instruction. Although some gurus lived years earlier or never left India, their writings were available here. Other gurus, swamis, and yogis traveled and lectured widely, visited America and, in some instances, relocated. The implication for the paranormal is obvious: If you were willing to embrace Hindu philosophy and practices, you were also open to the existence of psychic powers and mysticism, in marked contrast with conservative American religious attitudes. Within the limits of space, here are just a few of the better-known gurus in the 1960s and '70s, with no disrespect intended to the many others not included.

Sri Swami Sivananda (1887–1963) was one of the most respected gurus whose prolific writing totaled more than three hundred books. His disciples came from many different faiths and parts of the world. There was Swami Satchidananda, a disciple of Swami Sivananda, who visited America in 1966, brought here by the artist Peter Max, famous for his colorful psychedelic era "pop art" posters with cartoon hippies and messages of "peace, love, and harmony." Max was also a student of Eastern mysticism.

One of the most popular gurus in twentieth-century India has been Sai Baba, revered by countless Hindus much as a saint is in the Roman Catholic faith. Sai Baba died in 1918, but his devotees believe that several years later his spirit reincarnated into a young boy who was proclaimed the living embodiment of Sai Baba. His following through the 1960s and '70s was immense in India; he became world-known for his miraculous healings, psychic powers, and even restoring the dead to life.

During his too-brief lifetime, Swami Vivekananda (1863–1902) made an indelible contribution in his travels around the world, including to America, with his message of "spiritual consciousness and social responsibility," Peter Lorie wrote in *The Quotable Spirit*.[22] Vivekananda was also the founder of the Vedanta Society that brought to America a philosophy that believes in the "unity of all faiths"; in other words, all religions are basically the same, unlike Christianity, divided by denominations and factionalism. Among the well-known figures who joined the Vedanta Society was famed author Aldous Huxley.

Jiddu Krishnamurti (1895–1986) was only thirteen years old in 1908 when he was "discovered" by Annie Besant, then the head of the Theosophical Society. She pronounced him the "World Teacher" or the "returned Buddha." Later, however, he left the Theosophists and "questioned the value of spiritual teachers," claiming that the search for truth can only be accomplished by the individual. In numerous lectures over the years to millions of people, he urged them to avoid the strictures of "religious organizations."

One of the better-known gurus who moved to the United States during the 1960s to teach meditation was Sri Chinmoy. Born in India in 1931, he entered an ashram at age twelve, studied for twenty years, and then settled in New York in 1964. Four decades later he was still going strong with his teachings, world travels, and a prolific output of music, art, poetry, and athletic endeavors. A frequent guest on the *Joel Martin Show* on radio and TV, Chinmoy also led meditations at the United Nations for many years. His psychic abilities, including telepathy and clairvoyance, are astounding; yet he does not regard them as his most significant achievement. His celebrity devotees have included musician Carlos Santana, singer-songwriter Roberta Flack, and Olympic athlete Carl Lewis.[23]

Other noteworthy Hindu figures whose teachings are considered influential were Sri Ramakrishna, regarded as a nineteenth-century "religious genius" who also concluded that "all religions were directed toward the same God but used different paths," explained author Peter Lorie; and Ramana Maharshi (1879–1950), one of the twentieth century's "greatest enlightened masters and yogis." There was also the mystic Meher Baba (1894–1969), another "enlightened master," who counted among his followers rock star Pete Townshend of the Who.

One curious figure to emerge in the sixties as a self-proclaimed guru was not Indian, but an American in his thirties named Richard Alpert, who later adopted the name Baba Ram Dass. At Harvard University, where he taught psychology, he joined his colleague Timothy Leary in the early 1960s in the research of "mind-altering drugs," mainly LSD, and together they studied the mystical qualities of hallucinogens.

"For centuries mystics and philosophers from all cultural traditions have held that people may attain 'higher' states of consciousness through meditation techniques," wrote Dr. Harold Bloomfield.[24] In the late nineteenth century William James, the highly insightful American philosopher and psychologist who investigated the paranormal, surmised there was value in yoga when he pondered "whether the yoga discipline may not be . . . a methodical way of waking up deeper levels of will power than are habitually used, and thereby increasing the individual's vital tone and energy." With remarkable foresight James anticipated yoga as a means of expanding human consciousness, noting that people typically use only a small amount of their potential.

For sheer popularity during the 1960s craze over Eastern teachings, the Maharishi Mahesh Yogi who first brought Transcendental Meditation (TM) to the United States had no equal. But a great deal of TM's success here was initially due to the Beatles' interest in it. Far beyond their music, the Beatles were a cultural phenomenon with incredible influence during the sixties; whether they sang or spoke millions of America's youth took notice. When the "Fab Four" made their American network TV debut on the *Ed Sullivan Show* in February 1964, more than seventy-three million viewers watched. Overnight, millions of American teenagers were prompted to grow their hair long, and learn to play guitars and drums; hundreds of musical groups sprouted to imitate the Beatles' sound.

Many of the older generation were completely thrown by the Beatles, just as they were by the revolution in styles, tastes, and the fascination with Eastern beliefs. One night in 1964 on the popular TV game show, *What's My Line?* a guest was Brian Epstein, the Beatles' legendary manager. When the panel eventually guessed Epstein's occupation, one panel member, the middle-aged, erudite Random House publisher Bennett Cerf, revealed how out of touch he and many adults were with the stunningly rapid changes occurring. Cerf asked Epstein, "Are you sorry for what you've done?" referring to the Beatles' phenomenal success in America.

When the Beatles traveled to India during the mid-sixties and met personally with the Maharishi, the group was enthused by TM, and became among its biggest boosters—although not for long. TM literally would not have been able to pay for the publicity generated by the Beatles. TM exploded in popularity—and membership.[25]

As a spokesman for TM, the Maharishi couldn't have been a better choice if he'd been cast by Hollywood. Behind his bearded face and wispy, long hair were a friendly smile and an exuberant personality. In 1967 when the Maharishi toured the United States he was an immediate hit on the TV talk show circuit; a combination of mystical bearing and charm that attracted people from all walks of life to TM, "the simplest of all yogic techniques." The Maharishi's message had universal appeal: Our lives could be more joyful and productive, through the practice of Transcendental Meditation.

The basic goal of all meditation is to reduce external "distractions." During TM, "a person allows his mind to experience a relaxed and enjoyable state which draws his attention inward. He experiences a state in which the mind becomes very quiet, but extraordinarily alert," explained Dr. Harold Bloomfield. TM utilizes a "power word" or sound called a mantra that is repeated to aid concentration during meditation. Each TM student receives his or her own particular mantra. Once the person learns to utilize the mantra correctly, "mental activity is reduced" during TM, leading to "profound rest during the meditation period," according to Bloomfield.

In the process of meditating, "paranormal phenomena may be produced," parapsychologist Richard Broughton explained. "Most common [is] a feeling of clairvoyant omniscience but sometimes they include physical effects such as levitation, the movement of objects, and healing."[26]

The Maharishi's promise to teach levitation proved controversial, since there was never incontrovertible evidence that TM produced levitation. There were some allegations that photos purporting to show people levitating were created by individuals jumping up and down, rather than floating on air.

"The purpose of TM is not only to relax but to prepare for efficient creative ability," wrote Dr. Hans Selye. A number of rock stars must have agreed during the sixties for there is an impressive list of performers from that era who either explored or practiced TM including the Beach Boys, the Beatles, Mick Jagger and Brian Jones from the Rolling Stones, Robby Krieger and Ray Manzarek of the Doors, and Maurice and Verdine White of Earth, Wind, and Fire, as well as actresses Jane Fonda and Mia Farrow.

Later, former Beatle George Harrison turned to a belief in Krishna, the Hindu god.[27] His 1970s hit song, "My Sweet Lord," reflected that belief. He was always "identified in the public mind as an avatar of Eastern mysticism," Josh Ozersky wrote.

Had you moved among the counterculture types or on college campuses during the sixties, you'd surely have overheard someone mentioning Zen, reading about it, or perhaps you'd have seen an advertisement for the nearest Zen center. Zen actually came from a Chinese word that, in turn, originated in Sanskrit, meaning "meditation." As the Chinese and Japanese Buddhist form of meditation, it dates back to the sixth century and also recognizes the value of intuition.

Many American youth were captivated by the concept of Zen in the sixties. Those who practice it typically sit on a pillow or pad with their legs crossed in what is called the "lotus position." The Zen meditator is taught to "still the mind" from unnecessary or digressive thinking. "The goal of Zen practice is . . . enlightenment, an awareness of the ultimate reality beyond the limits of individual consciousness," Nathaniel Lande explained.[28] Ultimately, the hope is that "the mind is freed from its past conditioning." Zen encourages each person to learn from within, rather than from unyielding and intolerant religious dictates. That idea was especially appealing to those young people seeking spirituality without the restraints imposed by traditional Judeo-Christian practices.

Some serious parapsychologists by the mid-1960s were also devoting time and thought to Eastern beliefs, studying the implications for psychical research. One of them was parapsychologist Charles Honorton at the Maimonides Dream Laboratory, who was particularly interested in Eastern religions in which meditation was practiced. He hoped to observe and study the range of paranormal abilities that occurred as a result of meditation, author Richard Broughton explained. Probably the most substantial connection is given in the ancient Hindu scriptures, the Vedas, "in which paranormal powers, known as siddhis, were considered to be undesirable side effects of meditation," Broughton said. "Undesirable because of their tendency to distract the meditator from the true purpose of his or her exercises."[29]

It didn't take long for scientists and medical doctors to become curious about meditation. For centuries, there were only two known states of consciousness: awake and asleep. However, with the invention of electroencephalography, subtle changes in brain wave activity could be measured by use of an EEG machine. Electrodes were attached to a subject's head and connected to the EEG device as it showed the person's brain waves functioning in different states. Beta waves are the most rapid or active, as when a person is thinking, concentrating, or experiencing tension. Alpha waves are slower, indicating a state of relaxation. Theta, slower still, and seen when someone is drowsy or falling asleep, has also been linked to creativity and tranquility or contentment. Delta, the slowest of the four brain wave states, occurs when one is sleeping soundly or deeply.

Specifically, doctors sought to determine what brain wave changes would occur during meditative states. They found more alpha wave activity, and an increase in theta waves, as well, when a person meditates, suggesting that brain wave activity quieted to a more relaxed state during meditation. In the years ahead, science would study the efficacy of meditation, and discover its positive effects on reducing stress, even lowering blood glucose levels and blood pressure, beneficial to the heart.

In one experiment conducted in the mid-1960s, dozens of Zen Buddhists had their brain waves monitored. The results showed that in less than a minute after beginning to meditate, alpha waves were recorded. Similar changes have been observed in psychics and mediums whose brain waves have been tested.[30]

Serious paranormal interest in Eastern teachings was also found in various journal articles. One detailed paper appeared in the *International Journal of Parapsychology* in its winter 1965 issue, titled "Naturalism and Supernaturalism in East and West." It was published by the Parapsychology Foundation, based in New York, whose founder and president was the medium Eileen Garrett. The author, a college professor, examined and compared Eastern and Western thought, noting the "distinction between natural and supernatural . . . knowledge," suggesting the latter is more commonly found in Eastern belief. The author concluded,

"The primary characteristic of the devotee of the supernatural is spirituality" and recognized the philosophical "conflict" between East and West. The journal article was certainly timely, published as American interest in Hinduism and Zen Buddhism skyrocketed.

What precipitated the easy availability of Eastern belief systems in the 1960s that conservative Christian denominations viewed as exotic but "pagan"? One part of the answer was deceptively simple: a change in U.S. immigration law, specifically the Immigration and Nationality Act of 1965 that repealed a quota system which had kept Asian immigration here at a virtual trickle. Where there had been just several thousand Hindus and Buddhists in the United States before the quota was lifted, after 1965 each group could boast numbers in the hundreds of thousands throughout America, and still climbing in the 1990s.

The assimilation between cultures helped expose Western youth to Eastern philosophies in unprecedented numbers, and many liked what they heard; in Eastern religions there was an "emphasis on avoiding authority," author George Lipsitz noted. As well, Hinduism was open to psychic phenomena—considered "wicked," even satanic, by many fundamentalist Christian sects.

The Roman Catholic Church recognized the winds of change, hence the creation of the Second Vatican Council (1962–65), charged with responsibility for liturgical reform. That moved the Church to increase interfaith dialogue, replace Latin with English, and introduce folk music to Masses designed to attract alienated young people back to church.

It also became increasingly common to see radical clergy protest the Vietnam War, as Daniel and Philip Berrigan, both priests, and Yale chaplain William Sloane Coffin, Jr. did, becoming nationally reviled or respected depending upon which side of the demonstration you stood. There were also activist clergy who worked in inner cities, among minorities and the poor. Reform-minded ministries placed more emphasis on social change than liturgical nuances, and in the process were often more tolerant about a diversity of beliefs—including the paranormal—as the following true incident shows. To protect the priest's identity, we have changed his name.

Father "John," a young Roman Catholic priest serving in a large city parish, became curious about the place of the paranormal in Christian belief, motivated by the stories of the saints, Marian apparitions, and a revered Italian friar, Padre Pio, who was said to have considerable psychic and miraculous gifts. To study such abilities more closely, Father John discreetly observed—but did not participate in—several sessions or séances conducted by a popular medium in his community. The priest wore street clothes, so as not to call attention to his vocation. John was never certain who recognized him, but apparently someone had, and reported his activity as "dabbling in the occult" to his bishop. The priest was admonished in no uncertain terms by his superiors to cease his paranormal studies.[31]

It was an example of the kind of division between generational attitudes, even within the clergy, that escalated in the mid-1960s and beyond. The medium, a Catholic, spoke of embracing all religious beliefs, sounding an Eastern note. Many of those who attended the medium's sessions were also Catholic, and although some expressed guilt, right or wrong, they felt a need to seek bereavement help from a psychic, hoping to receive messages from departed loved ones. Like a mighty river changing its course, there was a momentum under way that would force shifts in American religious thinking, even concerning long condemned paranormal beliefs. If conservative church hierarchies were opposed, great numbers of young people—even some liberal clergy—were less resistant. Was it possible to be spiritual but not religious? What was the difference between the two, and was there a place for psychic and metaphysical experiences within traditional religion? As the times changed, so did the questions—and answers.

In 1962 when the Esalen Institute was founded in scenic Big Sur, on the California coast, between Los Angeles and San Francisco, it couldn't have chosen a better time and place. Its goal was to "explore trends in the behavioral sciences, religion, and philosophy" with the purpose of developing a means to increase human potential, according to the *Encyclopedia of Occultism and Parapsychology*.[32]

The founder of Esalen was Michael Murphy, a Californian who'd studied in India for several years, practiced meditation, and lived for a time in an Indian ashram, a Hindu retreat. The idea for Esalen resulted from conversations Murphy had in 1961 with like-minded friends, including novelist Aldous Huxley. Esalen's aspirations fit perfectly with the mood and attitude of the decade, just as the emerging youth culture was searching for new ways of thinking and problem solving. The institute quickly developed a national reputation and with its high profile, attracted many well-known and respected figures as lecturers.

Looking over some of the names that visited Esalen provides an interesting overview of the diversity of subjects taught there—no one philosophy or doctrine ruled—and a dazzling roster of some of the most significant "thinkers" of the 1960s and '70s.

Among them were noted mythologist Joseph Campbell; Timothy Leary; Aldous Huxley; Abraham Maslow, advocate of humanistic psychology, described as "psychology's most positive evaluation of human potential," and a critic of Freud; Theodore Roszak, who wrote about the counterculture; and Alan Watts, prolific author on Zen and spirituality. "The spiritual is not to be separated from the material, nor the wonderful from the ordinary," Watts opined. There were also Ken Kesey, author of *One Flew Over the Cuckoo's Nest*; Nobel laureate Dr. Linus Pauling; B. F. Skinner, noted psychologist; and Carlos Castaneda, bestselling author, who wrote, "Modern man has left the realms of the unknown and the mysterious, and has settled down in the realm of the functional. He has turned his back to the world of the foreboding and the exulting and has welcomed the world of boredom." As well, Esalen hosted historian Arnold Toynbee; John Lilly, expert on dolphin communication; and Episcopalian Bishop James Pike, one of the most controversial figures of the decade for his heretical views and a televised séance.

"Esalen's catalogue shows a . . . smorgasbord of human programs and the blending of Eastern and Western thought," author Nathaniel Lande observed in *Mindstyles/Lifestyles*.[33] Topics included expanding consciousness, psychotherapy, mysticism, and meditation. One of Esalen's lasting contributions to the popular vocabulary was the concept of the "encounter group."

Esalen became a target for critics of the Human Potential Movement, especially because of its influence on those who espoused tapping unrealized human capability. Many found the status quo satisfactory, and radical new ideas represented unwanted and unnecessary change. For those who opted not to move any further than their traditional religious convictions, the sixties' schools of thought that mixed psychology with the occult, supernatural, mysticism, and Eastern philosophy were greeted with disdain, even hostility; for some they represented confusing and largely irrelevant nonsensical ideas promoted by long-haired hippies and radicals. The rush to revolutionize beliefs was at the crux of many of the decade's confrontations. For alienated youth and the counterculture, change in the traditional American way of life couldn't come fast enough while others condemned the social, political, and cultural rebellions sweeping the country from Berkeley to Boston as the ravings of spoiled kids—unwashed, promiscuous, bearded hippies with no discipline, responsibility, or respect for authority.

It was a decade when an array of leftist politics and pacifist philosophies and ideas were being read and discussed by young people, on and off the campuses: Karl Marx, Lenin, Thoreau, Walt Whitman, Gandhi, and Martin Luther King, Jr. Later in the sixties, the tone grew angrier; so did the exemplars. Revolutionaries and militants replaced the gentle poets and pacifists as heroes and role models. Meanwhile, there were an increasing number of books that dealt with psychic phenomena—from author Jess Stearn's biography of Edgar Cayce, *The Sleeping Prophet* to New Age author Ruth Montgomery, whose string of bestsellers began in 1965 with *A Gift of Prophecy: The Phenomenal Jeane Dixon and A Search for the Truth* (1967) and continued into the 1980s—a total of nearly a dozen books about a range of New Age subjects that attracted millions of readers.

Television did not ignore interest in the supernatural. However, as veteran TV producer Margaret Wendt observed, the networks were too timid to seriously explore anything paranormal. So, the subject had to be packaged with "an element of fantasy," lest scientists, skeptics, and fundamentalist Christians be overly offended. Therefore, in the 1960s, TV series about psychic phenomena, the occult and supernatural included comedic elements, such as *I Dream of Jeanie, Bewitched, The Addams Family, The Munsters,* and *Lost in Space*. On a more serious note were *The Twilight Zone* and *Star Trek*. In the afternoons, many kids raced home from school to watch *Dark Shadows,* about the vampire Barnabas Collins and his occult doings; it was probably closest to the real interests of the counterculture: astrology, the I Ching, and tarot. There were also witches and werewolves, and episodes about time travel. It was fun, except to the inevitable handful of fundamentalist Christian leaders who vigorously opposed *Dark Shadows*. Wendt said TV networks would never have shown that occult subject matter in prime time; on daytime TV it was easier to get away with it during the 1960s.[34]

The 1960s also marked a time of dramatically increasing drug use among America's youth. "There was a sense that nothing like this generation had ever existed before—and never would again. For one thing, its members had discovered so much—including the mystical properties of chemically induced experiences. This was a new age. The age of freedom—freedom from convention, from limitations, from authority," wrote Mark Miller in *Bad Trips*.[35]

In their search for other realms or dimensions of consciousness, millions of young people turned to hallucinogenic drugs, especially LSD. There was a connection between the mystical states produced by meditation and psychedelic drugs. The late astronomer Carl Sagan, no friend of the paranormal, was sufficiently open-minded to conjecture that both meditation and hallucinogenic drugs might put a person in an altered state that seems to "induce a sense of union with the universe . . ."

Whether through psychedelic drugs or meditation, every person shares the same description of "heaven and God," Sagan wrote in *Broca's Brain*. "Then must there not be a sense in which Western as well as Eastern religions are hard-wired in the neuronal structure of our brains?" he asked. "Can it really be that the Hindu mystical experience is prewired into us, requiring only two hundred milligrams of LSD to be made manifest?" The question had a serious implication for parapsychology. Was the human brain equally hardwired for psychic, as well as religious experiences? In the decades ahead, scientists would discover some surprising answers that we'll explain later.

Hallucinogenic and psychoactive drugs have a history that dates back thousands of years, taken in a quest for "spiritual enlightenment" in India, ancient Greece, and Rome. Native American tribes have long included peyote cactus in their religious ceremonies. Mescaline, another hallucinogenic employed by some tribes, is extracted from peyote cactus. The Aztecs of Mexico used hallucinogenic drugs to both communicate with and receive messages from the gods.

But of all the drugs associated with the turbulent sixties' counterculture, LSD was the most widely publicized and debated. To some, LSD or "acid" as it was often called on the street, came to represent the decade. However, LSD wasn't invented in some hippie hideaway in Haight-Ashbury during the stormy 1960s. Credit for its discovery actually goes to a Swiss chemist named Dr. Albert Hoffmann. In 1938, he was experimenting with lysergic acid diethylamide (LSD) hoping to find a new medication to relieve headaches. The lysergic acid, a component of LSD, came from the ergot fungus, a parasite that grows on rye plants. For hundreds of years there were epidemics of ergot poisoning across Europe. Among the results were severe pain, loss of hands and feet, hallucinations and delirium that led to hysterical accusations of witchcraft. Hundreds of thousands, mainly women, were burned at the stake throughout Europe; for many of them, their visions of strange and frightening beings, thought to be demonic, were actually the consequence of ergot poisoning. There were also "occult practitioners," who centuries ago secretly and intentionally ingested ergot to "explore psychic realms," wrote Dr. Paul Gahlinger.

When Hoffmann was unable to produce an analgesic from LSD, he set aside the effort, not realizing that he'd discovered "the most potent psychoactive drug ever known," according to *LSD: Visions or Nightmares?* One day in 1943, Hoffmann returned to the bottle of LSD that he'd stored away five years earlier, and accidentally ingested or absorbed some when he spilled a small amount on his hands. Hoffmann's next experience, inadvertently, was an "acid trip" that lasted for several hours. He recorded the experience in his journal:

"As I lay in a dazed condition with my eyes closed there surged up a succession of fantastic, rapidly changing imagery of a striking reality and depth, alternating with a vivid kaleidoscopic play of colors." Hoffmann continued, "There was an uninterrupted stream of fantastical images . . . [and] . . . visual disturbances."

Alterations in perception and coordination became hallmarks of LSD use. Although it was not addictive, it was unpredictable. Different people had markedly different reactions to taking LSD; there were "good trips" and "bad trips." One person would tell of having an exhilarating and inspiring, even mystical experience. Someone else would, in the lingo of the time, "freak out," after seeing frightening and distorted hell-like images that left the disoriented user grasping for control. Still others claimed they had the sensation of being removed from their bodies.

LSD first arrived in the United States in 1949 and scientists initiated animal experiments; every species given LSD exhibited behavioral changes. In the 1950s, experiments with humans were begun to treat addictions and mental illness, but they proved ineffective. Then the government surreptitiously moved in. The U.S. military and intelligence establishment sought to use LSD for purposes of mind control and brainwashing. The CIA allotted millions of dollars to test LSD on thousands of people, including college students. Perhaps foreign agents given hallucinogenic drugs would become confused, and more easily overpowered. The CIA plan went awry when some test subjects became psychotic, and at least one leapt to his death. LSD proved too unstable.

One college student who partook in LSD at the time was a fellow named Ken Kesey. While he attended Stanford University in Palo Alto, California, he worked nights at a local VA hospital. There he found all kinds of psychedelic drugs, apparently on hand for medical research. Late one night, Kesey, while "tripping" on LSD, wrote his bestseller about life in a mental hospital, *One Flew Over the Cuckoo's Nest*, published in 1962.

Meanwhile, famed British novelist Aldous Huxley (1894–1963), author of the remarkably prescient *Brave New World*, about a dehumanized society and the danger technology posed to individual freedom, wrote a slim volume in 1954 titled *The Doors of Perception*. It would prove to have immense influence on the 1960s drug culture. Huxley said his purpose was to discuss "the relationship between drug experiences and mysticism." He described what occurred to him a year earlier, in 1953, when he took "four-tenths of a gram" of mescaline, the hallucinogen found in peyote cactus. Huxley excitedly claimed that mescaline allowed him to see "what he had only written about before."

Huxley originally became fascinated with Eastern mysticism in the 1930s, especially Buddhism and Hinduism. By then he'd met the famed British occult and magic practitioner Aleister Crowley who introduced him to mescaline. After Huxley moved to Los Angeles in 1937, he continued his pursuit of mystical experiences and the occult. He began drug use in 1953 for a very specific reason: He'd hoped he could chemically imitate the "mystical state." His quest led him to become one of the first to take LSD, and his writings about it became influential on the acid-dropping counterculture of the sixties. Huxley concluded that, "all religions owed their basic beliefs to visions inspired by hallucinogenic experiences." He considered hallucinogenic drugs a means of expanding one's consciousness, and his vivid descriptions of their effects motivated the 1960s' leading LSD proselytizer, Dr. Timothy Leary, among many others. Even Huxley's title, *The Doors of Perception* was an influence on the sixties rock group, the Doors, who took their name from Huxley's book.

Huxley experienced hundreds of LSD and mescaline "trips" and encouraged others to do the same, especially creative types—artists, writers, and musicians. At some point in the 1950s, after Huxley began his drug taking, he met a brilliant young Canadian engineer named D. C. Webster, known to his friends as Ben. Webster was a graduate of Princeton University with a degree in engineering and a solid knowledge of chemistry. He was destined to become one of Canada's wealthiest men, an inventor of Velcro, and a powerful business leader and investor. In the 1960s, Webster founded the Toronto Society of Psychical Research (TSPR) that in the decades ahead made many substantial contributions to paranormal research. Webster, like Huxley, had a deep curiosity about mysticism and the occult, inspired by the teachings of the ancient shamans. Unbeknown to most Americans and Canadians, for many years, Webster quietly donated huge amounts of money into serious psychic research, projects, and discoveries that impacted generations to come, thanks to his funding.

Together the two men shared taking hallucinogenic drugs, including mescaline and LSD. Their goal was to expand their consciousness so that they might discover "new realities," Webster explained years later. During one LSD trip, Webster said he "saw God." Although he was unable—or unwilling—to articulate exactly what God looked like, the encounter left him exhilarated and inspired. Acting purely out of intellectual curiosity, having seen God, Webster continued taking LSD so that he might glimpse God's polar opposite: Satan.

Webster's LSD encounters continued, but once he witnessed the "dark side," there was no turning back. If the hallucinogenic experience opened doors to dimensions that led to spiritual enlightenment, and even God, it could also descend one into negative realms from which the mind could not easily recover, if at all. Webster's hallucinogenic encounters seemed to crumble the fragile wall that separates the good from evil. Having breached that dimension, there was no easy return. Despite

Webster's enormous professional success, he'd made a terrible error in believing the mind and spirit could enter a deeply negative space and then escape unscathed. Eventually it contributed to tormenting satanic visions years later when he was on his deathbed.

Huxley had written several books with occult themes in the 1950s, but he was never an advocate for the random use of LSD. In fact, by the early sixties, Huxley realized the dangers of haphazardly taking hallucinogenic drugs. He became aware that their use "would not bring liberation and understanding to everyone," said his brother, the eminent scientist Sir Julian Huxley. In the last book he wrote, *Island*, in 1962, the year before his death, Aldous Huxley warned of LSD's "potential danger." But by then, it was too late. The hallucinogenic demon had been loosed and "acid trips" would be a symbol of the psychedelic sixties.

For sheer, mind-bending audacity where LSD was concerned, no one could match Timothy Leary (1920–1996), the self-anointed "LSD Guru" who promoted the use of hallucinogens with the fervor of a crusading evangelist. Nor was anyone more identified with LSD in the sixties than Leary, far and away one of the most controversial and influential figures of the decade. In the early sixties, Leary taught psychology at Harvard University. By then he'd read Huxley's *The Doors of Perception* and was impressed with its claim that mystical experiences could be achieved through the use of hallucinogenic drugs. Author Joel Martin first met Leary in New York in the 1960s, and subsequently heard him speak publicly several times; then in the early 1980s he interviewed him on radio. The following, in addition to researched material, is based on personal knowledge and conversation with Leary.

In 1960, Timothy Leary literally had his first taste of a psychedelic drug when he experienced the so-called "Magic Mushroom." Certain mushrooms contain a hallucinogen known as psilocybin, used centuries ago in religious rituals by the Aztecs of Mexico. It was all Leary needed to convince him of the potential value in hallucinogenic or psychedelic drugs. He enthused that taking the "sacred mushroom" was "the deepest religious experience of my life." As Leary explained it, he'd had his epiphany, and made a solemn promise to dedicate himself to researching how hallucinogens could be used for psychological purposes, such as treating alcohol addiction and mental illness. However, Leary's major thrust became working with psilocybin and mescaline to learn more about their mind-expanding potential and effects on perception. To perform his experiments he enlisted a colleague, Dr. Richard Alpert. Together the two psychology professors constructed a series of tests. They were their own subjects, along with others they knew at Harvard, including willing students.

When Leary discovered LSD, it was love at first taste. From that moment on, in 1961, he concentrated all his efforts to understanding the effects and uses of LSD. It didn't take him very long to develop a following, especially among students. By 1962 "acid trips" had become a favorite—if clandestine—pastime, especially among radicals on many college campuses, as word of LSD's psychedelic effects spread. At the forefront of the LSD movement was Timothy Leary. If there was one thing he craved it was being in the spotlight. When Leary faced criticism that students were using LSD irresponsibly and for amusement, Leary argued back that it was fine with him. It seemed a particularly hypocritical response from a forty-something professor with a PhD to encourage students to "turn on, tune in, and drop out."

In 1963, Leary and Alpert's unauthorized hallucinogenic experiments with students resulted in the pair being fired from their Harvard teaching positions. Ironically, it was later revealed that the funding for Leary and Alpert's psilocybin research had come from the federal government. The public was never told about covert government interest in psychedelics, any more than it was informed about military and intelligence agency investigations of psychic phenomena, UFOs, or mind control.

Hallucinogens were another potential weapon during the Cold War. But that was not for the American people to know. All the public needed to be reminded of was that flying saucers and the occult were the beliefs of the eccentric and "unhinged," drugs were bad, and mind control experiments were to be kept top-secret—so no explanation was necessary. The government's duplicity was sometimes stunning.

For the ever-optimistic Leary, a little thing like being fired from a prestigious university was not going to impede his LSD crusade. He and Alpert had already accumulated a substantial amount of material about the drug's effects on the human psyche. Their next move was to create a privately funded foundation so they could continue their research. They relocated to a donated estate in Millbrook, New York, and there went back to work unencumbered by academic restrictions.

Meanwhile, Leary never missed a chance to promote what he considered LSD's spiritual value, and when he spoke people listened. The man had an innate gift for self-promotion; as a zealot for LSD he'd arrived at the right time, when many young people were increasingly restless and questioning virtually everything. By 1965, half of America's population was under thirty. What could be better than taking illicit drugs to confront and unnerve the "older" generation? Leary also attracted a number of intellectual lights—well-known literary figures, curious about the effects of psychedelic drugs. His reputation grew quickly; it wasn't long before Dr. Timothy Leary was a national figure, in the major media, and basking in his celebrity status.

In interview after interview, Leary proclaimed that LSD was "a part of the process of the evolution of the human mind toward higher consciousness." In 1965 Leary traveled to India where he converted to Hinduism. That, he said, added a "spiritual dimension" to his advocacy of LSD use. "I see my work as basically religious . . ." he commented in a *Playboy* interview in 1966. Combining the use of psychedelics with Eastern beliefs became widespread among many American youth through much of the 1960s, and once Leary latched onto the idea, he made it his own.

In 1964, Leary, Richard Alpert, and Ralph Metzner wrote *The Psychedelic Experience: A Manual Based on the Tibetan Book of the Dead*. The title made clear Leary's purpose: to compare the effects of hallucinogenic drugs with the ancient Buddhist concept of the afterlife. A couple of years later, in 1966, Leary wrote *Psychedelic Prayers After the Tao Te Ching*, inspired by an ancient Chinese book that explains Taoism, the Chinese philosophy that advocates humility and religious piety, and also includes "mystical contemplation." Those two, and a third Leary book, *The Psychedelic Reader* comprised what many LSD users regarded as essential.

But as the number of Leary followers grew, so did the discomfort among more traditional and older Americans, many of them parents, relatives, or neighbors of long-haired hippies and acid-dropping freaks who numbered several million strong by 1966–1967 when the counterculture hit its peak. Leary, with impunity, took every opportunity to preach the gospel of LSD, as the number of users rose.

"LSD was a pathway to divinity," Leary proclaimed. To those who knew him, whether he believed what he said was in doubt, for he was as much a charming con man as he was a guru. But, in addition to millions of young people, some quite famous Americans surprisingly supported Leary's claims about psychedelic spiritual enlightenment. Among them, motion picture star Cary Grant, comedian Steve Allen, jazz great Maynard Ferguson, even *Time* magazine publisher Henry Luce.

In 1967, at the height of his fame, Leary boasted about "the new LSD generation," and told one national magazine that a "social revolution" was under way. The goal was to "bring down" American society with its penchant for materialism, mechanization, and conformity; and he claimed that he found nothing wrong with young people interrupting their educations to "experience" LSD. He may have incensed older people and the so-called establishment, but he was revered by growing numbers of the youth.

In January 1967, a crowd of fifty thousand gathered in San Francisco to hear Leary and Beat poet Allen Ginsberg speak. Leary said he was especially pleased that bright college students were "turning on." His rosy vision of America's future was a society that achieved its enlightenment via LSD. But Dr. Tim's outrageous rants were about to catch up with him. LSD had been illegal across the country since President Lyndon Johnson forcefully called for a federal ban on it in 1967. It had been against the law in California since October 1966. Once LBJ realized that acid use, as well as pot, was rampant at antiwar demonstrations, he went on the attack against hallucinogens; likely more of his anger was against the anti-Vietnam war protesters than LSD.

However, Johnson only further enraged millions of young drug users, and countless thousands turned out in San Francisco for what was dubbed the "Summer of Love" in 1967. Even *Time* magazine recognized the psychedelic counterculture with a cover story in July about hippies. But there was a disturbing amount of drug-related crime, wild behavior, and unrestrained drug taking. There wasn't much love to be found, and very little LSD went toward expanding consciousness or enhancing spiritual enlightenment. It seemed as if the movement that Leary so strongly touted was spinning out of control; many blamed him for prodding and persuading naïve kids to take "powerful drugs" for which they were woefully unprepared.

Perhaps Leary could boast that he was the subject of a 1968 song, "Legend of a Mind" by the popular rock group, the Moody Blues. The lyrics began by saying Timothy Leary was dead. The song then went on to explain that no, he wasn't dead, but watching from out of his body, as he soared through a star-filled realm, ready to take followers on journeys through their minds—an obvious reference to LSD encounters. But the song was also prophetic, for, by 1969, Leary's LSD steamroller was sputtering to a stop. In addition to laws against hallucinogen use, more kids were learning about "bad trips," those frightening acid-induced descents to strange and distorted dimensions that were anything but mystical or insightful. Some experienced LSD-induced psychosis; others died. Several plunged to their death when they believed they could fly or walk on air, or through clouds, a result of LSD-produced hallucinations.

Leary was called a "faded guru" in a March 1969 *Washington Post* article, and in June 1969, less than a thousand turned out in the Midwest for a Leary public appearance. The promise that was "flower power" hadn't bloomed very long. One writer observed, "It quickly wilted." As the colorful, but short-lived, psychedelic era came to an end, so too did Leary's position as America's LSD guru; it had been a meteoric rise and fall.

Richard Nixon, who despised Leary, was in the White House when the law finally caught up with Dr. Tim. He was found guilty on drug charges and sent to prison in 1970, but escaped with the help of the radical Weather Underground. For a time he remained in Algeria, where he was granted political asylum. He was recaptured in 1973 in Afghanistan, of all places. Once back in the United States, he served three years in prison, and was then freed in 1976 after agreeing to testify against those who helped him escape.

His former colleague, Richard Alpert, left the country for India after Leary was jailed. When he returned it was as Baba Ram Dass, an unlikely guru with shoulder-length hair, beard, and mustache. But, by all accounts, an effective New Age teacher and author. When Alpert wrote *Journey of Awakening* in 1978, he distanced himself from his psychedelic years, and instead encouraged the practice of meditation.

Leary never again publicly encouraged drug use, but neither did he accept responsibility, apologize, or find fault with any of his earlier LSD experiences or having aggressively proselytized on its behalf. Although he'd always claimed that LSD was not physically dangerous, it was apparent in his last years that too much use had taken its toll on his mental health. Leary died of prostate cancer in 1996, but true to his outrageous ego, he'd even arranged his final trip—to the afterlife. In 1997, his ashes were sent into orbit around the Earth.

How many people gained mystical insights from acid trips that Huxley and Leary encouraged we'll never know. Perhaps some genuinely experienced psychic or spiritual enlightenment. More certain is that many who indulged heavily in LSD during its heyday reaped not the reward of the paranormal or religion, but instead endured disturbing "flashbacks" of their acid trips, even years later.

"The most remarkable recent discovery—something that those who practice yoga, meditation, prayer, or other mind-altering techniques have always known—is that all effects of psychoactive drugs can be produced naturally and spontaneously," wrote Dr. Paul Gahlinger. In other words, although certain drugs have long been considered gateways to other realities and dimensions, the human mind is capable of accessing those same altered states without the use of hallucinogens.

Rock music was one force that kids coalesced around, and some lyrics made obvious references or allusions to psychedelic drugs. Probably the best known was the Beatles' song "Lucy in the Sky with Diamonds." It's generally assumed the title was a play on LSD. Another Beatles' psychedelic tune was "Strawberry Fields Forever." One of the street terms for "acid" during the sixties was "strawberry fields." Another slang term for LSD at the time was "Purple Haze," the title of a hit song by guitarist Jimi Hendrix. Then there was "White Rabbit," by the 1960s group Jefferson Airplane. Hallucinogenic drug taking is compared to the strange, mind-altering experiences of *Alice's Adventures in Wonderland,* hence the song title "White Rabbit." You may recall that in the Lewis Carroll classic, once Alice follows a white rabbit wearing a waistcoat and carrying a pocket watch, down a large rabbit hole, her adventures begin in a surreal world with an assortment of strange characters. For example, she grows very tall, then becomes small again; a sensation not unlike psychedelic experiences in which time and space are distorted. The Doors' hit song "Break on Through (to the Other Side)," is an allusion to LSD as a way of reaching another dimension.

In real life, such as it was in the turmoil of the mid and late '60s, many popular rock stars and other celebrities made no secret of their mind-altering drug use; among some it was rampant. Influenced by the psychedelic drug gurus Tim Leary, Ken Kesey, Aldous Huxley, and Carlos Castaneda, the drug culture extended far beyond the hard-core hippies; they numbered only a couple of hundred thousand, at most. But by some estimates, as many six million American kids were engaged in marijuana smoking or "dropping acid," that is, experimenting with LSD and other mind-altering chemicals—by the mid-1960s. When California made LSD illegal in October 1966, it did little to discourage psychedelic drug use. In fact, it served as a battle cry for Leary and Kesey, who strongly protested the ban, and millions of young people openly defied the law. Demonstrations against drug prohibitions joined massive anti-war protests until the two movements were practically inseparable.

In a decade when spiritual and mystical exploration through meditation, psychedelic drugs, and occult practices consumed millions of American youth, it was not surprising that a "Death of God" movement would also emerge. But no philosophical questions seemed beyond bounds during the sixties. Besides the counterculture wasn't the first to ask where God was—if He was.

Just in time for Easter, in April 1966, *Time* magazine's cover became one of the best known of the entire decade.[36] In large gray letters on a stark black background was the foreboding question, "Is God Dead?" Although it sent many clergy reeling, and the movement was not numerically large, it attracted considerable attention and controversy. In the late nineteenth century, the German philosopher Friedrich Nietzsche had proclaimed, "God is dead." As far back as ancient Greece, the philosopher Plato struck a cynical note when he said, "He was a wise man who invented God." Yet every major Eastern and Western religion was centered on the concept of a deity. "The sole purpose of this human life is nothing but the realization of God," said the Indian mystics. "Meditate on Him with as much reverence and love as you can . . ."

But it wasn't that simple for many intellectuals. America's preeminent psychologist, philosopher, and parapsychologist William James (1842–1910) had some thoughts that echoed what others wondered, whether they dared admit it or not. "Whatever the God of earth and heaven is . . . his menial services are needed in the dust of our human trials, even more than his dignity is needed in the [heavens]," James concluded.

The question of God's existence and intervention in human life was part of a larger movement called "secular theology." It would have profound implications for the New Age that emerged in the 1960s, and continued into the decades ahead when an increasing number of Americans described themselves as more "spiritual" than "religious." Greater numbers of young people accepted psychic, mystical, and supernatural experiences, while rejecting centuries-old dogma, rituals, strictures, and prohibitions long promulgated by Christianity and Judaism that based their tenets largely on interpretations of the Old and New Testaments. But was the historic God of our fathers and forefathers still relevant in the changing sixties? The philosophers of the Age of Reason had asked much the same question. "If god did not exist, it would be necessary to invent him," Voltaire said in the eighteenth century.

"The premise [of secular theology] was that for modern individuals, traditional religion, Christian or otherwise, with all its doctrines, mythologies, pious feelings, and esoteric rites, was no longer accessible," explained Robert S. Ellwood. Especially jarring to the faith of many were the horrors of World War II and the slaughter of six million Jews during the Holocaust. How could a loving God allow atrocities of that magnitude? Why didn't He intervene? What had centuries of devotion and veneration to God meant? Where was God now during the turmoil of the sixties? In that frame of mind, secularism, unconcerned with religious belief, seemed a positive option for many. For secularists, "the ethical choices they make are human, not 'churchly,'" Ellwood said.

At the extreme end of "secular theology" were those who went beyond the argument that the traditional God was dead to conclude God never existed at all; they were the atheists. For them, there was no possibility an omniscient God ever dwelled in the sky, or answered us personally, rewarding us with heaven, punishing the sinners, or condemning the wicked to an eternity in hell's inferno. For those who conceived of such a universe, psychical events were equated with the miraculous and supernatural; all were flatly rejected. People were responsible for their own actions; morality or rightness was a matter of human determination. It had nothing to do with the concept of sin or transgression in the old religious sense.

Secular theology had some powerful champions throughout the

twentieth century, Sigmund Freud and Karl Marx among them. "Religion is an illusion," Freud believed; while Marx declared that "Religion is the sign of the oppressed creature . . . It is the opium of the people." Some hard-left extremists in the counterculture were drawn to Marxism; it was another form of protest.

The officially atheistic Soviet Union did not consider parapsychology in a religious context, and so psychic research conducted behind the Iron Curtain, throughout the Cold War years, was unencumbered by theological considerations or prohibitions. We, in America, linked the two so closely that Christianity's opposition to the paranormal was a major impediment to its study throughout the twentieth century. But, ironically, atheists and agnostics in America also rejected psychic phenomena for the same reason; they too considered it to be of a religious nature. "Irrevocable commitment to any religion is not only intellectual suicide; it is positive unfaith because it closes the mind to any new vision of the world," insisted Zen writer Alan Watts.

Perhaps those who predicted that the secularization of America was on the horizon ignored the emerging alternate spiritual beliefs of the sixties. If New Age teachings, metaphysics, and mysticism were considered, spirituality was thriving; it depended on how one defined God and religion. But the churches had no interest in being a part of the Age of Aquarius, the search for Atlantis, crystal healing, magical charms, or the life of the clairvoyant Edgar Cayce—subject of one of the decade's bestselling books, *The Sleeping Prophet*. Orthodox Christianity understood sin, not Zen.

Perhaps God lived within each of us; an idea posited by many who held to Eastern philosophies. Had the sixties generation given up on God? In 1966, *Time* magazine, reflecting concern about the changes in beliefs occurring across the country featured an article titled, "On Tradition or What's Left of It." The truth is most Americans needed God— and spirituality—despite the worldview of secularists; for example, author Harvey Cox who wrote *Secular City* in 1966. "Secularization is the liberation of man from religious and metaphysical tutelage, the turning of his attention away from other worlds and toward this one," he said. But in the final analysis, the "God is Dead" movement faded. God hadn't been killed by America's youth, as many feared. But He had changed by the end of the sixties. Christian mystic and author Jim Marion later wrote, "God isn't dead—but maybe our conception of God is . . . what has really died is our myth of God."

More people by the end of the sixties who'd become conscious of, or involved in the emerging New Age realized that to include such beliefs without entirely forsaking their traditional Christian or Jewish upbringing would require redefining religion; that meant contradicting biblical prohibitions against the so-called "occult." That debate continues to this day. Strict Christian fundamentalist denominations still warn against any involvement with psychic phenomena. What people do privately, however, even in Bible Belt states, is another matter. For example, the acceptance of mediums to contact the spirits of deceased loved ones has become widespread throughout the country, much of the change in consciousness originating with the generation of the 1960s and 1970s.

Many young people during the sixties were not fearful of condemnation from priests or ministers, as their parents likely were. Hundreds of years had passed since psychic gifts sent people to the stake for execution, as was Joan of Arc's fate. There had been a time in the Middle Ages when the Church frowned on dreams of departed loved ones or dreams that warned of future events, maintaining they were images from the devil. Cats that could have killed plague-carrying rats were instead believed to work for witches, and were destroyed in medieval Europe. Slowly over the centuries such superstitious attitudes had evolved into somewhat more tolerant thinking.

By the 1960s, Americans were open to new avenues of spiritual enlightenment, led not by scientists or the traditional clergy, but by young people—kids, hippies. But, as the writer Alan Watts once said, "There was never a spiritual movement without its excesses and distortions." That was, unfortunately, just as true when untold numbers of Americans turned to gurus, yogis, and swamis in the 1960s and later decades. In his thoughtful book, *The Death of the Mythic God*, Jim Marion imparts some valuable cautions about gurus who've acted less than responsibly; some of their behavior involved a misuse of their abilities, as well as abuse of their devotees.

During the 1960s and 1970s, there arose considerable controversy about cults in America, some created and led by disreputable gurus. There was damage done to many vulnerable minds of those who joined cults that taught pseudo-Eastern beliefs, sometimes muddled with the occult, and concocted only to financially enrich the gurus. There is reason to question whether members ever achieved higher consciousness or mystical states. The most visible were devotees of the Krishna Consciousness Society; its often emaciated-looking young members with shaved heads, except for a lock of hair in the back, wore long saffron-colored robes, danced and chanted "Hare Krishna" on the streets of cities—and in airports—seeking donations. But they were hardly the only group in the country popularly painted as brainwashing, abusing, or neglecting their gullible followers; most were less conspicuous, but no less notorious.[37] Several well-known gurus have also been accused of inappropriate sexual behavior with devotees; some of the charges have been reported in the media, others have been hushed up.

A number of gurus have been accused of virtual tyranny toward their followers, behaving more like petty dictators than loving teachers and guides. "Of course, some of these so-called enlightened gurus may not be enlightened at all," concluded Jim Marion.[38] He told of author and mystic Andrew Harvey who was warned that, "Many gurus now are not enlightened beings but black magicians, occult masters, manipulating millions of seekers . . . All of the serious mystical systems know of the existence of these occult powers, but modern seekers are naïve and uninformed and so vulnerable to them."

"The contemporary guru scene is deeply corrupted by gurus who are black magicians, that is, unenlightened frauds who use psychic powers to draw and keep disciples and are primarily interested in power, money, sex, and fame," Jim Marion explained, paraphrasing Andrew Harvey in *The Sun at Midnight*.[39]

"These gurus have failed the test that Jesus passed in the desert when Jesus refused occult powers," Jim Marion wrote, adding, "Avoid any spiritual movement based upon the glorification of any human . . . You cannot become enlightened if you have given away your power by projection onto guru or pope. Spiritual teachers and others can help, but we must do the work ourselves."

The 1960s opened the doors to the New Age. But some of what was behind those doors should never have been allowed out. The stereotypical fortune-teller who places a curse on some hapless victim, then charges a small fortune to remove it is a familiar story throughout history. Incredibly it still occurs. Skeptics see it as a criticism of the paranormal, but it is no more the fault of psychic phenomena than it is the fault of faith and prayer that some deceptive religious leaders or gurus misuse the teachings of Jesus, Buddha, or Krishna. In fact, the Bible got it right: "Beware of false prophets."

There are some appalling stories within recent history in which some claiming psychic powers have seriously hurt people psychologically and economically under the guise of spiritual enlightenment and psychic development. One such individual was Frederick Lenz, an avaricious and manipulative cult leader, who first became interested in Eastern beliefs when he was in his late teens at the end of the 1960s.

Born in California in 1950, and raised in Connecticut, Lenz earned a PhD in English, taught college for a time, and by 1980 had written his first book, *Lifetimes: True Accounts of Reincarnation*.[40] But Lenz had far loftier goals. He left New York for California where he briefly taught meditation, and soon after began his own organization in the Los Angeles area. By 1983, he'd changed his name to Rama, and then founded Rama Seminars. Claiming he'd been a Zen master in past lives, Lenz elevated his position and title to Zen Master Rama. Throughout the 1980s, Rama advertised and aggressively promoted himself throughout the country. Tall, lean, with angular features, piercing eyes, and wavy brown hair peppered with blond highlights, Rama always appeared in high-priced clothing; no one could ever accuse him of modesty or humility. But, although his Zen seminars were expensive, he attracted followers. And made plenty of money.

Then, in 1987, several former students and devotees accused Rama of coercing them into sex and drug use; charges he strongly denied. In the aftermath of the scandal, Rama assumed a much lower public profile; however, he was still very much in the guru business. That's when his sordid story went further downhill.

By 1996, Zen Master Rama was, once again, Frederick Lenz. He no longer taught meditation; he'd stopped doing that in 1994. Now he was in the computer software business and a New Age author; he'd written a book, *Surfing the Himalayas,* which became a bestseller. His computer seminars were costly, and he was making a fortune from his computer companies. Lenz had become a millionaire and moved to an expensive estate in an upscale Long Island, New York, community.

"I can't say anything good about that son of a bitch," one student's father said in a 1996 New York *Daily News* article about Lenz. The angry parent told how his daughter was a student of Lenz from 1984 until 1989 when she vanished. She likely committed suicide; depressed because she was unable to afford Lenz's seminars, according to her father.

The *Daily News* said, "There remain parents who accuse [Lenz] of stealing their children." Some claimed, "Lenz has ruined their lives—siphoning their money and stealing their minds." One young man, a former Lenz student for two years admitted, "I completely believed he had powers to alter people's state of consciousness." Others charged, "He abuses people," and accused Lenz of taking "advantage of them, either monetarily or sexually." A police detective described Lenz as a con man. Several other Lenz devotees went missing, and at least two more committed suicide. As with other scandal-plagued gurus, Lenz seemed to "mesmerize" his students; he was able to make his female followers feel "special" so they'd agree to have sex with him.

In the same newspaper article, Lenz was eerily prescient about his future, predicting his own death at the hands of his enemies. His carnal pleasures and greed eventually did end in tragedy when Lenz was found dead, the apparent victim of an accidental drowning—or if it was suicide, at the hands of his worst enemy: himself.

Another misguided soul, born and raised in New York City, was Frederick Von Mieres, a name he apparently gave himself because it sounded authoritarian. He also professed a strong devotion to Eastern philosophy and teachings, especially Hinduism. Von Mieres became accomplished in Hindu astrology, and combined with his considerable psychic powers, was able to persuade a number of "students," as he called them, to slavishly follow him in a hodgepodge of theosophical and occult teachings.

With his chiseled good looks, charismatic personality, and considerable cunning, by the 1980s his reputation had grown with frequent media appearances. His devotees and clients included some very wealthy people who sometimes received mean-spirited "wisdom" and instruction. For example, he once angrily chided a young blind woman that it had been her karma to lose her sight because, he claimed, she'd been "evil" in a past life. Hearing that, the young woman became inconsolable. In an astrology reading, he predicted to a teenage boy that he faced thirty years of "hell," traumatizing the boy for years to come. There were rumors that some students were driven to the verge of suicide.

Then Von Mieres found a means by which he could further con a small fortune from his naïve followers. He insisted that everyone he gave an astrology reading to must wear a specific crystal or gem—purchased only from a certain individual—in order to grow and heal spiritually from the alleged energy of the gemstones. His scam was uncovered when the district attorney charged that he and the jewelry dealer were in collusion to split the money from those who purchased the gems. Before he could be prosecuted, Von Mieres, only in his forties, died from natural causes in the early 1990s.[41]

Many young people had their first introduction to New Age ideas about past life memories and therapy, as well as the mind-body connection by reading a book called *Dianetics,* written by L. Ron Hubbard (1911–1986), the founder of the Church of Scientology. Originally a science fiction writer, Hubbard once admitted there was much more money to be made in starting his own religion, and so he did—charging substantial fees for counseling. Among his unorthodox theories of psychotherapy is the concept of the engram. All emotional and physical health problems are caused by engrams, Hubbard proclaimed, some of which go back to our past lives. The goal is to clear engrams through Scientology's teachings. Critics say it's in the business of "mind control."

Scientology was controversial from its beginning in the 1950s. Critics have harshly attacked it, and there is a debate whether it is "science" or "occult." The organization has spent years fighting an alphabet soup of federal agencies, and some judges have called Scientology "corrupt, sinister, and dangerous." Still, it has a strong following—although the precise number of members is not known—and became more appealing in the 1960s and the decades since. The most vexing question Scientology has persistently faced is whether it is a genuine religion—or as *Time* magazine once alleged—"the cult of greed."[42]

Parapsychology is not the same as the occult, although the two have long been confused—sometimes deliberately to discredit or stigmatize psychic abilities as evil. However, there are practitioners of the occult, "dark, hidden, and secret" areas of belief. During the 1960s, as many life-affirming New Age ideas percolated, the decade also produced some bizarre—even dangerous—individuals who had no fear of diving into the raging fire of hell, so to speak. One of them was Anton LaVey. Born in Chicago in 1930, he was fascinated by magic and the occult all his life. In 1966, LaVey created and became high priest of the First Church of Satan in San Francisco, and brought a touch of the theatrical to his new enterprise. He shaved his head and donned "black ritual garb," as one reporter described LaVey's somewhat macabre appearance.

All he needed to create a minor media sensation was the name he gave his organization: the Church of Satan. Most people were repulsed by the idea that a church was formally dedicated to the worship of Satan. It only added to confusion about the New Age by many traditional Americans. But LaVey was not bashful about his dark beliefs. In fact, in the 1968 occult screen thriller, *Rosemary's Baby*, starring Mia Farrow, LaVey happily played the part of the devil. The next year, 1969, LaVey authored *The Satanic Bible*, in which he provided his ideology, religious convictions, rites, and ceremonies, such as the "Black Mass." One of the holidays he included on his satanic calendar was Halloween.

LaVey realized the obvious: The mere perception of Satan was sufficient to frighten Christians. He wanted them to ease up on their attitude that "sex and pleasure" were sinful or evil. At one time, LaVey claimed he had as many as one hundred thousand followers and he knew how to garner national publicity for an event. He conducted funerals, and "worship services"—once with a naked young woman on the altar. When LaVey appeared on the *Tonight Show* with Johnny Carson years ago, he wore a hood adorned with horns at the top and carried a sword.

In 1967, the beautiful blond actress Jayne Mansfield was decapitated in a horrific automobile accident. She supposedly joined LaVey's group only the year before. Even if the two events were entirely coincidental, LaVey had no problem allowing people to draw a connection between Mansfield's untimely death and her interest in the Church of Satan. By the 1970s, LaVey's church membership was in a steep decline.[43]

On June 5, 1968, only ten days before *Rosemary's Baby* was released, the movie's director, Roman Polanski, and his wife, actress Sharon Tate, dined in Los Angeles with Senator Robert Kennedy, Democratic presidential aspirant. Then Kennedy left for the Ambassador Hotel to await the result of the day's California primary vote. That night, Kennedy was struck down; shot and killed by an assassin.

The next year, in August 1969, Tate was one of several murder victims "brutally stabbed and mutilated" by the deranged Charles Manson family of drug-crazed hippies. Manson admitted to authorities and the media he was a satanist. "All my women are witches, and I'm the devil," he boasted to reporters.

Rosemary's Baby, about a couple who inadvertently become involved with a witches' coven, was filmed at the Dakota, a landmark Manhattan apartment building with a gothic look and feel, where former Beatle John Lennon later lived and was murdered. In the late 1960s, right behind the Dakota on West Seventy-second Street, were the headquarters of the American Society for Psychical Research at Five West Seventy-third Street.

Were these all coincidences—or was there some peculiar synchronicity with an occult connection?

The 1960s and Bishop James Pike were perfectly suited to each other.[44] However, his liberal views on religion sat poorly with many of his more orthodox ecclesiastical colleagues within the Episcopalian Church and among his radical positions was a belief in communication with the dead. Throughout the sixties, Pike's name was often in the news, and once on the cover of *Time* magazine, the result of his challenges to Church doctrine; his venture into spiritualism, including a televised séance; and the accusations of heresy brought against him by Church officials. Through it all, Pike was seldom at a loss for some provocative or shocking comment or opinion.

James Albert Pike was born in Oklahoma City in 1913, and raised a Roman Catholic. He actually began his career as an attorney and taught at several law schools prior to his religious conversion. Ordained an Episcopalian priest in 1944, he rose quickly through the clerical ranks thanks to his keen mind and likeable personality. By 1951, he was the dean of the prestigious Cathedral of St. John the Divine in New York. Then, in 1958, Pike was named the Episcopal Bishop of California.

Although conservative in appearance—clean-shaven with short, dark hair, and black rimmed glasses—it was his political outspokenness and radical ideas to streamline the Church that led to confrontation with the Episcopal hierarchy. For instance, Pike dared to question the Virgin birth, and the Holy Trinity, both clearly heretical positions. He had a definite flair for calling attention to himself, never reticent about making his controversial opinions known. He eventually was accused of heresy by Church officials, but never convicted. Finally, in 1966, Pike resigned as bishop to take a position as "theologian in residence" at the Center for Democratic Institutions in Santa Barbara, California.

But in February of that year, Pike suffered an unspeakable personal tragedy when his son, James, Jr., committed suicide. The young man was only twenty-two when he shot himself to death, after taking LSD in a New York hotel room. The news devastated the elder Pike, cast a pall over the remainder of his life, and led to his interest in spiritualism as a way to find comfort.

About two weeks after his son's passing, the grieving bishop returned to the flat in Cambridge, England, that they'd shared while James, Jr. attended school. There he unexpectedly encountered evidence of psychic phenomena, specifically psychokinetic or PK events. Pike's secretary, and another clergyman, the Reverend David Barr, who had no interest in the paranormal, also witnessed many of the incidents.

For example, one morning, Pike noticed the clocks in the apartment abruptly stopped on their own—at precisely 8:19. He surmised that the time indicated when Jim, Jr. had taken his life. In another incident, safety pins were inexplicably found in the residence, and positioned to represent hands on a clock set at 8:19. Books that related to Jim, Jr. mysteriously moved by their own force from one place to another. Prayer books inexplicably opened themselves to passages that dealt with the subject of "eternal life."

On another occasion, Pike, his secretary, and a visiting cleric heard a clamor emanate from within a closet. When they looked, to their surprise, all of the clothing inside had been tossed around and was in complete disarray. One day, Pike was with visitors in the apartment talking about some of the mysterious events when suddenly a hand mirror that had belonged to Jim, Jr. lifted itself from the top of a dresser and slowly glided to the floor below—without breaking. Those watching were stunned.

When Pike confided the paranormal events to a bishop knowledgeable about psychic phenomena, the colleague suggested it was a result of the younger Pike's spirit desperately trying to make contact with his father. The bishop advised Pike to visit one of England's best-known mediums, Mrs. Ena Twigg, in London. Pike heeded the suggestion, accompanied by another priest to act as a witness. Although Twigg did not know Pike, the reading brought forth accurate communication from his son. Through Mrs. Twigg, Jim, Jr. apologized for taking his life, and regretted his terrible act—but said that he'd been under a great deal of stress at exam time, mentioned drugs, and thought his mind had snapped. "Dad, I wanted out and found there is no out. I wished I'd stayed and worked out my problems . . ." He sent love to his father, but was indignant the elder Pike had been treated harshly by the orthodox Episcopalian hierarchy. Another spirit contact came from Paul Tillich; he'd been a highly regarded theologian and philosopher, who died in 1965, and was godfather to James, Jr.

Once back in the United States, Pike also quietly consulted a medium named George Daisley in California. In September 1967, Pike and the medium Arthur Ford found themselves in Toronto, Canada, where both were appearing on TV in connection with a book about psychic phenomena that had been written by the religious editor of the *Toronto Star*, Allen Spraggett, a former minister. There have been several versions offered of the circumstances that led to Pike's appearance on a televised séance. The following is taken from Arthur Ford's account of the events in his autobiography *Unknown but Known*; Pike's book, *The Other Side*; and private interviews with the late D. C. Webster, founder of the Toronto Society for Psychical Research, who knew Ford and Spraggett at the time.

Ford said as he and Pike spoke privately at the Canadian Broadcasting Corporation's Toronto TV station, Pike asked if a "sitting" might be arranged so that he could receive messages from his late son. Ford said the two men "had previously agreed that a séance would be a good thing." However, the details and time were never worked out. "What's the matter with right now?" Ford inquired. Pike concurred. "We went into the studio and made the tape," Ford explained. The moderator was Allen Spraggett. The videotaped sitting took place on September 3, 1967, and was seen on Canadian TV on September 17, with portions also televised in the United States.

During the séance, Ford said he brought forth, through his spirit control, Fletcher, new information for Pike. Much of it came from Pike's son who told his father that his suicide was "the result of a bad [LSD] trip."

He said he "got mixed up with the thing in California," while at college. When he returned to New York he'd "fallen in with some of the same crowd," meaning counterculture and hippie types who irresponsibly "dropped acid."

There were also messages from others Pike knew in life, and who'd since passed on. One was described as "an old gentleman . . . who's with your son on the other side." Ford continued, "He has two cats with him that were pets of his son, who bears the same name he does—Donald MacKinnon. The present MacKinnon now lectures at Cambridge. James, Jr. used to drop in at his lectures." Ford's information was later verified as accurate.

Then Ford's spirit control, Fletcher, told of an "elderly man of Slavic and Jewish background." He'd helped Jim, Jr. make the transition to the "other side."

"Correct," Bishop Pike acknowledged. It was Jim's maternal grandfather, a Russian Jew. Another discarnate entity that communicated through Fletcher was Louis Pitt. Pike immediately recognized the name as that of the chaplain who preceded him at Columbia University. A former Bishop of California, Karl Block, also made contact and told of several real estate matters he'd dealt with for the Church that only he could have known.

At the end of the séance, James, Jr. once again came through and spoke of "a delightful elderly lady" he identified as Carol Rede. Pike's son said his father had once worked with her at the Cathedral of St. John the Divine. Jim, Jr. relayed a message from her, "She asks that you look up her brother, a retired major living in Carmel, when you go back to California."

"That was a shocker," Bishop Pike acknowledged. "I remember Carol Rede well, but didn't know she had died!"

Following the séance, Pike phoned as many people as he could to confirm the details Ford gave him. Ford said he found it interesting that among the messages from the Other Side was that "two long-deceased pet cats" were there. The medium regarded this as evidence that animals also survive death. That has long been a contentious issue in many Christian denominations: whether animals, like humans, have souls.

Bishop Pike's reaction to the séance was as controversial as his attendance in the first place. In addition to hordes of disapproving clergy, there were the inevitable—but understandable—questions from skeptics. Might the medium, Arthur Ford, have obtained the information from prior research of Pike who, after all, was very much a public figure? Could he have engaged in mental telepathy, that is "mind reading" rather than discarnate communication?

Pike replied that he didn't think so. "Some of the material was of such an intimately personal nature it had to be erased from the film," a reference to the videotape of the séance. "It certainly could not have been published and still is not published. Yet it checked out. Some details that proved correct were definitely beyond anything I could have known in my conscious mind—and I suspect, in some cases, in my unconscious," the bishop concluded.

The fallout from the televised séance was enormous. The fact that a man who had been a priest and bishop of the Episcopal Church would dare participate in a séance—and one that was televised—was absolute heresy to many of the faithful. What's more, Pike had not shown any regrets for taking part; he actually acknowledged Ford's accuracy, affirming that he felt the messages were from his late son. The story was fodder for an eager media, but considerably more grave for the ecclesiastical community. For many, Pike's dabbling in the "occult" was an intolerable sacrilege. On the other hand, among parapsychology's supporters, it sparked debate and interest in a subject that rarely made such headlines. The Church hierarchy was furious.

Not only did Pike withstand the controversy, he wrote about his experiences with spiritualism in a popular book, *The Other Side*, in 1968. He made no secret that he believed in the possibility of discarnate communication and the book became a topic of much debate. In 1969, Pike and his wife, Diane Kennedy Pike, began their own foundation dedicated to removing what they considered the mythical elements from Christianity. He remained passionate about "social change," and voiced strong opposition to the Vietnam War.

Pike also had a deep interest in the Dead Sea Scrolls, among the most important discoveries in recent archeology—found in caves of the Judean desert in 1947. The scrolls, or manuscripts, revealed a great deal about Jewish life immediately prior to and after Christ's life on earth, greatly helping to comprehend early Christianity. In pursuit of further study about the scrolls, and to research a future book about the "historical" Jesus, he and Diane journeyed to the Holy Land, Israel, in August 1969. She was Pike's third wife, twenty-five years his junior, and they were not yet married a year. But she shared his enthusiasm for learning and discovery. Once there, on September 1, the couple impulsively decided to take a side trip through the desert of Judah, southeast of Bethlehem. They'd driven about twenty-five miles when, after mistakenly taking a wrong turn, their car broke down. They agreed that Diane should seek help. That left James Pike alone with the stalled car. She eventually found assistance the next morning at a "road-building" site, although by then she was in a state of exhaustion. But Bishop Pike somehow became lost in the fiercely hot desert.

Israeli police launched a massive search on the ground, as well as with helicopters and aircraft. When there was no sign of the bishop, the army took over the rescue; even volunteers joined the search. Several days elapsed, but there was still no sign of Pike. Meanwhile, the story of the controversial cleric's mysterious disappearance made news in both the Israeli and American press. Some noted that it occurred in the same region where Jesus had gone into the desert for "forty days and forty nights" to fast and pray.

The *New York Times*, no fan of the paranormal, nonetheless reported that Diane Pike had consulted two Israeli mediums and one of them described the area where the bishop might be found. Other newspapers made only brief mention of the use of psychics, if at all. At one point, Diane said she'd spoken with the medium Arthur Ford and he'd reassured her, suggesting her husband was still alive, having found refuge in a desert cave. The California medium George Daisley claimed he had a premonition before the tragedy that the bishop would pass on in an accident. Many of the mediums and psychics who jumped on the story said their impression was that Pike was still alive, although several days had gone by since he'd been last seen. In *The Psychic World of Bishop Pike*, author and parapsychologist Hans Holzer quoted Diane Pike as saying, "We both have very good ESP and we're able to pass messages to each other," suggesting that she too held out hope he'd be found alive. But it was not to be. On Sunday, September 7, Pike's body was found in the "craggy hills of Judea."

Psychics had become involved from the moment of Pike's disappearance in the Israeli desert, including the British medium Ena Twigg.

According to *Psychic News,* a popular British weekly, Mrs. Twigg revealed the tragic news to Diane Pike that her husband had died, contradicting nearly every other medium's prediction. She also said the bishop's message was that he'd been choked. However, no official reports suggested foul play.

The *Jerusalem Post* reported, "It appeared that [Pike] had fallen from the cliff above, and met instant death." From a paranormal perspective, it meant many of the mediums that foretold Pike was alive were dead wrong.

"Jim did not fear death and now he is at peace," Diane was quoted by the Associated Press. "There was no more appropriate place for Jim to die, if he had to die," she said pensively. Pike's body was buried in Jaffa, Israel. The autopsy report concluded that he died six days earlier, only hours after his wife left to seek help. Despite the puzzling circumstances, the official determination was that Pike died of natural causes. However, Holzer wrote that several mediums suggested Pike's death was not accidental and his death "remains a mystery."

There is also the question of Diane Pike's visions. In January 1970, four months after her husband's untimely death, the *Jerusalem Post* reported, "The widow of Dr. James Pike said yesterday in Jerusalem that she had a vision of her husband dying in the Judean desert the night before his body was found there last September." She said the vision awakened her, and had been accompanied by "voices." Then there was a second vision; in that one she saw her husband's spirit breaking free from his body.

Once Diane Pike returned home to the United States, she received many letters from mediums, all claiming to have messages from her late husband. However, she found none of them to be accurate. She added that she did not think he wanted to communicate to her through mediums, so she never sought their help.

The debate between opposing camps in the Pike controversy about spiritualism never really ended. As with most controversies in the history of psychic phenomena, the outcome was inconclusive; each side believed as it wished. Pike apparently received a measure of comfort believing he'd been in contact with his late son's spirit. But skeptics mounted a determined campaign to discredit Arthur Ford. After Ford's death in 1971, Allen Spraggett, who'd moderated the televised séance, said that among

Ford's materials were found many articles about Bishop Pike, suggesting Ford might have researched his subject prior to their séance. But, if that was true, why did Pike acknowledge that there was information Ford gave him that had never been published? Might Ford have employed telepathy, in other words, mind reading rather than receiving discarnate communication? While that's a possibility, Pike said he'd received messages revealing circumstances he knew nothing about, such as the passing of a former colleague. The Pike séance demonstrated the continuing official animosity of the Christian churches against the paranormal.

The Vietnam War had taken a growing and terrible toll on America in the 1960s. If President Kennedy had lived, one could only speculate that events might have moved in a different direction. Lyndon Johnson completed JFK's term, then was elected in his own right in 1964, just as the noted medium Arthur Ford, through his spirit control Fletcher, had predicted.

It was Johnson who, after the assassination, reversed the Kennedy policy of pulling U.S. military advisors out of Vietnam and increased the American presence there. As the war escalated, the number of casualties mounted, and the country became bitterly polarized between those opposed to, and those who supported the war. It was the sixties' most divisive issue, and antiwar demonstrations disrupted college campuses from coast to coast. But it was no longer just the hippies, and other angry, frightened, and alienated youth who opposed U.S. involvement; more Middle Americans were questioning Johnson's war policy as they watched the carnage on the nightly news—the first time a war had been televised. In 1968, Johnson refused to run for a second term after American public opinion turned against the Vietnam War, especially after the success of the North Vietnamese Tet Offensive.

What most people did not know was that, second to Lincoln, Johnson was one of our nation's most psychic presidents. Since his childhood in Texas, Johnson was plagued by frightening dreams and nightmares, which, as president, he often shared with Doris Kearns, who worked for him and later wrote *Lyndon Johnson and the American Dream*.[45] In one recurring dream, he saw himself "sitting . . . in a big straight chair." Then a "stampede of cattle" headed toward him as he struggled to move, but he discovered his muscles were frozen and he couldn't budge.

The paralysis dream worsened in 1968 after the North Vietnamese Tet Offensive. In the dream, Johnson said he was transformed into the late president Woodrow Wilson. Although LBJ said his head was his own, "from the neck down his body was paralyzed." One night, to be certain that he was alive and Wilson was the one who was deceased, Johnson ran his hands over Wilson's portrait. LBJ became intensely fearful that his dream was a portent that he would suffer a stroke in his next term. "He couldn't get rid of the suspicion that a mean God had set out to torture him in the cruelest manner possible," Kearns wrote.

By late 1967, Johnson faced growing public pressure to deescalate the Vietnam War, find a solution to an inflationary economy that was spinning out of control, and address the danger of race riots in the inner cities. As he watched war casualties mount and presided over a nation divided by issues of war and race, he increasingly considered leaving politics for good. The vision he had of eliminating poverty in America was all but buried beneath the statistics of body counts, aerial sorties, and the rising number of American POWs. In 1968, antiwar advocate Senator Eugene McCarthy scored impressive numbers in the New Hampshire Democratic primary, numbers that would have embarrassed any incumbent president in the same party as the challenger. At that point, although he realized he could not remain in office, stubborn pride interfered. Johnson didn't want to be thought cowardly by leaving the presidency or serving a second term and becoming politically impotent by the deepening social morass. His feelings of hopelessness worsened as he sought an honorable way out. His situation, Kearns said, was a "total impossibility."

Then, as often happens, Johnson's answer arrived in a dream that was different from any he'd ever had before. LBJ "saw himself swimming in a river." He swam from the middle of the water to one shore, and then to the other. However, no matter how much he swam, he could not reach the shore, but was simply swimming round and round. LBJ concluded the dream's message was that he must free himself from politics. So the beleaguered president changed his strategy and ordered an end to bombing north of the twentieth parallel, a major shift in Vietnam War policy. A short while later, Johnson announced to the nation that he would not seek reelection in 1968.

Thus, Johnson's "decision to withdraw from . . . Vietnam . . . was influenced by a dream that clarified for him the impossible no-win situation he was in," wrote Peter and Elizabeth Fenwick in *The Hidden Door: Understanding and Controlling Dreams*.[46] Had Johnson experienced a problem-solving dream that was drawn from his subconscious mind—as skeptics would argue—or was it psychic? One paranormal theory suggests the dream state "makes the mind more receptive to outside input," such as telepathy or after-death communications. Psychics suggest that LBJ might have experienced a psychic dream in which a departed loved one, or a former president, communicated to him the course of action he needed to take in his desperate circumstance. Interestingly, while many military figures throughout history gained advice for battle from paranormal dreams, Johnson's dream helped initiate the pursuit of a negotiated solution to the Vietnam War even though the final peace would elude him and its pursuit would destroy the administration of the president who succeeded him.

Despite Johnson's passionate commitment to the cause of civil rights and the elimination of poverty in the United States, he will always be associated with the disaster of the Vietnam War, a war he described in the audiotapes he secretly recorded in the Oval Office as one America could not win no matter what the military did. It is no wonder his beleaguered psyche sought answers in the visions of dreams. These were visions that came to him at night, torturing his soul.

Johnson was a psychic individual living in a residence filled with the active spirits of those who had come before him. Thus, it's not surprising that the spirits of the departed who occupied the White House were especially active during LBJ's tenure. Many times spirits may not be seen or heard, even though their presence, very much with us, can be sensed. As it happened, among the spirits most agitated by the presence of the Johnson family in the White House were Abraham Lincoln and his young son Willie.

Also reported during the LBJ White House years were "phone calls from the departed." According to one author and paranormal researcher, presidential family members received phone calls but found no one at the other end of the line. When questioned, White House operators said they'd not been responsible for ringing the phones on those occasions. During the Johnson era in the 1960s, the White House phone system was not the digital system of today; it was controlled completely by operators, who routed calls to the president or other family members by hand according to a strict set of rules. If the operators had not rung the phones of family members and an investigation uncovered no malfunctions to the phone system, who was responsible? Phone calls from the departed may sound far-fetched but are actually quite common. It takes only a tiny electrical charge to make a phone ring and the spirit is actually some form of energy. It is not so unreasonable for a spirit to use electronic means to communicate with the living.

Outrageous and audacious were only two of the descriptions given Abbie Hoffman.[47] During the 1960s, he was one of the counterculture's brashest figures, and the radical founder of an antiwar movement called the Yippies at a time when peace demonstrations and draft card burnings were on the upswing. When Hoffman's mind churned with a new antic in the autumn of 1967, it would call attention to one of the paranormal's oldest purported abilities: levitation. Not content to leave the phenomenon of floating in the air to mystics and yogis or saints of the Catholic Church, Hoffman's newest attention-getting stunt would be an attempt to levitate the Pentagon building as a way to end the Vietnam War.

On October 21, the "March on the Pentagon" made national news when some hundred thousand youth gathered at the Lincoln Memorial in Washington. Later that day, about thirty thousand proceeded across the bridge to nearby Arlington, Virginia, to assemble closer to the Pentagon. For the most part it was a peaceful demonstration, but there were several hundred arrests when radicals threw bottles and pelted eggs in an attempt to rush Defense Department headquarters.

While the protest and draft card burnings were under way, Abbie Hoffman directed his followers to levitate and exorcise the Pentagon. More than a thousand hippies in full counterculture regalia—including love beads and sandals—formed a huge circle, and began chanting. The plan was to ring the building and exert sufficient energy to raise it far into the air. If Hoffman were to be believed—a risky proposition—the Pentagon would magically tremble and resonate until every bit of its destructive, war-making ability was gone. Needless to say, the Pentagon remained firmly in place. But Hoffman and his antiwar cohorts, such as Jerry Rubin, garnered another media publicity coup.

If there had been a spirit across the country that carried the promise of peace and harmony, the events of 1968 and 1969 whipped the spirit into a furious storm, whirling the Age of Aquarius out of its orbit, carrying us with it, but who knew to where. Had Americans ever known a year like 1968? If the decade until then was racked with unprecedented social change and turmoil, then 1968 would also be remembered for assassination and agony. The sunshine of spiritual enlightenment was quickly overshadowed by unspeakable tragedy. The antiwar movement had, for all practical purposes, forced Lyndon Johnson not to seek reelection in 1968. Several psychics and mediums were on record forecasting tragedy around two of the decade's icons: Dr. Martin Luther King, Jr. and United States Senator Robert F. Kennedy, brother of the slain president. Bobby Kennedy was enormously popular with young people and minorities, as he sought the Democratic presidential nomination. Dr. King, in 1967, spoke out forcefully against the Vietnam War, much to President Johnson's displeasure.

Once again, predictions and premonitions could not change an unalterable destiny. When Jeane Dixon warned in advance that she felt danger around King and Kennedy, her pleadings were ignored. In early April 1968, King was in Memphis, Tennessee, to support striking sanitation workers. There, Dr. King was gunned down by an assassin as he stood on a motel balcony. In the aftermath of King's death, riots exploded in many minority neighborhoods around the country. Before the country could catch its collective breath, in early June, Bobby Kennedy, newly victorious in the California Democratic presidential primary was shot and killed by an assassin in a Los Angeles hotel. Americans, especially the youth, were crushed. Two of the decade's most charismatic and progressive leaders who represented change were gone in a blink. And, in the eyes of millions of young people, there was despair and disillusionment. The singer Dion summed up much of the pain many felt after the assassinations in one of 1968's most popular songs, "Abraham, Martin, and John."

Then at the Democratic National Convention in Chicago in August, hordes of antiwar demonstrators broke into an open frenzy. In the mayhem that followed, Chicago police were ordered to move in and break up the protests. They did, with riot gear and nightsticks, and demonstrators, mostly kids, were left beaten and bloodied. America's opinions about the police response were sharply divided; conservative Middle America was satisfied that a blow had been struck against the antiwar hippies and counterculture. Liberals railed against what they saw as the excesses of a "police state."

On Election Day in November 1968, Middle America spoke with their votes: Republican Richard Nixon defeated Democrat Hubert Humphrey. Nixon despised the antiwar movement and the counterculture with every fiber of his being. He appealed to America's "silent majority," the hard-working middle class, repelled by the extremes of the counterculture, and the threat it posed to the country's stability and traditions. On the other hand, the Nixon administration failed to recognize slowly growing opposition to the Vietnam War even among the millions of people he counted as his supporters. As the war dragged on, the death toll by decade's end moved past fifty thousand, amidst a U.S. military strategy that left increasing numbers of Americans wondering why we were fighting in Southeast Asia—and how much longer we'd be there. Nearly half a million of our young men and women were serving in Vietnam.

The tumultuous decade was running out of breath by 1969, a year of highs and lows, literally. The antiwar protests and draft card burnings continued unabated. In July, three American astronauts made a successful voyage to the Moon, just as JFK had pledged. It was one of the few accomplishments that brought Americans together in a rare showing of unity and pride, when astronaut Neil Armstrong made that first step on the lunar surface. From hippies on the left, to conservatives on the far right, and millions in between, it was a crowning achievement, a metaphysical moment, albeit muted by the tragedies and failures that overshadowed the decade.

In July, Senator Ted Kennedy, the bearer of the Kennedy dynasty flame, as the sole surviving brother, was involved in a tragic automobile accident that killed his secretary and was followed by a disturbing obfuscation of the circumstances. It effectively ended Kennedy presidential aspirations and some wondered aloud about a "Kennedy curse."

When, in August, seven innocent people were brutally butchered in the Tate–La Bianca murders by the Charlie Manson "family"—a gang of Satan-worshipping, drug-crazed, hippie types, the country understandably reacted with revulsion and fear. It revealed the excesses of the counterculture many felt. One of the victims was actress Sharon Tate, pregnant wife of director Roman Polanski. In *The Haunting of America* we detailed her premonition of bloody tragedy involving her former boyfriend Jay

Sebring in his Benedict Canyon home. Sebring was also one of the victims, murdered as Tate had chillingly forewarned.

Just as ominously, the peace and love themes of the counterculture were giving way to an angrier, more revolutionary tone among black militant movements—flower power had been replaced by Black Power, harder drug use combined with a sharp uptick in crime, even violent elements in the antiwar movement—and several more brutal crimes attributed to satanists. No wonder Middle America had become increasingly tense, and welcomed the Nixon opposition to the "dissidents and subversives," as many called the disenchanted generation of sixties' kids. Even among young people, there was a reaction to some of the excesses of the decade in a renewed evangelical religious movement that saw many former hippies become "Jesus freaks," turning back to Christ for answers.

There was one final hurrah for the 1960s counterculture at a huge music festival in August 1969 near Woodstock, New York, that attracted more than four hundred thousand young people for a weekend of rock and protest songs performed by some thirty of the decade's best-known rock stars, including Joan Baez; Crosby, Stills, Nash and Young; the Grateful Dead; Jimi Hendrix; Jefferson Airplane; Janis Joplin; and the Who. It marked a culmination for the counterculture, as both its apex and the beginning of the end of the hippie generation that soon would begin to fade.

Nixon's secret decision to invade Cambodia in 1970 expanded the war, and led to even angrier protests on the nation's college campuses. The worst resulted when four student demonstrators were shot and killed by National Guardsmen at Kent State University in Ohio. Two of rock music's young icons died of drug overdoses that year: the powerful, raspy-voiced Janis Joplin and the brilliantly innovative guitarist Jimi Hendrix.[48]

As the decade was ending, there was one contribution that would have a profound impact on the paranormal in the years ahead, and on every American who wondered about life after death. It was the result of the tireless efforts of Dr. Elisabeth Kübler-Ross (1926–2004) who became a world authority on death and dying, and after-death states. She was a Swiss-born psychiatrist who moved to the United States, and in 1965 began working formally with dying patients, an interest sparked by the horrors she witnessed during a visit to a Nazi death camp at the end of World War II.

In 1969, Kübler-Ross wrote *On Death and Dying*; the critically acclaimed book became a bestseller, and is regarded as a classic in its field.[49] In it, she'd stirred America to face one of its last great taboos: facing and talking honestly about death. In earlier centuries, people had been closer to death and dying. Infant and child mortality rates were higher, and life spans were considerably shorter. During the nineteenth century, and before, more people died at home and their bodies were often laid out in the family parlor room. But as we moved toward the mid-twentieth century, death and dying had become an impersonal and profitable industry that kept the living at a distance from the departed. More people passed on in hospitals, especially as medical technology became increasingly sophisticated. Wakes or other services for the dead were held at funeral homes—or parlors—as they're still called. As these changes occurred, people talked less about the issues of death and dying, steering clear of the subject, if they could.

Kübler-Ross fulfilled a huge need with her landmark book. In it, she detailed the five stages the dying person faces: denial and isolation; anger; bargaining; depression; and finally, acceptance. She recognized, however, that death has always been "distasteful" and "probably always will be." In her many writings and lectures, she'd urged more honest communication between the living and their dying loved ones, advising and encouraging "a dialogue on questions of death and dying . . . to help people to live less fearfully until they die." In raising many provocative questions, Kübler-Ross had moved Americans to confront a subject they'd increasingly avoided.

Kübler-Ross directed her later research toward proving the existence of life after death. Her studies involved accounts by patients who reported out-of-body travel. When Kübler-Ross confined her research within traditional boundaries of psychology and bereavement, she was praised and applauded by peers. However, once she began exploring the age-old question of life after death, the accolades dwindled, and she became the target of considerable criticism and derision by those same colleagues who'd previously praised her work. Some went so far as to question her mental stability: How dare Kübler-Ross step beyond the line that separates the visible from the invisible world. Nonetheless, she would have a profound impact on the exploration of near-death experiences and questions about an afterlife in the years ahead. We'll talk more about the contributions Kübler-Ross made in our next book.

Meanwhile, as the dizzying sixties ended, and the New Age dawned, it was reasonable to ask what had been accomplished for parapsychology in one of the most eventful decades this country had ever known. Had we moved forward—or merely rediscovered ancient beliefs and practices? Without question, the 1960s opened millions of minds to new ways of seeking spirituality, beyond traditional Christianity and Judaism. Eastern practices, such as meditation and yoga would find a permanent and useful place in America. The archaic and negative term, "occult," applied to all things psychic, and was slowly giving way to the more positive and all-inclusive term "New Age." Many young people who grew up in the sixties would, in later years, be more open-minded about ESP, past lives, and life after death. Astrology enjoyed a resurgence of popularity that continues, as does interest in Kabbalah.

The sixties also produced false prophets, from self-serving gurus and cult leaders, to individuals such as Timothy Leary, who proved more showman than shaman. But, more important, millions realized they could be spiritual without submitting to unyielding religious dogma. At the same time, there was a profound sense that faith and spirituality were necessary, and God was very much alive; perhaps He/She understood the "spiritual awakening" of the sixties better than many had thought.

In a decade that professed altruism and idealism to effect social change, many young people learned there was no quick path—or fix—to utopia. If every effort from astrology to Zen could not improve society, end war and poverty, then what purpose was there in the new approaches? Perhaps New Age beliefs could not magically elevate us as a nation. However, they could be turned inward to help the individual. In the decades to come, much of the interest in New Age ideas, including psychic development, spiritual growth, and efforts to contact the departed, would move in the direction of helping oneself.

The 1970s would find the paranormal churning forward through an explosion of interest in near-death experiences, and "channeling," a New Age term for mediumship. Americans would also learn that the Soviets were diligently experimenting with the paranormal, while a U.S. astronaut, Edgar Mitchell, conducted ESP tests from outer space. More psychic healers were being scientifically tested. Skeptics and debunkers were becoming better organized in their efforts to topple New Age thinking.

What is the challenge to them? We already know that today's debunking has become tomorrow's science. Ideas once rejected by the establishment as preposterous become establishment thinking in the ensuing generation. But the challenge to the status quo was such that the debunkers decreed that parapsychology must never become complacent, for around every corner awaited a new controversy. However, by the 1970s, even the United States Army would become New Age, dabbling in aspects of parapsychology that even the parapsychologists would deem science fiction. Only this time, it had become a weapon.

Preface: The Turn of the Twentieth Century

1. Nicola Tesla (1856–1943), developer of alternating current, often experienced psychic visions that led to his inventions.
2. Lael Wertenbaker, *The World of Picasso* (New York: Time-Life Books, 1969), 13A. The mural *Guernica* was painted by Pablo Picasso (1881–1973) for the Paris World Exhibition, 128, 135.
3. Marcel Proust, famed French novelist (1871–1922).
4. Irish playwright Abraham "Bram" Stoker (1847–1912). J. Gordon Melton, *The Vampire Book* (Detroit: Visible Ink Press, 1999), 649–654.

Chapter 1: The Dark Side of the Paranormal: The Nazis and the Occult

1. Paul Roland, *The Nazis and the Occult* (Edison, New Jersey: Chartwell Books, 2009), 9, 15.
2. There were seven adult victims of the Manson family murders. However, actress Sharon Tate was eight months pregnant. Her unborn child would count as the eighth murder victim.
3. *Helter Skelter* was taken from the lyrics to a Beatles' song. It was also the title of a best-selling book about the Manson family murders by prosecutor Vincent Bugliosi.
4. The idea for Robert Louis Stevenson's story of *Dr. Jekyll and Mr. Hyde* (1886) came to him in a dream. Robert Van de Castle, *Our Dreaming Mind* (New York: Random House, 1994),16.
5. Michael Howard, *The Occult Conspiracy* (Rochester, Vermont: Destiny Books, 1989).
6. Ibid, 1.
7. Roland, *The Nazis and the Occult*, 12, 16, 17. Howard, *The Occult Conspiracy*, 113.
8. *Malleus Maleficarum* (*The Witches' Hammer*). Both Sprenger and Kramer belonged to the Dominican order.
9. J. Gordon Melton (ed.), *Encyclopedia of Occultism and Parapsychology* (Detroit, MI: Gale Research, 1996), 162–163, 529–530.
10. Dusty Sklar, *Gods and Beasts: The Nazis and the Occult* (New York: T. Y. Crowell, 1977); Jim Marrs, *Rule by Secrecy* (New York: Harper Perennial, 2000), 262–263, 331, 348–350; *Encyclopedia of Occultism & Parapsychology*, 529–530.
11. *Encyclopedia of Occultism & Parapsychology*, 644; Howard, *The Occult Conspiracy*, 87–92, 97.
12. Ibid, 97.
13. Rosemary Ellen Guiley, *The Encyclopedia of Ghosts and Spirits* (New York: Checkmark Books, 2000), 183–186; Howard, *The Occult Conspiracy*, 105–106.
14. Howard, *The Occult Conspiracy*, 106.
15. Ibid, 109–110.
16. Madame Helena Petrovna Blavatsky has been written about in many books. This section about her was compiled from several books, including: Peter Washington, *Madame Blavatsky's*

Baboon (New York: Schocken Books, 1995); *Encyclopedia of Occultism & Parapsychology*, 158–160; and James Lewis, ed., *Encyclopedia of Afterlife Beliefs and Phenomena* (Detroit: Gale Research, 1994). There were also author interviews conducted with several self-proclaimed Theosophists.

17. Among the books written by Edward Bulwer Lytton was *The Coming Race*. See also Howard, *The Occult Conspiracy*.

18. Roland, *The Nazis and the Occult*, 47–48; Howard, *The Occult Conspiracy*, 109; *Encyclopedia of Occultism & Parapsychology*, 1379.

19. Jon Ronson, *Men Who Stare at Goats* (New York: Simon & Schuster, 1996).

20. *Flash Gordon* was a popular science fiction character in a comic strip. During the 1930s, it became a network radio serial.

21. "Nordic warrior magicians": Roland, *The Nazis and the Occult*, 17.

22. Aleister Crowley (1875–1947): *Encyclopedia of Occultism & Parapsychology*, 286–287; Howard, *The Occult Conspiracy*; Roland, *The Nazis and the Occult*, 50, 53–54, 122–129; 198; George Pendle, *Strange Angel* (Orlando, FL: Harcourt, 2005).

23. For more about the Armanen and Armanenschaft: Roland, *The Nazis and the Occult*, 17–19, 47.

24. Toland, John, *Adolf Hitler* (Garden City, NY: Doubleday, 1976), 81, 85, 86, 103, 105, 124; Roland, 20–23.

25. Howard, 125; Roland, 23.

26. *Great Events from History, Modern European Series*, Volume 3, 1245–1248.

27. *Encyclopedia of Occultism & Parapsychology*, 1080; Howard, 119–122.

28. *Great Events from History, Modern European Series*, Volume 3, 1283–1288.

29. Ibid.

30. Toland, John, *Adolf Hitler*. Also, author interview with Toland; Shirer, William L., *The Rise and Fall of Adolf Hitler* (New York: Random House, 1961).

31. Toland, 7.

32. Ibid, 7–9.

33. Wistrich, Robert, *Who's Who in Nazi Germany* (New York: Bonanza Books, 1982), 145.

34. Ibid.

35. Ibid.

36. Toland, 52–53.

37. Author interview with John Toland, 1976.

38. Wistrich, 146.

39. Ibid; Toland, 77.

40. *Great Events from History, Modern European Series*, Volume 3, 1295–1298.

41. Wistrich, 146.

42. Toland, 146–177, 181–204; Shirer, 32–40.

43. *Great Events, Worldwide Twentieth Century Series*, Volume 1, 188–195.

44. Rogo, D. Scott, *Miracles* (New York: Dial Press, 1982), 221–223; Walsh, William T., *Our Lady of Fatima* (New York: MacMillan, 1947).

45. Shirer, *The Rise and Fall of Adolf Hitler*, 57.

46. *Great Events, Modern European Series*, Volume 3, 1377–1381.

47. Shirer, 69.

48. Shirer, 18, 139.

49. Goldston, Robert, *The Great Depression: The United States in the Thirties* (New York: Fawcett, 1968), 12, 233–236.

50. During the 1930s Father Charles Coughlin, a rabid anti-Semite and racist, broadcast a radio program spewing his hateful commentary. He was one of the most controversial figures of the decade, with millions of listeners. By the early 1940s, Coughlin was off the air.

51. Author interview with John Toland, 1976.

52. The authors interviewed several survivors of Auschwitz and other Nazi death and concentration camps to learn about the atrocities against the Jews. Especially revealing were conversations between Joel Martin and Auschwitz survivor Hyman Berman, to whom we are especially grateful; and interviews with Ruth Minsky Sender, who wrote of her horrific experiences in three books, *The Cage*, *To Life*, and *The Holocaust Lady*, all published by Macmillan.

53. Hitler's prescience was the subject of an author interview with John Toland, 1976.

54. Author interview with John Toland.

55. This section about the Nazi UFOs, the Bell, or *Die Glock* is based on extensive research and interviews conducted by Bill Birnes for the History Channel TV series *UFO Hunters*.

56. Toland, 124.

57. Wistrich, 126; Roland, 72–76, 121.

58. Infield, Glen B., *Hitler's Secret Life* (New York: Stein and Day, 1979), 199–200; Toland, 659–666, 668.

59. Roland, 120.

60. Ibid, 121.

61. Ibid, 74.

62. Ibid.

63. Although "Volk" translates from German to "people," within the anti-Semitic, racist, and nationalistic context of Nazi mentality, the word had a more sinister meaning. Volk referred to the *Aryan* people, but excluded Jews as "inferior." Thus the Volk were considered racially superior, and their goal, as Hitler decreed, was to "fight their common enemy—the Jew."

64. Wistrich, 97; Evans, Richard J., *The Coming of the Third Reich* (New York: Penguin Books, 2003); Toland, *Adolf Hitler*.

65. Cheetham, Erika, ed., *The Man Who Saw Tomorrow: The Prophecies of Nostradamus* (New York: Berkley Books, 1981), 5, 14.

66. The quatrain believed to refer to "Hister" as an anagram for Hitler is Century II, quatrain 24.

67. Lemesurier, Peter, *Nostradamus: The Next 50 Years* (New York: Berkley Books, 1994), 43, 272.

68. Wistrich, 101–105; Evans; Toland.

69. Bernard, Raymond, *The Hollow Earth* (Secaucus, NJ: Lyle Stuart, 1969); Roland, 153–154; author interview with paranormal expert and author Max Toth.

70. Wistrich, 138–142; Evans, 226–229, 454; Toland.

71. Evans, 227–228.

72. Sklar, Dusty, *Gods and Beasts: The Nazis and the Occult* (New York: T. Y. Crowell, 1977). This same theme, that the "Nazis took the occult seriously," was also the subject of author interview with John Toland.

73. Roland, 32, 154–155, 158–161.

74. Wulff, Wilhelm, *Zodiac and Swastika* (Barker, 1973).

75. Wistrich, 140.

76. *Great Events from History, Modern European Series,* Volume III (G. F. Putnam).

77. Roland, 97–99. Also the topic of author interview with John Toland.

78. The testing and observation of mediums is examined in several previous books by the authors.

79. Roland, 88.

80. Speer, Albert, *Inside the Third Reich* (London: Weidenfeld and Nicholson, 2003).

81. Shirer, *The Rise and Fall of Adolf Hitler.*

82. *Encyclopedia of Occultism & Parapsychology,* 554.

83. Roland, 88.

84. Biddles, Wayne, *Dark Side of the Moon;* Wernher Von Braun, *The Third Reich and the Space Race* (New York: W. W. Norton, 2009).

85. Cousineau, Philip, *UFOs: A Manual for the Millennium* (New York: HarperCollins, 1995).

Chapter 2: *New Orleans: A Haunted History*

1. Smith, Susy, *Prominent American Ghosts* (Cleveland: World Publishing, 1967), 139–144.

2. The highlights of the Hurricane Katrina story given here were compiled from a number of news sources including: wire service reports, Internet sites, network TV reports, *Time, Newsweek, New York Times, New York Post, New York Daily News,* and *USA Today* in the aftermath of the devastating storm.

3. Ward, Martha, *Voodoo Queen: The Spirited Lives of Marie Laveau* (Jackson: University Press of Mississippi, 2004), 82.

4. *Encyclopedia of Occultism & Parapsychology,* 1379.

5. The history and practice of Voodoo given here was compiled from several sources including the *Encyclopedia of Occultism & Parapsychology; Reader's Digest: Into the Unknown;* Davis, Rod, *American Voudou* (Denton, Texas: University of North Texas Press, 1998); Ward, Martha, *Voodoo Queen,* 2004; Tallant, Robert, *Voodoo in New Orleans* (New York: Macmillan, 1946); *Fate,* December 1976, 81–84; author interviews with several Voodoo experts and practitioners in New York and Los Angeles. In the mid-1990s, Joel Martin attended a major Voodoo exhibition at UCLA, Los Angeles. Martin once taught public school in a Haitian neighborhood in New York City; the authors have visited New Orleans.

6. Elwood, Ann, *Weird and Mysterious* (New York: Globe Book Company, 1979), 14–17; Norman and Scott, *Haunted America,* 143–145; Guiley, *Encyclopedia of Ghosts and Spirits,* 213–216; Ward, *Voodoo Queen.*

7. *Life,* March 1994 (author's private collection).

8. Dossey, Larry, M.D., *Be Careful What You Pray For* (HarperSanFrancisco, 1997).

9. The section about Marie Laveau was compiled from sources including: Guiley, Rosemary, *Encyclopedia of Ghosts and Spirits* (New York: Checkmark Books, 2000), 192–196; Guiley, *Encyclopedia of Demons and Demonology,* 202–203; Scott, Beth and Michael Norman, *Haunted America* (New York: Tom Doherty Associates, 1994), 143–145; Hauck, Dennis William, *Haunted Places: The National Directory* (New York: Penguin Books, 2002), 194; *New Orleans City Guide* (2009), 74, 112–113; Brandon, Jim, *Weird America* (New York: Dutton, 1978), 96–97; Ward, *Voodoo Queen.*

10. La Pharmacie Francaise is referenced in Kaczmarek, Dale, *National Register of Haunted Locations* (Oak Lawn, Illinois: Ghost Research Society); Hauck, *Haunted Places,* 194; Ward, 42–43.

11. Ward, 32; *New Orleans Directions* (travel guide).

12. The Lalaurie House is often claimed to be the most haunted house in New Orleans. Hauck,

194; Scott and Norman, 149–157; Brandon, 98; Kaczmarek; Winer, Richard and Nancy Osborn, *Haunted Houses* (New York: Bantam Books, 1981), 95–98.

13. *Frommer's New Orleans* 2009, 98; Karlin, Adam and Lisa Dunford, *New Orleans City Guide*, (Oakland, CA: Lonely Planet Publications, 2009), 203.

14. Frances Kermeen, *Ghostly Encounters* (New York, Warner Books, 2002), 202–208.

15. Hauck, *Haunted Places*, 193; Norman and Scott, 148–149; Brandon, 97–98; Ogden, Tom, *The Complete Idiot's Guide to Ghosts and Hauntings* (Indianapolis, Alpha Books, 2004), 173; Frommer, 178–179, 223.

16. Hauck, 193; Norman and Scott, 148; Ogden, 173.

17. Norman and Scott, 145–148.

18. Author interviews with parapsychologist and vampire expert Stephen Kaplan.

19. Frommer, 179–180; Ward, 25, 26, 29, 30, 45, 79; Melton, J. Gordon, *The Vampire Book: The Encyclopedia of the Undead* (Canton, Michigan: Visible Ink Press, 1999), 489–492; Wood, Marilyn, *Eyewitness Travel: New Orleans* (London: Dorling Kindersly, 2008), 70–71; Dickinson, Joy, *Haunted City* (New York: Citadel Press, 1995), 160–161; Arthur, Stanley Clisby, *Old New Orleans* (New Orleans: Harmanson, 1937), 168–171.

20. Author interview with Kaplan.

21. Dickinson, 261.

22. In Spring 2010, the New Orleans area was again struck by tragedy in the infamous "Gulf oil spill" when millions of gallons of oil from a broken well leaked into the Gulf of Mexico following an oil rig explosion that killed eleven workmen.

23. Asfar, Dan and Edrick Thay, *Ghost Stories of America* (Edmonton, Alberta: Ghost House Books, 2001), 76–79.

Chapter 3: *The Age of Spiritualism and Predictions of Disaster*

1. Broughton, Richard, *Parapsychology the Controversial Science* (New York: Ballantine, 1991), 18.

2. Birnes, William J. and Joel Martin, *The Haunting of America: From the Salem Witch Trials to Harry Houdini* (New York: Forge, 2009), 111–112, 274; Fuller, Robert C., *Religious Revolutionaries* (New York: Palgrave Macmillan, 2004), 70.

3. Fuller, 69.

4. Erdoes, Richard, *A.D. 1000: Living on the Brink of Apocalypse* (New York: Barnes & Noble, 1995); Berlitz, Charles, *Doomsday 1999 A.D.* (Garden City, NY: Doubleday, 1981).

5. This section about prophecies and predictions was compiled from sources including: Allan, Tony, *Prophecies* (London, UK: Thorsons, 2002); *Encyclopedia of Occultism & Parapsychology*; Sherden, William A., *The Fortune Sellers* (New York: John Wiley and Sons, 1998); Broughton, Richard, *Parapsychology: The Controversial Science* (New York: Ballantine Books, 1991); Fisher, Joe with Peter Commins, *Predictions* (New York: Van Nostrand Reinhold, 1980); Timms, Moira, *Prophecies and Predictions: Everyone's Guide to the Coming Changes* (Santa Cruz, CA: Unity Press, 1980); and author interview with Dean Radin, Ph.D., scientist and parapsychologist, Institute of Noetic Sciences, Sausalito, California.

6. Guiley, Rosemary, *Encyclopedia of Ghosts and Spirits*, 315–316; R. Fuller, *Revolutionaries*, 95–96, 109, 139; Swedenborg, *Heaven and Hell* (New York: Swedenborg Foundation, 1979).

7. The Salem woman who uttered the eerily prophetic words just before she was hanged in July 1692 was Sarah Good, the first to be executed in the Salem witchcraft hysteria. Hansen, Chadwick, *Witchcraft at Salem* (New York, George Braziller, 1969).

8. Andrew Jackson Davis was to have great influence on America's "Great Age of Spiritualism" in the nineteenth century. Guiley, 82–85; *Encyclopedia of Occultism & Parapsychology*, 301–302; *Into the Unknown*, 132; Fisher and Commins, 122.

9. Broughton, 54; Haynes, Renee, *Philosopher King: The Humanist Pope Benedict XIV* (London: Weidenfeld and Nicolson, 1970).

10. Fuller, 72–74; Fisher, 168–171.

11. Author (Martin) was witness to predictions of major world events made by acclaimed psychic medium George Anderson during 1980s and early 1990s.

12. *The Essential Joseph Smith* (Salt Lake City: Signature Books, 1995); Fuller, *Religious Revolutionaries*, 76–79.

13. Fuller, 76–79.

14. Allan, 42–43.

15. In addition to Mark Leone, *Roots of Modern Mormonism*, there are countless books and other sources conveying the belief that life is unending. It is a tenet of major religions, as well as the basis of spiritualism.

16. Broughton, 51–52.

17. Martin, Joel and William J. Birnes, *The Haunting of the Presidents* (New York: Signet, 2003); Allan, 46.

18. Martin and Birnes, 52–53.

19. Ibid, 53–54.

20. Broughton, 11–14.

21. Melton, J. Gordon, *Encyclopedia of American Religions* (Farmington Hills, MI: Thomson Gale, 2003).

22. Martin and Birnes, *Presidents*, 227–272; Martinez, Susan, *The Psychic Life of Abraham Lincoln* (Franklin Lakes, NJ: New Page Books, 2007).

23. Herndon, William H. and Jesse W. Weik, *Herndon's Life of Lincoln* (Cleveland: World Publishing Company, 1930. Originally written 1888).

24. Maynard, Nettie Colburn, *Was Abraham Lincoln a Spiritualist?* (Philadelphia: Rufus C. Hartranft, 1891).

25. Martin, Joel and William J. Birnes, *Haunting of the Presidents* (New York: Signet Books, 2003), 260.

26. Birnes, William J. and Joel Martin, *Haunting of America* (New York: Forge Books, 2009), 217–219.

27. Martin and Birnes, 133–134.

28. Ibid, 53.

29. Ibid, 179–186.

30. Van de Castle, Robert L., Ph.D., *Our Dreaming Mind* (New York: Ballantine Books, 1994), 408.

31. Allan, 60.

32. This section about *Titanic* premonitions and subsequent disaster was compiled from several sources, including Allan, 66–67; Van de Castle, 408; *Into the Unknown*, 132; *New York Times*, April 16, 1912 (author's private collection).

33. Stevenson, Ian, "A Review and Analysis of Paranormal Experiences Connected with the Sinking of the Titanic," *Journal of the American Society for Psychical Research*, volume 54, 1961.

34. Fisher, Joe with Peter Commins, *Predictions* (New York: Van Nostrand Reinhold Company, 1980), 180–181; Allan, 67.

35. Robertson, Morgan, *The Wreck of the Titan or, Futility* (Cutchogue, New York: Buccaneer Books, 1994); Fisher, Joe, *Predictions* (New York: Van Nostrand Reinhold Company, 1980), 179–181; Allan, 66–67.

36. Fisher and Commins, 118–122; also see their "Prediction Timetable," 212–217; Allan, 142–143; Sherden, 160–161; *Encyclopedia of Science, Technology, and Ethics*.

37. Fisher and Commins, 114, 118, 120–121; see "Prediction Timetable;"Allan, 144–145, 150; Sherden, 161, 205, 211–212; *Encyclopedia of Science, Technology, and Ethics*; *St. James Guide to Science Fiction Writers*, 1996.

38. Fisher and Commins, 129–130, 133–137; *Encyclopedia of World Biography* (1998).

39. Allan, 135, 138–140; "Utopia," *Wikipedia*.

40. Fisher and Commins, 132–133.

41. Ibid, 133.

42. Jung, C. G., *Memories, Dreams, Reflections* (New York: Random House, 1961), 175–176.

43. Bertone, Tarcisio, *The Last Secret of Fatima: My Conversations with Sister Lucia* (New York: Doubleday, 2008); Allan, 48–49; *The Message of Fatima*, www.vatican.va/roman (Congregation for the Doctrine of the Faith).

Chapter 4: *Edgar Cayce: The Sleeping Psychic*

1. This chapter about Edgar Cayce was compiled from a number of books, articles, online sources, and author interviews. Authors also visited the Association for Research and Enlightenment in Virginia Beach, Virginia. There, Joel Martin studied some of the thousands of Cayce readings that are on file at the Edgar Cayce Library.

2. Kirkpatrick, Sidney, *Edgar Cayce: An American Prophet* (New York: Riverhead Books, 2000).

3. Bro, Harmon, *A Seer Out of Season* (New York: New American Library, 1989) 330–332, 361.

4. Some details about Edgar Cayce's life as a young man (1904–1910) were drawn from Stearn, Jess, *A Prophet in His Own Country: the Story of the Young Edgar Cayce* (New York: Morrow, 1974).

5. Carter, Mary Ellen and William A. McGarey, M.D., *Edgar Cayce on Healing* (New York: Warner Books, 1972); Kirkpatrick, 270–271, 272, 278.

6. McGarey, William A., M.D., *The Edgar Cayce Remedies* (New York: Bantam Books, 1983) 32–34,38–41, 85–89. Stearn, Jess, *The Sleeping Prophet* (Garden City, NY: Doubleday, 1967).

7. McGarey, 168. Acupuncture became a popular treatment with many Americans following the historic 1972 visit to China by then-president Richard M. Nixon.

8. Some 14,500 Cayce readings are "indexed and catalogued" (Mary Ellen Carter) at the A.R.E. library in Virginia Beach. Approximately 9,000 of them "dealt with human illness."

9. Carter, *Edgar Cayce on Healing*.

10. The reader or serious student of Cayce should note the era in which Cayce's unorthodox remedies were prescribed. Cayce's trance readings were given at a time before many medical advances, modern drugs, and sophisticated medical technology. Thus, his treatments now often seem outdated. Yet, Cayce's medical knowledge while in trance could be remarkable. For instance, Cayce's cold remedies still work (Stearn, *The Sleeping Prophet*, 190–191; Carter, 101). Cayce also understood the nature of cancer at a time when less was known by doctors (Stearn, 161–162).

11. Stearn, 186.

12. McGarey, 5, 25.

13. Ibid, 2–7.
14. Stearn, *A Prophet in His Own Country: The Story of the Young Edgar Cayce*; Stearn, *The Sleeping Prophet*, 118–142.
15. Bro, 18.
16. Kirkpatrick, Sidney, *Edgar Cayce: An American Prophet*; see also McGarey, 251–252.
17. *The New York Times*, October 9, 1910.
18. Bro, 285, 295; Kirkpatrick, 165–166; 200.
19. Bro, 138.
20. Martin and Birnes, *Haunting of the Presidents* (New York: Signet, 2003), 69–72.
21. Bro, 293.
22. Bro, 312–314; Kirkpatrick, 253–254, 256–258, 267, 270–273, 298–299; Sugrue, 199–211, 217–8.
23. Furst, Jeffrey, *Edgar Cayce's Story of Jesus* (New York: Berkley, 1968); Sugrue, 298–9, 305–322. Kirkpatrick, 532.
24. Langley, Noel, *Edgar Cayce on Reincarnation* (New York: Warner Books, 1967), 11–13; Stearn, *Sleeping Prophet*, 47–51, 224–241.
25. Kirkpatrick, 6.
26. Langley 10, 11, 16–18.
27. Van de Castle, 372.
28. Berlitz, Charles, *The Mystery of Atlantis* (New York: Leisure Books, 1969), 22–25; Bro, 128, 210–213; Langley, 119, 134–138; Stearn, *Sleeping Prophet*, 47–51, 224–241.
29. Stearn, 230.
30. Berlitz, 11, 240.
31. Bro, 330–332, 361.
32. Ibid, 346–347.
33. Ibid, 350–351.
34. Ibid, 18, 113–114, 354.
35. Ford, Arthur, *Unknown But Known* (New York: New American Library, 1968); Bro, 107.
36. Bro, 145.
37. For those interested in the theory that Bruno Hauptmann did not act alone in the Lindbergh baby kidnapping, an excellent book is *Scapegoat* by Anthony Scaduto (New York: G. P. Putnam's Sons, 1976).
38. Edgar Cayce: *Modern Prophet* (four volumes in one). Section on prophecy, 11–144.
39. Allan, Tony, *Prophecies*, 128–129.
40. Stearn, Jess, *Edgar Cayce on the Millennium* (New York: Warner Books, 1998).
41. Sugrue, Thomas, *There is a River: The Story of Edgar Cayce* (New York: Holt, Rinehart and Winston, 1942). This book has been reprinted numerous times since it was originally published.
42. *The Sleeping Prophet* has also been reprinted numerous times since its original publication in 1967. During the 1990s, Joel Martin interviewed Jess Stearn and had a number of private conversations with him about his Cayce books.
43. Martin, during the 1970s, interviewed several individuals who either personally knew or received clairvoyant health readings from Cayce. They insisted they were greatly helped by his advice. One young man, a chiropractor, more recently told us about his successful use of a Cayce remedy—as a last resort—for a chronic condition that did not respond to traditional medical treatment.

Chapter 5: *The Subconscious, Relativity, Surrealism, and the Paranormal*

1. Fodor, Nandor, *Freud, Jung, and Occultism* (New Hyde Park, NY: University Books, 1971), 9.

2. Our review of obituaries and tributes to Carl G. Jung following his death in 1961 confirmed that few, if any, references were made to Jung's deep interest in the paranormal. However, as the author and psychoanalyst Dr. Nandor Fodor noted, "Jung's psychic life was kept secret most of his life."

3. Lewis, James R., *The Astrology Encyclopedia* (Detroit: Visible Ink, 1994), 311.

4. Jung, C. G., *Memories, Dreams, Reflections* (New York: Pantheon Books, 1961), 389–390 (collective unconscious); Jung, 388–389 (synchronicity); author interviews with John Gschwendtner, Ph.D., in 1980s. The late Dr. Gschwendtner, who became a professor of physics, was once a student of Carl Jung in Switzerland. More about Gschwendtner is told in *We Don't Die* by Joel Martin and Patricia Romanowski (New York: G. P. Putnam's Sons, 1988), 175–181.

5. Jung, C. G., *Memories, Dreams, Reflections*, 96–97.

6. Jung earned his doctoral dissertation in 1899, and it was first published in German in 1902. It was published in England in 1916 and then in the United States in 1920.

7. Van de Castle, Robert L., Ph.D., *Our Dreaming Mind* (New York: Ballantine Books, 1994), 158–165, 169–170, 175–176.

8. Fodor, 120.

9. Fodor, 9, 120–121; "The Occult World of C. G. Jung," www.forteantimes.com.

10. Broughton, 26.

11. George Boas (1891–1980) was a writer and a professor of philosophy at Johns Hopkins University.

12. Fuller, Robert C. *Religious Revolutionaries* (New York: Palgrave Macmillan, 2004), 124–125; Fodor, *Freud, Jung and Occultism*, 9–10.

13. Fodor, 13.

14. Ibid.

15. Ibid, 12–13.

16. Jung, *Memories, Dreams, Reflections*, 170–199, 302–303, 311, 326; Fodor, 169–170; "Carl Gustav Jung," (Detroit: Macmillan Reference USA, 2005); Gale Biography in Context, Ic.galegroup.com/ic/bicl/.

17. Woods, Richard, *The Occult Revolution* (New York: Herder and Herder, 1971), 207.

18. Wilson, Colin, *Mysteries* (New York: G.P. Putnam's Sons, 1978) 133, 558; Mack, John, *Abduction: Human Encounters with Aliens* (New York: Ballantine Books, 1995), 434.

19. Lewis, *Astrology Encyclopedia*, 497–498.

20. Martin and Romanowski, *Love Beyond Life* (New York: Harper, 2009), 81–87.

21. From author's files.

22. Fodor, 41, 44–45.

23. Fodor, Nandor, *Between Two Worlds* (West Nyack, NY: Parker Publishing Company, 1964), 39.

24. Fodor, *Freud, Jung, and Occultism*, 70–76.

25. Freud, Sigmund, *Studies in Parapsychology* (New York: Collier Books, 1963), 63–88.

26. Fodor, *Freud, Jung, and Occultism*, 137.

27. Ibid, 139–141.

28. Martin and Romanowski, *Love Beyond Life* (New York: Harper, 1997).

29. Freud, Sigmund, *The Interpretation of Dreams* (1900) [reprinted, New York: Basic Books, 1953].

30. Jung, *Memories, Dreams, Reflections,* 175.

31. Peter, Laurence, *Peter's Quotations: Ideas for Our Time* (New York: Bantam, 1979), 213.

32. Wilson, Colin, *Mysteries: An Investigation into the Occult* (New York: G.P. Putnam's Sons, 1978), 272; Fodor, *Occultism,* 167, 171, 175, 180–181, 182; Van de Castle, 148.

33. Fodor, 46–51.

34. Jung, *Memories,* 289–292; Fodor, *Occultism,* 183–186; Moody, Raymond A., Jr. *Life After Life* (Atlanta: Mockingbird Books, 1975); Fodor, *Between Two Worlds* (West Nyack, New York: Parker Publishing, 1964), 44.

35. Lewis, James R., *Encyclopedia of Afterlife Beliefs and Phenomena* (Detroit: Gale, 1994), 214–216; Birnes and Martin, *Haunting of America* (New York: Tor Books, 2009); Fodor, *Occultism,* 211–218.

36. Fodor, *Between Two Worlds,* 43; Fodor, *Occultism,* 88–90.

37. Jung, *Memories,* 299–326; Fodor, *Occultism,* 118–125.

38. Fodor, *Occultism,* 233.

39. Gould, Stephen Jay, *The Hedgehog, the Fox, and the Magister's Pox: Mending the Gap Between Science and the Humanities* (New York: Harmony Books, 2003).

40. Thomas Jay Hudson (1843–1903) was an American author and lecturer who became known for his theories about the paranormal. *The Law of Psychic Phenomena* was reprinted in 1969.

41. Henry Addington Bruce (1874–1959), author and journalist, once served as a trustee with the American Society for Psychical Research (ASPR). He wrote books and articles about the paranormal.

42. Fuller, Robert C., *Spiritual but not Religious* (New York: Oxford University Press, 2001), 34.

43. McHargue, Georgess, *Facts, Frauds, and Phantasms* (Garden City, NY: Doubleday, 1972); Birnes and Martin, *Haunting of America,* 2009.

44. The Society for Psychical Research (SPR) was founded in 1882. The American Society for Psychical Research (ASPR) was founded in 1885.

45. William James (1842–1910) was one of the founders of the ASPR. He discovered and studied the medium Leonora Piper during the 1880s. James taught at Harvard University for many years.

46. Among interviews conducted by coauthor (Martin) were those with Wayne Dyer and Leo Buscaglia (1970s–80s).

47. Aniela Jaffe, Jung's secretary, wrote *The Psychic World of C. G. Jung* (1960), originally in German. It was translated into English the following year. It is reprinted in Nandor Fodor, *Freud, Jung, and Occultism,* 202.

48. Fodor, *Occultism,* 188, 211. Jung was still a student in 1897 when he began reading about spiritualism, which was then a popular topic of interest.

49. Jung, *Memories,* 387; Fodor, 218–220,221.

50. Fodor, *Occultism,* 118–119; Jung, *Memories,* 312–313.

51. Jung, *Memories,* 300; Fodor, *Occultism,* 219.

52. Birnes and Martin, *The Haunting of America.*

53. Lewis, *Afterlife Beliefs,* 214–216.

54. Fodor, 9.

55. Ibid, 215. This was written as a review by Martin Ebon in the *International Journal of Parapsychology,* Autumn 1963.

56. Author interview with Dean Radin, Ph.D.

57. Freud made these comments in a letter to psychic researcher Hereward Carrington. Reprinted in the *Encyclopedia of Occultism and Parapsychology*, 498.

58. Van de Castle, *Our Dreaming Mind*, 11.

59. *Contemporary Hispanic Biography*, volume I, Gale 2002.

60. Author interview with film historian Thomas Santorelli, Long Island Film Festival.

61. "Solving a Spellbound Puzzle: Salvador Dali Designed Dream Sequence in Hitchcock's Film," James Bigwood, *American Cinematographer*, June 1991.

62. "Salvador Dalí," *Contemporary Hispanic Biography*, volume 1, Gale 2002. So popular was Dalí that famed comedian Bob Hope once showed up at a "Salvador Dalí party" in California "dressed as a bad dream" (Robin Langley Sommer, *Hollywood: the Glamour Years (1919–1941)* [New York: Gallery, 1987] 183).

63. Van de Castle, 13–19, 37; Panati, Charles, *Supersenses* (New York: *Quadrangle/New York Times Books*, 1974) 136,137; Greenhouse, Herbert B., *The Book of Psychic Knowledge* (New York: Taplinger, 1973), 89.

64. Van de Castle, 37; Greenhouse, 89.

65. Panati, 136–139.

66. Ibid, 138.

67. Ibid, 11–12.

68. Van de Castle, 11; Goldwater, Robert and Marco Treves (eds.),*Artists on Art* (New York: Pantheon Books, 1945), 258.

69. Pendle, George, *Strange Angel* (Orlando, FL: Harcourt, 2005), 67–68.

70. Davies, Paul, *God and the New Physics* (New York: Simon & Schuster, 1983).

71. Capra, Fritjof, *The Tao of Physics* (Boston: Shambhala, 2000), 62.

72. Targ, Russell and Keith Harary, *The Mind Race* (New York: Villard, 1984), 168–169.

73. Broughton, Richard S., Ph.D., *Parapsychology the Controversial Science* (New York, Ballantine Books, 1991), 303.

74. Hines, Brian, *God's Whisper, Creation's Thunder*.

75. Einstein wrote the introduction for the German edition of Upton Sinclair's *Mental Radio*.

76. Capra, 62.

77. Fuller, John G., *The Airmen Who Would Not Die* (New York: G.P. Putnam's Sons, 1979).

78. Ibid.

79. Ibid.

80. Targ, Russell and Keith Harary, *The Mind Race* (New York: Villard Books, 1984) 53; Panati, 214.

81. Capra, Fritoj, *The Tao of Physics*.

82. Peter, Laurence, *Peter's Quotations: Ideas for Our Time* (New York: Bantam, 1979)

83. Hoffmann, Banesh, *Albert Einstein: Creator and Rebel*. Hoffmann was Einstein's highly respected biographer.

84. Barr, Stephen, *Modern Physics and Ancient Faith* (Notre Dame, IN: University of Notre Dame Press), 102; Capra, 200–201.

85. Hoffmann, Frank W, and William G. Bailey, *Arts & Entertainment Fads* (New York: Harrington Park Press, 1990).

86. Panati, 116–118.

87. Leshan, Lawrence, *The Medium, the Mystic, and the Physicist* (New York: Viking, 1966).

88. Barr.

89. Capra.

90. Barnett, Lincoln, *The Universe and Dr. Einstein* (New York: William Sloane Associates, 1948).

91. Moore, William L. with Charles Berlitz, *Philadelphia Experiment* (New York: Fawcett Crest, 1980). Author interview with Charles Berlitz, 1980.

92. *Great Events of History.*

93. Moore and Berlitz; Cohen, Daniel, *The Encyclopedia of the Strange* (New York: Avon, 1985).

94. Jessup, Morris, *The Case for the UFO* (New York: Citadel Press, 1955). Two years later, Jessup wrote a sequel, *The Expanding Case for the UFO* (Citadel, 1957).

95. Author interviews with Jim Lorenzon and Dick Ruhl, *APRO*, UFO organization, 1970s–90s.

96. Author interview with Gray Barker, 1973.

97. Moore and Berlitz, *Philadelphia Experiment.*

98. Author interview with *APRO* investigator Dick Ruhl; author interview with Charles Berlitz.

99. Moore and Berlitz, *Philadelphia Experiment.*

100. Author interview with Ruhl.

101. Nichols, Preston B. with Peter Moon, *The Montauk Project Experiments in Time* (Westbury, NY: Sky Books, 1992). Author interviews with Preston Nichols, 1980s.

Chapter 6: *America's Search for Past Lives*

1. This chapter is based on a compilation of books, author and expert interviews, experiments, and interviews with subjects.

2. Bernstein, Morey, *The Search for Bridey Murphy* (Garden City, NY: Doubleday, 1956), 27, 134.

3. Ibid, 112.

4. Ibid, 112, 114.

5. Highlights of Bernstein's tape recorded sessions with Bridey Murphy/Virginia Tighe are from his book.

6. Bernstein, 119.

7. Ibid, 119–120.

8. Ibid, 114.

9. Ibid, 183.

10. Ibid, 181.

11. Ibid, 46.

12. The taped sessions with Bridey/Tighe begin in Bernstein, 108.

13. Edwards, Paul, *Reincarnation: A Critical Examination* (Amherst, NY: Prometheus Books, 1996), 65.

14. "Bridey Search Ends at Last," *Life*, June 25, 1956 (author's private collection).

15. Edwards, 65. Although Edwards was an outspoken skeptic of the Bridey Murphy story, he still regarded the Hearst "exposé" of it as "an extremely shoddy piece of journalism."

16. Edwards, 17. C. J. DuCasse had earned a reputation as a "leading philosophical supporter of reincarnation in recent decades," Edwards wrote. See also Noel Langley, *Edgar Cayce on Reincarnation* (Springfield, Illinois: Charles Thomas, 1961).

17. Edwards, 59.

18. Gardner, Martin, *Fads and Fallacies*, 316.

19. Gerber, William, *The Mind of India* cited in *The Quotable Spirit*, 114–115.

20. Plato, *Phardo*; *Into the Unknown*, 155.

21. Virgil, *Eclogues.*

22. Spinoza, *Tractatus Politicus*.

23. *Into the Unknown*, 155.

24. Author interviews about reincarnation and karma with Sri Chinmoy, Hindu guru and teacher, between 1977 and 1990s.

25. Greenhouse, Herbert B., *The Book of Psychic Knowledge*(New York: Taplinger, 1973), 273; interview with Greenhouse, 1973; Morey Bernstein, 99.

26. *Encyclopedia of Occultism & Parapsychology*, 927.

27. *The Quotable Spirit*, 114.

28. Besant, Annie, *Reincarnation* (Adyar, India: Theosophical Publishing House, 1892). Reprinted, 1972.

29. Langley, Noel, *Edgar Cayce on Reincarnation* (New York: Warner Books, 1967).

30. Ibid, 16.

31. Stearn, Jess, *Edgar Cayce on the Millennium* (New York: Warner Books, 1998), 91, 123.

32. Langley, *Cayce on Reincarnation*.

33. Stearn, *Cayce on the Millennium*.

34. Ibid.

35. Hence the great number of books, online sources, and other media about reincarnation that have appeared in recent years, although the subject remains anathema to traditional Christianity.

36. Broughton, Richard, *Parapsychology the Controversial Science*, 262–265; Stevenson, Ian, *Ten Cases in India, Cases of the Reincarnation Type* (Charlottesville, VA: University Press of Virginia, 1975), 144–173. Author had private conversations with Stevenson, 1988–90.

37. Broughton, 264.

38. Dr. Ian Stevenson died in 2007 at the age of eighty-nine.

39. Stevenson's books were published by the University Press of Virginia, Charlottesville, VA.

40. Broughton, 265.

41. Albert Einstein, Ph.D., *What I Believe*.

42. Fenwick, Peter and Elizabeth Fenwick, *Past Lives: An Investigation into Reincarnation Memories* (New York: Berkley Books, 2001), 11–17, 25, 145, 301; Stevenson, *Twenty Cases Suggestive of Reincarnation* (University Press of Virginia, 1974).

43. Heaney, John J., *The Sacred and the Psychic: Parapsychology and Christian Theology* (Ramsey, NJ: Paulist Press, 1984), 203–205.

44. Edwards, 256–258.

45. *Encyclopedia of Occultism*, 45.

46. Stevenson quoted in Broughton, 266.

47. Private conversation between author and Dr. Sagan, 1982.

48. Case study from author files.

49. Bowman, Carol, *Return from Heaven* (New York: HarperTorch, 2003), p. xv.

50. From author's personal files.

51. Case study from author files.

52. Bowman, *Children's Past Lives* (New York: Bantam, 1998); *Return from Heaven*, 55.

53. Case study from author files.

54. Case study from author files.

55. *Joel Martin Show* (radio), 1980.

56. From author's personal files.

57. From author's personal files.

58. Davies, Paul, *God and the New Physics* (New York: Simon & Schuster, 1983).

59. Mozart, during his short life on earth, wondered where his musical talent came from, uncertain if it was from within him or from somewhere beyond.

60. Jung, Carl G., *Memories, Dreams, Reflections*; Fodor, Nandor, *Freud, Jung, and Occultism*.

61. Tanous, Alex and Katherine Fair Donnelly, *Is Your Child Psychic?* (New York: Macmillan, 1979). Author interview with Tanous, 1980.

62. *On Death and Dying* was originally published in 1969. Author had private conversation with Dr. Kübler-Ross, 1980s.

63. *Life After Life* was originally published in 1975. Author interview with Dr. Moody, 1999.

64. The reference here is to what we call today the "near-death experience."

65. Fodor, *Occultism*, 46–51.

66. The experiment referred to here was actually a series of radio broadcasts aired during the early 1980s on the *Joel Martin Show*. The regressive hypnosis sessions were performed by experienced hypnotherapists, guided by Max Toth. Parapsychologists, a psychologist, physicist, medical doctor, psychic medium, and an astrologer who specialized in past lives also participated. In one experiment, the identical twins were young women, nineteen years old, who were regressed and questioned separately. Both purported they were "best friends" during the 1870s, living in Brooklyn, New York. A historian researched details given in the recorded sessions and found remarkable similarities and historical accuracies in the twins' accounts.

67. Dr. Wambach's books included *Reliving Past Lives* (New York: Bantam, 1978); *Life Before Life* (New York: Bantam, 1979).

68. Leading the national charge against the paranormal was the Committee for the Scientific Investigation of Claims of the Paranormal (CSICOP). The name has since been changed to the Committee for Skeptical Inquiry.

69. Pendle, George, *Strange Angel* (Orlando, FL: Harcourt, Inc. 2005), 25. Author interview with Pendle on public radio, 2005.

70. Author interview with Maria Moreno, 1997. See also Stearn, Jess, *A Matter of Immortality* (New York: Atheneum, 1976).

71. Stearn, Jess, *The Search for a Soul: Taylor Caldwell's Past Lives* (New York: Berkley, 1994). Author interview with Stearn, 1997.

72. Fiore, a psychologist, is largely credited as among the first to "popularize past-life therapy, through hypnotic regressions." Her best known book was *You Have Been Here Before* (New York: Ballantine, 1978).

73. Despite later personal controversy that led to Lenz's untimely death, his book *Lifetimes* (Indianapolis: Bobbs-Merrill Company, 1979) prodded memories of many *Joel Martin Show* listeners when Lenz questioned their recall of past-life experiences. Lenz used some of those phone-in responses in *Lifetimes*. Author interviews with Lenz, 1979–1980.

74. Whitton, Joel, M.D., and Joe Fisher, *Life Between Life* (New York: Warner Books, 1986).

75. Moody, Raymond, M.D., *Coming Back: A Psychiatrist Explores Past-Life Journeys* (New York: Bantam, 1991).

76. Cockell, Jenny, *Across Time and Death: A Mother's Search for Her Past Life Children* (New York: Simon & Schuster, 1993). This is regarded by many as "one of the most amazing and well-documented cases of spontaneous past life recalls" (Hammerman, 97–98).

77. Author and respected UFO researcher Bill Birnes extensively examined the Betty and Barney

Hill UFO abduction case that occurred in New Hampshire in 1961 and the regressive hypnosis of them that followed. Birnes interviewed Mrs. Hill. The story was featured on Birnes's popular network TV series *UFO Hunters*. Martin separately interviewed Betty Hill (1975) on radio, as well as John G. Fuller, author of *The Interrupted Journey* (New York: Dial Press, 1966) about the Hills's story.

78. Mack, John, *Abduction: Human Encounters with Aliens* (New York: Ballantine, 1994), 42.

79. Weiss, Brian L., M.D., *Many Lives, Many Masters* (New York: Fireside/Simon & Schuster, 1988); author interview with Weiss, 1999.

80. Displeased that Voltaire made this statement implying he was open to reincarnation, some skeptics quickly derided the remark, insisting Voltaire did not believe in the subject.

Chapter 7: *All the Presidents' Prophets: Americans and Astrology*

1. Regan, Donald T., *For the Record* (New York: Harcourt Brace Jovanovich, 1988).

2. Martin, Joel and William J. Birnes, *The Haunting of the Presidents* (New York: Signet, 2003), 227–272.

3. Paul Kurtz, founder of the Committee for the Scientific Investigation of Claims of the Paranormal (CSICOP) in 1976, is a humanist and was a professor of philosophy at the State University of New York at Buffalo.

4. Gleick, James, *Isaac Newton* (New York: Pantheon Books, 2003), 32.

5. Regan, *For the Record*, 70–71, 73–74, 290, 359.

6. Ibid, 367.

7. Regan, 74; Reagan, Nancy with William Novak, *My Turn: the Memoirs of Nancy Reagan* (New York: Random House, 1989), 50; author interview with Thomas Santorelli, film historian; author interview with Margaret Wendt, Hollywood-based TV producer/reporter; personal research and interviews with psychic practitioners and astrologers by authors Birnes and Martin in Los Angeles. Two famed silent movie stars who consulted astrologers were Charlie Chaplin and Mary Pickford. Movie star Mae West and Natacha Rambova, the wife of silent movie star Rudolph Valentino, were both mediums.

8. Kelley, Kitty, *Nancy Reagan: The Unauthorized Biography* (New York: Simon & Schuster, 1991), 147–149.

9. Ibid, 148.

10. Regan, 359.

11. Quigley, Joan, *"What Does Joan Say?" My Seven Years as White House Astrologer to Nancy and Ronald Reagan* (New York: Birch Lane Press, 1990), 24, 81.

12. Cousineau, Phil, *UFOs a Manual for the Millennium* (New York: HarperCollinsWest, 1995), 115.

13. Ibid, 223.

14. The guru was the late Sri Chinmoy, an international figure, based in New York for many years. Coauthor Joel Martin maintained a professional relationship with Chinmoy for more than two decades.

15. Regan, *For the Record*, 367.

16. Regan, 4; Reagan, 48; Quigley, 40–48.

17. Regan, 370.

18. Reagan, 44.

19. Martin and Birnes, *The Haunting of the Presidents*, 52–55.

20. Reagan, 46; Quigley, 46.

21. Reagan, 47.
22. Ibid, 44–54.
23. Quigley, 28, 70.
24. Reagan, 47, 48, 50.
25. Quigley, 5.
26. Reagan, 51.
27. Ibid, 53.
28. Ibid, 55.
29. Quigley, 21–22.
30. Reagan, 47.
31. Quigley, 66–69.
32. Ibid, 30, 162.
33. Ibid, 27–28.
34. Ibid, 55, 77, 123.
35. Ibid, 72.
36. Ibid, 24.
37. Ibid, 72.
38. Ibid, 68.
39. Ibid, 72–73.
40. Ibid, 129–133.
41. Ibid, 57, 165.
42. Ibid, 80–81.
43. Ibid, 12, 84–85.
44. Ibid, 91.
45. Ibid, 113–115, 120.
46. Ibid, 201–204.
47. This section about the history of astrology is compiled from books including: *Into the Un-known* (Pleasantville, New York: Reader's Digest Associates, 1981); *Encyclopedia of Occult-ism and Parapsychology* (Detroit: Gale Research, 1996); Lewis, James R., *The Astrology Encyclopedia* (Detroit: Visible Ink Press, 1994); Bobrick, Benson, *The Fated Sky: Astrology in History* (New York: Simon & Schuster, 2005); Adams, Evangeline, *The Bowl of Heaven* (New York: Dodd, Mead, 1924); Melton, Gordon, Jerome Clark, and Aidan A. Kelly, *New Age Encyclopedia* (Detroit: Gale Research, 1990); Pelton, Robert W., *Lost Secrets of Astrology* (New York: Cornerstone Library, 1973); Lee, Dal, *Dictionary of Astrology* (New York: Pa-perback Library, 1969); *Fate* (magazine), October 1981.
48. The profile of Evangeline Adams is drawn from: *Into the Unknown*; *Encyclopedia of Occultism and Parapsychology*; Adams, *The Bowl of Heaven*; Bobrick, *The Fated Sky*.
49. The highlights of Llewellyn George's career are from the *Encyclopedia of Occultism and Para-psychology*; Lewis, *The Astrology Encyclopedia*; Bobrick, *The Fated Sky*.
50. Author interview with John Toland about Hitler and the occult, 1976.
51. Howard, Michael, *The Occult Conspiracy* (Rochester, Vermont: Destiny Books, 1989).
52. For a thorough discussion of the Nazis and their involvement with the occult, see Chapter I in this book.
53. Books used to profile Dixon include: Martin and Birnes, *The Haunting of the Presidents*;

Montgomery, Ruth, *A Gift of Prophecy: the Phenomenal Jeane Dixon* (New York: Bantam, 1966); Dixon, Jeane, *My Life and Prophecies: Her Own Story* (1969). Coauthor Martin had personal conversation with Jeane Dixon, 1973.

54. The profile of Dane Rudhyar is based on research from *Encyclopedia of Occult and Parapsychology*; *New Age Encyclopedia*; *The Astrology Encyclopedia*; Rudhyar, Dane, *The Practice of Astrology* (New York: Penguin Books, 1970).

55. Geller, Larry and Joel Spector with Patricia Romanowski, *If I Can Dream: Elvis' Own Story* (New York: Simon & Schuster, 1989); Martin had subsequent private conversations with Geller's coauthor Romanowski about Presley's metaphysical interests.

56. The Michel and Francoise Gauquelin story known as the "sTARBABY expose" was featured in *Fate*, October 1981, 67–98; *The Humanist*, September/October 1975; *The Skeptical Inquirer*, Spring 1983, 77–82; *New Age Encyclopedia*; author interviews with Paul Kurtz, founder of CSICOP; Bill Marshall, astrologer; Stephen Kaplan, parapsychologist.

57. *Hair*, the rock musical, opened Off-Broadway in 1967, and had its Broadway premiere on April 29, 1968. Cooper, John Charles, *Religion in the Age of Aquarius* (Philadelphia: The Westminster Press, 1971); Woods, Richard, *The Occult Revolution* (New York: Herder and Herder, 1971); Howard, Gerald, ed., *The Sixties* (New York: Washington Square Press, 1982); Feinstein, Stephen, *The 1960s From the Vietnam War to Flower Power* (Berkley Heights, NJ: Enslow Publishers, 2000). Author interview with 1960s activist and author David Harris; author interview with journalist Albert Goodman, who wrote about 1960s popular culture. Both interviews were conducted during the 1980s.

58. Bobrick, *The Fated Sky*.

Chapter 8: *Ghosts, Spirits, and Demons in America*

1. Bodine, Echo, *Relax, It's Only a Ghost* (Boston: Element Books, 2000); author interviews with Bodine, 1999–2000.

2. Hans Holzer was the author of more than one hundred books, many of them about ghosts and hauntings. Author interviews and private conversations with Holzer during the 1980s and early 1990s.

3. Steiger, Brad, *Real Ghosts, Restless Spirits, Haunted Places* (Canton, MI: Visible Ink Press, 2003).

4. Holzer, author interview.

5. Bodine, author interview.

6. Martin, Joel and Patricia Romanowski, *Love Beyond Life* (New York: HarperCollins, 1997); Guggenheim, Bill and Judy Guggenheim, *Hello From Heaven* (New York: Bantam, 1996); Elliot, Nancy with John G. Elliot, *David's Message: Love and Life Are Eternal* (Penfield, NY: Enlightened Print, 2008); David Elliot's story seen on *Unsolved Mysteries* network TV show, 1993; author and Elliots had subsequent private conversations; LaGrand, Louis E., *Messages and Miracles: Extraordinary Experiences of the Bereaved* (St. Paul, MN: Llewellyn, 1999).

7. I Samuel 28 (Old Testament).

8. Greenhouse, Herbert, *The Book of Psychic Knowledge* (New York: Taplinger, 1973); author interview with Greenhouse, 1973.

9. Elwood, Ann, *Weird and Mysterious* (New York: Globe Book Company, 1979).

10. Guiley, Rosemary Ellen, *The Encyclopedia of Ghosts and Spirits* (New York: Checkmark Books, 2000), 312–314.

11. Guiley, 53–57; *Proceedings of the Society for Psychical Research*, Volume 51, Part 186, January 1956. "The Haunting of Borley Rectory, a Critical Survey of the Evidence" by Eric J. Dingwall, Kathleen M. Goldney, and Trevor H. Hall, Society for Psychical Research, London, UK.

12. Tuchman, Barbara W., *A Distant Mirror: the Tumultuous 14th Century* (New York: Alfred A. Knopf, 1978).

13. Swedenborg, Emanuel, *Heaven and Hell* (New York: Swedenborg Foundation, 1972); Guiley, 375–376.

14. Somerlott, Robert, *Here, Mr. Splitfoot: An Informal Exploration into Modern Occultism* (New York: Viking Press, 1971); Birnes, William J. and Joel Martin, *The Haunting of America*, 2009; Brown, Slater, *The Heyday of Spiritualism* (New York: Hawthorn, 1970); Weisberg, Barbara, *Talking to the Dead* (New York: HarperSanFrancisco, 2004); Brandon, Ruth, *The Spiritualists: The Passion for the Occult in the Nineteenth and Twentieth Centuries* (New York: Alfred Knopf, 1983).

15. Martin, Joel and William J. Birnes, *The Haunting of the Presidents* (New York: Signet, 2003); Belanger, Jeff, *Who's Haunting the White House?* (New York: Sterling, 2008).

16. Martin and Birnes, *The Haunting of the Presidents*; Martinez, Susan, *The Psychic Life of Abraham Lincoln* (Franklin Lakes, NJ: New Page Books, 2007); Coleman, Christopher K., *Ghosts and Haunts of the Civil War* (New York: Barnes & Noble Books, 2003).

17. Martin and Birnes, *The Haunting of the Presidents*.

18. Ibid.

19. Ibid.

20. West, J. B., *Upstairs at the White House* (New York: Warner Books, 1973). Author interview with Mr. West in 1973.

21. Martin and Birnes, *The Haunting of the Presidents*.

22. Ibid.

23. Ibid.

24. Ibid.

25. Ibid.

26. Ibid.

27. Alexander, John, *Ghosts: Washington Revisited* (Atglen, PA: Schiffer, 1998).

28. *Good Housekeeping*, May 1979.

29. *Presidential Prophecies* (TV documentary), History Channel, 2005.

30. Hauck, Dennis William, *Haunted Places: The National Directory* (New York: Penguin Books, 2002); author interview with former Nixon official Maurice Stans.

31. Hauck, *Haunted Places*.

32. Time-Life Books (eds.), *Hauntings* (New York: Barnes & Noble, 1997), 108–109.

33. Alexander, John, *Ghosts: Washington Revisited*.

34. Martin and Birnes, *Haunting of the Presidents*; Hauck, *Haunted Places*.

35. Holzer, Hans, *True Ghost Stories* (New York: Bristol Park Books, 1992), 351–355; Guiley, 267–268; Hauck, 267–268. Martin and Birnes, *Haunting of the Presidents*; Myers, Arthur, *Ghosts of the Rich and Famous* (Chicago: Contemporary Books, 1988); author interviews with Anne Gehman, psychic-medium; Priscilla Baker, former National Park Service official; author visit to Gettysburg, Pennsylvania.

36. Author interview with Donna DiBiase, 2005.

37. Martin and Birnes, *Haunting of the Presidents*, 153–162; author interviews with Dorothy and Pamela Mallone, owners of former Garfield residence, Hiram, Ohio, 2002.

38. Guiley, 358; *Time-Life Hauntings*, 26; *Encyclopedia of Occultism and Parapsychology*, 891; Somerlott, 148–149.

39. Cheroux, Clement, Andreas Fischer, et al., *The Perfect Medium: Photography and the Occult* (New Haven, CT and London, UK: Yale University Press, 2004). Companion book to exhibit at Metropolitan Museum of Art, New York, 2004. Author visit to museum exhibit.

40. Holzer, Hans, *True Ghost Stories*, 263–274; interview with Tracy Abbott who photographed spirit in Merchant House, 1995; author visit to Merchant House, 1998.

41. Fuller, John G., *The Ghost of Flight 401* (New York: G. P. Putnam's Sons, 1976); author interview with John G. Fuller, 1976; author interviews with several former Eastern Airlines employees.

42. Hauck, 425–428; author visit to Fredericksburg, VA during 1970s.

43. Author (Birnes) research in New Hope and Bucks County, PA.

44. Kaczmarek, Dale, *National Register of Haunted Locations* (Oak Lawn, IL: Ghost Research Society.)

45. Hauck, 297; Pressing, R. G., *Rappings That Startled the World: Facts About the Fox Sisters* (Lily Dale, NY: Dale News, 1940); Wicker, Christine, *Lily Dale: The True Story of the Town that Talks to the Dead* (New York: HarperSanFrancisco, 2003).

46. Kermeen, Frances, *Ghostly Encounters: The True Stories of America's Haunted Inns and Hotels* (New York: Warner Books, 2002). Author interviews (1995) with Sally Gaines and Annie R. who claimed they experienced haunting activities in the Battery Carriage House in 1987.

47. Author visits to Salem, Massachusetts, during 1970s and 1980s; Birnes and Martin, *The Haunting of America*, 63–101; Hauck, *Haunted Places*, 223–224; *Into the Unknown*, 167–168.

48. Myers, Arthur, *A Ghost Hunter's Guide to Haunted Public Places* (Chicago: Contemporary Books, 1993); Hauck, 22.

49. Hauck, *Haunted Places*; Holzer, Hans, *Haunted Hollywood* (Indianapolis: Bobbs-Merrill, 1974); Steiger, Brad and Sherry Steiger, *Hollywood and the Supernatural* (New York: St. Martin's Press, 1990).

50. Holzer, *Elvis Speaks From Beyond and Other Celebrity Ghost Stories* (New York: Dorset, 1993); Moody, Raymond, Jr., M.D., *Elvis After Life* (Atlanta: Mockingbird Books).

51. Winer, Richard, and Nancy Osborn, *Haunted Houses* (New York: Bantam Books, 1979), 157–169; Hauck, 70; Guiley, 3.

52. Winer and Osborn, 51–59; Holzer, *True Ghost Stories*, 473–498; Holzer, *The Ghost Hunter's Favorite Cases* (New York: Dorset, 2003), 447–481; Hauck, 69; Guiley, 398; Riccio, Dolores, and Joan Bingham, *Haunted Houses USA* (New York: Pocket Books, 1989).

53. Guiley, 136–137; Hauck, 402.

54. Guiley, 293–294; Roll, William, *The Poltergeist* (Garden City, NY: Doubleday, 1972).

55. Winer and Osborn, *Haunted Houses*, 13–31; *Into the Unknown*, 177–181; Birnes and Martin, *Haunting of the Presidents*, 109–118; Guiley, 40–43; Hauck, 384–385; Somerlott, Robert, *Here, Mr. Splitfoot*, 173, 209–223; Monahan, Brent, ed., *The Bell Witch: an American Haunting* (New York: St. Martin's Press, 1977).

56. Jarvis, Sharon, ed., *Dead Zones* (New York, Warner Books, 1992), 162–167; author interview in 1988 with David Kahn, *Newsday* reporter who covered Seaford poltergeist story in 1958; William Roll, *The Poltergeist*; Somerlott, 204–205.

57. Elwood, Ann, *Weird and Mysterious* (New York: Globe Books, 1979), 38–42; Hauck, 124.

58. Rogo, D. Scott, *Miracles: A Parascientific Inquiry into Wondrous Phenomena* (New York: The Dial Press, 1982); author interview, 1983.

59. *Into the Unknown*, 182–183; Owen, Iris M., and Margaret Sparrow, *Conjuring up Philip* (New York, Harper & Row, 1976); *Encyclopedia of Occultism and Parapsychology*, 1005; author interviews with D. C. Webster, founder of the Toronto Society for Psychical Research (TSPR) under whose auspices the Philip experiment was conducted in 1973. Webster died in 1997 at the age of sixty-seven.

60. Rogo, *Miracles*, 117–119, 122–123, 205–206.

61. Pauli, Hertha, *Bernadette and the Lady* (New York: Farrar, Straus and Cudahy, 1956); Trouncer, Margaret, *Saint Bernadette: the Child and the Nun* (New York: Sheed and Ward, 1958); author interviews with several visitors to Lourdes.

62. Rogo, *Miracles*, 221–236; *Psychic World* (magazine), Spring 1997, 72–76, 116–119.

63. Minutoli, Armando, *Medjugorje: a Pilgrim's Journey* (Medford, NY: The Morning Star Press, 1991); author interviews with Medjugorje pilgrims and visitors throughout early 1990s.

64. Bugliosi, Vincent, *Helter Skelter*.

65. Cuneo, Michael W., *American Exorcism* (New York: Doubleday, 2001); Hauck, 213; Guiley, *The Encyclopedia of Ghosts and Spirits*.

66. Martin, Malachi, *Hostage to the Devil* (New York: Harper & Row, 1976); author interview, 1980.

67. Cuneo, 27.

68. Curran, Robert with Jack and Janet Smurl and Ed and Lorraine Warren, *The Haunted: One Family's Nightmare* (New York: St. Martin's Press, 1988). The Warrens became well-known for their investigation of the *Amityville Horror* story. Author interviews with Ed and Lorraine Warren, 1970s–80s; author interviews with Peter Jordan, paranormal researcher who wrote about *Amityville Horror* in *Fate* magazine, 1970s; Stephen Kaplan, coauthor, *Amityville Horror Conspiracy*, 1995. Joel Martin was the first reporter at the scene of the Amityville murders, 1974, and had nationally exclusive broadcast interview with William Weber, attorney, revealing *Amityville Horror* hoax, 1979.

69. Cuneo, 61–63, 65, 243.

70. Heaney, *The Sacred and the Psychic*.

71. Dossey, *Be Careful What You Pray For*.

72. Jung, *Memories, Dreams, Reflections*.

73. Guiley, *The Encyclopedia of Ghosts and Spirits*.

Chapter 9: *New Age, Psychic Dreams, and Revolutions*

1. Feinstein, Stephen, *The 1960s From the Vietnam War to Flower Power* (Berkley Heights, NJ: Enslow Publishing, 2000).

2. Kelly, Mary Olsen, *Treasury of Light* (New York: Fireside Simon & Schuster, 1990).

3. Brian, Denis, *Jeane Dixon: The Witnesses* (Garden City, NY: Doubleday, 1976).

4. Ford, Arthur, *Known But Unknown* (New York: New American Library, 1968).

5. For a sense of the prevailing media attitude toward the paranormal and supernatural during the 1950s and early 1960s, see the book *Way Out World* by the late New York radio talk show host "Long" John Nebel who considered himself the ultimate skeptic, despite delving into the occult and psychic on the air from 1956–1978.

6. Author interview with singer Barry McGuire, 1980.

7. Kelly, *Treasury of Light*.

8. *Encyclopedia of Occultism and Parapsychology*, 88–90.

9. Author interviews with several Kabbalah experts including two orthodox rabbis (1979–1991); *Encyclopedia of Occultism and Parapsychology*, 697–698; Scholem, Gershom, *Kabbalah* (New York: Quadrangle, 1974).

10. Ullman, Montague, M.D., *Working With Dreams* (New York: Delacorte Press, 1979), 25, 37–38, 64–65, 294–314.

11. Van de Castle, Robert, *Our Dreaming Mind*.

12. *Encyclopedia of Occultism and Parapsychology*, 722.

13. Ibid, 892.

14. Broughton, *Parapsychology: the Controversial Science*, 89–99, 101–2, 124, 130, 134, 140, 148; Ebon, Martin, *The Signet Handbook of Parapsychology* (New York: Signet, 1978), 393–422; Dossey, Larry, M.D., *The Science of Premonitions* (New York: Plume Books, 2009).

15. Allan, Tony, *Prophecies*, 65.

16. Author interview with Ullman, 1980.

17. Van de Castle, 423–424.

18. Ibid, 414–416, 418–425, 427, 429–430, 436.

19. Elwood, Robert S., *The Sixties: Spiritual Awakening* (New Brunswick, NJ, 1994).

20. Devi, Indra, *Yoga for Americans* (1959).

21. Lande, Nathaniel, *Mindstyles/Lifestyles* (Los Angeles: Price, Stern, Sloan, 1976), 293–303.

22. Lorie, Peter, *The Quotable Spirit*, 9, 154, 208.

23. Sri Chinmoy died in 2007.

24. Bloomfield, Harold, M.D., *T. M.* (New York: Delacorte Press, 1975). Author interview, 1975.

25. Author interviews with many TM practitioners.

26. Broughton, 103, 180.

27. Author interview with former Beatle George Harrison, 1977.

28. Lande, 287, 304.

29. Broughton, 103.

30. Coauthor Joel Martin has observed brain wave tests of psychic mediums, some with startling results. For an example see Martin and Patricia Romanowski, *We Are Not Forgotten* (New York: Berkley Books, 1992); *Appendix One: The Electroencephalogram Test*, 303–309.

31. This account is from authors' files and interviews with priest, 1980s and 1990s. Certain identifying details have been changed to protect the priest's identity.

32. *Encyclopedia of Occultism and Parapsychology*, 420.

33. Lande, *Mindstyles/Lifestyles*, 116, 118, 198.

34. Author interviews with Margaret Wendt, 1980s to present.

35. The following section concerning the use of LSD and other hallucinogenic drugs during the 1960s was compiled from sources including: Miller Mark S., *Bad Trips* (New York: Chelsea House, 1988); Sagan, Carl, *Broca's Brain: Reflections on the Romance of Science* (New York: Random House, 1979); Huxley, Aldous, *The Doors of Perception* (New York: Harper & Row, 1956, 1963); Guiley, Rosemary Ellen, *The Encyclopedia of Demons & Demonology* (New York: Checkmark Books, 2009), 44–48; *Encyclopedia of Occultism and Parapsychology*, 286–287; *Time* magazine, "The Hippies," July 7, 1967; Castaneda, Carlos, *The Active Side of Infinity* (New York: HarperCollins, 1998); Hofmann, Albert, M.D., *LSD, My Problem Child* (New York: McGraw-Hill, 1980); Hofmann and Richard Evans Schultes, *Plants of the Gods* (Rochester, VT: Healing Arts Press, 1992); Trulson, Michael E., *LSD: Visions or Nightmares* (New

York: Chelsea House, 1985); Leary, Timothy, *Flashbacks: An Autobiography* (Los Angeles: J. P. Tarcher, 1983); author interview with Dr. Timothy Leary, 1983; Sugerman, Danny, *No One Here Gets Out Alive* (New York: Warner Books, 1980); author interview with Sugerman, who worked for the rock group The Doors, 1980; author interviews with D. C. Webster, 1997. Webster and Aldous Huxley experimented with LSD together during the 1950s and 1960s.

36. The section about "secular theology," and the "death of God" question, was drawn from several sources: Fodor, Nandor, *Freud, Jung, and Occultism*; Elwood (sometimes given as Ellwood), Robert S., *The Sixties Spiritual Awakening* (New Brunswick, NJ: Rutgers University Press, 1994); Marion, Jim, *The Death of the Mythic God* (Charlottesville, VA: Hampton Roads 2004); Cox, Harvey, *Secular City*; Woods, Richard, *The Occult Revolution*; Anderson, Walter Truett, *The Upstart Spring: Esalen and the American Awakening* (Reading, MA: Addison-Wesley, 1983); Kripal, Jeffrey J., *Esalen: America and the Religion of No Religion* (Chicago: University of Chicago Press, 2007); *Time*, "Is God Dead?" April 8, 1966 (cover story). Joel Martin served as a volunteer in a New York inner-city Catholic mission where he witnessed firsthand priests and nuns who embraced liberation theology (1969–71).

37. Author interviews about various cults and movements during 1970s and 1980s with leaders and disciples, included: Divine Light Mission, flying saucer cults, Jonestown, Krishna Consciousness, Church of Scientology, Unification Church. Interview with Steve Allen, TV personality and author on subject of cults; interview with Ted Patrick, nationally known cult deprogrammer.

38. Marion, Jim, *The Death of the Mythic God* (Charlottesville, VA: Hampton Roads, 2004).

39. Ibid.

40. Lenz, Frederick, *Lifetimes*. Author interviews with Lenz, 1979–80.

41. Author interviews with Frederick Von Mieres, throughout 1980s.

42. Hubbard, L. Ron, *Dianetics: The Modern Science of Mental Health* (Los Angeles: Bridge Publications, 1950, 1978; Garrison, Omar V., *The Hidden Story of Scientology* (Secaucus, NJ: Citadel Press, 1974); *What is Scientology?* (Los Angeles: Bridge Publications, 1992); Lande, 126–133; *Encyclopedia of Occultism & Parapsychology*, 1140–41.

43. Barton, Blanche, *The Secret Life of a Satanist: the Authorized Biography of Anton Lavey* (Los Angeles: Feral House, 1990); LaVey, Anton, *The Satanic Bible* (New York: Avon Books, 1969); *Encyclopedia of Occultism & Parapsychology*, 738; Lande, 271.

44. Ford, Arthur, *Unknown But Known*, 66–69; Pike, James A. and Diane Kennedy, *The Other Side* (New York: Doubleday, 1968); Pike, Diane Kennedy, *Search: The Personal Story of a Wilderness Journey* (New York: Doubleday, 1970); Spragett, Allen, *Arthur Ford: The Man Who Talked with the Dead* (New York: New American Library, 1973); Twigg, Ena with Ruth Hagy Brod, *Ena Twigg: Medium* (London: W. H. Allen, 1973); Holzer, Hans, *The Psychic World of Bishop Pike* (New York: Crown, 1970); *Encyclopedia of Occultism & Parapsychology*, 1011; Guiley, Rosemary, *Encyclopedia of Ghosts and Spirits*, 256–8; Lewis, James R., *Encyclopedia of Afterlife Beliefs*, 288. Private interviews with D. C. Webster, 1997.

45. Kearns, Doris, *Lyndon Johnson and the American Dream* (New York: Harper & Row, 1976).

46. Fenwick, Peter, and Elizabeth Fenwick, *Hidden Door: Understanding and Controlling Dreams*.

47. Author interview with the late antiwar radical and Yippies founder Abbie Hoffman, 1983.

48. The authors have had contact with or interviewed well-known 1960s figures including rock musicians Joan Baez, Grateful Dead, John Sebastian, Richie Havens, Peter, Paul and Mary;

Clive Epstein, brother of Beatles' manager Brian Epstein; civil rights leader and colleague of Dr. Martin Luther King, Jr., Bayard Rustin; convicted assassin of Dr. King, James Earl Ray; 1960s political activist David Harris; student radical leader Jerry Rubin; former congressman and RFK assassination researcher Allard Lowenstein; attorney, author, JFK and MLK assassinations researcher Mark Lane; former U.S. Attorney-General Ramsey Clark; Nixon speechwriter Ray Price; LSD guru Dr. Timothy Leary; consumer advocate Ralph Nader; Nixon administration and Watergate figure Maurice Stans; author Myra Freidman, *Buried Alive* (Janis Joplin); author Michael Harrington, *The Other America*; Vietnam Veterans of America founder, Bobby Muller; Vietnam War veteran, author, and subject of motion picture *Born on the Fourth of July,* Ron Kovic.

49. Kübler-Ross, Elisabeth, *On Death and Dying* (New York: Macmillan, 1969); subsequent private conversation with Kübler-Ross, 1980s.

Books

Alexander, John. *Ghosts: Washington Revisited*. Atglen, PA: Schiffer, 1998.

———. *Washington's Most Famous Ghost Stories*. Washington, DC: Washington Books, 1975.

Allan, Tony. Prophecies: *4000 Years of Prophets, Visionaries, and Predictions*. London, England: Thorsons, 2002.

Anderson, Jean. *The Haunting of America*. Boston: Houghton Mifflin, 1973.

Anderson, Jeffrey E. *Hoodoo, Voodoo, and Conjure: A Handbook*. Westport, CT: Greenwood Press, 2008.

Anson, Jay. *Amityville Horror*. Englewood Cliffs, NJ: Prentice Hall, 1977.

Aronson, Marc. *Witch-Hunt Mysteries of the Salem Witch Trials*. New York: Atheneum Books, 2003.

Bankston, John. *Sigmund Freud: Exploring the Mysteries of the Mind*. Berkley Heights, NJ: Enslow, 2006.

Barnett, Lincoln K. *The Universe and Dr. Einstein*. New York: W. Sloan Associates, 1948.

Bartlett, Laile. *PSI Trek*. New York: McGraw-Hill, 1981.

Baumer, Franklin L. *Religion and the Rise of Scepticism*. New York: Harcourt, Brace & Company, 1960.

Bellamy, Edward. *Looking Backward 2000-1887*. Charleston, SC: Bibliobazaar, 2007.

Berlitz, Charles. *The Mystery of Atlantis*. New York: Grosset and Dunlap, 1969.

———. *Atlantis the Eighth Continent*. New York: G. P. Putnam's Sons, 1984.

———. *Doomsday, 1999 A.D.* Garden City, NY: Doubleday, 1981.

———, and William Moore. *The Philadelphia Experiment: Project Invisibility*. New York: Grosset & Dunlap, 1979.

Bernard, Raymond, Ph.D. *The Hollow Earth*. Secaucus, NJ: Lyle Stuart, 1969.

Bernstein, Morey. *The Search for Bridey Murphy*. Garden City, NY: Doubleday, 1956.

Best of New Orleans. New York: Zagat Survey, 2007. (Travel guide).

Birnes, William J., and Joel Martin. *The Haunting of America: From the Salem Trials to Harry Houdini*. New York: Forge Books, 2009.

Bishop, Jim. *The Day Lincoln Was Shot*. New York: Harper & Row, 1955.

Blatty, William Peter. *The Exorcist*. Cutchogue, New York: Buccaneer Books, 1971. (Reprint.)

Blavatsky, Helena Petrovna. *Isis Unveiled*. 2 vols. New York: J. W. Bouton, 1877.

Bloom, Harold, ed. *William Blake*. New York: Chelsea House, 2008.

Bloomfield, Harold, M.D. *TM: Discovering Inner Energy and Overcoming Stress*. New York: Delacorte Press, 1975.

Bobrick, Benson. *The Fated Sky: Astrology in History*. New York: Simon & Schuster, 2005.

Bodian, Stephan. *Meditation for Dummies*. New York: Wiley, 2006.

Bodine, Echo. *Relax, it's Only a Ghost*. Boston: Element, 2000.

Booth, Sally Smith. *The Witches of Early America*. New York: Hastings House, 1975.

Bowman, Carol. *Children's Past Lives*. New York: Bantam Books, 1998.

———. *Return From Heaven: Beloved Relatives Reincarnated Within Your Family*. New York: HarperCollins, 2001.

Boyer, Paul, and Stephen Nissenbaum. *Salem Possessed*. Cambridge, MA: Harvard University Press, 1974.

Bradbury, Will, ed. *Into the Unknown*. Pleasantville, NY: Reader's Digest Associates, 1981.

Brandon, Ruth. *The Spiritualists: The Passion for the Occult in the Nineteenth and Twentieth Centuries*. New York: Alfred Knopf, 1983.

Brian, Denis. *Jeane Dixon: The Witnesses*. Garden City, NY: Doubleday, 1976.

Brill, A. A., ed. *The Basic Writings of Sigmund Freud*. New York: Modern Library, 1995.

Brinkley, Dannion. *Saved By the Light*. New York: Villard Books, 1994.

Bro, Harmon. *Edgar Cayce on Religion and Psychic Experience*. New York: Warner Books, 1970.

———. *Edgar Cayce on Dreams*. New York: Warner Books, 1988 [c1968].

Brodie, Fawn M. *No Man Knows My History: The Life of Joseph Smith the Mormon Prophet*. New York: Vintage Books, 1995.

Broughton, Richard, Ph.D. *Parapsychology: The Controversial Science*. New York: Ballantine Books, 1991.

Brown, Slater. *The Heyday of Spiritualism*. New York: Hawthorn Books, 1970.

Buckland, Raymond. *Doors to Other Worlds*. St. Paul, MN: Llewellyn, 1993.

Bulwer-Lytton, Sir Edward. *The Coming Race*. Middletown, CT: Wesleyan University Press, 2005.

Burnham, Sophy. *A Book of Angels*. New York: Ballantine Books, 1990.

Capra, Fritjof. *The Tao of Physics: An Exploration of the Parallels between Modern Physics and Eastern Mysticism*. Boston: Shambahala, 2000.

Carrington, Hereward, and Nandor Fodor. *Haunted People: Story of the Poltergeist Down the Centuries*. New York: E. P. Dutton, 1951.

Carter, Mary Ellen. *My Years with Edgar Cayce: The Personal Story of Gladys Davis Turner*. New York: Harper & Row, 1972.

——— and William A. McGarey. *Edgar Cayce on Healing*. New York: Warner Books, 1972.

Castaneda, Carlos. *The Teachings of Don Juan: A Yaqui Way of Knowledge*. Berkley, CA: University of California Press, 1996. (Originally published in 1968).

Cavendish, Marshal, ed. *Man, Myth and Magic*. North Bellmore, NY: Cavendish, 1995.

Cayce, Hugh Lynn, and Edgar Cayce. *God's Other Door and the Continuity of Life*. Virginia Beach, VA: A.R.E. Press, 1958.

Cerminara, Gina. *Many Mansions: The Edgar Cayce Story on Reincarnation*. New York: Signet, 1950.

Cheetham, Erika. *The Final Prophecies of Nostradamus*. New York: Perigee, 1989.

———. *The Man Who Saw Tomorrow: The Prophecies of Nostradamus*. New York: Berkley Books, 1973.

Cheroux, Clement, Andreas Fisher, Pierre Apraxine, Denis Canguilhem, and Sophie Schmit. *The Perfect Medium: Photography and the Occult*. New Haven, CT: Yale University, 2005.

Chinmoy, Sri. *Beyond Within: A Philosophy for the Inner Life*. Jamaica, NY: Agni Press, 1974.

———. *Death and Reincarnation*. Jamaica, NY: Agni Press, 1974.

Cockell, Jenny. *Across Time and Death: A Mother's Search for Her Past Life Children*. New York: Simon & Schuster, 1994.

Cohen, Daniel. *Civil War Ghosts*. New York: Scholastic Books, 1999.

————. *The Encyclopedia of the Strange*. New York: Avon Books, 1985.

————. *The Manhattan Project*. Brookfield, CT: Millbrook Press, 1999.

Cohn, Norman. *Warrant for Genocide: The Myth of the Jewish Conspiracy and the Protocols of the Elders of Zion*. Chico, CA: Scholars Press, 1981.

Coleman, Christopher K. *Ghosts and Haunts of the Civil War*. New York: Barnes & Noble, 2003.

Cook, Nick. *The Hunt for Zero Point: Inside the Classified World of Anti-Gravity Technology*. New York: Broadway Books, 2002.

Cox, Harvey. *Secular City*. New York: Macmillan, 1966.

Cuneo, Michael W. *American Exorcism*. New York: Doubleday, 2001.

Davies, Paul. *God and the New Physics*. New York: Simon & Schuster, 1983.

Dickinson, Alice. *The Salem Witchcraft Delusion: 1692*. New York: Franklin Watts, 1974.

Dickinson, Joy. *Haunted City: An Unauthorized Guide to the Magical, Magnificent New Orleans of Ann Rice*. Secaucus, NJ: Carol Publishers, 1995.

Donald, David Herbert. *Lincoln*. London: J. Cape, 1995.

Donnelly, Ignatius. *Atlantis: The Antediluvian World*. New York: Gramercy, 1949. (Originally published in 1882.)

Dossey, Larry, M.D. *Be Careful What You Pray For, You Just Might Get It*. San Francisco: HarperSanFrancisco, 1997.

————. *The Power of Premonitions*. New York: Dutton, 2009.

Doyle, Arthur Conan. *The History of Spiritualism*. New York: George H. Doran Company, 1926.

Dreher, Diane. *The Tao of Inner Peace*. New York: HarperCollins, 1991.

Dyer, Wayne W. *Your Erroneous Zones*. New York: Avon Books, 1976.

Ebon, Martin. *Communicating with the Dead*. New York: New American Library, 1981.

————. *Miracles*. New York: Signet Books, 1981.

Edmonds, I. G. *D. D. Home: The Man Who Talked with Ghosts*. Nashville, TN: Thomas Nelson, 1978.

Elliot, Nancy B. with John Elliot. *David's Message: Love and Life Are Eternal*. Penfield, NY: Enlightened Print, 2008.

Elwood, Ann. *Weird and Mysterious*. New York: Globe Books, 1979.

Estabrooks, G. H.: *Hypnotism*. New York: Dutton, 1957.

Estep, Sarah Wilson. *Voices of Eternity*. New York: Fawcett Gold Medal Books, 1988.

Evans, Richard. *The Coming of the Third Reich*. New York: Penguin Books, 2003.

Farber, David, ed. *The Sixties: From Memory to History*. Chapel Hill: The University of North Carolina Press, 1994.

Federal Writers Project. *New Orleans City Guide: 1938*. New Orleans: Garrett County Press, 2009.

Feinstein, Stephen. *The 1960s from the Vietnam War to Flower Power*. Berkley Heights, NJ: Enslow Publishers, 2006.

Fiore, Edith. *You Have Been Here Before: A Psychologist Looks at Past Lives*. New York: Coward, McCann, and Geoghegan, 1978.

Fisher, Joe with Peter Commins. *Predictions*. New York: Van Nostrand Reinhold Company, 1980.

Fitzsimmons, Raymund. *Death and the Magician: The Mysteries of Houdini*. New York: Atheneum, 1981.

Fodor, Nandor. *Between Two Worlds*. New York: Parker Publishing Company, 1964.

———. *Freud, Jung and Occultism*. New Hyde Park, NY: University Books, 1971.

Ford, Arthur. *Unknown but Known*. New York: Signet Books, 1968.

Fuller, John G. *The Airmen Who Would Not Die*. New York: G. P. Putnam's Sons, 1979.

———. *The Ghost of Flight 401*. New York: G. P. Putnam's Sons, 1976.

Fuller, Robert C. *Mesmerism and the American Cure of Souls*. Philadelphia: University of Pennsylvania Press, 1982.

———. *Religious Revolutionaries*. New York: Palgrave Macmillan, 2004.

Gaddis, Vincent. *Invisible Horizons*. Philadelphia: Chilton, 1965.

Garrett, Eileen J. *Many Voices*. New York: G. P. Putnam's Sons, 1968.

———. *My Life as a Search for the Meaning of Mediumship*. New York: Oquaga Press, 1939.

Garrison, Omar V. *The Hidden Story of Scientology*. Secaucus, NJ: Citadel Press, 1974.

Gauld, Alan. *The Founders of Psychical Research*. New York: Schocken Books, 1968.

Gleick, James. *Isaac Newton*. New York: Pantheon Books, 2003.

Godwin, Doris Kearns. *Lyndon Johnson and the American Dream*. New York: Harper & Row, 1969.

Godwin, Malcolm. *Angels: An Endangered Species*. New York: Simon & Schuster, 1990.

Goldsmith, Thomas. *Dawn of Modern Science*. Boston: Houghton Mifflin, 1980.

Goldston, Robert. *The Great Depression: The United States in the Thirties*. New York: Fawcett, 1968.

Gordon, Mary. *Joan of Arc*. New York: Viking Books, 2000.

Gould, Stephen Jay. *The Hedgehog, the Fox, and the Magister's Pox: Mending the Gap Between Science and the Humanities*. New York: Harmony Books, 2003.

Greenhouse, Herbert. *The Book of Psychic Knowledge*. New York: Taplinger, 1973.

Guggenheim, William, and Judy Guggenheim. *Hello from Heaven*. New York: Bantam Books, 1996.

Guiley, Rosemary Ellen. *The Encyclopedia of Demons and Demonology*. New York: Checkmark Books, 2009.

———. *The Encyclopedia of Ghosts and Spirits*. New York: Facts on File, 2000.

Hansen, Chadwick. *Witchcraft at Salem*. New York: George Braziller, 1969.

Hauck, Dennis William. *Haunted Places: The National Directory*. New York: Penguin Books, 1996.

Hayden, Tom. *The Long Sixties: From 1960 to Barack Obama*. Boulder, CO: Paradigm, 2009.

———. *Reunion: A Memoir*. New York: Random House, 1988.

Heaney, John J. *The Sacred and the Psychic: Parapsychology & Christian Theology*. Ramsey, NJ: Paulist Press, 1984.

Herndon, William H., and Jesse W. Welk. *Herndon's Life of Lincoln*. Cleveland, OH: World Publishing Company, 1930. (Originally written in 1888. Herndon was Lincoln's law partner.)

Hilgard, Ernest R. *The Experience of Hypnosis*. New York: Harcourt, Brace, Jovanovich, 1965.

Holzer, Hans. *The Ghosts that Walk Washington*. Garden City, NY: Doubleday, 1971.

———. *The Psychic World of Bishop Pike*. New York: Crown, 1970.

———. *Travel Guide to Haunted Houses*. New York: Black Dog & Leventhal, 1998.

———. *Where the Ghosts Are: The Ultimate Guide to Haunted Houses*. Secaucus, NJ: Carol Publishing Group, 1995.

Home, D. D. *Incidents in My Life*. London, England: 1863.

Houdini, Harry. *A Magician among the Spirits*. New York: Arno Press, 1972. (Originally published 1924.)

Howard, Gerald, ed. *The Sixties: The Art, Attitudes, Politics, and Media of Our Most Explosive Decade*. New York: Washington Square Press, 1982.

Howard, Michael. *The First World War*. New York: Oxford University Press, 2003.

———. *The Occult Conspiracy*. Rochester, Vermont: Destiny Books, 1989.

Hurley, Jennifer A. *The 1960s: Opposing Viewpoints*. San Diego, CA: Greenhaven Press, 2000.

Huxley, Aldous. *Brave New World*. Garden City: Doubleday, Doran & Company, 1932.

———. *The Doors to Perception, and Heaven and Hell*. New York: Perennial Classics, 2004. (Originally published in 1956.)

Isaacson, Walter. *Einstein: His Life and Universe*. New York: Simon & Schuster, 2008.

Jackson, Herbert G. *The Spirit Rappers*. Garden City, NY: Doubleday, 1972.

Jacobson, Laurie. *Hollywood Haunted*. Santa Monica, CA: Angel City Press, 1994.

James, William. *The Varieties of Religious Experience*. New York: Penguin Books, 1982.

Jarvis, Sharon, ed. *Dead Zones*. New York: Warner Books, 1992.

Jenkins, Elizabeth. *The Shadow and the Light: A Defence of Daniel Dunglas Home the Medium*. London: Hamish Hamilton, Ltd., 1982.

Jenkins, Philip. *Mystics and Messiahs: Cults and New Religions in American History*. New York: Oxford University Press, 2000.

Jung, Carl G. *Memories, Dreams, Reflections*. New York: Vintage Books, 1965.

———. *Psychology and the Occult*. Princeton, NJ: Princeton University Press, 1977.

———, ed. *Man and His Symbols*. New York: Dell, 1968.

Kaczmarek, Dale. *National Registry of Haunted Locations*. Chicago: Ghost Research Society.

Kahn, David E. *My Life with Edgar Cayce*. Garden City, NY: Doubleday, 1970.

Kallen, Stuart A. *Voodoo*. San Diego, CA: Lucent Books, 2005.

Kaplan, Fred. *The Singular Mark Twain*. New York: Doubleday, 2003.

Kaplan, Stephen, and Roxanne Salch Kaplan. *Amityville Horror Conspiracy*. Laceyville, PA: Belfry, 1995.

Kaplan, Stephen, with Carol Kane. *Vampires Are*. Palm Springs, CA: ETC Publications, 1984.

Kaye, Marvin. *Haunted America*. New York: Barnes & Noble Books, 1990.

Keller, Helen. *My Religion*. New York: Pyramid Books, 1974. (Originally published in 1960.)

Kelley, Kitty. *Nancy Reagan: The Unauthorized Biography*. New York: Simon & Schuster, 1991.

Kermeen, Frances. *Ghostly Encounters: The True Stories of America's Haunted Inns and Hotels*. New York: Warner Books, 2002.

Kerr, Howard. *Mediums and Spirits*. Urbana, IL: University of Illinois Press, 1972.

——— and Charles L. Crow. *The Occult in America*. Urbana, IL: University of Illinois Press, 1983.

Kesey, Ken. *One Flew Over the Cuckoo's Nest*. New York: Penguin Books, 2007. (Originally in 1962.)

Kirkpatrick, Sidney. *Edgar Cayce: An American Prophet*. New York: Riverhead Books, 2000.

Klein, Edward. *The Kennedy Curse*. New York: St. Martin's Press, 2003.

Kubler-Ross, Elisabeth. *On Death and Dying*. New York: Macmillan, 1969.

Langley, Noel. *Edgar Cayce on Reincarnation*. New York: Warner Books, 1967.

Leadbeater, C. W. *A Textbook of Theosophy*. Madras, India: Theosophical Publishing House, 1956.

Leary, Timothy, Richard Alpert, and Ralph Metzner. *The Psychedelic Experience: A Manual Based on the Tibetan Book of the Dead*. Secaucus, NJ: Citadel Press, 1964.

Lemesurier, Peter. *Nostradamus: The Next Fifty Years*. New York: Berkley Books, 1993.

Lenz, Frederick. *Lifetimes: True Accounts of Reincarnation*. Indianapolis: Bobbs-Merrill, 1979.

————. *Surfing the Himalayas: A Spiritual Adventure*. New York: St. Martin's Press, 1995.

Leoni, Edgar. *Nostradamus and His Prophecies*. New York: Bell Publishers, 1982.

LeShan, Lawrence. *The Medium, the Mystic, and the Physicist*. New York: Viking, 1966.

Lewis, James R. *Encyclopedia of Afterlife Beliefs and Phenomena*. Detroit: Gale Research, 1994.

Lycett, Andrew. *The Man Who Created Sherlock Holmes: The Life and Times of Sir Arthur Conan Doyle*. New York: Free Press, 2007.

MacLaine, Shirley. *Out on a Limb*. New York: Bantam Books, 1983.

Manvell, Roger, and Heinrich Fraenkel. *Inside Adolf Hitler*. New York: Pinnacle Books, 1973.

Martin, Joel, and William J. Birnes. *The Haunting of the Presidents: A Paranormal History of the U. S. Presidency*. New York: Signet Books, 2003. (Reprinted by Konecky & Konecky, Old Saybrook, CT.)

Martin, Joel, and Patricia Romanowski. *Love Beyond Life*. New York: HarperCollins, 1997.

Martin, Malachi. *Hostage to the Devil*. San Francisco: HarperSanFrancisco, 1976.

Martinez, Susan B. *The Psychic Life of Abraham Lincoln*. Franklin Lakes, NJ: New Page Books, 2007.

Maynard, Nettie Colburn. *Was Abraham Lincoln a Spiritualist?* Philadelphia: Rufus C. Hartranft, 1891.

McGarey, William A. *The Edgar Cayce Remedies*. New York: Bantam Books, 1983.

McHargue, Georgess. *Facts, Frauds, and Phantasms: A Survey of the Spiritualist Movement*. Garden City, NY: Doubleday, 1972.

Melton, J. Gordon: *The Vampire Book: The Encyclopedia of the Undead*. Canton, MI: Visible Ink Press, 1999.

Monahan, Brent, ed. *The Bell Witch: An American Haunting*. New York: St. Martin's Press, 1977.

Montgomery, Ruth. *Gift of Prophecy: The Phenomenal Jeane Dixon*. New York: Morrow, 1965.

————. *Herald of the New Age*. Garden City, NY: Doubleday, 1986.

————. *Strangers Among Us*. New York: Coward, McCann, and Geoghegan, 1979.

————. *A World Beyond*. New York: Ballantine Books, 1988.

Moody, Raymond A., M.D. *Life after Life*. Atlanta: Mockingbird Books, 1975.

———— with Paul Perry. *Coming Back: A Psychiatrist Explores Past Life Journeys*. New York: Bantam Books, 1991.

Murphy, Gardner. *Challenge of Psychical Research*. New York: Harper & Brothers, 1961.

Neame, Alan. *The Happening at Lourdes*. New York: Simon and Schuster, 1967.

Nesbitt, Mark. *Ghosts of Gettysburg*. Gettysburg, PA: Thomas Publications, 1991.

Nichols, Preston. *The Montauk Project: Experiments in Time*. Westbury, NY: Sky Books, 1992.

Norman, Michael, and Beth Scott. *Haunted America*. New York: Tor Books, 1994.

————. *Historic Haunted America*. New York: Tor Books, 1995.

Orwell, George. *1984*. New York: Knopf, 1992. (Reprint.)

Ostrander, Shelia, and Lynn Schroeder. *Psychic Discoveries Behind the Iron Curtain*. Englewood Cliffs, NJ: Prentice-Hall, 1970.

Panati, Charles. *Supersenses: Our Potential for Parasensory Experience*. New York: Quadrangle, 1974.

Park, Robert L. *Superstition: Belief in the Age of Science*. Princeton, NJ: Princeton University Press, 2008.

————. *Voodoo Science: The Road from Foolishness to Fraud*. New York: Oxford University Press, 2000.

Parks, Lillian Rogers. *My Thirty Years Backstairs at the White House*. New York: Fleet, 1961.

Perry, Michael. *Psychic Studies: A Christian's View*. Wellingborough, Great Britain: The Aquarian Press, 1984.

Pike, James. *The Other Side: An Account of My Experiences with Psychic Phenomena*. New York: Doubleday, 1968.

Price, Hope. *Angels: True Stories of How They Touch Our Lives*. New York: Avon, 1993.

Prose, Francine. *Marie Laveau*. New York: Berkley Books, 1977.

Quigley, Joan. *"What Does Joan Say?" My Seven Years as White House Astrologer to Nancy and Ronald Reagan*. Secaucus, NJ: Birch Lane, 1990.

Reagan, Nancy with William Novak. *My Turn: The Memoirs of Nancy Reagan*. New York: Random House, 1989.

Regan, Donald. *For the Record*. San Diego, CA: Harcourt Brace Jovanovich, 1988.

Rhine, J. B. *New Frontiers of the Mind*. New York: Farrar & Rinehart, 1937.

Rhodes, Jewell Parker. *Voodoo Season: A Marie Laveau Mystery*. New York: Atria Books, 2005.

Rinn, Joseph F. *Sixty Years of Psychical Research*. New York: Truth Seeker Company, 1950.

Roberts, Nancy. *Civil War, Ghosts and Legends*. Columbia, SC: University of South Carolina Press, 1992.

Robertson, Morgan. *The Wreck of the Titan, or Futility*. Cutchogue, NY: Buccaneer Books, 1994. (Reprint of original published in 1898.)

Rogo, D. Scott. *Miracles: A Parascientific Inquiry into Wondrous Phenomena*. New York: The Dial Press, 1982.

Roland, Paul. *The Nazis and the Occult: The Dark Forces Unleashed by the Third Reich*. Edison, NJ: Chartwell Books, 2007.

Ronson, Jon. *Men Who Stare at Goats*. New York: Simon & Schuster, 2006.

Sagan, Carl. *The Demon-Haunted World: Science as a Candle in the Dark*. New York: Random House, 1996.

Shermer, Michael. *Why People Believe Weird Things*. New York: W. H. Freeman, 1977.

Shirer, William L. *The Rise and Fall of the Third Reich*. New York: Simon & Schuster, 1959.

Sinclair, Upton. *Mental Radio*. C. C. Thomas, 1962. (Originally published in 1930.)

Sklar, Dusty. *Gods and Beasts: The Nazis and the Occult*. New York: T. Y. Crowell, 1977.

Smith, Susy. *Prominent American Ghosts*. Cleveland: World Publishing Company, 1967.

Speer, Albert. *Inside the Third Reich*. London: Weidenfeld and Nicholson, 2003.

Spitz, Robert Stephen. *Barefoot in Babylon: The Creation of the Woodstock Music Festival 1969*. New York: The Viking Press, 1979.

Stearn, Jess. *Edgar Cayce: The Sleeping Prophet*. New York: Doubleday & Company, 1967.

————. *A Matter of Immortality*. New York: Atheneum Publishers, 1976.

————. *A Prophet in His Own Country: The Story of the Young Edgar Cayce*. New York: Morrow, 1974.

————. *The Search for a Soul: Taylor Caldwell's Psychic Lives*. Garden City, NY: Doubleday, 1973.

————. *Soul Mates*. New York: Bantam Books, 1984.

Steiger, Brad. *Real Ghosts, Restless Spirits, and Haunted Places*. Canton, MI: Visible Ink Press, 2003.

Stein, Gordon. *The Sorcerer of Kings: The Case of Daniel Dunglas Home and William Crookes*. Buffalo, NY: Prometheus Books, 1993.

Stevenson, Ian. *Twenty Cases Suggestive of Reincarnation*. Charlottesville, VA: University Press of Virginia, 1974.

Sugrue, Thomas. *There Is a River: The Story of Edgar Cayce*. New York: Holt, Rinehart, and Winston, 1942.

Swedenborg, Emanuel. *Heaven and Hell*. New York: Swedenborg Foundation, 1972. (Originally published in Latin, London, 1758.)

Time-Life Books, eds. *Hauntings*. New York: Barnes & Noble Books, 1989.

Toland, John. *Adolf Hitler*. Garden City, NY: Doubleday, 1976.

Trouncer, Margaret. *Saint Bernadette: The Child and the Nun*. New York: Sheed and Ward, 1958.

Turlington, Shannon R. *The Complete Idiot's Guide to Voodoo*. Indianapolis, IN: Alpha Books, 2002.

Twigg, Ena, with Ruth Hagy Brod. *Ena Twigg: Medium*. New York: Manor Books, 1973.

Ullman, Montague, and Stanley Krippner. *Dream Studies and Telepathy*. New York: Parapsychology Foundation, 1970.

Van de Castle, Robert. *Our Dreaming Mind*. New York: Ballantine Books, 1994.

Vogel, Dan. *Joseph Smith: The Making of a Prophet*. Salt Lake City: Signature Books, 2004.

Waite, Robert G. L. *The Psychopathic God: Adolf Hitler*. New York: Basic Books, 1977.

Walsh, William Thomas. *Our Lady of Fatima*. New York: Doubleday, 1990.

Wambach, Helen. *Reliving Past Lives: The Evidence Under Hypnosis*. New York: Harper & Row, 1978.

Ward, Martha. *Voodoo Queen: The Spirited Lives of Marie Laveau*. Jackson: University Press of Mississippi, 2004.

Warren, Ed, and Lorraine Warren, with Robert Curran. *The Haunted: One Family's Nightmare*. New York: St. Martin's Press, 1988.

Washington, Peter. *Madame Blavatsky's Baboon: A History of the Mystics, Mediums, and Misfits Who Brought Spiritualism to America*. New York: Schocken Books, 1995.

Weible, Wayne. *Medjugorje: The Message*. Orleans, MA: Paraclete Press, 1989.

Weiss, Brian, M.D. *Many Lives, Many Masters*. New York: Simon & Schuster, 1988.

Whitton, Joel L., M.D., Ph.D., and Joe Fisher. *Life Between Life*. New York: Warner Books, 1986.

Wicker, Christine. *Lily Dale: The True Story of the Town that Talks to the Dead*. New York: HarperSanFrancisco, 2003.

Williams, Dinah. *Spooky Cemeteries*. New York: Bearport Publishers, 2008.

Winer, Richard, and Nancy Osborn. *Haunted Houses*. New York: Bantam Books, 1979.

Wistrich, Robert. *Who's Who in Nazi Germany*. New York: Macmillan, 1982.

Witkowski, Igor. *Truth About the Wunderwaffer*. Warsaw, Poland: European History Press, 2008.

Woods, Richard. *The Occult Revolution*. New York: Herder and Herder, 1971.

Reference Books

Amplified Bible, expanded edition: The Lockman Foundation. Grand Rapids, MI: Zondervan, 1987.

Asimov, Isaac. *Asimov's Biographical Encyclopedia of Science and Technology*. Second Revised Edition. Garden City, NY: Doubleday, 1964.

Great Events from History: American Series (three volumes). Frank N. Magill (ed.) Englewood Cliffs, NJ: Salem Press, Incorporated, 1975.

Great Events from History: Modern European Series (three volumes). Frank N. Magill (ed.) Englewood Cliffs, NJ: Salem Press, 1973.

Grun, Bernard. *The Timetables of History: A Horizontal Linkage of People and Events*. New York: Simon & Schuster, 1975.

Lande, Nathaniel. *Mindstyles/Lifestyles*. Los Angeles: Price/Stern/Sloan, 1976.

Lorie, Peter, and Manuela Dunn Mascetti. *The Quotable Spirit: A Treasury of Religious and Spiritual Quotations from Ancient Times to the Twentieth Century*. Edison, NJ: Castle Books, 1996.

Melton, J. Gordon. *Encyclopedia of Occultism & Parapsychology*. Fourth edition. Two volumes. Detroit: Gale Research, 1996.

Oxford Desk Dictionary and Thesaurus, American Edition. New York: Berkley Books. *Time Almanac with Information Please*. Boston: Time, Inc. (annual publication). *World Almanac Book of the Strange*. New York: Signet Books, 1977.

Periodicals
Magazines

America, American Psychologist, Art Digest, Atlantic Monthly, Contemporary Hispanic Biography, Coronet, Economist, Fate, Guideposts, Humanist, Intuition, Liberty, Life, Nation, National Geographic Traveler, New Orleans Directions, New York, Newsmakers, Newsweek, Omni, Parade, Playboy, Psychic News, Psychic World, Psychology Today, Scientific American, Skeptic, Skeptical Inquirer, Smithsonian, Time, Travel Weekly (New Orleans), *UFO Magazine, U.S. News & World Report, Vanity Fair*.

Newspapers

Albany Evening Times (NY), *Banner of Light, The Boston Globe, The Tablet* (UK), *Chicago American, Chicago Daily News, The Christian Science Monitor, The Denver Post, Frank Leslie's Illustrated, The Globe and Mail* (Toronto), *The New Orleans Bee, Daily News* New York, *New York Herald Tribune, New York Journal American, New York Post, The New York Times, Newsday* (NY), *San Francisco Chronicle, San Francisco Examiner, The Times* (London), *The Times-Picayune* (New Orleans), *The Toronto Star, USA Today, The Washington Post, Washington Star*.

Journals

The A.R.E. Journal, The Christian Parapsychologist, CQ Researcher, Exceptional Human Experience, The Journal of the American Society for Psychical Research, The Journal of Parapsychology, Journal of Religion and Psychical Research, Journal of the Society for Psychical Research, Proceedings of the American Society for Psychical Research.

Articles

Accurso, Lina. "The Lady and the Peasant Girl: Saint Bernadette and the Miracle of Lourdes." *Psychic World*: Spring 1998.

Accurso, Lina. "The Miracle of Fatima: Will the Last Secret be Revealed?" *Psychic World*: Spring 1997.

Fate. "Psychic Adventures of Mark Twain." June 2004.

Fate. "My Sittings with Arthur Ford." July 1974.

Freud, Sigmund. "Dreams and Telepathy." Paper presented, 1922.

Journal of the American Society for Psychical Research. "An Attempt to Relate Creativity to Possible Extrasensory Empathy as Measured by Physiological Arousal in Identical Twins." *ASPR*: 1968.

Journal of the American Society for Psychical Research. "Mark Twain's Premonition." *ASPR*: 1913.

Journal of the American Society for Psychical Research. "Honesty and Dishonesty of Mediums." *ASPR*: 1914.

Journal of the American Society for Psychical Research. "Hypnosis in Modern Medicine," book review. *ASPR*: 1953.

Journal of the American Society for Psychical Research. "The Mystical and the Paranormal." *ASPR*: 1954.

Journal of the American Society for Psychical Research. "Experiences of the Supernatural in India." *ASPR*: 1937.

Journal of the American Society for Psychical Research. "Yoga, a Scientific Evaluation." *ASPR*: 1937.

Journal of the American Society for Psychical Research. "Nostradamus." *ASPR*: 1937.

Journal of the American Society for Psychical Research. "War Prophecies." *ASPR*: 1939.

Journal of the American Society for Psychical Research. "Mr. Sludge the Medium." ASPR: 1954.

Journal of the American Society for Psychical Research. "A Review and Analysis of Paranormal Experiences Connected with the Sinking of the Titanic." *ASPR*: 1960.

Lawrence L. LeShan. "The Vanished Man: A Psychometry Experiment with Mrs. Eileen J. Garrett." *Journal of the American Society for Psychical Research*. *ASPR*: 1968.

Murphy, Gardner. "Progress in Parapsychology." *Journal of the American Society for Psychical Research*. *ASPR*: 1959.

————. "William James on Psychical Research." *Journal of the American Society for Psychical Research*. *ASPR*: 1962.

Rhine, J. B. "What Do Parapsychologists Want to Know?" *Journal of the American Society for Psychical Research*. *ASPR*: 1959.

Rhine, Louisa E. "ESP in Life and Lab." *Journal of Parapsychology*. December 1967.

Ullman, Montague, M.D. "On the Occurrence of Telepathic Dreams." *Journal of the American Society for Psychical Research*. *ASPR*: April 1959.

Tart, Charles T. "A Parapsychological Study of Out-of-the-Body Experiences in a Selected Subject." *Journal of the American Society for Psychical Research*. *ASPR*: January 1968.

Journal of the Society for Psychical Research. "A Survey of Reported Premonitions and of Those Who Have Them." *SPR*: 1984.

Life. "Visions of Life After Death: The Ultimate Mystery." March 1992.

New York. "The Believer." July 16, 2007.

New York Daily News. "Winston Churchill and Dwight Eisenhower Covered Up UFO Letter Claims." August 5, 2010.

New York Times. "Awful Event—President Lincoln Shot by an Assassin." April 15, 1865.

New York Times. "In Work on Intuition, Gut Feelings Are Tracked to Source: The Brain." March 4, 1997.

Newsday. "The Search for Scientific Proof" [of mediumship]. January 5, 1997.

Proceedings of the American Society for Psychical Research. "Lily Dale." *ASPR*: 1908.

Publishers Weekly. "New Age Is All the Rage." March 10, 1997.

River Bender. "Meet Rhea A. White." February 7, 1996.

Scientific American. "Darwin and Associates, Ghostbusters." October 1996.

Ian Stevenson, M.D. "Telepathic Impressions: A Review and Report of Thirty-Five New Cases." *Proceedings of the American Society for Psychical Research*. ASPR: 1970.

Tablet. "Research Shows Lincoln Was a Religious Man." February 15, 1992.

Toronto Globe-Mail. "Thibault explains talks with deceased." February 1, 1997.

Vanity Fair. "Elisabeth Kubler-Ross's Final Passage." June 1997.

Libraries and Other Collections

American Society for Psychical Research, NY
Association for Research and Enlightenment: Edgar Cayce Foundation, Virginia Beach, VA
Axinn Library of Hofstra University, Hempstead, NY
East Meadow (NY) Public Library
Exceptional Human Experience, New Bern, NC
Hopkinsville-Christian County (KY) Public Library
Metropolitan Museum of Art (NY)
New York Public Library
Rochester (NY) Public Library
Toronto Society for Psychical Research
West Babylon (NY) Public Library

Web sites and Online Sources

Afterlife research
    www.theafterlifeinvestigations.com
American Ghost Society
    www.prairieghosts.com
American Society for Psychical Research
    www.aspr.com
Amityville Horror
    www.amityville.com
    www.amityvillemurders.com
    www.amityvillerecord.com
Atlantic Paranormal Society
    www.the-atlantic-paranormal-society.com
Bell Witch
    www.bellwitch.org
Borley Ghost Society (UK)
    www.borleyrectory.com
Carol Bowman/Past Life Center
    www.childpastlives.org
Edgar Cayce/Association for Research and Enlightenment
    www.edgarcayce.org
Edgar Cayce birthplace
    www.visithopkinsville.com
Edgar Cayce grave site
    www.roadsideamerica.com
The Committee for Skeptical Inquiry
    www.csicop.org
Jeane Dixon
    www.skepdic.com/dixon.html
    www.catholicrevelations.org
Exceptional Human Experience Network
    www.ehe.org

Fate magazine
  www.fatemag.com
Arthur Ford
  www.spiritwritings.com/ArthurFord.html
Fortean Times
  www.forteantimes.com
Eileen Garrett
  www.parapsychology.org
Ghost Research Society
  www.ghostresearch.org
Haunted Hollywood
  http://gothic.vei.net/hollywood
Haunted Places in Chicago
  www.hauntedchicago.com
Haunted Places in the District of Columbia
  www.theshadowlands.net
Haunted Places in New Orleans
  www.hauntedneworleans.com
  www.neworleansghosts.com
  www.marieleveau.com
International Association for Near-Death Studies
  www.iands.org
Institute of Noetic Sciences
  www.noetic.org
Institute for Parapsychology
  www.instituteforparapsychology.org
Journal of Parapsychology
  www.journalparapsychology.com
Carl G. Jung
  www.cgjungpage.org
Lily Dale Spiritualist Assembly (NY)
  www.lilydale.com
Abraham Lincoln
  www.lincolnghost.org
Loving Light (various religious views of afterlife)
  www.lovinglight.com
Merchant House Museum
  www.merchanthouse.com
Mind Science Foundation
  www.mindscience.org
New England Society for Psychic Research (Lorraine Warren)
  www.warrens.net
Parapsychology Association
  www.parapsychologyassociation.org

Parapsychology Foundation
 www.parapsychologyfoundation.com
Psychical Research Foundation
 www.afterlife-psychical.org
J. B. Rhine
 www.rhine.org
Salem Witch Trials of 1692/Salem Witch Museum
 www.salemwitchmuseum.com/education/index/.shtml
Ian Stevenson
 www.reluctant-messenger.com/reincarnation-proof
Theosophical Society in America
 www.theosophical.org
Brian Weiss, M.D. (past lives regressive hypnosis)
 www.brianweiss.com
Whaley House
 www.whaleyhouse.com
White House ghosts
 www.whitehouse.gov/ghosts